THE LIFE AND WORKS OF GEORGE PEELE

VOLUME 3

CHARLES TYLER PROUTY

GENERAL EDITOR

The Dramatic Works of

GEORGE PEELE

THE ARAYGNEMENT OF PARIS

Edited by R. Mark Benbow

DAVID AND BETHSABE

Edited by Elmer Blistein

THE OLD WIVES TALE

Edited by Frank S. Hook

NEW HAVEN AND LONDON: YALE UNIVERSITY PRESS, 1970

CONTENTS

THE ARAYGNEMENT
OF PARIS

ACKNOWLEDGMENTS

In its original form this edition was a dissertation presented to the faculty of the Department of English, Yale University, in partial fulfillment of the requirements for the doctoral degree. Since then the edition has been revised and augmented.

I owe much to Professor C. T. Prouty, the general editor of this series, and to Professor Carl J. Weber of Colby College. The former directed the research; the latter offered encouragement and example as a senior colleague. While specific indebtedness to previous scholars is noted, many have contributed indirectly to this edition. I am grateful to Richard Harrier of New York University and to Howard L. Koonce for reading the manuscript and to those of my colleagues whose discussions helped to clarify the problems of the play. Thanks are also due Colby College for faculty research grants.

R. M. B.

Colby College
January 1969

ABBREVIATIONS AND SHORT TITLES

Arber   *A Transcript of the Registers of the Company of Stationers of London, 1554–1640 A.D.*, ed. Edward Arber, 5 vols., London, 1875–94.

B   *The Works of Peele*, ed. A. H. Bullen, 2 vols., London, 1888.

Baskervill   Baskervill, C. R., V. B. Heltzel, and A. H. Nethercot, eds., *Elizabethan and Stuart Plays*, New York, 1934.

BM   British Museum copy of Quarto.

Brooke   Brooke, C. F. T., and N. B. Paradise, eds., *English Drama 1580–1642*, Boston, 1933.

Chambers   Chambers, E. K., *The Elizabethan Stage*, 4 vols., Oxford, 1923.

Cheffaud   Cheffaud, P. H., *George Peele (1558–1596?)*, Paris, 1913.

Child   *The Araygnement of Paris*, ed. H. H. Child, Malone Society Reprint, Oxford, 1910.

Daniel   Daniel, P. A., Notes included in Bullen's edition (See B, above).

Dyce   *The Works of Peele*, ed. Alexander Dyce, 2d ed., 3 vols., London, 1829–39.

Dyce 1   *The Dramatic and Poetical Works of Robert Greene and George Peele*, ed. Alexander Dyce, London, 1861.

EH   *England's Helicon*, ed. H. E. Rollins, 2 vols., Cambridge, Mass., 1935.

Feuillerat, *Edward*   Feuillerat, A., *Documents Relating to the Office of the Revels in the Time of King*

	Edward and Queen Mary, Vol. 44 of Materialen zur Kunde des Alteren Englischen Dramas, ed. W. Bang (Louvain, 1914).
Feuillerat, *Elizabeth*	Feuillerat, A., *Documents Relating to the Office of the Revels in the Time of Queen Elizabeth*, Vol. 21 of Materialen zur Kunde des Alteren Englischen Dramas, ed. W. Bang (Louvain, 1908).
H	Henry E. Huntington Library copy of Quarto.
Horne	Horne, David H., *The Life and Minor Works of George Peele*, New Haven, 1952.
Jeffrey	Jeffrey, N., "Italian and English Pastoral Drama of the Renaissance," *Modern Language Review*, *19* (1924), 175–187.
Larsen	Larsen, Thorleif, "The Early Years of George Peele, Dramatist, 1558–1588," *Transactions of the Royal Society of Canada*, *22* (1928), 271–318.
Nicholson	Nicholson, Brinsley, Notes included in Bullen's edition (See B, above).
OED	*Oxford English Dictionary*.
P	Pforzheimer copy of Quarto.
Q	Collated Quartos.
SD	Stage Direction.
Smeaton	*The Arraignment of Paris*, Ed. O. Smeaton, London, 1905.
T	Trinity College copy of Quarto.
( )	Broken or missing letter.

References to Shakespeare are to the edition of W. A. Neilson and C. J. Hill, those to Chaucer to the edition of F. N. Robinson, those to Spenser to the Oxford editions of E. de Selincourt and J. C. Smith. For Peele I have used the Yale edition where available or the Malone Society reprints. All references to classical authors are to the Loeb Library editions unless otherwise noted.

INTRODUCTION

1. Authorship and Date

The only edition of George Peele's *The Araygnement of Paris* is the quarto of 1584. While there is no entry in the Stationers' Register, there is no evidence that this is a surreptitious edition. Though unusual, the lack of an entry at this specific period is not unprecedented. Lyly's *Campaspe* appeared in the same year but was unrecorded until 1597, when it was transferred from Thomas Cadman to Mistress Brome.[1] Likewise in 1584, Ward printed Wilson's *Three Ladies of London* without entry.[2] We can only conclude that even if the printing of the *Araygnement* was irregular, it is not suspect.

The title page does not mention Peele's name, but his authorship is established by Nashe's statement in the letter "To the Gentlemen Students," prefaced to Greene's *Menaphon* (1589). Having lavishly praised Spenser, Nashe continues:

Neither is he [Spenser] the onely swallow of our Summer, (although *Apollo*, if his Tripos were up againe, would pronounce him his *Socrates*,) but he being forborne, there are extant about London many most able men to revive Poetry, though it were executed tenne thousand times, as in *Platoes*, so in Puritans Common-wealth; as, namely, for example, *Mathew Roydon, Thomas Achlow*, and *George Peele* . . . and for the last, though not the least of them all, I dare commend him unto all that know him, as the chiefe supporter of pleasance now living, the *Atlas* of Poetrie, and *primus verborum Artifex:* whose first

1. Arber, *3*, 82.
2. Further instances may be noted in Chambers, *4*, appendix L.

increase, the arraignement of *Paris*, might pleade to your opinions his pregnant dexterity of wit, and manifold varietie of invention; wherein (*me iudice*) he goeth a steppe beyond all that
write.[3]

This ascription is corroborated by the appearance of the two lyrics
"Colin's Lament" and "Oenone's Complaint," above the signature
"Geo. Peele" in *England's Helicon* (1600).[4]

The problem of dating the *Araygnement* is complex, and on the
whole the arguments must be inferential. The title page furnishes
the only direct evidence, first in the publication date, 1584,[5] and
second in the reference to the Children of the Chapel. The play,
although by nature a court drama, is nevertheless closely connected
with Peele's university studies. In this respect it is like Marlowe's
Dido, and since some scholars believe that *Dido* was written at
Cambridge before Marlowe came to London,[6] it is possible that
the *Araygnement* was written at Oxford. Decisive evidence is
lacking. As for Peele's dramatic interests during his university
career, we know through Gager's testimony that Peele had translated an *Iphigenia* of Euripides into English,[7] although there is
no evidence in the university records that the play was ever performed. Besides this dramatic effort, Peele's discursive poem *The
Tale of Troy* may reasonably be assigned to the university period.[8]
The subject matter of the poem and of the *Araygnement* suggests
that the two were conceived at the same time. Aside from this

3. *The Works of Thomas Nashe,* ed. R. B. McKerrow (London, 1904–
10), *3,* 323.

4. *EH,* nos. 148, 149, in *1,* 197–198.

5. The play probably could not have been printed before February 2,
1583/4, when Henry Marsh was admitted freeman *per patronagium* in the
Stationers' Company (Arber, *2,* 690).

6. J. Bakeless, *The Tragical History of Christopher Marlowe* (Cambridge, Mass., 1942), *2,* 54–58. F. S. Boas, *Christopher Marlowe* (Oxford,
1940), pp. 49–51.

7. Among Gager's manuscript poems are two in Latin: "In Iphigeniam
Georgii Peeli Anglicanis versibus redditam," and "In eandem." Reprinted in
Horne, pp. 43–45.

8. Horne, pp. 183–202. This poem was appended to *A Farewell to Norris
and Drake,* printed in 1589; however, in the prefatory letter Peele calls
The Tale "an old poem."

conjectural evidence and the fact that between 1579 and 1581 Peele had the leisure to write, there is no reason to believe that the *Araygnement* was written in Oxford. It is more likely that the play was composed between 1581, the date of Peele's arrival in London, and 1584, the publication date of the quarto.

During this period the Children of the Chapel acted at Court six times: February 5, 1580/1, December 31, 1581, February 27, 1581/2, December 26, 1582, January 6, 1583/4, and February 2, 1583/4. On December 26, 1582, the Children of the Chapel performed a "Comodie or Morrall devised on A game of the Cardes"; [9] and the play on February 5, 1580/1, was:

A Storie of ———— . . . whereon was ymployed . . . one citty, one pallace and xviij paire of gloves.[10]

The first of these performances is obviously not the *Araygnement*, and the "citty" and the "pallace" do not fit its stage requirements. Feuillerat has suggested that Lyly's *Campaspe* and *Sapho and Phao* were produced on December 31, 1581, and February 27, 1581/2,[11] but in the light of the warrant for payment to the "Erle of Oxford his servaunts, Johon Lilie" on November 25, 1584, these plays may have been produced January 1 and March 3, 1583/4.[12]

We have little definite information concerning the plays of the season 1581/2; however, the Revels Accounts for the period November 1, 1581, to October 31, 1582, record two or three items of interest. Under "Emptiones and Provicions" there is an entry for "Pearles Spangles fflowers ffrutage and braunches," which suggests the gifts offered by Flora, Pomona, and Sylvanus in I.4.[13] Later entries mention "silke floweres" and "fruytadge" but imply that the "braunches" were "garnishinges for the hall," probably for lighting.[14] A hitherto unnoticed item first appears in the

9. Feuillerat, *Elizabeth*, p. 349.

10. Ibid., p. 336.

11. In *John Lyly, Contribution à l'histoire de la renaissance en Angleterre* (Cambridge, 1910), p. 574.

12. Chambers, 2, 39.

13. Feuillerat, *Elizabeth*, table II. This connection was first noted by Cheffaud (p. 33).

14. Feuillerat, *Elizabeth*, p. 346.

"Declaration of the Charges . . ." under "Tasque work," where John Rose was paid £100 for:

> a Mount with a Castle upon the toppe of it a Dragon and a Artificiall Tree . . .[15]

The "Artificiall Tree," which reappears in the accounts as a "tree with shyldes,"[16] suggests either Juno's *Tree of gold laden with Diadems and Crownes of golde*" (l. 456 SD) or the poplar tree upon which Paris hangs his vows (l. 285).

Assuming that the Children of the Chapel ceased to play in 1582, Cheffaud dated the *Araygnement* in the season of 1581/2, citing for support the evidence of the Revels Accounts.[17] The Children of the Chapel, however, continued to appear in Court until 1584, when the troupe known as the Queen's Players was formed. Fascinating as the items from the Revels Accounts may be, there is no other evidence to support the ascription of the *Araygnement* to either December 31, 1581, or February 27, 1581/2.

On the other hand, biographical evidence seems to indicate that the Children of the Chapel performed the *Araygnement* in 1583/4. In 1582 Peele contributed the last of the prefatory verses to Watson's *Hecatompathia or the Passionate Century of Love*. As Larsen suggests, if Peele had written the *Araygnement* prior to the publication of Watson's volume, he would, in all probability, have preceded such men as Acheley, Downhalus, and Roydon; but since Peele is last, we may assume that he was relatively unknown.[18]

In 1583 Peele was at Oxford, and the Account Books there list two payments to him:

> To *Mr Peele* for provisions for the playes at Christ-churche   xviij li [19]

15. Ibid., table II.

16. Ibid., p. 345.

17. Cheffaud, pp. 32–33. Cf. F. S. Boas, *University Drama in the Tudor Age* (Oxford, 1914), p. 180, and F. G. Fleay, *Biographical Chronicle of the English Drama* (London, 1891), 2, 152.

18. Larsen, p. 296.

19. Dyce 2, 3, vii. Boas notes that this item, communicated by Bliss to Dyce, "is not in the bill of accounts but is doubtless genuine" (*University Drama*, p. 180).

It[e]m the chardges of a Comedye and a Tragedye and a shewe
of fi[r]e works as appeareth by the particular bill[e]s of Mr
Vice Chauncelor Mr Housone Mr Maxie and Mr Pille
lxxxvj li xviij s ij d [20]

The comedy and the tragedy were respectively the *Rivals* and
the *Dido* of Gager, provided for the entertainment of Albertus
Alasco in June 1583.[21] That Peele was summoned from London
suggests that he may have had some previous theatrical experience.
He might have obtained such experience during the London years
for which we have no records, but it is equally possible that the
translation of Euripides praised by Gager was performed at Cambridge. The exact nature of Peele's connection with these performances remains questionable, and he may have been asked
merely because he was a friend of Gager.

One other pertinent fact relating to the date of the *Araygnement*
is its literary relationship to such plays as *Sapho and Phao* and the
lost pastoral *Phyllida and Choryn* played by the Queen's Men on
December 26, 1584.[22] Not only do *Sapho and Phao* and the
Araygnement present a pastoral world involving mythological
characters, but both plays are attempts at royal flattery.[23] Furthermore, it must be noted that the *Araygnement*, as it stands, is
obviously not a play for the public or even the private theaters.
The publication of such a play would normally follow its per-

---

20. A. L[ane] P[oole], "A University Entertainment in 1583," *Oxford
Magazine, 30* (1911–12), 86; first cited by Dyce.

21. Boas, *University Drama*, pp. 179–191.

22. Feuillerat, *Elizabeth*, p. 365.

23. The *Araygnement* is also like Lyly's two plays in that its cast is a
large one: 32 speaking parts and perhaps 19 walk-ons. As might be expected
in a children's play, the number of feminine roles in high, 15. There is in
addition a remarkable demand for musical talents, with double choirs used
in two instances. The play, even with doubling, requires a minimum of 14
or 15 actors plus extras. Lyly's plays demand a similar number. Actors
would have been most available during the last years of the period under
consideration, when the Children of the Chapel were associated with those
of Windsor, Paul's, and the Earl of Oxford (M. C. Bradford, "Silk? Satin?
Kersey? Rags?—The Chorister's Theater under Elizabeth and James,"
Studies in English Literature 1500–1900, 1, 1961, 59–60, and Chambers, *2*,
15–18, 36–37, 63).

formance.[24] It seems probable, therefore, that the court performance was on either January 6 or February 2, 1583/4.[25]

There is some reason to believe, however, that the *Araygnement*
was written somewhat earlier and that the text as it now exists is
a revision of an earlier version. From a purely practical viewpoint
the Children of the Chapel could not have profited much by a
single performance of the play at court. For the two plays produced by the Chapel in the season of 1583/4, the Master was paid
£15,[26] and not much would have remained for the company after
it had paid the playwright for his endeavor. Since the Children of
the Chapel were playing at Blackfriars, it is plausible that the
Araygnement existed in some form suitable for the private theater.
Evidence of the earlier form may perhaps be seen in Ate's prologue,
which promises "the Tragedie of Troie," and in the foreboding
dismissal of Paris from the council of the gods.[27] Moreover, Oenone
disappears at the end of the third act with no dramatic solution. The
nature of the tragedy is uncertain, and it may have been concerned
not with the Troy story in its entirety but merely with the tragic
love affair of Paris and Oenone. The publication of a play still on
the boards may be explained by the closing of the Blackfriars early
in 1584 and by the company's attempt to turn its plays into ready
cash.[28] In any case, the existence of an earlier version of the
Araygnement must remain conjectural until more substantial
evidence can be advanced in its support, and there is no reason
to suppose that the play was not written in its extant form shortly
before its court performance in 1584.

2. SOURCES

The sources of the *Araygnement* lie in a complex of classical and
medieval material. They can be divided into the general categories

24. Such is the case with Peele's Lord Mayor's pageants, and a similar
practice was followed by Churchyard.

25. Child, p. v; C. W. Wallace, *The Evolution of the English Drama*
(Berlin, 1912), pp. 180–181, 209; Larsen, p. 296.

26. Wallace, p. 224.

27. Cf. ll. 979–981, 985, 988–991; also ll. 786–787.

28. A similar reason may explain the publication of Lyly's *Campaspe* and
Sapho and Phao.

of mythology and pastoral, though these classes are not mutually exclusive. It will be convenient to consider the various plot elements separately and to suggest in each case the possible source or sources. The five elements are the judgment of Paris, the arraignment of Paris, the love affair of Paris and Oenone, the pastoral subplot of Colin and Thestilis, and, finally, the presentation of the golden apple to Elizabeth. After determining Peele's classical and medieval sources, we shall consider the relation of the *Araygnement of Paris* to the Italian play *Il Giuditio de Paride*, which Miss V. M. Jeffrey has advanced as the principal source of the *Araygnement*.[1]

Elizabethan interest in the Troy story was not limited to medieval Troy romances or pseudo-historical accounts of the Trojan War. In early miscellanies such as Tottel's or *The Paradise of Dainty Devices*, for example, the Trojan material has become one of the conventions of love poetry. Paris is transformed into a Petrarchan lover; and if Helen is in many poems a second Cressid, in other poems her beauty serves as a foil for that of the poet's lady. Most frequent are the references to the judgment of Paris, for the Elizabethan poetaster often praised his lady by claiming that had she been on Mount Ida, the golden apple would have been her due reward. The constant recurrence of these motifs reveals a familiarity not only with the medieval but also with the classical accounts and further illustrates the Renaissance adaptation of old materials to new conventions.

In classical accounts of the Troy story, the center of interest was the war and the heroes who were immortalized in the conflict. Virgil's epic of Trojan fortunes after the war was augmented by two spurious works that appeared in the period of Roman decadence. The first of these, the *Historia de excidio Trojas*, was attributed to one Dares Phrygius, mentioned by Homer in the *Iliad* (5.9); the other, *Ephemeria belli Trojani*, was supposedly written by Dictys of Crete, a companion of Idomeneus and Merion. Both works championed the Trojan cause and claimed to be eyewitness accounts of the war. Under the influence of Dares and Dictys, medieval writers expanded and embellished the legend until the account of the war was dwarfed in comparison to the treatment given the preceding legendary periods. Having accepted the

1. See list of Short Titles for full reference.

Trojan point of view, medieval authors transformed the legend
into a chivalric romance of warring knights.[2] Within the chivalric
framework, the judgment of Paris was metamorphosed into a
dream vision that came to Sir Paris hunting on a Friday in India.
Occasionally, as in the Harley manuscript of the *Seege or Batayle
of Troye*,[3] the medieval trappings are discarded, but what the
Harley manuscript indicates is less a new tradition than a freedom
in the handling of traditional materials, which also characterizes
Peele's treatment of his mythological material.

Peele's first treatment of the Troy story, his narrative poem the
Tale of Troy, looks back to the medieval histories of the Trojan
War.[4] The *Tale* deals in a cursory manner with the traditional
Troy story, limiting itself to the war and the events immediately
preceding it. Cheffaud traces this material to Ovid's *Metamorphoses*
(13) and *Heroides* (5, 16, 17), noting the incidental influence of
the *Aeneid* and of Dares and Dictys;[5] but Tatlock has shown that
the Ovidian material supplements the accounts given in Caxton's
Recuyell of the Historyes of Troye and Lydgate's *Troy Book*.[6]
Though Peele's poem, like its medieval predecessors, is predominantly chivalric, it significantly introduces the Ovidian fusion of
mythological and pastoral elements into the judgment episode and
into the Paris and Oenone love affair. Moreover, in these sections
the influence of the *Shepheardes Calender* is evident. The archaic
diction is more pronounced here, and Paris becomes the "shepherd's swayne" who beguiles "nymphes and shepherd's trulls." [7]

2. The main ME versions are found in the *Geste Hystoriale of the
Destruction of Troye*, the *Laud Troy Book*, and Caxton's *Recyuell of the
Historyes of Troye*. Although a sixteenth-century translation and much
abbreviated, Thomas Paynell's *The Faythfull and True Storye of the Destruction of Troye* . . . , 1533, might well be included.

3. Ed. M. E. Barnicle, Early English Text Society (OS), 172 (1927),
appendix A, ll. 417–452 and pp. lxviii–lxx.

4. Horne, pp. 183–202.

5. Cheffaud, p. 156.

6. J. S. P. Tatlock, "The Siege of Troy in Elizabethan Literature, Especially in Shakespeare and Heywood," *PMLA*, 30 (1915), 679–682; cf. Larsen,
p. 280. Larsen's study of Peele's early career includes a convenient and
comprehensive study of the sources of the *Tale* and the *Araygnement* and
is the basis for the present discussion.

7. The Spenserian influence was first noted by Dyce in a note to l. 70,

The rejection of the chivalric mode for the pastoral-mythological anticipates Peele's later treatment of the material in the *Araygnement*.

The *Tale* presents an epitome of most of the material found in the *Araygnement*; in fact, as Larsen observes, the *Tale* "reads in part like a first draft" of the play.[8] In recasting this narrative poem for dramatic purposes, Peele develops many details into whole scenes. The suggestion of Flora decking the earth in "yellow, blew and greene" (l. 76) is probably the germ of Flora's descriptive speeches in I.3; and the essential dramatic situation of Paris' chance meeting with the goddesses is already present in the poem (ll. 91–96).

Perhaps the most interesting instance of revision concerns the origin of the apple and the cause of the Trojan War. In the 1589 version of the *Tale* the cause of the war and of Troy's fall is Paris' supposed impartiality; the apple itself was thrown by some "fell furie." Although the allusion to Hecuba's dream in ll. 37–57 implies that Paris is predestined to destroy Troy, the concept of fate and destiny is only vaguely defined in the poem. In the *Araygnement*, however, Ate, as Prologue, announces that Troy must fall "so bidde the gods above," since Tellus has complained to them of the earth's overpopulation. Paris is thus destined to be the organ of that destruction, and the fall of Troy is decreed even before the judgment. H. M. Dowling contends that the play confuses the issue here by the introduction of Tellus, who appears to be "the more essential cause."[9] It would seem that Peele is merely developing the situation implicit in the original version of the *Tale*. Although he draws upon the usual Renaissance mythographers, the identification of the "fell furie" with Ate is seemingly Peele's invention, and the introduction of Tellus is a logical extension of the myth to explain Ate's action.[10] Peele's extension complicates the

which parallels l. 36 of the April Eclogue (Bullen, *2*, 244); cf. Larsen, p. 285. It is possible that the archaisms that Larsen notes reflect Caxton or Lydgate, but the presence of pastoral elements strengthens the case for a direct Spenserian influence.

8. Larsen, p. 294.

9. "Miscellaneous Notes on Peele," *Notes and Queries, 165* (1933), 273.

10. J. D. Reeves, "The Cause of the Trojan War," *Notes and Queries,* n.s. *2* (1955), 333, notes that the suggestion for such an extension may have

myth, but it does not necessarily confuse it, as Dowling argues. Peele is uninterested in the tragic implications of the myth, and his development of the details is essentially decorative. Such revisions suggest Peele's interest in the classical-mythological as opposed to the medieval-chivalric tradition.

When we turn to the *Araygnement*, the variations between the play and the medieval accounts of the judgment story are perhaps best explained by referring to classical treatments of the episode. Paris' judgment is only alluded to in the *Iliad* (24.25–30) and the *Aeneid* (1.25–28); and, though in Euripides the references are more frequent,[11] they are still allusions. These allusions differ fundamentally from the medieval accounts in that Paris is a herdsman, and the first major treatment establishes the incident in a pastoral setting. Lucian, who devotes an entire dialogue to the story,[12] presents Mercury taking the golden apple to the herdsman Paris because Zeus cannot honestly or expediently resolve the quarrel. In the course of the debate Paris demurs because of his rustic background. The dialogue attempts some differentiation among the characters, and the quibbling of the goddesses suggests the quibbling found in II.1, of the *Araygnement*. The tone of the dialogue, at times almost flippant in its satire, is also closer to the *Araygnement* than to the medieval accounts.

The judgment incident is also referred to in Ovid's *Heroides*, where Paris gives a full account in his letter to Helen.[13] This version is basically the same as Lucian's, with additional emphasis on

come from Euripides, who twice (*Orestes*, ll. 1639–42 and *Helen*, ll. 36–40) attributes the cause of the war to the desire to relieve the earth's overpopulation.

11. *Hecuba*, ll. 643–645; *Andromacha*, ll. 262–302; *Iphigenia at Aulis*, ll. 1282–1310; *Helen*, ll. 23–30. Since Peele had translated one of the *Iphigenias*, there is a good possibility that he was familiar with the plays as a whole; cf. A. H. Gilbert, "The Source of Peele's *Arraignment of Paris*," *Modern Language Notes*, 41 (1926), 39.

12. "The Judgement of the Goddesses," *Lucian*, ed. A. M. Harmon (Loeb Library, London, 1921), 3.384–409. Lucian's influence was first noted by Cheffaud, p. 39.

13. *Heroides*, ed. G. Showerman (Loeb Library, London, 1921), V (Oenone to Paris), ll. 33–38; XVII (Helen to Paris), ll. 115–118, cf. ll. 131–134; XVI (Paris to Helen), ll. 53–88, 165–168.

the pastoral setting; however, the satiric elements and the quibbling of the goddesses are omitted.

Perhaps the most interesting of the classical accounts is that found in Apuleius' *Golden Ass*.[14] Here the story of the judgment is seen as a brilliant ballet or masque. The scene opens on Mount Ida with Paris tending a flock of goats. Mercury enters, bringing with him the golden apple and the three goddesses. Juno is accompanied by Castor and Pollux, and she offers to make Paris lord of all Asia. Attended by two young men, Terror and Fear, Pallas promises to make Paris strong and victorious. Finally, Venus, surrounded by little cupids and a multitude of fair maidens representing the Graces and the Seasons, promises the fairest maiden as a reward. As Cheffaud points out, the important additions are the attendants of each goddess, who suggest the "showes" of the *Araygnements*.[15]

In most classical accounts of the judgment story the basic episode is the same: Mercury brings the goddesses to the herdsman Paris, and the goddesses offer their gifts of empire, victory, and the fairest spouse or Helen. In this respect there is little difference between the medieval and the classical traditions, though the classical accounts make no mention of the feast at which the apple was found, and the bribe Pallas offers is victory rather than wisdom. The most essential difference is a matter of treatment, mythological as opposed to chivalric. It must be said that no one of the accounts, classical or medieval, is the source of the *Araygnement;* but if both traditions are evident, as in Peele's handling of Pallas, *The Araygnement of Paris* is closer to the classical than to the medieval.

While there are numerous treatments of the judgment episode, the idea of the arraignment of Paris before a council of the gods is generally attributed to Peele. The council motif is, of course, traditional; and in the anonymous play *The Rare Triumphs of Love and Fortune* (ca. 1582) it had already been put to dramatic use. Both the *Araygnement* and the *Rare Triumphs*, however, draw upon a

14. Trans. William Aldington (1566), ed. T. Seccombe (London, 1913), Bk. X, chap. XLVI, pp. 250–253.
15. Cheffaud, p. 39.

larger tradition. The council motif was common in eulogistic verse, and in the poetry of the period there was a tradition of "arraignment" poems. Undoubtedly, the tradition stems from Petrarch's *canzone* "Quell' antique mio dolce empio Signore," where the poet brings suit against Love in the court of reason.[16] Petrarch's *canzone* was translated by Wyatt, and the arraignment poem became a conventional variant of the lover's complaint to his lady. The arraignment episode in Peele's play is therefore not an invention but rather an adaptation of a literary tradition for dramatic purposes.

It is possible that Peele took some hints for this episode from Lucian's dialogue. Although the tone has changed and Jove is no longer in control of the situation, there is some suggestion of Lucian's portrayal of Zeus as the unwilling judge. Furthermore, some of the details and arguments in Paris' defense are similar to those in Lucian's account. Both shepherds object to being chosen judge on the ground that they are herdsmen, and both argue that if they err it is because their sight is at fault.[17] Beyond these similarities there seems to be little else that can be traced to any specific source. Once the idea of the arraignment was conceived, however, traditional accounts would have furnished adequate materials for its development.

The Oenone story is not mentioned in Homer, Euripides, Apuleius, Lydgate, or Caxton, and there is only an allusion to Oenone in Lucian's dialogue, where Mercury refers to her as "a woman from Mount Ida, well enough, but countrified and unsophisticated." [18] The basic story of Oenone and Paris rests ultimately upon Ovid's fifth epistle in the *Heroides*, in which Oenone recalls their earlier life on Mount Ida and laments Paris' infidelity. While the account in the *Araygnement* is prior in narrative time to that of the *Heroides*, Oenone's recollection of the earlier days furnishes Peele's fundamental situation. There is a difference, however, between the Ovidian story and that which appears in the *Araygnement:* in Ovid, Oenone is Paris' wife; in the *Araygnement* she is his love. Peele is probably responsible for this alteration of the myth since

16. *Sonnets and Songs,* ed. A. M. Armi (New York, 1946), pp. 500–508.
17. Cf. *Lucian,* p. 395, and the *Araygnement,* ll. 913–918; *Lucian,* p. 397 and the *Araygnement,* ll. 873–878, 893, 897, 898–899.
18. *Lucian,* p. 387.

Turberville's translation of the *Heroides* preserves the marital relationship found in Ovid,[19] and Cooper's *Thesaurus* merely cites Oenone as Paris' "concubine." Peele's changes result from the adaptation of the story to the love conventions of the pastoral; and the Oenone story is a good example of Peele's method: given the narrative account in Ovid, he has created a dramatic situation in a new convention.

Besides the Paris-Oenone episode, Peele introduces a second pastoral element in the Colin-Thestilis love affair. While this affair's pastoral nature allies it to a wide literary tradition, the use of the same pastoral names as in the *Shepheardes Calender* suggests the *Calender* as a possible source. Cheffaud notes the similarity of "Colin's Lament" and the "Argument" to Spenser's January Eclogue, where "Colin Cloute a shepheardes boy complaineth him of his unfortunate love." [20] Although there is a striking similarity in the two situations, apart from the common pastoral theme of unrequited love, their authors treat them differently. Unlike the *Shepheardes Calender*, Peele's poetry reflects the diction and tone of the early sonneteers. In the *Araygnement* a Petrarchan Colin addresses "gentle love" and ends by dying at the feet of Venus; Spenser's Colin, on the other hand, seems more rustic. Peele's specific debt to Spenser is further lessened by the fact that the pastoral names he popularized were drawn from Virgil, Mantuan, and other writers. This is not to deny Peele's knowledge of the *Calender*, for there are distinct echoes of it in the play; but, while it is possible that "in the pastoral scenes of this play we have the *Shepheardes Calender* dramatized," [21] it seems more probable that Peele's debt to Spenser's pastoral is general rather than specific.

In Act V, by a neat twist of the myth, Peele turns the entire play into a compliment to Queen Elizabeth. It is generally recognized that this twist was not Peele's own invention; in fact, the

19. G. Turberville, *The Heroycall Epistles*, ed. F. S. Boas (London, 1928). Turberville retains Ovid's basic relationships, though even in his translation the trend toward pastoral love conventions is present.

20. Cheffaud, p. 41.

21. Larsen, p. 300. Both Malone's belief that Colin was a portrait of Spenser (*Life and Works of Shakespeare*, London, 1821, 2, 249) and Fleay's interpretation of the play as court allegory (*Biographical Chronicle*, 1, 152) seem unfounded; cf. Larsen, p. 305, n. 131.

presentation of the golden apple to the Queen and the resolution of
the judgment story by this means is a commonplace of Renaissance
flattery. The motif had an illustrious career even before Elizabeth's
reign. T. S. Graves notes that the motif appears in a pageant cele-
brating the marriage of Henry VII's daughter to James IV of Scotland and again in a pageant for Ann Boleyn's coronation.[22] The
judgment motif also appears in a masque at the wedding of Fran-
ces, daughter of Henry Ratcliffe, Lord Fitzwaller and Earle of
Sussex, to Mr. Myldwaye of Lincoln's Inn, in June 1566.[23] Besides
these dramatic presentations, the theme was reiterated in contemporary art and poetry. Miss Jeffrey notes the occurrence of the
compliment in Ariosto,[24] and the theme again appears in Gascoigne's manuscript poem "The vanities of Bewtie." [25] While several scholars have advanced one or another of these pageants and
poems as the source of Peele's compliment, the frequency and
diversity of the theme indicate that the theme was a traditional
mode of compliment.[26]

The preceding survey of sources for individual plot elements
clearly illustrates the essential eclecticism of the *Araygnement*, for
no one source includes all the elements. It is possible to recognize
Ovid, Lucian, and Apuleius in the judgment story, to trace the
Oenone-Paris episode to Ovid, to cite Spenserian influence in the
pastoral subplot, and to point out the conventionality of the presentation scene. Yet there is always a fundamental difference in

22. "*The Arraignment of Paris* and Sixteenth Century Flattery," *Modern
Language Notes*, 28 (1913), 49.

23. Bodlian MS Rawl. Poet. 108, transcribed in the *Britisher Bibliographer*,
ed. E. Brydges and J. Haslewood (London, 1812), 2, 612–617.

24. *Orlando Furioso*, ll. 70 (Jeffrey, p. 176, n. 2).

25. *The Grief of Joye* in *The Complete Works of George Gascoigne*, ed.
J. W. Cunliffe (Cambridge, 1910), 2, 526; cf. F. E. Schelling, "The Source
of the 'Arraignment of Paris,'" *Modern Language Notes*, 8 (1893), 103–
104.

26. I. Ekeblad, "On the Background of Peele's *Araygnement*," *Notes and
Queries*, n.s. 3 (1956), 246–249. J. D. Reeves, "The Judgment of Paris as
a Device of Tudor Flattery," ibid., 2 (1954), 7–11. E. C. Wilson suggests a
further development of the theme, where the contention is no longer for
the apple but for the Queen herself; Lyly's Latin poem "Jovis Elizabeth" is
perhaps the model for this type (*England's Eliza*, Cambridge, Mass., 1939,
p. 238).

Peele's treatment of the materials. The difference lies ultimately in the combination of the elements into an integrated plot and perhaps more specifically in the Renaissance tendency toward independent mythologizing.

The appearance of the compliment motif in pageants and a masque, noted above, suggests that Peele was not the first to use the judgment story for dramatic purposes. There are scattered references to continental plays based on the same material;[27] and in her study of the relations between Italian and Elizabethan drama Miss Jeffrey discovered a trilogy of plays on the Trojan War by a little-known playwright, Anello Paulilli.[28] The first of these plays, *Il Giuditio di Paride*, deals with the judgment story and introduces pastoral elements into the classical story. Although Miss Jeffrey argues that the play is the source of the *Araygnement*, there are serious objections. In the first place, *Il Giuditio* is a minor play of a practically unknown dramatist; and, while it is not impossible that Peele might have read the play, it is highly improbable. Secondly, there are fundamental differences in structure and situations between the two plays, and their similarities in diction and content may more easily be explained by the use of common sources and traditions.

Although *Il Giuditio* is the first play of a trilogy, Paulilli attempted to give it a unity of its own. Its climax is of course the judgment; but because Paulilli has chosen to follow the principles of Senecan structure, he is faced with a paucity of material to fill

27. In *Das Geschichte des Neueren Dramas* (Halle, 1893–1923), W. Creizenach notes the following continental plays: *Paris von Troja und die drie Gotterinnin* in 1455 at the Lubecker Fastnachtsspiele (*1*, 426); Jacob Locher's *Judicum Paradis* in 1522 at Ingolstadt and Krakau (*2*, 40–41, 88); and Hans Sachs' *Das Judicum Paradis* in 1532 (*3*, 417 ff.). Another play on the subject was performed in Brittany in 1505 on the visit of Queen Anne of France (A. Le Braz, *Essai sur l'histoire du Théâtre Celtique*, Paris, 1904, p. 262).

28. Paulilli was evidently a Neopolitan lawyer whose only literary work was this trilogy, which appeared with the following title page: IL GIVDITIO / DI PARIDE. / TRAGICOMEDIA. / A cui sieque l'altra del Ratto d'Helena, con / la Tragedia dell' Incendio di Troia. / DI ANELLO PAVLILLI NAP. / SECUNDO L'ANTICHE FAVOLE. / . . . Con Priuilegio per anni diece. / IN NAPOLI. / Appresso Gio. Maria Scotto, *1566*.

the first four acts. In Act I the problem is stated in the dialogue between Jove and Peleus, at whose ill-fated feast the apple was thrown; and a solution is proposed by Jove. In Act II the suggested action is undertaken, but since this action will bring about the climax, Paulilli must of necessity introduce a subplot to fill the space. Thus in Act II the pastoral plot of the happy lovers is interpolated into the main action and brought to one stage of completion in the disclosure of lovers' identity. Act III, while it introduces the protagonist, does not advance the main plot; instead the pastoral plot is complicated by the addition of the disdained lover and resolved with the final union of the happy lovers. The entrance of the goddesses in Act IV brings the climax nearer, but the greater part of the act is concerned with the foreboding soliloquy of Peleus, Paris' dream, and the Second Shepherd's ironic hymn of joy. The weakness of this structure is apparent, for there is no real action outside of the judgment in the main plot. Moreover, the pastoral subplot is only tenuously connected with the main plot—by means of the master-servant relationship of Paris and the shepherds. Finally, the presentation of the apple to Clarice is an epilogue and remains unconnected with the play.

There is obviously a fundamental difference between *Il Giuditio* and the *Araygnement* from the point of view of structure. As we shall see in the following section, the *Araygnement* is primarily an expository play on the theme of beauty, and the narrative plot is subordinate to the exposition. Furthermore, Peele has chosen to incorporate the compliment into the play and to make it the resolution of the conflict. The situations also are different from those in Paulilli. For example, by allowing the goddesses to discover the apple and to elect Paris as their judge, Peele has seriously modified Jove's role as the controlling agent, and at the same time he has tightened the inciting action by ignoring Peleus and his ill-fated feast. Peele further tightens the plot by making Paris one of the lovers and by using the pastoral subplot of Colin and Thestilis as a counterpoint to the love affair of Paris and Oenone.

Although Miss Jeffrey cites a number of specific parallels between the pastoral triangle which forms the subplot of Paulilli's play and the *Araygnement*, her parallels seem inconclusive.[29] Her

29. Jeffrey, p. 177.

contention that the dumb show of Thestilis and the "croked churl" has its exact counterpart in Italian popular drama does not demonstrate Peele's dependence upon *Il Giuditio*. Moreover, the plays are often similar because they draw upon widely used conventions. The appearance of singing matches in both seems natural for pastoral drama, and that Oenone's catalogue of mythological stories should recall the mythological riddles of Flori and Florido is not unexpected.[30] There is no reason to assume that Peele must have known this play in order to have introduced a pastoral subplot; as Gilbert emphasizes, the judgment of Paris is a "ready-made pastoral," and the portrayal of Oenone and Paris as happy lovers is an inherent feature of the mythological story told by Ovid.[31] It may be said that the pastoral plots of the *Il Giuditio* are fundamentally dissimilar from those in the *Araygnement*.

Even if it could be granted to Miss Jeffrey that the pastoral plots were directly related, her arguments concerning the judgment and presentation scenes are weak. The parallel passages that she quotes are indeed reminiscent of each other, but the resemblance probably owes more to the use of common sources than to Peele's knowledge of the Italian play. In fact Peele is much closer to the classical sources than he is to Paulilli. Finally, the presentation of the apple to Clarice is but another example of the traditional motif discussed earlier. To claim this similarity between Peele and Paulilli is to disregard Peele's more obvious sources.

To deny Peele's knowledge of *Il Giuditio* does not, of course, deny his knowledge of Italian or of Italian traditions, for Peele owes much, directly or indirectly, to the Italian theater. Nevertheless the sources of the *Araygnement* are predominantly classical; Lucian, Apuleius, and Ovid provided the basic materials from which Peele created his play. This strong classical influence is not surprising, for training in both secondary school and university was primarily classical. At Christ's Hospital, Peele undoubtedly read Ovid among other Latin authors, and at Oxford he would have become familiar with both Greek and Latin works. That he used the classics in his first play is but another manifestation of the

30. Larsen, p. 302.

31. A. H. Gilbert, "The Source of Peele's *Arraignment of Paris*," *Modern Language Notes, 41* (1926), 36.

Renaissance interest in the classics; and, as we shall see in the next section, the classical elements in the *Araygnement* link it to contemporary dramatic developments.

3. DRAMATIC TRADITION

When Peele returned to London in 1581 after his university career, he found a lively and growing interest in drama. This interest was not new, for its roots reached back into the early years of the century. Even a cursory survey of the relevant documents reveals more dramatic activity than is often recognized. As early as 1549 items occur in the Minutes of the Aldermen's Court in London prohibiting plays, and in 1569 the City went so far as to issue a general precept prohibiting innkeepers, tablekeepers, taverners, hallkeepers, and brewers from sponsoring, either openly or privately, "any mannour of stage play, enterlude, or other disguising whatsoever" in their mansion houses, yards, courts, gardens, orchards, or other places.[1] This was seven years before the building of The Theater; and when not only The Theater but The Curtain and the first Blackfriars were built or converted in the late seventies specifically for dramatic performances, we have clear indication of the demand for theatrical entertainment of whatever quality. Moreover, the continual chorus of criticism from pulpit and pamphlet serves to support the other documentary evidence. John Stockwood's sermon at Paul's Cross (1578) attacking filthy plays and bawdy interludes as well as less dramatic entertainments may be puritanical, but his reference to "eight ordinarie places in the Citie" playing at least once and sometimes two and three times a week indicates contemporary interest in the theater.[2] A reading of the Revels Accounts and Court records reveals similar interests at court. We must see the *Araygnement of Paris* in relation to this growth of dramatic interest and to the corresponding growth of the drama itself.

Although the dramatic activity of the period was widespread, we must recognize and differentiate its various aspects. In *Shakespeare and the Rival Traditions* Harbage defines two vital dramatic

1. Chambers, *4*, 267.
2. Ibid., p. 200.

traditions: one was popular and stretched back to medieval drama; the other, growing out of the interludes of the early Tudors, was essentially private.[3] The establishment of the first Blackfriars in 1576, the same year as the erection of The Theater, emphasizes the distinction between private and public drama. The enclosed theater of the Blackfriars called for methods of production different from those used at the public theaters, and the higher admission fees created a specialized audience that demanded a somewhat different dramatic fare. The differentiation between private and public theaters is probably much older than existing records show. The use of Trinity Hall for theatrical performances during 1557–68 suggests an earlier adventure in private theater, and the activity of Paul's Boys and the Children of the Chapel warrants the assumption that theatrical facilities were available to them for production.[4] If these two traditions existed side by side, the Court served as a meeting place where both were received. In the early years of Elizabeth's reign, the children's companies predominated; in the latter years the adult companies had the lion's share of court performances. Neither performed to the exclusion of the other at any time. Moreover, the Court fostered its own dramatic tradition in masques and pageants. Although Peele's *Araygnement* was played by the Children of the Chapel and reflects the traditions of the private theaters, it combined this heritage with the court traditions and developed both in its own manner.

This combination and its particular elements deserve more detailed comment, for part of the historical importance and artistic achievement of the *Araygnement* lies in its synthesis. The pastoral motif of the play reflects the contemporary interest in the pastoral,

3. Harbage's study of the "rival traditions" (New York, 1952) has been supported by D. M. Bevington's study of "the growth and structure of popular drama in Tudor England," *From Mankind to Marlowe* (Cambridge, Mass., 1962). Bevington demonstrates the existence of a repertory of popular plays whose structure can be clearly differentiated from that of the private theater plays. Whether the Tudor interludes were entirely the product of a private theater movement is perhaps debatable in the light of Rastell's stage in Finnsbury Fields, but Rastell's stage may have been an outside private theater.

4. C. T. Prouty, "An Early Elizabethan Playhouse," *Shakespeare Survey*, 6 (1953), 64–67; and Harbage, pp. 30–41.

both dramatic and nondramatic. Likewise, the mythological and classical subject matter is not new but currently popular. The use of masque materials and techniques is firmly based on court traditions. Finally, the quasi-intellectual quality of the play, its questioning of the nature of beauty, is related to the more serious didactic interests of the earlier moralities and interludes. What is new in the *Araygnement* (as well as in Lyly's *Sapho and Phao* and, to an extent, *Campaspe*) is the combination of these elements, which marks the emergence of a new form of drama, the pastoral comedy of ideas. While such a form did not exclude other drama from the court stage or seriously invade the public theaters, during the eighties it did achieve a notable popularity both at the Court and in the private theaters.

One of pastoral drama's fundamental problems is its definition. W. W. Greg defines it in terms of Tasso's *Aminta* and Guarini's *Pastor Fido* and their dramatization of the theme of unrequited love.[5] In neither Tasso nor Guarini do we have actual deities or mythological characters although a satyr appears in *Pastor Fido*. Instead we have their derivatives in the oracles, romantic shepherdesses, and huntresses. In those plays the subject is strictly limited to the theme of unrequited love treated as tragicomedy; chasity and lust are repudiated and the thematic pattern ends in marriage.

If pastoral drama is defined by Tasso and Guarini, it is difficult to explain the widespread use of the term "pastoral." For example, the *Araygnement* is called a "pastorall" on its title page although only one act is concerned with shepherds and their loves; and on the title page of Lyly's *Loves Metamorphoses* that play is described as "a wittie and courtly pastorall." Greg's definition by subject matter is too limiting, for pastoralism is not merely the presence of shepherds in an idealized world talking about love. The essential element is indeed an Arcadian existence outside of reality, but this world is not defined with any exactitude.

As Cheffaud points out, the fundamental relationship of the pastoral world to Ovid's *Metamorphoses* and to the classical concept

5. In *Pastoral Poetry and Pastoral Drama* (London, 1906) Greg traces the development of Italian pastoral drama from the dramatic eclogue, the *sacre representzsione,* and the Arcadian romance.

of the Golden Age cannot be overlooked.[6] The pastoral shepherds
are basically sylvan gods, and the chaste women of the later pastorals are no more than the chaste nymphs of Diana. Any analysis
of the pastoral world leads ultimately to familiar mythological
types. What is suggested by such a relationship is that both mythological and pastoral worlds may have been used for similar purposes.

Citing Guarini, who uses "pastoral" as an adjective rather than a
noun, J. H. Summerell suggests that, strictly speaking, there is no
pastoral genre; the term merely defines a setting. What does characterize pastoral literature is its intent "to affirm by means of its
pastoral elements the validity of the pastoral ideal." [7] To define that
ideal solely in terms of the theme of unrequited love or of the blessings of humility and contentment seems questionable, however;
pastoralism is also a way of embodying the Platonic idealism which
underlies the Renaissance world view. In Edmund Bolton's "The-
orello: a Sheepheards Edillion," [8] for example, the lady Cosma,
who is celebrated in the song, comes to symbolize the ordered
world which lies behind the surface reality, and the shepherd's
love is the love of order. In the opening stanza Bolton establishes
the relation between the pastoral vision of order and coherence and
the complexities of reality by comparing the shepherds who sit on
their hillocks to princes sitting on their thrones. In such a poem
the pastoral mode is a means of fitting the complexities of real life
into an aesthetic perspective. Whether the artist satirically contrasts real conditions with the ideal or seeks to mirror the real in
the ideal, the characteristic features of pastoral literature are its
idealized Arcadian world and its affirmation of an idealistic view of
life. Defined thus, pastoral poetry is perhaps only a variation of
mythological poetry; both are symbolic representations.

English pastoral drama developed through experimentation,
which combined traditional elements into new forms that were
then subject to further adaptation. Although Greg argues for an
independent development in England parallel to that of Italy, it

6. Cheffaud, pp. 45–46.
7. J. H. Summerell, "Backgrounds of Elizabethan Pastoral Drama" (dissertation, Columbia University, 1958), p. 244.
8. *EH, 1*, 9–12.

seems evident that England knew the Italian tradition and was probably influenced by it.[9] Travel on the Continent was common, and Gascoigne in his dedication to *The Tale of Hemetes the Here-myte* refers to the ease with which Italian could be learned in London. The Revels Accounts record payments to the Italian actors who followed the Queen's progress in 1574 and "made pastyme fyrst at Wynsor and afterwardes at Reading." Interestingly enough, the performance at Reading was clearly pastoral, as the properties listed in the Revels Accounts indicate.[10] Another Italian play was presented before the Privy Council at Durham Place in April 1577,[11] and on January 13 the Privy Council issued a memorandum to the Lord Mayor permitting "one Drousiano, an Italian, a commediante and companye" to play in London.[12] Determining the extent of Italian influence is difficult, but to claim that the English pastoral is a mere importation is to overlook the evidence of a native tradition. There is undoubtedly an ultimate and general debt to Italian tradition, and the subsequent development of the genre in England is not unrelated to the Italian development.

As in Italy, experiments with pastoral elements appeared early in England. Rustic lovers are traditional, and rustic settings are used in May games and wooing songs. Drawing their themes from the medieval *pastourelle*, the songs and games often involve dialogue and elementary intrigue plots.[13] It is debatable how fre-

9. Jeffrey, pp. 56–62, 175–187, 435–444; A. H. Thorndike, "The Pastoral Element in English Drama before 1605," *Modern Language Notes, 14* (1899), 118.

10. Feuillerat, *Elizabeth*, p. 225.

11. Chambers, *2*, 262; *4*, appendix A, 93. Chambers also notes (*2*, 264) that payment was made to Alfruso Ferrabolle for a play on February 22, 1576. "Alfruso Ferrabolle" is probably a clerical error for Alfonso Ferrabosco, who contributed intermittently to court activities.

12. As Miss Jeffrey points out (p. 61), Catherine de Medici had summoned to Paris in 1576 an Italian Company known as the "comici gelosi." This company, headed by Drusiano Martinelli, had performed Tasso's *Aminta* at its premiere in Ferrara. If the Privy Council's "Drusiano" is Martinelli, it is possible that England may have seen the *Aminta* in the original.

13. C. R. Baskervill, "Some Evidences for Early Romantic Plays in England," *Modern Philology, 14* (1916–17), 229–251, 467–528.

quently these works became formal drama and whether we are dealing with pastoralism or merely with rusticity. In the masques and entertainments produced during royal progresses, there is clearer evidence of mythological and pastoral motifs; and it is in these traditions that the dramatic potential of pastoralism was developed.

Essentially the masque was an amateur performance done in disguise for the purpose of entertainment. At times it was a mere pretext for dancing; at other times the masque functioned as the setting for a complimentary speech or gift. Originally mere pageantry, the masque often became something more than a spectacular show. The masque poems of John Lydgate suggest the transition.[14] Two of his six "devyces for disguysings" are in the *debat* tradition; dramatically they present a single idea and achieve thematic unity. The other four "mommynges" are pageants explained by a Presentor or Trunchman. These poems may be taken as the norm for fifteenth-century masquing, with its diverse elements of dancing, pageantry, and simple dramatic action or representation through monologue or dialogue.

The famous festivities at the wedding of Prince Arthur and Catherine of Aragon in 1501 reveal both the variety and the dramatic possibilities of the masque: on "the Fryeday at Night after the first Justs Royall" three great pageants were wheeled into Westminster Hall. The first, drawn by four beasts, was a castle inhabited by eight ladies; the second was a ship and its mariners who brought Hope and Desire to the castle as ambassadors from eight knights of the Mount of Love which was the third pageant. When their ambassadors were disdainfully dismissed, the knights assaulted the castle; the ladies readily capitulated and danced with the knights. John Leland records that "the Masters of the Shippe and their Company, in ther Counteynaunces, Speeches, and Demeanor, used and behaved themselves after the Manner and Guyse of Mariners . . ." which suggests the development of a dramatic situation. The later masques of these festivities were less spectacular; on the following Sunday the pageants represented an arbor

14. R. Brotanek, *Die Englischen Maskenspiele* (Vienna and Leipzig, 1902), p. 309; E. P. Hammond, "Lydgate's Mumming at Hertford," *Anglia*, 22 (1899), 364–374.

and a lanthorn and on Tuesday two mountains. The festivities
were concluded on the second Sunday with a masque whose pageant wagon was "a glorious Towre or Tabernacle made like a
goodly Chapell." [15] These masques range from the occasional
achievement of simple dramatic form to mere pageantry and dancing.

Throughout its career the masque retained a large degree of flex-
ibility and encouraged innovation, though at no time were the
earlier forms discarded: new and old simply existed side by side.
Similarly, although themes and materials from medieval dream and
court-of-love allegories remained popular well into the reign of Elizabeth, new subject matter appeared. The Revels Accounts for the
reigns of Edward and Mary reveal an increasing interest in mythical and classical subjects. In 1551/2 there was a masque of Amazons
and one of Argus, in 1552/3 a masque of the Women of Diana and
a masque of "covetuous" men with satyrs for torchbearers, in 1553
a masque of Greek Worthies, in 1554 a masque of Hercules, and
in 1554/5 a masque of "Venusses" and Cupids.[16] There was a
concurrent interest in masques portraying people of other countries, Almains, Polanders, Venetians, etc. Though characters from
various trades and social classes were used, they usually appeared
as torchbearers. In only one instance was a masque concerned with
allegorical figures: in 1553 a masque of "medioxes being half
deathe, half man" was produced for the Easter or the May Day
revels.[17]

Perhaps the most interesting Elizabethan masques from a dramatic viewpoint are those designed in anticipation of the meeting
between Queen Elizabeth and Mary Queen of Scots at Nottingham
in 1562. Although the meeting was canceled and the masques never
performed, a description of the proposed masques is preserved
among the Burghley papers.[18] On the first night False Report and
Discord were to be put in the prison of Extreme Oblivion by Tem-

15. E. Hall, *The union of the two noble and illustre famelies York and
Lancaster 1542*, ed. C. Whibley (London, 1904), *1*, 57.

16. Feuillerat, *Edward*, pp. xii–xv.

17. Ibid., p. 145.

18. "Dramatic Records from the Lansdowne Manuscripts," ed. W. W.
Greg and E. K. Chambers, Malone Society, *Collections, 1* (1908), 144–148.

perance and Prudence, aided by the goddess Pallas. On the second night Peace, in a chariot drawn by an elephant, was to be presented by Friendship at the castle called the Court of Plenty as a companion to Temperance and Prudence. Finally, on the third night Disdain, riding a wild boar and accompanied by Malice "in the similitude of a great serpent," was to attempt the rescue of False Report and Discord. Valiant Courage, otherwise known as Hercules, was to give battle and, aided by Discretion, to kill Malice and force Disdain to flee. This extended entertainment appears at first glance to be merely another moral interlude on a political theme, but actually it is a series of masques in which the allegorical or mythological characters Pallas, Friendship, and Discretion act as presenters. The action described by them is performed in pantomime by the main characters. The masquers or dancers who accompany each of the main characters have no real part in the play itself, but after the action is completed they take out the Scotch nobility and introduce the usual period of dancing and gallantry. As Miss Welsford notes, the weakness of the entertainment as drama lies in its failure to make the masquers an integral part of the performance.[19] This combination of morality play and masque is significant not only for its dramatic quality but also for the ease with which disparate elements could be combined into a single entertainment without straining the imagination of the audience.

A similar amalgam is represented in George Ferrers' triumph or "play of cupid" presented as part of the Twelfth Day revels in 1552/3. In this "play" Venus enters in a triumphal chair with a masque of ladies seeking to rescue Cupid from the Lord Marshall with his band of men. With her come Mars and his attendants. In one of the letters concerning the preparation of the entertainment, Ferrers writes that Ydelnes and Dalyaunce are to be "two Ladies straungely attyred"; and it is probable that these two abstractions were two of Venus' attendants.[20] Allegorical and mythological elements are combined here to produce some sort of mock combat.

In the masques we have considered thus far we have not encountered the Arcadian world of the pastoral. While the Arcadian world is not unrelated to the bowers and gardens of love found in

19. E. Welsford, *The Court Masque* (Cambridge, 1937), p. 154.
20. Feuillerat, *Edward*, pp. 93–94.

the early masques, there is an essential difference. In the masques we have the garden of the *Romance of the Rose* although the various mounts used in the Tudor revels suggest mythological sources. When we turn to consider the entertainments produced during the Queen's progresses, we find the pastoral elements coming to the fore. One reason for this undoubtedly lies in the outdoor nature of these entertainments. At Kenilworth the Queen was greeted with speeches by Sibylla, Hercules, and the Lady of the Lake. Later the Queen heard an outdoor dialogue between a Savage Man and Echo, but the highlight of the entertainment was an aquatic show portraying the delivery of the Lady of the Lake.[21] A similar water show was produced at Elvetham in 1591 where Silvanus, Neptune, Nereus and others delivered gifts to the Queen. At Elvetham the Queen also witnessed early morning pastorals, in one Phyllida and Corydon sang a pastoral song, in another Aureola and her fairies danced.[22]

The pastoral nature of these devices goes beyond setting and characters, for the themes and conventions that we noted in the Italian pastoral reappear here. The chastity motif was a common one; it was used as a compliment to Elizabeth, or it was contrasted with marital bliss in order to induce the Queen to marry. Other pastoral conventions such as the singing match, unrequited love, and rustic wooing scenes appear frequently. By 1560 the Arcadian world with its mixture of allegorical, mythical, and rustic characters had become a part of the English tradition of court entertainment.

The pastoral elements we have noted in the masque and country entertainments are also present in the early drama. In *Sir Clyomon and Sir Clamydes* Neronis in her grief over the supposed death of Clyomon wanders into the company of the shepherd Corin. Her rustic adventure remains, however, within the context of the romance, and the rustic world of the play is not the Arcadian world of the pastoral. The "pastorell or historie of a Greeke maide" per-

21. G. Gascoigne, *The Princelye Pleasures, at Kennelwoorth Castle* in *Complete Works*, 2, 91–131.

22. *The Honorable Entertainment . . . at Elvetham in Hampshire, 1591,* in J. Nichols, *Progresses and Public Processions of Queen Elizabeth* (London, 1788), 2, 91–131.

formed at Richmond by the Earl of Leicester's men in 1578/9 [23] and the enigmatic "lusus pastorales newly compyled" recorded in the Stationers' Register for 1565/6 [24] suggest that the pastoral had invaded the popular stage. The existence of such plays helps explain Munday's comment about "wanton wives fables and pastorical songes of love." [25]

The mythological elements popular in the masque were also present in early drama. Classical allusions and metaphors are, of course, common in plays otherwise unrelated to mythology. More important is the introduction of mythological characters, although they are often less mythological than allegorical.[26] Further evidence suggests that mythological plays were acted on the Tudor stage: on Shrove Tuesday 1546/7 the Revels Accounts record that a play of Orpheus was performed before King Edward,[27] and the Revels Accounts for Elizabeth's reign list mythological plays during the seventies. On Twelfth Night, 1571/2, the Children of the Chapel presented *Narcissus*, and on March 2, 1578/9, they performed the *History of Loyaltie and bewtie*.[28] Nothing more is known about either play; the former may have been based on the account in the fourth book of the *Metamorphoses*. The title of the *History of Loyaltie and bewtie* suggests a morality, but the entry in the Revels Accounts of "a garland of grapes and Leaves for Baccus and other of roses for . . ." implies a sumptuously produced mythological play.[29] One of the children's companies, probably Paul's Boys under the supervision of Wescott, is cited by Gosson in 1582 as performing a play on the subject of Cupid and Psyche.[30]

23. Feuillerat, *Elizabeth*, p. 286. The phrase "pastorell or historie" suggests that some of the plays recorded merely as "histories" may be examples of other genres.

24. Arber, *1*, 313.

25. [A. Munday?], *A second and third blast of retrait from plaies and Theaters* (1580), in *The English Drama and Stage under the Tudor and Stuart Princes 1543–1664*, ed. W. C. Hazlitt (London, 1869), p. 145.

26. Cf. Heywood's *Play of the Weather* and *Thersites* for allegory, and *Cambyses*, where Venus and Cupid symbolize the action.

27. Feuillerat, *Edward*, p. 3 n.

28. Feuillerat, *Elizabeth*, pp. 145, 303.

29. Ibid., p. 308.

30. S. Gosson, *Playes Confuted in Five Actions*, in Hazlitt, *English Drama and Stage*, p. 188. Cf. J. P. Brawner, "Early Classical Narrative Plays by

All these plays presumably presented a combination of deities and humans in a dramatization of some problem of love; the mythological Arcadianism of the *Araygnement* was undoubtedly anticipated in them. Mythological plays may well have been produced on the public stage by the adult companies, but they seem to have been more characteristic of the children's companies playing at Court or in the private theater.

Two plays that are basically mythological probably belong to the public theater. *The Rare Triumphs of Love and Fortune* (ca. 1582), performed before the Queen by the Queen's Men, starts with a debate between Love and Fortune before the council of the Olympic gods. The romantic plot, which follows in the succeeding acts, is merely an illustration of the relative powers of Venus and Dame Fortune. Likewise, the *Cobbler's Prophecy*, printed in 1594 but undoubtedly much older, has a mythological framework. Venus' "bower of bliss" in the latter play suggests some aspects of the Arcadian world; but, on the whole, the play is closer to the older moralities.

In addition to these strictly mythological plays, the Revels Accounts record several plays based on classical heroic legends. Paul's Boys presented "Effigenia" on December 28, 1571, and *Ajax and Ulysses* on New Year's Night 1571/2. On Shrove Tuesday, 1573/4, Mulcaster's Boys performed *Persius and Andromeda*.[31] Latin plays on similar subjects were common at both universities during the period, although they were usually Senecan tragedies.

While the scarcity of evidence often obscures the fundamental relation of the *Araygnement* to previous traditions, it is obvious that the play's mythological and pastoral elements had already appeared in masques, court entertainments, and early drama. Undoubtedly Italian practices had influenced the English development, but the *Araygnement*, while not entirely independent of the Italian traditions, was not the result of direct importation. Moreover, Peele's handling of the mythological and pastoral world

Sebastian Wescott and Richard Mulcaster," *Modern Language Quarterly,* 4 (1943), 456, n. 4.

31. Feuillerat, *Elizabeth*, pp. 145, 213. Another play, presumably on the Trojan War, *The History of Agamemnon and Ulysses*, is listed as having been performed on December 27, 1585 (p. 365).

follows and develops contemporary dramatic traditions; it is to these traditions that we must now turn our attention.

A close examination of extant plays and of the Revels Accounts points to the emergence of a new kind of dramatic entertainment in the sixties and seventies, culminating in the work of Lyly and Peele. Growing out of the earlier tradition of expository drama exemplified in the Tudor interludes and moralities, the new drama can be distinguished from its predecessors by its limited, private audience and its specialized subject matter and approach. While the popular forms of drama—the moralities, the romances, the intrigue comedies—frequently appeared at court, they were written with an eye toward production on the popular stage. The new expository drama, on the other hand, seems to have developed partly to meet the increased demands for court entertainment in the sixties and partly to fill out the repertories of the private theaters. The opening of the Blackfriars in the seventies increased the demand for intellectual and sophisticated drama.

Two extant plays suggest the subject matter and approach that seem to have characterized the "new drama." Richard Edwardes' *Damon and Pithias*, probably produced at court during the Christmas season of 1564/5 and printed in 1571, is the earlier of the two; the second, *The Wars of Cyrus*, exists only in an edition printed in 1594. At first glance the *Wars* appears to be a post-*Tamburlaine* play, but J. P. Brawner in his edition advances convincing arguments for considering it a Blackfriars' play produced about 1576, although perhaps not in its present form.[32] Essentially these plays are expository drama stemming from the older moralities. Although they are based on incidents drawn from ancient and legendary history, they are not history plays in the same sense that *Gorboduc* is. The emphasis is not on the sequence of events, the rise or fall of an

32. Introduction, *The Wars of Cyrus*, in Illinois Studies in Language and Literature (1942), 10–20. I. Ribner suggests that Brawner overemphasizes the romantic element of the *Wars* and argues that the play in its present form contains historical elements. For Ribner, "far from being an imitation of Marlowe's play, *The Wars of Cyrus* was probably printed at the height of *Tamburlaine's* popularity as an antidote to dangerous political heresy" ("*Tamburlaine* and *The Wars of Cyrus*," *Journal of English and Germanic Philology*, 53, 1954, 573). The different intent in the original and revised versions may account for structural differences in the extant text.

historical character, or the historical or political moral behind such events; rather, the authors have used historical material to illustrate an ethical or intellectual problem that is discussed and analyzed throughout the play. In this respect the new expository drama is similar to the morality; and the rhetorical debates on love, honor, and friendship recall the tirades and exhortations of the virtues in the moralities. The basic allegoric structure of the morality is disguised by the historical story, and the use of the historical framework is supported by the substitution of concrete characters for the older personifications. In *Damon and Pithias*, for example, although the characters are basically type characters and at times might assume allegorical names, they are more concrete and possess some aura of the historical setting.

The tendency to disguise the moral framework of the morality was not new but was evidenced as early as Skelton's *Magnificence* (c. 1515) and the play *Godly Queen Hester* (?1525–29). A comparison of *Lusty Juventus* and *Nice Wanton*, both probably written between 1547 and 1553, illustrates the tendency. In the former the characters are abstractions, with the exception of the Devil, a Messenger, and Little Bess, a "Curtisane," though even these are but one remove from abstraction. In the latter play the dramatis personae are a heterogeneous group, including a Messenger, Barnabas, Ismael, Dalila, Eulalia, Iniquity, Baily Errand, Xantippe, Worldly Shame, and Daniel. There are fewer abstractions per se here although in the case of Barnabas and Eulalia the concreteness may be illusory. In both plays current theological controversies structure the allegoric tenor; but the contemporary settings give the abstractions greater immediacy, and the pseudo-biblical setting of *Nice Wanton* masks its contemporary portrayal of life in historical concreteness. Nevertheless, although both plays attempt to submerge the moral framework in concrete detail, both remain essentially moralities.

The fundamental difference between these moralities and the later expository drama like *Damon* and the *Wars* lies in the subject matter. The later plays pose ethical rather than religious problems and draw upon conventional literary themes. In this respect the expository drama of the sixties and seventies is a development of the Tudor interludes written by Medwall and John Heywood. Like Edwardes and the author of the *Wars*, these men were writ-

ing for a well-defined audience, and they were dramatizing intellectual or social problems of contemporary interest. Essentially
their plays are *debats* and belong to the tradition of expository
drama. In Heywood's *Witty and Witles*, for example, James, John,
and Jerome argue whether it is better to be wise or foolish, while
in *A Play of Love* Heywood applies the *debat* technique to the
problem of love. While Medwell's *Fulgence and Lucres* is more
successful as drama, it remains nonetheless an exposition of the
relative merits of wealthy nobility and virtuous poverty. The
interest in these stereotyped problems of love and conduct was by
no means limited to the interludes, for throughout the Tudor and
Elizabethan periods new treatments of these conventional materials
continued to appear. Castiglione's *The Courtier* presents one
aspect, the numerous courtesy books another, and the novelli were
often told as illustrations or examples of specific problems. Even in
Sidney's *Arcadia* interest in the old themes is ever present, and the
novel itself is a vehicle for serious exposition. The tendency toward
expository literature perhaps results from or is concomitant to a
critical theory that stressed the didactic element of literature.

The new expository drama brought together the morality and
the interlude to produce a hybrid that manifests characteristics of
each. In terms of dramatic technique, the new drama gives far
greater attention to structure and plot development, not from the
viewpoint of action or portrayal of character, but rather from that
of the central idea or theme, thus making the play fundamentally
expository.

In *Damon and Pithias* the theme is the nobility of friendship,
and the story of the two friends shows "a rare ensample of friendship true." The play's expository structure embodies both the main
plot and the subplot of Aristippus and Carisophus; for the subplot
is related to the main plot by Carisophus' intrigues against Damon,
and it also thematically complements the main plot. While Damon
and Pithias represent true friendship, the plotting and counterplot-
ting of Aristippus and Carisophus illustrate sham friendship based
on self-interest. As Bradner notes, the subplot actually functions as
the framework for the main plot, and the entire play becomes an
expanded exposition on the nature of friendship.[33] Applying the

33. L. Bradner, *The Life and Poems of Richard Edwardes,* Yale Studies
in English, No. 74 (New Haven, 1927), pp. 63–65.

doctrine of friendship to the problem of tyranny extends the general problem into the political realm and is integral to the play because it resolves the difficulties and averts the impending tragedy. Dionysius' pardon is more than a mere solution of the narrative plot. It is only by the example of Damon and Pithias that Dionysius accepts the doctrine of friendship, and his conversion becomes part of the exposition. Thus *Damon and Pithias* is essentially an expository drama in which the theme of friendship unifies the play and provides its basic structure.

The Wars of Cyrus, ending in the tragedy of Panthea, is a more serious play than *Damon*. The expository element underlies the two main plots of Panthea and the "wars of Cyrus." As in *Damon and Pithias*, the political "wars" plot is subordinate and acts as a frame for Panthea's tragic story. What is not obvious at first is the tragedy's motivating force, which lies in the problem debated by Araspas and Cyrus in Act I, scene 3: the respective powers of love and will. Cyrus declares that since the will is weaker, love should be avoided; Araspas argues that love is resistible. The succeeding scenes illustrate the power of love as Araspas falls in love with the beautiful captive, Panthea. He is disdained, for Panthea is in love with her husband Abradatas; and her love is too strong to be moved by her captivity or by the entreaties of Araspas. When Cyrus sends Araspas to outwit King Antiochus, Panthea misinterprets the gambit and assumes that Araspas has revolted against Cyrus because of her disdain. To compensate, Panthea offers to aid Cyrus by sending for her husband. In the final battle between Cyrus and Antiochus, Abradatas is slain. The catastrophe cannot be averted, and Panthea commits suicide. The two plots, expositions of the relative powers of love and will, demonstrate the overwhelming and destructive power of love.

The extent of the episodic material added to the Xenophon account obscures at times the expository nature of the *Wars* and suggests that the author is interested in narrative rather than expository drama.[34] While Ctestiphon's story serves a functional purpose in the "wars" plot, the stories of Gobryas, Alexandra, Libanio, and Dinon are unrelated to the Panthea plot and only tenuously related to that of the "wars." Sometimes these stories serve to illustrate the

34. Brawner, *The Wars of Cyrus*, pp. 39–40.

nature of lust or to point out, directly or indirectly, the character of a good ruler. And again the ultimate nature of the dramatic action is expository.

Besides these two extant plays, the Revels Accounts record a number of plays probably of the same genre presented by the childrens' companies. During 1573/4 the Boys of Windsor presented *Quintus ffabius* and the Merchant Taylors' School performed *Timoclia at the sege of Thebes;* in 1576/7 the Boys of Windsor and the Children of the Chapel combined to perform *The Historye of Mutius Sceuola,* and Paul's Boys produced *The historye of Titus and Gisippus.* The Children of the Chapel presented *A historye of Alucius* in 1579, and Paul's Boys performed *The history of Cipio Africanus* the following season and *A storie of Pompey* in 1580/1. There was also a play on "Xerxes" in 1574/5;[35] and perhaps *A history of the foure sonnes of ffabyous,* produced by the Earl of Warwick's men on January 1, 1579/80, should be included.

With the exception of *Titus and Gisippus,* the sources of these plays are probably classical.[36] Two of them, *Quintus ffabius* and *Mutius Sceuola* (i.e. *Scaevola*) are possibly from Livy; *Titus and Gisippus* was well-known either in Elyot's version in the *Governor* (II.12) or in Boccaccio's original tale in the *Decameron* (X.8). Not only did these plays have classical sources and settings, which characterize the children's plays of the period, but the stories chosen offered the opportunity to pose some conventional literary problems. If *Quintus ffabius* was drawn from the story of Quintus Fabius Maximus Rullianus, as seems probable, the central problem would have been whether willful disobedience to authority can be justified. The plays about Xerxes may have treated the problem of love versus fraternal loyalty in the relationship between Xerxes and his brother's wife, while in *Mutius Scaevola* the conflict could have been between loyalty and gratitude. Finally, *Alucius,* similar to *The Wars of Cyrus* and *Campaspe,* may have presented the theme of love versus war. If we are right in suggesting that these plays involved ethical questions and serious situations, the plays would

35. Feuillerat, *Elizabeth,* pp. xiii–xvii, 244.
36. Brawner has traced the sources, and the following account is based on his discussion (pp. 52–55).

fall into the kind of expository drama we have described above. *The Wars of Cyrus* and *Damon and Pithias* would, therefore, not be solitary examples but part of a contemporary dramatic tradition. This was the tradition Peele and Lyly inherited and transmuted in the eighties into a pastoral comedy of ideas.

The early drama of Lyly and Peele reveals the continuity of the tradition. In the Blackfriars' prologue to *Campaspe*, Lyly writes:

> But howsoeuer we finish our worke, we craue pardon, if we offend in matter, and patience if we transgresse in manners. We haue mixed mirth with counsell, and discipline with delight, thinking it not amisse in the same garden to sowe pot-hearbes, that we set flowers.[37]

The aim of *Campaspe* is obviously the Horatian mixture of instruction and delight, and the emphasis on the didactic element is part of the tradition we have noted previously. This aim is reiterated in the Prologue to *Sapho and Phao:*

> Our intent was at this time to moue inward delight, not outward lightnesse, and to breede (if it might bee) soft smiling, not loude laughing: knowing it to the wise to be as great pleasure to heare counsell mixed with witte, as to the foolish to have sporte mingled with rudenesse. They were banished the Theater at Athens, and from Rome hyssed, that brought parasites on the stage with apish actions, or fooles with vnciuill habites, or Curtesans with immodest words. We haue endeauored to be as farre from vnseemely speaches, to make your eares glowe, as wee hope you will bee from vnkinde reportes to make our cheekes blush.[38]

What was new in the plays of Lyly was not the mixture of instruction and delight, but the manner of presenting the subject matter. While Edwardes calls *Damon* a "tragical comedy" and the author of the *Wars* warns his audience that the story of Panthea is "writ in sad and tragicke tearmes," Lyly emphasizes the non-serious nature of his drama. Because the extravagant love conceits and the revels of the pages and low-comedy figures are cast in the same sophisticated mold, it is difficult for the modern audience to

37. J. Lyly, *Complete Works*, ed. R. W. Bond (Oxford, 1902), 2, 315.
38. Ibid., p. 371.

discern the serious element behind the action. Frequent use of lyrics and attention to wit and euphuistic style further emphasize the nonserious aspects, and this polished surface makes serious analysis difficult. But above all, it is the world in which the action takes place that supplies the nonserious atmosphere. Although *Campaspe* reflects the historical reality of its source, its atmosphere approaches the mythical Arcadianism of *Sapho and Phao* and the remaining plays of the canon, excluding *Mother Bombie*. This Arcadian world, as defined in such plays as *Sapho and Phao* and *Gallathea*, possesses the mixture of rustic and mythological elements that we noted in the masque and court entertainments and that are prominent in the *Araygnement*.

If the plays of Lyly are an innovation in the sense that with them the earlier expository drama acquired a new sophistication and became essentially nonserious, his drama does reveal characteristics of the tradition, namely surface characterization and careful attention to structure. In *Campaspe* the central question is whether Alexander should choose love or arms; what is important is not the actual conflict on the narrative level between Alexander and Apelles but the treatment of the ideas that cause the conflict. If we are not moved by the characters and their difficulties, it is because the characters as such are not important. What matters is that Campaspe would not be a proper wife for Alexander because of her low birth and that Alexander himself is a warrior rather than a lover. In the play the conflict between love and arms is within Alexander, and the two structures, the expository and the narrative, coincide.[39] In *Sapho and Phao*, however, where the conflict is between chastity and love, some difficulty arises from the failure to integrate the expository and the narrative levels. Venus is not only the anagonist in the narrative plot but also the representative of love on the expository level. In this situation Sapho, the protagonist of the narrative plot, must represent the opposing force of chastity. As a result, Lyly has failed either to focus the opposition within his heroine by giving her a choice or to represent dramatically the opposition of love and chastity in a separate plot. This difficulty is worked out in *Gallathea*, for the narrative and exposition are kept

39. T. W. Baldwin, *Shakespere's Five Act Structure* (Urbana, Ill., 1947), p. 512.

separate; the plot centers not on the love triangles involving
Gallathea and Phillida but rather on the rivalry of Diana and
Venus. The exposition is embodied in a separate plot, and the conflict between love and chastity is portrayed dramatically without
interrupting the narrative. In each of these plays the expository
plot ultimately controls the play.

Using the expository structure as the basis for his plays links
Lyly with the earlier playwrights of the tradition; but, as in their
plays, its adoption entails serious dramatic difficulties and limitations. Structurally, Lyly's plays are weak because the comic plot is
unrelated to the expository and narrative plots. The pages in
Campaspe, the courtiers and pages in *Sapho,* and the three brothers
in *Gallathea* contribute nothing to the development of either the
narrative or expository plots. These characters provide good
comedy, but they momentarily obstruct the play's movement.
Furthermore, as we have noted before, there is no serious dramatic
conflict in these plays; dramatic action is desired not for itself but
as an illustration of the central idea. Finally, there is no interest in
character development, and characterization is limited. Where
Campaspe substitutes historical characters for abstractions, *Sapho
and Phao* and *Gallathea* use the mythological equivalents of abstractions. In minor characters who have no connection with the
expository plot, characterization is a matter of type, although there
is some individualization. Nevertheless, as expository plays of contemporary or literary interest they successfully combine exposition
with a sophisticated style and a mythological world.

Turning to *The Araygnement of Paris*, we recognize immediately a surface similarity to the work of Lyly. That is not surprising, for the *Araygnement* was probably produced during the same
season as *Campaspe* and *Sapho and Phao;*[40] and Peele's play anticipates *Gallathea* by at least one year.[41] The importance of the similarity lies not so much in their influence upon each other as in their
simultaneous interest in using an exotic world for the dramatic

40. The date is uncertain, but the "Court Prologue" to *Campaspe* implies
that it had already been produced at the Blackfriars; cf. above, p. 11, and
Chambers, *3,* 413–415.

41. Although *Gallathea* was not published until 1592, the entry "A Com-
moedie of Titrirus and Galathea" in the Stationers' Register for April 1,
1585, may refer to Lyly's play. Cf. Chambers, *3,* 415.

purposes of court comedy. The Arcadian world of the *Araygnement* is the same mythical world of Lyly's *Sapho and Phao* and *Gallathea*, whose rustic elements never shatter the dramatic illusion. Moreover, there is obviously a close relation between the complimentary allegory of *Sapho* and the presentation of the golden apple to Elizabeth in the *Araygnement*. Finally, the sophistication and emphasis on style that characterize Lyly's plays are also present in Peele's "first encrease."

Although Peele does not use Lyly's euphuistic prose, he clearly attempts to develop a stylized verse modeled after Surrey and those who were emphasizing smoothness and regularity. There is little complexity in Peele's style, but he achieves the effect of complexity by using rhetorical devices. For example, in the Prologue Ate announces that:

> Proude Troy must fall, so bidde the gods above,
> And statelie Iliums loftie towers be racet
> By conquering handes of the victorious foe:
> King Priams pallace waste with flaming fire,
> Whose thicke and foggie smoake peircing the skie,
> Must serve for messenger of sacrifice
> T'appeaze the anger of the angrie heavens,
> And Priams younger sonne, the sheepeherde swaine,
> Paris th'unhappie organ of the Greekes.
>
> [ll. 8–16]

This entire passage consists of a series of parallel statements. Rhetorically it is an example of amplification ending with the elliptical prophecy of Paris' role in the Trojan War. The ellipsis itself is a further rhetorical device, one of the many variations of zeugma. But the statements are not merely parallel, for there is a gradual particularization of the catastrophic nature of Troy's fall implied in the order of the verbs. The city must fall; the towers must be razed; and the palace wasted. Surface complexity is also achieved by such devices as the use of the nominal and adjectival forms "anger" and "angrie" within the same line. The play is further characterized by puns and the smart talk of the sophisticated courtier who indulges in bawdy repartee and innuendo.

Rhymed fourteeners are the predominant verse form; but

although at times they retain their earlier awkwardness, Peele has transformed them into supple dialogue. Perhaps outstanding in this respect are the passages of stichomythia, where Peele avoids both the ponderous regularity that accompanies linear speech division and the doggerel achieved by breaking the line at the medial caesura (e.g. ll. 626–640). There is, furthermore, a consciousness of verse decorum. Fourteeners are used throughout the play indiscriminately for rustic and mythical characters where situations and tone are "low"; rhymed couplets are used for those situations which are more "serious." For heightened effect Peele introduces blank verse. The use of dramatic blank verse is historically important, for it is an innovation, having been used before only in *Gorboduc* and *Jocasta*. More important is the verse itself; for the first time it becomes a flexible medium of poetic expression. The verse is primarily end-stopped, but there are passages where run-on lines create larger rhythmical patterns (e.g. ll. 872–881). Peele shows skill in phrasing and in adapting sentence structure to verse form, both lacking in earlier attempts at dramatic blank verse. Although Peele's blank verse often achieves dignity—for example, in Paris' oration—it lacks the force and intensity that later characterized Marlowe's "mighty line."

Besides the fourteeners, decasyllabic couplets, and blank verse, Peele experiments with various lyric forms. The lyrics are remarkable both in number, twelve in all, and in quality. Two of them—the "woing of Colman" in III.5 and the song "Hey Downe downe downe" in IV.3—are no longer extant. Of the remainder, one is in Italian and one in Latin; both are pedantic and mere *tours de force*. The English lyrics, however, reveal Peele's true craftsmanship, for they are characterized by an easy control of the verse and by a freshness that is hard to match in the preceding period. Lamb's praise of "Cupid's Curse" is well-known; [42] and "Colin's Lament" and "Oenone's Complaint" were popular enough to find their way into *England's Helicon* (Nos. 148, 149). The use of rhyme throughout the play and the frequent introduction of songs emphasizes the artificiality of the verse and makes it an integral part of the atmosphere. While the result is less stylized than the euphuistic prose of Lyly's plays, Peele's verse achieves a sophistication and a

42. "Dramatic Specimens and the Garrick Plays," *The Works of Charles and Mary Lamb,* ed. E. V. Lucas (London, 1904), *4,* 443.

texture which differentiate it both from previous dramatic verse and from the language of reality.

The relation of the *Araygnement* to Lyly's work is closer than these surface similarities would indicate. Although Peele has altered the tradition by adding to it features of the masque, the *Araygnement* belongs essentially to the tradition of expository drama. The resulting synthesis is best seen in a consideration of the structure of the *Araygnement*. Peele partially disregards the five-act structure basic to Lyly's plays, but he retains the dual structure of narrative and expository plots. He compresses the narrative plot, the love story of Paris and Oenone into four acts, reserving the fifth for resolution of the expository plot. Schematically, the narrative plot is introduced in I.5, where Paris and Oenone pledge their vows of undying love. In II.2 Paris is faced with the judgment of the goddesses. His judgment, however, is not the turning point but the beginning of the narrative action; for by giving the apple to Venus, Paris is forsaking Oenone and arousing the anger of Juno and Pallas, who become the force of opposition. Act III reveals the growing separation of the lovers and brings the climax when Juno and Pallas are successful in summoning Paris to trial. The catastrophe following the climax is resolved in Act IV, with Paris' defense and his acquittal. Through his choice Paris has lost Oenone; and though the narrative plot is comic, there are tragic overtones. Act II seems at first structurally weak, for it introduces new characters who appear to have no functional purpose; but the Colin-Thestilis story is actually integral to the development of the narrative plot. It is in fact the reversal of the Paris-Oenone-Venus triangle and functions as a commentary on that triangle. The love of Paris and Oenone is doomed from the beginning; and their choice of the poplar tree as the symbol of their love is prophetic, for the poplar is the symbol of inconstancy. The unfortunate affair of Colin and Thestilis serves as a variation on the theme of unrequited love; and although Paris is acquitted and the lovers disappear from the scene, the tragedy of their love is anticipated both in the burial of Colin and in Paris' departure from the pastoral world and his return to Troy. Because of his emphasis on the pastoral elements of the Paris and Oenone story, Peele is able to introduce the pastoral interlude without violating the mythical mode.

The narrative plot is governed by the expository plot, which poses the academic question whether majesty, wisdom, or love is the most beautiful. The development of the expository plot follows the traditional classic formula used by Lyly. Act I gives the necessary exposition, and the problem itself is stated in II.1, where each of the goddesses presents her claim to the golden apple. Juno, chosen Queen of Heaven because of her majesty, equates that majesty with beauty, while Venus argues that the apple is hers alone, since "the name of Venus is in deede but beautye." Pallas subtly shifts the question to the inner aspect of beauty and contends that the beauty of the mind exceeds that of the body. In the second scene of Act II argumentation is replaced by a show of power, and, as in the narrative plot, the action begins when Paris awards the apple to Venus. The two plots converge in Act III, where opposition to Paris is indirectly opposition to Venus. Although Mercury's search for Paris carries the expository plot forward, the catastrophe of the expository plot is not reached until Act V, for Act IV serves only to restate the central problem and to bring the goddesses into direct opposition. When the catastrophe is brought about by the necessity for a final decision, Peele neatly makes the compliment to Elizabeth the solution to the problem of beauty. He thus avoids any real decision of the theoretical problem and averts as well the tragic decision of the Troy story. The introduction of Elizabeth as Eliza is, of course, in the masque tradition; and, while Peele has escaped the restrictions of court allegory that hindered Lyly in *Sapho and Phao*, the compliment remains integral to the play as a whole.

Commenting upon the *Araygnement*, Cheffaud finds it difficult to accept the eulogy of Elizabeth as a suitable climax; not only does he find the climax of the play weak, but "l'intérêt de la pièce tend à languir après le 3ᵉ acte." [43] His objection is due to a misinterpretation of the fundamental structure of the play; he has overlooked the fact that the play's central concern is the problem of beauty rather than the narrative story of Paris and Oenone. A more serious objection is that of Miss Welsford, who argues that by introducing Elizabeth, Peele has violated dramatic detachment, a weakness that Lyly avoided by the use of allegory.[44] This violation is not so

43. Cheffaud, p. 48.
44. Welsford, *Court Masque*, p. 287.

serious as Miss Welsford contends inasmuch as court drama and
the tradition of the masque were closely connected. One characteristic of the masque was its inclusion of the audience in the revels as
manifested in the common practice of "taking out," and the masque
itself was often merely an elaborate presentation of some gift to the
Queen. Moreover, in Elizabethan drama, dramatic detachment was
often disregarded. There was a closer relationship between the
audience and the actors than exists today; prologues and epilogues
were addressed to the audience, and throughout the play the
actors were constantly in touch with their auditors by means of
soliloquies and direct addresses. Thus, the introduction of Elizabeth
as a silent character was not an innovation, and the audience would
have accepted it without losing the dramatic illusion.

If the culmination of the play is seen as a ritual action, much of
our embarrassment is eliminated. Rossiter notes that "the apparently abject flattery of Spenser's references to Queen Elizabeth
becomes something different if they are recognized as part of a ritual
of order." [45] In the *Araygnement* Peel transforms his flattery into
ceremony. The scene opens with the formal oath swearing, followed by Diana's description of *"the Nymph Eliza a figure of the
Queene."* This description fuses the contemporary world with the
idealized pastoral world. Time is neatly telescoped so that past and
present coexist.[46] With the entrance of the Fates and the singing
of their Latin song a new dimension is added to the ritual, for the
action is seen in terms of eternity and the Fates offer to Eliza their
"properties"—the distaff, the spindle, and the knife. The scene then
culminates with the presentation of the golden apple. The formality
of the action reinforces the ritual of the scene. In the final scene

45. A. P. Rossiter, *English Drama from Early Times to the Elizabethan*
(London, 1950), p. 18.
46. A similar telescoping of time is present in the eleventh canto of the
first book of *The Faerie Queene*. In "The Structural Significance of Myth
and Flattery in Peele's *Arraignment of Paris*" (*Studies in Philology, 65,*
1968, 168) Henry Lesnick notes Peele's emphasis in V,1 upon England as
a second Troy and upon the idyllic environment of Elizabeth's realm which
links England to the pastoral, mythological world of Mount Ida. Thus, there
is a telescoping of place as well as time. Lesnick's argument that the play is
to be seen as a Christian fall and redemption myth in which the second
Troy is a paradise regained by an Elizabeth-Christ figure is questionable.

Peele achieves the intent of pastoralism: in mirroring the real in the ideal, he suggests the order and coherence which lie behind the mutable reality. The academic question of which is most beautiful —majesty, wisdom, or love—is resolved through the idealization of Queen Elizabeth within the Arcadian golden world.

The use of expository and narrative plots in the *Araygnement* links the play with the preceding tradition of expository drama. Although Larsen denies more than a superficial relation between Lyly and Peele, it is obvious that the two men were concurrently attempting to create the same kind of drama.[47] This is not, of course, the relation of master and disciple; for Lyly and Peele were independently developing in much the same manner the dramatic traditions at their disposal. The work of the two, if fundamentally similar in technique and approach, differs in execution. Earlier we noted Peele's use of verse in contrast to Lyly's euphuistic prose, and the emphasis on comedy per se varies between the two. While Larsen's contention that there is "hardly a touch of comedy" in the *Araygnement* is an overstatement,[48] comedy is restricted, and Peele's use of comedy differs from Lyly's. Where Lyly focused the comedy in an episodic and unrelated subplot, Peele tends to integrate it with the play as a whole. Moreover, Peele's comedy is less that of situation than of intellectual repartee and bawdy innuendo. The influence of the masque in the *Araygnement* also differentiates it from Lyly's plays, for there is a greater emphasis on spectacle.

As an example of court entertainment in the eighties, the *Araygnement* represents a culminating point in the development of that specialized genre. One of the major difficulties of the earlier expository drama is solved in the *Araygnement:* for the first time an expository drama achieves total unity. The expository plot is portrayed dramatically in the contention of the goddesses, while the narrative plot centers upon the relationship between Paris and Oenone; and, although the two plots converge in Act III, they retain their identity and can be resolved separately. Where earlier the comic plots remained unrelated to the play as a whole, Peele has succeeded in tying the individual elements together. This arises partly from the use of the Arcadian world with its inclusiveness

47. Larsen, p. 305.
48. Ibid., p. 306.

and partly from the fact that the Colin-Thestilis story is functional rather than decorative. Although the *Araygnement* achieves a unity, it possesses the other weaknesses which characterize the genre. As a play, it lacks the conflict arising from characters in action; for Peele was no more successful than Lyly in the creation of complex characterization. But if the goddesses are little more than mythical abstractions, they do achieve some individualization as types, and Paris and Oenone hold some interest as characters.

The weaknesses of the *Araygnement* lie less in the play itself than in the genre to which it belongs; for the dramatic presentation of literary and conventional problems in a world removed from reality limits the appeal and the ultimate value of such a tradition. The failure of these plays to arouse modern interest should not, however, obscure the achievement of Lyly and Peele, although it must qualify that achievement. Writing for a specialized audience, these men developed the genre of expository drama into a sophisti-cated comedy of ideas. While Lyly might claim to instruct as well as delight, it is that latter claim that predominates and charac-terizes these plays as fundamentally nonserious.

In the years that followed publication of the *Araygnement* the fortunes of the new pastoral comedy of ideas were varied. During the time when the children's companies were performing (1587–90), there is evidence that the pastoral comedy of ideas continued to appeal. The Stationers' Register records that on July 26, 1591 a "booke intituled the Huntinge of Cupid and written by George Peele . . ." was entered for publication.[49] From the evidence of Drummond and the songs printed in *England's Helicon,* the play was a mythological pastoral, probably similar to the *Araygnement;* beyond that we cannot say. Lyly's *Endymion, Midas,* and *Love's Metamorphoses* are essentially expository drama cast in the form of pastoral comedy. Set in a mythological world, they preserve the dual structure of narrative and expository plots and pose conven-tional problems. In them we sense the exhaustion of what was a rich if shallow vein of ore.

Lyly's last play, *The Woman in the Moon,* apparently was writ-ten after the dissolution of Paul's Boys and seems to have been an attempt to adapt the genre to the public stage and to an adult

49. Arber, 2, 591.

company. Although the play retains the Arcadian world, the atmosphere of its Arcadia is different. There is no longer innocent mirth; for in its satire on women, the play suggests the pastoral world after the fall. The play is more of an exposé than a presentation of an ideal world. Whether or not the change in tone mirrors a change in Lyly's attitude toward his earlier work and an evaluation of it, *The Woman in the Moon* stands as the last of Lyly's plays and the last example of the pastoral mythological comedy of ideas.

In the hands of others, the tradition of Lyly and Peele received varied treatment. During the seasons of 1584 and 1585 the Queen's Men performed two pastorals: the "pastorall of phillyda and Choryn" and the "history of felix and philomena." [50] If the latter dramatizes an incident in Montemayor's *Diana*, the emphasis in these plays may have been on the pastoral as distinct from the mythological. In Marlowe's *Dido*, on the other hand, the classical mythological elements are emphasized to the exclusion of the pastoral, and the play is not an expository drama. Marlowe has accepted the Arcadian world but used it for other purposes. It remained for Shakespeare to create great drama from the Arcadian world. In *Two Gentlemen of Verona* Shakespeare experiments with the comedy of ideas using the conflict between love and friendship to structure the play. Shakespeare, however, coalesces the narrative and expository elements. *Love's Labour's Lost* retains interest in intellectual problems, although here the pastoral world becomes courtly. Finally, in *As You Like It* the Arcadian world is stripped of its mythological trappings and becomes a means of examining the romantic problems of the real world. The old academic questions are inherent in Shakespeare's plays, but the interest no longer lies in the abstract intellectual problem but in the characters who pose the problem. The sophisticated comedy of ideas of Peele and Lyly has become high comedy.

4. THE TEXT

The bibliographical description of the collated quarto upon which an authoritative text must be based is as follows:

50. Feuillerat, *Elizabeth*, p. xvii.

[Within lace border] *The Araygnement of Paris* / A PASTO-
RALL. / Presented before the Queenes / Maiestie, by the Children
/ of her Chappell. / [Ornament] / Imprinted at London by / Henrie Marsh. / ANNO. 1584. /

HT] THE ARAIGNEMENT / *OF PARIS.* /
RT] The Araygnement / of Paris.[1]
Collation] A–E4
Contents] A1 title page; A1ᵛ blank; A2 head title, "Ate Prologus";
A2ᵛ–E4ᵛ text.

Catchwords] Omitted from A2 and E2; elsewhere inaccurate:
A3ᵛ A dain-, *Sil.* A deintie; A4 *The*, An Eccho . . . / The
songe . . . ; B3ᵛ and, And; C1ᵛ *Act.*, *ACT.*; D1 yf, Yf; D1ᵛ
Vulcan, ACT . . . . / *Vulcan* . . . ; E3ᵛ *The*, The. These
variations are not unusual since the practice was never stan-
dardized, but their frequency corresponds with the inferior
presswork throughout the quarto.
Copies] The four extant copies of the quarto have been collated
for the present edition:
British Museum
Huntington
Pforzheimer
Trinity College, Cambridge [2]
(running titles and speech prefixes badly mutilated in re-
binding)
Variants] Significant variants listed below show at least two states
of correction.[3]

1. See below, pp. 57–59, for a discussion of the running titles.
2. W. W. Greg attributes a copy to Harvard (*Bibliography of the English Printed Drama*, Oxford, 1939, item 83). The late W. A. Jackson informed me that no such copy exists.
3. Because of faulty presswork numerous doubtful letters occur: *e.g.*,
l. 111 hea[d] BM, H, T, head P; l. 334 tru[l]l BM, H, T, trull P; l. 529
[s]weete BM, H, P, sweete T. The use of these as evidence in determining
correction is questionable in the light of their frequent occurrence. Two
cases, however, may be of some value as corroborative evidence: i.e., A2ᵛ
(l. 55) thinke[s]t H, T, thinkest, BM, P; A3 (l. 73) se[r]vice H, service
BM, P, T.

		State 1	State 2
A[o]			
A2^v	[l. 51 SD]	*Pomōna* (H)	*Pomona* (BM,P,T)
	[l. 52]	hadthe (H,T)	had the (BM,P)
A3	[l. 85]	that (H,T)	That (BM,P)
	signature missing, (H,T)		Aiij (BM,P)
A4^v	[l. 168]	to *o Ida* (H,T)	to *Ida* (BM,P)
A[i]			
A4	[l. 152]	marche (H)	marche (,) (T)
			marche, (BM,P)
B[o]			
B1	[l. 224]	*Iuno:* (T)	*Iuno.* (BM,H,P)
B4^v	[l. 467]	worthines, (H,P,T)	worthines. (BM)
B[i]			
B2	[l. 294]	fore (BM)	for (H,P,T)
B3^v	[l. 364]	*Pulherrimae* (BM)	*Pulcherrimae* (H,P,T)
	[l. 369]	giue (BM)	giuen (H,P,T)
B4	[l. 436]	thie (BM)	this (H,P,T)
C[o]			
C2^v	[l. 581]	náme (H)	name (BM,P,T)
	[l. 593]	therebín (H)	therebin (BM,P,T)
C4^v	[l. 717]	died (BM,H,T)	died. (P)
C[i]			
C3^v	[l. 635]	loúe (H)	loue (BM,P,T)
C4	[l. 682]	stav(t)e (H)	starte (BM,P,T)
D[i]			
D1^v	[l. 761]	that- selfsame (BM,H,T)	that selfesame (P)
E[i]			
E1^v	[l. 1047]	sacredpowre (H,P,T)	sacred powre (BM)
E3^v	[l. 1190]	beāutifull (H)	beautifull (BM,P,T)

The corrections were at best haphazard and diminished in frequency as printing proceeded. In no case was it necessary for the proofreader to resort to the copy or to make independent emendation since the errors are on the whole typographical and such as would normally be corrected by the printer.

Of the four copies of the quarto, P preserves the text in its most corrected state. Formes A[o], B[i], C[o,i], and D[i] represent the final stages of correction; E[i] and B[o] manifest an intermediary stage. BM has formes A[o], B[o], C[i] and E[i] in their final stages, but formes B[i] and D[i] are uncorrected while C[o] is in an intermediary stage. T has only forme B[i] in a final stage; four, A[o], C[o,i], and E[i], are intermediary; and two, B[o] and D[i], are uncorrected. The text of H is the least corrected. Forme B[i] is in the final stage; formes D[i] and B[o] are intermediary, while formes A[o], C[o,i] and E[i] are uncorrected.[4]

Neither the inner forme of A nor the outer formes of D and E appears to have been corrected. The one variant in the inner forme of A [A4 (l. 152) marche H; marche (,) T; marche, BM, P] can be attributed to deterioration of type rather than to actual correction. The impression of a space at the beginning of the line in H suggests that the comma has dropped out and that the type is loose. On the same page in ll. 159 and 160, P and BM clearly print "Ladie" and "Is here"; in H and T, however, the "L", "s" and "h" are damaged probably because of loose type, evidenced by the space mark at the beginning of l. 159. Similar deterioration would account for many of the doubtful readings.

The text for this edition has been prepared from a collation of P with photostatic copies of BM, H, and T; all variants are listed in the textual notes. Where it was necessary to emend, the source of the emendation and the quarto reading have been duly cited. While no attempt has been made to collate later editions of the play, such editions have been consulted on all difficult passages; textual notes cite emendations by the editor who introduced them.

4. Child collated BM and T for the Malone Society Reprint and noted that T had formes A[o], E[i] uncorrected while BM had an uncorrected inner forme of B. The state of the outer forme of B was uncertain; Child suggested that it was uncorrected (p. vi).

The conjectures of other editors are cited in the notes only when illuminating.

The quarto text is reproduced except that *i, j, u,* and *v* are changed to conform with modern usage, long *s* is replaced by short *s, vv* by *w, æ* by *ae,* and *œ* by *oe.* Where typographical abbreviations were used to save space, they have been silently expanded. Distinctions between italic and roman type have been disregarded except on the title page. Unless otherwise noted, the punctuation is that of the quarto. Typographical errors have been corrected and the original reading given; broken type is noted only in extreme instances where the letter is doubtful in all quartos. Frequently the compositor in pointing a line did not provide a space after a comma but allowed the comma to function as a space. Such failures have not been noted although failures to provide spacing between unpunctuated words have been recorded.

The line numbering is consecutive throughout the play, excluding stage directions, which are given the number of the last line of dialogue preceding the direction. Signatures are given in square brackets to the right of the text. Act and scene divisions are retained; in one instance—Act III, scene 4—the scene division omitted by the printer has been supplied by the editor. The stage directions are printed as in the quarto. Speech prefixes have been regularized, though the use of *Iup.* for *Ioue* throughout Act IV is an obvious variation and has therefore been retained.

The exact nature of the printer's copy is debatable, but certain literary features of the quarto suggest that it was closely related to the autograph manuscript. Most important in this respect are the extraneous comments that precede several of the songs: for example, Colin's lament, which opens Act III, is titled *"Colin thenamored sheepeherd singeth his passion of love. / The songe."* and Oenone's song in scene 4 of the same act is headed "OENONES COMPLAINT." In the first act the country gods answered the singing of the birds with a song captioned *"An Eccho to their song. / The songe. A quier within and without."* (l. 166 SD).[5] To

5. It is possible that this is a repetition of the phrase from the preceding line (l. 166, "Pomona, if we nil bestowe an Eccho to their songe.") and thus a printer's error, although the practice of composing by pages makes this seem improbable.

these examples might be added the titles that head the two set pieces: *"Paris oration to the Councell of the gods."* (l. 852 SD); *"Diana describeth the Nymphe Eliza a figure of the Queene."* (l. 1137 SD). Finally, the note appended to the close of the dialogue between Thestilis and the shepherds, *"The grace of this song is in the Shepherds Ecco to her verse."* (l. 742 SD), characterizes the nondramatic nature of these stage directions.

The inclusion of these nondramatic comments in a dramatic document is at first puzzling, but a comparison of the descriptive method here with the conventions of the anthologies of the period reveals a striking similarity. A contemporary anthology, *A Handful of Pleasant Delights*, demonstrates the widespread use of the caption not merely as a title but as a description of the contents; for example, No. 8, "A proper sonet, wherein the Louer dolefully sheweth his grief to his L. and requireth pity," or No. 32, "The Louer compareth him self to the painful Falconer." [6] In an earlier collection, *The Paradise of Dainty Devices*, epigrammatic couplets and short maxims serve as titles, but even here we find among the love poems such captions as "A lover disdained, complaineth" and "Not attainyng to his desire, he complaineth." [7] The convention also appears in the prose romances of Greene and Lodge, where the captions serve to link the songs with the narrative. [8] In all of these instances we are concerned with a definite literary con-

6. [C. Robinson et al.], *A Handful of Pleasant Delights* (1584), ed. H. E. Rollins (Cambridge, Mass., 1924).

7. [R. Edwardes et al.], *The Paradise of Dainty Devices* (1576–1606), ed. H. E. Rollins (Cambridge, Mass., 1927), pp. 81, 84.

8. While in Gascoigne's prose tale, *The Adventure of Master F. J.*, the descriptive caption as such does not appear, the convention is present in the introductory paragraph to the sixth song, "A Moonshine Banquet." As C. T. Prouty points out, this poem has two introductions: "The first is part of the narrative, while the second . . . is similar to the introductory comments prefaced to the separate poems . . ." (*George Gascoigne*, New York, 1942, p. 195). The latter was probably marked for deletion, but in the printing of the *Hundreth Sundrie Flowres* the deletion mark was overlooked. This oversight was corrected in the *Posies*. In any case, the prefatory paragraph is an extended example of the descriptive caption. More interesting in connection with the *Adventures* are the narrator's comments after the songs on their literary merit. This practice sheds light on Peele's stage direction *"The grace of this song . . ."* (l. 742 SD).

;vention. The similarity of the extraneous comments in the *Araygnement* to this convention suggests that Peele was attempting to emphasize the literary rather than the dramatic nature of his play. In so doing, Peele was conforming to the sixteenth-century conception that poetry but not drama was proper to the gentleman.

There is, furthermore, some evidence to support the conjecture that the copy for the quarto represents a revision of the performed play. The stage directions following the captions to the three "showes" suggest in two cases that the directions were added after the performance:

> *Heereuppon did rise a Tree of gold laden with Diadems and Crownes of golde.* (l. 456 SD)
> *Hereuppon did enter. 9. knights in armour, treading a warlike Almaine, by drome and fife, and then having march't foorth againe, Venus speaketh.* (l. 478 SD)

The use of the past tense in these directions is in contrast to the use of the present in Venus' show and in the stage directions throughout the play. The significance of this variation is evident upon an examination of Peele's Lord Mayors' pageants. Both pageants appear to have been prepared for publication after their performance; the revision required was inconsequential, involving the addition of a few explanatory and descriptive directions.[9] Such a "revision" for publication in the case of the *Araygnement* would possibly explain the occurrence of stage directions in the past tense and the inclusion of the extraneous comments.

In addition to the evidence that strongly suggests an autograph origin of the copy, a few stage directions seem to come from the prompt book. For example, the direction "*Gods daunce.*" is placed to the left of ll. 177–178, and similarly the direction "*Mercurie taketh her fan.*" to the left of ll. 783–784. If the position of stage

9. For example: "A speech spoken by him that rid on a Luzarne before the Pageant apparelled like a Moore," "Spoken by the Children in the Pageant . . ." (Horne, pp. 209–213); "The Presenters Speech," "In the hinder part of the Pageant did sit a Child, representing Nature . . ." (ibid., pp. 214–219). D. M. Bevington notes a similar use of literary stage directions in *Gorboduc* and argues that "the use of the past tense in these descriptions [of the dumbshows] suggests literary intent rather than dramaturgic instruction to actors" (*From "Mankind" to Marlowe*, p. 37).

directions to the left of the text indicates prompt copy, these directions might well be traced to the prompter.[10] It is also possible that the directions *"Pallas reades."* and *"Venus reades."* at ll. 367 and 369 were originally prompt directions at the left of the text which the compositor transposed to the right of the text. This would explain the absence of the speech prefixes at this point. Even more important, however, are the directions which anticipate their action, e.g., those at ll. 494 and 1077 that duplicate later directions and serve as cues. Prompt book origin might also explain the repetitive directions found at ll. 508 and 531, where the prompter has merely abbreviated the original directions.

To summarize, the evidence concerning the printers' copy indicates that it was probably either the autograph manuscript or a careful transcript of it that served as the prompt book. Furthermore, the copy may or may not have undergone superficial revision before publication.

The other bibliographical peculiarity of the quarto, namely, the variations in the running titles, warrants some explanation. The origin of the spelling irregularity is at first baffling, since the running titles are usually considered part of the furniture and, therefore, remain unaltered in the process of printing. However, as Fredson Bowers has demonstrated, it was not unusual for the printer to use two skeletons.[11] If the running titles for the *Araygnement* are arranged as they would appear in their formes on the stone, the irregularity is explicable.

A[i]

A4 of Paris.	A3ᵛ The Araygnement
A1ᵛ (Blank)	A2 Head Title

A[o]

A3 of Paris	A4ᵛ The Araygnement
A2ᵛ The Araygnement	A1 Title Page

B[i]

B4 of Paris.	B3ᵛ The Araygnment
B1ᵛ The Araygnement	B2 of Paris.

10. W. W. Greg, *Elizabethan Dramatic Documents* (Oxford, 1931), *1*, 213.

11. F. Bowers, "Notes on Running Titles as Bibliographical Evidence," *Library*, Ser. 4, *19* (1938–39), 315–338.

B[o]

B3 of Paris.	B4^v The Araygnment
B2^v The Araygnement	B1 of Paris.

C[i]

C4 of Paris.	C3^v The Araygnement
C1^v The Araygnement	C2 of Paris.

C[o]

C3 of Paris	C4^v The Araygnement
C2^v The Araygnement	C1 of Paris.

D[i]

D4 of Paris.	D3^v The Arayngment
D1^v The Araygnement	D2 of Paris.

D[o]

D3 Of Paris	D4^v The Araygnment
D2^v The Araygnement	D1 of Paris.

E[i]

E4 of Paris.	E3^v The Araygnement
E1^v The Araygnement	E2 of Paris.

E[o]

E3 Of Paris.	E4^v The Araygnement
E2^v The Araygnment	E1 of Paris.

In printing the quarto, Henry Marsh employed two skeletons, which we shall label I and II. Skeleton I was used for printing sheets A and C and the inner forme of B. In all probability the inner forme of A was printed first.[12] When it was time to impress A[o], the skeleton was transferred piece by piece to the new forme. In the process, the head title was replaced by the title page and a running title, "The Araygnement", added on A2^v. For the printing of C, the title page was removed and the correct running title, "of Paris.", substituted. The printing of the outer forme of C and the inner forme of E proceeded regularly. The omission of the period on C3 is probably due to the displacement of type either in the transferring process or during printing; the correction on E4 was automatic. Skeleton II, set up for the inner forme of B, was transferred with the variant spelling "Araygnment" to the outer forme and was subsequently used for D and for the outer forme of

12. Ibid., pp. 335–338.

E. The misspelling on D3^v, "Arayngment", resulted either from an accident in transference or from an erroneous attempt at correction. If the running title had been reset from new type, we could reasonably expect to find the spelling with "e" as on D1^v. The error was corrected on the outer forme (D4^v) and a further correction, the capitalization of "of", was made on D3. In transferring the skeleton to the outer forme of E, the running titles for E2^v and E4^v, i.e., D2^v and D4^v, were accidentally interchanged.

This use of two skeletons, one per sheet instead of per forme, though unusual, is paralleled in the printing of *The Wars of Cyrus* (1594).[13] In both cases two presses were probably involved, each press printing and perfecting alternate sheets. Since the second press would have started later than the first, by the time D was perfected the first press would have begun printing E. To complete the job efficiently, the second press would normally perfect E. The irregularity of the running titles and the possible use of two presses confirms to some extent the previous evidence of haste and faulty workmanship.

No seventeenth or eighteenth editions are known to exist, but the play has been frequently reprinted in the nineteenth and twentieth centuries.

1. In Vol. I of *The Works of George Peele: Now First Collected*, ed. Alexander Dyce, 2 vols., London, 1828. (This edition has not been available.)

2. In Vol. I of *The Works of George Peele*, ed. Alexander Dyce, 2nd ed., 2 vols., London, 1829. A third volume was added in 1839. Spelling and punctuation are modernized. The text has been checked against a copy of the quarto, probably the BM copy; and there are occasional textual notes and glosses.

3. In *The Dramatic and Poetical Works of Robert Greene and George Peele*, ed. Alexander Dyce, London, 1861. Reprinted in 1874 with the date of reprinting on the title page. Although the text is substantially that of the earlier edition, Dyce introduces into the text as emendations readings which before were only queries. Moreover, Dyce has simplified the act-scene divisions and added extensively to the notes.

13. Ibid., pp. 332–333.

4. In *Plays and Poems by George Peele*, ed. Henry Morley, London, 1883. There is no mention of the source of the text, and there are no notes or textual apparatus.

5. In Vol. I of *The Works of George Peele*, ed. A. H. Bullen, 2 vols., London, 1888. If Bullen follows Dyce's text, he has collated it with the quarto, and his textual notes are fuller. He includes notes by P. A. Daniel and Brinsley Nicholson.

6. *The Arraignment of Paris*, ed. Oliphant Smeaton. Temple Classics, London, 1905. Although Smeaton refers to the work of Dyce, identified as Robert Dyce, no indication is given as to the source of the text. A glossary is appended as well as notes which occasionally refer to textual problems.

7. *The Arraignment of Paris. 1584*, ed. H. H. Child. Malone Society Reprints, Oxford, 1910. The text is based upon a collation of the BM and TC quartos. Variants are listed, and Child notes the presence of uncorrected formes.

8. In *English Drama 1580–1642*, ed. C. F. T. Brooke and N. B. Paradise, New York, 1933. The text is apparently based upon the H quarto although there is no attempt to provide textual notes. Annotations are given.

9. In *Elizabethan and Stuart Plays*, ed. C. R. Baskervill, V. B. Heltzel, and A. H. Nethercot, New York, 1934. The text is based upon Child's collation of the BM and TC quartos. Some textual notes are given, but most of the annotation consists of glossing.

&.

The Araygnement of Paris

A PASTORALL.

Prefented before the Queenes
Maieftie, by the Children
of her Chappell.

Ge. Peele, as Tremells

Imprinted at London by
Henrie Marfh.
ANNO. 1584.

[LIST OF CHARACTERS

PASTORAL CHARACTERS
Paris
Colin
Hobbinol
Diggon
Thenot
Oenone
Pastores

COUNTRY GODS
Pan
Faunus
Silvanus
Shepherd, Hunter, Woodman, attendants to the country gods
Flora
Pomona
Choir of Muses

OLYMPIAN GODS
Jupiter
Apollo
Bacchus
Mars
Mercury
Neptune
Pluto
Saturn
Vulcan
Pyracmon and Vulcan's Cyclopes

Ate, Prologus
Diana
A Nymph of Diana
Juno
Pallas
Rhanis
Venus
The Three Fates
  Clotho
  Lachesis
  Atropos
Choir of Muses

MASQUES AND DUMB SHOWS
The Nine Knights
Helen and the Four Cupids
Thestilis and a Foul Crooked Churl
Eliza or Zabeta, Queen Elizabeth]

Ate Prologus.

Condemned soule Ate, from lowest hell,
And deadlie rivers of the infernall Jove,
Where bloudles ghostes in paines of endles date
Fill ruthles eares with never ceasing cries,
Beholde I come in place, and bring beside
The bane of Troie: beholde the fatall frute
Raught from the golden tree of Proserpine.
Proude Troy must fall, so bidde the gods above,
And statelie Iliums loftie towers be racet
10   By conquering handes of the victorious foe:
King Priams pallace waste with flaming fire,
Whose thicke and foggie smoake peircing the skie,
Must serve for messenger of sacrifice
T'appeaze the anger of the angrie heavens,
And Priams younger sonne, the sheepeherde swaine,
Paris th'unhappie organ of the Greekes.
So loath and weerie of her heavie loade
The Earth complaynes unto the hellish prince,
Surcharged with the burden that she nill sustaine.
20   Th'unpartiall daughters of Necessitie
Bin aydes in her sute: and so the twine
That holdes olde Priams house, the threede of Troie
Dame Atropos with knife in sunder cuttes.
Done be the pleasure of the powers above,

2   *of the*] ofthe Q
14   *T'appeaze*] T'appeaz e Q
21   *aydes*] Q; aiders Dyce1
23   *Atropos*] Dyce *Atrops* Q

Whose hestes men must obey: and I my parte
Performe in Ida vales: Lordinges adieu,
Imposing silence for your taske, I ende,
Till just assemblie of the goddesses
Make me beginne the Tragedie of Troie.

Exit Ate cum aureo pomo.

ACT. I. SCENA I.   [A2ᵛ]

*Pan, Faunus, and Silvanus with their attendants enter to
give welcome to the goddesses: Pans sheepeherd hath a
lambe, Faunus hunter hath a faune, Silvanus woodman
with an oken bowe laden with acornes.*

Pan incipit.

30 *Pan.*   Silvanus, either Flora doth us wronge,
Or Faunus made us tarrie all to longe,
For by this morning mirth it shoulde appeere,
The Muses or the goddesses be neere.
Faun.   My faune was nimble, Pan, and whipt apace,
Twas happie that we caught him up at last,
The fattest fairest fawne in all the chace,
I wonder how the knave could skip so fast.
Pan.   And I have brought a twagger for the nonce,
A bunting lambe: nay, pray you feele no bones.
40 Beleeve me now, my cunning much I misse,
If ever Pan felt fatter lambe then this.
Sil.   Sirs, you may boast your flockes and herdes that bin
both fresh and faire,
Yet hath Silvanus walkes ywis that stand in holsome ayre:
And loe the honor of the woodes, the gallant Oken-bowe,
Do I bestowe laden with Acornes and with mast enough.
Pan.   Peace man for shame, shalt have both lambes and dames
and flockes and herdes and al,
And all my pipes to make the glee, we meete not now to
brawle.

29   SD *Pans sheepeherd*] Pans*sheepeherd* Q

Faun.   Theres no such matter, Pan, we are all friendes assembled hether,

To bid Queene Juno and her pheeres most humblie welcome hether.

50   Diana mistresse of our woodes, her presence will not want,

Her curtesie to all her friends we wot is nothing skant.

ACT. I. SCENA. II.

Pomona entereth with her fruite. Manentibus Pan cum reliquis.

Pom.   Yee Pan, no farther yet, and had the starte of me,

Why then Pomona with her fruite comes time enough I see:

Come on a while, with countrie store like friendes we venter forth,

Thinkest Faunus that these goddesses will take our giftes in woorth.

Faun.   Yea doubtles, for shall tell thee dame, twere better give a thing,

A signe of love, unto a mightie person, or a king:

Then to a rude and barbarous swayne but bad and baselie borne,   [A₃]

For gentlie takes the gentleman that oft the clowne will scorne.

60   *Pan.*   Saist trulie Faunus, I my selfe have given good tidie lambes,

To Mercurie may saie to thee, to Phoebus and to Jove:

When to a countrie mops forsooth, chave offred all their dames,

And pypt and prayed for little worth and raunged about the grove.

Pom.   God Pan that makes your flocke so thin, and makes you looke so leane,

To kisse in corners.

51   SD *Pomona*] BM, P, T; *Pomōna* H
52   *had the*] had (t)he BM, P; hadthe H, T
55   *Thinkest*] BM, P; Thinke(st) H, T
60   *selfe*] selse Q

Pan.   Wel-sed wench some other thing you meane.

Pom.   Yea jest it out till it goe alone, but marvell where we mysse

Faire Flora all this merrie morne.

Faun.   Some newes, see where she is.

ACT. I. SCENA. III.

Flora entereth to the countrie gods.

Pan.   Flora well met, and for thy taken payne,
     Poore countrie gods thy debters we remaine.
70 *Flo.*   Beleeve me, Pan, not all thy lambes and yoes,
     Nor, Faunus, all thy lustie buckes and does,
     (But that I am instructed well to knowe,
     What service to the hills and dales I owe,)
     Could have enforcet me to so straunge a toyle,
     Thus to enrich this gaudie gallant soyle.
  Faun.   But tell me wench hast don't so trick in deede,
     That heaven it selfe may wonder at the deede.
  Flo.   Not Iris in her pride and braverie,
     Adornes her arche with such varietie:
80   Nor doth the milke white way in frostie night,
     Appeare so faire and beautifull in sight:
     As done these fieldes, and groves, and sweetest bowres,
     Bestrewed and deckt with partie collord flowers.
     Alonge the bubling brookes and silver glyde,
     That at the bottome doth in sylence slyde,
     The waterie flowers and lillies on the bankes,
     Like blazing cometes burgen all in rankes:
     Under the Hathorne and the Poplar tree,
     Where sacred Phoebe may delight to be:

65   *Wel-sed*] wel-sed Q
67   *Some*] some Q
73   *service*] BM, P, T; ser(r)uice H
74   *Could*] Could Q
85   *That*] BM, P; that H, T
86   *waterie flowers*] Q; water-flowers Dyce1

90   The Primerose and the purple Hyacinthe,
        The dayntie Violet and the holsome Minthe:
        The dooble Daisie, and the Couslip queene   [A3ᵛ]
        Of sommer floures, do over peere the greene:
        And rounde about the valley as ye passe,
        Yee may ne see for peeping flowers the grasse:
        That well the mightie Juno and the rest,
        May boldlie thinke to be a welcome guest
        On Ida hills, when to approve the thing,
        The queene of flowers prepares a second spring.
100 *Silv.*   Thou gentle Nymphe, what thankes shall we repaie
        To thee, that makest our fieldes and woodes so gaie?
     Flo.   Silvanus, when it is thy hap to see,
        My workemanship, in portraying all the three,
        First stately Juno with her porte and grace,
        Her roobes, her lawnes, her crounet and her mace:
        Would make thee muse this picture to beholde,
        Of yellow Oxslips bright as burnisht golde.
     Pom.   A rare device, and Flora, well perdie,
        Did painte her yellow for her jellozie.
110 *Flo.*   Pallas in flowers of hue and collowers red,
        Her plumes, her helme, her launce, her Gorgons head,
        Her trayling tresses that hang flaring rounde,
        Of Julie-flowers so graffed in the grounde,
        That trust me Sirs, who did the cunning see,
        Would at a blush suppose it to be shee.
     Pan.   Good Flora, by my flocke twere verie good,
        To dight her all in red resembling blood.
     Flo.   Faire Venus of sweete Violetts in blue.
        With other flowers infixt for chaunge of hue,
120   Her plumes, her pendants, bracelets and her ringes,
        Her dayntie fan and twentie other thinges:
        Her lustie mantle waving in the winde,
        And everie part in collor and in kinde:
        And for her wreath of roses she nil dare,

96   *Juno*] B; *Iono* Q
107   *Oxslips*] B; Oxstips Q   *burnisht*] burnish t Q
116   *twere*] Q 'twas Dyce

With Floras cunning counterfet compare.
So that what lyving whight shall chaunce to see,
These goddesses, eche placed in her degree,
Portrayed by Floraes workemanshipe alone,
Must say that Arte and nature met in one.

130   *Sil.*   A deintie draught to lay her downe in blue,   [A4]
The collour commonlie betokening true.

Flo.   This peece of worke compact with many a flowre,
And well layde in at entraunce of the bowre,
Where Phoebe meanes to make this meeting royall,
Have I prepared to welcome them withall.

Pom.   And are they yet dismounted, Flora, saie:
That we may wende to meete them one the way.

Flo.   That shall not neede: they are at hand by this,
And the conductor of the trayne hight Rhanis.

140   Juno hath left her chariot longe agoe,
And hath returned her Peacocks by her rainebowe.
And bravelie as becommes the wife of Jove,
Doth honour by her presence to our grove.
Faire Venus shee hath let her sparrowes flie,
To tende on her and make her melodie:
Her turtles and her swannes unyoked bee,
And flicker neere her side for companie.
Pallas hath set her Tygers loose to feede,
Commaunding them to waite when shee hath neede.

150   And hitherward with proude and statelie pace,
To doe us honor in the Silvan chace
They marche, like to the pompe of heaven above,
Juno the wife and sister of king Jove,
The warlicke Pallas, and the Queene of love.

Pan.   Pipe Pan for joy and let thy sheepeherdes sing,
Shall never age forget this memorable thing.

Flo.   Clio the sagest of the sisters nine,
To do observaunce to this dame devine,
Ladie of learning and of chyvalrie,

150   *hitherward*] Hitherward Q
152   *marche,*] BM, P; marche(,) T; marche H
159   *Ladie*] BM, P; (L)adie H, T

160   Is here aryved in faire assemblie,
        And wandring up and downe th'unbeaten wayes,
        Ringe through the wood sweete songes of Pallas prayse.
Pom.   Harke Flora, Faunus, here is melodie,
        A charme of birdes and more then ordinarie.

        An artificiall charme of birdes being harde within, Pan
        speakes.

Pan.   The sillie birdes make mirth, then shoulde we doe them
            wronge,
        Pomona, if we nil bestowe an Eccho to their songe.

                    An Eccho to their song.   [A4ᵛ]

            The songe. A quier within and without.

Gods.   O Ida, o Ida, o Ida happie hill,
        This honour done to Ida may it continue still.
Muses.   Yee countrie gods, that in this Ida wonne,
170   Bring downe your giftes of welcome:
                    For honor done to Ida.
Gods.   Beholde in signe of joye we sing,
        And signes of joyfull wel-come bring.
                    For honor done to Ida.
Muses.   The *Muses* give you melodie to gratulate this chaunce,
        And Phoebe cheife of silvan chace commaundes you all to
            daunce.
Gods.   The rounde in a circle our sportance must be,
        Holde handes in a hornepype all gallant in glee.

                    Gods daunce.

Muses.   Reverence, reverence, most humble reverence.
180   *Gods.*   Most humble reverence.

    160   *Is here*] BM, P; I(s h)ere H, T
    164   *birdes and*] birdesand Q
    168   *to Ida*] BM, P; to o Ida H, T
    173   *wel-come*] BM, T; wel(-)come H. P
    177   *Gods. The rounde*] *Gods* The rouude Q; *Gods.* Then rounde Dyce؛
must be,] Dyce; must must be, Q
    178   SD *Gods daunce.*] See Explanatory Notes.

ACT. I. SCENA. IIII.

Pallas, Juno, and Venus enter, Rhanis leading the way,
Pan alone sings.

The songe.

The God of sheepeheardes and his mates,
With countrie chere salutes your states:
Faire, wise, and worthie as you bee,
And thanke the gracious Ladies three,
    For honour done to Ida.

The birdes singe.

The songe being done, Juno speakes.

Juno.   Venus, what shall I saie, for though I be a dame devine,
   This welcome and this melodie exceedes these wittes of mine.
Ven.   Beleeve me, Juno, as I hight the soveraigne of Love,
   These rare delightes in pleasures passe the banquets of king
    Jove.
190 *Pal.*   Then, Venus, I conclude, it easelie may be seene,
   That in her chaste and pleasaunt walkes fayre Phoebe is a
    Queene.
Rhan.   Divine Pallas, and you sacred dames,
   Juno and Venus, honoured by your names:
   Juno, the wife and sister of kinge Jove,
   Faire Venus, Ladie president of love:
   If any entertaynment in this place,   [B1]
   That can afford but homely, rude and base,
   It pleaze your godheads to accept in gree,
   That gratious thought our happinesse shalbe.
200 My mistresse Dian, this right well I know,
   For love that to this presence shee doth owe,

185 SD *The birdes singe.*] See Explanatory Notes.
188 *the*] thee Q
189 *pleasures*] Q; pleasure Dyce1
192 *Divine*] Q; Divinest B
195 *Venus*] Venns Q

Accountes more honoure done to her this day,
Then ever whilom in these woods of Ida.
And for our countrey gods, I dare bee bolde,
They make such cheere, your presence to beholde,
Such jouysaunce, such myrth and merryment,
As nothing els their minde might more content:
And that you doe beleeve it to bee so,
Fayre goddesses, your lovely lookes doe showe:
210   It rests in fine, for to confirme my talke,
Yee dayne to passe alonge to Dians walke:
Where shee amonge her troupe of maydes attends
The fayre aryvall of her welcome friends.
Flo.   And wee will wayte with all observance due,
And doe just honour to this heavenly crue.
Pan.   The god of sheepheardes, Juno, ere thou goe,
Intends a lambe on thee for to bestowe.
Faun.   Faunus, high raunger in Dianas chace,
Presents a fawne to lady Venus grace.
220   *Sil.*   Sylvanus gives to Pallas deitye,
This gallant bowe raught from the Oken tree.
Pom.   To them that doth this honour to our fieldes,
Her mellowe apples poore Pomona yeildes.
Juno.   And gentle gods, these signes of your goodwill
Wee take in worth, and shall accept them still.
Ven.   And Flora, this to thee amonge the rest,
Thy workmanship comparinge with the best,
Let it suffize thy cunninge to have power,
To call kinge Jove from forth his heavenly bowre:
230   Hadst thou a lover, Flora, credit mee,
I thinke thou wouldst beedecke him gallantly.
But wende we on, and, Rhanis, leade the way,
That kens the paynted pathes of pleasunt Ida.

Exeunt omnes.

228   *to have power,*] Dyce; to haue, Q

ACT. I SCENA V. *and ultima.*   [B1ᵛ]

Paris and Oenone.

Par.   Oenone, while we bin disposed to walke,
    Tell me what shall be subject of our talke:
    Thou hast a sorte of pretie tales in stoore,
    Dare saye no Nymphe in Ida woods hath more:
    Againe, beside thy sweete alluring face,
    In telling them thou hast a speciall grace.
240   Then preethee sweete, afforde some pretie thing,
    Some toie that from thy pleasaunt witte doth springe.
Oen.   Paris, my hartes contentment, and my choice,
    Use thou thy pype, and I will use my voyce,
    So shall thy just request not be denyed.
    And time well spent and both be satisfied.
Par.   Well gentle Nymphe although thou do me wrong,
    That can ne tune my pype unto a songe,
    Me list this once, Oenone, for thy sake,
    This idle taske on me to undertake.

They sit under a tree togeather.

250 *Oen.*   And whereon then shall be my Roundelay:
    For thou hast harde my stoore long since, dare say,
Fabu- How Saturne did devide his kingdome tho,
la.   *1* To Jove, to Neptune, and to Dis below,
      2 How mightie men made foule succesles warre,
        Against the gods and state of Jupiter:
      3 How Phorcias ympe that was so tricke and fayre,
        That tangled Neptune in her golden haire,
        Became a Gorgon for her lewde misdeede,
        A pretie fable Paris for to reade,
260   A peece of cunning trust me for the nonce,
        That wealth and beautie alter men to stoones.
      4 Howe Salmacis resembling ydlenes,

256 *Phorcias ympe*] Q; Phorcys' imp Dyce
257 *That tangled*] Thattangled Q
260 *cunning*] cunnig Q

Turnes men to women all through wantonnes.

5 How Pluto raught Queene Ceres daughter thence,
And what did followe of that love offence.

6 Of Daphne turned into the laurell tree,   [B2]
That shewes a myror of virginitie.

7 How faire Narcissus tooting on his shade,
Reproves disdayne, and tells how forme doth vade.

270   *8* How cunning Philomelaes needle tells,
What force in love, what wit in sorrow dwelles.

9 What paynes unhappie soules abyde in hell,
They say because on earth they lived not well.

10 Ixions wheele, proude Tantals pyning woe.

11 Prometheus torment, and a many moe.

12 How Danaus daughters plie their endles taske.

13 What toyle the toyle of Sysiphus doth aske.

All these are olde and knowne I knowe, yet if thou wilt
have anie,

Chuse some of these, for trust me else Oenone hath not
manie.

280   *Par.*   Nay what thou wilt: but sith my cunning not compares
with thine,

Beginne some Toy, that I can play upon this pipe of mine.

Oen.   There is a pretie sonnet then, we call it Cupids curse:
They that do chaunge olde love for new, pray gods they
chaunge for worse.

The note is fine and quicke withall, the dittie will agree,
Paris, with that same vowe of thine upon our Poplar tree.

Par.   No better thing, begine it then, Oenone thou shalt see
Our musicke, figure of the love that growes twixt thee and
me.

They sing: and while Oenone singeth, he pypeth.

Incipit Oenone.   Faire and fayre and twise so faire,
As fayre as any may be:

265   *of that*] ofthat Q
273   *They*] T hey Q
285   *with*] With Q

290   The fayrest sheepeherd on our grene,
                      A love for anie Ladie.

Paris.   Faire and faire and twise so fayre,
                      As fayre as anie may bee:
                 Thy love is fayre for thee alone,
                      And for no other Ladie.

Oenone.   My love is faire, my love is gaie,
                      As fresh as bine the flowers in May,
                 And of my love my roundylaye,   [B2ᵛ]
                 My merrie merrie roundelaie
300   Concludes with Cupids curse:
                 They that do chaunge olde love for newe,
                 Pray Gods they chaunge for worse.
Ambo. simul.   They that do chaunge, etc.
Oenone.   Faire and faire, etc.
Paris.   Faire and faire, etc. Thy love is faire etc.

Oenone.   My love can pype, my love can sing,
                      My love can manie a pretie thing,
                 And of his lovelie prayses ring
                 My merry merry roundelayes:
310   Amen to Cupids curse:
                 They that do chaunge, etc.
Paris.   They that do chaunge, etc.
Ambo.   Faire and fayre, etc.   *Finis Camoenae.*

The songe being ended they rise, and Oenone speakes.

Oen.   Swete sheepeherd, for Oenones sake be cunning in this
            songe,
        And kepe thy love, and love thy choice, or else thou doest
            her wrong.

290   *The*] Oenone. *The* Q
294   *for*] H, P, T; *fore* BM
299   *merrie merrie*] B; *merrie merrie merrie* Q
309–310   *My . . . curse:*] See Explanatory Notes.
310   *curse*] cnrse Q
313   SD *ended they*] endedthey Q

Par. My vowe is made and witnessed, the Poplar will not
  starte,
 Nor shall the nymphe Oenones love from forth my breathing hart.
 I will goe bring the one thy way, my flocke are here behinde,
 And I will have a lovers fee: they saie, unkist, unkinde.

Exeunt ambo.

ACT. II. SCENA I.

Venus, Juno, Pallas.

320 *Ven.* (*ex abrupto.*) But pray you tell me, Juno was it so,
 As Pallas tolde me here the tale of Eccho.
Juno. Shee was a nymphe indeede, as Pallas tels,
 A walker, such as in these thickets dwells:
 And as shee tolde what subtill jugling prankes
 Shee playde with Juno, so she tolde her thankes:
 A tatling trull to come at everie call,
 And now foresooth nor tongue nor life at all.
 And though perhaps shee was a helpe to Jove,   [B3]
 And held me chat, while he might court his love:
330 Beleeve me, dames, I am of this opinion,
 He tooke but little pleasure in the minion.
 And what so ere his scapes have bene beside,
 Dare saie for him a never strayed so wyde:
 A lovely nutbrowne lasse, or lustie trull,
 Have power perhaps to make a god a bull.
Ven. Gramercie gentle Juno for that jest,
 Ifaith that item was worth all the rest.
Pal. No matter, Venus, how so ere you skorne,
 My father Jove at that time ware the horne.
340 *Juno.* Had everie wanton god above, Venus, not better
  lucke,

320 *Ven.* (*ex abrupto.*) *But*] See Explanatory Notes.
322 *Shee*] S hee Q *nymphe*] nympe Q
324 *shee tolde*] sheetold Q
334 *A lovely*] Alouely Q

Then heaven would be a pleasaunt parcke, and Mars a lustie
   bucke.

Ven.   Tut Mars hath hornes to butte withall although no bull
   a showes,

A never needes to maske in nets, a feares no jellous froes.

Juno.   Forsooth the better is his turne, for if a speake to
   loude,

Must finde some shifte to shadowe him, a net, or else a
   cloude.

Pal.   No more of this, fayre goddesses, unrip not so your
   shames,

To stand all naked to the world, that bene such heavenly
   dames.

Juno.   Nay, Pallas, that's a common tricke with Venus well
   we knowe,

And all the Gods in heaven have seene her naked, long agoe.

350   *Ven.*   And then she was so faire and bright, and lovelie and so
   trim,

As Mars is but for Venus tooth, and shee will sporte with
   him.

And but me list not here to make comparison with Jove,

Mars is no raunger, Juno, he in everie open grove.

Pal.   To much of this: we wander farre, the skies begine to
   skowle,

Retire we to Dianas bowre, the weather will be foule.

*The storme being past of thunder and lightning, and Ate
having trundled the ball into place, crying* Fatum Troie,
Juno taketh the bal up and speaketh.

Juno.   Pallas, the storme is past and gon, and Phoebus cleares
   the skies,

And loe, beholde a ball of golde, a faire and worthie prize.

Ven.   This posie wils, the apple to the fayrest given be,

Then is it mine: for Venus hight the fayrest of the three.

360   *Pal.*   The fayrest here as fayre is ment, am I, ye do me
   wronge:

350   *and lovelie*] Q; so lovelie Dyce1
358   *fayrest*] fayre st Q

And if the fayrest have it must, to me it doth belong.

Juno.   Then Juno may it not enjoy, so every one sayes no,
But I will prove my selfe the fayrest, er I lose it so.
The breyfe is this, *Detur Pulcherrimae*.   [B3ᵛ]

They reade the posie.

Let this unto the fayrest gyven bee,
The fayrest of the three, and I am shee.

[*Pal.*]   *Detur Pulcherrimae*. Let this unto the fayrest gyven
be,   *Pallas reades.*

The fayrest of the three, and I am shee.

[*Ven.*]   *Detur Pulcherrimae*. Let this unto the fayrest given
bee   *Venus reades.*

370   The fayrest of the thre, and I am shee.

Juno.   My face is fayre, but yet the majestye
That all the gods in heaven have seene in me,
Have made them chuse me of the Planetes seaven,
To bee the wyfe of Jove, and Queene of heaven.
Yf then this prize be but bequeathed to beautye,
The only shee that wins this prize, am I.

Ven.   That Venus is the fayrest, this dothe prove,
That Venus is the lovely Queen of love.
The name of Venus is in deede but beautye,

380   And men me fayrest call, per excellencye.
Yf then this prize be but bequeathed to beautye,
The only shee that wins this prize, am I.

Pal.   To stand on tearmes of beautye as yow take it,
Beeleve me, Ladies, is but to mystake it:
The beautye that this subtill prize must win,

364   *Pulcherrimae*] H, P, T; *Pulherrimae* BM
367   *Pal.*] Q omits   SD *Pallas reades.*] See Explanatory Notes.
369   *Ven.*] Q omits   *given*] H, P, T; give BM   SD *Venus reades.*] See Explanatory Notes.
371   *majestye*] maistye Q
374   *wyfe*] w yfe Q
375   *Yf then*] Yfthen Q
378   *of love*] oflove Q
379   *beautye*] bautye Q

No outwarde beautye highte, but dwels within.
And syfte it as yow please, and yow shall finde,
This beautye, is the beautye of the minde.
This fayrenes, Vertue highte, in generall,
390 That many braunches hathe in speciall:
This beauty wysdom hight, whereof am I,
By heaven appointed, goddesse worthelye.
And looke how muche the minde, the better parte,
Doth overpasse the bodye in deserte:
So much the mistris of those guyfts devine,
Excells thy beautie, and that state of thine.
Then yf this prize bee thus bequeathed to beautye,
The only she that wins this prize, am I.
Ven.   Nay, Pallas, by your leave, yow wander cleane,
400 Wee must not conster heereof as yow meane:
But take the sense as it is plainly ment,
And let the fayrest ha't, I am content.   [B4]
Pal.   Our reasons wil be infinite, I trowe,
Unles unto some other point we grow.
For first heres none mee thinkes disposed to yeelde,
And none but will with wordes maintaine the fielde.
Juno.   Then if you will to avoyde a tedious grudge,
Refer it to the sentence of a judge,
Who ere he be that commeth next in place,
410 Let him bestowe the ball, and ende the case.
Ven.   So can it not go wronge with me at al.
Pal.   I am agreed how ever it befall.
And yet by common doome, so may it bee,
I may be sayde the fayrest of the three.
Juno.   Then yonder loe that sheepeherde swaine is he,
That must be umpier in this controversie.

387 *yow please*] y ow please Q
397 *prize bee*] prizebee Q
400 *conster*] Q; construe Dyce1
402 *ha't,*] Child; hate, Q
403 *wil be*] wilbe Q
411 *me at al*] Dyce; me not at al Q

ACT. II. SCENA II.

Paris alone. Manentibus Pal. Junone, Venere.

Ven.   Juno, in happie time, I do accept the man,
It seemeth by his lookes, some skill of love he can.
Par.   The nymphe is gone, and I all solitarie,
420   Must wend to tend my charge, opprest with melancholy.
This day (or else me fayles my sheepeherdes skill)
Will tide me passing good, or passing ill.
Juno.   Sheepeherd, abash not, though, at sudden thus,
Thou be aryved by ignorance among us,
Not earthlie but devine, and goddesses all three,
Juno, Pallas, Venus, these our titles be,
Nor feare to speake, for reverence of the place,
Chosen to ende a harde and doubtfull case.
This apple loe (nor aske thou whence it came)
430   Is to be given unto the fayrest dame.
And fayrest is, nor shee, nor shee, but shee,
Whom, sheepeherd, thou shalt fayrest name to be.
This is thy charge, fulfill without offence,
And shee that winnes shall give thee recompence.
Pal.   Dreade not to speake for we have chosen thee,
Sith in this case, we can no judges be.
Ven.   And, sheepeherd, say that I the fayrest ame,
And thou shalt win good guerdon for the same.
Juno.   Nay, shepherde, looke uppon my stately grace,   [B4ᵛ]
440   Because the pompe that longs to Junoes mace,
Thou mayst not see: and thincke Queene Junoes name,
To whome olde shepherds title workes of fame,
Is mightye, and may easily suffize,
At Phebus hande to gaine a golden prize.
And for thy meede, sythe I ame Queene of riches,

419   *nymphe*] ny mphe Q
426   *Juno*] *Iune* Q
436   *this*] T, H, P; thie BM
441   *Thou*] Dyce They Q
444   *Phebus*] Q; Phoebe's Dyce₁, Paris N   *prize*] p(r)ize Q

Shepherde, I will rewarde thee with greate monarchies,
Empires, and kingdomes, heapes of massye golde,
Scepters and diadems, curious to beholde,
Riche robes, of sumpteous workmanship and cost,
450 And thowsand thinges whereof I make no boast
The moulde whereon thowe treadest shall be of Tagus
    sandes,
And Xanthus shall runne liquid golde for the to wash thy
    handes:
And yf thou lyke to tend thy flock, and not from them to
    flie,
Their fleeces shalbe curled gold to please their masters eye.
And last, to sett thy harte one fire, gyve this one fruite to
    me,
And, shepherd, lo this Tree of Golde will I bestowe on
    thee.

JUNOES SHOWE.

*Heereuppon did rise a Tree of gold laden with Diadems
and Crownes of golde.*

The grownde whereon it growes, the grasse, the roote of
    golde,
The body and the bark of golde, all glistringe to beholde,
The leaves of burnysht golde, the fruites that thereon
    growe
460 Are diadems sett with pearle in golde in gorgeous glistringe
    showe:
And yf this Tree of Golde, in lue may not suffize,
Require a grove of golden trees, so *Juno* beare the prize.

The Tree sinketh.

Pal. My lyst not tempt thee with decayinge wealthe,
    Which is embaset by want of lusty healthe:

450 *boast*] bo(a)st Q
456 *shepherd*] s(h)epherd Q
457 *growes*] groes Q
459 *of burnysht*] ofburnysht Q
461 *yf this*] yfthis Q

But yf thou have a minde to fly above,
Ycrowned with fame neere to the seate of Jove:
Yf thou aspire to wysdomes worthines,
Whereof thow mayst not see the brightnes
Yf thou desyre honor of chyvallrye,
470   To bee renouned for happy victorie,
To fighte it out, and in the champaine feilde,
To shrowde thee under Pallas warlike sheilde,
To praunce on barbed steedes, this honor loe,
My selfe for guerdon shall on thee bestowe.   [C1]
And for encouragement, that thou mayst see,
What famous knightes dame Pallas warriers be,
Beholde in Pallas honour here they come,
Marching alonge with sounde of thundring drom.

PALLAS SHOW.

*Hereuppon did enter. 9. knights in armour, treading a
warlike Almaine, by drome and fife, and then having
march't foorth againe, Venus speaketh.*

Ven.   Come sheepeherde, come, sweete sheepeherde looke
on me,
480   These bene to hoat alarams these for thee:
But if thou wilt give mee the golden ball,
Cupide my boy shall ha't to playe withall,
That when so ere this apple he shall see,
The god of love himselfe shall thinke on the,
And bid thee looke and chuse, and he will wounde,
Whereso thy fancyes object shalbe founde,
And lightlie when he shootes he doth not misse:
And I will give the many a lovelie kysse,
And come and play with thee on Ida here,
490   And if thou wilt a face that hath no peere,
A gallant girle, a lustie minion trull,

467   *Yf thow*] Y fthow Q   *worthines,*] H, P, T; worthines. BM
468   *not*] n(o)t Q
472   *Pallas*] pallas Q
482   *ha't*] Child; hate Q

That can give sporte to thee thy bellyfull,
To ravish all thy beating vaines with joye,
Here is a lasse of Venus court, my boy,

Helen entreth with 4. Cupides.

Here gentle sheepeherde, heres for thee a peece,
The fayrest face, the flower of gallant Greece.

VENUS SHOW.

Here Helen entreth in her braverie, with 4. Cupides
attending on her, each having his fan in his hande to
fan fresh ayre in her face. Shee singeth as followeth.

> *Si Diana nel cielo è una stella*
> *Chiara, è lucente piena di splendore*
> *Che porge luc' all' affanato cuore:*
> 500 *Si Diana, nel ferno è una dea,*
> *Che da conforto all' anime dannate,*
> *Che per amor son morte desperate:*
> *Si Diana ch' in terra è delle nimphe*   [C1ᵛ]
> *Reina, imperative di dolce fiori*
> *Tra bosch' e Selve da morte a pastori.*
> *Io son un Diana dolce e rara*
> *Che con Le guardi Io posso far guerra*
> *A Dian' in fern' in cielo, et in terra.   Exit.*

The song being ended Helen departeth, and Paris
Speaketh.

Par.   Most heavenly dames, was never man as I
510   Poore shepherde swaine, so happy and unhappy:
      The least of these delights, that you devyse,
      Able to wrape and dazle humaine eyes.
      But since my silence may not pardoned bee,

496   *fayrest face*] fayrestface Q   SD *Shee*] *shee* Q
501   *da conforto*] *daconforto* Q
507   *Che*] *Chle* Q
508   *in fern'*] infern' Q
512   *wrape*] Q; rape Dyce1

And I appoint which is the fayrest shee,
Pardon, most sacred dames, sythe one not all,
By Paris doome must have this golden ball.
Thy beautye, stately Juno, dame devine,
That lyke to Phoebus golden beames doth shine,
Approves it selfe to bee most excellent,
520   But that fayre face that dothe me most content,
Sythe fayre, faire dames, is neyther shee nor shee,
But shee whome I shall fairest deeme to bee.
That face is hers that hight the Queene of Love,
Whose sweetenes dothe bothe gods and creatours move.

He giveth the golden Ball to Venus.

And if the fayrest face deserve the ball,
Fayre Venus, Ladyes, beares it from yee all.
Ven.   And in this ball dothe Venus more delight,
Then in her lovely boy faire Cupids sighte.
Come shepherd comme, sweete Venus is thy frend,
530   No matter how thow other gods offend.

Venus taketh Paris with her.   *Exeunt.*

Juno.   But he shall rue, and ban the dismal day
Wherein his Venus bare the ball away:
And heaven and earth just witnesses shall bee,
I will revenge it on his progenye.
Pal.   Well, Juno, whether wee bee leyfe or lothe,
Venus hathe got the aple from us bothe.

Exeunt ambo.

523   *of Love*] ofLoue Q
524   *Whose*] whose Q   SD *giveth*] guieth Q   *Venus*] venus Q
530   SD *Paris*] paris Q
532   *Wherein*] wherein Q
535   *Well*] well Q   leyfe or] Dyce; leyseor Q
536   SD *ambo.*] *Ambo* Q   *Colin thenamored sheepeherd singeth his
passion of love.*] Q; *Colin the enamoured sheepheard, singeth this passion of
loue. EH* See Explanatory Notes.

ACT. III. SCENA. I.   [C2]

Colin thenamored sheepeherd singeth his passion of love.

The songe.

O gentle love, ungentle for thy deede,
    Thou makest my harte
    A bloodie marke
540   With pearcyng shot to bleede.

Shoote softe sweete love, for feare thou shoote amysse,
    For feare too keene
    Thy arrowes beene,
And hit the harte, where my beloved is.

To faire that fortune were, nor never I
    Shalbe so blest
    Among the rest
That love shall ceaze on her by simpathye.

Then since with love my prayers beare no boot,
550   This doth remayne
    To cease my payne,
I take the wounde, and dye at Venus foote.

Exit Colin.

ACT. III. SCENA. II.

Hobinol, Digon, Thenot.

Hob. Poore Colin wofull man, thy life forespoke by love,
  What uncouth fit, what maladie is this, that thou dost
    prove.
Dig. Or love is voide of phisicke cleane, or loves our com-
    mon wracke,
  That gives us bane to bring us lowe, and let us medicine
    lacke.

551 *cease*] Q; ease *EH*

Hob.   That ever love had reverence 'mong sillie sheepeherd
swaines,

Belike that humor hurtes them most that most might be
their paines.

The.   Hobin, it is some other god that cheerisheth her sheepe,

560   For sure this love doth nothing else but make our herdmen
weepe.

Dig.   And what a hap is this I praye, when all our woods
rejoyce,

For Colin thus to be denyed his yong and lovely choice.

The.   She hight in deede so fresh and faire that well it is for
thee,

Colin and kinde hath bene thy friends, that Cupid coulde
not see.   [C2ᵛ]

Hob.   And whether wendes yon thriveles swaine, like to the
striken deere.

Seekes he Dictamum for his wounde within our forrest
here.

Dig.   He wendes to greete the Queene of love, that in these
woods doth wonne,

With mirthles layes to make complaint to Venus of her
sonne.

The.   A Colin thou art all deceived, shee dallyes with the
boy,

570   And winckes at all his wanton prankes, and thinkes thy
love a toy.

Hob.   Then leave him to his luckles love, let him abide his
fate,

The sore is ranckled all to farre, our comforte coms to late.

Dig.   Though Thestilis the Scorpion be that breakes his
sweete assault,

Yet will Rhamnusia vengeance take, on her disdainefull
fault.

557   *sheepeherd*] sheepeheed Q
559   *cheerisheth her*] cheerishethher Q; cherisheth their Dyce1
564   *friends,*] friende, Q
566   *Dictamum*] Q; Dictamnum Dyce

The. Lo yonder comes the lovely Nymphe, that in these
　　　Ida vales,
　　Playes with Amintas lustie boie, and coyes him in the dales.
Hob. Thenot, me thinks her cheere is changed, her mirthfull
　　　lookes are layd,
　　She frolicks not: pray god the lad have not beguilde the
　　　mayde.

ACT. III. SCENA. III.

Oenone entreth with a wreath of popular on her heade.
Manent Pastores.

Oen. Beguilde, disdayned, and out of love: live longe thou
　　　Poplar-tree,
580　And let thy letters growe in length, to witnes this with mee.
　　A *Venus,* but for reverence, unto thy sacred name,
　　To steale a sylly maydens love, I might account it blame.
　　And if the tales be true I heare, and blushe for to receite,
　　Thou dost me wrong to leave the playnes, and dally out of
　　　sight.
　　False *Paris,* this was not thy vow, when thou and I were
　　　one,
　　To raung and chaung old love for new: but now those
　　　dayes be gone.
　　But I will finde the goddesse out, that shee thy vow may
　　　reade,
　　And fill these woods with my lamentes, for thy unhappy
　　　deede.
Hob. So faire a face, so foule a thought to harbour in his
　　　breast,
590　Thy hope consum'd, poore Nymphe, thy hap is worse then
　　　all the rest.
Oen. A sheepeherdes, you bin full of wiles, and whet your
　　　wits on bookes.

575　*comes*] co(m)es Q
578　*beguilde*] Dyce; beguide Q
581　*name*] BM, P, T; náme H

And wrap poore maydes with pypes and songes, and sweete
    alluring lookes.

Dig. Mispeake not al, for his amisse, there bin that keepen
    flocks,

That never chose but once, nor yet beguiled love with
    mockes.

Oen. False Paris he is none of those, his trothles doble deede,
    Will hurte a many sheepeherds else that might go nigh to
    speede.

The. Poore Colin, that is ill for thee, that art as true in trust
    To thy sweete smerte, as to his Nymphe Paris hath bin
    unjust.   [C3]

Oen. A well is she hath Colin wonne, that nill no other love:
600   And woo is me, my lucke is losse, my paynes no pytie
    moove.

Hob. Farewell faire Nymphe, sith he must heale alone that
    gave the wound.

There growes no herbe of such effect upon Dame Natures
    ground.

Exeunt Pastores.

[ACT. III. SCENA. IIII.]

Manet Oenone. Mercu. entr. with Vulcans Cyclops.

Mer. Here is a Nymphe that sadlie sittes, and shee belike
    Can tell some newes, Pyracmon, of the jolly swaine we
    seeke.

Dare wage my winges the lasse doth love, she lookes so
    bleak and thin,

And tis for anger or for griefe: but I will talke beginne.

592 *wrap*] Q; wrape Dyce rape B   *sweete*] Dyce; swee(t)e Q
593 *there bin*] therebin BM, P, T; therebín H
595 *those*] tho(s)e Q
599 *A well*] Awell Q
601 *alone*] alone Q
602 *Dame Natures*] dame natures Q   SD *ACT. III. SCENA. IIII.*]
Q omits
  603 *belike*] beleek Dyce1

Oen. Breake out poore harte, and make complaint the moun-
taine flocks to move,
What proude repulse and thanckles scorne thou hast received of love.

Mer. She singeth, sires, be husht awhile.

Oenone singeth as shee sitts.

OENONES COMPLAINT.

610 Melpomene, the muse of tragicke songes,
With moornefull tunes in stole of dismall hue,
Assist a sillie Nymphe to wayle her woe,
And leave thy lustie companie behinde.

Thou luckles wreath, becomes not me to weare
The Poplar tree for triumphe of my love.
Then as my joye my pride of love is lefte,
Be thou uncloathed of thy lovelie greene,

And in thy leaves my fortune written bee,
And them some gentle winde let blowe abroade,
620 That all the worlde may see how false of love,
False Paris hath to his Oenone bene.

The songe ended, Oenone sitting still. Mercurie speaketh.

Mer. Good-day fayre mayde, werie belike with following
of your game,
I wish thee cunning at thy will, to spare or strike the same.

Oen. I thanke you sir, my game is quick and rids a length of
grounde,
And yet I am deceaved or else a had a deadlie wounde.

---

609 SD *OENONES COMPLAINT.*] Q; Oenones *complaint in blanke
verse. EH* See Explanatory Notes.
610 *Melpomene,*] *EH; Melponie,* Q
614 *Thou*] Q; This *EH*
618 *fortune*] Q; fortunes *EH*
619 *them*] Q; then *EH*

Mer.	Your hand perhaps did swarve awrie.
Oen.	Or else it was my harte. [C3ᵛ]
Mer.	Then sure a plyed his fotemanship.
Oen.	A played a raunging parte.
Mer.	You should have given a deeper wound.
Oen.	I could not that for pity.
Mer.	You should have eyd him better then.
Oen.	Blind love was not so witty.

630 *Mer.*   Why tell me, sweete, are you in love.

Oen.   Or would I were not so.

Mer.   Yee meane because a does ye wrong.

Oen.   Perdie the more my woe.

Mer.   Why meane ye love, or him ye loved?

Oen.   Wel may I meane them both.

Mer.   Is love to blame?

Oen.   The queene of love hath made him false
his troth.

Mer.   Meane ye indeede the queene of love.

Oen.   Even wanton Cupids dame.

Mer.   Why was thy love so lovely then?

Oen.   His beautie hight his shame,
The fairest sheepeherde one our greene.

Mer.   Is he a sheepeherd than.

Oen.   And sometime kept a bleating flock.

Mer.   Enough, this is the man.
Where woons he than?

Oen.   About these woods: far from the Poplar tree.

Mer.   What Poplar meane ye?

626 *awrie*] Dyce; awarie Q   *Or*] or Q
627 *A*] a Q
629 *Blind*] blind Q
630 *Why*] why Q   *Or*] or Q; O Daniel
631 *does ye*] H, P; do(e)s ye BM; do( ) s ye T   *Perdie*] perdie Q
632 *Wel*] wel Q
633 *blame*] bIame Q   *The*] the Q   *of love*] ofloue Q
634 *of love*] ofloue Q   *Even*] euē Q
635 *love*] BM, P, T; loúe H   *His*] his Q
636 *Is*] is Q
637 *Enough*] enough Q
638 *Where*] Mer. Where Q   *About*] about Q

Oen.   Witnes of the vowes betwixt him and me.
640   And come and wend a little way and you shall see his skill.
Mer.   Sirs tarrie you.
Oen.   Nay let them goe.
Mer.   Nay not unles you will.
     Stay Nymphe, and harke what I say of him thou blamest so,
     And credit me, I have a sad discourse to tell thee ere I go.
     Know then, my pretie mops, that I hight Mercurie,
     The messenger of heaven, and hether flie
     To cease upon the man whom thou dost love,
     To summon him before my father Jove,
     To answere matter of great consequence,
     And Jove himselfe will not be longe from hence.
650 *Oen.*   Sweete Mercurie, and have poore Oenons cryes,
     For Paris fault, ypeirced th'unpertiall skyes.
Mer.   The same is he, that jolly sheepeherdes swaine.
Oen.   His flocke do grase upon Auroras plaine,
     The colour of his coate is lustie greene,
     That would these eyes of mine had never seene,
     His tycing curled hayre, his front of yvorie,
     Then had not I poore I bin unhappie.
Mer.   No marvell wench, although we cannot finde him,
     When all to late the queene of heaven doth minde him,
660 But if thou wilt have physicke for thy sore,
     Minde him who list, remember thou him no more:
     And find some other game, and get thee gon,
     For here will lustie suters come anon,
     To hoat and lustie for thy dyeing vaine,   [C4]
     Such as nere wont to make their sutes in vaine.
                    Exit Merc. cum Cyclop.
Oen.   I will goe sit and pyne under the Poplar tree,
     And write my answere to his vow, that everie eie may see.
                    Exit.

639 *Witnes*] witnes Q   *betwixt*] Q; 'twixt Dyce 1
641 *Nay . . . Nay*] nay . . . nay Q
642 *of him*] ofhim Q
646 *whom*] whon Q
651 *ypeirced*] Dyce; ypeircest Q
665 *nere wont*] Dyce; were monte Q

ACT. III. SCENA V.

Venus, Paris, and a companie of sheepeherdes.

Ven.   Sheepeherdes, I am contente, for this sweete sheepeherdes sake,

  A straunge revenge upon the maide and her disdaine to
take.

670   Let Colins corps be brought in place, and burned in the
plaine,

  And let this be the verse. *The love whom Thestilis hath
slaine.*

  And trust me I will chide my sone for parciallitie,

  That gave the swaine so deepe a wound, and let her scape
him by.

Pastores.   Alas that ever love was blinde, to shoote so farre
amisse.

Ven.   *Cupid* my sonne was more to blame, the fault not
mine, but his.

Pastores exeunt, Manent. Ven. cum Par.

Par.   O madam, if your selfe would daine the handling of
the bowe,

  Albeit it be a taske, your selfe more skill, more justice
knowe.

Ven.   Sweete sheepeherde, didst thou ever love.

Par.   Lady, a little once.

Ven.   And art thou changed.

Par.   Faire queene of love I loved not al attonce.

680   *Ven.*   Well wanton, wert thou wounded so deepe as some
have ben,

  It were a cunning cure to heale and rufull to be seene.

Par.   But tell me, gracious goddesse, for a starte and false
offence,

670 *burned*] Q; buried Dyce
675 *the fault*] thefault Q
679 *Faire*] faire Q
682 *starte*] BM, P, T; stav(te) H

Hath Venus or her sonne the power, at pleasure to dispence.
Ven. My boy, I will instruct thee in a peece of poetrie,
That happly erst thou hast not heard: in hel there is a tree,
Where once a day doe sleepe the soules of false foresworen
    lovers,
With open hartes, and there aboute in swarmes the number
    hovers
Of poore forsaken ghostes, whose winges from of this tree
    do beate
Round drops of firie Phlegiton to scorch false hartes with
    heate.
690 This payne did Venus and her sonne, entreate the prince of
    hell,
T'impose to such as faithles were, to such as loved them
    well.
And therefore this, my lovely boy, faire Venus doth advise
    thee,
Be true and stedfast in thy love, beware thou doe disguise
    thee.
For he that makes but love a jest, when pleaseth him to
    starte,
Shall feele those firye water drops consume his faithles
    harte.   [C4ᵛ]
Par. Is Venus and her sonne so full of justice and severytye.
Ven. Pittie it weare that love shoulde not be lincked with
    indifferencie.
Howe ever lovers can exclaime for harde successe in love,
Trust me, some more then common cause that painfull hap
    dothe move.
700 And Cupids bowe is not alone his triumphe, but his rod,
Nor is he only but a boy: he hight a mighty god.
And they that do him reverence, have reason for the same,
His shafts keepe heaven and earth in awe, and shape re-
    wardes for shame.

684 *of poetrie*] ofpoetrie Q
688 *forsaken*] forsa ken Q
700 *Cupids*] cupids Q
703 *for*] Q; or Daniel

Par.   And hathe he reason to mantayne why Colin died for
    love.

Ven.   Yea reason good I warrant thee, in right it might
    beehove.

Par.   Then be the name of love adored, his bowe is full of
    mighte,

    His woundes are all but for desert, his lawes are all but
    right.

Ven.   Well for this once me lyst apply my speeches to thy
    sense,

    And Thestilis shall feele the paine for loves supposed
    offence.

*The shepherds bring in Collins Hearce singing [to the
tune] Welladay Welladay.*

710   Poore Colin thow arte going to the grounde:
         The love whome Thestilis hathe slaine,
         Harde harte, faire face fraughte with disdaine:
         Disdaine in love a deadlie wounde.
         Wounde her swete love so deepe againe,
         That shee may feele the dyeing paine
         Of this unhappie shepherds swaine,
         And dye for love as Colin died, as Colin died.

Finis Camoenae.

Ven.   Shepherdes abyde, let Colins corps bee wittnes of the
    paine

    That Thestilis endures in love, a plague for her dysdaine.
720   Beholde the organ of our wrathe, this rusty churle is hee,
    She dotes on his yllfavored face, so muche accurst is shee.

706 *of love*] oflove Q
707 *right.*] Dyce; right: Q
708 *Ven. Well*] Dyce; well Q
709 SD–710 See Explanatory Notes.
711 *Thestilis*] *Thestis* Q
715 *dyeing*] dyeng Q
717 *died,*] *died.* Q   *died.*] P; *died* BM, H, T   SD *Finis*] *finis* Q

She singeth an old songe called the woing of Colman. A foule croked Churle enters, and Thestilis a faire lasse wooeth him. He crabedly refuzeth her, and goethe out of place. She tarieth behinde.

Par. A poore unhappy Thestilis, unpitied is thy paine.

Ven. Her fortune not unlyke to hers whome cruell thow hast slaine.

Thestilis singeth, and the Shepherds replie.

The songe. [D1]

The straunge affects of my tormented harte,
Whome cruell love hathe wofull prisoner caughte,
Whome cruel hate hathe into bondage broughte,
Whome wit no way of safe escape hath taughte,
Enforce me say in wittnes of my smarte,
There is no paine to foule disdaine in hardy sutes of love.

730   *Shep.*   There is no paine etc.

     Thest.   Cruell, farewell.

     Shep.   Cruell, farewell.

     Thest.   Moste cruell thow, of all that nature framed.

     Shep.   Moste cruell etc.

     Thest.   To kill thy love with thy disdaine.

     Shep.   To kill thy love with thy disdaine.

     Thest.   Cruell disdaine soe live thow named.

     Shep.   Cruell disdaine etc.

     Thest.   And let me dye of Iphis paine.

     Shep.   A life to good for thy disdaine.

740   *Thest.*   Sithe this my stars to me allot,

  721   SD *He*] *he* Q

  722   *Thestilis*] Dyce; Thestlis Q

  723   *hers*] Dyce; his Q   SD *songe.*] ( )onge. Q See Explanatory
Notes.

  724   *affects*] B; *effects* Q

  725   *hathe*] *hat he* Q

  731   *Shep.*] *Shep* Q

  733   *cruell*] *creull* Q

  738   *Iphis paine*] *Iphispaine* Q

  739   *life*] Q; *death* Daniel

And thow thy love hast all forgot.

Exit Thest.

Shep.   And thow etc.

The shepherds carie out Colin.

The grace of this song is in the Shepherds Ecco to her verse.

Ven.   Now shepherds, bury Colins corps, perfume his herce
with flowers,
And write what justice Venus did amid these woods of
yours.
How now, how cheeres my lovely boy, after this dump of
love.

Par.   Such dumpes, sweete Lady, as bin these are deadly
dumpes to prove.

Ven.   Cease shepherde, there are other nues, after this mel-
ancholye.
My minde presumes some tempest toward upon the speache
of Mercurie.

ACT III. SCENA. VI.

*Mercurye with Vulcans Cyclops enter. Manentibus Ven.
cum Par.*

Mer.   Faire lady Venus, let me pardoned bee
750   That have of longe bin well beloved of thee,
Yf as my office bids, my selfe first brings   [D1ᵛ]
To my sweete Madame these unwellcome tydings.

Ven.   What nues, what tydings, gentle Mercurie,
In midest of my delites to troble me.

Mer.   At Junoes sute, Pallas assisting her,

745   *cheeres my*] cheeresmy Q   *lovely*] Louely Q
747   *there*] Dycei; these Q
748   *Mercurie.*] Mercurie Q   SD *ACT . . . Par.*] ACT. III. SCEN
A.VI. *Mercurye with Vulcans / Cyclops enter. Manentibus Ven. cum Par.* Q
750   *well beloved*] wellbeloued Q
752   *sweete*] swee(t)e Q

Sythe bothe did joyne in sute to Jupiter.
Action is entred in the court of heaven,
And me, the swyftest of the Planets seaven,
With warant they have thence despatcht away,
760   To apprehende and finde the man, they say,
That gave from them that selfesame ball of golde,
Which I presume I do in place beeholde,
Which man, unles my markes bee taken wyde,
Is hee that sytts so neere thy gracious syde.
This beinge so, it rests he go from hence,
Before the gods to answere his offence.
Ven.   What tale is this, dothe Juno and her mate
Pursue this shepherde with such deadly hate.
As what was then our generall agrement,
770   To stande unto they nil be nowe content.
Let Juno jet, and Pallas play her parte,
What heere I have, I woonne it by deserte:
And heaven and earthe shall bothe confounded bee,
Ere wronge in this be donne to him or me.
Mer.   This litle fruite, yf Mercury can spell,
Will sende I feare a world of soules to hell.
Ven.   What meane these Ciclops, Mercurie, is Vulcan waxt
   so fine,
   To sende his Chimnysweepers forth, to fetter any freinde
   of mine.
   Abashe not shepherd at the thinge, my self thy baile wilbe,
780   He shalbe present at the courte of Jove, I warrant thee.
Mer.   Venus, gyve me your pledge.
Ven.   My Cestone, or my fan, or bothe.
Mer.   Nay this shall serve: your worde to mee as sure as is
   your othe.

Mercurie taketh her fan.

757   *of heaven*] ofheauen Q
761   *that selfesame*] P; that(-)selfesame BM, H, T
777   *Vulcan*] vulcan Q
779   *thinge*] thing e Q
780   *Jove,*] Ioue(,) Q
781   *My*] my Q
782   SD *Mercurie taketh her fan.*] See Explanatory Notes.

At Dianas bowre: and Lady, yf my witt or pollycie
May profit him for Venus sake, let him make bolde with
   Mercury.

Exit.

Ven.   Sweete Paris, whereon doest thow muse?
Par.   The angrye heavens for this fatall jar,
Name me the instrument of dire and deadly war.

Explicit. Actus Tertius. Exeunt Venus and Paris.

ACT. IIII. SCENA I.   [D₂]

Vulcan following one of Dianas Nymphes.

Vul.   Why nymphe, what need ye run so fast? what though
   but black I be?
I have more preetie knackes to please, then everie eye doth
   see.
790   And though I goe not so upright, and though I am a smythe,
To make me gratious you may have some other thinge
   therewith.

ACT. IIII. SCENA II.

Bacchus, Vulcan, Nymphe.

Bac.   Yee Vulcane, will yee so in deede: nay turne and tell
   him, trull,
He hath a mystresse of his owne to take his belly full.
Vul.   Why sir, if Phoebes dainty nymphes please lustie Vul-
   cans tooth,
Why may not Vulcan treade awry, aswell as Venus dooth?

784   SD *Exit.*] (*Exit* Q
786   *Par.*] P r Q
787   SD *Explicit*] *Explici* (). Q
788   *be?*] H, P; b(e) BM, T
792   *Yee*] Q; Yea Dyce

Nym. Ye shall not taynt your trothe for me: you wot it
verie well,

All that be Dians maides are vowed to halter apes in hell.

Bac. Ifaith, Ifaith, my gentle mops, but I do know a cast,
Leade apes who list, that we would helpe t'unhaltar them
as fast.

800 *Nym.* Fy, fy, your skill is wondrous great, had thought the
god of wine,

Had tended but his tubbes and grapes, and not ben haulfe so
fine.

Vul. Gramercie for that quirke, my girle.

Bac.   That's one of dainties frumpes.

Nym. I pray sir tak't with all amisse, our cunning comes by
lumpes.

Vul. Sh'ath capt his aunswere in the Q.

Nym.   How sayes a, has shee so?

Aswel as shee that kapt your head to keepe you warme
below.

Vul. Yea then you will be curst I see.

Bac.   Best let her even alone.

Nym. Yea gentle gods, and finde some other stringe to harpe
upon.

Bac. Some other string, agreed Ifayth, some other pretie
thing,

Twere shame fayre maydes should idle be, how say you,
wil ye sing.

810 *Nym.* Some roundes or merry roundylaies, we sing no other
songes,

Your melancholick noates not to our countrie myrth be-
longes.

Vul. Here comes a crue will helpe us trimme.

797 *apes*] Dyce; apples Q
798 *Ifaith, Ifaith,*] Ifaith Ifaith, Q
800 *Fy, fy,*] Fy fy Q
802 *That's*] Thats Q
804 *How sayes*] how sayes, Q
806 *Best*] best Q
811 *countrie myrth*] countriemyrth Q

ACTUS IIII SCENA III.

Mercurie with the Cyclops.

Mer.   Yea now our taske is done.
Bac.   Then merry Mercurie more then time, this rounde were
          well begone.

They sing Hey Downe, downe, downe, etc.
The songe done, she windeth a horne in   [D2ᵛ]
Vulcans eare and runneth out.

                  Manent. Vulc. Bac. Mer. Cyclops.

Vul.   A harletrie I warrant her.
Bac.   A peevish elvish shroe.
Mer.   Have seene as farre to come as neare, for all her raung-
          ing so.
          But, Bacchus, time well spent I wot, our sacred father Jove,
          With Phoebus and the god of warre are met in Dians grove.
Vul.   Then we are here before them yet, but stay the earth
          doth swell,
          God Neptune to, (this hap is good) doth meete the prince
          of hell.

Pluto ascendeth from below in his chaire. Neptune
entreth at an other way.

820   *Plut.*   What jarres are these, that call the gods of heaven and
                hell beloe.
       Nep.   It is a worke of wit and toyle to rule a lustie shroe.

ACT. IIII. SCENA. IIII.

Enter Jupiter, Saturne, Apollo, Mars, Pluto, Neptune, Bacchus,
Vulcan, Mer. Juno, Pallas, Diana, Cyclops.

                      Jupiter speaketh.

Jup.   Bring forth the man of Troie that he may heare,

814   *A*] a Q

Whereof he is to be araigned here.
Nep.   Lo where a comes prepared to pleade his case,
Under conduct of lovely Venus grace.
Mer.   I have not seene a more alluring boy.
Apol.   So beautie hight the wracke of Priams Troy.

The gods being set in Dianaes bower: Juno, Pallas,
Venus, and Paris stand on sides before them.

Ven.   Loe sacred Jove, at Junoes proude complaynte,
As erst I gave my pledge to Mercurie,
830   I bring the man whom he did late attaint,
To aunswere his inditement orderlie:
And crave this grace of this immortall senate,
That yee allowe the man his advocate.
Pal.   That may not be, the lawes of heaven denie,
A man to pleade or answere by atturney.
Ven.   Pallas, thy doome is all too peremptorie.
Apol.   Venus, that favour is denyed him flatlie,
He is a man and therefore by our lawes,
Him selfe, without his ayd, must plead his cause.   [D3]
840   *Ven.*   Then bashe not, sheepeherde, in so good a case,
And friendes thou hast as well as foes in place.
Juno.   Why, Mercurie, why doe yee not indite him.
Ven.   Softe gentle Juno, I pray you do not bite him.
Juno.   Nay, gods, I troe you are not like to have great silence,
Unles this parrot be commaunded hence.
Jup.   *Venus*, forbeare, be still: speake, Mercurie.
Ven.   If Juno jangle, Venus will replie.
Mer.   Paris, king Priams sonne, thou art araygned of par-
ciallitie,
Of sentence partiall and unjust, for that without indiffer-
encie,
850   Beyonde desert or merit far, as thine accusers say,

823   *Whereof he*] Whereofhe Q
825   *Under*] vnder Q
827   SD *Juno*] *Inno* Q   *Pallas, Venus*] B; *Pallas, Diana, Venus* Q
843   *gentle*] gentle, Q
844   *you are not like*] you are like Q

From them, to Lady Venus here, thou gavest the pryze
    away.
What is thine answere?

Paris oration to the Councell of the gods.

Par.   Sacred and just, thou great and dreadfull Jove,
And you thrise reverende powers, whom love nor hate,
May wrest awry, if this to me a man,
This fortune fatall bee, that I must pleade,
For safe excusall of my giltles thought,
The honour more makes my mishap the lesse,
That I a man must pleade before the gods,
Gratious forbearers of the worldes amisse,
For her, whose beautie how it hath enticet,
This heavenly senate may with me aver.
But sith nor that, nor this may doe me boote,
And for my selfe, my selfe must speaker bee,
A mortall man, amidst this heavenlie presence:
Let me not shape a longe defence, to them,
That ben beholders of my giltles thoughtes.
Then for the deede, that I may not denie,
Wherein consists the full of myne offence,
I did upon commaunde: if then I erde,
I did no more then to a man belong'd.
And if in verdit of their formes devine,
My dazled eye did swarve or surfet more
On Venus face, then anie face of theirs: [D3ᵛ]
It was no partiall fault, but fault of his
Belike, whose eysight not so perfect was,
As might decerne the brightnes of the rest.
And if it were permitted unto men
(Ye gods) to parle with your secret thoughtes,
There ben that sit upon that sacred seate,
That woulde with Paris erre in Venus prayse.
But let me cease to speake of errour here:
Sith what my hande, the organ of my harte,

860

870

880

853   *Par.*] Q omits

Did give with good agreement of myne eye,
My tongue is vow'de with processe to maintaine.
Plut. A jolly sheepeherde, wise and eloquent.
Par. First then arraign'de of parciallitie.
Paris replyes unguiltie of the fact:
His reason is, because he knewe no more
Faire Venus Ceston, then dame Junoes mace,
Nor never sawe wise Pallas cristall shielde.
Then as I looked I loved and likte attonce,
And as it was referd from them to me,
To give the pryze to her, whose beautie best
My fancie did commend, so did I prayse
And judge as might my dazled eye decerne.
Nep. A peece of art, that, cunninglie pardie,
Refers the blame to weakenes of his eye.
Par. Now (for I must adde reason for my deede)
Why Venus rather pleased me of the three:
First, in the intrayles of my mortall eares,
The question standing upon beauties blaze,
The name of her that height the queene of love,
Me thought in beautie should not be exceld.
Had it bene destyned to majestie,
(Yet will I not rob Venus of her grace,)
Then stately Juno might have borne the ball.
Had it to wisedome bine entituled,
My humaine wit had given it Pallas then.
But sith unto the fayrest of the three,
That power, that threw it for my farther ill,
Did dedicate this ball: and safest durst   [D4]
My sheepeherdes skill adventure, as I thought,
To judge of forme and beautie, rather then
Of Junos state, or Pallas worthynes,
That learnd to ken the fayrest of the flocke,
And praysed beautie but by natures ayme:

885 *vow'de*] Daniel; *voyde* Q   *maintaine*] mainta(i)ne Q
903 *of love*] oflove Q
904 *Me*] Dyce; My Q

Behold to Venus Paris gave this fruite,
A dayesman chosen there by full consent,
920 And heavenly powers should not repent their deedes.
Where it is sayde, beyonde desert of hers,
I honoured Venus with this golden prize:
(Yee gods) alas what can a mortall man
Decerne, betwixt the sacred guiftes of heaven.
Or, if I may with reverence reason thus:
Suppose I gave, and judgd corruptly then,
For hope of that, that best did please my thought,
This apple not for beauties prayse alone:
I might offende, sithe I was gardoned,
930 And tempted, more than ever creature was,
With wealth, with beautie and with chivalrie:
And so preferred beautie before them all,
The thing that hath enchaunted heaven it selfe.
And for the one, contentment is my wealth:
A shell of salte will serve a sheepeherde swayne,
A slender banquet in a homely skrip,
And water running from the silver spring,
For armes, they dreade no foes that sit so lowe,
A thorne can keepe the wind from off my backe,
940 A sheepe-coate thatcht, a sheepeherdes pallace hight:
Of tragicke Muses sheepeherdes con no skill,
Enough is them, if Cupid ben displeased,
To sing his prayse on slender oten pipe.
And thus, thryse reverend, have I tolde my tale,
And crave the torment of my guiltles soule
To be measured by my faultles thought.
If warlicke Pallas, or the queene of heaven
Sue to reverse my sentence by appeale,
Be it as please your majesties devine,
950 The wronge, the hurte not mine, if anie be,   [D4ᵛ]
But hers whose beautie claymed the prize of me.

Paris having ended, Jupiter speaketh.

920 *repent*] rep( )nt Q
929 *gardoned*] B; pardoned Q
951 SD *speaketh*] speakeeh Q

Jup.   Venus, withdrawe your sheepeherde for a space,
    Till he againe be called for into place.

Exeunt Venus and Paris.

Juno, what wil ye after this reply
But doome with sentence of indifferencie.
And if you will but justice in the cause,
The man must quited be by heavens lawes.
Juno.   Yea gentle Jove, when Junoes sutes are mooved,
    Then heaven may see how well shee is beloved.
960   *Apol.*   But, Madam, fits it majestie devine,
    In anie sorte from justice to decline?
Pal.   Whether the man be guiltie yea or noe,
    That doth not hinder our appeale, I troe?
Juno.   Phoebus, I wot, amid this heavenly crue,
    There be that have to say as well as you.
Apol.   And Juno, I with them, and they with me,
    In lawe and right, must needefully agree.
Pal.   I graunt ye may agree, but be content
    To doubt upon regarde of your agrement.
970   *Plut.*   And if yee markt, the man in his defence.
    Saide thereof as a might with reverence.
Vul.   And did hee verie well I promise yee.
Juno.   No doubt, sir, you could note it cunninglie.
Sat.   Well, Juno, if ye will appeale yee may,
    But first dispatch the sheepeherde hence away.
Mars.   Then Vulcans dame is like to have the wronge.
Juno.   And that in passion doth to Mars belonge.
Jup.   Call Venus and the sheepeherde in againe.
Bac.   And rid the man that he may knowe his payne.
980   *Apol.*   His payne, his payne, his never dying payne,
    A cause to make a many moe complaine.

Mercurie bringeth in Venus and Paris.

965 *you.*] you Q
967 *agree.*] agree: Q
971 *thereof as*] thereofas Q
972 *hee*] yee Q
977 *doth*] dot h Q

Jup.   Sheepeherd, thou hast ben harde with equitie and law,
        And for thy stars do thee to other calling drawe,
        We here dismisse thee hence, by order of our senate:
        Goe take thy way to Troie, and there abide thy fate. [E1]
Ven.   Sweete shepherde, with such luck in love while thow
        dost live,
        As may the Queene of Love to any Lover give.
Par.   My lucke is losse howe ere my love do speede,
        I feare me Paris shall but rue his deede.

Paris exit.

990   *Apol.*   From Ida woods now wends the shepherds boye,
        That in his bosome caries fire to Troy.
Jup.   Venus, these Ladies do appeale yow see,
        And that they may appeale the gods agree,
        It resteth then that yow be well content
        To stande in this unto our finall judgment:
        And if king Priams sonne did well in this,
        The Lawe of heaven will not leade amysse.
Ven.   But, sacred Jupiter, might thy daughter chuse,
        Shee might with reason this appeale refuse:
1000   Yet, if they bee unmoved in their shames,
        Bee it a staine and blemysh to their names:
        A deede to far unworthy of the place,
        Unworthy Pallas Launce, or Junoes mace:
        And, if to beauty it bequeathed be,

She layeth Down the ball.

        I doubte not but it will returne to me.
Pal.   Venus, there is no more adoe then soe,
        It restethe where the gods doe it bestowe.
Nep.   But, Ladies, under favour of your rage,
        How ere it be, yow play uppon the vauntage.
1010 *Jup.*   Then dames, that wee more freely may debate,
        And heere th'indifferent sentence of this senate,
        Withdrawe yow from this presence for a space,

995   *judgment*] indgment Q
1004 SD *She layeth Down the ball.*] See Explanatory Notes.

Till wee have throughtly questioned of the cace:
Dian shalbe your guyde, nor shall yow neede
Your selves t'enquire how things do heere succeede,
Wee will, as wee resolve give yow to knowe,
By generall doome, how every thinge doth goe.
Dian.   Thy will, my wish. Faire Ladies, will yee wende?
Juno.   Beshrewe her whome this sentence doth offende.
1020   *Ven.*   Now *Jove* be just, and gods you that bee Venus freindes,
Yf yow have ever donne her wronge, then may yow make amends.

   Manent Dii. Exeunt Diana, Pallas, Juno, Venus.

Jup.   Venus is faire, Pallas and Juno toe.   [E1ᵛ]
Vul.   But tell me now without some more adoe,
Who is the fairest shee, and do not flatter.
Plut.   Vulcan, uppon comparison hanges all the matter:
That donne the quarrell and the stryfe were ended.
Mars.   Because tis knowne, the quarrell is pretended.
Vul.   Mars, you have reason for your speeche perdie:
My dame (I troe) is fairest in your eye.
1030   *Mars.*   Or (Vulcan) I shold do her doble wronge.
Sat.   About a toy wee tary heere so longe.
Gyve it by voices, voices give the odds:
A trifle so to troble all the gods.
Nep.   Beleve me, Saturne, be it so for me.
Bac.   For me.
Plut.   For me.
Mars.   For me, yf Jove agre.
Mer.   And gentle gods, I am indifferent:
But then I knowe whoose lykely to be shent.
Apol.   Thryse reverend gods, and thow immortall Jove.

1013   *throughtly*] through()ly Q
1018   *Faire*] faire Q
1021   *ever*] ev er Q
1031   *so*] Q; to Dyce1
1033   *to*] Dyce; to to Q
   1035   *Bac. . . . agre.*] Bac. For me, *Pluto.* for me *Mars.* for me, yf *Ioue*
agre. Q

Yf Phoebus may, as him doth much behove,

1040   Be licensed, accordinge to our Lawes,

To speake uprightly in this doubted cause,

(Sythe womens witts woorke mens unceasinge woes)

To make them freindes, that now bin frendles foes,

And peace to keepe with them, with us, and all

That make their title to this golden ball:

(Nor thincke yee gods my speeche doth derogate

From sacred powre of this immortall senate,)

Refer this sentence where it doth belonge,

In this say I fayre Phoebe hathe the wronge.

1050   Not that (I meane) her beautye beares the prize:

But that the holly Lawe of heaven denies,

One god to medle in an others powre.

And this befell so neere Dianas bowre,

As for thappeazinge this unplesant grudge,

(In my conceyte) shee hight the fittest judge.

Yf Jove comptroll not Plutoes hell with charmes,

Yf Mars have sovraigne powre to manage armes:

Yf Bacchus beare no rule in Neptune sea

Nor Vulcans fire dothe Saturnes sythe obay:

1060   Suppresse not then, 'gainst lawe and equitie,   [E2]

Dianas power in her owne territorie:

Whose regiment, amid her sacred bowers,

As proper height as anie rule of yours.

Well may we so wipe all the speeche awaie,

That Pallas, Juno, Venus hath to say,

And aunswere that by justice of our lawes,

We were not suffred to conclude the cause.

And this to me most egall doome appeares,

A woman to be judge amonge her pheeres.

1070   *Mars.*   Apollo hathe founde out the onely meane,

To rid the blame from us and trouble cleane.

     Vul.   We are beholding to his sacred wit.

     Jup.   I can commend and well allow of it,

And so derive the matter from us all,

1047   *sacred powre*] BM; sacredpowre H, P, T
1063   *as anie*] asanie Q

That Dian have the giving of the ball.

Vul.   So Jove may clearly excuse him in the case,
Where Juno else woulde chide and braule apace.

All they rise and goe foorth.

Mars.   And now, it were some cunning to devine,
To whom Diana will this pryze resigne.
1080   *Vul.*   Suffizeth me, it shall be none of mine.
Bac.   Vulcan, though thou be blacke, thart nothing fine.
Vul.   Goe bathe thee, Bacchus, in a tub of wine,
The balls as likely to be mine as thine.

Exeunt omnes: explicit. Act. 4.

ACT. V. *and ultimi*, SCENA I.

Diana, Pallas, Juno, Venus.

Dian.   Lo, Ladyes, farre beyonde my hope and will, you see,
This thankles office is imposd to me:
Wherein if you will rest aswell content,
As Dian wilbe judge indifferent,
My egall doome shall none of you offende,
And of this quarrell make a finall ende:
1090   And therefore, whether you be liefe or loath,
Confirme your promise with some sacred othe.
Pal.   Phoebe, chiefe Mistresse of this silvan chace,
Whom gods have chosen to conclude the case,   [E2ᵛ]
That yet in ballance undecyded lies.
Touching bestowing of this golden prize.
I give my promise and mine othe withall,
By Stix, by heavens power imperiall,
By all that longes to Pallas deytie,
Her shilde, her launce, ensignes of chivalirie,
1100   Her sacred wreath of Olive, and of Baye,
Her crested helme, and else what Pallas may,
That where so ere this ball of purest golde,

1078   *cunning*] cunnning Q
1090   *or*] Dyce; of Q

That chast Diana here in hande doth holde,
Unpartially her wisedome shall bestowe,
Without mislike or quarrell any moe,
Pallas shall rest content and satisfied,
And say the best desert doth there abide.
Juno.   And here I promise and protest withall,
By Stix, by heavens power imperiall,
1110   By all that longes to Junoes deitie,
Her crowne, her mace, ensignes of majestie:
Her spotles mariage-rites, her league divine,
And by that holy name of Proserpine,
That wheresoere, this ball of purest golde,
That chast Diana here in hande doth holde,
Unpartially her wisedome shall bestowe,
Without mislike or quarrell anie moe,
Juno shall rest content and satisfied,
And say the best desert doth there abyde.
1120   *Ven.*   And lovely Phoebe, for I knowe thy dome
Wilbe no other then shall thee become,
Beholde I take thy daintie hande to kisse,
And with my solemne othe confirme my promise,
By Stix, by Joves immortall emperie,
By Cupids bowe, by Venus mirtle-tree,
By Vulcans gifte, my Ceston, and my fan,
By this red rose, whose colour first began,
When erst my wanton boy (the more his blame)
Did drawe his bowe awry and hurt his dame,
1130   By all the honour and the sacrifice,
That from Cithaeron and from Paphos rise: [E3]
That wheresoere this ball of purest golde,
That chast Diana here in hande doth holde,
Unpartially her wisedome shall bestowe,
Without mislike or quarrell any moe,
Venus shall rest content and satisfied,

1107   *abide.*] ab(i)de. Q
1117   *anie*] ani e Q
1132–37   *That wheresoere . . . doth there abyde.*]; See Explanatory
Notes.

And say the best desert doth there abyde.

Diana having taken their othes speaketh.
Diana describeth the Nymphe Eliza a figure of the
Queene.

Dian.   It is enough, and goddesses attende:
  There wons within these pleasaunt shady woods,
1140 Where neither storme nor Suns distemperature
  Have power to hurte by cruell heate or colde,
  Under the clymate of the milder heaven,
  Where seldome lights Joves angrie thunderbolt,
  For favour of that soveraygne earthly peere:
  Where whystling windes make musick 'mong the trees,
  Far from disturbance of our countrie gods,
  Amids the Cypres springes a gratious Nymphe,
  That honour Dian for her chastitie,
  And likes the labours well of Phoebes groves:
1150 The place Elizium hight, and of the place,
  Her name that governes there Eliza is,
  A kingdome that may well compare with mine.
  An auncient seat of kinges, a seconde Troie,
  Ycompast rounde with a commodious sea:
  Her people are ycleeped Angeli,
  Or if I misse a lettre is the most.
  She giveth lawes of justice and of peace,
  And on her heade as fits her fortune best,
  She weares a wreath of laurell, golde, and palme:
1160 Her robes of purple and of scarlet die,
  Her vayle of white, as best befits a mayde.
  Her auncestors live in the house of fame,
  Shee giveth armes of happie victorie,
  And flowers to decke her lyons crowned with golde.
  This peereles nymphe whom heaven and earth beloves,
  This Paragon, this onely this is shee,
  In whom do meete so manie giftes in one,
  On whom our countrie gods so often gaze,

1145 *musick*] musi(c)k Q
1148 *honour*] Q; honours Dyce

In honour of whose name the Muses singe.
1170   In state Queene Junos peere, for power in armes,
And vertues of the minde Minervaes mate: [E3ᵛ]
As fayre and lovely as the queene of love:
As chast as Dian in her chast desires.
The same is shee, if Phoebe doe no wronge,
To whom this ball in merit doth belonge.
Pal.   If this be shee whom some Zabeta call,
To whom thy wisedome well bequeathes the ball
I can remember at her day of birthe,
Howe Flora with her flowers strewed the Earth,
1180   How everie power with heavenlie majestie,
In person honored that solemnitie.
Juno.   The lovely graces were not farre away,
They threw their balme for triumph of the day.
Ven.   The fates against their kinde beganne a cheerefull
songe,
And vowed her life with favour to prolonge.
Then first gan Cupids eysight wexen dim,
Belike Elisas beautie blinded him.
To this fayre Nymphe, not earthly but devine:
Contents it me my honour to resigne.
1190 *Pal.*   To this fayre Queene so beautifull and wise,
Pallas bequeathes her title in the prize.
Juno.   To her whom Junoes lookes so well become,
The queene of heaven yeildes at Phoebes doome.
And glad I am Diana found the arte,
Without offence so well to please desart.
Dian.   Then marke my tale the usuall time is nie,
When wont the dames of life and destinie,
In robes of cheerfull collours to repayre,
To this renowned Queene so wise and fayre,
1200   With pleasaunt songes this peereles nimphe to greete,
Clotho layes downe her distaffe at her feete.
And Lachesis doth pull the threed at length,
The thirde with favour gives it stuffe and strength

1190   *beautifull*] BM, P, T; beáutifull H
1193   *Phoebes*] Dyce; *Phoebus* Q
1197   *dames*] dame s Q

> And far contrarie kinde affordes her leave,
> As her best likes her web of life to weave.
> This time we will attend, and in the meane while
> With some sweete songe the tediousnes beguile.

The Musicke sounde and the Nimphes within singe [E4]
or solfa with voyces and instrumentes awhile. Then enter
Clotho, Lachesis and Atropos singing as followeth: The
state being in place.

The songe.

Cloth.   *Humanae vitae filum sic volvere Parcae.*
Lach.   *Humanae vitae filum sic tendere Parcae.*
1210   Atrop.   *Humanae vitae filum sic scindere Parcae.*
Cloth.   *Clotho colum baiulat.*
Lach.   *Lachesis trahit.*
Atrop.   *Atropos occat.*
Tres simul.   *Vive diu foelix votis huminúmque deúmque:*
              Corpore, mente, libro, doctissima, candida, casta.

They lay downe their properties at the Queenes feete.

Cloth.   *Clotho colum pedibus.*
Lach.   *Lachesis tibi pendula fila.*
Atrop.   *Et fatale tuis manibus ferrum Atropos offert.*
        Vive diu foelix, etc.

The song being ended Clotho speakes to the Queene.

Cloth.   Gracious and wise, fayre Queene of rare renowne,
      Whom heaven and earth beloves amyd thy trayne,
1220   Noble and lovely peeres: to honour thee
      And doe thee favour, more then may belong,
      By natures lawe to any earthly wight,
      Beholde continuance of our yearely due,
      Th'unpartiall dames of destenie we meete,
      As have the gods and we agreed in one,
      In reverence of Elizas noble name,

1204   *far*] for Q
1205   *weave.*] Child; weaue Q
1206   *in the meane*] Q in mean Dyce1
1207   *the tediousnes*] thetediousnes Q   SD *followeth:*] follloweth: Q

And humblie loe her distaffe Clotho yeeldes.

Lach.   Her spindle Lachesis and her fatall reele,
Layes downe in reverence at Elizas feete.

1230   *Te tamen in terris unam tria numina Divam*
          Invita statuunt naturae lege sorores,
          Et tibi non aliis didicerunt parcere Parcae.

Atrop.   Dame Atropos according as her pheeres
To thee fayre Queene resignes her fatall knife:
Live longe the noble Phoenix of our age,   [E4ᵛ]
Our fayre Eliza our Zabeta fayre.

Dian.   And loe beside this rare solemnitie,
And sacrifice these dames are wont to doe,
A favour far in deed contrarie kinde,
1240   Bequeathed is unto thy worthynes.

*Shee delivereth the ball of golde to the Queenes owne
hands*

This prize from heaven and heavenly goddesses,
Accept it then, thy due by Dians dome,
Praise of the wisedome, beautie and the state,
That best becomes thy peereles excellencie.

Ven.   So fayre Eliza, Venus doth resigne,
The honour of this honour to be thine.

Juno.   So is the queene of heaven content likewise,
To yelde to thee her title in the prize.

Pal.   So Pallas yeeldes the prayse hereof to thee,
1250   For wisedome, princely state, and peerelesse beautie.

EPILOGUS.

          Vive diu foelix votis hominúmque Deúmque.
Omnes simul.
          Corpore, mente, libro, doctissima, candida, casta.

          Exeunt omnes.

FINIS.

1229   *Layes downe*] Layesdowne Q   *Elizas*] Elizaas Q
1233   *Atropos*] Atrops Q

EXPLANATORY NOTES

Ate Prologus]   The usual accounts of the mythographers state that Eris or Discord threw the apple during the feast of the gods (e.g., Hyginus, *Fabulae, The Myths of Hyginus,* trans. and ed. M. Grant, Lawrence, Kansas, 1960, pp. 82–83). There is, however, some basis for Peele's invention. Thomas Cooper (*Thesaurus linguae Romanae & Britannicae,* London, 1578) cites Ate as "in latine *Noxa detrimentum,* the name of a hurtfull spirite, always working yll to men"; and Hesiod (*Theogony,* l. 230) lists Ate as a daughter of Eris, goddess of discord. In the *Iliad* (19.128) Ate is the daughter of Jove. Spenser makes the same identification as Peele in the *Faerie Queene,* II.7.55 and IV.1.22. Ate evidently enters with the golden apple (l. 5). The apple's size is uncertain. The SD at l. 355 speaks of the ball's being "trundled . . . into place," implying that the ball is too large to be carried; if this is true, it is another indication of the masque tradition and the spectacular quality of the play.

1   *Condemned*]   Q has an initial block letter followed by capital *O.*

2   *deadlie rivers*]   Resembling or suggestive of death in darkness, gloom, silence; perhaps also in the sense that only the dead can cross the rivers.

6–7   *fatall . . . Proserpine*]   Although no specific source has been found for this connection between Ate's apple and Proserpina's garden, Peele's account is acceptable in an age of independent mythologizing. He may be drawing upon the compilations of Renaissance mythographers such as Natale Conti. A similar allusion to the golden apple appears in Spenser's *Faerie Queene,* II.7.55.

7   *Raught*]   Taken from, snatched from; archaic past participle of "reach." In using archaic forms such as this, Peele may be imitating Spenser.

9   *racet*]   Torn, snatched down.

16   *Paris . . . organ*]   Dyce, B, and Smeaton note an obscurity of meaning here. B suggests the transposition of ll. 15–16 to follow l. 10, but this is not entirely satisfactory. The problem is clarified if the lines are considered elliptical and ll. 8–16 are seen as a series of parallels. Not only must Troy fall, but "statelie *Iliums*" lofty towers must be razed, "*Priams* pallace" must be wasted, and Paris must be "th'unhappie organ of the *Greekes*"—i.e., his abduction of Helen will precipitate the Trojan

War. The relative clause "whose thicke and foggie smoake . . ." is a
continuation and expansion of the parallelism.   organ] A person or
body of persons by which some particular purpose is carried out (*OED*,
"organ," sb., III, 7); cf. E. Halle, *The Union of the two noble and illustrious families York and Lancaster* (London, 1548), Henry VI, f. 113b,
"an enchantresse, an orgayne of the diuill, sent from Sathan."). A similar use of the word occurs at l. 720.

20 *unpartiall*] Unbiased   *daughters of Necessitie*] I.e., the Fates.
The genealogy alluded to is probably based on Hesiod, *Theogony*,
ll. 901 ff. "Necessity" is used in the sense of "law" or "justice" and is
thus equivalent to the goddess Themis. K. Frey, *Die Klassische Gotter-
und Heldensaga* (Karlsruhe, 1909), pp. 58–59, cites Plato's *Laws*, XII
(Loeb ed., p. 537).

21 *aydes*] Since the word may be dissyllabic, there is no reason to emend
to "ayders" as does D; cf. W. Franz, *Die Sprache Shakespeares in Vers
und Proza* (Halle, 1939), p. 188.

25 *hestes*] Commands.

26 *Ida vales*] This phrase may have been suggested by Ovid's "vallebus
Idae," *Heroides* 16.15; see A. Gilbert, "The Source of Peele's *Arraignment of Paris*," *Modern Language Notes, 41* (1926), 38.

30 *Silvanus*] Q has an initial block letter and capitals.

32 *morning mirth*] The specific reference is unclear; the phrase may
mean no more than "joy" or "happiness." Although there is no SD
here, it is possible that Pan, Sylvanus, and Faunus enter to music.

38 *twagger*] This word occurs only here. *OED* suggests as a meaning
"a (?big or fat) lamb"; but it is quite possible that this is a misprint
for "twigger" which had a contemporary meaning "a vigorous, pro-
lific breeder" (*OED*, "twig," v²).

39 *bunting lambe*] A plump lamb.

43 *walkes*] Tracts of forest lands.

45 *mast*] Nuts, used to refer to food for swine.   *enough*] In many
dialects "enow" was the plural form. When the distinction was vague,
the two forms and their pronunciations were interchangeable; hence,
the rhyme here is "bowe" and "enow."

46 Dyce and B both note the unusual length of this line. At first glance,
the difficulty could be alleviated by considering "and al" anticipatory
of l. 47, but this would destroy the rhyme. It is possible, however, that
"flockes and herdes" is an erroneous repetition of the phrase from
l. 42.   *dames*] Variant form of dams (ewes); cf. l. 62.

47 *to make the glee*] If "the" is "thee," the phrase is the archaic "to
make glee," meaning "to be glad, merry" (*OED*, "glee," sb., 3b; Spenser, *Shepheardes Calander*, May Eclogue, l. 282. "Being within, the
Kidde made him [the fox] good glee"). If "the" is the article, the
phrase means "to make music, melody" (*OED*, "glee," sb., 2a). The
former seems preferable.

49 *pheeres*] Companions; a variant spelling of "fere."

52 *had the starte*] To have the advantage gained by starting first, i.e., you had a head start but have got no farther (*OED*, sb.², 6; J. Lyly, *Euphues and his England*, (*Euphues* ed. E. Arber, London, 1868), p. 418, "Those, who hauing gotten the starte in a race, thinke none to be neere their heeles").

55 *Thinkest*] The imperfect ligature in H and T may have been replaced when the spacing was corrected in l. 52. Cf. above, p. 51 note 3.
take . . . woorth] To take at their proper value.

59 *clowne*] Countryman, ill-bred man, rustic.

60 *tidie*] In good condition; plump or fat.

62 *mops*] Wench; a term of endearment.   *chave*] Southern or Southwestern dialectal form of "I have." Peele follows Elizabethan stage convention in using Southern dialect to suggest rustic speech and manners.   *dames*] Variant form of dam (ewe). The point lies in the contrast between the sacrifices made to gods and those to maids—lambs and dams. The rhyme is with l. 60; the couplets give way in ll. 60–63 to a ballad stanza.

63 *pypt . . . worth*] I.e., piped and prayed to little or no avail.

65 *To kisse in corners*] To kiss covertly. The phrase may be proverbial and in the context suggests the enervating effects of love-making.

67 SD*Flora*] Ovid's account of Flora as the goddess of spring and of flowers in the *Fasti* 5.183–378, may have contributed to this scene. The welcome of the goddesses by the rural deities, the muses, and the birds recalls the April Eclogue of the *Shepheardes Calender*.

68 The verse changes here from rhymed fourteeners to iambic couplets; similar shifts occur throughout the play: e.g., ll. 278 and 339. The shift in verse form indicates a shift in subject matter and tone. Fourteeners are not restricted to the rustics.

70 *yoes*] Dialectal form of "ewes" used for the sake of rhyme.

73 *service*] If this is a correction, it was made when the spelling in l. 51 SD was corrected; cf. note to l. 55.

76 *don't*] Contraction of "done it."   *trick*] Cleverly.

82 *done*] Archaic plural form of "do"; cf. Peele's *Descensus Astraeae*, l. 83: "With hir lives wane done Englands joyes decrease."

84 *glyde*] Stream; the gliding portion of a stream, a shallow; cf. Peele's *Devices of the Pageant, etc.*, l. 82, "With silver glide my pleasant streames doo runne." Although Peele may intend to contrast brooks and streams, the clause of l. 85 suggests that "glide" is the current of the "bubling brookes."

87 *burgen*] Burgeon, burst forth.

90 *Hyacinthe*] The wild hyacinth or bluebell. Thus all the flowers are small, and the imagery is consistent.

90–94 Cf. Spenser's catalogue of flowers in *Shepheardes Calender*, April Eclogue, ll. 136–144.

109 *yellow for her jellozie*]   The color symbolism here and in ll. 117 and
     131, common throughout the Renaissance, is an inheritance from the
     Middle Ages (cf. M. Turmann, *Die Farbenbezeichnunge in der Dich-
     tung der englischen Renaissance*, Reval, 1934). Yellow for jealousy
     occurs in Chaucer's "Knight's Tale" (ll. 1928–30) and frequently in
     Shakespeare, e.g., *Merry Wives*, I.3.110. The use of blue for Venus
     is perhaps ironic since blue is the color not only of true lovers but
     also of prostitutes; cf. G. Whetstone's *Promos and Cassandra* (1578),
     Part II, V (Kjᵛ, Kij), where Cassandra wears blue, "the weeds of
     shame." The association of red with Pallas is probably related to her
     role as the warrior goddess; cf. her "show," l. 478.

110 *collowers*]   This spelling seems to combine two distinct spellings of
     the second syllable: *ow* for *o* or *ou* and *er* for the phonetic ər or syl-
     labic *r*; the first is essentially orthographic, the second phonetic. H. C.
     Wylde (*History of Modern Colloquial English*, Oxford, 1936, p. 265)
     cites "faver" as a sixteenth-century spelling of "favor."

111 *Gorgons head*]   One of the traditional symbols associated with Pallas;
     it appears on her breastplate or on her "aegis." Here the phrase may
     stand for Pallas' shield, which would complete her armor.

113 *Julie-flowers*]   A variant of "gillyflower," referring to a species of
     wallflowers or pinks, often an alternate term for carnations.

115 *at a blush*]   At a glance.

116 *twere*]   B, following the suggestion of Daniel, emends this to "twas,"
     but plural verbs with singular subjects are not uncommon in Peele.

117 *dight*]   Clothe, array.

118 *blue.*]   The use of a period for a comma is common throughout Q,
     e.g., ll. 173, 244, 970, 1095, 1152.

120 *pendants*]   In H, P, and T the quad following the *s* has become loose
     and has left a mark resembling an apostrophe. Space marks are frequent
     because of faulty presswork, e.g., ll. 180 SD, 775, 984, 1113, 1127. Cf.
     above, p. 53.

122 *lustie*]   Handsome, beautiful. The modern German "lustig" preserves
     the earlier meaning of the word in English.

126 *whight*]   Variant spelling of "wight," creature or human being.

130 *deintie*]   Variant form of dainty, meaning not only "pleasing, valu-
     able" but also "made with delicate taste"; cf. Spenser, *Shepheardes
     Calender*, June Eclogue, l. 6: "The grassye ground with daintye Day-
     sies dight."   *draught*]   A representation, delineation.

132 *This peece of worke*]   Refers to the flower portraits which Flora
     has been describing. These, as Flora says, are in Diana's bower, which
     is offstage. The reference to Flora's workmanship (l. 227) is probably
     to the "second spring" which she has created for the goddesses (ll.
     78 ff.).

138 *That . . . neede*]   It is not needful or necessary; the negative form
     of the usual construction "It needs."

139 *Rhanis*] Barnabe Googe in *Cupido Conquered* (*Eglogs, Epytaphes, and Sonettes,* 1563, ed. E. Arber, London, 1871, p. 116) lists Rhanis among Diana's ladies. The ultimate source of identification is Ovid's account of Actaeon in *Metamorphoses* 3.171.

140–149 The mythological details Peele uses are conventional and essentially decorative. The source of Juno's famous golden chariot, drawn by peacocks, is probably Ovid, *Metamorphoses* 2.553. The peacocks bear Argus' hundred eyes, which were placed there by Juno (*Metamorphoses* 1.601). Venus is traditionally accompanied by sparrows and doves, which were noted for their lechery (R. Graves, *The Greek Myths,* Baltimore, 1955, *1,* 112). The swans are associated with Venus by Horace, *Carmina* 4.1, and Ovid, *Metamorphoses* 10.708. The association of tigers with Pallas appears to be another instance of independent mythologizing by Peele.

141 *by*] By means of; cf. Latimer, *Sermon on the Ploughers,* (*English Reprints,* No. 2, ed. E. Arber, London, 1868), p. 34, "Christe . . . draweth soules unto hym by his bloudy sacrifice." Perhaps the preposition is also used in the sense of motion over a course; cf. A. Guevara, *The Golden boke of Marcus Aurelius,* trans. J. Bourchier (London, 1546), Ciij: "To goo by the stretes as vacabundes."

142 *bravelie*] Handsomely, gaily.

152 *marche*] The space mark at the beginning of the line suggests that the type was loose and that the variants are due to deterioration of type. A similar case of deterioration occurs in ll. 159–160. Cf. above, p. 53.

157 Peele may call Clio "the sagest of the sisters nine" because she is the muse of history and knows what has happened in recorded time, or he may attribute her wisdom to the fact that she is the oldest of the muses; cf. Spenser, *Tears of the Muses* (l. 53).

164 *charme*] Blended singing or noise of many birds.

166 SD*A quier . . . without*] Twice in the play Peele uses two singing groups. Here the inner group identifies itself as the Muses; in l. 1207 SD the inner group is called the Nimphes. The availability of many voices is, of course, a characteristic of the children's companies.

173 *wel-come*] The misprint in P and H is a broken hyphen. A hyphen is clearly printed in the other copies. Cf. l. 761.

178 SD*Gods daunce*] This SD is printed to the left of ll. 177–178 in Q, the speech prefix serving as the subject of the direction. The position to the left of the text may indicate prompt copy; cf. above, pp. 56–57, and note to l. 367 SD.

185 SD*The birdes singe*] This SD is printed as part of the song in Q.

198 *accept in gree*] Accept with good will or favor.

206 *jouysaunce*] Festivity, joyousness.

210 *in fine*] In short.

236 *sorte*] Collection, set.

252–279   Although Ovid refers to only some of the stories in Oenone's list, the "Fabula" are ultimately derived from the *Metamorphoses*. In the "Epistle to Leicester" prefixed to his translation of the *Metamorphoses* (London, 1567), Golding commends the *Metamorphoses* for its moral value: "in all the tales are pitthye, apt and pleyne / Instructiones which import the prayse of vertues, and the shame / Of vices, with the due rewardes of eyther of the same" (ll. 64–66). Oenone's "fabula" are likewise moral examples. Dyce believes that "Peele had an eye to Golding's translation"; and he cites the following passages from the "Epistle to Leicester" which he finds parallel to ll. 262–263, 266–267, and 268–269 of the *Araygnement:* "Hermaphrodite and Salmacis declare that idlenesse / Is cheefest nurce and cherisher of all volupteousnesse" (ll. 133–134); "As for example, in the tale of Daphnee turn'd to Bay / A myrror of virginitie appeere untoo us may" (ll. 68–69); "Narcissus is of scornfulnesse and pryde a myrror cleere, / Where beawties fading vanitie most playnly may appeere" (ll. 105–106). Perhaps a closer parallel in the last case is found in 3.632–34: "And afterward when into Hell receyved was his spright, / He goes me to the Well of Styx, and there both day and night, / Standes tooting on his shadow still as fondely as before." While these parallels suggest a knowledge of Golding's translation, Peele would have been familiar with the *Metamorphoses* in the original.

252   *Saturne*]   In classical accounts Saturn (Cronus) was overcome by Jove, e.g., Hesiod, *Theogony*, ll. 453–506; in *Myths* (p. 115) Hyginus mentions only Jove, Pluto (Orcus) and Neptune. Jove's victory is alluded to in *Metamorphoses* 1.113–114.

254   *mightie men*]   The Titans (Hesiod, *Theogony*, ll. 615–735) or the Giants (*Metamorphoses* 1.151–153), both of whom made war on Olympus. Peele, like Hyginus, may have confused the two (*Myths*, p. 122).

256   *Phorcias ympe*]   Medusa, the daughter of Phorcys. The reference is to the story of Medusa and Neptune (*Metamorphoses* 4.65–79). Previous editors have unnecessarily emended to "Phorcys'." The Q spelling, however, is probably phonetic. In Shakespeare, nouns ending in "y" form their genitive in "ies" or "yes"; "as" for "es" is an acceptable phonetic spelling if the ending is syllabic. Possibly the misprint "Elizaas" (l. 1229) is a similar example of phonetic spelling.

260   *for the nonce*]   For the particular purpose, i.e., to illustrate, prove.

262   *Salmacis*]   The nymph who pursued the disdainful Hermaphroditus, the son of Mercury and Venus, into a pool. In answer to her prayer, they were united into one body while the pool, in answer to his prayer, was cursed with enervating waters (*Metamorphoses* 4.285–388).

264   *Pluto*]   Ovid tells the story of the rape of Proserpina by Pluto in *Metamorphoses* 5.385–571. Ceres sought to recover her daughter, but Jove decreed that since Proserpina had eaten of a pomegranate in Hades

she could return to earth for only six months each year. Seasonal change is the result of "that love offence."

266 *Daphne*] A nymph who in fleeing from Apollo's love was changed into a laurel tree (*Metamorphoses* 1.425–567).

268 *Narcissus*] The self-centered boy whose rejection of Echo's love caused her to become a disembodied voice (*Metamorphoses* 3.339–510). *tooting*] Peeping, prying.

269 *disdayne*] anger (OED "disdain", sb. 2); i.e., Narcissus chides the nymph's anger.   *vade*] Fade; this dialectal form appears frequently in printed books of the period, cf. W. Horn, *Historische Neuenglischen Grammatik* (Strasbourg, 1908), §165.

270 *Philomelaes needle*] The daughter of Pandion revealed through her tapestry her rape by Tereus, the husband of Procne, her sister (*Metamorphoses* 6.424–674).

274 *Ixions wheele*] For boasting of an affair with Juno, Ixion was bound to an ever-turning wheel in Hades (Hyginus, *Myths*, p. 63).   *Tantals pyning woe*] For betraying the counsel of the gods, Tantalus was tortured in Hades by standing in a river from which he could never drink and reaching for fruit which was unattainable (Hyginus, *Myths*, pp. 76–77).

275 *Prometheus torment*] For stealing fire from heaven, Prometheus was chained to a cliff where during the day an eagle devoured his heart, which then grew back at night (Hyginus, *Myths*, pp. 118–119).

276 *Danaus daughters*] The fifty daughters of Danaus who, with the exception of Hypermnestra, murdered their husbands on their wedding night to evade the prophecy of the oracle that Danaus would be killed by a husband of his daughter. As a punishment the daughters were sentenced to fill with water a great barrel full of holes (Hyginus, *Myths*, pp. 131–132).

277 *Sysiphus*] For his crimes Sisyphus was condemned to roll a stone up a hill in Hades; when he reached the top, the stone would fall down again and renew his labor (Hyginus, *Myths*, 62–63).

285 *Poplar tree*] Choice of the poplar as the symbol of their love is prophetic, since the poplar is conventionally a symbol of inconstancy. Cheffaud, p. 38, notes the passage in Ovid's *Heroides* where Oenone recalls: "pulviali consita rivo / est in quia nostri littera scripta memor. / et quantum trunci, tantum mea nomina crescunt. / crescite et in titulos surgite recta meos: / popule, vive, precor, quae consita margine ripae / hoc in rugoso cortice carmen habes: / CUM PARIS OENONE POTERIT SPIRARE RELICTA, / AD FONTEM XANTHI VERSA RECURRET AQUA" (Loeb ed., 5.21–30). Cf. ll. 579–580 and note.

299 *merrie merrie*] The triple repetition of "merrie" in Q is probably a printer's error. The line is correctly printed in the refrain, ll. 309 ff.

303 *Ambo. simul.*] Both together.

309–310 *My . . . curse*] Q prints these two lines as one.

313 SD*Finis Camoenae*] End of song.
316 *starte*] Move, depart; J. Heywood, "A Dialogue Containing Prov-
     erbs," *John Heywood's "Works"*, ed. B. A. Milligan in Illinois Studies
     in Language and Literature 41 (1956), 25. "Who hopeth in Gods helpe,
     his helpe can not starte."
320 SD(*ex abrupto*)] This SD is printed to the left of ll. 320–321 in Q.
     Cf. note to l. 178 SD.
321 *Eccho*] Cf. Ovid's account in *Metamorphoses*, 3.338–510.
323 *walker*] Apparently used here in a pejorative sense.
325 *tolde her thankes*] Literally the phrase means "expressed her grati-
     tude" (*OED*, "Thank," sb., 4b); but if, as Baskervill suggests, "she"
     refers to Juno, the phrase means "Juno thanked her," i.e., "dismissed
     her."
329 *held me chat*] Kept me engaged in talk.
343 *maske in nets*] "Nets" is a variant spelling of "neat" (cattle). There
     is perhaps a pun on "nets" and an allusion to the expression "to dance
     or walk in a net," meaning "to think oneself unseen when covered by
     a net through which all can see." The reference to the Europa story
     in the preceding line makes the phrase ironic: "Jove might as well
     be as open as Mars since his disguises are transparent."   *froes*]
     Women. The word was often applied to the Maenads or Bacchants
     of classical paganism; cf. T. Nashe, *The Returne of the renowned Cava-
     liero, Pasquill of England* (1589), in *Works, 1, 95*: "Some gadded vppe
     and downe the streetes, like Bacchus Froes, franticke for the time."
344 *turne*] Subtle device, artifice. "His turne" refers to Mars; "for if a
     speake" refers, of course, to Jove.
351 *tooth*] Taste.   *and*] If.
364 *breyfe*] Device, motto.   *Detur Pulcherrimae*] Tatlock (*PMLA*,
     30, 724–725) notes that the Latin inscription is not in the classical ac-
     counts of the judgment. It is probably a translation of Caxton's "and
     ther was wreoton aboute thys apple in the grekysh langage be hit
     gyven to the fayreste" (*Recuyell of the Historyes of Troye*, ed. H. O.
     Sommer, London, 1894, *2, 521*).   SD*They . . . posie*] This SD
     is printed to the right of ll. 365–366.
367 SD*Pallas reades*] This SD is printed to the right of ll. 367–368. The
     absence of the speech prefix in l. 367, and in l. 369 where a similar
     SD occurs, suggests that these were originally prompt directions at
     the left of the text that the compositor transposed to the right. In the
     process the speech prefix was incorporated into the SD and transposed
     with it. Cf. above, p. 57, and note to l. 178 SD.
369 SD*Venus reades*] Cf. note to l. 367 SD.
373 *Planetes seaven*] This identification of Juno with the planets is un-
     usual. In the Ptolemaic system the planets were the moon, Mercury,
     Venus, the sun, Mars, Jupiter, and Saturn. Cf. l. 758.

380 *per excellencye*] As *OED* notes, the Latin, Italian, and Old French "per" became practically an English preposition. Peele may be anglicizing the French phrase.

383 *stand on tearmes*] Insist upon conditions. Pallas' claim to the apple based upon her inward beauty—"the beautye of the minde"—is essentially medieval. In the medieval tradition Pallas is associated with the contemplative life and contemplative virtues. Here Peele combines medieval and classical treatments of the goddess. In her bribe (ll. 463 ff.) Pallas refers to "wysdomes worthines," but she dwells upon the "honor of chyvallrye" and "happy victorie." Moreover, her show is martial. The classical tradition is reflected in ll. 931 ff., and 1099; the medieval in ll. 908–909. Cf. D. Bush, *Mythology and the Renaissance Tradition in English Poetry* (Minneapolis, 1932), p. 17, and above, p. 17.

385 *subtill*] Artfully designed or executed.

386 *highte*] Means, purports; cf. Spenser, *Shepheardes Calender,* September Eclogue, ll. 172–173: "Say it out, Diggon, whateuer it hight, For not but well mought him betight."

387 *syfte*] Examine closely.

389–390 *in generall . . . speciall*] With reference to a class as a whole ("fayrenes"); with reference to the particular members ("braunches" is here used as the divisions of a subject).

399 *cleane*] Completely; perhaps also in the sense of "cleverly," "dextrously" (*OED*, "clean," adv., 3).

400 *conster*] Construe; this spelling results from a shift of accent so that the final syllable is unaccented.

418 *skill . . . can*] He has knowledge of or discriminates.

421 *skill*] Science, art.

423 *abash*] Stand dumb with confusion or astonishment.

442 *olde shepherds*] Used in the pastoral sense to mean poets.   *title*] Ascribe, assign.

443 *suffize*] Satisfy the requirements.

444 *Phebus*] There is much dispute over this reading. Dyce in 1861, and Smeaton have accepted "Phoebe's" (cf. l. 1193), and Nicholson has proposed "Paris's." B, Daniel, and the more recent editors have retained the Q reading. Daniel explains the passage by referring to ll. 356–357 and the mysterious appearance of the apple. Since the goddesses did not know that Ate had brought the apple, they assumed that Phoebus left it when he cleared the skies after the storm.

451 *moulde*] The earth.   *Tagus*] The river famous for its golden sand, which flows through Spain and Portugal into the Atlantic; cf. Ovid, *Metamorphoses* 2.251 and Wyatt's epigram "Of his returne from Spaine" (*Tottel's Miscellany (1557–1587)*, ed. H. Rollins (Cambridge, Mass., 1965), 1, 81).

452 *Xanthus*] A river near Troy which was said to have been set on fire when Troy fell. Cooper in his *Thesaurus* notes that "if sheepe did drinke [thereof], the fleese became yellowe."

464 *embaset*] Debased, corrupted.

471 *champaine*] Level, open.

473 *barbed*] Armed or caparisoned with metal or leather armor known as a barb or bard.

478 SD9. *knights*] As Nicholson suggests, this is probably an allusion to the Nine Worthies, i.e., Joshua, David, Maccabeus, Hector, Alexander, Julius Caesar, Arthur, Charlemagne, and Godfrey of Bouillon. The Worthies appear frequently in the masques and pageants of the period, most notably in *Love's Labours Lost*, V.2. Cf. L. Ellison, *The Early Romantic Drama at the English Court* (Menasha, Wis., 1917), pp. 30–33, and the "Maske of Greek Worthies," which included Hercules, Jason, Perseus, Pirithous, Achilles, and Theseus (Feuillerat, *Edward*, pp. 53, 81).

480 *hoat*] Hot.

487 *lightlie*] Merrily, in a good humor.

488 *lovelie*] Loving.

493 *vaines*] Veins.

497–508 *Si Diana . . . et in terra*] Baskervill's edition:

> If Diana is a star in heaven,
> bright and shining, full of splendor,
> giving light to the grieving heart;
>
> If Diana is a goddess in hell,
> who gives comfort to the tormented souls
> who on account of love have died in despair;
>
> If Diana, who on earth is of the nymphs
> the reigning queen of sweet flowers,
> amid woods and groves gives death to shepherds;
>
> I am Diana gentle and rare
> for with my glances I can make war
> upon Diana in hell, in heaven, and on earth.

This Italian song is puzzling in its context. Helen, the representative of Venus, compares herself to Diana. Although no source has been found for the song, Peele may have borrowed it rather than composed it himself. The song, though crude, reflects the contemporary interest and delight in the Italian language. The Revels Accounts record several payments for the translation of verses and speeces into Italian for use in court entertainments: in 1578/9 "To Patruchius Vbaldinas as by the comaundment of the Lord Chamberlayne for the translating of certen speeches into Italian to be used in the maske . . ." (Feuillerat, *Elizabeth*, p. 301).

512 *wrape*] To transport, ravish, or delight; *OED* quotes Q as an erroneous spelling of "rape," v², 4.

531 *ban*] Curse.

535 *leyfe or lothe*] Willing or unwilling; an idiomatic antithetical construction, cf. l. 1090.

536 SD *Colin . . . love*] In collating this poem and "Oenones Complaint" with the *EH* (Nos. 148, 149) versions, no variations in spelling and punctuation have been noted.

539 *marke*] Target.

548 *ceaze*] Variant spelling of "seize."

549 *beare no boot*] Have no avail.

552 *take*] Receive, suffer.

553 *forespoke*] Renounced (*OED*, "forspeak," v, 2); the verb is formed with the prefix "for" (*OED*, "for-," I, 5) "implying destructive, painful, or prejudicial effect;" cf. "fordeem" and Spenser, *Shepheardes Calender*, May Eclogue, l. 82: "Sike worldly sovenance he must foresay."

559 *cheerisheth*] Holds dear, guards.   *her*] Their.

564 Previous editors have interpreted "kinde" as Nature and have punctuated the line: "Colin, and nature hath bene thy friende, that Cupid could not see." They have assumed that the lines are addressed to Colin and that Colin is in apposition to "thee" in l. 563; but Colin has left the stage at l. 552. The Q punctuation suggests that the line means: "Diggon, be happy that Cupid could not see you because Colin and other men hid you from his sight." The singular "friende" may reflect the spelling of the preceding "kinde" although lack of agreement is common; see note to l. 116.

565 *thriveles*] Unsuccessful.

566 *Dictamum*] Variant spelling of "dictamnum," an herb said to cure deer when they were wounded: J. Grange, *Golden Aphroditis*, London, 1577, Fiij: "no, no, if I had (faire Dame) that hearbe *Dictamus*, or Tragion, planted in my bosome, the growth whereof should touche my lippes, yet would I not taste thereof: although in deede they auayled as much in man as in the Harte or Deare, who so soon as they feele the arrowe sticke amiddst their ribbes, straightfoorth (tastyng therof) can shake it foorth."

567 *wonne*] Dwell.

572 *ranckled*] Festered.

573 *Scorpion*] A military engine for hurling stones, darts, and other missiles, used primarily in defense of the walls of a town.   *breakes*] Stops, cuts short.

574 *Rhamnusia*] Nemesis, the goddess of vengeance. Cooper (*Thesaurus*, "Nemesis") derives "Rhamnusia" from "Rhamnus, a village where hir [Nemesis] temple was"; cf. Ovid, *Metamorphoses* 3.406; *Tristia*, V.8.9.

576 *Amintas*] This pastoral name may be an allusion to Tasso's *Aminta*, produced in 1573 but not published until 1581 (Venice). Thomas

Watson published a Latin translation of the play in 1585, and Peele might have seen the manuscript before publication. Peele alludes to Watson's *Amyntas Gaudia* (1593) in the prologue to *The Honour of the Garter*, and he had written a prefatory poem for Watson's sonnet sequence, *The Hecatompathía* (1582). There is no reason to assume, however, that the reference in the *Araygnement* is to Tasso's play, since such an allusion has no meaning in context. The name is ultimately derived from Virgil's *Eclogues*, and probably used here in a general pastoral sense. Cf. Barnabe Googe, "Egloga Prima" (*Eglogs, Epytaphes, and Sonettes*, p. 31) where Amintas is one of the shepherds.   *coyes*] Blandishes, courts, caresses.

577   *are layd*] Put away; perhaps in the sense of subsided.

579–580   Cf. Ovid, *Heroides* 5.25–28 (Oenone to Paris). The use of the poplar is ironic, since it was a symbol of inconstancy (G. Gascoigne, *Complete Works, 2, 125*).

582   *blame*] Blameworthy.

592   *wrap*] Surround, encompass, or beset with; cf. l. 512 and note.

593   *Mispeake*] Speak evil of, calumniate.

596   *speede*] Prosper.

598   *smerte*] I.e., Thestilis.

600   *woo*] Woe.   *my lucke is losse*] This is a common poesie; e.g., in *The Paradise of Dainty Devices* five poems are signed with this phrase. Cf. l. 988, where it also occurs.

601–602   Cf. Ovid, *Heroides* 5.149, 153–154.

604   *Pyracmon*] Cooper, *Thesaurus*, identifies him as one of the cyclopes; cf. *Aeneid* 8.424–448, where Pyracmon, Brontes, and Steropes are described as the cyclopes who manufacture Jove's thunderbolts.

609   SD *OENONES COMPLAINT*] See note to l. 536 SD.

624   *rids*] Covers ground.

627   *plyed*] Applied.   *fotemanship*] Skill in running; cf. "to lay on fotemanship," to run quickly.

629   *eyd*] Aimed.   *witty*] Cunning, artful.

630   *Or*] Dyce and Baskervill have suggested "O"; but it is equally possible that "or" is used here as an introductory particle in the sense of "now" (*OED*, "or," adv.²). Cf. Kyd, *Spanish Tragedy* (1602), Malone Society Reprint (Oxford, 1925), ll. 1180–81: "Say treacherous Villupo, tell the King? / Or wherein hath Alexandro used thee ill?"

633   *false*] Break, violate.

635   *hight*] Heightens.

646   *cease*] Cf. l. 548, "ceaze."

651   *ypeirced*] Q's "ypeircest" is probably a misreading of the manuscript "ypeirct" or "ypeirst," variant forms of the archaic past participle. The compositor, not recognizing the form, possibly mistook the "st" for the second person and corrected the word to "ypeircest."

658 *although*] If.

659 *all to late*] All too recently.   *minde*] Pay attention to, care for.

670 *burned*] Dyce's emendation, "buried," is based on l. 743: "Now shepherds, bury Colins corps. . . ." Though "burned" may be a printer's error, Dyce's emendation, generally accepted by later editors, is unnecessary except for the sake of consistency.

682 *starte*] A sudden fit of passion; a beginning.

689 *Phlegiton*] A river bounding Tartarus with waves of torrent fire (*Aeneid* 6.551).

691 *impose to*] "To" is used here idiomatically instead of the more normal "upon"; cf. *OED*, "impose" v, 2b.

693 *beware . . . thee*] I.e., "beware if you dissemble or misrepresent yourself."

694 *starte*] Swerve from love.

703 *for*] Daniel's suggestion of "or" seems unnecessary. "Rewardes" is used ironically for "punishments."

705 *behove*] Is proper.

709SD–710 Q ends SD at "singing," and the two words "Welladay Welladay" are included in the opening line of the lyric. John Long has called my attention to the fact that Chappell and Wooldridge (*Old English Music*, New York, 1893, *1*, 130–131) give the music for the ballad "Welladay," which they found in Sir John Hawkins' *Transcripts of Virginal Music*. They comment that the original ballad to this tune is lost but that there were other extant ballads written to be sung to this tune. It appears that Peele's lyric "Poore Colin . . ." is one of these. The opening line of the lyric, as given in Q, is hypermetric. The first two words are extraneous and are not repeated elsewhere in the lyric. Peele is too much of a craftsman to mar irrationally or irregularly the metrical flow of his lyrics. By the removal of "Welladay Welladay" the line becomes regular; and the extraneous words are recognized as the title of the tune. The lyric, as emended, fits the music as given in Chappell and Wooldridge; and it is the only lyric in the play for which the contemporary music can be supplied. If the name of the tune had been jotted in the margin at the beginning of the lyric, perhaps by the prompter, it might easily have been incorporated into the lyric erroneously by the compositor. For a related textual error cf. l. 178 SD and note.

710 *going . . . grounde*] Being buried.

720 *rusty*] Rude, churlish.

721 *She*] It is uncertain to whom "she" refers, but it is probably Venus, who sings the ballad; Thestilis then woos the churl in pantomime. No trace of the ballad remains.

721 SD This SD appears to be out of place. Venus in l. 720 refers to the "rusty churl" as being on stage, and probably this direction should

follow l. 717 SD: *"Finis Camoenae."*   *crabbedly*] Crossly, ill-temperedly.

723 SD*The songe*] This SD is printed to the left of ll. 724–725 in Q; cf. note to l. 178 SD.

724 *affects*] Passions.

733 *cruell*] Q's inversion "creull" probably reflects dissyllabic pronunciation.

738 *Iphis paine*] In *Metamorphoses* 14.699–764 Ovid recounts the story of Iphis, who, spurned by Anaxarte, hanged himself while she looked on contemptuously.

739 *life*] Daniel suggests the emendation "death." The ambiguity of "life," its reference not only to this life but to the life to come, makes the Shepherd's reply ironic and meaningful.

745 *dump*] Mournful song.

748 *toward*] Threatening.

761 *that selfesame*] The misprint in BM, H, and T is probably a broken hyphen; cf. l. 173.

762 *in place*] Present, at hand.

763 *unles . . . wyde*] Unless I err. Such archery metaphors are common in Petrarchan love poetry.

771 *jet*] Strut, swagger.

775 *spell*] Guess, suspect.

781 *Cestone*] Cestus. Cooper, *Thesaurus*, records that the cestus is "a marriage gyrdle full of studdes, wherewyth the husbande gyrded his wife at hir first wedding." Venus' cestus had the special power of inciting love (*Iliad* 14.217 ff.).

782 SD*Mercurie . . . fan*] This SD is printed to the left of ll. 782–784 in Q, the speech prefix serving as the subject of the direction; cf. note to l. 178 SD.

786 *jar*] Quarrel, dissension.

789 *knackes*] Trinkets, toys; tricks.

790 *upright*] The reference is to Vulcan's limp, caused by Jove's throwing him off Olympus and breaking his legs.

797 *halter apes in hell*] The proverbial punishment of spinsters.

798 *cast*] Trick, device.

801 *fine*] Accomplished, skillful.

802 *frumpes*] Jeers, mocking speeches.

803 *take't . . . amisse*] To err or mistake it, i.e., "I pray you sir, you err withal."   *by lumpes*] Piecemeal; cf. Gascoigne, *Philomene, Works*, 2, 184: "Common people love by lumpes, And fancie comes by bits."

804 *capt his aunswere in the* Q] "She has answered him better in the same disposition or humour."

805 *kapt your head*] I.e., with the horns of cuckoldry.

806 *curst*] Shrewish.

812 *trimme*] The exact meaning of this word is uncertain. Brooke interprets it in the adverbial sense of "finely," but the context suggests
that the word is an infinitive. If so, the word might mean to "thrash,
or scold," and the reference then is to repaying the Nymph for her
impertinence. Baskervill suggests the word means to "balance the parts
(of the song)."

814 *shroe*] A dialectal form of "shrew."

815 "I might as well have seen her far off as to have seen her close."

827 *hight*] Directs (*OED*, "hight," v.¹, III, 6).

839 *ayd*] Assistant, i.e., his advocate; cf. l. 21.

844 The sense of the line requires a negative. The scansion will be irregular; but if "you are" is contracted, the line will have a feminine
ending like l. 842. Note the metrical irregularity of l. 842.

860 *forbearers*] One who is patient with, indulgent.

862 *aver*] Affirm.

863 *doe me boote*] To render help, to be of service.

870–871 *if . . . belong'd*] The lines echo the proverbial "to err is human"; cf. M. P. Tilley, *Elizabethan Proverb Lore in Lyly's "Euphues"
and in Pettie's "Petite Pallace"* (New York, 1926), No. 192.

872 *verdit*] Verdict.

885 *vow'de with processe*] Baskervill interprets the Q reading "voyde
with processe" to mean "unable to explain in a detailed story"; but
Paris proceeds to defend himself following the rules of logic. B's
emendation, "vow'de," restores coherence to the passage as a whole.
"Processe" may be used here in the distinctly legal sense of "the
course or method of carrying on an action" (*OED*, sb., 7a). Throughout this scene there is extensive use of legal terminology, part of the
arraignment convention. Cf. above, pp. 17–18.

919 *dayesman*] Mediator.

929 *gardoned*] The Q reading, "pardoned," is unsatisfactory in any interpretation of the passage as a whole. "Gardoned" and "tempted" are
parallel verbs governing the prepositional phrases of l. 931. In such a
construction "pardoned" has no meaning. While "tempted" may seem
redundant in connection with "gardoned," it actually qualifies the latter and suggests that the gifts are intended not only as rewards but
also as bribes. Cf. ll. 438 and 474, where the gifts are referred to as
"guerdon."

935 *shell*] A shell or a dish resembling one which was used for eating.

936 *skrip*] Bag or wallet carried by pilgrims.

961 *decline*] Deviate.

969 *doubt upon*] To suspect, be uncertain. The use of "upon" is unusual.
regarde] Motive; J. Calvin, *Sermons on The Epistles to Timothy*, trans.
L. Tomson (London, 1579), p. 188; "Therefore must we have an other
regard to cause us to come nigh to God."

979 *rid*] Acquit, dispatch. There is also a suggestion of the legal meaning

"to advise or counsel," "payne" in this instance being interpreted as punishment.

988 *My lucke is losse*] Cf. note to l. 600.

1004 SD*She . . . ball*] This SD is printed to the right of ll. 1004–05.

1013 *Throughtly*] Completely, thoroughly.

1019 *Beshrewe her*] Curse her.

1037 *shent*] Injured.

1059 *sythe*] Scythe.

1062 *regiment*] Rule, government.

1074 *derive*] Divert.

1088 *egall*] Fair, just.

1100 *Olive*] As protectoress of agriculture, Pallas is said to have created the olive in her contest with Poseidon over the possession of Athens (Hyginus, *Myths*, p. 128).   *Baye*] There is no obvious reason to connect the bay or laurel with Pallas; it is usually associated with Apollo.

1109 *By Stix*] The most sacred oath among the Olympic deities; cf. *Aeneid* 6.324.

1124 *emperie*] Authority.

1127 *red rose*] Peele's account of the rose's change appears to be another example of independent mythologizing, cf. note on ll. 140–149. Classical authors link the change to the death of Adonis (Bion, "Idyl I" (*Theocritus, Bion, and Moschus*, trans. A. Lang, London, 1906, pp. 173–174) or to Cupid's spilling a bowl of nectar at his wedding feast (Constantine, Agricult. 11, 18 quoted by R. Burton, *Anatomy of Melancholy*, 3, 2, 3, ed. F. Dell and P. Jordan-Smith, New York, 1938, p. 756).

1131 *Cithaeron*] An island sacred to Venus which was believed to be near the spot where the goddess arose from the waves; cf. Ovid, *Heroides* 7.60.   *Paphos*] Site of a famous temple of Venus; cf. *Aeneid* 10.51.

1132–37 *That wheresoere . . . abyde*] Q omits these lines, printing instead the following abbreviation:

The conclu-⎱ That wheresoere, &c.⎰*vt supra.*
sion aboue.⎰ Venus shall rest, &c.⎱

The reason for this abbreviation is unclear. The printer may have been following his copy where the abbreviation was made to save time, or the printer may have thought he was going to need another gathering and therefore sought to crowd his material. This precaution proved unnecessary, since he had enough extra space on E4ᵛ.

1137 SDPraise of Queen Elizabeth and of England was a commonplace of both incidental verse and drama. It was the usual practice in the early drama to end the play with a prayer for Elizabeth; cf. the encomium of Elizabeth in Peele's *The Battle of Alcazar*, ll. 667–705. In the

masque tradition and in court drama the Queen was directly addressed.
For a further discussion see E. C. Wilson, *England's Eliza*.

1147   *springes*] copses.

1162   *house of fame*] Probably a reference to Chaucer's House of Fame,
although Smeaton suggests an allusion to Westminster Abbey; cf.
Peele's *The Order of the Garter*, ll. 164, 252, 340, 369.

1176   *Zabeta*] This name for Elizabeth was popularized by Gascoigne in
The Princely Pleasures at Kennelworth Castle.

1183   *triumph*] Joy.

1184   *against their kinde*] Contrary to their nature. This was a common
theme of eulogistic verse; cf. Kyd, *Soliman and Perseda*, *Works*, ed.
F. S. Boas (Oxford, 1901), V.5.34 ff., where it is Death rather than the
Fates who spares "Cynthia's friend."

1204   *far*] The Q reading, "for," is obscure. Brooke glosses "and for" as
"because"; but this does not really clarify the problem. Baskervill
suggests the emendation in a footnote and calls attention to the occurrence of the same phrase in l. 1239 and its Latin equivalent in l. 1231;
cf. l. 1184.

1207   SD*The state*] The chair of state.

1208–17   *Humanae vitae . . . Vive diu foelix, etc.*] Baskervill's edition:

Cloth.   Thus the Fates spin the thread of human life.
Lach.   Thus the Fates measure the thread of human life.
Atrop.   Thus the Fates cut the thread of human life.
Cloth.   Clotho bears the distaff.
Lach.   Lachesis measures.
Atrop.   Atropos cuts.
The three together.   Live long, happy in the prayers of men and gods,
    Chaste in body, pure in mind, most skilled in learning.
Cloth.   Clotho places the distaff at thy feet,
Lach.   Lachesis gives thee the pendent threads,
Atrop.   And Atropos puts into your hands the fateful shears.
The three together.   Live long, happy *etc.*

1211   This line also occurs in the gloss to l. 148 of the November Eclogue
of the *Shepheardes Calender*. Alice A. Sawtele notes that the line is
ultimately drawn from the *Anthologia Latina* (*Origin of Spenser's
Classical Mythology*, New York, 1896, p. 55).

1230–32   *Te tamen . . . parcere Parcae*] Baskervill's edition:

The three divine sisters, despite the law of nature,
appoint thee a goddess unique, though on earth; and thee
and no others have the Fates learned to spare.

DAVID AND BETHSABE

ACKNOWLEDGMENTS

In its original form and many years ago this edition was a dissertation submitted to the faculty of the Department of English, Brown University, in partial fulfillment of the requirements for the doctoral degree. The editorial sections now bear small resemblance to the original form, and the text of the play now shows many more emendations than I permitted myself earlier. Despite the emendations, the text still contains a number of unresolved problems.

In addition to the obligations indicated in the notes, I am indebted to several friends, many of them teachers and colleagues of mine. The late Robert Gale Noyes and the late Ben W. Brown were invariably kind and helpful; William T. Hastings, Leicester Bradner, and Charles T. Prouty, the general editor, always had the right suggestions at the right time; Lawrence C. Wroth and Paul M. Chalmers provided me with much needed information; I. J. Kapstein helped to interpret thorny images. To all of them I am grateful. Finally, to David A. Jonah and his staff at the John Hay and John D. Rockefeller, Jr. Libraries of Brown University, I owe special thanks.

E. M.B.

Brown University
January 1969

ABBREVIATIONS AND SHORT TITLES

Arber   *A Transcript of the Registers of the Company of Stationers of London, 1554–1640 A.D.*, ed. Edward Arber, 5 vols., London, 1875–94.

B   *The Works of Peele*, ed. A. H. Bullen, 2 vols., London, 1888.

Bod   Bodleian Library copy of Q.

BM   British Museum copies of Q (when necessary, the call number is given to distinguish between the two copies).

BPL   Boston Public Library copy of Q.

Chambers, *ES*   Chambers, E. K., *The Elizabethan Stage*, 4 vols., Oxford, 1923.

Chambers, *MS*   Chambers. E. K., *The Mediaeval Stage*, 2 vols., Oxford, 1903.

Cheffaud   Cheffaud, P. H., *George Peele (1588–1596?)*, Paris, 1913.

D   Dyce copy of Q (Victoria and Albert Museum).

Diary   *Henslowe's Diary*, ed. W. W. Greg, 2 vols., London, 1904–08.

Dyce 2   *The Works of Peele*, ed. Alexander Dyce, 2d ed., 3 vols., London, 1829–39.

Dyce 3   *The Dramatic and Poetical Works of Robert Greene & George Peele*, ed. Alexander Dyce, London, 1861.

Dyce +   Indicates concurrence of both Dyce editions.

E   Elizabethan Club copy of Q (Yale University).

F   Folger Shakespeare Library copy of Q.

Greg   *The Love of King David and Fair Bethsabe by George Peele*, ed. W. W. Greg, Malone Society Reprints, 1912 (editor's note dated Feb. 1913).

H	Henry E. Huntington Library copy of Q.
HCL	Harvard College Library copy of Q.
Hawkins	Hawkins, Thomas, *The Origin of the English Drama*, 3 vols., London, 1773.
Horne	Horne, David H., *The Life and Minor Works of George Peele*, New Haven, 1952.
Manly	Manly, John Matthews, *Specimens of the Pre-Shaksperean Drama*, 2 vols., Boston, 1897.
OED	*Oxford English Dictionary.*
P	Pforzheimer copy of Q.
Q	Quarto of 1599.
SD	Stage Direction.
STC	Pollard, A. W., and Redgrave, C. R., *A Short-Title Catalogue of Books Printed in England, Scotland, & Ireland and of English Books Printed Abroad 1475–1640*, London, 1926.
Young	Young, Karl, *The Drama of the Medieval Church*, 2 vols., Oxford, 1933.

References to Shakespeare are to the Yale edition. References to Marlowe are to the Case edition. Peele's minor works, *Edward I*, and *The Battle of Alcazar* are cited from the first two volumes of the Yale edition. For Spenser I have used the Oxford Standard Authors edition.

INTRODUCTION

1. AUTHORSHIP AND DATE

The problem of authorship has never disturbed students of *David and Bethsabe*. The title page of the 1599 quarto prints Peele's name in full:

THE / LOVE OF KING / DAVID AND FAIR / BETH-SABE. / With the Tragedie of Absalon. / As it hath ben diuers times plaied on the stage. / *Written by George Peele.* / [Ornament: not in McKerrow] LONDON, / Printed by Adam Islip. / 1599.

Three passages from *David and Bethsabe*, corresponding to ll. 77–81, 555–565, and 1727–29, were reprinted in Robert Allott's *England's Parnassus* (London, 1600). Allott assigns these passages, which differ from the quarto only in the spelling habits of the compositors, to Peele. All seventeenth-century play lists, bibliographies, and biographies, with the exception of the list of Rogers and Ley (1656), assign the play to Peele: Archer (1656), Kirkman (1661 and 1671), Winstanley (1687), Langbaine (1687 and 1691), Anthony à Wood (1691–92), and Gildon (1698–99). No subsequent scholar or antiquary has questioned the authorship, although the fact that the play was not published until some three years after the death of Peele might have given some cautious scholar occasion to pause. Since the external evidence of the title page and *England's Parnassus* is strong, and since the internal evidence, that is, stylistics and metrical tests, does not preclude Peele's authorship, there seems to be little reason to doubt for the sake of doubting. *David and Bethsabe* definitely belongs in the Peele canon.

No such critical unanimity is present, and no such postiveness is possible when we attempt to assign a date of composition to the play. The Stationers' Register gives us a *terminus ad quem* of May 14, 1594 (Arber, 2, 649). To try to discover the earliest possible date of composition is a frustrating chore. No external evidence aids in dating, and the internal evidence is confined to metrical tests and stylistics, questionable aids at best. Critics and scholars from Hawkins on have made attempts to date the play with singular lack of success. Some of these attempts have been ingenious, some ingenuous, and some merely willful.

Thomas Hawkins cautiously dates the play, "about the close of the sixteenth century,"[1] but Thomas Warton's statement, "George Peele had also published his tragedy in blank-verse of David and Bethsabe, about the year 1579,"[2] is a spectacular error. Warton gives no evidence for his statement, and there is little reason to suppose that Peele wrote *David and Bethsabe* in the year he received his M.A. from Oxford. The play does not seem to be an academic exercise, and since Peele remained in Oxford until 1581,[3] he had had no connection with the public theaters by 1579. We may assume that the error is typographical and that Warton intended to give us the publication date of the quarto, 1599. This assumption may be too charitable, since it takes no account of Warton's use of the word "about."

Dyce, Keltie, Bullen, and Ward followed the cautious line set by Hawkins and said either that the date of composition was unknown, or that it was unascertainable. Fleay, in 1878, decided quite arbitrarily that the play was written in 1585.[4] In 1891, however, inspired by his love for political allegory, he changed his mind: *"The Love of King David and Fair Bethsabe . . .* may fairly be dated c. 1588. The situations in the play are strikingly suggestive of Elizabeth and Leicester as David and Bethsheba, Uriah as Leicester's first wife, and Absalom as Mary Queen of Scots. The disguise of political allusions by a change of sex was not

1. Hawkins, *1*, xi.

2. Thomas Warton, *The History of English Poetry from the Close of the Eleventh Century to the Commencement of the Eighteenth Century* ed. Richard Price (rev. ed. London, 1840), *3*, 70.

3. Chambers, *ES*, *3*, 458; Horne, pp. 53, 57.

4. Frederick G. Fleay, *Shakespeare Manual* (London, 1878), p. 88.

unknown to the early stage; witness Lyly's plays and the representations of Elizabeth as Richard II." [5] Chambers (*ES, 3, 461*), is overly kind, although undoubtedly right, when he describes these political allusions as "not very plausible."

Fleay took thirteen years to change his mind from 1585 to 1588. Schelling took only three years to change his mind from a "perhaps" to a "was." In 1911, Schelling said that the play was "perhaps written as early as 1589." [6] In 1914, he said: "in 1589, Peele's by no means ineffective *David and Bethsabe* was on the stage." [7] Thorndike assumes the play was "acted about 1591." [8] Allardyce Nicoll and Henry W. Wells date the play "c. 1593." [9] Aronstein [10] and Chambers (*ES, 3, 461*), commendably cautious, say the play was written before 1594. Gerrard offers as a date, "sometime between 1583 and 1588"; [11] Gassner says it was "produced about the same time as Marlowe's first play," [12] which he had previously dated 1587; and T. W. Baldwin suggests "a date of 1590." [13] Arthur Acheson believes, if I interpret his reasoning correctly, that the play was composed between 1582/3 and 1589." [14]

Arguing from resemblances that he discerns between *David and Bethsabe* on the one hand, and *L'Eden, Les Artifices, L'Arche*, and *Les Trophées* of the Huguenot poet, Guillaume de Saluste, Seigneur du Bartas on the other, Cheffaud (pp. 129–131) believes that the play was written and produced in 1591 or 1592. Cheffaud's arguments have something to commend them. A study of the

5. Frederick G. Fleay, *A Biographical Chronicle of the English Drama 1559–1642* (London, 1891), *2*, 153–154.

6. Felix E. Schelling, *Elizabethan Drama 1558–1642* (Boston, 1911), *1*, 43.

7. Felix E. Schelling, *English Drama* (New York, 1914), p. 31.

8. Ashley H. Thorndike, *Tragedy* (Boston, 1908), p. 110.

9. Allardyce Nicoll, *British Drama* (New York, 1925), p. 75; Henry W. Wells, *Elizabethan and Jacobean Playwrights* (New York, 1939), p. 300.

10. Philipp Aronstein, *Das Englische Renaissancedrama* (Leipzig, 1929), p. 12.

11. Ernest A. Gerrard, *Elizabethan Drama and Dramatists 1583–1603* (Oxford, 1928), p. 181.

12. John Gassner, *Masters of the Drama* (New York, 1940), p. 201.

13. T. W. Baldwin, *On the Literary Genetics of Shakspere's Plays 1592–1594* (Urbana, Ill., 1959), p. 172.

14. Arthur Acheson, *Shakespeare, Chapman and "Sir Thomas More"* (London, 1931), pp. 14, 266.

sources will show that Peele is indebted to du Bartas much more than would have been the case if the two writers were merely working from the same source materials. In short, it seems definite that Peele had read du Bartas somehow, somewhere, and in some form.

Although Cheffaud's arguments concerning du Bartas are not unreasonable, there is no evidence to insure the accuracy of his dating of the play. Conceivably the play was written in 1591 or 1592, but we can't be certain. There is one point that seems to argue strongly against 1591 or 1592 as the date of the play. Cheffaud (p. 23) indicates by his chronological table that he thinks *David and Bethsabe* is Peele's last play. There is, of course, no rule that a man has to be writing plays until the day of his death, but it seems strange that Peele should have stopped writing plays over four years before he died. Even if Cheffaud is correct that *David and Bethsabe* was Peele's last play, a date as close to 1594 as possible would be convincing, for it would be strange if a man with an excellent reputation as a dramatist would not try to earn some money by his acknowledged skill at a time when he was obviously short of funds.

The scholar who has devoted the greatest amount of time and effort to the problem of dating Peele's plays is Harold M. Dowling. His argument is too long to be quoted in full, but it should be noted that he attempts to place *David and Bethsabe* far earlier in the Peele canon than most other scholars. Leaning heavily on Peele's indebtedness to du Bartas and on metrical statistics, he arrives at a date "near 1586," and "before 1588." [15] So far as the metrical statistics are concerned, I am in agreement with the enlightened scholar who said something to the effect that the metrical test resembled expert testimony in a court of law: it was always expected; it was always delivered; and it was always disregarded. So far as Dowling's cleverness and ingenuity are concerned, I am not convinced that *David and Bethsabe* was written as early in Peele's career as Dowling concludes. In the absence of any external evidence for establishing an earliest possible date of composition, and in the absence of any internal evidence that stands up under objective examination, it seems safest to date the play as close to its entry

15. Harold M. Dowling, "The Date and Order of Peele's Plays," *Notes and Queries, 164* (1933), 167.

in the Stationers' Register, May 14, 1594, the one definite date we have. I feel therefore that the play was composed sometime during the winter and spring of 1593/4.

Ordinarily in a study such as this, several pages are devoted to the stage history of the play under consideration. Suffice it to say that most contemporary critical judgment feels that the reference in Henslowe's *Diary* (*1*, 182; *2*, 232),

$$\left.\begin{array}{l}\text{pd for poleyes \& worckmanshipp for to}\\ \text{hange absolome} \dots\dots\dots\dots\dots\dots\dots\dots\dots\end{array}\right\} \text{xiiij}^{\text{d}}$$

probably does not refer to Peele's *David and Bethsabe*. Except, then, for the title page bromide, "As it hath ben diuers times plaied on the stage," which was accepted as gospel by the seventeenth- and eighteenth-century dramatic bibliographers but by nobody else, I have been unable to find any evidence that *David and Bethsabe* was ever performed.[16]

2. SOURCES

A short answer and a long answer are available to the question of the source of *David and Bethsabe*. The short one states simply that the play is based upon the biblical story of David, Bethsabe, and Absalon found in the Second Book of Samuel. The short answer should also include some mention of the First Book of Kings, and of du Bartas and his *Semaines*. Until the twentieth century this short answer was considered adequate; indeed the seventeenth-century bibliographers and biographers frequently gave an even shorter answer: "Plot from Holy Scripture."

Such cursory treatment has proved inadequate for the twentieth-century scholar. Neitzel, in 1904, and Sampley, in 1928, attempted to ascertain what version of the Bible Peele used for a source.[1] Dyce realized by 1861 that part of one chorus of *David and Bethsabe* imitated a passage in du Bartas (Dyce 3, pp. 469–470), but not

16. See Baldwin, *Genetics . . . Plays*, p. 173; Lily B. Campbell, *Divine Poetry and Drama in Sixteenth-Century England* (Cambridge, 1959), p. 253; and Chambers, *ES*, *3*, 48–49.

1. Bruno Neitzel, *George Peele's "David and Bethsabe"* (Halle, 1904); Arthur M. Sampley, "The Version of the Bible Used by Peele in the Composition of *David and Bethsabe*," *University of Texas Studies in English*, *8* (1928), 79–87.

until the researches of Cheffaud in 1913 (pp. 129–130, 137–141, 176–185), and Sykes in 1924,[2] has Peele's indebtedness to du Bartas been examined in detail. Important as the du Bartas influence upon Peele is, it must take second place to the Bible in any examination of Peele's sources.

Neitzel and Sampley, who were, as far as I can discover, the only scholars to make a systematic study of the relation of *David and Bethsabe* to the Bible, arrived at totally different conclusions. Neitzel cautiously decided that it was impossible to discover which versions of the Bible Peele used. Sampley decided that Peele had used the Bishops' Bible and some edition of the Vulgate. Neitzel, while using in his study six versions of the Bible, seemed to limit himself to the Coverdale, Bishops', and four editions of the Geneva. Sampley contended that only three English Bibles "were in general use in Peele's day: the Great Bible, the Bishops' Bible, and the Geneva Bible." He therefore limited himself in his study to these three and the Vulgate.[3]

We cannot, however, leave out of consideration other sixteenth-century versions of the Bible. Coverdale's, Matthew's, and Taverner's versions were not so common as editions of the Great, Bishops', and the Geneva, but they did exist and should be considered. Between 1535, the date of the first complete Bible in English, and 1594, the date of the Stationers' Register entry, there appeared 89 editions of the six versions that contained either the Old Testament or those parts of the Old Testament germane to our study. Of these 89 editions, there are five of the Coverdale Bible, four of Matthew's Bible, three of Taverner's Bible, 20 of the Great Bible, 41 of the Geneva Bible, and 16 of the Bishops' Bible. To eliminate the three early versions from consideration would be unsound from a scholarly standpoint because editions of Matthew's and Taverner's versions were still being published in 1551, an edition of Coverdale's was published as late as 1553, and finally, because to do so would eliminate unique verbal parallels.[4]

2. H. Dugdale Sykes, "Peele's Borrowings from Du Bartas," *Notes and Queries*, *147* (1924), 349–351, 368–369.

3. Neitzel, pp. 7–9; Sampley, pp. 79–81, 86–87.

4. *Historical Catalogue of the Printed Editions of the Holy Scripture in the Library of the British and Foreign Bible Society*, comp. T. H. Darlow and H. F. Moule (London, 1903–11), *1*, 6–109.

The last consideration is most important to this study. In the search for verbal parallels, I have discovered ninety occasions where Peele's word choice is identical with that of one of these six versions of the Bible. These ninety parallels do not, perhaps, exhaust all of the possibilities for comparison; I have omitted other passages that were echoes rather than precise correspondences. I have also omitted those few passages in which Peele's wording agreed with all six of the collated versions. In addition to these conscious omissions, I may have unwittingly made others. Many of the echoes are discussed in the Explanatory Notes. The following tables show in brief the results of my collations.

Table 1.

VERSION	NUMBER OF PARALLELS	UNIQUE PARALLELS
Coverdale	28	4
Matthew's	47	0
Taverner's	47	0
Great	49	0
Bishops'	66	0
Geneva	56	3

Sampley, on the basis of variation in the spelling of proper names, dismisses the Geneva version from consideration. Yet that version, as Table 1 shows, is second only to the Bishops' in number of parallels and has, in addition, three unique parallels. On the basis of twelve examples, Sampley also dismisses the Great Bible from consideration, maintaining that any reading found in the Great Bible and *David and Bethsabe* could be reconstructed by use of the Bishops' Bible and the Vulgate. Such reasoning has little save ingenuity to recommend it. The Great Bible, source of 49 parallels, cannot be treated so lightly.[5]

The versions of Matthew and Taverner are, for all practical purposes, identical. Each has 47 parallels, and each has only two readings which the other does not have. Since these two versions are so much alike, we may safely treat them as a single version. In that combined version, we see six unique parallels. The Coverdale Bible, the earliest complete English Bible, is not kept in this colla-

5. Sampley, p. 86.

tion merely because of sentimental leanings towards antiquity. It has only 28 parallels, to be sure, but four of them are found in no other version. If we should, then, dismiss from consideration the Coverdale Bible, Matthew's Bible, Taverner's Bible, and the Geneva Bible, as Sampley indicates we should, we should be disregarding 13 unique parallels which the Great Bible, the Bishops' Bible, and the Vulgate cannot provide. Here is additional proof that there is a need to collate all six of the versions that could have been available to Peele if we are to attempt to ascertain which Bible Peele used as his source.

Table 2.

VERSION OR VERSIONS	NUMBER OF PARALLELS
M, T, Gr, B, Ge	18
B, Ge	13
M, T	6
M, T, Gr, B	6
Gr, B, Ge	6
C, M, T, Gr, B	5
C, B, Ge	5
C	4
C, Gr, B, Ge	4
M, T, Gr	4
C, M, T, B	3
M, T, B	3
Ge	3
C, T	2
C, Ge	2
Gr, Ge	2
C, M, Gr, B, Ge	1
C, Gr, B	1
C, Gr, Ge	1
M, Gr, B, Ge	1

A collation of these six versions with *David and Bethsabe* produces the results summarized in Table 2. The frequency of occurrence determines the order in which the versions are ranked. The versions of the Bible used in this collation were a Coverdale Bible of 1537 (STC 2065), a Matthew's Bible of 1537 (STC 2066), a Taverner's Bible of 1539 (STC 2067), a Great Bible of 1539 (STC 2068), a Bishops' Bible of 1572 (STC 2107), and a Geneva Bible of 1583 (STC 2136). The abbreviations used are the obvious ones: C for Coverdale, M for Matthew's, T for Taverner's, Gr for Great, B for Bishops', and Ge for Geneva.

A careful study of the collation and its results leads inevitably to the belief that Neitzel was cautiously right and Sampley was bravely wrong. It seems impossible to ascertain which version of the Bible Peele used as his source. Because of unique parallels, it is impossible to omit the Coverdale, Matthew's, Taverner's, and the Geneva; it is equally impossible to omit the Great and the Bishops' since three times as many editions of these versions were published before Peele's death than were published of all three of the earlier versions. Accessibility precludes their omission. No matter where we turn, then, we find evidence that Peele's source was the Bible rather than any particular version of the Bible. To attempt to go further would involve such niceties of research as the psychology of memory and the sociology of book ownership during the six-teenth century.

While the conclusion is negative, the collation of the various versions of the Bible with *David and Bethsabe* is not a completely fruitless task. Peele either possessed a remarkable memory or had some version of the Bible before him during composition. It is hard to believe that John Hailes, the usher at Christ's Hospital who probably taught Peele his catechism (Horne, p. 29), would have emphasized—if, indeed, he taught his students the Bible at all—such portions of the Bible as the seduction of Bethsabe, the rape of Thamar, or Absalon's rebellion and attempted patricide-regicide. It is equally hard to believe that Peele's studies at Christ Church would have involved emphasis on such portions. It is, however, easy to believe that a student with ready access to the Bible would be more interested in the salacious than in the morally didactic. Churchmen, poets, and scholars, from St. Augustine through John Milton to C. S. Lewis, have always had to contend with the fact that to many minds evil is far more attractive than good. Many a person who possesses only a just-passing-through knowledge of Bethlehem possesses, when he sets out to describe Sodom or Go-

morrah, accuracy and knowledge which would do credit to a Bae-
deker. Such a conclusion is not necessarily unfair to Peele. Peele
was a dramatist and chose his subjects from those available to him.
The All-Good and the All-Bad lie in the province of the theolo-
gian not the playwright. Perfection merits awe, not applause.

And so, while we are unable to determine which version of the
Bible Peele used as his source, we are sure he used the Bible. In
addition, we may safely say that Peele used that portion of the
Bible which was most admirably suited to his abilities and tastes.
Horne remarks that the "two principal elements of Peele's later
works [are] the martial and the pastoral" (p. 56). Surely nowhere
else in the Bible could Peele have found a story more agreeable to
his talents than the account of David, shepherd and warrior, psalmist and king. In dramatizing this account, Peele did not, I believe,
rely wholly upon either his memory or close and constant reference. *David and Bethsabe* seems to be a combination of both. Perhaps the unevenness of the finished play may be traced to this dual
approach to source material. I am not, however, convinced that the
failures should be blamed upon a faulty memory; neither am I
convinced that the excellences should be attributed to the source
rather than to the playwright. The weight of the biblical tradition
would engulf the play were it not for the light and dextrous hand
of a genuine poet and a developing dramatist.

Peele's indebtedness to the Bible would be obvious if we possessed only the title of his play. For all practical purposes then, the
knowledge that Peele's play was based on biblical sources dates
from the Stationers' Register entry. Almost three centuries were to
pass before Dyce noted that Peele had a source other than the
Bible: the works of the Huguenot poet du Bartas (Dyce 3, pp.
469–470). Dyce noticed that the simile of the "fatall Raven" bore
more than a passing resemblance to a simile from the first part of
the Second Day of the Second Week, the part that du Bartas
entitled *L'Arche*.[6]

6. Like as the fatall Raven, that in his voice
   Carries the dreadful summons of our deaths,
   Flies by the faire Arabian spiceries,
   Her pleasant gardens, and delightsome parkes,
   Seeming to curse them with his hoarse exclaimes,

Sykes (p. 349) had this comment to make about Dyce's discovery: "That Dyce should have discovered the source of this particular passage is somewhat strange, since it is one of the least conspicuous of the plagiarisms from Du Bartas in Peele's play. As these plagiarisms, numerous and flagrant though they are, seem to have escaped the notice of Peele's editors, I propose to draw attention to them here." Sykes is right when he says that the "plagiarisms" had not been noticed by Peele's editors. Cheffaud was, after all, a biographer rather than an editor. Sykes may have considered Dyce's discovery "strange," but I think it even stranger that Sykes was unaware that Cheffaud had done an extremely close and thorough job on Peele's indebtedness to du Bartas in 1913, eleven years before Sykes's article appeared. Perhaps we should be more charitable than Sykes and agree with Horne who says that the two men "worked out the relationship independently" (p. 93).[7]

The similarities between the studies of Cheffaud and those of Sykes are far greater than the differences, but the differences should be noted. Sykes (p. 349) maintains that, with the exception of the "fatall Raven" passage, all of Peele's borrowings from du Bartas come from "the first and fourth Parts of the First Day [Second Week], i.e., from Book i. (entitled 'Eden') and Book iv. ('Les Artifices')." Cheffaud is in fundamental agreement, but he also stresses Peele's indebtedness to the First Part of the Fourth Day

---

And yet doth stoope with hungrie violence
Upon a peece of hatefull carrion . . .
                              [*David and Bethsabe*, ll. 555–561]
Ainsi que les corbeaux, d'une penne venteuse,
Passent les bois pleurans de l'Arabie heureuse,
Mesprisent les jardins et parcs delicieux
Qui de fleurs esmaillez vont parfumant les cieux,
Et s'arrestent, gloutons, sur la salle carcasse
D'un criminel rompu n'a guere à coups de masse . . .
                              [*L'Arche*, ll. 521–526]
Dyce, 3, 469–470, also points out a similar figure in Chapman and Shirley's *Chabot, Admiral of France*, IV.1:
                    like crows and carrion birds,
     They fly o'er flowery meads, clear springs, fair gardens,
     And stoop at carcasses . . .
7. Baldwin, *Genetics . . . Plays*, p. 172 n., agrees with Horne.

of the Second Week, the part called *Les Trophées*. Cheffaud believes that this part provided Peele with the entire plan of his play
(pp. 137–138):

> Les épisodes avaient déjà été choisis at isolés pour lui, le lien
> qui les réunit, indissolublement attaché par du Bartas dans une
> partie de sa "Seconde Semaine" intitulée "les Trophées." La
> conception générale du drame peelien,—l'expiation d'un péché
> par d'infinis malheurs,—est aussi celle du poème français. . . .

Cheffaud has made a strong case and has tied it up in a neat little
package. The principal difficulty is that the package is just a little
too neat. In the first place, the theme of the passage cited by Cheffaud was at least as well known to Peele as it was to du Bartas. The
source of the passage, Nathan's conversation with David in II
Samuel 12:1–15, especially verses 9–14, was equally known to
both. Peele's acquaintance with it was more than cursory since I
find 19 verbal parallels from 14 of the verses. I think, therefore,
that Cheffaud is overly eager in his attempt to establish a relationship, and I feel that Horne is, perhaps, overstating the case when he
says (p. 93 n.): "Du Bartas' *Les Trophées* is, apart from the Bible,
the main source of the play." [8]
Despite Cheffaud's minor lapse, his study of the relation between
du Bartas and Peele is certainly thorough and complete. I have
been unable to discover that Sykes adds anything of importance to
Cheffaud's work. Sykes insists (p. 349), and I think rightly, that
Peele worked directly from the French original and not from any
translation. Cheffaud never states a definite belief that Peele
worked from the original, but his list (p. 130) of editions of du
Bartas' works and translations of them implies that Peele could not
have had access to translations of those sections of du Bartas that
had so strong an influence on him. For all practical purposes,
Cheffaud's thoroughness precludes the listing of parallel passages
here,[9] but after comparing the two works, it is difficult not to
agree with Cheffaud (p. 141), "La différence la plus grande entre

8. Cf. also Baldwin, *Genetics . . . Plays,* pp. 172–173.

9. In addition to the simile cited above, two of Cheffaud's other passages should be cited to show the close relation between Peele and du
Bartas. Cheffaud (pp. 138–139) modernizes spelling and uses Bullen's scene

le poème française et sa traduction anglaise est une différence de
mètre,—le vers blanc se substitutant, dans la copie, aux alexandrine
de l'original." The words *"traduction"* and *"copie"* may be irritat-
ing, but they seem justified. It is interesting to note that the parallels, with the exception of the "fatall Raven," are found either
at the very beginning or the very end of the play: ll. 58–123 of
David and Bethsabe are indebted to *L'Eden,* and ll. 1641–1770,
1897–1916 are indebted to *Les Artifices.* Cheffaud also notes (p.
138) that both du Bartas and Peele had a penchant for compound
words.

In summary, then, Peele's sources for *David and Bethsabe* include
the Bible (although we are unable to determine which version),
and du Bartas' *L'Eden* and *Les Artifices* with perhaps a hint from
Les Trophées. One simile in *David and Bethsabe* (ll. 825–833)
seems to echo Spenser's *Faerie Queene* (I.5.2), but the simile is
common enough,[10] and Peele also used it in *Edward I* (I.263 ff.).
While the influence of the Bible is more important than the influence of du Bartas, the latter is helpful in understanding some points
of Peele's style, and in pointing up the closeness of Anglo-French
literary relations at the end of the sixteenth century.

---

division and line numbers; I have added in brackets the line numbers of the
present edition.

> Let all the grasse that beautifies her bower,
> Beare Manna every morne in steed of dew.
>
> Sc. i. 44–45 [ll. 67–68]
>
> Si je dis qu'an matin des champs la face verte
> étoit, non de rosée, mais de manne, couverte.
>
> 2e Sem. 1er J. v. 73–74
>
> Seated in hearing of a hundred streames, . . .
> And with their murmure summon easfull sleepe.
>
> Sc. i. 95, 100 [ll. 118, 123]
>
> Le bruit de cent ruisseaux semond le doux sommeil.
>
> 2e Sem. 1er J. v. 43

10. Baldwin in *Genetics . . . Plays,* pp. 414–415, and in *The Literary
Genetics of Shakspere's Poems and Sonnets* (Urbana, Ill., 1950), pp. 4–8,
sees echoes in *3 Henry VI,* II.1.21–24; *Venus and Adonis,* ll. 1–3; *Titus
Andronicus,* II.1.1–17; *Descensus Astraeae,* l. 4; *Anglorum Feriae,* l. 24;
Ps. 19:1–6; Cant. 5:2. J. M. Robertson, *An Introduction to the Study of the
Shakespeare Canon* (London, 1924), pp. 176 ff. has, as Baldwin notes,
"gathered together most of these parallels."

As far as the biblical influence is concerned, I should speculate that because of availability and the number of verbal parallels, it seems likely that Peele's source was either the Bishops' Bible or the Great Bible.[11] In a choice between these two versions, I should lean along with Sampley to the Bishops' Bible. My agreement with Sampley would be only a surface one since he feels that Peele definitely used the Vulgate. Although I am aware that the Universities had special dispensation to use a Latin Bible for their services,[12] I think no Latin Bible was a source for *David and Bethsabe*.[13] Sampley feels that the Bishops' Bible was definitely a source; I feel that it may have been.

11. The Great Bible and the Bishops' Bible were the Bibles "apoynted to the use of the churches." Of the first Great Bible of 1539, Darlow and Moule say (*1*, 21): "The first edition of the 'Great Bible,' *the holy byble of the largyest volume*, which Thomas Cromwell, as the King's viceregent, in an injunction to the clergy (September, 1538), ordered to be *set vp in sum conuenient place wythin the said church that ye haue cure of, where as your parishoners may most commodiously resorte to the same and reade it*." The second edition of the Great Bible, the first with Cranmer's Prologue, bears on its title page the words, "This is the Byble apoynted to the use of the churches" (Darlow and Moule, *1*, 26). The last edition of the Great Bible was published in 1569. The first edition of the Bishops' Bible was published in 1568; of this edition Darlow and Moule say (*1*, 69): "In April 1571 the Convocation of the Province of Canterbury ordered that copies of this edition should be placed in every cathedral, and as far as possible in every church; and enjoined every ecclesiastical dignitary to exhibit a copy in a prominent place in his house for the use of his servants and guests." Obviously, then, the Great Bible and the Bishops' Bible would have been the versions most readily available in Peele's lifetime.

12. John H. Blunt, *The Annotated Book of Common Prayer* (London, 1866), pp. 18–19.

13. Despite Sampley, it does not seem feasible to search for verbal parallels in a foreign tongue, no matter how fascinating and interesting the search. The problem of the du Bartas influence is different. No English translation of much of the germane material was available to Peele. If we do not use a foreign language source in this case, we have nothing to work with. Neither do I find it feasible to use the Vulgate to compare the spellings of proper names, for the orthography of the sixteenth-century printer was notoriously erratic. Further, Sampley's table (pp. 80–81) seems to show that in the spellings of proper names, *David and Bethsabe* come closer to the Great Bible and the Bishops' Bible than it does to the Vulgate.

3. The Critical History

On May 14, 1594, Edward White or Adam Islip entered five plays in the Stationers' Register: *Friar Bacon, King Leir, John of Gaunt, David and Bethsabe,* and *Robin Hood and Little John.* The *David and Bethsabe* entry reads (Arber, 2, 649):

~~Adam Islip . /.~~   Entred for his Copie vnder th[e h]andes
Edward White . / .   of bothe the wardens a booke called *the booke of DAVID and BETHSABA* . vjᵈ C . / .

In all five entries Adam Islip's name is canceled in favor of Edward White's. Why the cancellation took place is not known. Perhaps Edward White intended to publish the five plays and hired Adam Islip as the printer. Islip, deputized by White, proceeded to enter the plays in the Register. The wardens or clerk who made the entry probably assumed that Islip was entering them for himself, and so indicated in the Register until corrected later by Islip or White. Other conjectures can, of course, be offered, but no definite reason for the cancellation can be ascertained.[1]

In addition to the cancellation problem, this entry provides a history in brief of the problems confronting a student of dramatic publication in England from 1586 to 1616. During these thirty years, 237 plays were entered in the Stationers' Register (Chambers, *ES, 3,* 181). Of these, Chambers notes only 22 "in which the

1. Edward White does not seem ever to have printed a play. See Chambers, *ES, 4,* 382–388. See also W. W. Greg, *A Bibliography of the English Printed Drama to the Restoration* (London, 1939–59), *1,* 11: "The alteration of name in these entries, though in the original hand, is in a different ink, and was probably made later." Of the five entries, *Friar Bacon* belonged to the Queen's Men, and *King Leir* probably did (Chambers, *ES, 2,* 114; *3,* 328; *4,* 25). *John of Gaunt* was described by Chambers (*ES, 4,* 401) as "Probably not a play," despite Arber's contention that it was (*5,* 176). *David and Bethsabe* and *Robin Hood and Little John* may have been, then, Queen's Men plays too, but there is no definite evidence. Interesting material on copyright problems is in W. W. Greg, *Some Aspects and Problems of London Publishing Between 1550 and 1650* (Oxford, 1956), and in C. J. Sisson, "The Laws of Elizabethan Copyright: The Stationers' View," *The Library,* Ser. 5, *15* (1960), 8–20.

earliest print known falls in a calendar year later than the next after that of entry" (*ES, 3,* 175–176 n.); of the five plays in this entry, only *Friar Bacon,* published in 1594, falls within this time span. *David and Bethsabe* was not published until 1599, and *Leir* was re-entered May 8, 1605 (Arber, *3,* 289), before being published in that year. Of these 237 plays, Chambers notes that 214 are extant (*ES, 3,* 181). *John of Gaunt* and *Robin Hood* are among the 23 plays missing (*ES, 4,* 401, 402).

Despite the cancellation of Islip's name, Islip printed *David and Bethsabe* in 1599 and gave no indication of a publisher. This is the only known edition of the play until 1773 when Thomas Hawkins included it in his *Origin of the English Drama* (*2,* 123–193). Some 14 copies of the 1599 quarto are extant.[2] The possibility that another sixteenth-century edition was published is very slight. As has been mentioned above, three passages from *David and Bethsabe* were reprinted in 1600 in *England's Parnassus* (sigs. Cc7, O2, T6). Only 29 very minor differences between the two versions exist, and such differences probably indicate different spelling habits of the compositors rather than the existence of another pre-1600 edition. Of the 29 differences, only two cannot be completely accounted for by spelling, punctuation, and capitalization. Line 79 of *David and Bethsabe* reads, "Sweeter then flames of fine perfumed myrrhe." *England's Parnassus* (sig. Cc7) reads, "Sweeter than flames of fire-perfumed Mirrhe," but the difference between "fine" and "fire" could be typographical, not editorial. Line 558 of *David and Bethsabe* reads, "Her pleasant gardens, and delightsome parkes," while *England's Parnassus* (sig. O2) reads, "Her pleasant gardens and delightfull parts." These two variants, both possibly typographical like the other 27, are not enough to support a theory that two pre-1600 editions were published.

Although Adam Islip printed *David and Bethsabe* without indicating a publisher, the play may have remained Edward White's property. White died some time between August 21, 1612, when he made his last entry in the Register (Arber, *3,* 493), and January 12, 1612/13, when his widow, Sara, made her first entry (Arber, *3,* 511). White's copies probably passed to his widow and then to

2. Greg, *Bibliography, 1,* 262, lists 12 copies; Thorleif Larsen, "A Bibliography of the Writings of George Peele," *Modern Philology, 32* (1934), 155–156, lists 14 copies.

his son, Edward Junior, whose wife assigned to Edward Aldee the rights to some twenty books on June 29, 1624 (Arber, *4, 120*). Nineteen of the twenty books assigned to Aldee were originally entered to Edward White. The twentieth, "The Threasury of hidden secrettes," seems to have no previous entry. Included in the list is a play called *Salomon and Bersheba*. We could assume that *Salomon* and *Bersheba* meant *David and Bethsabe*, especially since three of the four remaining plays from the May 14, 1594, entry follow *Salomon and Bersheba* in the June 29, 1624, entry. Only *John of Gaunt* is omitted. One flaw detracts from the force of such an assumption: Edward White, according to an entry of November 20, 1592 (Arber, *2, 622*), also owned *Soliman and Perseda*. Since precise spelling of titles was not the strong suit of either the wardens or the clerks of the Stationers Company, the 1624 entry could refer to either *David and Bethsabe* or *Soliman and Perseda*. An early publication of either play following the 1624 entry might have solved the problem, but neither play appeared in print again until Hawkins reprinted them both in 1773 (*2, 123–284*).

The first definite reference to *David and Bethsabe* after the 1599 quarto and *England's Parnassus* is found in 1656. In that year Richard Rogers and William Ley appended a list of plays they had for sale to their edition of Thomas Gosse's *The Careless Shepherdess*. Edward Archer did the same thing in the same year in his edition of the Massenger-Middleton-Rowley play, *The Old Law*. Francis Kirkman appended play lists to his editions of *Tom Tyler and His Wife* (1661), and Dancer's translation of Corneille's *Nicomede* (1671). These four lists are of more interest to the student of book sales than they are to one interested in the history of the drama. The men who compiled these lists were booksellers; as a result we learn little from their lists except that certain plays were on sale between 1656 and 1671, and that later compositors had as much difficulty spelling Bethsabe's name as did the compositors in Adam Islip's shop.[3]

David and Bethsabe continued to attract notice in catalogs, bib-

---

3. But Kirkman at least seems to have had a genuine antiquarian interest. See W. W. Greg, "Notes on Dramatic Bibliographers," *Malone Society Collections, 1* (1911), 329–330. See also the "Advertisement" to the catalogue appended to *Nicomede*.

liographies, and play lists during the century following the publication of Kirkman's 1671 list. Most of the references were incomplete, some were inaccurate, and some were condescending. In *Theatrum Poetarum* (London, 1675), Edward Phillips, Milton's nephew, mentioned Peele but not his plays. William Winstanley mentioned Peele and three of his plays, including *David and Bethsabe*, in *The Lives of the Most Famous English Poets, or the Honour of Parnassus* (London, 1687). Gerard Langbaine, the Younger, a man whom Greg considers to be the father of English dramatic bibliography,[4] mentions *David and Bethsabe* in all three of his works: *Momus Triumphans* (London and Oxford, 1688), *A New Catalogue* (London and Oxford, 1688),[5] and *An Account of the English Dramatick Poets* (Oxford, 1691).

David and Bethsabe was noticed at least twice more before the seventeenth century had run its course. Anthony à Wood mentioned it in *Athenae Oxonienses* (London, 1691–92), and "a Careful Hand," thought to be Charles Gildon, mentioned it in *The Lives and Characters of the English Dramatic Poets* (London, 1699). All these seventeenth-century notices are cursory and, with rare exception, the same is true of references to the play in the eighteenth and nineteenth centuries. *David and Bethsabe* is mentioned by Giles Jacob (1719–20); in play lists appended to a volume containing three plays by Ben Jonson (1732) and a volume containing Thomas Whincop's *Scanderbeg* (1747); and by Thomas Tanner (1748), William Rufus Chetwood (1750), Colley Cibber (1756), and David Erskine Baker (1764).

Other fugitive mentions of the play are found in Thomas Warton's *History of English Poetry* (London, 1774–81), John Berkenhout's *Biographia Literaria* (London, 1777), Isaac Reed's *Biographia Dramatica* (London, 1782), Edward Capell's *Notitia Dramatica* (London, 1783), Ames's and Herbert's *Typographical Antiquities* (London, 1785–90), and *Egerton's Theatrical Remembrancer* (London, 1788). The type of critical snobbery that refuses to consider dramatic poetry as poetry seems to have existed

4. Greg, "Notes," p. 332.
5. For bibliographical details concerning these volumes, see Greg, "Notes," pp. 331–332, and Sidney Lee in *DNB*, *s.v.* "Langbaine, Gerard, the Younger."

in England as late as the beginning of the nineteenth century. Joseph Ritson, in his *Bibliographia Poetica* (London, 1802), devoted three pages to a discussion of Peele's poetry, but passed off his dramatic works by a casual reference to *Biographia Dramatica*.

Critical nausea, if not critical snobbery, is evidenced by the not-so-gentle Charles Lamb. In his *Specimens of English Dramatic Poets Who Lived About the Time of Shakespeare* (London, 1808), pp. 13-15, he quotes ll. 23 SD-93, 115-124 from *David and Bethsabe*, and then has the following uncharitable comment: "There is more of the same stuff, but I suppose the reader has a surfeit; especially as this Canticle of David's has never been suspected to contain any pious sense couched underneath it, whatever his Son's may. The Kingly bower 'seated in hearing of a hundred streams' is the best of it."

Stephen Jones in his *Biographia Dramatica* (London, 1812) enlarged and corrected the work of David Erskine Baker and Isaac Reed, and naturally mentioned *David and Bethsabe*. Nathan Drake, M.D., left his patients long enough to produce a large work in two volumes, *Shakespeare and His Times* (London, 1817). He devotes slightly more than a page to Peele, deciding, "The pastoral and descriptive parts of his plays are the best, which are often clothed in sweet and flowing verse; but as dramas they are nerveless, passionless, and therefore ineffective in point of character" (2, 240). To prove his point about "sweet and flowing verse," he quotes ll. 34-48 of *David and Bethsabe*.

Perhaps because he did not feel that morality was everything in literature, Thomas Campbell was far more appreciative of *David and Bethsabe* than was Charles Lamb. In his *Specimens of the British Poets* (London, 1819), *1*, 140-141, he claims that in versification and imagery Peele was the chief of Shakespeare's predecessors:

> His "David and Bethsabe" is the earliest fountain of pathos and harmony that can be traced in our dramatic poetry. His fancy is rich and his feeling tender, and his conceptions of dramatic character have no inconsiderable mixture of solid veracity and ideal beauty. There is no such sweetness of versification and imagery to be found in our blank verse anterior to Shakespeare.

David's character—his passion for Bethsabe—his art in inflaming the military ambition of Urias, and his grief for Absalom, are delineated with no vulgar skill.

Robert Watt's *Bibliotheca Britannica; A General Index to British and Foreign Literature* (Edinburgh, 1824), mentions *David and Bethsabe* twice, once under the author and once under the title. Watt's work is mentioned here because it is a literary encyclopedia; the general biographical dictionaries like Lempriere's, Chalmers', and Lord's edition of Lempriere, mention Peele and *David*, but add nothing of critical, bibliographical, or biographical interest to the admittedly meager offerings of the literary encyclopedists.

As mentioned above, there was no edition of *David and Bethsabe* after the quarto until Thomas Hawkins edited the play in 1773. Hawkins' edition was excellent for his time. A twentieth-century critic may complain that Hawkins made some silent emendations and omissions, and that he frequently regularized spelling and punctuation, yet he followed the quarto text rather carefully. He made no attempt to insert act or scene divisions, although he did assist the reader by including a dramatis personae. Hawkins was a scholar, and he recognized the need for accurate texts. A section from his Preface will demonstrate his critical tenets (*1*, xvi–xvii):

> The beauties, which he discovered in some of these old plays being greatly obscured by the inaccuracy of modern editors, he was induced to make inquiries after the earliest and most correct impressions of them: in which pursuit he received assistance from many persons of note in the literary world, and particularly from Mr. Garrick, who very politely communicated to him the treasures of his large and invaluable Collection. . . .
>
> The editor has avoided the tedious pomp of too many philological notes, and . . . has chosen to suppress all those, which might disturb the attention without assisting the judgment, and to give no more than might tend to elucidate a few particular passages, or to explain some contemporary writer. Wherever he has presumed to deviate from the copies before him, many of which he found exceedingly incorrect, he has printed the Original Reading at the bottom of the page; and, if in any passage he has not been happy enough to discover the true one, he hopes the candid reader will excuse the boldness of his conjectures.

But his principal care, through the whole work has been to admit no composition, how ancient or elegant soever, in which the author has not payed the strictest regard to virtue, and morality; for without these the finest productions of human genius are of no value and deserve no attention.

Hawkins' critical theory resembles that of his great contemporary, Samuel Johnson. Many of the ideas in Hawkins' preface seem to echo those found in Johnson's *Preface* to his edition of Shakespeare. Whatever his practice turned out to be, Hawkins' theory of criticism seemed to follow the strict editorial course set by Johnson in his insistence on morality in literature, on the necessity for using the earliest available texts, and on the fact that an emendation is a presumption. In one major respect, however, the two men differed: Hawkins loved ornate and flowery language; Johnson did not.

With the notable exception of Hawkins' *Origin*, the only references to *David and Bethsabe* for over two and one-quarter centuries were fugitive mentions and scraps of critical, but not always judicious, opinions. This situation was remedied in 1828 by the appearance of *The Works of George Peele*, in two volumes, collected and edited by that indefatigable Elizabethan scholar, The Reverend Alexander Dyce, B. A. Dyce's 1828 edition was followed the next year by a "second edition with additions." The second edition concerns us here. It has everything the first edition has, and a little more. Its prefatory note on *David and Bethsabe* is excellent for the time, citing the opinions of Warton, Hawkins, and Campbell. For obvious reasons, the opinion of Charles Lamb is omitted. Dyce considers *David and Bethsabe* Peele's chef-d'oeuvre, and while he does not feel that Peele is equal to Marlowe, he does feel that *David and Bethsabe* "vies in tenderness and poetic beauty with any of the tragedies of his sublime associate" (Dyce 2, *1*, xxxiv, xxxviii).

More important than the kind critical remarks that Dyce bestows upon *David and Bethsabe* is the excellent text that he provides. It is extremely close to the quarto and, almost invariably, he indicates in a footnote any deviations from what he terms the "old copy." In this respect alone his text would demonstrate a vast improvement on Hawkins' text, but Dyce goes much further. He gives examples of other uses of strange words; his emendations occur rarely and demonstrate commendable caution; and, although this commendation is perhaps owed to Pickering and not to Dyce, the text is clear, well printed, and easy to read.

In 1839, Dyce issued a third volume supplementary to the 1829 edition. It contains little of interest to the student of *David and Bethsabe* except a gentle rejoinder to Rev. John Mitford, whose comments on ll. 1829–30 of *David* in Dyce's 1829 edition had appeared in the *Gentleman's Magazine* for February 1833 (*103*, 99–104):

> We omitted to say, that in *David and Bethsabe*, p. 76, there is an expression that to our ears sounds as unmusical as a Roman trumpet to a Volscian soldier.
>
> > "O help, my David! help thy Bethsabe
> > Whose heart is pierced with *thy breathy swords*."
>
> We suggest whether it should not be, "breathed words;" but, if the text is suffered to remain, we can only say, that "breathy swords," for the "swords of thy breath," is more barbaric than anything which we have met with in Peele.

Dyce's answer is succinct: "Barbaric as the expression may be, I nevertheless believe that it is the genuine reading" (Dyce 2, 3, 197). In Dyce's answer is the summary of a complete theory of editing, a theory that Dr. Johnson held but took many words to describe: "As I practised conjecture more, I learned to trust it less; and after I had printed a few plays, resolved to insert none of my own readings in the text. Upon this caution I now congratulate myself, for every day encreases my doubt of my emendations. . . . But I have always suspected the reading is right, which requires many words to prove it wrong; and the emendation wrong, that cannot without so much labour appear to be right. The justness of a happy restoration strikes at once." [6] Dyce was to change his mind about emendation before he published his 1861 edition, and it is interesting to note that he was closer to twentieth-century standards of editing in 1829 than he was in 1861.

6. Samuel Johnson, "Preface to Shakespeare," in *Johnson on Shakespeare*, ed. Walter Raleigh (Oxford, 1931), pp. 58–59.

The next appearance in print of *David and Bethsabe* was in Dyce's 1861 edition. The introduction, insofar as it concerns *David and Bethsabe*, differs little from that of the 1829 edition, but the texts show a tremendous change. In the 1861 edition there is emendation on a scale not even hinted at in the earlier text. Dyce is too much of a scholar not to indicate most of his changes, but occasionally his emendations are silent; nevertheless, the text is a good one. Especially valuable are some of his explanatory notes and source references. Any editor who follows Dyce owes him a tremendous debt. To accept all of Dyce's tremendous Elizabethan research and then carp because he emended overmuch, is to swallow the camel and strain at the gnat. To give some idea of the difference in the number of emendations in the two texts, we need look at only a few figures. In his 1829 edition, not counting normalization of spelling or emendations suggested in the notes but not included in the text, Dyce made 60 emendations; in his 1861 edition, following the same conditions, Dyce made 168 emendations. Only 43 are common to both texts; the 1829 edition contains only 17 changes not found in the 1861 edition, but the 1861 edition contains 125 emendations not found in the earlier text.

Dyce himself summed up succinctly the nature of the snare that attends the editor who is too frequently tempted to emend. In a letter to John Forster, he writes, "Unfortunately, after all the pains I took to amend the texts, much remains, in Greene and Peele especially, in a most wretched state, and must ever remain so, owing to the frightful mutilation they have undergone." [7] To the editor who emends, there are always more emendations to make.

Perhaps the most serious charge against Dyce for overemending in his 1861 edition is that three other editors, Keltie in 1870, Morley in 1878, and Thorndike in 1910, followed him slavishly as far as text is concerned. John Scott Keltie's *The Works of the British Dramatists* (Brooklyn, 1870) gives due credit to Dyce for most of the borrowed notes and emendations. Keltie's edition of the play, however, is influenced by an idea that dates back not to Dyce's 1861 edition but to Thomas Bowdler's edition of Shakespeare in 1818. One long scene and several small passages in *David and Beth-*

7. Cited by John Forster, "A Word on Alexander Dyce," *The Fortnightly Review*, 23 (1875), 739.

sabe were considered by Keltie or his publisher to be too indelicate for mid-Victorian ears and eyes. As a result, the Thamar rape scene, ll. 244 SD–319, and ll. 344–345, 375–376, 460–464, 731–732 are omitted. That the omission of the Thamar rape scene deprives Absalon of his motive in slaying Ammon didn't seem to bother Keltie at all.

Henry Morley's text of *David and Bethsabe*, included in his *Plays and Poems by George Peele* (London, 1887), has even less to recommend it than Keltie's. He bowdlerizes less, omitting only ll. 339–340 and changing slightly only ll. 462 and 737, but he never gives the source of his emendations or changes. His division of the play into acts and scenes is peculiar and inaccurate. His text has no scholarly value whatsoever. Light in weight, handy in size, clear and large in print, it is a fair reading text; and that probably is just what Morley was striving to accomplish.

A. H. Bullen's text of *David and Bethsabe*, included in his edition of *The Works of George Peele* (London, 1888), is an excellent one. He admits that he has availed himself of all the researches of Alexander Dyce (*1*, ix), but he is not guilty of slavish imitation or unconsidered acceptance. P. A. Daniel assisted him in his edition (*1*, ix), and Bullen carefully indicates whenever he uses one of Daniel's suggestions. Bullen divides the play into a prologue (which he obviously considers a chorus since his first and second choruses are referred to as Second Chorus and Third Chorus respectively), two choruses, and fifteen scenes. His scene division is more accurate than Morley's, but it falls somewhat short of Greg's excellent division. For his critical opinion of the play, Bullen follows Lamb rather than Dyce or Hawkins (*1*, xli):

> *David and Bethsabe* was first printed in 1599; but the date of its composition is unknown. It has been highly praised by critics of distinction, but I confess that I do not care two straws for it. . . . the play is exasperatingly insipid,—a mess of cloying sugar-plums. As being the only Elizabethan play extant that deals with a purely scriptural subject, it has a special interest of its own; but judged on its literary merits it is surely a failure.

Bullen may be lacking in critical charity, but he did not let his personal distaste for the play prevent him from producing the best edition of it up to 1888. No more can be asked of either editor or critic.

The closest approach to a variorum edition of *David and Bethsabe* is that of John Matthews Manly in his *Specimens of Pre-Shakesperean Drama* (Boston, 1897). Unfortunately, the variorum aspect of Manly's work is confined to the text, where he carefully records readings from Dyce (1861), Bullen, and Hawkins. He also records the quarto reading on the rare occasions that he deviates from it. Although he did modernize the punctuation, he was the only editor up to his time to leave the original spelling. His edition probably would have been variorum in explanatory notes and interpretation as well as in text had his promised third volume ever materialized. The introduction, notes, and glossary are not available. Since many of Manly's footnote discussions end with a reference to this nonexistent third volume, the loss is obviously a great one.

The only peculiarity of Manly's edition is his division of the play into acts and scenes. His scene division resembles Bullen's, but his act division resembles nothing known to the Elizabethan stage. He divides the play into three acts because "The CHORUS and the express statements of the author" (2, 422) insist on such a division.[8] The Chorus that Manly refers to is obviously the second Chorus of the play ("5 Chorus" in the quarto), which contains the frequently debated ll. 1580–85:

> Now since this storie lends us other store,
> To make a third discourse of Davids life,
> Adding thereto his most renowmed death,
> And all their deaths, that at his death he judgd,
> Here end we this, and what here wants to please,
> We will supplie with treble willingnesse.

Manly may have interpreted "third discourse" to mean third act, but since the rest of the play has nothing about David's death, and nothing about the deaths of those he judged just before he died, such an interpretation has little to sustain it. Perhaps, though, Manly meant that the Prologue marked the beginning of Act I, the

8. Campbell, *Divine Poetry*, p. 254; Baldwin, *Genetics . . . Plays*, p. 523; and Chambers, *ES*, 3, 461, seem to agree with Manly's division.

First Chorus the beginning of Act II, and the Second Chorus the
beginning of Act III. If so, he could have stated it more clearly.
But the play as we have it is undoubtedly corrupt. To play Pro-
crustes to an already mutilated corpus is misdirected energy. Nonetheless, despite his arbitrary act division, and despite the nonappear-
ance of his volume of introduction, glossary, and notes, Manly
produced the finest nineteenth-century edition of *David and
Bethsabe*. Precise, searching, and informative, it is a thoroughly
scholarly job.

Ashley Thorndike's version of *David and Bethsabe* in *The
Minor Elizabethan Drama* (London, 1910) has nothing to recommend it. The text is a verbatim copy of Dyce's 1861 edition, and
the introduction adds nothing to our knowledge.

It is a pleasure to turn from Thorndike's edition to the excellent
reprint of the quarto prepared by W. W. Greg for the Malone
Society Reprints (Oxford, 1912). Greg has done a masterful job of
making the quarto text available to the general reader. A careful
collation of Greg's text shows but one misprint: in l. 152, for
"conversant in" Greg (l. 159) reads "inconversant." He has prefixed to his edition a list of doubtful readings (pp. vii–viii), and a
list of characters (p. ix). He also prints photostatic copies of the
title page, and sigs. B1, and B1ᵛ from the Bodleian copy of the
quarto. By means of marginal annotations, he has divided the play
into seventeen scenes, but wisely makes no attempt at act division.
Since the Malone Society is primarily interested in bibliographical
and textual matters, there is, perhaps unfortunately, no lengthy
introduction to Greg's excellent edition of the text of *David and
Bethsabe*.

In 1912 the critical history of Peele's *David and Bethsabe*, for
all practical purposes, comes to an end. From its mention in the
Stationers' Register in 1594, to a reprint of its quarto in 1912, its
history has been an active one. Eight modern editors have produced
nine modern editions; Hawkins in 1773 and Greg in 1912 stand at
opposite chronological poles. *David and Bethsabe* has been praised
and damned, and has been the subject, in whole or in part, of at
least one French and four German doctoral dissertations.[9] The

9. R. Lämmerhirt, *George Peele, Untersuchungen über sein Leben und
seine Werke* (Rostock, 1882); Emil Penner, *Metrische Untersuchungen zu*

history is a long and full one, especially for a play which, in the mutilated state that it has come down to us, is really only a promise of what might have been, not a fulfillment.

4. DAVID IN THE DRAMA BEFORE 1600

A. DAVID IN THE MEDIEVAL CHURCH

Before discussing David's place in the Medieval Church, it might be well to comment on the nature of drama and the nature of liturgy. We generally speak about the influence the liturgy of the Roman Church has had on the development of modern drama, just as we speak about the rise of Greek drama from Greek religious ritual. While Greek religious ritual gave a direct impetus to Greek drama, Karl Young (*1*, 84–85) feels that the liturgy of the Roman Church had no such direct effect:

> The impossibility of there being impersonation in the liturgy of the Eucharist arises from the fact that since the early Christian centuries this rite has been regarded as a true sacrifice. The central act is designed not to represent or portray or merely commemorate the Crucifixion, but actually to repeat it . . . The consecrated elements *are* Christ, and through the words and acts of the celebrant, Christ accomplishes His own immolation, being Himself, in reality, both the victim and the priest. The celebrant remains merely the celebrant, and does not undertake to play the part of his Lord. He is only the instrument through which Christ acts.

> The Mass, then, has never been a drama, nor did it ever directly give rise to drama . . . the liturgy itself in its ordinary observances, remained always merely worship.

In the above quotation, Young takes direct issue with Chambers, for Chambers (*MS, 2*, 3–4) insists on the essential dramatic quality of the liturgical service:

George Peele (Halle, 1890); Bruno Neitzel, *George Peele's "David and Bethsabe"* (Halle, 1904); Max Dannenberg, *Die Verwendung des biblischen Stoffes von David und Bathseba im englischen Drama.* [*G. Peele: David and Bethsabe; Ch. W. Wynne: David and Bathshua; St. Phillips: The Sin of David.*] (Königsberg, 1905); P. H. Cheffaud, *George Peele* (Paris, 1913).

The dramatic tendencies of Christian worship declared themselves at an early period. At least from the fourth century, the
central and most solemn rite of that worship was the Mass, an
essentially dramatic commemoration of one of the most critical
moments in the life of the Founder . . . And when the conception of the Mass developed until instead of a mere symbolical
commemoration it was looked upon as an actual repetition of the
initial sacrifice, the dramatic character was only intensified.

The last clause of the last sentence cited here is the one to which
Young objects. The point need not be labored, but Young provides a most telling answer to Chambers' argument when he says:
"The celebrant remains merely the celebrant, and does not undertake to play the part of his Lord. He is only the instrument through
which Christ acts." Were the celebrant to "undertake to play the
part of his Lord," he would be most presumptuous. Pride is, after
all, the chief of the Seven Deadly Sins.

But what of David's part in this liturgy? We know, of course,
that Jesus and David have a common ancestor in Jesse, and for that
reason, if for no other, we should expect that David's place would
be an important one. On examination, however, we find that the
Psalms of David are important in the liturgy of the Roman Church;
David the King is not. When David does appear in the liturgical
drama, he appears as a Prophet rather than as a king; he speaks as
a Psalmist rather than as a warrior. For example, the influence of
David the Psalmist is seen in the dramatic representations of the
Harrowing of Hell theme. Young points out that while the story
came from the section of the Gospel of Nicodemus commonly
called *Descensus Christi ad Infernos,* the dramatic effects of the
story may well be derived from the last four verses of the twenty-
fourth Psalm (Young, *1,* 149–150; see also 151–177).

Attollite portas, principes, vestras, et elevamini, portae aeter-
nales, et introibit rex gloriae.
Quis est iste rex gloriae? Dominus fortis et potens, Dominus
potens in praelio.
Attollite portas, principes, vestras, et elevamini, portae aeter-
nales, et introibit rex gloriae.

Quis est iste rex gloriae? Dominus virtutum, ipse est rex gloriae.

In the Gospel of Nicodemus, David is mentioned several times by name, but the words he speaks are most often derived from his Psalms. So far as I have been able to discover, David is never mentioned in any dramatic representation of the Harrowing of Hell.

David's part in the various versions of the *Ordo Prophetarum* is also a very minor one. The function of the *Ordo Prophetarum* was to convert Jews and Gentiles to a belief in Christ. Presented during the Christmas Season, it summoned as witnesses some thirteen Jewish and pagan prophets, who testified to the divinity of Christ (Young, *2*, 125–171). David is invariably summoned. After Moyses (Moses) and before Abachuc (Habbakkuk), the Lector summons David in the Lectio of the Cathedral of Salerno (Young, *2*, 134):

Lector: Prophetam dictum Christum, ipsum Christum audi in Evangelio dicentem: Non est propheta sine honore, nisi in patria sua. Accedat enim David Sanctus testis fidelis, ex cuius semine processit ipse cui lex et prophete testimonium dicunt; dicat et ipse de Christo. Dic et tu, David, propheta, testimonium Christo.

David: Adorabunt eum omnes reges terrae, omnes gentes servient ei.

Lector: Cui servient? Dic, cui servient?

David: Vis audire cui?

Lector: Volo.

David: Dixit Dominus Domino meo: Sede ad dexteram meam, donec ponam inimicos tuos scabellum pedum tuorum.

The version from the monastery of St. Martin at Limoges has David appear between Abacuc (Habakkuk) and Simeon. Instead of the question-and-answer method of the Salerno version, the Limoges version asks one question and gets one answer (Young, *2*, 140):

[Cantor:]   Dic tu, David, de nepote
             causas que sunt tibi note.

Responsum: Universus
                    grex conversus
              adorabit Dominum,
                    cui futurum
                    serviturum
              omne genus hominum.
              Dixit Dominus Domino meo:
                    Sede a dextris meis.

In the Laon version, David appears between Moses and Habakkuk, as he had in the Salerno version. The Laon version is most interesting because of its costume suggestions: "David: regio habitu," and "Elizabeth: femineo habitu, pregnans." Moses is to be represented carrying the tablets of the Law, and Virgil carrying writing materials. Even Balaam's Ass is not forgotten (Young, *2*, 145). David's speech is almost identical with that of the Limoges version. The "grex" of the Limoges version becomes "rex" in the Laon, and the two concluding lines of David's Limoges answer are omitted in the Laon (Young, *2*, 148).

The *Festum Asinorum* from the Cathedral of Rouen may properly be considered here since in the sections that concern us, it differs little from the Limoges and Laon versions of the *Ordo Prophetarum*. David, "ornatus regalibus ornamentis," appears between Samuel and Osee (Hosea). The "grex" of the Limoges version is restored, but the two concluding lines of the Limoges version are still missing (Young, *2*, 159).

David, then, is of minor importance in the liturgy of the Roman Church. As mentioned above, however, whatever importance he does possess, he possesses as a Psalmist and Prophet; despite the regal attire prescribed for him in the Laon *Ordo Prophetarum* and the Rouen *Festum Asinorum*, David the King and warrior is subordinated to David the Psalmist and Prophet.

B. DAVID IN ENGLISH DRAMA BEFORE 1600

Although David did not figure very prominently in the liturgy of the Medieval Church, he did figure prominently enough so that we might expect some treatment of his many-sided career in the

English miracle plays. According to Chambers (*MS*, 2, 425), David's fight with Goliath provided the subject of a play in the Norwich Cycle, but that play is no longer extant.[1] The only surviving miracle play that deals with the David story, so far as I have been able to discover, is *Ordinale de Origine Mundi*. This play should be considered British rather than English, for its locale was Cornwall, and its language Cornish.

Some of the cycles, to be sure, contained a play similar in conception and purpose to the *Ordo Prophetarum*, but most of the cycles, if they ever left Genesis as a source of Old Testament plays, never went any further than Exodus (Chambers, *MS*, 2, 407–435). The Cornish play is, in a sense, unique. Those portions which deal with the biblical David story may be found in Appendix B. I say "biblical David story" because some of the material to be found in the Cornish cycle has legendary but not biblical authority. In speaking of the Cornish plays, Chambers says (*MS*, 2, 127): "But their most remarkable legendary addition is an elaborate treatment of the history of the Holy Rood, which provides the motives for the scenes dealing with Seth, Moses, David, Solomon, Maximilla, and the Bridge upon Cedron."

Whatever the reason for its existence, we do have a British miracle play that deals with the David-Bethsabe-Uriah story. The scene in which they appear is, like the rest of the play, primitive in conception and execution. It is, however, not without interest. Because character motivation seems to have been an unknown art to the Cornish writer, we see the strange spectacle of David merely suggesting an alliance, and Bethsabe accepting without demur. After accepting, Bethsabe immediately suggests that Uriah be disposed of before he causes any trouble. David thinks her suggestion is a splendid one, and sends Uriah off to the wars. In the Cornish play, in short, Bethsabe resembles a minor-league Clytemnestra rather than her biblical original; she is, without doubt, more sinning than sinned against. But despite the lack of motivation, the

1. Hardin Craig, *English Religious Drama of the Middle Ages* (Oxford, 1955), pp. 300–301, says of this cycle: "The Old Testament plays are normal, except for the inclusion of an elsewhere unknown subject of David and Goliath."

play does contain some sense of drama, and a definite sense of the value of dramatic irony.[2]

From the Cornish *Ordinale de Origine Mundi* to Bishop Bale's *God's Promises* (1538) is a jump of at least two centuries but, so far as I am able to discover, David makes no appearance in English drama during that time.[3] *God's Promises* is important to this discussion because one of the promises is made to David. The play starts with a prologue by Bale. Then "Pater Coelestis" speaks in turn to Adam, Noah, Abraham, Moses, David, Esias, and Johannes Baptista. The discourse between "Pater Coelestis" and David may be found below in Appendix C. To my mind, there is no more evidence that Peele borrowed from Bale's work, or that he was even aware of its existence, than there is that Peele was aware of or borrowed from the Cornish play. The sections of *God's Promises* and *Ordinale de Origine Mundi* that deal with David are interesting as predecessors, but not as sources, of *David and Bethsabe*.

The next item to be mentioned is both tantalizing and frustrating. Sometime between July 22, 1561, and July 24, 1562, the following entry appears in the Stationers' Register (Arber, *1*, 181):

> Recevyd of Thomas hackett for his lycense for pryntinge an new interlude of the ij synmes [sins] of kynge *DAVYD* . . . iiij[d].

The entry is frustrating because it is only a promise; the interlude is no longer extant. We are forced to speculate when we should like to compare.

A peculiar now-you-have-it-now-you-don't situation confronts us when we turn to a play called *Absalon*. We first hear of it in Roger Ascham's *The Scholemaster* (1570): [4]

> Whan *M. Watson* in S. Johns College at Cambrige wrote his excellent Tragedie of *Absalon, M. Cheke,* he and I, for that part of trew Imitation, had many pleasant talks togither, in

2. See especially ll. 2174, 2178, 2187–89.

3. While Craig, *Religious Drama*, p. 364, is undoubtedly correct when he says, "David with the various events in his career appears in many dramas in many languages," it might be well to add that English is not one of those "many languages."

4. Ed. Edward Arber (London, 1870), pp. 139–140.

comparing the precepts of *Aristotle* and *Horace de Arte Poetica*, with the examples of *Euripides, Sophocles,* and *Seneca.* Few men, in writyng of Tragedies in our dayes, have shot at this marke. Some in *England,* moe in *France, Germanie,* and *Italie,* also have written Tragedies in our tyme: of the which, not one I am sure is able to abyde the trew touch of *Aristotles* preceptes, and Euripides examples, save onely two, that ever I saw, *M. Watsons Absalon,* and *Georgius Buckananus Jephthe.* . . . *M. Watson* had an other maner [of] care of perfection, with a feare and reverence of the judgement of the best learned: Who to this day would never suffer, yet his *Absalon* to go abroad, and that onelie, bicause, in *locis paribus, Anapestus* is twise or thrise used in stede of *Iambus.* A smal faulte, and such [a] one, as perchance would never be marked, no neither in *Italie* nor *France.*

Ascham speaks with firsthand knowledge of the play, even though his literary judgment may leave something to be desired.[5] Gabriel Harvey also speaks of the play, but as Boas remarks, he does little more than quote Ascham.[6] Francis Meres in *Palladis Tamia* (1598) also demonstrates the direct influence of Ascham: "As Georgius Buchananus' *Jepthae* amongst all moderne Tragedies is able to abide the touch of Aristotle's precepts and Euripides's examples: so is Bishop Watson's *Absalon.*"[7] In 1788, *Egerton's Theatrical Remembrancer* refers to a play called *Absalon,* "not printed," by Bishop John Watson.[8] To be sure, Ascham's friend was Thomas Watson, not John, and was Bishop of Lincoln, not Winchester (Chambers, *MS, 2,* 458), but the possibility remains that the

5. See the comment of John E. B. Mayor, ed. *The Scholemaster, by Roger Ascham* (London, 1895), p. 260.

6. F. S. Boas, *University Drama in the Tudor Age* (Oxford, 1914), p. 64 n.

7. Cited by Chambers, *ES, 4,* 246. John Hazel Smith, *A Humanist's "Trew Imitation": Thomas Watson's Absalom,* Illinois Studies in Language and Literature, *52* (Urbana, Ill., 1964), 13, says, "Meres had no firsthand knowledge: even his simile and his spelling of Buchanan's name are based upon Roger Ascham" Smith is, of course, correct. See also Boas, *University Drama,* p. 64 n.

8. T. and J. Egerton, *Egerton's Theatrical Remembrancer* (London, 1788), p. 269.

Egertons' *Absalon* is the same as that of Ascham, Harvey, and Meres.

The problem that now arises is if Ascham, Harvey, Meres, and the Egertons are talking about the same play, is this play to be identified with the play contained in the British Museum Stowe Manuscript 957? Boas (pp. 63–64) doesn't think so:

> But there is a unique MS. in the British Museum (Stowe 957) which preserves for us either Watson's play or another neo-classic treatment of the same subject. It is written in a sixteenth-century hand, but has no title-page nor even title, nor any indication of authorship, date, or provenance. The numerous corrections in the text by the original hand suggest that the MS is autograph, and show that the writer had the faculty of self-criticism which Ascham attributes in so full a measure to Watson. In constructive power and psychological insight the anonymous work, as a detailed examination of it shows, would not be unworthy of the Cambridge humanist. But one hesitates, without any external evidence, to make so fastidious a scholar responsible for its tasteless rhetoric and monotonous versification, though the Renaissance standard in such matters was different from our own. On the whole, it seems improbable that an auto-graph copy, with the author's own corrections, of Watson's jealously guarded play should have come down in this haphazard fashion, without any outward sign of its origin. Moreover if, as is probable, Ascham included the observance of the Unities amongst "Aristotles preceptes," though the immediate reference is to "Imitation," the extant *Absalon* could not have earned his commendation, for that of Time, in particular, is set at defiance.

It seems to me that Boas has made his argument suspiciously weak. Since Watson did not "suffer yet his *Absalon* to go abroad," but devoted much time, as Boas implies, to correcting it, it is not at all strange that the play bears no "outward sign of its origin." After all, an author's name and a play's title are frequently not affixed until a manuscript goes to press. In the Tudor period, many academic plays were not printed, and gentlemen rarely published anything, let alone plays. So far as Boas' argument about unities is concerned, it might be remarked that Ascham speaks of "Euripides examples," as well as "Aristotles preceptes." Euripides frequently sets the unity of time "at defiance." T. W. Baldwin feels that Boas' argument concerning the unities is "anachronistic," and argues that "Ascham and his friends would certainly not have found the unities of time and place in or around Aristotle . . . when they were studying his precepts." Baldwin goes on to say: "I think it highly probable that the surviving *Absalon* is Bishop Watson's." [9]

But the strongest evidence for Bishop Watson's authorship of Stowe MS 957 has been provided by John Hazel Smith. Smith has compared the handwriting of Stowe MS 957 with the handwriting in a letter from Watson to Lord Burghley, October 6, 1578, and that in a voucher dating from the period 1553–57 found in the College, University of Durham, and has found all three hands—allowing of course for the infirmities of age—to be similar. He has reproduced specimen pages of the manuscript, the letter, and the voucher. After examining his specimen pages, I find it difficult to dispute either his opening statement on the authorship problem, "the Absolom preserved in Stowe MS. 957 was written by Thomas Watson," or his concluding statement, "the identity of the handwriting of all three manuscripts is . . . unmistakable." [10]

Whatever the case for Watson's authorship of Stowe MS 957, and I think the case is strong, there can be no doubt that the *Absalon* play, as Boas has remarked (p. 363), "presents instructive points of comparison with George Peele's English play on the same subject." Boas' comparison is admirably thorough, and his summation of the problem (p. 365) deserves quotation:

> On the whole, the Latin play profits by comparison with the English. Peele had far more sense of beauty and a finer ear for rhythm than the academic dramatist, and he was free from his cardinal sin of diffuseness. But in dextrous arrangement of material, in concentration of interest, and, above all, in psychological

9. T. W. Baldwin, *William Shakspere's Five-Act Structure* (Urbana, 1947), pp. 362, 364. Although Baldwin is probably correct, I should point out that Buchanan's *Jephthes* (1554) does observe the unities of time and place.

10. Smith, *A Humanist's "Trew Imitation,"* p. 12.

insight, *Absalon* is the work of an abler and more original play-wright than Peele.

I find it difficult to understand how a dramatist who suffered from the "cardinal sin of diffuseness" could succeed in obtaining a "concentration of interest," but perhaps I am merely quibbling. Boas' work of comparison is complete enough to preclude any elaborate discussion here. One point should be made: there are no feminine characters in the Latin play, and practically no feminine interest. In this sense *Absalon*, as Boas remarks (p. 363), loses in "moral import, for the rebellion and death of Absalon have their deepest significance as incidents in the divine chastisement of David for his son." Boas therefore believes, and it is impossible to disagree wtih him, that Peele's *David*, despite Peele's association with the university stage, shows no influence of the *Absalon* play. The Latin play is interesting as an analogue, not as a source, of *David and Bethsabe*, and "the contrast between them is an instructive example of the varied results obtained by two dramatists of different temper, and working under different influences, from identical materials" (Boas, p. 363).

David, then, plays a small part in the English drama before 1600. We should not be surprised, for biblical drama as a whole seemed to interest neither the Elizabethan dramatist nor his audience. Bullen is more right than wrong when he says (*1*, xli), "as being the only Elizabethan play extant that deals with a purely scriptural subject, it [*David and Bethsabe*] has a certain interest of its own." Aside from the very few plays mentioned above, I can discover only five plays based partially or completely on the Bible that were entered in the Stationers' Register or printed during the reign of Elizabeth. *Goodly Queen Hester* was entered in 1560/1, and printed in 1561. *Jacob and Esau*, although not printed until 1568, was entered in the Stationers' Register in 1557/8. *Susanna*, by Thomas Garter, was entered in the Register in 1568/9 and printed in 1578.[11] In 1575, Arthur Golding translated Theodore Beza's *Abraham Sacrifant* from French into English. Although the translation undoubtedly belongs in the period, the original antedates

11. Thomas Garter, *Susanna*, ed. B. Ifor Evans and W. W. Greg (Malone Society Reprints, 1937), p. v.

the reign of Elizabeth (Chambers, *ES, 3, 322; 4, 382*). Beza, according to Creizenach, wrote the original in 1550.[12] Finally, we should consider in this connection *A Looking Glass for London and England* (c. 1590) by Robert Greene and Thomas Lodge. It was entered in the Stationers' Register on March 5, 1593/4 (Arber, *2, 645*), and printed in 1594, 1598, 1602, and 1617 (Chambers, *ES, 3, 328*). Perhaps other plays on biblical subjects were written during the reign of Elizabeth,[13] but they were neither entered in the Stationers' Register nor, so far as we are able to discover, printed. In short, *David and Bethsabe* stands alone in the Elizabethan period as an extant English play based completely on the Bible.

C. DAVID IN CONTINENTAL DRAMA BEFORE 1600

While David plays but a small part in the English drama before 1600, he plays a major part in the continental drama of the same period. I find, either by reference or by examination, some 60 plays written on the Continent before 1600 in which David figures. These 60 plays include thirteen Latin, twelve French, four Italian, twenty German (ten by Hans Sachs), one Dutch, nine Spanish, and one Portuguese. Some of these plays apparently are not extant, some are not available in modern editions, and some are available only in manuscript. So far as possible, I have examined these plays in any editions available; I drew titles from many sources.[14]

Of the 60 plays, only thirteen cover approximately the same ground as Peele does in *David and Bethsabe*. Of these thirteen,

12. Wilhelm Creizenach, *Geschichte des Neueren Dramas* (Halle, 1893–1923), 2 (1918), 426.

13. See Chambers, *ES, 4*, 389–404; Campbell, *Divine Poetry*, pp. 240–242; C. F. Tucker Brooke, *The Tudor Drama* (Cambridge, Mass., 1911), p. 144; and Craig, *English Religious Drama*, pp. 376–377.

14. Among the most important sources: Wilhelm Creizenach, *Geschichte des Neueren Dramas* (5 vols., Halle, 1893–1923); Baron James de Rothschild, with Emile Picot, *Le Mistére du Viel Testament* (6 vols., Paris, 1878–91); Leicester Bradner, "A Check-List of Original Neo-Latin Dramas by Continental Writers Printed Before 1650," *PMLA, 58* (1943), 621–633; Leicester Bradner, "List of Original Neo-Latin Plays Printed Before 1650," *Studies in the Renaissance, 4* (1957), 55–70; *Hans Sachs*, ed. Adelbert von Keller and E. Goetze (26 vols., Tübingen, 1870–1908).

four are French, two are Italian, six are German, and one is Spanish. Ten of the thirteen, so far as I have been able to discover, were in print before Peele's death. I have examined the text of eight of these plays, and I do not think it at all possible that Peele used material from any of them. Peele's source was the Bible; the continental dramatists' source was the Bible.

5. THE PLAY

Most criticism of *David and Bethsabe* has been neither critical nor judicious; its propounders seem motivated either by enthusiasm or distaste. Such men as Hawkins, Campbell, Halliwell-Phillips, Saintsbury, and Gerrard deviate from praise only to enthuse; Lamb, Bullen, and Creizenach deviate from condemnation only to deplore. Some critics, like Swinburne and Keltie, attempting to be judicious, are merely fatuous. "There is not much of a plot, little art is displayed in the conduct of the story, and none of the characters can be said to be distinctly marked; still, on the whole, it is pleasant and readable." [1] "It is a poor thing on the whole; yet there is the mark of a real though certainly not a great poet on the earlier scenes." [2] So Keltie and Swinburne: on such scales, as Arthur Koestler once remarked in a similar context, a ton weighs the same as an ounce.

These same critics, after displaying varying degrees of enthusiasm, distaste, or fatuousness, join other critics in the fascinating game of pinning a label on the play. Martha Bellinger believes that it is a "morality surviving out of season." [3] Boas calls it a "Miracle Play" on one occasion, "a scriptural play . . . cast in the mould of a Revenge tragedy," on another, and a "Scriptural chronicle-history" on still a third. [4] Brawley, Schelling, and Thorndike believe that it is a chronicle play; Keltie and Symonds think it is

1. [John Scott Keltie], *The Works of the British Dramatists*, p. 59.

2. Algernon Charles Swinburne, *The Complete Works*, ed. Edmund Gosse and Thomas J. Wise (London, 1926), *12*, 132.

3. Martha F. Bellinger, *A Short History of the Drama* (New York, 1927), p. 218.

4. Frederick S. Boas, *Shakespeare and his Predecessors* (New York, n.d.), pp. 75–76; *Introduction to Tudor Drama* (Oxford, 1933), p. 157; *University Drama*, p. 363.

a miracle play. Agnes Mackenzie agrees with both sides: "In theme it thus suggests the miracles, but the treatment is that of the 'history' or chronicle-play like Henry VI." [5] T. W. Baldwin dismisses most labels, but implies, if he does not state, one of his own: "In fact, Peele is not interested in drama as drama at all, but in story presented in pageant form. This is as true in the two plays [*The Araygnement of Paris* and *The Battle of Alcazar*] where Peele uses the five-act formula overtly as it is in the others [*Edward I, David and Bethsabe,* and *The Old Wives Tale*]." [6] Lily B. Campbell has an interesting classification as she provides both a species and a genus: "Peele seems to me to stand as the lone poet of the age to undertake a divine play conscious of its place in divine literature and aware of traditions and practices of the poets who were writing divine poems." [7]

Important as a label is, it should be merely the beginning, not the sole object, of criticism. Important as value judgments are, they are more accurately determined by examination and analysis than by impression and intuition. The play deserves neither the great praise of Campbell, nor the severe censure of Bullen.

Even the newest of the new critics would admit that it is helpful, even necessary, to possess the literary work as the author wrote it if we are to understand the work's intention and render a valid judgment of it. Despite the excellent editing of Dyce, Bullen, Manly, and Greg, we do not have an accurate text. The quarto is very corrupt. Along with the errors of spelling and punctuation customarily found in Elizabethan publications, we find the quarto of *David and Bethsabe* marked by errors of both omission and commission. The play contains two choruses, but the second is marked "*5. Chorus.*" [8] The numeral "*5*" could, I suppose, be a typographical error for the numeral *2* (or, if we call the *Prologue, 1. Chorus,* a typographical error for the numeral *3*), but it is equally easy to believe that two or three of the intervening choruses are missing. In this conection, it should be noted that the

5. *The Playgoer's Handbook to the English Renaissance Drama* (London, 1927), p. 44.
6. *Genetics . . . Plays,* p. 523.
7. *Divine Poetry,* p. 260.
8. See l. 1573 SD and note.

Chorus which starts at l. 551 SD has no numerical designation.

The "5. *Chorus*" is the source of another problem. The eighth line, "to make a third discourse of Davids life," may be variously interpreted. Perhaps it means that Peele is promising to treat the death of David within this play. The first two "discourses" would then be (1) the love of King David and fair Bethsabe, and (2) the tragedy of Absalon. If the line is so intended, this promise is never fulfilled. A. M. Sampley, however, suggests that Peele is promising another play to follow this one.[9] He bases his position on the fact that the play's title is *The Love of King David and Fair Bethsabe. With the Tragedie of Absalon.* He argues that, since the two stories mentioned in the title are treated, Peele was following a common Elizabethan practice of preparing for a second play within the text of a first. I feel that Sampley's literal conclusion has much to commend it, but I also feel that the conclusion should be stated more cautiously. When dealing with corrupt texts, it is always advisable to proceed with wariness if not with fear.[10]

The fact that "5. *Chorus*" is located in the play where an undoubted corruption (the misplaced fragment) appears should increase our hesitancy, for the misplaced fragment appears immediately following its conclusion. It consists of a stage direction, three lines and a catchword (ll. 1585 SD–1588):

> *Absalon with three or foure of his servants or gentlemen.*
> *Abs.*   What boots it Absalon, unhappie Absalon,
> Sighing I say what boots it Absalon,
> To have disclos'd a farre more worthy wombe
>
> > Then

Since Absalon had been killed in the scene immediately preceding the Chorus, his entrance at this time is little short of startling. The misplaced fragment and the catchword that follows it probably belong to an omitted section of the play. The fragment bears no relation to any of the scenes preceding or following it; the catch-

9. "The Text of Peele's *David and Bethsabe*," *PMLA*, 46 (1931), 667–669.

10. See Campbell, *Divine Poetry*, p. 254; Baldwin, *Genetics . . . Plays*, pp. 173, 523; and Chambers, *ES*, 3, 48, for other approaches to the problem of the "third discourse."

word should not be "Then," but "*Trumpets.*" Suffice it to say
here that the misplaced fragment is the most cogent argument that
we are dealing with a corrupt text. The rest of the evidence lets us
assume that we are; the fragment enables us to know that we are.

Two other episodes may be cited to indicate possible textual
omissions. When Thamar first comes to minister to the feigned
needs of Ammon, she says that she comes by the King's command
(l. 278) when, according to the text, the King neither has heard
of Ammon's "illness," nor has asked Thamar to minister to his
needs. A similar episode occurs when the Widow from Thecoa, at
Joab's instigation, seeks audience with David to urge him in parable
to call home the banished Absalon (ll. 880 ff.). Prior to her
entrance, David has neither banished Absalon nor attempted to
punish him for his killing of Ammon.

The Thamar episode is handled properly in the biblical narrative
(II Sam. 13):

> 6. So Amnon lay down, and made himself sick: and when the
> king was come to see him, Amnon said unto the king, I pray
> thee, let Tamar my sister come, and make me a couple of cakes
> in my sight, that I may eat at her hand.
> 7. Then David sent home to Tamar, saying, Go now to thy
> brother Amnon's house, and dress him meat.

Conceivably, of course, Peele could have overlooked the biblical
passage because the verses, especially verse 7, are short. A more
likely solution to the problem is that several speeches are missing
between l. 272 and l. 273 of Jonadab's insidious speech.

The biblical handling of the Widow from Thecoa episode is
not so explicit as its handling of the Thamar episode. Because it is
not explicit, Harold M. Dowling does not believe that any textual
lacunae are present:

> In 2 Sam. xiii, 37, we hear that Absalon fled the country after
> the murder of Amnon, and that David, far from banishing him,
> mourned for him and longed for his return. Yet in 2 Sam. xiv,
> 13, the Widow of Thecoa reproves the King for not allowing
> his "banished one" to return, pointing out that to God alone
> belongs revenge. Thus the attempts of Manly and Daniel to

explain the passage were really unnecessary. It is only another illustration of the fidelity with which Peele habitually followed his source—a fidelity that was usually uncritical and often absurd.[11]

Dowling has looked at the Bible in an attempt to explain away an evident lacuna, but he has not looked at it closely enough. The pertinent passages from II Samuel 13 and 14 follow:

> 37. But Absalom fled, and went to Talmai, the son of Anmihud, king of Geshur. And *David* mourned for his son every day.
> 38. So Absalom fled, and went to Geshur, and was there three years.
> 39. And the *soul of* king David longed to go forth unto Absalom: for he was comforted concerning Amnon, seeing he was dead.

> 21. And the king said unto Joab, Behold now, I have done this thing: go therefore, bring the young man Absalom again.
> 24. And the king said, Let him turn to his own house and let him not see my face. So Absalom returned to his own house, and saw not the king's face.
> 28. So Absalom dwelt two full years in Jerusalem, and saw not the king's face.

Dowling is right in that the Bible makes it perfectly clear that David did not banish Absalon and did, indeed, mourn for him. What Dowling seems to forget is that under the eye-for-an-eye code, the sentence of death was already upon Absalon. An absconding bank clerk today doesn't have to see the warrant for his arrest to be aware that he has committed a crime. David didn't have to pass a sentence of death or banishment upon Absalon before Absalon realized that he had sinned. David's immediate reaction was, indeed, to mourn for Absalon, but three years were to pass before Absalon was allowed to return to Jerusalem, and two more years before he was allowed once more in the king's presence. The eye-for-an-eye code may have nothing to say about a statute of

11. "Miscellaneous Notes on Peele," *Notes and Queries*, 165 (1933), 273.

limitations, but human memories are short, paternal love is strong, and Absalon's provocation had been great.

For all practical purposes then, Dowling, although he fails to discriminate between mourning for a son's absence and condoning the crime that necessitated that absence, is right in his insistence that no textual lacunae are present here. Peele may be guilty of abbreviating the time carelessly, but neither he nor the compositor is guilty of omitting pertinent material. Peele could probably expect that his audience would bring with it some knowledge of the Bible, but he could not expect it to fill in all of the gaps. The lack of dramatic motivation for Thamar's presence in Ammon's chamber may be attributed to textual corruption; the lack of dramatic motivation for the presence of the Widow from Thecoa may be attributed to an injudicious condensation of time.

Although the text is admittedly corrupt, it is far less corrupt than some editors would have us believe. Episodic construction combined with Peele's sometimes unreasonable contraction of time have tended to foster the belief that the text is hopelessly corrupt. We have already seen how condensation of time can hint at lacunae which may not be present; episodic construction can also hint at lacunae, particularly in a play whose events move as rapidly as they do in this one. The play is fairly short for an Elizabethan play, yet it manages to have three distinct plots in only 1920 lines: the David and Bethsabe love story; the Thamar-Ammon-Absalon incest and revenge story; and the story of Absalon's rebellion. It could be argued that the incest-revenge plot is used to balance the adultery plot. If we believe that when a father eats a sour grape the teeth of his children are set on edge, there is some validity to such an argument. Surely, however, more than one plot still remains, for there seems to be only thematic motivation for the incest plot, and only a suggestion of dramatic motivation for the rebellion plot. It may be argued that the scene in which Solomon appears and in which the regal succession is settled coordinates the plots, but, if so, the concluding scene is anticlimactic.

If it were possible to ascertain definitely what scenes and lines have been omitted from the text, it would be far easier to discuss the problems of plot construction indicated above. Under the circumstances it seems safer to say that Peele's sometimes imprudent condensation of time occasionally deprives his characters and events of proper motivation.[12] In short, causal linking of scenes frequently gives way to a loose, episodic method of presenting materials.

The characterization is generally adequately handled, even though it never attains perfection. Peele seldom indicates the grandeur that marks David in the biblical narrative, but it might well be argued that Peele's David had few occasions for grandeur. If David in the play is weak, vacillating, almost puerile in his indulgence of his emotions, it must be remembered that he is essentially a human being, and he reacts humanly if not grandly to the situations that confront him. At the beginning of the play Bethsabe is weakly human. She seems at first to give some evidences of character strength as she resists the blandishments of David, but then suddenly she becomes a party to the plot (ll. 149–150):

> Then let the King be cunning in his cure,
> Least flattering both, both perish in his hand.

Nevertheless, she is strongly maternal in her successful fight to have her son succeed David as king. Bethsabe accepts misfortune fatalistically, but before misfortune strikes she demonstrates strength in her attempts to avoid it. Absalon is, in general, a consistent, well-developed character. His motivation for rebellion could be more explicitly stated, but he is implicitly revealed as longing for fame and adulation, conscious and proud of his masculine beauty. The irony underlying his characterization is brilliantly, if not particularly subtly, presented when his golden hair, praised in ecstatic

---

12. For a discussion of time in the play see Mable Buland, *The Presentation of Time in the Elizabethan Drama*, Yale Studies in English, 44 (New York, 1912), 14, 229–232. Horne's statement (p. 93), "The action which in the play requires less than a year is spread over 55 years in the Bible," must be inexact. Even allowing for his undoubted precocity, Solomon must be about ten years old at the time of his scene with David (ll. 1640 SD–1780). Solomon's birth, of course, followed the conception, birth, and death of the first child of David and Bethsabe. Although Peele is careless about time, he should not be accused of condensing 55 years into one. I assume that the play's action covers a period of about twelve years.

terms by Joab and David, causes his death. If his speeches while hanging by his hair seem ridiculous to the reader in the library, one could argue that if the play were ever presented the audience in the pit would find them theatrically effective.

Some of the minor characters, notably Urias, Joab, and Ammon, aspire to the third dimension. Urias is consistently convincing; his drunkenness, his repetition of words, and his determination not to swerve from his decision are essentially realistic. Joab is excellently portrayed as the thoroughly courageous, loyal soldier. His character does not break when he changes his attitude toward Absalon. The Absalon whom Joab befriends is an erring son of his king; the Absalon whom he kills is his king's deadly enemy. Although Ammon appears only briefly, he possesses, I believe, both psychological and dramatic motivation when, in disgust, he thrusts Thamar from his bed.

The dialogue of *David and Bethsabe*, since it is essentially descriptive and narrative, is not always dramatically sound. David, however, when he is courting Bethsabe, mourning the death of the child born to him and Bethsabe, and talking to Urias and the Widow of Thecoa, speaks naturally. So, too, speak Thamar in her distress and Urias in his drunkenness. Even some of the long speeches, although not dramatic, are both flexible and poetic compared to similar speeches in the *Battle of Alcazar* and *Edward I*. The mingling of biblical, classical, and natural imagery seems integral to the dramatic lines rather than mere surface ornamentation.[13] If some of the speeches, like Absalon's while he is hanging by his hair and Solomon's precocious outpourings, leave much to be desired, they are more than balanced by the genuinely dramatic and poetic speeches already mentioned.

David and Bethsabe, then, has much to commend it. Its characterization and dialogue are adequate; its poetry is frequently brilliant.

---

13. In this connection see Campbell, *Divine Poetry*, p. 260: "The comparisons are drawn from Biblical story,—Adam and Eve, Isaac and Rebecca, Pharaoh and the Red Sea, the cedars of Lebanon. The epithalamium and the elegy are treated as ornaments of divine poetry. Joab's great speeches are kept in the mood as they echo the language of the Bible." Certainly the biblical imagery is present and in abundance, but imagery from other sources is also present.

Though its plot is sometimes faulty, we do well to remember that our text is corrupt. If my value judgment of the play places it in the happy middle ground of drama with plays that neither aspire to greatness nor sink to oblivion, so, too, my label of the play is in the middle ground. I do not believe that *David and Bethsabe* is an attempt in the tradition of the miracle play. I think its roots go much deeper: perhaps to the warning of the Lord in Exodus 20:5–6, "For I the Lord thy God am a jealous God, visiting the iniquity of the fathers upon the children, upon the third and upon the fourth generation of them that hate me"; perhaps to the tragedies of Sophocles that deal with the curse on the house of Labdacus; perhaps to the tragedies of Aeschylus that deal with the curse on the descendants of Pelops. Just as Orestes expiated the curse on his house, so in this play is it hinted that Solomon will expiate the curse on his.

David and Bethsabe is proof enough, if we need any proof, that Peele was familiar with the themes and attitudes of biblical stories as well as with the stories themselves. Peele's familiarity with Greek literature, particularly the tragedy, is another problem. It would be pleasant to believe that Peele used Homer as a source for his *Tale of Troy*, but there is nothing in that work that could not have been derived from Ovid or Caxton. We do have, however, a contemporary account that tells us that Peele had successfully translated one of Euripides' *Iphigenia* plays.[14] William Gager wrote two verses of commendation about this translation.[15] Although the translation has not survived, there is no reason to doubt Gager's authority. Since, therefore, Peele was familiar with Euripides, only a confirmed skeptic would be unwilling to believe that Peele was also acquainted with the tragedies of Sophocles and Aeschylus.

One further bit of information should, perhaps, be mentioned. According to Horne (p. 65), Peele was friendly with Thomas Watson in 1581, about the same time that Watson's translation of

14. Horne (p. 42) makes the reasonable suggestion that the translation was of *Iphigenia in Aulis*.

15. For the verses see Horne, pp. 43–45. For an account of Gager see C. F. Tucker Brooke, "The Life and Times of William Gager (1555–1622)," *Proceedings of the American Philosophical Society*, 95 (1951), 401–431.

Sophocles' *Antigone* was entered in the Stationers' Register and published.[16] He was so friendly, in fact, that he composed a commendatory poem for inclusion in Watson's *Hekatompathia* (1582).[17] It would be strange indeed if Peele could have avoided knowledge of Sophocles and his art. When two men, scholars and poets, are friends, it is very difficult for one not to know what the other is doing. This evidence along with Gager's testimony concerning Peele's *Iphigenia* is proof enough, I believe, that Peele was acquainted with the Greek tragic dramatists. In Peele's case I believe that acquaintance led to emulation.

From the point of view of theme and mood, then, *David and Bethsabe* is a tragedy in the tradition of Sophocles and Aeschylus; [18] from the point of view of plot construction, the play is, in effect if not in conception, a chronicle play that substitutes the Second Book of Samuel for the *Chronicles* of the earthly Raphael Holinshed.

6. THE TEXT

A. EARLY EDITION

THE / LOVE OF KING / DAVID AND FAIR / BETHSABE. / With the Tragedie of Absalon. / As it hath ben diuers times plaied on the stage. / *Written by George Peele.* / [Printer's device: not in McKerrow] / LONDON, / Printed by Adam Islip. / 1599.

HT] [Ornament] The Loue of *Dauid* and faire *Bersabe*, / with the Tragedie of *Absalon*.

RT] *Dauid and Bethsabe.* [*Bersabe* on B2ᵛB3C1C2ᵛC3C4ᵛD1D2ᵛ D3D4ᵛE1E2ᵛE3E4ᵛF1F2ᵛF3F4ᵛG1G2ᵛG3G4ᵛH1ᵛH2H3ᵛ H4I1I1ᵛ; *Bersahe* on B4ᵛ; *Bet hsabe* on D1ᵛ]

Explicit] *FINIS.*

16. Thomas Watson, *Poems*, ed. Edward Arber (London, 1870), pp. 5–6.
17. Watson, *Poems*, pp. 9, 36; see Horne, p. 203.
18. For a David play in the tradition of Seneca, see Brunetto's *David Sconsolato* (Fiorenza, 1586). This play, which does not observe the unities, contains five acts divided into 34 scenes. It has twenty characters including the "Ombra del figliuolo adulterino di David," who speaks the Prologue. Since this son of David and Bethsabe was only seven days old when he died, the appearance of his "ombra" as the Prologue is mildly surprising.

Collation] 4to. A2, B1–H4, I2. 32 leaves unnumbered.

Contents] A1, blank; A2, title; A2ᵛ, blank; B1, text with ornament, HT, and initial; B1ᵛ, text, RT, and initial; I1ᵛ, *Explicit;* I2, blank.

Catchwords] B3 *Enter;* C3 And; D3 Water; E3 *Dauid;* F3 Will; G3 Tenne; H3 Lifting.

Typography] 36 ll. plus headline and direction line. Roman 20 ll. = 85 mm.

Copies] Bodleian
     British Museum C.34.d.54
     British Museum 162.d.52
     Boston Public Library
     Dyce Collection (Victoria and Albert Museum)
     Elizabethan Club (Yale University)
     Folger
     Harvard
     Huntington
     Pforzheimer [1]

Variants]

F2	[l. 1135]	out-pace (Bod, BM—both, D, E, H, HCL)
		out pace (BPL, F)
H1ᵛ	[l. 1622]	reverence (Bod, BM—both, BPL, D, E, HCL, P)
		residence (F, H)
H2	[l. 1667]	Shee, shee, (Bod, BM 162.d.52, BPL, D, E, HCL)
		Shee, shee (BM C.34.d.54, F, H)
H2	[l. 1679]	Israel: (Bod, BM C.34.d.54, BPL, D, E, HCL)
		Israel (BM 162.d.52, F, H)
H2ᵛ	[l. 1714]	first (All except Bod)
		sirst (Bod—ligature between the "f" and "i" may not have inked well in this copy)

1. Of the extant copies of the Q, the first nine listed here were available for collation. The Pforzheimer copy was also checked on certain points. To these repositories I am grateful.

H4 [l. 1808] wretched (All except BPL)
wtetched (BPL—so Manly, but close examination indicates that the letter in
question is probably "r")

H4 [ll. 1810–11] . . . shade (the thunder slew, . . .
blacke) (Bod, BM C.34.d.54, BPL, D, E,
HCL)
. . . shade the thunder slew, . . .
blacke (BM 162.d.52, F, H)

The quarto was printed with two sets of running titles. In sigs. B through G the spellings *Bersabe* and *Bethsabe* alternate regularly. The outer forme has the spelling *Bersabe* in the running title, and the inner forme has the spelling *Bethsabe* in the running title. In sig. H the order is reversed with *Bethsabe* on the outside and *Bersabe* on the inside. Sig. I, consisting of only one printed leaf, has *Bersabe* on both sides. The only exceptions are a misprint, *Bersahe* for *Bersabe*, in the running title of B4ᵛ, and a spacing error, *Bet hsabe* in the running title of D1ᵛ.

B. THE PRESENT EDITION

The Boston Public Library copy of the 1599 quarto is the copy text.[2] This text follows the original, except that *i, j, u,* and *v* are changed to conform with modern usage, long *s* is altered to modern *s*, and diphthongs are expanded. Ampersands are silently expanded, and obvious printer's errors in spacing have been corrected. Editorial insertions are enclosed in square brackets and noted. In spelling proper names I have always followed the quarto, even when the quarto spells the same name two different ways in the same line, as in l. 943. The spelling of speech ascriptions has been regularized throughout.

I have not attempted to make a complete revision of the punctuation, but I have substituted some periods, interrogation marks, and colons for commas in an attempt to improve the intelligibility of the quarto text. All such changes are noted.

No scene divisions have been added. Line numbers are consecutive throughout, excluding stage directions, which are given

2. The photograph of the 1599 quarto title page is reproduced with permission of the Boston Public Library.

the number of the last line of dialogue preceding the direction. Page signatures of the original edition are indicated in brackets at the right margin of the text. I have included the misplaced fragment (ll. 1585 SD–1588) even though I have made no attempt to account for its presence.

In the collations, variant readings are separated by a semicolon. Punctuation readings include the word immediately preceding the mark.

THE
LOVE OF KING
DAVID AND FAIR
BETHSABE.

With the Tragedie of Abſalon.

As it hath ben diuers times plaied on the ſtage.

Written by George Peele.

LONDON,
Printed by Adam Iſlip.
1599.

[CHARACTERS OF THE PLAY

I. Speaking Parts
   Prologue
   Bethsabe, Urias' wife
   David, King of Israel
   Cusay, a follower of David
   Joab ⎫
   Abisay ⎭ captains in David's army
   Urias, a soldier in David's army
   Hanon, King of Ammon
   Machaas, King of Gath
   Jonadab, follower of Ammon
   Ammon, son of David
   Thamar, daughter of David
   Jethray, Ammon's servant
   Absolon, son of David
   Chorus
   Nathan, a prophet
   A slave of David's
   Adonia, son of David
   Widow from Thecoa
   Sadoc, high priest
   Ahimaas, his son
   Jonathan, son of Abiathar
   Ithay, a follower of David
   First Concubine
   Second Concubine
   Achitophel, follower of Absolon
   Amasa, captain in Absolon's army
   Abiathar, a priest

Semei, David's accuser
First Soldier
Second Soldier
Salomon, son of David and Bethsabe
A messenger

II. WALK-ONS
Bethsabe's maid
Soldiers
A page
Attendants
Shepherds
Chileab, son of David]

THE LOVE OF
DAVID AND FAIRE *BERSABE,*
WITH THE TRAGEDIE OF *ABSOLON.*

Prologus.

Of Israels sweetest singer now I sing,
His holy stile and happie victories,
Whose Muse was dipt in that inspiring deaw,
Arch-angels stilled from the breath of Jove,
Decking her temples with the glorious flowers,
Heavens raind on tops of Syon and Mount Synai.
Upon the bosome of his yvorie Lute,
The Cherubins and Angels laid their brests,
And when his consecrated fingers strooke
10   The golden wiers of his ravishing harpe,
He gave alarum to the host of heaven,
That wing'd with lightning, brake the clouds and cast
Their christall armor, at his conquering feet.
Of this sweet Poet Joves Musition,
And of his beauteous sonne I prease to sing.
Then helpe devine Adonay to conduct,
Upon the wings of my well tempered verse,
The hearers minds above the towers of Heaven,
And guide them so in this thrice haughty flight,
20   Their mounting feathers scorch not with the fire,
That none can temper but thy holy hand:

6 *Synai.*] Synai, Q
15 *his*] Hawkins, Dyce+, B, Manly; bis Q

To thee for succour flies my feeble muse,
And at thy feet her yron Pen doth use.

He drawes a curtaine, and discovers Bethsabe [B1ᵛ]
with her maid bathing over a spring: she sings, and
David sits above vewing her.

The Song.

Hot sunne, coole fire, temperd with sweet aire,
Black shade, fair nurse, shadow my white haire.
Shine sun, burne fire, breathe aire, and ease mee,
Black shade, fair nurse, shroud me and please me.
Shadow (my sweet nurse) keep me from burning,
Make not my glad cause, cause of mourning.
30　　Let not my beauties fire,
Enflame unstaied desire,
Nor pierce any bright eye,
That wandreth lightly.

Beth.　Come gentle Zephire trickt with those perfumes
That erst in Eden sweetned Adams love,
And stroke my bosome with thy silken fan:
This shade (sun proofe) is yet no proofe for thee.
Thy body smoother then this wavelesse spring,
And purer then the substance of the same,
40　　Can creepe through that his launces cannot pierse;
Thou and thy sister, soft and sacred aire,
Goddesse of life, and governesse of health,
Keep every fountaine fresh and arbor sweet;
No brasen gate, her passage can repulse,

23　SD *The Song.*] In left margin of Q; some copies are so cut that
The is missing; H lacks *The Song.*
　25　*haire.*] haire Q
　26　*breathe*] Hawkins, Dyce+, B, Manly; breath Q
　27　*me.*] me Q
　28　*burning,*] burning Q
　36　*thy*] Dyce 3, B, Manly; the Q
　37　*thee.*] thee, Q
　40　*pierse;*] pierse, Q
　41　*sister,*] sister Q
　43　*Keep*] Dyce 3; Keepes Q　　　*sweet;*] sweet, Q

Nor bushly thicket, bar thy subtle breath.
Then decke thee with thy loose delightsome robes,
And on thy wings bring delicate perfumes,
To play the wantons with us through the leaves.

David.   What tunes, what words, what looks, what wonders
     pierce

50   My soule, incensed with a suddain fire?
What tree, what shade, what spring, what paradise
Enjoyes the beautie of so faire a dame?
Faire Eva plac'd in perfect happinesse,
Lending her praise-notes to the liberall heavens,   [B2]
Strooke with the accents of Arch-angels tunes,
Wrought not more pleasure to her husbands thoughts,
Then this faire womans words and notes to mine.
May that sweet plaine that beares her pleasant weight,
Be still enameld with discoloured flowers,

60   That precious fount, beare sand of purest gold,
And for the Peble, let the silver streames
That pierce earths bowels to mainteine the sorce,
Play upon Rubies, Saphires, Chrisolites,
The brims let be imbrac'd with golden curles
Of mosse that sleepes with sound the waters make,
For joy to feed the fount with their recourse.
Let all the grasse that beautifies her bower,
Beare Manna every morne in steed of dew,
Or let the dew be sweeter far then that

70   That hangs like chaines of pearle on Hermon hill,
Or balme which trickled from old Arons beard.
Cusay, come up and serve thy lord the King.

Enter Cusay.

Cusay.   What service doth my lord the King command?
David.   See Cusay see, the flower of Israel,
    The fairest daughter that obeies the King,

45   *breath.*] breath, Q
48   *leaves.*] leaves, Q
50   *fire?*] fire, Q
66   *recourse.*] recourse, Q

In all the land the lord subdued to me.
Fairer then Isacs lover at the well,
Brighter then inside barke of new hewen Caedar,
Sweeter then flames of fine perfumed myrrhe,
80 And comelier then the silver clouds that dance
On Zephires wings before the king of heaven.
Cusay.   Is it not Bethsabe, the Hethites wife,
Urias, now at Rabath siege with Joab?
David.   Goe know, and bring her quickly to the King,
Tell her, her graces have found grace with him.
Cusay.   I will my lord.

Exit Cusay to Bethsabe.

David.   Bright Bethsabe shall wash in Davids bower,
In water mix'd with purest Almond flower,
And bath her beautie in the milke of kids.
90 Bright Bethsabe gives earth to my desires,   [B2ᵛ]
Verdure to earth, and to that verdure flowers,
To flowers, sweet Odors, and to Odors wings,
That carrie pleasures to the hearts of Kings.

Cusay to Bethsabe, she starting as something afright.

Cusay.   Faire Bethsabe, the King of Israell
From forth his Princely tower hath seen thee bath,
And thy sweet graces have found grace with him.
Come then and kneele unto him where he stands,
The King is gracious and hath liberall hands.
Beth.   Ah what is Bethsabe to please the King,
100 Or what is David, that he should desire
For fickle beuties sake his servants wife?
Cusay.   David (thou knowest faire dame) is wise and just,
Elected to the heart of Israels God,
Then doe not thou expostulate with him

79 *fine perfumed*] fire-perfumed *England's Parnassus*   *myrrhe,*]
myrrhe. Q
  82 *Bethsabe,*] Bethsabe Q   *wife,*] wife Q
  85 *have*] Hawkins, Dyce+, B; hath Q
  89 *kids.*] kids, Q
  96 *him.*] him, Q

For any action that contents his soule.

Beth.   My lord the King, elect to Gods owne heart,
Should not his gracious jelousie incense,
Whose thoughts are chast. I hate incontinence.

Cusay.   Woman thou wrongst the King, and doubtst his honour,
110   Whose truth mainteines the crowne of Israel,
Making him stay, that bad me bring thee strait.

Beth.   The Kings poore handmaid will obey my lord.

Cusay.   Then come and doe thy dutie to his grace,
And doe what seemeth favour in his sight.

Exeunt.

David.   Now comes my lover tripping like the Roe,
And brings my longings tangled in her haire.
To joy her love Ile build a kingly bower,
Seated in hearing of a hundred streames,
That for their homage to her sovereine joies,
120   Shall as the serpents fold into their nests,
In oblique turnings wind their nimble waves,
About the circles of her curious walkes,
And with their murmure summon easeful sleepe,   [B₃]
To lay his golden scepter on her browes.
Open the dores, and enterteine my love,
Open I say, and as you open sing,
Welcome faire Bethsabe King Davids darling.

Enter Cusay with Bethsabe.

David.   Welcome faire Bethsabe King Davids darling.
Thy bones faire covering, erst discovered faire,
130   And all mine eyes with all thy beuties pierst,
As heavens bright eye burnes most when most he climes
The crooked Zodiake with his fierie sphere,

108   *chast.*] chast, Q
112   *lord.*] lord, Q
116   *haire.*] haire, Q
121   *their*] Dyce+, Manly; the Q
124   *browes.*] browes, Q
128   *darling.*] darling, Q

And shineth furthest from this earthly globe:
So since thy beautie scorcht my conquerd soule,
I cald thee neerer for my neerer cure.

Beth.   Too neere my lord was your unarmed heart,
When furthest off my haplesse beautie pierc'd,
And would this drerie day had turnd to night,
Or that some pitchie cloud had clok'd the Sun,
140   Before their lights had caus'd my lord to see
His name disparag'd, and my chastitie.

David.   My love, if want of love have left thy soule,
A sharper sence of Honor then thy King,
(For love leads Princes sometimes from their seats,)
As erst my heart was hurt, displeasing thee,
So come and tast thy ease, with easing me.

Beth.   One medicine cannot heale our different harmes,
But rather make both ranckle at the bone,
Then let the King be cunning in his cure,
150   Least flattering both, both perish in his hand.

David.   Leave it to me my deerest Bethsabe,
Whose skill is conversant in deeper cures,
And Cusay hast thou to my servant Joab,
Commanding him to send Urias home
With all the speed can possibly be used.

Cusay.   Cusay will flie about the Kings desire.

Exeunt.

Enter Joab, Abisay, Urias, and others, with drum   [B3ᵛ]
and ensigne.

Joab.   Courage ye mightie men of Israel,
And charge your fatall instruments of war
Upon the bosomes of prowd Ammons sonnes,
160   That have disguisd your Kings Embassadors,
Cut halfe their beards, and halfe their garments off,
In spight of Israel, and his daughters sonnes.
Ye fight the holy battels of Jehova,
King Davids God, and ours and Jacobs God

162   *sonnes.*] sonnes, Q

That guides your weapons to their conquering strokes,
Orders your footsteps, and directs your thoughts
To stratagems that harbor victorie:
He casts his sacred eiesight from on high,
And sees your foes run seeking for their deaths,
170 Laughing their labours and their hopes to scorne,
While twixt your bodies, and their blunted swords,
He puts on armor of his honors proofe,
And makes their weapons wound the sencelesse winds.
Abisay.   Before this citie Rabath we will lie,
And shoot forth shafts as thicke and dangerous
As was the haile that Moises mixt with fire,
And threw with furie round about the fields
Devouring Pharoes friends, and Egypts fruits.
Urias.   First mighty captains, Joab and Abisay,
180 Let us assault and scale this kingly Tower,
Where all their conduits and their fountaines are,
Then we may easily take the citie too.
Joab.   Well hath Urias counseld our attempts,
And as he spake us, so assault the Tower.
Let Hanon now, the king of Ammons sonnes,
Repulse our conquering passage if he dare.

Hanon with King Machaas and others, upon the wals.

Hanon.   What would the shepheards dogs of Israel
Snatch from the mighty issue of King Ammon,
The valiant Amonites, and haughty Syrians?
190 Tis not your late successive victories,   [B4]
Can make us yeeld, or quaile our courages,
But if ye dare assay to scale this Tower,
Our angrie swords shall smite ye to the ground,
And venge our losses on your hatefull lives.
Joab.   Hanon, thy father Nahas gave releefe
To holy David in his haplesse exile,
Lived his fixed date, and died in peace:
But thou in steed of reaping his reward,

184   *Tower*.] Tower, Q
185   *now*,] now Q   *sonnes*,] Dyce+, B, Manly; sonne, Q

Hast trod it under foot, and scornd our King,
200   Therefore thy daies shall end with violence,
      And to our swords thy vitall bloud shall cleave.
Mach.   Hence thou that bearst poor Israels shepherds hook,
      The prowd lieutenant of that base borne King,
      And kep within the compasse of his fold,
      For if ye seeke to feed on Ammons fruits,
      And stray into the Syrians fruitfull Medes,
      The mastives of our land shall werry ye
      And pull the weesels from your greedy throtes.
Abisay.   Who can indure these Pagans blasphemies?
210 *Urias.*   My soule repines at this disparagement.
Joab.   Assault ye valiant men of Davids host,
      And beat these railing dastards from their dores.

Assault, and they win the Tower, and Joab speakes above.

Thus have we won the Tower, which we will keepe,
Maugre the sonnes of Ammon, and of Syria.

Enter Cusay beneath.

Cusay.   Where is lord Joab leader of the host?
Joab.   Here is lord Joab, leader of the host.
      Cusay come up, for we have won the hold.

He comes.

Cusay.   In happie hower then is Cusay come.
Joab.   What news then brings lord Cusay from the king?
220 *Cusay.*   His majestie commands thee out of hand
      To send him home Urias from the wars,
      For matter of some service he should doe.
Urias.   Tis for no choler hath surpris'd the King,   [B4ᵛ]
      (I hope lord Cusay) gainst his servants truth.
Cusay.   No rather to prefer Urias truth.

207   *land*] land, Q   *ye*] ye, Q
209   *blasphemies?*] blasphemies, Q
219   *king?*] king, Q
222   *doe.*] doe, Q
223   *Urias.*] Urias, Q; see also c.w. on B4

Joab.   Here take him with thee then, and goe in peace,
And tell my lord the King that I have fought
Against the citie Rabath with successe,
And skaled where the royall pallace is,
230   The conduit heads and all their sweetest springs.
Then let him come in person to these wals,
With all the souldiers he can bring besides,
And take the city as his owne exploit,
Least I surprise it, and the people give
The glory of the conquest to my name.
Cusay.   We will Lord Joab, and great Israels God
Blesse in thy hands the battels of our King.
Joab.   Farewell Urias, hast away the King.
Urias.   As sure as Joab breathes a victor here,
240   Urias will hast him, and his owne returne.

Exeunt.

Abisay.   Let us descend, and ope the pallace gate,
Taking our souldiors in to keepe the hold.
Joab.   Let us Abisay, and ye sonnes of Juda,
Be valiant, and mainteine your victory.

Exeunt.

Ammon, Jonadab, Jethray, and Ammons page.

Jonad.   What meanes my lord, the Kings beloved son,
That weares upon his right triumphant arme,
The power of Israel for a royall favor,
That holds upon the Tables of his hands,
Banquets of honor, and all thoughts content
250   To suffer pale and grisely abstinence
To sit and feed upon his fainting cheekes,
And sucke away the bloud that cheeres his lookes?
Ammon.   Ah Jonadab it is my sisters lookes,
On whose sweet beutie I bestow my bloud,

230   *springs.*] springs, Q
238   *Farewell*] Earewell Q
239   *breathes*] Hawkins, Dyce+, B; breaths Q
252   *lookes?*] lookes. Q

That make me looke so amorously leane.
Her beautie having seasd upon my heart,
So merrily consecrate to her content,   [C1]
Sets now such guard about his vitall bloud,
And viewes the passage with such piercing eyes,
260   That none can scape to cheare my pining cheekes,
But all is thought too little for her love.
Jonad.   Then from her heart thy lookes shall be releeved,
And thou shalt joy her as thy soule desires.
Ammon.   How can it be my sweet friend Jonadab,
Since Thamar is a virgine and my sister?
Jonad.   Thus it shall be: lie downe upon thy bed,
Faining thee fever sicke, and ill at ease,
And when the king shall come to visit thee,
Desire thy sister Thamar may be sent
270   To dresse some deinties for thy maladie:
Then when thou hast her solely with thy selfe,
Enforce some favour to thy manly love:
See where she comes, intreat her in with thee.

Enter Thamar.

Thamar.   What aileth Ammon with such sickly lookes,
To daunt the favour of his lovely face?
Ammon.   Sweet Thamar sick, and wish some wholesome
cates
Drest with the cunning of thy daintie hands.
Thamar.   That hath the King commanded at my hands.
Then come and rest thee, while I make thee readie
280   Some dainties, easefull to thy crased soule.
Ammon.   I goe sweet sister, eased with thy sight.

Exeunt. Restat Jonadab.

Jonad.   Why should a Prince, whose power may command,
Obey the rebell passions of his love,

255   *make*] Dyce 3, B; makes Q   *leane.*] leane, Q
266   *be:*] be, Q
278   *hands.*] hands Q
281   SD *Restat*] Hawkins, Dyce 2; *Restet* Q

When they contend but gainst his conscience,
And may be governd or supprest by will.
Now Ammon lose those loving knots of bloud,
That sokte the courage from thy kingly heart,
And give it passage to thy withered cheekes:
Now Thamar ripened are the holy fruits
290   That grew on plants of thy virginitie,   [C1ᵛ]
And rotten is thy name in Israel.
Poore Thamar, little did thy lovely hands
Foretell an action of such violence,
As to contend with Ammons lusty armes,
Sinnewd with vigor of his kindlesse love.
Faire Thamar now dishonour hunts thy foot,
And followes thee through every covert shade,
Discovering thy shame and nakednesse
Even from the valeyes of Jehosophat,
300   Up to the loftie mounts of Libanon,
Where Caedars stird with anger of the winds,
Sounding in stormes the tale of thy disgrace,
Tremble with furie, and with murmure shake
Earth with their feet, and with their heads the heavens,
Beating the clouds into their swiftest racke,
To beare this wonder round about the world.

Exit.

Ammon thrusting out Thamar.

Ammon.   Hence from my bed, whose sight offends my soule
As doth the parbreake of disgorged beares.
Thamar.   Unkind, unprincely, and unmanly Ammon,
310   To force, and then refuse thy sisters love:
Adding unto the fright of thy offence,
The banefull torment of my publisht shame.
O doe not this dishonor to thy love,
Nor clog thy soule with such increasing sinne.

291   *Israel.*] Israel, Q
295   *love.*] love, Q
304   *Earth*] Eearth Q
312   *shame.*] shame, Q
314   *sinne.*] sinne, Q

This second evill far exceeds the first.

Ammon.   Jethray come thrust this woman from my sight,
And bolt the dore upon hir if she strive.

Jethray.   Go madame goe, away, you must be gone,
My lord hath done with you, I pray depart.

He shuts her out.

320 *Thamar.*   Whether alasse, ah whether shall I flie
With folded armes, and all amased soule,
Cast as was Eva from that glorious soile
(Where al delights sat bating wingd with thoughts,
Ready to nestle in her naked breasts)   [C2]
To bare and barraine vales with floods made wast,
To desart woods, and hils with lightening scorcht,
With death, with shame, with hell, with horrour sit.
There will I wander from my fathers face,
There Absolon, my brother Absolon,
330 Sweet Absolon shall heare his sister mourne,
There will I lure with my windie sighs,
Night Ravens and Owles to rend my bloudie side,
Which with a rustie weapon I will wound,
And make them passage to my panting heart:
Why talkst thou wretch, and leavst the deed undone?

Enter Absolon.

Rend haire and garments as thy heart is rent,
With inward furie of a thousand greefes,
And scatter them by these unhallowed dores,
To figure Ammons resting crueltie,
340 And Tragicke spoile of Thamars chastitie.

Abs.   What causeth Thamar to exclaime so much?

Thamar.   The cause that Thamar shameth to disclose.

Abs.   Say, I thy brother will revenge that cause.

Thamar.   Ammon our fathers son hath forced me,
And thrusts me from him as the scorne of Israel.

327 *sit.*] sit, Q
331 *lure*] Dyce+, B, Manly; live Q
334 *make*] makee Q
335 *thou*] thon Q   *undone?*] undone. Q

Abs.   Hath Ammon forced thee? by Davids hand,
       And by the covenant God hath made with him,
       Ammon shall beare his violence to hell,
       Traitor to Heaven, traitor to Davids throne,
350   Traitor to Absolon and Israel.
       This fact hath Jacobs ruler seene from heaven,
       And through a cloud of smoake, and tower of fire
       (As he rides vaunting him upon the greenes)
       Shall teare his chariot wheeles with violent winds,
       And throw his body in the bloudy sea.
       At him the thunder shall discharge his bolt,
       And his faire spouse, with bright and fierie wings,
       Sit ever burning on his hatefull bones.   [C2ᵛ]
       My selfe as swift as thunder, or his spouse,
360   Will hunt occasion with a secret hate,
       To worke false Ammon an ungracious end:
       Goe in my sister, rest thee in my house,
       And God in time shall take this shame from thee.
Thamar.   Nor God nor Time will doe that good for me.

           Exit Thamar. restat Absolon.
           Enter David with his traine.

David.   My Absolon, what makst thou here alone,
       And beares such discontentment in thy browes?
Abs.   Great cause hath Absolon to be displeasd,
       And in his heart to shrowd the wounds of wrath.
David.   Gainst whom should Absolon be thus displeased?
370 *Abs.*   Gainst wicked Ammon thy ungracious sonne,
       My brother and faire Thamars by the King,
       My stepbrother, by mother, and by kind.
       He hath dishonoured Davids holinesse,
       And fixt a blot of lightnesse on his throne,
       Forcing my sister Thamar when he faind
       A sickenesse, sprung from root of heinous lust.

355   *sea.*] sea, Q
357   *wings,*] wings Q
358   *bones.*] bones, Q
364   SD *Thamar*] *Tham.* Q
372   *kind.*] kind, Q

David.   Hath Ammon brought this evill on my house,
    And suffered sinne to smite his fathers bones?
    Smite David deadlier then the voice of heaven,
380   And let hates fires be kindled in thy heart,
    Frame in the arches of thy angrie browes,
    Making thy forehead like a comet shine,
    To force false Ammon tremble at thy lookes.
    Sin with his sevenfold crowne and purple robe,
    Begins his triumphs in my guiltie throne,
    There sits he watching with his hundred eyes,
    Our idle minuts, and our wanton thoughts,
    And with his baits made of our fraile desires,
    Gives us the hooke that hales our soules to hell:
390   But with the spirit of my kingdomes God,
    Ile thrust the flattering Tyran from his throne,   [C3]
    And scourge his bondslaves from my hallowed court
    With rods of yron, and thornes of sharpened steele:
    Then Absolon revenge not thou this sin,
    Leave it to me, and I will chasten him.
Abs.   I am content, then graunt my lord the king
    Himselfe with all his other lords would come
    Up to my sheepe feast on the plaine of Hazor.
David.   Nay my faire sonne, my selfe with all my lords
400   Will bring thee too much charge, yet some shall goe.
Abs.   But let my lord the king himselfe take paines,
    The time of yeare is pleasant for your grace,
    And gladsome Summer in her shadie robes,
    Crowned with Roses and with planted flowers,
    With all her nimphs shall enterteine my lord,
    That from the thicket of my verdant groves,
    Will sprinckle hony dewes about his brest,
    And cast sweet balme upon his kingly head:
    Then grant thy servants boone, and goe my lord.
410 *David.*   Let it content my sweet sonne Absolon,
    That I may stay and take my other lords.

378 *bones?*] bones, Q
383 *lookes.*] lookes, Q
408 *head:*] head, Q

Abs.   But shall thy best beloved Ammon goe?

David.   What needeth it that Ammon goe with thee?

Abs.   Yet doe thy sonne and servant so much grace.

David.   Ammon shall goe, and all my other lords,
  Because I will give grace to Absolon.

Enter Cusay, and Urias, with others.

Cusay.   Pleaseth my lord the king, his servant Joab
  Hath sent Urias from the Syrian wars.

David.   Welcome Urias from the Syrian wars,
420   Welcome to David as his deerest lord.

Urias.   Thankes be to Israels God, and Davids grace,
  Urias finds such greeting with the king.

David.   No other greeting shall Urias find,
  As long as David swaies the elected seat,
  And consecrated throne of Israel.   [C3ᵛ]
  Tell me Urias of my servant Joab,
  Fights he with truth the battels of our God,
  And for the honor of the Lords annointed?

Urias.   Thy servant Joab fights the chosen wars
430   With truth, with honour, and with high successe,
  And gainst the wicked King of Ammons sonnes,
  Hath by the finger of our sovereines God,
  Besieg'd the citie Rabath, and atchiev'd
  The court of waters, where the conduits run,
  And all the Ammonites delightsome springs:
  Therefore he wisheth Davids mightinesse
  Should number out the host of Israel,
  And come in person to the citie Rabath,
  That so her conquest may be made the kings,
440   And Joab fight as his inferior.

David.   This hath not God, and Joabs prowesse done,
  Without Urias valours, I am sure,

413   *thee?*] thee. Q
424   *David*] Davids Q
440   *And*] Aud Q

Who since his true conversion from a Hethite,
To an adopted sonne of Israel,
Hath fought like one whose armes were lift by heaven,
And whose bright sword was edgd with Israels wrath:
Goe therefore home Urias, take thy rest,
Visit thy wife and houshold with the joies
A victor and a favorite of the Kings
450   Should exercise with honor after armes.

Urias.   Thy servants bones are yet not halfe so cras'de,
Nor constitute on such a sickly mould,
That for so little service he should faint,
And seeke (as cowards) refuge of his home:
Nor are his thoughts so sensually stird,
To stay the armes with which the lord would smite
And fill their circle with his conquered foes,
For wanton bosome of a flattering wife.

David.   Urias hath a beauteous sober wife,
460   Yet yong, and framd of tempting flesh and bloud,
Then when the King hath summoned thee from
    armes,   [C4]
If thou unkindly shouldst refraine her bed,
Sinne might be laid upon Urias soule,
If Bethsabe by frailtie hurt her fame:
Then goe Urias, solace in her love,
Whom God hath knit to thee, tremble to lose.

Urias.   The King is much too tender of my ease,
The arke, and Israel, and Juda dwell
In pallaces, and rich pavillions,
470   But Joab and his brother in the fields,
Suffering the wrath of Winter and the Sun:
And shall Urias (of more shame then they)
Banquet and loiter, in the worke of heaven?
As sure as thy soule doth live my lord,
Mine eares shall never leane to such delight,
When holy labour cals me forth to fight.

David.   Then be it with Urias manly heart,
As best his fame may shine in Israel.

Urias.   Thus shall Urias heart be best content:
480   Till thou dismisse me backe to Joabs bands,
This ground before the king my masters dores,

He lies downe.

Shall be my couch, and this unwearied arme,
The proper pillow of a souldiours head.
For never will I lodge within my house,
Till Joab triumph in my secret vowes.
David.   Then fetch some flagons of our purest Wine,
That we may welcome home our hardie friend,
With full carouses to his fortunes past,
And to the honours of his future armes.
490   Then will I send him backe to Rabath siege,
And follow with the strength of Israel.

Enter one with the flagons of Wine.

Arise Urias, come and pledge the King.

He riseth.

Urias.   If David thinke me worthy such a grace,
I will be bold, and pledge my lord the king.   [C4ᵛ]
David.   Absolon and Cusay both shall drinke
To good Urias, and his happinesse.
Abs.   We will my lord to please Urias soule.
David.   I will begin Urias to thy selfe,
And all the treasure of the Ammonites,
500   Which here I promise to impart to thee,
And bind that promise with a full carous.
Urias.   What seemeth pleasant in my sovereines eyes,
That shall Urias doe till he be dead.
David.   Fill him the cup, follow ye lords that love
Your sovereines health, and doe as he hath done.
Abs.   Ill may he thrive or live in Israel,

479   *content:*] content, Q
483   *head.*] head, Q
489   *armes.*] armes, Q
503   *dead.*] dead Q

That loves not David, or denies his charge.
Urias, Here is to Abisais health,
Lord Joabs brother, and thy loving friend.

510   *Urias.*   I pledge lord Absolon and Abisais health.

He drinkes.

Cusay.   Here now Urias, to the health of Joab,
And to the pleasant journy we shall have,
When we returne to mightie Rabath siege.
Urias.   Cusay I pledge thee all, with all my heart,
Give me some drinke ye servants of the king,
Give me my drinke.

He drinkes.

David.   Well done my good Urias, drinke thy fill,
That in thy fulnesse David may rejoice.
Urias.   I will my lord.
520   *Abs.*   Now lord Urias, one carouse to me.
Urias.   No sir, Ile drinke to the King,
Your father is a better man then you.
David.   Doe so Urias, I will pledge thee straight.
Urias.   I will indeed my lord and sovereine,
I once in my daies be so bold.
David.   Fill him his glasse.
Urias.   Fill me my glasse.

He gives him the glasse.

David.   Quickly I say. *Urias.* Quickly I say.
Urias.   Here my lord, by your favour now I drinke to you.
530   *David.*   I pledge thee good Urias presently.

He drinkes.

Abs.   Here then Urias, once againe for me,   [D1]
And to the health of Davids children.
Urias.   Davids children?
Abs.   I Davids children, wilt thou pledge me man?

508–509 *Urias . . . friend*] Hawkins, Dyce+, B, Manly treat as two
lines, as the scansion requires; Q treats as one line.

Urias.   Pledge me man.

Abs.   Pledge me I say, or else thou lovest us not.

Urias.   What doe you talke, doe you talke?
  Ile no more, Ile lie downe here.

David.   Rather Urias goe thou home and sleepe.

540 *Urias.*   O ho sir, would you make me break my sentence?

He lies downe.

Home sir, no indeed sir. Ile sleepe upon mine arme,
Like a souldiour, sleepe like a man as long as I live in Israel.

David.   If nought will serve to save his wives renowne,
  Ile send him with a letter unto Joab
  To put him in the forefront of the wars,
  That so my purposes may take effect.
  Helpe him in sirs.

Exit David and Absolon.

Cusay.   Come rise Urias, get thee in and sleepe.

Urias.   I will not goe home sir, thats flat.

550 *Cusay.*   Then come and rest thee upon Davids bed.

Urias.   On afore my lords, on afore.

Exeunt.

Chorus.

O prowd revolt of a presumptious man,
Laying his bridle in the necke of sin,
Ready to beare him past his grave to hell.
Like as the fatall Raven, that in his voice
Carries the dreadful summons of our deaths,
Flies by the faire Arabian spiceries,
Her pleasant gardens, and delightsome parkes,
Seeming to curse them with his hoarse exclaimes,
560 And yet doth stoope with hungrie violence
Upon a peece of hatefull carrion:

540   *sentence?*] sentence. Q
541   *sir.*] sir? Q
554   *hell.*] hell, Q
558   *delightsome parkes*] delightfull parts *England's Parnassus*

So wretched man, displeasd with those delights,
Would yeeld a quickning savor to his Soule,
Pursues with eagre and unstanched thirst,   [D1ᵛ]
The greedie longings of his lothsome flesh.
If holy David so shoke hands with sinne,
What shall our baser spirits glorie in?
This kingly giving lust her raigne,
Pursues the sequell with a greater ill.
570   Urias in the forefront of the wars,
Is murthered by the hateful Heathens sword,
And David joies his too deere Bethsabe.
Suppose this past, and that the child is borne,
Whose death the Prophet solemnly doth mourne.

Enter Bethsabe with her handmaid.

Beth.   Mourne Bethsabe, bewaile thy foolishnesse,
Thy sinne, thy shame, the sorrow of thy soule.
Sinne, shame, and sorrow swarme about thy soule,
And in the gates and entrance of thy heart,
Sadnesse with wreathed armes hangs her complaint.
580   No comfort from the ten string'd instrument,
The tinckling Cymball, or the Yvorie Lute,
Nor doth the sound of Davids kingly Harpe,
Make glad the broken heart of Bersabe.
Jerusalem is fild with thy complaint,
And in the streets of Syon sits thy greefe.
The babe is sicke, sicke to the death I feare,
The fruit that sprung from thee to Davids house,
Nor may the pot of Honny and of Oyle,
Glad David or his handmaids countenance.
590   Urias, woe is me to thinke hereon,
For who is it among the sonnes of men,

565   *flesh.*] flesh, Q
567   *in?*] in. Q
572   *Bethsabe.*] Bethsabe, Q
576   *soule.*] soule, Q
578   *thy*] Hawkins, Manly; my Q
581   *tinckling*] Hawkins, Manly; twinckling Q

That sayth not to my soule, the King hath sind,
David hath done amisse, and Bersabe
Laid snares of death unto Urias life.
My sweet Urias, falne into the pit
Art thou, and gone even to the gates of hell,
For Bersabe, that wouldst not shrowd her shame.   [D2]
O what is it to serve the lust of Kings,
How Lyonlike they rage when we resist,
600   But Bersabe in humblenesse attend,
The grace that God will to his handmaid send.

Exit Bethsabe.

David in his gowne walking sadly. To him Nathan.

[*David.*]   The babe is sicke, and sad is Davids heart,
To see the guiltlesse beare the guilties paine.
David hang up thy Harpe, hang downe thy head,
And dash thy yvorie Lute against the stones.
The dew that on the hill of Hermon fals,
Raines not on Syons tops, and loftie towers:
The plaines of Gath and Askaron rejoice,
And Davids thoughts are spent in pensivenesse.
610   The babe is sicke, sweet babe, that Bersabe
With womans paine brought forth to Israel.

Enter Nathan.

But what saith Nathan to his lord the king?

Nathan to David.

Nathan.   Thus Nathan saith unto his Lord the King:
There were two men both dwellers in one towne,
The one was mighty and exceeding rich
In Oxen, sheepe and cattell of the field,

599   *they*] Dyce 3, B, Manly; *thy* Q
601   SD *Bethsabe*] *Beth.* Q
602   *David*] Q omits
607   *towers:*] towers, Q
608–609 Q transposes these lines; first noted in Dyce 3
608   *rejoice,*] rejoice. Q
609   *pensivenesse.*] pensivenesse, Q

The other poore having nor Oxe, nor Calfe,
Nor other cattell, save one little Lambe,
Which he had bought and nourisht by the hand,
620   And it grew up, and fed with him and his,
And eat and dranke as he and his were wont,
And in his bosome slept, and was to him
As was his daughter or his deerest child.
There came a stranger to this wealthy man,
And he refus'd and spar'd to take his owne,
Or of his store to dresse or make him meat,
But tooke the poore mans sheepe, partly poore mans store,
And drest it for this strangar in his house:
What (tell me) shall be done to him for this?

630   *David.*   Now as the lord doth live, this wicked man   [D2ᵛ]
Is judgd, and shall become the child of death,
Foure fold to the poore man shall he restore,
That without mercy tooke his lambe away.

Nathan.   Thou art the man, and thou hast judgd thy selfe,
David, thus sayth the Lord thy God by me:
I thee annointed King in Israel,
And sav'd thee from the tyranny of Saul.
Thy maisters house I gave thee to possesse,
His Wives into thy bosome did I give,
640   And Juda and Jerusalem withall,
And might (thou knowest) if this had ben too small,
Have given thee more.
Wherefore then hast thou gone so far astray,
And hast done evill, and sinned in my sight?
Urias thou hast killed with the sword,
Yea with the sword of the uncircumcised
Thou hast him slaine, wherefore from this day forth,
The sword shall never goe from thee and thine:
For thou hast tane this Hethites wife to thee,
650   Wherefore behold, I wil (saith Jacobs God)
In thine owne house stir evill up to thee,
Yea I before thy face will take thy Wives,

622   *him*] Dyce 3, B, Manly; live Q
637   *Saul.*] Saul, Q
640   *and*] aud Q

And give them to thy neighbor to possesse:
This shall be done to David in the day,
That Israel openly may see thy shame.
David.   Nathan, I have against the Lord, I have
Sinned, O sinned greevously, and loe
From heavens throne doth David throw himselfe,
And grone and grovell to the gates of hell.

He fals downe.

660   *Nathan.*   David stand up. Thus saith the Lord by me:
David the King shall live, for he hath seene
The true repentant sorrow of thy heart.
But for thou hast in this misdeed of thine
Stird up the enemies of Israel
To triumph and blaspheme the God of hosts,
And say, He set a wicked man to reigne,   [D3]
Over his loved people and his Tribes:
The child shall surely die, that erst was borne,
His mothers sin, his kingly fathers scorne.

Exit Nathan.

670   *David.*   How just is Jacobs God in all his workes!
But must it die that David loveth so?
O that the mighty one of Israel
Nill change his dome, and sayes the babe must die,
Mourne Israel and weepe in Syon gates,
Wither ye Caedar trees of Libanon,
Ye sprouting Almons with your flowering tops,
Droope, drowne, and drench in Hebrons fearefull streames.
The babe must die that was to David borne,
His mothers sin his kingly fathers scorne.

David sits sadly.

Enter Cusay to David and his traine.

660   *up.*] up, Q   *me:*] me, Q
662   *heart.*] heart, Q
677   *streames.*] streames, Q

680 *Servus.*   What tidings bringeth Cusay to the King?
Cusay.   To thee the servant of King Davids court,
  This bringeth Cusay, as the Prophet spake,
  The Lord hath surely striken to the death,
  The child new borne by that Urias wife,
  That by the sonnes of Ammon erst was slaine.
Servus.   Cusay be still, the King is vexed sore,
  How shal he speed that brings this tidings first,
  When while the child was yet alive, we spake,
  And Davids heart would not be comforted?
690 *David.*   Yea Davids heart will not be comforted.
  What murmure ye the servants of the King,
  What tidings telleth Cusay to the King?
  Say Cusay, lives the child, or is he dead?
Cusay.   The child is dead, that of Urias wife, David begat.
David.   Urias wife saiest thou?
  The child is dead, then ceaseth Davids shame.
  Fetch me to eat, and give me Wine to drinke,
  Water to wash, and Oyle to cleere my lookes.   [D3ᵛ]
  Bring downe your Shalmes, your Cymbals, and your Pipes.
700 Let Davids Harpe and Lute, his hand and voice,
  Give laud to him that loveth Israel,
  And sing his praise, that shendeth Davids fame,
  That put away his sinne from out his sight,
  And sent his shame into the streets of Gath.
  Bring ye to me the mother of the babe,
  That I may wipe the teares from off her face,
  And give her comfort with this hand of mine,
  And decke faire Bersabe with ornaments,
  That she may beare to me another sonne,
710 That may be loved of the Lord of hosts:
  For where he is, of force must David goe,

687   *first*] sirst Q
690   *comforted.*] comforted, Q
696   *shame.*] shame, Q
698   *lookes.*] lookes, Q
699   *Pipes.*] Pipes, Q
704   *Gath.*] Gath, Q

But never may he come where David is.

They bring in water, wine, and oyle, Musike, and a
banquet. [With them Bethsabe.]

Faire Bersabe, sit thou, and sigh no more,
And sing and play you servants of the King.
Now sleepeth Davids sorrow with the dead,
And Bersabe liveth to Israel.

They use all solemnities together, and sing, etc.

David.   Now armes, and warlike engins for assault,
Prepare at once ye men of Israel,
Ye men of Juda and Jerusalem,
720 That Rabba may be taken by the King,
Least it be called after Joabs name,
Nor Davids glory shine in Syon streets.
To Rabba marcheth David with his men
To chastise Ammon and the wicked ones.

Exeunt omnes.

Enter Absolon with two or three.

Abs.   Set up your mules, and give them well to eat,
And let us meet our brothers at the feast.
Accursed is the maister of this feast,
Dishonour of the house of Israel,   [D4]
His sisters slander, and his mothers shame.
730 Shame be his share that could such ill contrive,
To ravish Thamar, and without a pause
To drive her shamefully from out his house,
But may his wickednesse find just reward.
Therefore doth Absolon conspire with you,
That Ammon die what time he sits to eat,
For in the holy Temple have I sworne
Wreake of his villany in Thamars rape.

712 SD *With . . . Bethsabe*] Q omits
714 *King.*] King, Q
722 *streets.*] streets, Q
726 *feast.*] feast, Q

And here he comes, bespeake him gently all,
Whose death is deeply graved in my heart.

*Enter Ammon with Adonia and Jonadab, to Absolon
and his companie.*

740 *Ammon.* Our shearers are not far from hence I wot,
And Ammon, to you all his brethren
Giveth such welcome as our fathers erst
Were wont in Juda and Jerusalem,
But specially Lord Absolon to thee,
The honour of thy house and progenie.
Sit downe and dine with me King Davids sonne,
Thou faire young man, whose haires shine in mine eye
Like golden wyers of Davids yvorie Lute.
Abs. Ammon, where be thy shearers and thy men,
750 That we may powre in plenty of thy vines,
And eat thy goats milke, and rejoice with thee?
Ammon. Here commeth Ammons shearers and his men,
Absolon sit and rejoice with me.

*Here enter a company of sheepeheards, and daunce and
sing.*

Ammon. Drinke Absolon in praise of Israel,
Welcome to Ammons fields from Davids court.
Abs. Die with thy draught perish and die accurst,
Dishonour to the honour of us all, [D4ᵛ]
Die for the villany to Thamar done,
Unworthy thou to be King Davids sonne.

Exit Absolon.

760 *Jonad.* O what hath Absolon for Thamar done,
Murthered his brother, great king Davids sonne.
Adonia. Run Jonadab away, and make it knowne,
What cruelty this Absolon hath showne.
Ammon, thy brother Adonia shall

743 *wont*] Last letter unclear in all Q copies; could be *t* or *r*. Cf. l. 1808.
751 *thee?*] thee. Q
759 *King*] Kings Q SD *Absolon*] Absa. Q

Bury thy body among the dead mens bones,
And we will make complaint to Israel
Of Ammons death, and pride of Absolon.

Exeunt omnes.

Enter David with Joab, Abyssus, Cusay, with drum and
ensigne against Rabba.

[*David.*]   This is the towne of the uncircumcised,
            The citie of the kingdome, this is it,
770   Rabba where wicked Hannon sitteth king:
            Dispoile this King, this Hannon of his crowne,
            Unpeople Rabba, and the streets thereof,
            For in their bloud and slaughter of the slaine,
            Lyeth the honor of King Davids line.
            Joab, Abyshai, and the rest of you,
            Fight ye this day for great Jerusalem.
Joab.   And see where Hannon showes him on the wals.
            Why then do we forbeare to give assault,
            That Israel may as it is promised,
780   Subdue the daughters of the Gentils Tribes?
            All this must be performd by Davids hand.
David.   Harke to me Hannon, and remember well,
            As sure as he doth live that kept my host,
            What time our young men by the poole of Gibeon,
            Went forth against the strength of Isboseth,
            And twelve to twelve did with their weapons play,
            So sure art thou, and thy men of war
            To feele the sword of Israel this day,
            Because thou hast defied Jacobs God,   [E1]
790   And suffered Rabba with the Philistine
            To raile upon the tribe of Benjamin.
Hanon.   Harke man, as sure as Saul thy maister fell,
            And gor'd his sides upon the mountaine tops
            And Jonathan, Abinadab, and Melchisua

768   *David.*] Q omits
777   *wals.*] wals, Q
780   *Tribes?*] Tribes, Q
790   *Philistine*] Philistime Q

Watred the dales and deepes of Askaron
With bloudy streames that from Gilboa ran
In channels through the wildernesse of Ziph,
What time the sword of the uncircumcised
Was drunken with the bloud of Israel:
800   So sure shall David perish with his men,
Under the wals of Rabba, Hannons towne.

Joab.   Hannon, the God of Israel hath said,
David the King shall weare that crowne of thine,
That weighs a Talent of the finest gold,
And triumph in the spoile of Hannons towne,
When Israel shall hale thy people hence,
And turne them to the tile-kill, man and child,
And put them under harrowes made of yron,
And hew their bones with axes, and their lims
810   With yron swords devide and teare in twaine.
Hannon, this shall be done to thee and thine,
Because thou hast defied Israel.
To armes, to armes, that Rabba feele revenge,
And Hannons towne become king Davids spoile.

*Alarum, excursions, assault. Exeunt omnes. Then the
trumpets, and David with Hannons crowne.*

David.   Now clattering armes, and wrathfull storms of war,
Have thundred over Rabbaes raced towers,
The wreakefull ire of great Jehovaes arme,
That for his people made the gates to rend,
And clothed the Cherubins in fierie coats,
820   To fight against the wicked Hannons towne.
Pay thankes ye men of Juda to the King,   [E1ᵛ]
The God of Syon and Jerusalem,
That hath exhalted Israel to this,
And crowned David with this diademe.

Joab.   Beauteous and bright is he among the Tribes,
As when the sunne attir'd in glist'ring robe,

798   *uncircumcised*] uncircumsed Q
814   SD *assault.*] *assault,* Q
820   *towne.*] towne, Q

Comes dauncing from his orientall gate,
And bridegroome-like hurles through the gloomy aire
His radiant beames, such doth King David shew,
830 Crownd with the honour of his enemies towne,
Shining in riches like the firmament,
The starrie vault that overhangs the earth,
So looketh David King of Israel.
Abyshai.   Joab, why doth not David mount his throne,
Whom heaven hath beautified with Hannons crowne?
Sound Trumpets, Shalmes, and Instruments of praise
To Jacobs God for Davids victory.

Enter Jonadab.

Jonad.   Why doth the King of Israel rejoice,
Why sitteth David crownd with Rabbaes rule?
840 Behold there hath great heavinesse befalne
In Ammons fields by Absolons misdeed,
And Ammons shearers, and their feast of mirth
Absalon hath overturned with his sword,
Nor liveth any of King Davids sonnes,
To bring this bitter tidings to the King.
David.   Ay me, how soone are Davids triumphs dasht,
How suddenly declineth Davids pride,
As doth the daylight settle in the west,
So dim is Davids glory, and his gite.
850 Die David, for to thee is left no seed,
That may revive thy name in Israel.
Jonad.   In Israel is left of Davids seed.

Enter Adonia with other sonnes.

Comfort your lord, you servants of the King.
Behold thy sonnes returne in mourning weeds,   [E2]
And only Ammon, Absalon hath slaine.
David.   Welcome my sonnes, deerer to me you are

835   *crowne?*] crowne, Q
839   *rule?*] rule, Q
853   *King.*] King, Q
856   *deerer*] deeret Q

Then is this golden crowne, or Hannons spoile.
O tell me then, tell me my sonnes I say,
How commeth it to passe, that Absolon
860   Hath slaine his brother Ammon with the sword?
Adonia.   Thy sonnes O King went up to Ammons fields
To feast with him, and eat his bread and oyle,
And Absalon upon his mule doth come,
And to his men he sayth, When Ammons heart
Is merry and secure, then strike him dead,
Because he forced Thamar shamefully,
And hated her, and threw her forth his dores:
And this did he, and they with him conspire,
And kill thy sonne in wreake of Thamars wrong.
870   *David.*   How long shall Juda and Jerusalem
Complaine and water Syon with their teares?
How long shall Israel lament in vaine,
And not a man among the mighty ones
Will heare the sorrowes of King Davids heart?
Ammon thy life was pleasing to thy Lord,
As to mine eares the Musike of my Lute,
Or songs that David tuneth to his Harpe,
And Absalon hath tane from me away
The gladnesse of my sad distressed soule.

Exeunt omnes.

Manet David, Enter widdow of Thecoa.

880   *Widdow.*   God save King David, King of Israel,
And blesse the gates of Syon for his sake.
David.   Woman, why mournest thou? Rise from the earth,
Tell me what sorrow hath befalne thy soule.
Widdow.   Thy servants soule O King is troubled sore,
And greevous is the anguish of her heart,
And from Thecoa doth thy handmaid come.
David.   Tell me, and say, thou woman of Thecoa,
What aileth thee, or what is come to passe.   [E2ᵛ]

882   *thou?*] thou, Q   *Rise*] rise Q
885   *greevous*] greenous Q

Widdow.   Thy servant is a widdow in Thecoa,
890   Two sonnes thy handmaid had, and they (my lord)
Fought in the field, where no man went betwixt,
And so the one did smite and slay the other.
And loe behold the kindred doth arise,
And crie on him that smote his brother,
That he therefore may be the child of death,
For we will follow and destroy the heire.
So will they quench that sparkle that is left,
And leave nor name, nor issue on the earth,
To me, or to thy handmaids husband dead.

900   *David.*   Woman returne, goe home unto thy house,
I will take order that thy sonne be safe,
If any man say otherwise then well,
Bring him to me, and I shall chastise him:
For as the Lord doth live, shall not a haire
Shed from thy sonne, or fall upon the earth.
Woman to God alone belongs revenge,
Shall then the kindred slay him for his sinne?

Widdow.   Well hath King David to his handmaid spoke,
But wherefore then hast thou determined
910   So hard a part against the righteous Tribes
To follow and pursue the banished,
When as to God alone, belongs revenge?
Assuredly thou saist against thy selfe,
Therefore call home againe the banished,
Call home the banished, that he may live,
And raise to thee some fruit in Israel.

David.   Thou woman of Thecoa answere me,
Answere me one thing I shall aske of thee,
Is not the hand of Joab in this worke?
920   Tell me is not his finger in this fact?

Widdow.   It is my lord, his hand is in this worke,
Assure thee, Joab captaine of thy host,
Hath put these words into thy handmaids mouth,
And thou art as an angel from on high,   [E3]

912   *revenge?*] revenge. Q

To understand the meaning of my heart:
Lo where he commeth to his lord the King.

Enter Joab.

David. Say Joab, didst thou send this woman in
To put this parable for Absalon?
Joab. Joab my lord did bid this woman speake,
930 And she hath said, and thou hast understood.
David. I have and am content to do the thing,
Goe fetch my sonne, that he may live with me.

Joab kneeles.

Joab. Now God be blessed for King Davids life,
Thy servant Joab hath found grace with thee,
In that thou sparest Absolon thy child.
A beautifull and faire young man is he,
In all his bodie is no blemish seene,
His haire is like the wyer of Davids Harpe,
That twines about his bright and yvorie necke:
940 In Israel is not such a goodly man,
And here I bring him to entreat for grace.

Enter Absolon with Joab.

David. Hast thou slaine Ammon in the fields of Hazor
Ah Absalon my sonne, ah my sonne Absolon,
But wherefore doe I vexe thy spirit so?
Live and returne from Gesur to thy house,
Returne from Gesur to Jerusalem,
What boots it to be bitter to thy soule,
Ammon is dead, and Absolon survives.
Abs. Father I have offended Israel,
950 I have offended David and his house,
For Thamars wrong hath Absolon misdone,

925 *heart:*] heart, Q
928 *Absalon?*] Absalon. Q
935 *child.*] child, Q
942 *Ammon*] B, Manly; Q omits
944 *so?*] so, Q

But Davids heart is free from sharpe revenge,
And Joab hath got grace for Absalon.

David.   Depart with me you men of Israel,   [E3ᵛ]
You that have followed Rabba with the sword,
And ransacke Ammons richest treasuries.
Live Absalon my sonne, live once in peace,
Peace with thee, and with Jerusalem.

Exeunt omnes.

Manet Absolon.

Abs.   David is gone, and Absolon remaines,
960   Flowring in pleasant spring time of his youth.
Why liveth Absalon, and is not honoured
Of Tribes and Elders, and the mightiest ones,
That round about his Temples he may weare
Garlands and wreaths set on with reverence,
That every one that hath a cause to plead,
Might come to Absolon, and call for right?
Then in the gates of Syon would I sit,
And publish lawes in great Jerusalem,
And not a man should live in all the land,
970   But Absolon would doe him reasons due,
Therefore I shall addresse me as I may,
To love the men and Tribes of Israel.

Exit.

*Enter David, Ithay, Sadoc, Ahimaas, Jonathan, with
others, David barefoot, with some lose covering over his
head, and all mourning.*

David.   Proud lust the bloudiest traitor to our soules,
Whose greedie throte, nor earth, aire, sea, or heaven,
Can glut or satisfie with any store,
Thou art the cause these torments sucke my bloud,
Piercing with venome of thy poysoned eies,
The strength and marrow of my tainted bones:

956   *treasuries.*] treasuries, Q
960   *youth.*] youth, Q

To punish Pharoh, and his cursed host,
980   The waters shrunk at great Adonaies voice,
And sandie bottome of the sea appeard,   [E4]
Offering his service at his servants feet,
And to inflict a plague on Davids sinne,
He makes his bowels traitors to his breast,
Winding about his heart with mortall gripes.
Ah Absalon the wrath of heaven inflames
Thy scorched bosome with ambitious heat,
And Sathan sets thee on a lustie tower,
Shewing thy thoughts the pride of Israel
990   Of choice to cast thee on her ruthlesse stones,
Weepe with me then ye sonnes of Israel.

He lies downe, and all the rest after him.

Lie downe with David, and with David mourne,
Before the holy one that sees our hearts,
Season this heavie soile with showers of teares,
And fill the face of every flower with dew,
Weepe Israel, for Davids soule dissolves,
Lading the fountaines of his drowned eyes,
And powres her substance on the sencelesse earth.
Sadoc.   Weepe Israel, O weepe for Davids soule,
1000   Strewing the ground with haire and garments torne,
For tragicke witnesse of your heartie woes.
Ahim.   O would our eyes were conduits to our hearts,
And that our hearts were seas of liquid bloud,
To powre in streames upon this holy Mount,
For witnesse we would die for Davids woes.
Jonat.   Then should this mount of Olives seeme a plaine,
Drownd with a sea, that with our sighs should rore,
And in the murmure of his mounting waves,
Report our bleeding sorrowes to the heavens,
1010   For witnesse we would die for Davids woes.
Ithay.   Earth cannot weepe ynough for Davids woes,
Then weepe you heavens, and all you clouds dissolve,
That pittious stars may see our miseries,

980   *shrunk*] Hawkins, Dyce 3, Manly; shrinke Q

And drop their golden teares upon the ground,
For witnesse how they weepe for Davids woes.
Sadoc.   Now let my soveraigne raise his prostrate
      bones,   [E4ᵛ]
And mourne not as a faithlesse man would doe,
But be assurd, that Jacobs righteous God,
That promist never to forsake your throne,
1020   Will still be just and pure in his vowes.
David.   Sadoc high priest, preserver of the arke,
Whose sacred vertue keepes the chosen crowne,
I know my God is spotlesse in his vowes,
And that these haires shall greet my grave in peace:
But that my sonne should wrong his tendred soule,
And fight against his fathers happinesse,
Turnes all my hopes into despaire of him,
And that despaire feeds all my veines with greefe.
Ithay.   Thinke of it David, as a fatall plague,
1030   Which greefe preserveth, but preventeth not,
And turne thy drooping eyes upon the troupes
That of affection to thy worthinesse,
Doe swarme about the person of the King.
Cherish their valours, and their zealous loves,
With pleasant lookes, and sweet encouragements.
David.   Me thinkes the voice of Ithay fils mine eares.
Ithay.   Let not the voice of Ithay loth thine eares,
Whose heart would baulme thy bosome with his teares.
David.   But wherefore goest thou to the wars with us?
1040   Thou art a stranger here in Israel,
And sonne to Achis mightie king of Gath,
Therefore returne, and with thy father stay.
Thou camst but yesterday, and should I now
Let thee partake these troubles here with us?
Keepe both thy selfe, and all thy souldiors safe,
Let me abide the hazards of these armes,
And God requite the friendship thou hast shewd.

1028 *despaire*] despaire, Q
1033 *King.*] King, Q
1039 *us?*] us, Q
1042 *stay.*] stay, Q

Ithay.   As sure as Israels God gives David life,
What place or perill shall containe the King,
1050   The same will Ithay share in life and death.
David.   Then gentle Ithay be thou still with us,
A joy to David, and a grace to Israel.   [F1]
Goe Sadoc now, and beare the arke of God
Into the great Jerusalem againe.
If I find favour in his gratious eyes,
Then will he lay his hand upon my heart
Yet once againe before I visit death,
Giving it strength and vertue to mine eies,
To tast the comforts, and behold the forme
1060   Of his faire arke, and holy tabernacle.
But if he say my wonted love is worne,
And I have no delight in David now,
Here lie I armed with an humble heart,
T'imbrace the paines that anger shall impose,
And kisse the sword my lord shall kill me with.
Then Sadoc take Ahimaas thy sonne,
With Jonathan sonne to Abiathar,
And in these fields will I repose my selfe,
Till they returne from you some certaine newes.
1070 *Sadoc.*   Thy servants will with joy obey the King,
And hope to cheere his heart with happy newes.

Exeunt Sadoc, Ahimaas, and Jonathan.

Ithay.   Now that it be no greefe unto the King,
Let me for good enforme his majestie,
That with unkind and gracelesse Absalon,
Achitophel your auncient counsellor,
Directs the state of this rebellion.
David.   Then doth it aime with danger at my crowne.
O thou that holdst his raging bloudy bound,

1054   *againe.*] againe, Q
1060   *tabernacle.*] tabernacle, Q
1065   *with.*] with, Q
1071   SD *Exeunt*] Dyce 3, B, Manly; *Exit* Q
1077   *crowne.*] crowne, Q

Within the circle of the silver moone,
1080   That girds earths center with his watrie scarfe,
Limit the counsell of Achitophel,
No bounds extending to my soules distresse,
But turne his wisdome into foolishnesse.

Enter Cusay with his coat turnd, and head covered.

Cusay.   Happinesse and honour to my lord the King.
David.   What happinesse or honor may betide   [F1ᵛ]
His state that toiles in my extremities?
Cusay.   O let my gracious soveraine cease these greefes,
Unlesse he wish his servant Cusayes death,
Whose life depends upon my lords releefe,
1090   Then let my presence with my sighs, perfume
The pleasant closet of my soveraignes soule.
David.   No Cusay no, thy presence unto me,
Will be a burthen since I tender thee,
And cannot breake thy sighs for Davids sake:
But if thou turne to faire Jerusalem,
And say to Absalon, as thou hast been
A trusty friend unto his fathers seat,
So thou wilt be to him, and call him King,
Achitophels counsell may be brought to naught.
1100   Then having Sadoc and Abiathar,
All three may learne the secrets of my sonne,
Sending the message by Ahimaas,
And friendly Jonathan, who both are there.
[*Cusay*.]   Then rise, referring the successe to heaven.
David.   Cusay I rise, though with unweldie bones,
I carrie armes against my Absalon.

Exeunt.

*Absalon, Amasa, Achitophel, with the concubines of
David, and others in great state, Absalon crowned.*

Abs.   Now you that were my fathers concubines,
Liquor to his inchast and lustfull fire,

1103   *there*.] there, Q
1104   *Cusay*.] Q omits

Have seene his honour shaken in his house,
1110 Which I possesse in sight of all the world.
I bring ye forth for foiles to my renowne,
And to eclipse the glorie of your King,
Whose life is with his honour fast inclosd
Within the entrailes of a Jeatie cloud,
Whose dissolution shall powre downe in showers
The substance of his life and swelling pride:
Then shall the stars light earth with rich aspects,   [F2]
And heaven shall burne in love with Absalon,
Whose beautie will suffice to chase all mists,
1120 And cloth the suns spheare with a triple fire,
Sooner then his cleare eyes should suffer staine,
Or be offended with a lowring day.
[*1*] *Concub.*   Thy fathers honour, gracelesse Absalon,
And ours thus beaten with thy violent armes,
Will crie for vengeance to the host of heaven,
Whose power is ever armed against the prowd,
And will dart plagues at thy aspiring head,
For doing this disgrace to Davids throne.
2. [*Concub.*]   To Davids throne, to Davids holy throne,
1130 Whose scepter angels guard with swords of fire,
And sit as Eagles on his conquering fist,
Ready to prey upon his enemies.
Then thinke not thou the captaine of his foes,
Wert thou much swifter then Azahell was,
That could out-pace the nimble footed Roe,
To scape the furie of their thumping beakes,
Or dreadfull scope of their commanding wings.
Achit.   Let not my lord the King of Israel
Be angrie with a sillie womans threats,
1140 But with the pleasure he hath erst enjoied,
Turne them into their cabinets againe,

1119 *chase*] Hawkins, Dyce+, B; chast Q
1123 *1.*] Q omits
1129 *Concub.*] Q omits
1132 *enemies.*] enemies, Q
1135 *out-pace*] Bod, BM (both), D, E, HCL, H; out pace BPL, F
1138 *Achit.*] *Achip.* Q

Till Davids conquest be their overthrow.
Abs.   Into your bowers ye daughters of Disdaine,
Gotten by furie of unbridled lust,
And wash your couches with your mourning teares,
For greefe that Davids kingdome is decaied.
1. [*Concub.*]   No Absalon, his kingdome is enchaind
Fast to the finger of great Jacobs God,
Which will not lose it for a rebels love.

Exeunt.

1150 *Amasa.* If I might give advise unto the King,
These concubines should buy their taunts with bloud.
Abs.   Amasa no, but let thy martiall sword
Empty the paines of Davids armed men,   [F2ᵛ]
And let these foolish women scape our hands
To recompence the shame they have sustaind.
First Absalon was by the Trumpets sound
Proclaimd through Hebron King of Israel,
And now is set in faire Jerusalem
With complete state, and glorie of a crowne.
1160 Fiftie faire footmen by my chariot run,
And to the aire whose rupture rings my fame,
Where ere I ride they offer reverence.
Why should not Absolon, that in his face
Carries the finall purpose of his God,
That is, to worke him grace in Israel,
Endevour to atchieve with all his strength,
The state that most may satisfie his joy,
Keeping his statutes and his covenants pure?
His thunder is intangled in my haire,
1170 And with my beautie is his lightning quencht,
I am the man he made to glorie in,
When by the errors of my fathers sinne,
He lost the path that led into the land,

1147 *Concub.*] Q omits
1158 *in faire*] infaire Q
1168 *pure?*] pure, Q

Wherewith our chosen ancestors were blest.

Enter Cusay.

Cusay.   Long may the beautious King of Israel live,
To whom the people doe by thousands swarme.
Abs.   What meaneth Cusay so to greet his foe?
Is this the love thou shewdst to Davids soule,
To whose assistance thou hast vowed thy life,
1180   Why leavest thou him in this extremitie?
Cusay.   Because the Lord and Israel chuseth thee,
And as before I servd thy fathers turne,
With counsell acceptable in his sight,
So likewise will I now obey his sonne.
Abs.   Then welcome Cusay to king Absalon,
And now my lords and loving counsellors,
I thinke it time to exercise our armes
Against forsaken David and his host.   [F3]
Give counsell first my good Achitophel,
1190   What times and orders we may best observe,
For prosperous manage of these high exploits.
Achit.   Let me chuse out twelve thousand valiant men,
And (while the night hides with her sable mists
The close endevors cunning souldiers use)
I will assault thy discontented sire,
And while with weakenesse of their wearie armes,
Surchargd with toile to shun thy suddaine power,
The people flie in huge disordred troupes
To save their lives, and leave the King alone,
1200   Then will I smite him with his latest wound,
And bring the people to thy feet in peace.
Abs.   Well hath Achitophel given his advise,
Yet let us heare what Cusay counsels us,
Whose great experience is well worth the eare.

1175   *of*] os Q   *Israel*] Ifrael Q
1177   *foe?*] foe, Q
1180   *extremitie?*] extremitie. Q
1188   *host.*] host, Q
1195   *sire*] fire Q

Cusay.   Though wise Achitophel be much more meet
        To purchase hearing with my lord the King,
        For all his former counsels, then my selfe,
        Yet not offending Absolon or him,
        This time it is not good, nor worth pursute:
1210   For well thou knowest thy fathers men are strong,
        Chafing as shee beares robbed of their whelpes.
        Besides the King himselfe a valiant man,
        Traind up in feats and stratagems of warre,
        And will not for prevention of the worst
        Lodge with the common souldiers in the field:
        But now I know his wonted policies
        Have taught him lurke within some secret cave,
        Guarded with all his stoutest souldiers,
        Which if the forefront of his battell faint,
1220   Will yet give out that Absalon doth flie,
        And so thy souldiers be discouraged.
        David himselfe withall, whose angry heart
        Is as a Lyons, letted of his walke,
        Will fight himselfe, and all his men to one,   [F3ᵛ]
        Before a few shall vanquish him by feare.
        My counsell therefore, is with Trumpets sound
        To gather men from Dan to Bersabe,
        That they may march in number like sea sands,
        That nestle close in anothers necke:
1230   So shall we come upon him in our strength,
        Like to the dew that fals in showers from heaven,
        And leave him not a man to march withall.
        Besides if any citie succour him,
        The numbers of our men shall fetch us ropes,
        And we will pull it downe the rivers streame,
        That not a stone be left to keepe us out.
Abs.   What saies my lords to Cusaies counsell now?
Amasa.   I fancie Cusaies counsell better farre
        Then that is given us from Achitophel,
1240   And so I thinke doth every souldier here.

1234   *numbers*] nnmbers Q
1237   *lords*] Manly; lord Q

All.   Cusaies counsell is better then Achitophels.

Abs.   Then march we after Cusaies counsell all,
Sound trumpets through the bounds of Israel,
And muster all the men will serve the King,
That Absalon may glut his longing soule
With sole fruition of his fathers crowne.

Exeunt.

Achit.   Ill shall they fare that follow thy attempts,
That skornes the counsell of Achitophel.

[Exit.]

Restat Cusay.

Cusay.   Thus hath the power of Jacobs jealous God
1250   Fulfild his servant Davids drifts by me,
And brought Achitophels advise to scorne.

Enter Sadoc, Abiathar, Ahimaas, and Jonathan.

Sadoc.   God save lord Cusay, and direct his zeale
To purchase Davids conquest gainst his sonne.

Abia.   What secrets hast thou gleande from Absalon?

Cusay.   These, sacred priests that beare the arke of God:
Achitophel advised him in the night
To let him chuse twelve thousand fighting men,   [F4]
And he would come on David at unwares,
While he was wearie with his violent toile:
1260   But I advisd to get a greater host,
And gather men from Dan to Bersabe,
To come upon him strongly in the fields.
Then send Ahimaas and Jonathan
To signifie these secrets to the King,
And will him not to stay this night abroad,
But get him over Jordane presently,
Least he and all his people kisse the sword.

Sadoc.   Then goe Ahimaas and Jonathan,

1248 *Exit.]* Q omits
1254 *Absalon?]* Absalon. Q
1255 *These,]* Hawkins, Dyce+, B, Manly; These Q   *God:]* God, Q

And straight convey this message to the King.

1270 *Ahim.*　Father we will, if Absalons cheefe spies
Prevent not this devise, and stay us here.

Exeunt.

Semei solus.

Semei.　The man of Israel, that hath rul'd as King,
Or rather as the Tyrant of the land,
Bolstering his hatefull head upon the throne,
That God unworthily hath blest him with,
Shall now I hope, lay it as low as hell,
And be depos'd from his detested chaire.
O that my bosome could by nature beare,
A sea of poyson to be powr'de upon
1280 His cursed head that sacred baulme hath grac'd,
And consecrated King of Israel:
Or would my breath were made the smoke of hell,
Infected with the sighs of damned soules,
Or with the reeking of that serpents gorge,
That feeds on adders, toads, and venomous roots,
That as I opened my revenging lips
To curse the sheepeheard for his Tyrannie,
My words might cast rancke poyson to his pores,
And make his swolne and ranckling sinewes cracke,
1290 Like to the combat blowes that breake the clouds,
When Joves stout champions fight with fire,
See where he commeth, that my soule abhors.　　　[F4ᵛ]
I have prepard my pocket full of stones
To cast at him, mingled with earth and dust,
Which bursting with disdaine, I greet him with.

David, Joab, Abyshai, Ithay, with others.

Semei.　Come forth thou murtherer and wicked man:
The Lord hath brought upon thy cursed head
The guiltlesse bloud of Saule and all his sonnes,

1296　*man:*] man, Q

Whose royall throne thy basenesse hath usurpt,
1300 And to revenge it deepely on thy soule,
The Lord hath given the kingdome to thy sonne,
And he shall wreake the traitrous wrongs of Saule,
Even as thy sinne hath still importund heaven,
So shall thy murthers and adulterie
Be punisht in the sight of Israel,
As thou deservst with bloud, with death, and hell.
Hence murtherer, hence!

He throws at him.

Abisay. Why doth this dead dog curse my lord the King?
Let me alone to take away his head.
1310 *David.* Why medleth thus the son of Zervia
To interrupt the action of our God?
Semei useth me with this reproch,
Because the Lord hath sent him to reprove
The sinnes of David, printed in his browes,
With bloud that blusheth for his conscience guilt,
Who dares then aske him why he curseth me?
Semei. If then thy conscience tell thee thou hast sind,
And that thy life is odious to the world,
Command thy followers to shun thy face,
1320 And by thy selfe here make away thy soule,
That I may stand and glorie in thy shame.
David. I am not desperate Semei like thy selfe,
But trust unto the covenant of my God,
Founded on mercie with repentance built,
And finisht with the glorie of my soule.
Semei. A murtherer, and hope for mercie in thy end? [G1]
Hate and destruction sit upon thy browes
To watch the issue of thy damned ghost,
Which with thy latest gaspe theile take and teare,

1307 Q prints entire line as SD: "*Hence murtherer, hence, he threw at him.*"
1308 *this*] Hawkins, Dyce+, B, Manly; his Q   *King?*] King, Q
1326 *end?*] end Q

1330   Hurling in every paine of hell a peece.
Hence murtherer, thou shame to Israel,
Foule letcher, drunkard, plague to heaven and earth.

He throwes at him.

Joab.   What is it pietie in Davids thoughts,
So to abhorre from lawes of pollicie
In this extremitie of his distresse,
To give his subjects cause of carelesnesse?
Send hence the dog with sorrow to his grave.
David.   Why should the sons of Zervia seeke to checke
His spirit which the Lord hath thus inspir'd?
1340   Behold my sonne which issued from my flesh,
With equall furie seekes to take my life.
How much more then the sonne of Jemini,
Cheefely since he doth nought but Gods command?
It may be he will looke on me this day
With gracious eyes, and for his cursing blesse,
The heart of David in his bitternesse.
Semei.   What doest thou fret my soule with sufferance?
O that the soules of Isboseth and Abner,
Which thou sentst swimming to their graves in bloud,
1350   With wounds fresh bleeding, gasping for revenge,
Were here to execute my burning hate:
But I will hunt thy foot with curses still,
Hence Monster, Murtherer, Mirror of Contempt.

He throwes dust againe.

Enter Ahimaas and Jonathan.

Ahim.   Long life to David, to his enemies death.
David.   Welcome Ahimaas and Jonathan,
What newes sends Cusay to thy lord the King?
Ahim.   Cusay would wish my lord the King,

1336   *carelesnesse?*] carelesnesse, Q
1339   *inspir'd?*] inspir'd: Q
1343   *command?*] command, Q
1353   SD *Ahimaas*] Ahimaaas Q
1356   *King?*] King. Q

To passe the river Jordane presently,
Least he and all his people perish here.
1360   For wise Achitophel hath counsel'd Absalon
To take advantage of your wearie armes,
And come this night upon you in the fields.
But yet the Lord hath made his counsell skorne,
And Cusaies pollicie with praise preferd,
Which was to number every Israelite,
And so assault you in their pride of strength.
   Jonat.   Abiathar besides intreats the King
To send his men of warre against his sonne,
And hazard not his person in the field.
1370 *David.*   Thankes to Abiathar, and to you both,
And to my Cusay, whom the Lord require,
But tenne times treble thankes to his soft hand,
Whose pleasant touch hath made my heart to dance,
And play him praises in my zealous breast,
That turnd the counsell of Achitophel
After the praiers of his servants lips.
Now will we passe the river all this night,
And in the morning sound the voice of warre,
The voice of bloudie and unkindly warre.
1380 *Joab.*   Then tell us how thou wilt devide thy men,
And who shall have the speciall charge herein.
   David.   Joab, thy selfe shall for thy charge conduct,
The first third part of all my valiant men,
The second shall Abisaies valour lead,
The third faire Ithay, which I most should grace,
For comfort he hath done to Davids woes,
And I my selfe will follow in the midst.
   Ithay.   That let not David, for though we should flie,
Tenne thousand of us were not halfe so much
1390 Esteemd with Davids enemies, as himselfe:
Thy people loving thee, denie thee this.
   David.   What seemes them best, then that will David doe.
But now my lords and captaines heare his voice

1390   *himselfe:*] himselfe, Q
1392   *doe.*] doe, Q

That never yet pierst pittious heaven in vaine,   [G2]
Then let it not slip lightly through your eares,
For my sake spare the young man Absalon.
Joab thy selfe didst once use friendly words
To reconcile my heart incenst to him,
If then thy love be to thy kinsman sound,
1400   And thou wilt prove a perfit Israelite,
Friend him with deeds, and touch no haire of him,
Not that fair haire with which the wanton winds
Delight to play, and love to make it curle,
Wherein the Nightingales would build their nests,
And make sweet bowers in every golden tresse,
To sing their lover every night asleepe.
O spoile not Joab, Joves faire ornaments,
Which he hath sent to solace Davids soule.
The best ye see (my lords) are swift to sinne,
1410   To sinne our feet are washt with milke of Roes,
And dried againe with coales of lightening.
O Lord thou seest the prowdest sinnes, poore slave,
And with his bridle, pulst him to the grave,
For my sake then spare lovely Absalon.
Ithay.   Wee will my lord for thy sake favour him.

Exeunt.

Achitophel solus with a halter.

Achit.   Now hath Achitophel orderd his house,
And taken leave of every pleasure there.
Hereon depend Achitophels delights,
And in this circle must his life be closde.
1420   The wise Achitophel, whose counsell prov'd
Ever as sound for fortunate successe,
As if men askt the Oracle of God,
Is now usde like the foole of Israel.
Then set thy angrie soule upon her wings,

1403   *love*] Dyce+; loves Q
1417   *there.*] there, Q
1418   *depend*] Dyce+; depends Q
1423   *Israel.*] Israel, Q

And let her flie into the shade of death,
And for my death, let heaven for ever weepe,
Making huge flouds upon the land I leave,   [G2ᵛ]
To ravish them, and all their fairest fruits.
Let all the sighs I breath'd for this disgrace,
1430   Hang on my hedges like eternall mists,
As mourning garments for their maisters death.
Ope earth, and take thy miserable sonne
Into the bowels of thy cursed wombe,
Once in a surfet thou diddest spue him forth,
Now for fell hunger sucke him in againe,
And be his bodie poyson to thy vaines.
And now thou hellish instrument of heaven,
Once execute th'arrest of Joves just doome,
And stop his breast that curseth Israel.

Exit.

Absalon, Amasa, with all his traine.

1440   *Abs.*   Now for the crowne and throne of Israel,
To be confirmd with vertue of my sword,
And writ with Davids bloud upon the blade.
Now Jove let forth the golden firmament,
And looke on him with all thy fierie eyes,
Which thou hast made to give their glories light,
To shew thou lovest the vertue of thy hand,
Let fall a wreath of starres upon my head,
Whose influence may governe Israel,
With state exceeding all her other Kings.
1450   Fight lords and captaines, that your soveraignes face
May shine in honour brighter then the sunne,
And with the vertue of my beautious raies,
Make this faire land as fruitfull as the fields,
That with sweet milke and hony overflow'd.
God in the whissing of a pleasant wind,
Shall march upon the tops of Mulberie trees,

1431   *mourning*] monrning Q
1436   *vaines.*] vaines, Q
1442   *blade.*] blade, Q

To coole all breasts that burne with any greefes,
As whylome he was good to Moyses men.
By day the Lord shall sit within a cloud,
1460   To guide your footsteps to the fields of joy,
And in the night a piller bright as fire   [G3]
Shall goe before you like a second sunne,
Wherein the essence of his godhead is,
That day and night you may be brought to peace,
And never swarve from that delightsome path,
That leads your soules to perfect happinesse.
This shall he doe for joy when I am King:
Then fight brave captaines that these joies may flie
Into your bosomes with sweet victorie.

Exeunt.

The battell, and Absalon hangs by the haire.

1470   [*Abs.*]   What angrie angel sitting in these shades,
Hath laid his cruell hands upon my haire,
And holds my body thus twixt heaven and earth?
Hath Absalon no souldier neere his hand,
That may untwine me this unpleasant curle,
Or wound this tree that ravisheth his lord?
O God behold the glorie of thy hand,
And choisest fruit of Natures workemanship,
Hang like a rotten branch upon this tree,
Fit for the axe, and ready for the fire.
1480   Since thou withholdst all ordinarie helpe
To lose my bodie from this bond of death,
O let my beautie fill these sencelesse plants,
With sence and power to lose me from this plague,
And worke some wonder to prevent his death,
Whose life thou madst a speciall miracle.

Joab with another souldier.

Sould.   My lord I saw the young prince Absalon
Hang by the haire upon a shadie oke,

1470   *Abs.*] Q omits

And could by no means get himselfe unlosde.

Joab.   Why slewst thou not the wicked Absalon,
1490   That rebell to his father and to heaven,
That so I might haue given thee for thy paines
Tenne silver sickles, and a golden wast?   [G3ᵛ]

Sould.   Not for a thousand sickles would I slay
The sonne of David, whom his father chargd,
Nor thou, Abisay, nor the sonne of Gath,
Should touch with stroke of deadly violence.
The charge was given in hearing of us all,
And had I done it, then I know thy selfe,
Before thou wouldst abide the Kings rebuke,
1500   Wouldst have accus'd me as a man of death.

Joab.   I must not now stand trifling here with thee.

Abs.   Helpe Joab, helpe, O helpe thy Absalon.
Let not thy angrie thoughts be laid in bloud,
In bloud of him, that sometimes nourisht thee,
And softned thy sweet heart with friendly love.
O give me once againe my fathers sight,
My deerest father, and my princely soveraigne,
That shedding teares of bloud before his face,
The ground may witnesse, and the heavens record,
1510   My last submission sound and full of ruth.

Joab.   Rebell to nature, hate to heaven and earth,
Shall I give helpe to him, that thirsts the soule
Of his deere father, and my soveraigne lord?
Now see the Lord hath tangled in a tree
The health and glorie of thy stubborne heart,
And made thy pride curbd with a sencelesse plant.
Now Absalon how doth the Lord regard
The beautie whereupon thy hope was built,
And which thou thoughtst his grace did glorie in?

1488   *unlosde.*] unlosde, Q
1492   *wast?*] wast. Q
1495   *thou,*] Hawkins, Dyce+, B, Manly; thou Q
1502   *Absalon.*] Absalon, Q
1505   *love.*] love, Q
1516   *plant.*] plant, Q

1520   Findst thou not now with feare of instant death,
        That God affects not any painted shape,
        Or goodly personage, when the vertuous soule
        Is stuft with naught but pride and stubbornnesse?
        But preach I to thee, while I should revenge
        Thy cursed sinne that staineth Israel,
        And makes her fields blush with her childrens bloud?
        Take that as part of thy deservd plague,
        Which worthily no torment can inflict.   [G4]
    Abs.   O Joab, Joab, cruell ruthlesse Joab,
1530   Herewith thou woundst thy Kingly soveraignes heart,
        Whose heavenly temper hates his childrens bloud,
        And will be sicke I know for Absalon.
        O my deere father, that thy melting eyes
        Might pierce this thicket to behold thy sonne,
        Thy deerest sonne gor'de with a mortall dart:
        Yet Joab pittie me, pittie my father, Joab,
        Pittie his soules distresse that mournes my life,
        And will be dead I know to heare my death.
    Joab.   If he were so remorsefull of thy state,
1540   Why sent he me against thee with the sword?
        All Joab meanes to pleasure thee withall,
        Is to dispatch thee quickly of thy paine.
        Hold Absalon, Joabs pittie is in this,
        In this prowd Absalon is Joabs love.

                              He goes out.

    Abs.   Such love, such pittie Israels God send thee,
        And for his love to David pittie me.
        Ah my deere father, see thy bowels bleed,
        See death assault thy deerest Absalon,
        See, pittie, pardon, pray for Absalon.

                      Enter five or sixe souldiors.

1550   [*Souldier.*]   See where the rebell in his glorie hangs,
        Where is the vertue of thy beautie Absalon,

        1542   *paine.*] paine, Q
        1546   *me.*] me, Q
        1550   *Souldier.*] Q omits

Will any of us here now feare thy lookes?
Or be in love with that thy golden haire,
Wherein was wrapt rebellion gainst thy sire,
And cords prepar'd to stop thy fathers breath?
Our captaine Joab hath begun to us,
And heres an end to thee, and all thy sinnes.
Come let us take the beauteous rebell downe,
And in some ditch amids this darksome wood,
1560   Burie his bulke beneath a heape of stones,
Whose stonie heart did hunt his fathers death.

Enter in triumph with drum and ensigne, Joab,   [G4ᵛ]
Abyshai, and souldiers to Absalon.

Joab.   Well done tall souldiers take the Traitor downe,
And in this myerie ditch interre his bones,
Covering his hatefull breast with heapes of stones.
This shadie thicket of darke Ephraim
Shall ever lower on his cursed grave.
Night Ravens and Owles shall ring his fatall knell,
And sit exclaiming on his damned soule,
There shall they heape their preyes of Carrion,
1570   Till all his grave be clad with stinking bones,
That it may loth the sence of every man,
So shall his end breed horror to his name,
And to his traitrous fact eternall shame.

Exeunt.

5. Chorus.

Oh dreadfull president of his just doome,
Whose holy heart is never toucht with ruth
Of fickle beautie, or of glorious shapes,
But with the vertue of an upright soule,
Humble and zealous in his inward thoughts,
Though in his person loathsome and deform'd.

1564   *stones.*] stones, Q
1565   *Ephraim*] Ephrami Q
1573   SD *Exeunt.*] Hawkins, Dyce+, Manly; *Exit* Q
1577   *But*] Bur Q

1580   Now since this storie lends us other store,
        To make a third discourse of Davids life,
        Adding thereto his most renowmed death,
        And all their deaths, that at his death he judgd,
        Here end we this, and what here wants to please,
        We will supplie with treble willingnesse.

        Absalon with three or foure of his servants or gentlemen.

Abs.   What boots it Absalon, unhappie Absalon,
        Sighing I say what boots it Absalon,
        To have disclos'd a farre more worthy wombe

        Trumpets sound, enter Joab, Ahimaas, Cusay,   [H1]
        Amasa, with all the rest.

Joab.   Souldiers of Israel, and ye sonnes of Juda,
1590   That have contended in these irkesome broiles,
        And ript old Israels bowels with your swords:
        The godlesse generall of your stubborne armes
        Is brought by Israels helper to the grave:
        A grave of shame, and skorne of all the Tribes.
        Now then to save your honours from the dust,
        And keepe your blouds in temper by your bones,
        Let Joabs ensigne shroud your manly heads,
        Direct your eies, your weapons, and your hearts
        To guard the life of David from his foes.
1600   Error hath maskt your much too forward minds,
        And you have sind against the chosen state,
        Against his life, for whom your lives are blest,
        And followed an usurper to the field,
        In whose just death your deaths are threatened.
        But Joab pitties your disordered soules,
        And therefore offers pardon, peace, and love,
        To all that will be friendly reconcil'de
        To Israels weale, to David, and to heaven.
        Amasa, thou art leader of the host,
1610   That under Absalon have raisde their armes:

1585   SD–1588   See Introduction, pp. 178–179 and 188.
1594   *Tribes.*] Tribes, Q
1604   *threatened.*] threatened, Q

Then be a captaine wise and polliticke,
Carefull and loving for thy souldiers lives,
And lead them to this honourable league.
Amasa.   I will, at least Ile doe my best,
And for the gracious offer thou hast made,
I give thee thankes as much as for my head.
Then you deceiv'd poore soules of Israel,
Since now ye see the errors you incurd,
With thankes and due submission be appeasde,
1620   And as ye see your captaines president
Here cast we then our swords at Joabs feet,   [H1ᵛ]
Submitting with all zeale and reverence
Our goods and bodies to his gracious hands.

All stand up.

Joab.   Stand up and take ye all your swords againe,
David and Joab shall be blest herein.
Ahim.   Now let me go enforme my lord the King,
How God hath freed him from his enemies.
Joab.   Another time Ahimaas, not now,
But Cusay goe thy selfe, and tell the King
1630   The happie message of our good successe.
Cusay.   I will my lord, and thanke thee for thy grace.

Exit Cusay.

Ahim.   What if thy servant should goe to my lord?
Joab.   What newes hast thou to bring since he is gone?
Ahim.   Yet doe Ahimaas so much content,
That he may run about so sweet a charge.

Exit.

Joab.   Run if thou wilt, and peace be with thy steps:
Now follow, that you may salute the King
With humble hearts and reconciled soules.
Amasa.   We follow Joab to our gracious King,
1640   And him our swords shall honour to our deaths.

Exeunt.

1622   *reverence*] Bod, BM (both), BPL, D, E, HCL, P; residence F, H

David, Bethsabe, Salomon, Nathan, Adonia, Chileab,
with their traine.

Beth.   What meanes my lord, the lampe of Israel,
        From whose bright eyes all eyes receive their light,
        To dim the glory of his sweet aspects,
        And paint his countenance with his hearts distresse?
        Why should his thoughts retaine a sad conceit,
        When every pleasure kneeles before his throne,
        And sues for sweet acceptance with his grace?
        Take but your Lute, and make the mountaines dance,
        Retrive the sunnes sphere, and restraine the clouds,
1650   Give eares to trees, make savage Lyons tame,   [H2]
        Impose still silence to the loudest winds,
        And fill the fairest day with foulest stormes:
        Then why should passions of much meaner power,
        Beare head against the heart of Israel?
David.   Faire Bersabe, thou mightst increase the strength,
        Of these thy arguments, drawne from my skill,
        By urging thy sweet sight to my conceits,
        Whose vertue ever serv'd for sacred baulme
        To cheere my pinings past all earthly joies,
1660   But Bethsabe, the daughter of the highest,
        Whose beautie builds the towers of Israel,
        Shee that in chaines of pearle and unicorne,
        Leads at her traine the ancient golden world,
        The world that Adam held in Paradise,
        Whose breath refineth all infectious aires,
        And makes the meddowes smile at her repaire.
        Shee, Shee, my dearest Bethsabe,
        Faire peace, the goddesse of our graces here,
        Is fled the streets of faire Jerusalem,
1670   The fields of Israel, and the heart of David,
        Leading my comforts in her golden chaines,

    1647   *grace?*] grace, Q
    1652   *stormes:*] stormes, Q
    1654   *Israel?*] Israel. Q
    1667   *Shee, Shee,*] Bod, BM (162.d.52), BPL, D, E, HCL; Shee, shee BM
(C.34.d.54), F, H

Linckt to the life and soule of Absalon.
Beth. Then is the pleasure of my soveraignes heart,
So wrapt within the bosome of that sonne,
That Salomon, whom Israels God affects,
And gave the name unto him for his love,
Should be no salve to comfort Davids soule?
David. Salomon (my love) is Davids lord,
Our God hath nam'd him lord of Israel:
In him (for that, and since he is thy sonne)
Must David needs be pleased at the heart,
And he shall surely sit upon my throne:
But Absalon the beautie of my bones,
Faire Absalon the counterfeit of love,
Sweet Absalon, the image of content,
Must claime a portion in his fathers care,   [H2ᵛ]
And be in life and death King Davids sonne.
Nathan. Yet as my lord hath said, let Salomon raigne,
Whom God in naming, hath annointed King.
Now is he apt to learne th'eternall lawes,
Whose knowledge being rooted in his youth,
Will beautifie his age with glorious fruits,
While Absalon incenst with gracelesse pride,
Usurpes and staines the kingdome with his sinne.
Let Salomon be made thy staffe of age,
Faire Israels rest, and honour of thy race.
David. Tell me my Salomon, wilt thou imbrace
Thy fathers precepts graved in thy heart,
And satisfie my zeale to thy renowne,
With practise of such sacred principles
As shall concerne the state of Israel?
Salo. My royall father, if the heavenly zeale
Which for my welfare feeds upon your soule,
Were not sustaind with vertue of mine owne,
If the sweet accents of your cheerefull voice
Should not each hower beat upon mine eares

1680

1690

1700

1679 *Israel:*] Bod, BM (C.34.d.54), BPL, D, E, HCL; Israel BM (162.d. 52), F, H
1694 *sinne.*] sinne, Q

As sweetly as the breath of heaven to him
That gaspeth scorched with the Summers sunne,
I should be guiltie of unpardoned sinne,
1710   Fearing the plague of heaven, and shame of earth:
But since I vow my selfe to learne the skill
And holy secrets of his mightie hand
Whose cunning tunes the musicke of my soule,
It would content me (father) first to learne
How th'eternall fram'd the firmament,
Which bodies lead their influence by fire?
And which are fild with hoarie Winters yse?
What sign is raignie, and what starre is faire?
Why by the rules of true proportion
1720   The yeare is still divided into months,
The months to daies, the daies to certaine howers?
What fruitfull race shall fill the future world?   [H3]
Or for what time shall this round building stand?
What Magistrates, what Kings shall keepe in awe
Mens minds with bridles of th'eternall law?
   David.   Wade not too farre my boy in waves too deepe.
The feeble eyes of our aspiring thoughts
Behold things present, and record things past:
But things to come, exceed our humane reach,
1730   And are not painted yet in angels eyes:
For those, submit thy sence, and say, Thou power
That now art framing of the future world,
Knowest all to come, not by the course of heaven,
By fraile conjectures of inferiour signes,
By monstrous flouds, by flights and flockes of birds,
By bowels of a sacrificed beast,
Or by the figures of some hidden art:
But by a true and naturall presage,
Laying the ground and perfect architect
1740   Of all our actions now before thine eyes,
From Adam to the end of Adams seed.

1714 *first*] All Qq except Bod; sirst Bod (ligature between *f* and *i* may
not have inked properly.)
   1726 *deepe*.] deepe, Q

O heaven protect my weaknesse with thy strength,
So looke on me that I may view thy face,
And see these secrets written in thy browes.
O sun come dart thy raies upon my moone,
That now mine eyes eclipsed to the earth,
May brightly be refin'd and shine to heaven.
Transforme me from this flesh, that I may live
Before my death, regenerate with thee.
1750 O thou great God, ravish my earthly sprite,
That for the time a more than humane skill
May feed the Organons of all my sence,
That when I thinke, thy thoughts may be my guide,
And when I speake, I may be made by choice
The perfect eccho of thy heavenly voice.
Thus say my sonne, and thou shalt learne them all.
   Salo.   A secret fury ravisheth my soule,
Lifting my mind above her humane bounds,   [H3ᵛ]
And as the Eagle roused from her stand,
1760 With violent hunger (towring in the aire)
Seaseth her feathered prey, and thinkes to feed,
But seeing then a cloud beneath her feet,
Lets fall the foule, and is emboldened
With eies intentive to bedare the sun,
And stieth close unto his stately sphere:
So Salomon mounted on the burning wings
Of zeale devine, lets fall his mortall food,
And cheeres his sences with celestiall aire,
Treads in the golden starrie Labyrinth,
1770 And holds his eyes fixt on Jehovaes browes.
Good father teach me further what to doe.
   Nathan.   See David how his haughtie spirit mounts
Even now of height to wield a diademe,
Then make him promise, that he may succeed,
And rest old Israels bones from broiles of warre.
   David.   Nathan thou Prophet, sprung from Jesses root,
I promise thee, and lovely Bethsabe,

1770 *browes.*] browes, Q
1773 *height*] heigth Q

My Salomon shall governe after me.

Beth.   He that hath toucht thee with this righteous thought
1780   Preserve the harbour of thy thoughts in peace.

Enter Mess[enger].

Mess.   My lord, thy servants of the watch have seene
One running hitherward from forth the warres.
David.   If hee bee come alone, he bringeth newes.
Mess.   Another hath thy servant seene my lord,
Whose running much resembles Sadocs sonne.
David.   He is a good man, and good tidings brings.

Enter Ahimaas.

Ahim.   Peace and content be with my lord the King,
Whom Israels God hath blest with victory.
David.   Tell me Ahimaas, lives my Absalon?
1790   *Ahim.*   I saw a troupe of souldiours gathered,
But know not what the tumult might import.
David.   Stand by, untill some other may informe   [H4]
The heart of David with a happie truth.

Enter Cusay.

Cusay.   Happinesse and honour live with Davids soule,
Whom God hath blest with conquest of his foes.
David.   But Cusay lives the young man Absalon?
Cusay.   The stubborne enemies to Davids peace,
And all that cast their darts against his crowne,
Fare ever like the young man Absalon.
1800   For as he rid the woods of Ephraim
(Which fought for thee as much as all thy men)
His haire was tangled in a shadie oake,
And hanging there (by Joab and his men)
Sustaind the stroke of well deserved death.
David.   Hath Absalon sustaind the stroke of death?
Die David for the death of Absalon,
And make these cursed newes the bloudy darts,

1780   SD *Messenger*] Mess. Q
1799   *Absalon.*] Absalon, Q

That through his bowels rip thy wretched breast.
Hence David, walke the solitarie woods,
1810 And in some Caedars shade (the thunder slew,
And fire from heaven hath made his branches blacke)
Sit mourning the decease of Absalon,
Against the body of that blasted plant
In thousand shivers breake thy yvorie Lute,
Hanging thy stringlesse harpe upon his boughs,
And through the hollow saplesse sounding truncke,
Bellow the torments that perplexe thy soule.
There let the winds sit sighing till they burst,
Let tempest mufled with a cloud of pitch,
1820 Threaten the forrests with her hellish face,
And (mounted fiercely on her yron wings)
Rend up the wretched engine by the roots
That held my dearest Absalon to death.
Then let them tosse my broken Lute to heaven,
Even to his hands that beats me with the strings,
To shew how sadly his poore sheepeheard sings.

He goes to his pavillion, and sits close a while. [H4ᵛ]

Beth. Die Bethsabe to see thy David mourne,
To heare his tunes of anguish and of hell,
O helpe my David, helpe thy Bethsabe,

She kneeles downe.

1830 Whose heart is pierced with thy breathie swords,
And bursts with burthen of tenne thousand greefes.
Now sit thy sorrowes sucking of my bloud,
O that it might be poison to their powers,
And that their lips might draw my bosome drie,
So Davids love might ease him, though she die.
Nathan. These violent passions come not from above,
David and Bethsabe offend the highest,

1808 *wretched*] See Explanatory Notes.
1810-11 (*the thunder slew,* . . . *blacke*)] Bod, BM (C.34d.54), BPL, D,
E, HCL; BM (162.d.52), F, H omit parentheses.
1832 *sit*] Hawkins, Dyce+; sits Q

To mourne in this immeasurable sort.

David.   O Absalon, Absalon, O my sonne, my sonne,
1840   Would God that I had died for Absalon:
But he is dead, ah dead, Absalon is dead,
And David lives to die for Absalon.

He lookes forth, and at the end sits close againe.

Enter Joab, Abisay, Ithay, with their traine.

Joab.   Why lies the Queene so prostrate on the ground?
Why is this companie so Tragicke hew'd?
Why is the King now absent from his men?
And marcheth not in triumph through the gates?

He unfolds the pavillion.

David awake, if sleepe have shut thine eies,
Sleepe of affection, that thou canst not see
The honour offerd to the victors head.
1850   Joab brings conquest pierced on his speare,
And joy from all the Tribes of Israel.

David.   Thou man of bloud, thou sepulchre of death,
Whose marble breast intombs my bowels quicke,
Did I not charge thee, nay intreat thy hand,
Even for my sake to spare my Absalon?
And hast thou now in spight of Davids health,
And skorne to doe my heart some happinesse,   [I1]
Given him the sword, and spilt his purple soule?

Joab.   What? irkes it David, that he victor breaths,
1860   That Juda and the fields of Israel,
Should cleanse their faces from their childrens bloud?
What art thou wearie of thy royall rule?
Is Israels throne a Serpent in thine eyes,
And he that set thee there, so farre from thankes,
That thou must curse his servant for his sake?
Hast thou not said, that as the morning light,
The cloudlesse morning, so should be thine house,
And not as flowers by the brightest raine,

1849   *head.*] head, Q
1853   *intombs*] Hawkins, Dyce+, B, Manly; intombe Q

Which grow up quickly, and as quickly fade?
1870 Hast thou not said, the wicked are as thornes,
That cannot be preserved with the hand,
And that the man shall touch them, must be armd
With coats of yron, and garments made of steele,
Or with a shaft of a defenced speare?
And art thou angrie he is now cut off,
That lead the guiltlesse swarming to their deaths,
And was more wicked then an host of men?
Advance thee from thy melancholy denne,
And decke thy bodie with thy blisfull robes,
1880 Or by the Lord that swaies the heaven, I sweare,
Ile lead thine armies to another King,
Shall cheere them for their princely chivalrie,
And not sit daunted, frowning in the darke,
When his faire lookes, with Oyle and Wine refresht,
Should dart into their bosomes gladsome beames,
And fill their stomackes with triumphant feasts,
That when elsewhere sterne warre shall sound his trumpe,
And call another battaile to the field,
Fame still may bring thy valiant souldiers home,
1890 And for their service happily confesse
She wanted worthy trumpes to sound their prowesse.
Take thou this course and live, refuse, and die.
Abisay. Come brother, let him sit there till he sincke, [I1ᵛ]
Some other shall advance the name of Joab.

Offers to goe out.

Beth. O stay my lords, stay, David mournes no more,
But riseth to give honour to your acts.

Stay.

He riseth up.

David. Then happie art thou Davids fairest sonne,
That freed from the yoke of earthly toiles,

1869 *grow*] Hawkins, Dyce+, B; growes Q   *fade*] Hawkins,
Dyce+; fades Q
1891 *prowesse.*] prowesse, Q

And sequestred from sence of humane sinnes,
1900   Thy soule shall joy the sacred cabinet
Of those devine Ideas, that present
Thy changed spirit with a heaven of blisse.
Then thou art gone, ah thou art gone my sonne
To heaven I hope my Absalon is gone.
Thy soule there plac'd in honour of the Saints
Or angels clad with immortalitie,
Shall reape a sevenfold grace, for all thy greefes.
Thy eyes now no more eyes but shining stars,
Shall decke the flaming heavens with novell lampes.
1910   There shalt thou tast the drinke of Seraphins,
And cheere thy feelings with archangels food.
Thy day of rest, thy holy Sabboth day
Shall be eternall, and the curtaine drawne,
Thou shalt behold thy soveraigne face to face,
With wonder knit in triple unitie,
Unitie infinite and innumerable.
Courage brave captaines, Joabs tale hath stird,
And made the suit of Israel preferd.
   Joab.   Bravely resolvd and spoken like a King,
1920   Now may old Israel, and his daughters sing.

Exeunt.

FINIS.

1904   *gone.*] gone, Q
1907   *greefes.*] greefes, Q
1911   *food.*] food, Q
1916   *innumerable.*] innumerable, Q

EXPLANATORY NOTES

Characters of the Play] Q has no cast of characters. I list them in order of their speeches, not their appearance. I include both Prologus and Chorus, although one actor would probably play both parts. The First Soldier would speak ll. 1486–88, 1493–1500; the Second Soldier ll. 1550–61. These two parts normally would be assigned to one actor, but the attitudes of the speakers differ so markedly that I differentiate them here. Chileab is the only named character that I list among the walk-ons; I do so because he speaks no lines.

SD *Prologus*] Even though Leslie Hotson, *Shakespeare's Wooden O* (London, 1959), p. 212, believes that Stage Right is the "Prologue's side," the Prologue Speaker could enter from either side or, indeed, from the center. A. M. Nagler, *Shakespeare's Stage* (New Haven, 1958), p. 53, argues "The Prologue, in traditional black mantle and bearing a laurel wreath, comes and goes through the middle." Nagler is talking about the staging of *Romeo and Juliet,* but his word "traditional" enables us to carry over his suggestion to the Prologue in *David and Bethsabe.*

1 *Israels sweetest singer*] See Ps. 23:1. While most versions of the Bible refer to David as "the sweet Psalmist of Israel," the Geneva version does refer to him as "the swete singer of Israel."

2 *stile*] Not merely manner or form but, according to the *OED,* "a literary composition . . . spoken or sung." The derivation is probably from "stylus," which is "a symbol of literary composition." See Spenser, *Shepheardes Calender,* Jan. 10: "Well couth he tune his pipe, and frame his stile."

4 *stilled*] Distilled.   *Jove*] Not the Roman deity but the Hebrew Jehovah. The *OED* gives no sixteenth-century example of the identification of Jove with Jehovah, but does cite Wilkins, *Nat. Relig.* 51 (1672): "Believing but one supreme Deity . . . whom they called Jupiter or Jove, with plain reference to the Hebrew name Jehovah." While there may be some question about the identification in this line, the reference in l. 14 below is clear: David was Jehovah's "Musition," not Jove's. See note to l. 16 below.

9 *strooke*] Past tense of strike.
12 *brake*] Past tense of break.
15 *prease*] Endeavor, strive.
16–18 *Then helpe . . . Heaven*] Harold Bayley, *A New Light on the Renaissance Displayed in Contemporary Emblems* (London, [1909?]), pp. 172–175, 178–179, thinks that these lines are analagous to or based on certain emblematic headpieces used by printers. I should be more willing to be convinced if any of the headpieces he uses for illustration could be dated earlier than 1609.
16 *Adonay*] OED: "One of the names given to the Deity in the Old Testament . . . also substituted by the Jews, in reading, for the 'ineffable name' JHVH = JAHVEH or JEHOVAH." Jehovah "is said to owe its vowels to being 'pointed' by the Masoretes with those of Adonai." Although *Adonai* is used in English as early as 1483 (by Caxton), there seems to be no use of *Jehovah* in English until 1530 when Tyndale used it.
23 SD *He drawes . . . vewing her*] "He" is the Prologue Speaker, who exits after opening the curtain. Bethsabe, not her maid, sings the song; if the grammatical reference in SD is unclear, David's speech below, particularly ll. 49 and 57, is conclusive. No SD in the play has evoked so much critical comment. Chambers, *ES, 3,* 48, sounds almost plaintive as he remarks, "somewhat undue use has been made of the opening direction in speculations as to the configuration of the back wall of the public stage." Other discussions are: George F. Reynolds, *Some Principles of Elizabethan Staging* (Chicago, 1905), p. 11; Victor E. Albright, *The Shaksperian Stage* (New York, 1909), pp. 51–52, 66–67; Thornton S. Graves, *The Court and the London Theatres During the Reign of Elizabeth* (Menasha, Wis., 1913), p. 9 n.; Ashley H. Thorndike, *Shakespeare's Theater* (New York, 1916), p. 106; William J. Lawrence, *Pre-Restoration Stage Studies* (Cambridge, Mass., 1927), p. 36; Richard Hosley, "Shakespeare's Use of a Gallery Over the Stage," *Shakespeare Survey, 10* (1957), 77–89, "The Gallery Over the Stage in the Public Playhouse of Shakespeare's Time," *Shakespeare Quarterly, 8* (1957), 15–31, and "The Discovery-Space in Shakespeare's Globe," *Shakespeare Survey, 12* (1959), 35–46; Leslie Hotson, *Shakespeare's Wooden O* (London, 1959); William A. Armstrong, "Actors and Theatres," *Shakespeare Survey, 17* (1964), 191–204. Although Nagler in *Shakespeare's Stage* never mentions *David and Bethsabe,* his ideas concerning the "booth" or "tent" or "pavilion" on the Elizabethan stage make good sense. I am particularly impressed with his logical account of what scenes should be played close as possible to the audience. And when he suggests (p. 102) that pavilion scenes in the outdoor theaters became alcove scenes in the indoor theaters, he compels assent. I believe, then, that Bethsabe is discovered in a pavilion or tent probably placed against the tiring-house wall. David sits in the

Lords' Room at the side of the gallery where he can see her and the audience can see them both.

23   SD *The Song*] If music to Bethsabe's song ever existed, it is, to the best of my knowledge, no longer extant.

30–33   *Let not . . . lightly*] Bethsabe's fears are realized. As we learn from l. 130 below, the blaze of beauty does enter through the eyes.

33   *lightly*] Frivolously, with the connotation of wantonly, unchastely.

34   *Zephire*] Specifically the west wind, but by extension any soft, mild, gentle wind or breeze.

45   *bushly*] Bushy. Dyce 3: "Qy. 'busky' = bosky?" Although bushly has no lexicographical authority, it does not bother me. Either busky or bosky would be acceptable. Cf. *Edward I*, ll. 2133–34: "Hale him from hence and in this buskie wood, / Bury his corps," and *1 Henry IV*, V.i.1–2: "How bloodily the sun begins to peer / Above yon busky hill!"

46   *decke*] Adorn.

48   *play the wantons*] Dally, trifle. Cf. *Richard II*, III.3.164: "Or shall we play the wantons with our woes."

55   *Strooke*] See l. 9 and note.

59   *still*] Always.   *enameld*] *OED:* "beautified with various colors." *discoloured*] Variously colored. Cf. Spenser, *Epithalamium*, l. 51: "Diapred lyke the discolored mead."

61   *Peble*] *OED:* "A name for various gems or valuable stones." Certainly that definition is pertinent in light of l. 63.

63   *Chrisolites*] A name given to several different gems of a green color.

64   *imbrac'd*] Encircled, surrounded.

68   For a discussion of this line's indebtedness to du Bartas, see Introduction, pp. 150–151 n.

69–71   Cf. Ps. 133:2–3.

70   *Hermon hill*] With an altitude of about 9,200 feet, Mount Hermon is one of Israel's highest mountains. Snowcapped most of the year, its ample streams and melting snow feed the Jordan River and the Huleh plain. Since the Psalmist resided in a semi-arid country, he was naturally impressed with water as a source of fertility.

71   *balme . . . Arons beard*] Aaron, the brother of Moses, was the first anointed priest. There is a Rabbinical tradition that "two drops of ointment like two pearls hung upon the beard of Aaron." See William Braude, *The Midrash on Psalms* (New Haven, 1959), 2, 320.

72   SD *Enter Cusay*] Many editors have unnecessarily added "above" to the SD. As frequently happens in Elizabethan drama, the SD is in the text: "Cusay, come up . . ." Cusay would ascend by a stairway that Hosley ("Shakespeare's Use of a Gallery," p. 78) postulates was within the tiring house, and present himself to David in the Lords' Room.

77   *Isacs lover*] Rebekah. See Gen. 24:15–16. There may be a touch of irony in this reference since the marriage of Isaac and Rebekah was

considered to be a prime example of monogamy in an age when polyg-
amy was widely practiced.

79 *fine perfumed*] The reading "fire-perfumed" in *England's Parnassus*
is, as Manly remarks, an "attractive reading." It is so attractive that it
is almost certainly the correct reading.

82–83 Cf. II Sam. 11:3.

82 *Hethites*] Hittite's. "Heth" is the eponym of the Hittites. Only the
Geneva Bible uses "Hittite"; the Coverdale, Matthew's, Taverner's,
Great, and Bishops' versions use "Hethite."

83 *Rabath*] Rabbah, the capital city of the Ammonites.

86 SD *Exit Cusay to Bethsabe*] Peele provides seven lines of dialogue to
cover Cusay's descent to Bethsabe. Cusay would use the tiring-house
stairs for his descent.

90 *earth*] B remarks: "This word is suspicious; but Collier's proposed
correction 'birth' is not happy." Manly comments: "The reading has
been doubted, and *birth* (by Collier) and *heart* (by Sprenger) have
been proposed; but *earth* is right." "Earth" is a perfectly natural reading, and "earth," "verdure," "flowers," and "odors" make an excellent
poetical and, I may add, botanical, progression.

106–108 B suggests by his capitalization that "his" refers to God; by his
lack of punctuation he suggests that "whose" also refers to God. He
quotes a conjecture of P. A. Daniel, "Qy. 'Whose thoughts are chaste
and hate' &c?" K. Deighton, *The Old Dramatists* (Westminster, 1896),
pp. 109–110, suggests "ay" for "I" in l. 108. Manly provides a variorum note: "The text of this passage has been misunderstood by some
commentators and emended by others. *Keltie* (*Brit. Dram., p. 60*)
thinks *his* and *whose* refer to URIAS; *Sprenger* (*Engl. Stud., XVII,
319*) thinks *whose* refers to BETHSABE herself, and suggests that
a line has fallen out. *D.* and *B.*, to judge from their punctuation,
saw clearly that *his* and *whose* refer to God." "His" and "whose"
probably do refer to God, and probably there should be a semicolon or, even better, a period, for the comma after "chast" in l.
108. Despite the weight of critical opinion against it, Keltie's reading
is not lightly dismissed; it shows much psychologcal insight. Bethsabe's
thoughts would, in a situation like this, undoubtedly turn to her husband (see l. 101). From the point of view of the hierarchical principle,
however, only God would have the right to become incensed at the
actions of the King, and only God could do it "graciously."

107 *jelousie*] Indignation.

111 *strait*] Immediately.

114 SD *Exeunt*] Cusay and Bethsabe exit through the rear of the pavilion,
which is placed against the tiring-house wall. Presumably Bethsabe's
maid (see l. 23 SD) would close the curtained front of the pavilion.
The only problem this episode propounds is the meeting place of
David and Bethsabe. While the Lords' Room from which David has

observed Bethsabe at her bath would be large enough to hold David, Bethsabe, and Cusay, a scene of this importance should not be at such far remove from the audience. Possibly, then, David descends the tiring-room stairs during Cusay's dialogue with Bethsabe (ll. 94–114) and takes his position on the stage. Cusay and Bethsabe, exiting as suggested, enter the stage through one of the tiring-house doors. Such staging would give point to David's lines (ll. 125–127). David could be standing on the stage by l. 97.

115   Cf. Cant. 2:8–9.

117   *joy*] I.e., enjoy.

118   For a discussion of this line's indebtedness to du Bartas, see Introduction, pp. 150–151 n.

119   *sovereine*] Supreme, paramount. Cf. Spenser, *Faerie Queene*, II.7.16: "The gifts of soueraigne bountie did embrace."   *joies*] Dyce+ suggests "charms" or "eyes"; Sprenger wishes to read "sovereign's joy" as meaning Bethsabe; B suggests "eyes" but, along with Manly, thinks no emendation is necessary. I see no need for emendation.

121   *their*] Dyce 3 and Manly emend Q's "the," following W. S. Walker, *A Critical Examination of the Text of Shakespeare* (London, 1860), 2, 231.

122   *curious*] Skillfully, elaborately wrought.

124   *his*] I.e., sleep's.

125   *enterteine*] To give reception to; to receive. So *OED*, which compares *Comedy of Errors*, III.1.120: "Since mine own doors refuse to enterteine me."

127   *darling*] Probably used here in the ordinary sense of one dearly loved, but *OED* lists several sixteenth-century uses of the word in which there is a connotation of illicit relations. Perhaps, then, darling connotes minion.

129   *bones faire covering*] Peele frequently uses this metonymy in speaking of the body. See ll. 378, 451, 978, 1016, 1105, 1596, 1683, and 1775. Although strange, such usage is not uncommon. *OED* cites examples as early as 1398 and as late as 1873.   *erst*] Not long ago; a little while since. Cf. Spenser, *Faerie Queene*, I.5.9: "The armes, that earst so bright did show."

130   Cf. ll. 30–33 and note; and l. 137.   *And all*] B comments: "By reading 'Enthrall'd mine eyes,' we could make some sense of this corrupt passage." Dyce 3 says, "To connect this with what precedes, a friend would read 'Have all mine eyes,' &c.: but the probability is, that a line has dropt out." Manly reads "afar" and Deighton also desires to emend. Perhaps Dyce is correct, but B's emendation has much to commend it.

131–135   The metaphysical conceit here seems to be a strange mingling of Ptolemaic and Copernican astronomy. The Zodiac is "crooked" because the apparent path of the sun in the ecliptic is irregular. For the Zodiac as the path of the sun, cf. *Titus Andronicus*, II.1.5–7: "As when the golden sun salutes the morn, / And, having gilt the ocean with his beams, / Gallops the Zodiac in his glistering coach." See too *Descensus Astraeae*, ll. 4–5: "And heavens bright eie / Gallop the Zodiacke"; and *Anglorum Feriae*, ll. 23–24: "From where the risinge sune, / gallops the Zodiack in his fierie wayne."

135 *neerer . . . neerer*] This kind of word play is common with Peele. The word is first used as an adverb of place, i.e., closer; it is then used as a temporal adjective, i.e., more rapid.

138 *drerie*] B suggests "garish," perhaps because he is disturbed that the day could change so suddenly from sunny and bright (ll. 24, 26) to dismal and gloomy. According to *OED*, the first use of dreary to mean gloomy occurs in 1667, so there is no reason to emend. The day is sad and doleful—both common sixteenth-century meanings—and so is Bethsabe. There may, then, be a transferred epithet here: the day, though bright and sunny, saddens Bethsabe because, being bright, it has permitted David to see her and become inflamed with passion for her.

152 *conversant in*] Greg misprints as "inconuersant" for one of the rare errors in his Malone Society Reprint edition.

156 SD *Exeunt*] More point is given to this exit if David and Bethsabe leave through the curtained pavilion and Cusay through one of the tiring-house doors. Joab and the rest would enter through the opposite door immediately afterwards.

158 *charge*] Not an anachronism for "discharge a gun," but as *OED* says, "To place (a weapon) in position for action."

159 *Ammons sonnes*] I.e., the Ammonites, a Transjordanian Semitic tribe. See II Sam. 10:2–5, and ll. 185 and 431.

160–161 Cf. II Sam. 10:4.

160 *disguised*] Disfigured. See *Rape of Lucrece*, l. 1452: "Her cheeks with chaps and wrinkles were disguis'd."

170 *Laughing . . . scorne*] To "laugh to scorn" is very common biblical phraseology. See II Chron. 30:10, Neh. 2:19, Job 12:4, and Ezek. 23:32.

176–178 Cf. Ex. 9:23–25.

180–182 Urias' advice is sound. Polybius in his *Histories* V.71, describes how Antiochus in 218 B.C. brought about the surrender of this same city by capturing its water supply. See *The Histories of Polybius*, tr. Evelyn S. Schuckburgh (London, 1889), *1*, 422–423.

180 *Tower*] There could be a tower on the stage, but there is no definite need for one. The Lords' Room could represent the tower, and the tower could then be assaulted both from the stage ("scale") and the tiring-house stairs. The balcony would then represent the "wals" of l. 186 SD. The "wals" and "Tower" must be distinct, because even though the Israelites "win the Tower" (l. 212 SD), Hanon is still showing himself "on the wals" in l. 777. If the pavilion had a rigid roof, as

Nagler, *Stage*, p. 61, suggests, the roof of the pavilion as well as the balcony could represent the "wals." See note on l. 212 SD.

185   *Hanon*] Hanun, son of Nahash. See l. 195 and note.   *Ammons sonnes*] The Ammonites. Cf. ll. 159 and 431.

186   SD *Machaas*] I.e., Maacah. In II Sam. 10:6, the Ammonites hire the king of Maacah, a small Aramean kingdom in Gaulanitis, to aid them against David's forces. In this line and in II Sam. 10:8, Maacah and Tob seem to be distinguished from the other mercenaries, who were Syrians. In the account of the battle in II Sam. 10:9–14, however, all who are not Ammonites are called Syrians. See also I Chron. 19:6–15.

195   *Nahas*] I.e., Nahash, father of Hanun. The friendship between Nahash and David may have resulted from the fact that Saul was an enemy to both of them. Another reason for their friendship may be found in their conjectured common relationship to Abigail. See II Sam. 17:25 and I Chron. 2:16.

206   *Medes*] I.e., meads.

207   *werry*] I.e., worry. *OED* cites this line as illustrative of its definition, "To seize by the throat with the teeth and tear and lacerate . . . Said e.g. of . . . hounds when they seize their quarry."

208   *wessels*] Windpipes. *OED* cites this line.

210   *repines*] Frets, complains.

212   *dastards*] Cowards. See *Edward I*, l. 871: "And noble mindes all dastard feare defies." See also *Richard II*, I.1.189–190: "Or with pale beggar-fear impeach my height / Before this outdar'd dastard."

212   SD *Assault, . . . above*] See note on l. 180. Lawrence, *Pre-Restoration Stage*, p. 37, has an interesting, although not entirely accurate, note on this episode: "In the first act of *David and Bethsabe* there is a siege scene in which a tower is stormed and taken, though there is no slightest hint in text or direction of the use of scaling-ladders. [But see l. 180.] If to me it seems not improbable that the assault was made by means of the staircase leading to the gallery, it is because there is some indication, later in the scene, of the use of the staircase. Cusay makes his appearance below and is requested by Joab, the victorious, to come up. The direction which follows simply says, He comes." I see no need to assume the existence of a stairway on stage leading to the upper Lords' Room.

214   *Maugre*] In spite of, despite. Cf. *King Lear*, V.3.131–33: "Maugre thy strength, youth, place, and eminence, / Despite thy victor sword and fire-new fortune, / Thy valor and thy heart, thou art a traitor."

217   *hold*] I.e., stronghold.   SD *He comes*] If the Lords' Room is the Tower, Cusay uses the tiring-house stairs for his ascent, which must be very rapid since no lines cover the action.

220   *out of hand*] Immediately.

224   *truth*] Loyalty.

225   *prefer*] Favor, esteem.

231–235 Cf. II Sam. 12:28.

241 This line could be what Hosley refers to as a "fictional" rather than a "theatrical" stage direction. It need not, of course, be acted. After the exit of Abisay and Joab (Cusay and Urias having departed earlier) no one is present in the "tower," and the scene shifts to Ammon's house.

244 SD *Ammon*] Amnon. The son of David is Amnon, not Ammon. Perhaps either Peele or the compositor was confused by the similarity between Ammon, the people and the country (see l. 159), and Amnon, David's son. The confusion would be enhanced, of course, by the fact that Peele frequently refers to the Ammonites as Ammons sonnes (see ll. 159, 185, 431).

255 Cf. II Sam. 13:4.

256–260 Although William Harvey did not begin his lectures on the circulation of the blood until 1616, and did not publish *Exercitatio anatomica de motu cordis et sanguinis* until 1628, knowledge that the blood circulates goes back at least to Homer.

257 *merrily*] Wholly, absolutely. *OED* points out that "merely" is an old form of "merrily." The compositor, perhaps trying to bring Peele up to date, changed his "merely" to "merrily." The words "mere" and "merely" occasionally retain their Elizabethan meanings in the twentieth century. Cf. Yeats, "The Second Coming": "Mere anarchy is loosed upon the world."

263 *joy*] I.e., enjoy. See l. 117.

266–270 Cf. II Sam. 13:5.

272 *favour*] The word seems to be used euphemistically here. *OED* gives no example of such usage until 1676 when one example is found in Wycherley, *The Plain Dealer*, V.3: "She . . . granted you the last favour, (as they call it)." Yet here in context and in conjunction with the verb "enforce" and the adjective "some" meaning "a certain," the sexual connotation seems clear.

275 *favour*] Comeliness, beauty. Obviously there is an ironic echo of "favour" in l. 272 above.

276 *cates*] Choice viands, delicacies, dainties. Cf. *Taming of the Shrew*, II.1.189, "For dainties are all Kates."

278 *That . . . hands*] Thamar has not as yet seen the King. See discussion of this problem in the Introduction, p. 179.

280 *crased*] Diseased, infirm.

281 SD *Exeunt. Restat Jonadab*] Since Ammon says "bolt the dore" in l. 317, I propose that the exit of Ammon, Thamar, Jethray, and the page be made through the right tiring-house door, that Jonadab exit through the left tiring-house door (l. 306 SD), and that Ammon thrust Thamar out of the same door through which they had made their exit.

286–288 See ll. 256–260 and note.

286 *lose*] I.e., loose.

287 *sokte*] Drained, exhausted. Manly suggests: " 'lokte,' which comes very near 'sokte,' is attractive." "Knots" in l. 286 makes "lokte" attractive, perhaps, but "sokte" makes perfectly good sense.

289 *ripened*] B emends to "rifled" but no change is necessary. "Ripened" is the natural middle term in a progression that begins with "grew" in l. 290 and ends with "rotten" in l. 291. The conjunction of "ripe" and "rot" is common enough in Elizabethan literature. See *As You Like It*, II.7.26–27: "And so from hour to hour we ripe and ripe, / And then from hour to hour we rot and rot."

291 *rotten*] Morally corrupt.

295 *kindlesse*] Unnatural.

299–300 *Jehosophat . . . Libanon*] Jehosophat probably cannot be located exactly on any map, but since the fourth century it has been identified with a deep valley east of Jerusalem and between that city and the Mount of Olives. Lebanon is, of course, the very high, snow-covered, mountain range.

305 *racke*] Gale, storm.

308 *parbreake*] Vomit. See Marlowe, *1 Tamburlaine*, V.2.193: "Noisome parbreak of the Stygian snakes." See also Spenser, *Faerie Queene*, I.1.20: "Her filthy parbreake all the place defiled has."

309 *Unkind*] Unnatural, as often in Elizabethan literature, but here the word has a stronger connotation of ungentle than is customary.

311 *fright*] I.e., frightfulness.

316–319 Cf. II Sam. 13:16–18.

321 *amased*] Thoroughly confused, stunned. As Alexander Schmidt, *Shakespeare-Lexicon* (London and Berlin, 1886), puts it: "In confusion . . . in a state where one does not know what to do or to say or to think."

323 *bating*] According to *OED*: "The action of beating the wings, and (*spec.* in *Falconry*) fluttering off the fist or perch." See *Romeo and Juliet*, III.2.14: "Hood my unmann'd blood bating in my cheeks," and *Taming of the Shrew*, III.3.188–189: "To watch her as we watch these kites / That bate and beat and will not be obedient."

327 *sit*] Although B emends to "rife" and Dyce 3 believes the word to be an error, "sit" makes sense. If an emendation were necessary, I should suggest "live."

331 *lure*] Although I follow Dyce+, B, and Manly by emending Q, the Q reading "live" is certainly possible.

335 *thou*] The *n* in Q is probably a turned *u*. Greg, although he follows Q in other misprints, prints "thou" here. See notes on ll. 440, 640, and 885.

339 *figure*] To portray or represent by speech or action.   *resting*] Spoiling, becoming rancid or rotten. Dyce 3 may be right with his reading, "wresting," which here would mean "the action of taking away or obtaining by force."

361 *ungracious*] Devoid of spiritual grace.
370 *ungracious*] Impious, wicked. Cf. l. 361 and note.
372 *kind*] Nature.
374 *lightnesse*] Lewdness. Notice the word play in the phrase "blot of lightnesse."
378 *suffered*] Permitted, allowed.   *bones*] See note to l. 129.
381 *Frame*] Manly's emendation, "Flame," is so attractive that it almost certainly is correct, but "Frame" is not impossible.
384 *Sin . . . crowne*] The Seven Deadly Sins.
389 *Gives . . . hell*] The image is from fishing; see "baits" in l. 388.
391 *Tyran*] I.e., tyrant.
396–414 Cf. II Sam. 13:23–27.
400 *charge*] Expense, cost.
404 *planted*] Dyce 3, B, and Manly emend to "painted."
412 *best beloved*] Contrast ll. 370 and 383.
414 *doe . . . grace*] Do honor to.
424 *swaies*] Rules, governs.
426–551 Cf. II Sam. 11:7–15.
431 *Ammons sonnes*] The Ammonites, as in ll. 159 and 185.
432 *finger*] *OED*: "Viewed as 'the instrument of work' . . . as attributed to God." Cf. Ex. 8:19.
433 *atchiev'd*] Gained, won.
440 *And*] The "Aud" in Q probably results from a turned *n*. See notes to ll. 335, 640, and 885.
442 *valours*] Although Hawkins, Dyce 3, B, and Manly emend to *valour*, *valours* may well be right. See Kyd, *Spanish Tragedie*, I.2,39: "And captaines strove to have their valours tride." See also l. 1034.
451 *bones*] See l. 129 and note.   *cras'de*] See l. 280 and note.
458 *wanton*] Amorous.   *flattering*] Caressing.
462 *unkindly*] Unnaturally.
465 *solace*] Give oneself comfort, consolation, entertainment, or amusement.
467 *tender*] Considerate.
472 *shame*] Loss of reputation. Hence "more shame" = less reputation.
488 *carouses*] *OED*: "Cupfuls drunk 'all out'; toasts." Cf. *Taming of the Shrew*, I.4.276: "Quaff carouses to our mistress' health."
528 Hawkins and Dyce 2 print this line as David's speech, treating *"Urias"* as a vocative. Dyce 3, B, and Manly follow Q. I see no need for emendation. Urias is drunk, and it is natural for him to repeat both his own and others' words. See ll. 526–527, 534–535, and 537.
529 *Urias*] Greg: "Speaker's name repeated." If we follow Q in l. 528, this speech prefix is unnecessary.
530 *presently*] Immediately.
531–534 Absolon may be talking about "David's Children" in awareness of the affair between David and Bethsabe, although the play is not

specific on the point, and David's speech in ll. 543–546 may be an aside.

540 *sentence*] Word, decision.

551 SD *Chorus*] See note to Prologue, above.

553 *Laying . . . sin*] This line would cause no problem if the preposition were "on" instead of "in," since *OED* says " 'to lay the bridle on his neck' is to abandon control of him." Perhaps the problem is a twentieth-century one, for the earlier editors ignored it, and Schmidt, *Shakespeare-Lexicon*, gives many examples of the use of "in" for "on."

555–561 For a discussion of this simile's indebtedness to du Bartas, see Introduction, pp. 148–149 n. Dyce 3 and B cite Chapman and Shirley, *Chabot, Admiral of France*, and the anonymous *Distracted Emperor*, respectively, for comparable passages. Cf. also Marlowe, *The Jew of Malta*, II.i.1–2: "Thus, like the sad presaging raven, that tolls / The sick man's passport in her hollow beak."

566 *shoke*] I.e., shook.

568 *This . . . raigne*] This line has disturbed most editors. Dyce 2, "king by"; B, "kingly ruler"; Morley, "kingly spirit"; Manly, "This king by giving unto lust her raigne." Manly's reading is the most likely, even though the "unto" which he inserts to make the tetrameter line a pentameter may not be necessary. "King" must be subject of "Pursues" in l. 569. The substitution of *l* for *b* would be easy for the compositor since *l* and *b* occupy adjoining boxes in the font. See R. B. McKerrow, *Introduction to Bibliography* (London, 1927), p. 9.

572 *joies*] I.e., enjoys.

581 *tinckling*] The Q reading, "twinckling," is not impossible, but the influence of I Cor. 13:1 is strong.

589 *Glad*] Cause to rejoice. Using "glad" as a transitive verb is not uncommon in Elizabethan literature.

601 SD *David . . . Nathan*] This SD would seem clear enough were it not for *"Enter Nathan"* at l. 611 SD, *"Nathan to David"* at l. 635 SD, and the speech prefix *"Nathan"* in l. 613. Certainly Nathan enters by l. 611, and begins to speak in l. 613. The other directions are unnecessary.

614–669 For Nathan's parable, cf. II Sam. 12:1–14.

621 *eat*] I.e., ate. This is the common Elizabethan past tense of the verb. See *Taming of the Shrew*, III.3.190: "She eat no meat today, nor none shall eat."

622 *was to him*] This emendation by Dyce 3, B, and Manly is probably correct, but could the Q reading, "was to live" mean "lived"?

625 *spar'd*] Refrained from using. The Coverdale version of the Bible uses the form, "spared." Matthew's, Taverner's, and the Great Bible versions say, "coulde not fynde in his heart." The Bishops' Bible says "spared," but has a marginal gloss, "or refused." The Geneva version says "refused," but has as a marginal gloss, "or spared."

627 *But . . . store*] Both Dyce 3 and B say the line is hopelessly corrupt,

but suggest no emendation. Manly makes excellent sense with his emendation "the" for "partly." His emendation restores the pentameter line, which may not be important, but it also restores the sense, which is important. His reasoning, too, has much to commend it: "In Elizabethan English 'store' means all one has, as well as 'abundance.'"

640 *and*] The Q reading "aud" probably results from a turned *n*. See ll. 335, 440, and 855, and notes.

654 *day*] I.e., daylight.

668 *erst*] Not long ago, just recently. See l. 684.

673 *Nill*] Will not.   *dome*] I.e., doom in the sense of judgment, decision.

686–712 Cf. II Sam. 12:18–24.

694 *The . . . begat*] Hawkins, Dyce+, B, and Manly treat the last two words of the line as part of the following line, obviously for metrical reasons. Their treatment gives two pentameter lines rather than a heptameter and a trimeter.

699 *Shalmes*] According to *OED*, "Shalmes" is an alternate spelling of "shawm," a musical instrument "of the oboe class, having a double reed enclosed in a globular mouthpiece."

701 *laud*] Praise.

702 *shendeth*] Shields, defends. *OED* cites this line.

711 *he*] I.e., the dead child. See II Sam. 12:23.

712 SD *They . . . Bethsabe*] Both David and Bethsabe would be washed and annointed; meanwhile the tables could bet set up for the banquet. Music would probably begin when David gives the order in l. 714. The singing and dancing implied in the SD at l. 716 would accompany the eating and drinking. The eating and drinking could be either symbolic or actual, but Peele certainly relied upon such masque elements as singing and dancing in this play (see l. 753 SD and note). The play is short enough to permit time for two episodes of music, song, and dance.

716 SD *solemnities*] Formal ceremonies. These ceremonies are not necessarily grave and serious; indeed a solemnity is most often a joyous occasion. Cf. *Romeo and Juliet*, I.4.173, 179. David's speech (ll. 695–716) makes it clear that despite the death of the child, indeed because of it, this is an occasion for rejoicing not grief. See *OED* and C. S. Lewis, *A Preface to Paradise Lost* (London, 1942), pp. 15–16.

724 *Ammon*] Either the Ammonites, in which case "the wicked ones" refers to the Ammonites' mercenaries; or Hanun, son of Nahash and king of the Ammonites, in which case "the wicked ones" refers to the Ammonites.   SD *Exeunt omnes.*] Although all the characters exit here, the banquet tables could remain since they are used again in the next scene.

725 *mules*] The mules do not, of course, have to be on stage. Absalon could give this order over his shoulder as he enters.

727 *Accursed . . . feast*] Absalon, not Ammon, was supposed to be the
     host. See ll. 396–416.

737 *Wreake*] Revenge. See also l. 869 and note. Cf. *Titus Andronicus*,
     IV.3.33: "Take wreak on Rome for this ingratitude."

740 *wot*] Know. Cf. *Romeo and Juliet*, III.2.139: "I wot well where he is."

746 *Sit downe*] Presumably at the banquet tables left on stage after the
     previous scene. See note to l. 724.

747–748 *haires . . . wyers*] The Bible is clear that Absalon was an ex-
     ceedingly handsome man and that he had abundant hair, but no sug-
     gestion is present in the Bible that his hair was golden. The common
     notion, which Peele adopts (see l. 1469 SD), that Absalon was caught
     by his hair has no specific biblical authority, but in Rabbinic literature
     much is said about his beautiful and abundant hair, which grew so
     rapidly that even though he had taken the Nazarite vow (see Num.
     6:5), he was permitted to clip it slightly every week, as otherwise
     its weight would have become intolerable. *The Universal Jewish En-
     cyclopedia* (New York, 1939), s.v., "Absalom," says, "The Rabbis
     point to Absalom's fate as an example of poetic justice, since he re-
     ceived his punishment by way of those beautiful locks of which he
     was so vain." Peele, of course, takes the same point of view as the
     Rabbis. He may have been influenced by "The Fourth Part of the
     Homily Against Disobedience and Wilful Rebellion" (see G. E. Corrie,
     ed., *The Homilies* [Cambridge, 1850], pp. 579–580): "When . . . most
     men were afraid to lay their hands upon him, a great tree stretching
     out his arm, as it were for that purpose, caught him by the great and
     long bush of his goodly hair . . . and so hanged him up by the hair
     of his head in the air, to give an eternal document, that neither come-
     liness of personage, neither nobility, nor favour of the people, no nor
     favour of the king himself, can save a rebel from due punishment."

750 *vines*] Although Hawkins, Dyce+, and B emend to "wines," Manly
     says, "Kittredge points out that 'plenty of thy vines' (= 'the increase
     of thy vines,' i.e., 'wine') is better."

753 This nine-syllable line disturbs some of the editors. Dyce 3 in a note
     suggests the addition of "down" after "sit"; Morley inserts "now"
     after "and"; B inserts "Come" before "Absolon." I see no reason for
     change.

753 SD *Here . . . sing*] Two musical interludes in such a short space
     of time would not disturb the Elizabethan audience. The SD at ll. 712
     and 716 indicate instrumental and vocal music; here more masque ele-
     ments are used as there is a dance by the shepherds as well as songs.
     The pastoral element of the play is too important to be overlooked.
     See Introduction, p. 148.

756–759 *Die . . . sonne*] Absalon is probably the killer of Ammon, but
     the text does not suggest the means of killing. Presumably, Absalon
     would use a knife, but there is no evidence. One interpretation of ll.

734–735, "Therefore doth Absolon conspire with you, / That Ammon die what time he sits to eat," would suggest that Absalon's men, not Absalon, commit the murder, much as Achilles' Myrmidons kill Hector in *Troilus and Cressida*. I lean toward the use of a knife or sword because speed and surprise are important here, and neither strangulation nor poisoning ("Die with thy draught . . ." could be interpreted to suggest poisoning) would be so rapid as stabbing.

759   SD *Exit Absa.*] Presumably the "two or three" mentioned in l. 724 SD would exit along with Absalon. There would be no reason for them to stay and, indeed, it might be dangerous for them.

767   SD *Exeunt omnes*] Both Ammon's body and the banquet tables must be removed here.   *Enter . . . Rabba*] The four named characters plus the drummer and flag carrier would be enough to symbolize the host of Israel. See Nagler, *Stage*, p. 84.

771   *Dispoile*] Strip or deprive by violence.

777   *And . . . wals.*] Joab's forces have captured the tower (ll. 180, 212 SD, and notes), but the city remains to be subdued.

784–786   Cf. II Sam. 2:13–15.

792–797   Cf. I Sam. 31:1–4.

794   *Jonathan, Abinadab, and Melchisua*] All sons of Saul. Only the Bishops' and Geneva versions of the Bible have the form, "Jonathan"; the rest have "Jonathas." The form, "Melchisua," is in Matthew's, Taverner's, and the Bishops' versions; Coverdale reads "Malchisua"; The Great and Geneva versions read "Malchishua."

804   *Talent*] A measure of weight and of value. Since Hanun presumably did wear the crown and, according to II Sam. 12:30 and l. 814 SD, David also wore it, both were extremely stalwart men because the Babylonian talent weighed about 65 pounds.

807–810   Cf. II Sam. 12:31.

807   *tile-kill*] A kiln in which tiles are baked. Hawkins, Dyce+, and B read "tile-kiln"; the Great Bible reads "tylekele," and the Bishops' Bible reads "tylekil." The Coverdale Bible reads "tyle ovens," Matthew's and Taverner's Bibles read "fornaces," and the Geneva Bible reads "tyle kilne." *OED* cites *Letters and Papers of Henry VIII*, V.180: "A longe cart caryng of tylys from the tyle kill."

814   SD *Alarum . . . crowne*] Although nothing in the text describes an opposing army (only Hanun is mentioned as being present on the walls), the typical stage battle takes place here. Presumably David's forces drive the enemy into the tiring house on two levels, leaving a temporarily empty stage (*"Exeunt omnes"*) before the sound of the trumpets symbolizes victory. When David reenters with his forces, he is wearing Hanun's crown.

816   *raced*] Hawkins reads "rased." Dyce+ and B suggest "razed," but *OED* defines "raced" as scratched, cut, slashed. There may not then be any need for change.

817 *wreakefull*] Vengeful. See ll. 737 and 869. Cf. *Timon of Athens*, IV.229–230: "In all the spite / Of wreakful heaven."

825–833 For a discussion of the popularity of this simile, see Introduction, p. 151 n.

834 *Joab . . . throne*] Although David's throne could be anywhere on stage, I suggest that it should be in the pavilion with the curtains drawn back. Such placement would give visual point to David's complaints of being alone in his sorrow (ll. 873–874). Abisay's suggestion must be adopted with alacrity, since he mentions the throne in this line and David is obviously seated on the throne by Jonadab's entrance in l. 837 SD.

844 *Nor . . . sonnes*] This bit of psychological cruelty is not Peele's; it is dictated by II Sam. 13:30. In the Bible, however, Jonadab is not the dispenser of the falsehood: "tidings came to David."

849 *gite*] *OED*: "Used by Peele for: Splendour, magnificence." *OED* then cites this line and *The Tale of Troy*, l. 456: "Doone is thy pride, dim is thy glorious gite."

864–865 Cf. II Sam. 13:28.

869 *in wreake of*] In revenge of. *OED* cites this line.

879 SD *Exeunt omnes.*] David obviously remains seated on his throne despite this SD. Perhaps the line would have been too long had "*Manet David*" followed "*Exeunt omnes,*" so the compositor placed the last two words in the following line.

880–958 Cf. II Sam. 14:1–24,33.

880 The Widow of Thecoa must enter and throw herself on the ground before David's throne, even though there is no SD. David's order, "rise from the earth" in l. 882 makes that clear.

885 *greevous*] The Q reading "greenous" is an example of a turned *u*. Cf. ll. 335, 440, 640, and notes.

900 *Woman . . . house*] Despite David's command, the Widow does not exit at this point, for she has two more speeches (ll. 908–916, 921–926). I do not think, however, that her exit should be delayed until the "*Exeunt omnes*" of l. 958. Joab could readily wave her off stage while speaking l. 930. The problem of the number of people on stage during this episode is a vexing one. We know from l. 879 SD that David and the Widow of Thecoa are alone on stage until Joab enters at l. 926 SD. I suggest that the Widow exit at l. 930, and that Joab exit and return with Absalon at l. 941 SD. David, Absalon, and Joab would then be alone on stage. The problem revolves about the identity and whereabouts of "you men of Israel" whom David orders to depart with him in l. 954. The men are David's forces, and they are perhaps imagined to be just off stage. After Absalon's line (953), "And Joab hath got grace for Absalon," David gives the order for departure as he rises from his throne and goes to the tiring-house door. At the door he presumably turns, addresses Absalon in ll. 957–958, and

then he and Joab exit, leaving Absalon to deliver his soliloquy (ll. 959–972).

909–916   For a discussion of the fact that Absalon has not been banished, see Introduction, pp. 179–181.

947   *What boots it*] What good does it do, what avails it. Cf. Spenser, *The Teares of the Muses*, ll. 445–446: "What bootes it then to come from glorious / Forefathers, or to haue been nobly bredd?"

956   *Ammons*] The Ammonites. Cf. ll. 159, 185, 431.

968   *publish*] *OED:* "Announce in a formal or official manner; to pronounce (a judicial sentence), to promulgate (a law or edict)."

972   SD *Enter David . . . mourning*] For the head covered with a loose covering and for bare feet as signs of mourning, see Ezek. 24:17.

978   *marrow . . . bones*] Even though the word "marrow" would seem to restrict "bones" to its denotation, "bones" retains its broader, figurative meaning. See note to l. 129.

980   *shrinke*] Hawkins, Dyce 3, and Manly read "shrunk," but perhaps "shrinke" is the historical present.

984   *He . . . breast*] A clear violation of the hierarchical principle. Cf. *The Tempest*, I.2.468–469: "What, I say! / My foot my tutor?"

985   *gripes*] Grasp, grip. *OED* points out that the plural form was very common.

987   *ambitious heat*] The heat of ambition.

988–989   Cf. Matt. 4:8 and Luke 4:5.

988   *lustie tower*] Tower of lust. Dyce 3 and B read "lofty tower," but as Manly points out, "In Elizabethan English a *lustie tower* means a *tower of lust*, just as *ambitious heat* (see l. 987) means *the heat of ambition.*

991   SD *He . . . him*] During this episode every character would probably be prostrate on the stage except the one speaking, and he need only raise his head as he delivers his lines. See ll. 1063, 1104–05 and notes.

997   *Lading*] Emptying, draining, bailing. Cf. *3 Henry VI*, III.2.138–139: "And chides the sea that sunders him from thence, / Saying, he'll lade it dry to have his way."

1000   *garments torne*] For torn garments as a symbol of mourning, see II Sam. 13:19, 15:30.

1001   *heartie*] Although *OED* cites no such usage earlier than 1661, here "heartie" must mean "giving unrestrained expression to the feelings; vehement."

1016   *Now . . . bones*] Despite Sadoc's suggestion, David would not rise immediately, but he should not remain groveling much beyond l. 1021. When David rises, his followers also would rise and gather about him to comfort him (see ll. 1031–33).   *bones*] See note to l. 129.

1020 *still*] Always.

1025 *tendred soule*] Absalon in his fight "against his father's happinesse" (l. 1026), has wronged his God-given soul by violating the commandment concerning the honor and respect due a parent.

1031 *drooping*] Downcast. Cf. Shakespeare, *Sonnets*, 27.7: "And Keep my drooping eyelids open wide."   *troupes*] I.e., troops.

1037 *loth*] To be hateful, displeasing, or offensive. *OED* cites this line.

1038 *baulme*] Annoint.

1039–52 Cf. II Sam. 15:19–22.

1048–50 Ithay's protestations of affection and loyalty help to restore David's morale. Cf. ll. 1385–86.

1049 *What*] I.e., whatever.

1053–69 Cf. II Sam. 15:25–28.

1061 *worne*] Exhausted.

1063 *lie*] Remain. There is no reason to believe that David is still lying prostrate, but see ll. 1016, 1104–05 and notes.

1074 *unkind*] Unnatural.   *gracelesse*] Depraved, wicked, impious.

1078 *his . . . bound*] This phrasing caused the earlier editors no problems, but B was disturbed: "Very corrupt.—Qy. 'sea's ranging body bound'? That *raging* is a misprint for *ranging* I am convinced; but the rest is dark." Manly says: "Psalm 89 prevents me from sharing B's conviction in regard to *raging* [Psalm 89:9 speaks of the "raging of the sea"]. The rest is dark enough . . . but . . . *bloody* may, as B suggests, be a misprint for *body*, or *bloody bound* may be a distortion of *floody bound* (past participles with *y*- are not unknown in Elizabethan English)." Charles T. Prouty suggests: "God holds his raging bloody boundaries within the sublunary world, i.e., the world of men. Bloody deeds are natural to man."

1083 SD *Enter Cusay with his coat turnd, and head covered*] The word "turnd" poses a problem. II Sam. 15:32 makes it plain that the coat was "torn" not "turnd." I do not emend, even though I feel that Peele probably wrote "torne," since David in ll. 1095–99 suggests that Cusay become a spy or a "turncoat." *OED* cites examples as early as 1565 for such a meaning of "turncoat." For the covered head and torn coat as signs of mourning, see ll. 972 SD, 1000, and notes.

1085 *betide*] Happen, befall.

1092–1106 Cf. II Sam. 15:32–37.

1093 *tender*] Cherish, foster, take care of.

1094 *breake*] Hawkins, Dyce+, B, and Manly emend to "brook." They are probably correct, because the simple meaning seems to be "endure" or "bear." Yet David may be saying that he cannot make Cusay "breake" (i.e., stop) sighing.

1104 *rise*] I do not believe that David has been prostrate since l. 991 SD, but feel he has been on his throne within the pavilion since about l. 1021.

When Cusay suggests that he rise in this line and David agrees to in the next, he is merely leaving his throne preparatory to his exit. See ll. 991 SD, 1016, 1063, and notes.

1105   *bones*] See note to l. 129.

1106   SD *Absalon . . . crowned*] This scene with its crowded stage makes a fine spectacle. The curtains of the pavilion would be opened at Absalon's entrance, and he should be seated on the throne within as he delivers his speeches.

1107–49   Cf. II Sam. 16:21–22.

1111   *foiles*] *OED:* "Anything that serves by contrast . . . to adorn another thing or set it off to advantage." The Concubines, in Absalon's terms, set off his own brilliance and, at the same time, darken David's glory.

1114   *Jeatie*] I.e., jet black. Cf. *1 Tamburlaine*, IV.i.60–62: "Black are his colours, black pavilion; / His spear, his shield, his horse, his armour, plumes, / And jetty feathers menace death and hell."

1119   *chase*] Despite Hawkins, Dyce+, and B, the correct reading may will be Q's "chast" not "chase." According to *OED,* "chast" means to correct, reprove, rebuke, subdue, restrain. Manly's comment is pertinent: "Confusion of the verbs *chase* and *chaste* is so easy and some of the meanings of *chaste* are so appropriate that it seems possible that Peele wrote *chaste*." Although Manly is persuasive, the meaning probably is to chase away, dispel, disperse.

1123   *gracelesse*] Depraved, wicked, impious.

1134–35   Cf. II Sam. 2:18.

1137   *scope*] According to B, P. A. Daniel suggests "swoop"; according to Manly, Kittredge suggests "stoop," but thinks as Manly does that Peele wrote "scope." I see no need for emendation, particularly since in his *Shakespeare-Lexicon* Schmidt points out at least two occasions when Shakespeare uses "scope" to mean power, which clearly is the meaning here. Cf. Shakespeare, *Sonnets*, 29.7: "Desiring this man's art, and that man's scope." Cf. too *Measure for Measure*, I.i.64–65: "Your scope is as mine own, / So to enforce or qualify the laws."

1141   *cabinets*] Little rooms, boudoirs. *OED* says that these meanings run parallel to the meanings of "bower." See l. 1143 and note.

1143   *bowers*] Boudoirs, bedrooms.

1149   *lose*] I.e., loose.   SD *Exeunt*] The concubines would exit through the tiring-house door left. The pavilion has presented the illusion of a bower or cabinet earlier in the play (Bethsabe's bathing scene and the Thamar rape scene), but the idea of a throne within the pavilion is also important, and should be maintained here.

1153   *paines*] Hawkins, Dyce+, B, and Manly read "veins"; Dyce 2 suggests the even more attractive reading "plaines." "Paines" may be "panes," however. See l. 1330 and note.

1160   Cf. II Sam. 15:1.

1192–1241   Cf. II Sam. 17:1–14.

1194   *close*] Hidden, secret.

1197   *Surchargd*] Overwhelmed, oppressed.

1200   *latest*] I.e., last.

1205   *meet*] Suitable, proper.

1223   *letted*] Hindered, prevented.

1229   *in anothers*] Hawkins, Dyce+, B, and Manly insert "one" between these words, an emendation that seems essential metrically, but I suspect that Peele wrote "in anothers."

1234   *numbers*] The Q reading "nnmbers" is an example of a turned *u*. Cf. notes to ll. 335, 440, 640, and 885.

1246   *fruition . . . crowne*] Cf. *1 Tamburlaine*, II.7.29: "The sweet fruition of an earthly crown."   SD *Exeunt*] Absalon and his followers exit stage right through the tiring-house door. Achitophel delivers his lines (1247–48) and exits stage left, since his course will not be the same as that of Absalon and his followers. Cusay's lines (1249–51) following Achitophel's allow enough time to permit Sadoc and the rest to enter from the right.

1250   *drifts*] Intentions, schemes, plans.

1253   *purchase*] Strive for.

1258   *at unwares*] Without warning, suddenly.

1265   *will*] Urge, desire.

1266   *presently*] Immediately.

1271   SD *Semei solus*] Semei would deliver his speech as far stage front as possible both to add intensity to his words by the immediacy of his presence and to give David and his train enough space to enter (l. 1295 SD). The space also helps establish the gulf between Semei and David.

1272–1353   Cf. II Sam. 16:5–13.

1284   *reeking*] Exhalation. The word frequently carries the connotation of smoke (see l. 1282) and sighing (see l. 1283). According to *OED*, the connotation of "reeking" that implies unpleasant or unwholesome vapors or odors does not exist until the eighteenth century, but such a connotation seems to be present here.   *gorge*] Throat.

1288   *rancke*] Virulent. Cf. Douglas, *Aeneis*, II.4.37: "Full of vennome and rank poyson."

1289   *ranckling*] Festering.

1291   *Joves . . . fire*] For "Joves" see notes to ll. 4 and 16. Manly inserts "do" after "champions"; P. A. Daniel, according to B, would insert the words "in air" between "fight" and "with." While I see no need for any additions, Manly's suggestion seems more metrically sound since "champions" is trisyllabic.

1302   *wreake*] Avenge.

1307   See Textual Notes. Every time Semei throws dust at David (ll. 1332 SD and 1353 SD), David must endure it with stoicism.

1308 *this*] I follow Hawkins, Dyce+, B, and Manly in emending Q "his," because in all six sixteenth-century versions of the Bible II Sam. 16:9 reads, "this dead dogge [or dog]."

1309 *Let . . . head*] Presumably Abisay would grab Semei and draw his sword, only to be prevented by David in the next line.

1310 *medleth*] Interfere, probably, but the word did have the connotation of contend, mingle in fight. Cf. *Twelfth Night*, III.4.258–260: "Therefore on, or strip your sword stark naked; for meddle you must, that's certain, or forswear to wear iron about you." *Zervia*] Here the word seems to be trisyllabic, but in l. 1338 scansion requires that it be pronounced as two syllables.

1312 *useth*] According to *OED* an older meaning was prosecutes, and Peele may mean that here. The ordinary meaning of treats, i.e., deals with, also fits.

1322 *desperate*] Without hope. David, as the next line shows, has hope because he trusts in God.

1328 *issue*] Exit, outgoing.

1330 *paine*] I.e., pane, meaning "a piece, portion, or side of anything." See l. 1153 and note.

1336 *carelessnesse*] Negligence.

1353 SD Semei, frustrated by his inability to arouse David's wrath, must here exit unaccompanied, since David's followers would not disobey David's orders and drag him off stage.

1357 B expands this line to make it metrically correct by inserting "sovereign" before "lord"; Manly expands the line by inserting "my lord" before "would." I see no reason to expand, and agree with Manly when he says, "but it is by no means clear that in plays of this date metrically incomplete lines are to be filled out."

1378 *sound*] To give a signal by a trumpet or other instrument.

1379 Ahimaas and Jonathan could exit here or at the general exit in l. 1415 SD.

1382–1414 Cf. II Sam. 18:2–5.

1401–06 For a comment on the heavy-handed irony concerning Absalon's hair, see ll. 747–748 and note.

1407 *Joves*] See notes to ll. 4 and 16.

1410–11 These lines seem to indicate that sinning is easy at the beginning, that sin is as attractive and pleasant as having one's feet washed with the cooling and soothing milk of roes. Yet the punishment for sin is as drastic and violent as "coales of lightening." A contrast exists between "washt" and "dried," "milke" and "coales." In the latter pair, the contrast is not only between cool and hot but also between colors. Whether "coales" implies black or red (and with "lightening" I think red is implied), the contrast with the whiteness of milk is striking. Since lightning and fire are used almost interchangeably in the Bible, the connotation of "coals of fire" is probably also present.

1412–13 *O Lord . . . grave*] Most editors emend these lines. If I were
to emend, I should insert a comma after "Lord" and delete the comma
after the singular possessive "sinnes." Collier (cited by Dyce 3, p.
480 n.) complains that the passage "stands . . . as if David, addressing
the Lord, said, 'Thou pull'st man to the grave with the bridle of sin';
whereas the meaning is, that 'sin with his bridle pulls man to the
grave.' " I should tend to agree with Collier, but in II Kings 19:28 God
speaks a similar phrase: "I will put my hook in thy nose, and my
bridle in thy lips."

1415 SD *Exeunt*] David and his followers exit stage right.   SD *Achitophel . . . halter*] Achitophel would enter from stage left and exit
stage right after l. 1439. His suicide takes place off stage.

1418 *Hereon*] The halter mentioned in l. 1415 SD.   *depend*] There
could be a pun here; word play in the face of death was not uncommon in Elizabethan literature. Cf. *Romeo and Juliet*, III.1.100–101,
where the dying Mercutio says: "Ask for me tomorrow and you
shall find me a grave man."

1420–22 Cf. II Sam. 16:23.

1423 *usde*] Treated.

1428 *ravish*] B emends to "ravage," but since *OED* defines "ravish" as
ravage, destroy, I see no need for an emendation.

1430 *my*] B emends "my" to "thy," since "the word [is] being addressed
to the 'land I leave' [l. 1427]." I feel that l. 1431 makes it clear that
"my" is correct.

1431 *mourning*] Q "monrning" is an example of a turned *u*. Cf. ll. 335,
440, 640, 885, 1234, and notes.

1435 *fell*] Savage, ruthless.

1438 *Joves*] See ll. 4 and 14, and notes to ll. 4 and 16.   *doome*]
Judgment.

1439 *breast*] Dyce+ and B read "breath," but I suspect that Peele wrote
"breast."

1454 Cf. Ex. 3:8.

1455–56 Cf. I Chron. 14:15 and II Sam. 5:23–24.

1455 *whissing*] A sibilant sound made by the wind. *OED* cites Cooper,
Thesaurus: "The whissyng of the winde."

1459–62 Cf. Ex. 13:21, 40:36–38, Num. 9:15–18, and Deut. 1:33. See also
l. 352.

1465 *swarve*] Variant spelling of swerve.

1469 SD–1475 See note on ll. 747–748.

1469 SD *The battell, . . . haire*] This episode could be staged by having
the customary alarums and excursions of battle occur on stage with the
curtains of the pavilion closed. When the impression of battle is clear,
contending warriors could throw open the curtains of the pavilion and
discover Absalon hanging there. I believe that Absalon would hang
from a tree, agreeing with Nagler, *Stage*, p. 35, that trees were def-

inite parts of the scenery of some Elizabethan stages. The text refers
to a "tree" in ll. 1475, 1478, and 1514, to "sencelesse plants" in l. 1482,
to "a sencelesse plant" in l. 1516, and to "a shadie oke" in l. 1487.

1475 *ravisheth*] Seizes. Cf. note to l. 1428.

1486–1501 Cf. II Sam. 18:10–14.

1492 *sickles*] A variant spelling of shekels. See also l. 1493. Although
Hawkins, Dyce+, B, and Manly emend to shekels, this variant spelling
has authority.   *wast*] I.e., waist; girdle.

1501 *I . . . thee*] Here Joab turns to Absalon, and presumably the soldier
exits.

1510 *ruth*] Sorrow, regret, repentance, contrition.

1512 *thirsts*] Longs for. "To long for the soul" would be equivalent to
"to desire the death."

1521 *affects*] Likes, loves. Cf. *Twelfth Night*, II.5.24–27: "Maria once
told me she did affect me; and I have heard herself come thus near,
that should she fancy, it should be one of my complexion."

1527 *Take that*] At this point Joab undoubtedly stabs Absalon with
dagger or sword. If there be any doubt that Joab actually stabs him,
it is resolved by Absalon's speech, especially ll. 1530, 1535, 1547–48.

1539 *remorsefull*] Compassionate, full of pity.

1541 *pleasure*] To give pleasure, to please, to gratify.

1543 *Hold*] Could this be an error for "Bold"? "Hold" makes sense, but
the reading would be improved if a comma followed it. "Bold" would
require no mark of punctuation.

1553 See note to ll. 747–748.

1556 *begun to*] We should say "for" instead of "to," but there is an obvious parallel intended between "begun to us" and "end to thee" in
the next line.

1557 *heres an end to thee*] Here, presumably, the soldier who is speaking
delivers the coup de grace.

1558–61 *Come . . . death*] The soldiers could be taking Absalon down as
Joab and his men enter (l. 1561 SD). Joab, approving their action, repeats the soldiers' words with more detail in ll. 1562–73. As the soldiers
carry Absalon's body off right, the curtains of the pavilion would be
closed, and Joab and his troop would exit left.

1559–60 Cf. II Sam. 18:17–18.

1562 *tall*] Brave.

1565 *Ephraim*] The forest of Ephraim, a wooded area east of the Jordan
into which Joab's forces chased Absalon's forces. See II Sam. 18:6.
Q reading, "Ephrami," is a typographical error and should be emended.

1566 *lower*] A variant spelling of lour, meaning to look dark and threatening. Cf. Marlowe, *Edward II*, IV.6.62–63: "O my stars! / Why do
you lour unkindly on a king?" and *Richard III*, I.1.3–4: "And all the
clouds that lour'd upon our house / In the deep bosom of the ocean
buried."

1571 *loth*] Be hateful or displeasing to. See l. 1037 and note.

1573 SD *5.Chorus*] See Introduction, pp. 177–78, for a discussion of this problem. See also Manly, *2*, 475. The Chorus could use the pavilion for entrance and exit. See *Prologus* and note.

1574 *president*] Deity, guardian, according to *OED;* hence, God.

1575–76 *ruth Of*] Compassion for.

1581 *third discourse*] See Introduction, p. 178, for discussion of this problem.

1585 SD–1588 For discussion of this misplaced fragment, see Introduction, pp. 178–79, and Manly, *2*, 421, 476.

1588 SD *Trumpets . . . rest*] While this entire episode can take place on the platform, a better dramatic effect would be achieved if Joab, Ahimaas, and Cusay appeared on the balcony above; Joab then could address Amasa and the vanquished troops from a position of physical eminence.

1596 *in temper*] In proper condition.

1597 *shroud*] Shelter, protect.

1600 *forward*] Presumptuous. Cf. Marlowe, *Doctor Faustus*, Epilogue, ll. 7–8: "Whose deepness doth entice such forward wits / To practice more than heavenly power permits."

1608 *weale*] Welfare.

1614 Dyce+ and B wish to expand the line to make it metrically "correct." It seems a pity to expand a line of such natural dialogue. See note to l. 1357.

1615 *gracious*] Kind, courteous.

1620 *president*] A variant spelling of precedent, not to be confused with "president" in l. 1574.

1620–23 *And . . . hands*] As Amasa speaks, he would place his sword on the ground and either kneel or fall prostrate, his troops following his example.

1623 SD *All stand up*] This SD should follow l. 1624 or l. 1625.

1626–36, 1787–1804 Cf. II Sam. 18:19–23. Exigetes have devoted much time to the fact that Ahimaas leaves second, arrives first, and avoids giving the bad news about Absalon's death to David, allowing Cusay that doubtful privilege. For the purposes of this play it is important only to point out Peele's fidelity to his biblical source.

1640 SD *David, Bethsabe, Salomon . . . traine*] Solomon appears in the play for the first time in this SD. There has been no earlier mention of him, not even of his birth. As David and his train enter, an attendant would open the curtains of the pavilion, and David would ascend his throne placed within.

1643 *aspects*] Appearance, countenance, face.

1649 *retrive*] Bring back, cause to return; a variant spelling of "retrieve." *OED* cites this line.

1662 *unicorne*] Although Keltie suggests "ivory," the Q reading is correct.

OED cites this line along with the definition: "Horn reputed to be that of the unicorn prepared as an embellishment or ornament."

1665 *Whose . . . aires*] In Vol. 2 of the Yale ed. of Peele, Hook says (p. 187), "Bethsabe has this remarkable respiratory ability," as he comments on *Edward I*, ll. 1040–46.

1666 *repaire*] Arrival.

1667 Dyce 3 wishes to expand the line by inserting "alas" between "Shee" and "my." There is no reason to expand the line. Although it has but eight syllables, it does have five stresses. See note to l. 1357.

1675–76 *That . . . love*] According to II Sam. 12:25, Solomon was given the name Jedidiah, "beloved of the Lord." In the same verse, however, David calls him Solomon, probably derived from "shalom," meaning peace or prosperity. See also I Chron. 22:9, and l. 1689.

1675 *affects*] Loves. See l. 1521 and note.

1684 *counterfeit*] Image, portrait. Compare "image of content" in the next line and also *Merchant of Venice*, III.2.114–115: "What find I here?/ Fair Portia's counterfeit!"

1690 *apt*] Ready to learn, intelligent.

1694 The verbs are in the present tense because David and Nathan as yet do not know of Absalon's death. See also David's comment in ll. 1683–87.

1696 *rest*] Tranquillity, peace.

1711–25 Solomon's desire for knowledge is analogous to that of Faustus. David's warning and comments in ll. 1726–56 may well be necessary.

1716 *lead*] Although Dyce 3 and B emend to "lend," "lead" makes good sense.

1731–55 *Thou power . . . voice*] It would be an error in theology as well as in staging to have David kneel as he prays.

1737 *figures*] The word in this context could mean calculations, though *OED* does not give such a meaning at this early date. More likely it means one of the mystic symbols such as a pentacle.   *hidden art*] Esoterica.

1738 *presage*] Omen.

1739 *architect*] Although *OED* does not give such a meaning, the word in context clearly means architecture. Nonetheless, Manly (*Engl. Stud.*, *18*, 1893, 302) is convincing when he argues that "architect" is the correct reading, and that Dyce 3 "archetype," B "archi'ture," and Sprenger "a" instead of "and" before "perfect," are wrong. Manly would be even more convincing had Marlowe not written in *1 Tamburlaine*, II.7.21–22: "Our souls, whose faculties can comprehend / The wondrous architecture of the world." "Architect" must be Peele's form of "architecture."

1749 *regenerate*] Not simply born again, but "invested with a new and higher spiritual nature," according to *OED*.

1750 *ravish*] In l. 1428 the word clearly means ravage, destroy; but here and in l. 1757 it seems to have another *OED* meaning: "To carry away (esp. to heaven) in mystical sense; to transport *in spirit* without bodily removal."   *sprite*] Spirit.

1751   *humane*] Variant spelling of human. See also l. 1758.

1752   *Organons*] Bodily organs especially considered as the instruments of the soul or mind. *OED* cites this line and *2 Tamburlaine*, V.3.95–96: "The soul, / Wanting those organons by which it moves."

1757   *fury*] "Inspired frenzy, as of one possessed by a god or demon," is one definition in *OED*.   *ravisheth*] l. 1750 and note.

1758   *humane*] See l. 1751 and note.

1759   *stand*] *OED:* "A standing in ambush or cover," and cites *3 Henry VI*, III.1.3–4: "And in this covert will we make our stand, / Culling the principal of all the deer."

1764   *intentive*] Intently bent or directed.   *bedare*] Defy. The "be-" is an intensive, according to *OED*, which cites this passage.

1765   *stieth*] Ascends, mounts up, rises to a higher level. *OED* cites this line.

1772   *haughtie*] High-minded, aspiring.

1775   *broiles*] Tumults, turmoils. Cf. *1 Henry VI*, I.1.53: "Prosper this realm, keep it from civil broils!"   *bones*] See note to l. 129.

1781–1842   Cf. II Sam. 18:25–33, and note to ll. 1626–36.

1786   SD *Enter Ahimaas*] See ll. 1626–36 and note.

1789   *Tell me . . . Absalon?*] In his eagerness, David may well leave his throne and pavilion to come forward at this line.

1791   *tumult*] Commotion of a multitude, uproar. The Bishops' and Geneva versions of the Bible use the word "tumult"; Coverdale says "uproare"; Matthew's says "great ado," and the Great Bible says "much a doo"; but Taverner's version has the interesting reading, "great hurlee burlee."

1793   SD *Enter Cusay*] See ll. 1626–36 and note.

1807   *these cursed newes*] News was frequently considered a plural noun during the Elizabethan period. Cf. *Much Ado About Nothing*, II.1.182: "But hear these ill news."

1808   *wretched*] This reading is in all Qq except, possibly, BPL. Manly feels that BPL reads "wtetched," but close examination indicates that the letter in question is probably *r* not *t*. It is frequently difficult to distinguish between *r* and *t* in Islip's font. Cf. ll. 743, 856, and 1577.

1814   *shivers*] Fragments.

1819–21   *tempest . . . yron wings*] Many biblical passages refer to the wings of the wind. See II Sam. 22:11, Ps. 18:10 and 104:3. Why this tempest has "yron wings" is not so easy to explain. Perhaps Peele was thinking of an analogy between the destructive power of a tempest and that of iron instruments. See also l. 23.

1822   *engine*] Snare, trap. The word can also mean an instrument of torture, which, in a sense, the tree was to Absalon.

1826 SD *He goes . . . while*] David returns to his throne within the pavilion and either he or, more likely, an attendant would close the curtains.

1829 SD *She kneeles downe*] Bethsabe might approach the pavilion, but she certainly would not open it. From a kneeling position, she addresses her plea to the closed curtain.

1830 *breathie swords*] Mitford (*Gent. Mag., 103* 103) suggests "breathed words." Dyce 3 believes the Q reading, "Barbaric as the expression may be," is correct. B argues: " 'Breathy swords' is a horrible expression, but Mitford's correction 'breathed words' is insipid. 'Thy breath's keen swords' would be tolerable,—but it would not be what Peele wrote." I obviously lack Victorian sensibility and sensitivity, but "breathie swords," i.e., sharp sighs, or the word which David has just spoken, seems both correct and tolerable to me. See Introduction, p. 160.

1842 SD *He lookes . . . againe*] This SD, at least its first part, belongs between ll. 1838–39. David would open the curtain slightly, deliver ll. 1839–42, and close the curtain again.

1843 *prostrate*] Despite Joab's word, there is no reason to assume that Bethsabe has changed her kneeling position indicated in l. 1829 SD. In the sixteenth century, "prostrate" frequently meant in a position of humility, not necessarily prone.

1844 *Why . . . hew'd*] Why does this company appear so tragic? Hue means appearance in general, and is not necessarily confined to color.

1846 SD *He unfolds the pavillion*] When Joab opens the curtains, they remain open. David remains seated until l. 1896 SD.

1848 *Sleepe of affection*] Two meanings seem to be present: diseased sleep, i.e., sleep caused by a malady, and sleep caused by emotion as opposed to reason.

1850 *conquest pierced on his speare*] Campbell, *Divine Poetry*, p. 259 n., compares this line with *Henry V*, V. Chorus. 32: "Bringing rebellion broached on his sword."

1852–53 This is a fascinating metaphysical conceit, but the key problem is the interpretation of "quicke." It probably means the adjective "alive" rather than the adverb "quickly."

1857 *skorne*] I.e., scorning.

1859–92 Cf. II Sam. 19:1–7.

1866–74 Cf. II Sam. 23:4–7.

1871 *preserved*] Dyce 3 and B suggest "repressed," but a reference to II Sam. 23:6 clears up the problem: "But the sons of Belial shall be all of them as thorns thrust away, because they cannot be taken with hands." Hence the clause, "cannot be preserved with the hand," makes good sense if we adopt one of the *OED* meanings, "retained," for preserved.

1874 *defenced*] Protected. This strange use of the word is dictated by II Sam. 23:7 in the Bishops' version: "But the man, that shal touche them, must be defensed with iron or with the shaft of a speare," and the Geneva version: "But the man that shal touch them, must be defensed with yron, or with the shaft of a speare."

1894   SD *Offers to goe out*] Presumbably both Abisay and Joab start to leave, and are restrained by Bethsabe's speech (ll. 1895–96).

1897–1916   This long speech is almost a soliloquy, and should be delivered as such. David is, however, aware of his audience, and there is no sharp break in his delivery as he addresses Joab and the rest in ll. 1917–18.

1898   *toiles*] Snares, traps. Cf. *Antony and Cleopatra*, V.2.351–352: "As she would catch another Antony / In her strong toil of grace."

1899   *sequestred*] In the religious sense, according to *OED*, the word means set apart, consecrated to a particular service.

1908–09   *Thy eyes . . . lampes*] Campbell, *Divine Poetry*, p. 259 n., suggests a comparison with *Romeo and Juliet*, II.1.57–59: "Two of the fairest stars in all the heaven, / Having some business, do entreat her eyes / To twinkle in their spheres till they return."

1909   *novell*] Newly made or created.

1915   *triple unitie*] If this is a Trinitarian reference, it comes strangely from the lips of David. Campbell, *Divine Poetry*, p. 259, thinks that Saint Paul rather than David was in Peele's mind when he wrote these lines.

APPENDIX A

David and Bethsabe and *The Book of Common Prayer*

According to *The Book of Common Prayer* (1549), commonly known as *The First Book of Edward VI*, and *The Book of Common Prayer* (1559), commonly known as *The First Book of Queen Elizabeth*, the 24 chapters of the Second Book of Samuel were read at services according to the following table.

	Date	Matins	Evensong
April	24	1	2
	25	3	4
	26	5	6
	27	7	8
	28	9	10
	29	11	12
	30	13	14
May	1	15	16
	2	17	18
	3	19	20
	4	21	22
	5	23	24

On the sixth Sunday after Trinity, 2 Sam. 12 was read at Matins, and 2 Sam. 21 was read at Evensong. On the seventh Sunday after Trinity, 2 Sam. 22 was read at Matins, and 2 Sam. 24 was read at Evensong.

APPENDIX B

From the Cornish *Origo Mundi*

The Cornish *Origo Mundi* contains, exclusive of stage directions, 2846 lines. Of these 2846 lines, 472 lines (ll. 1899–2370) deal with King David, and only 150 lines (ll. 2105–2254) deal with the biblical David story. The David-Bethsabe-Urias episode is the only one with biblical authority. The first episode (ll. 1899–2104) deals with a dream of David's concerning the location of three rods which Moses had planted. David takes these rods, for in his dream he has been told that the rods will grow into a tree from which the Savior's cross will be constructed. The David-Bethsabe-Urias episode (ll. 2105–2254), given in full below, follows. The third episode (ll. 2255–2370) has little to do with the Bible. In it David asks a "Counsellor" what atonement can be made for his sinful treachery against Urias. He is ordered to have a "brilliant temple" constructed. David immediately sends for workmen, but when they are ready to start work, God appears and tells David that a man-killer cannot be allowed to build a temple sacred to Him. David wants to know who can build the temple. The answer is, of course, Solomon. David therefore requests that his son Solomon be allowed to rule after him. The request is granted and he dies.

The translation of the second episode is that of Edwin Norris's *Ancient Cornish Drama*, 1, 159–171.

And king David says to Bathsheba (washing her dress in the stream):—

KING DAVID

Damsel, on thy gentleness,
  Shew me how to love thee;

For never have I seen
   A woman who pleases me better,
     Yet in any place.
2110 I give thee my palace, hall, and chamber;
     I will be thy husband;
     Together we will live always.

BATHSHEBA

My dear loved lord,
   King thou art over all the world,
It would be a pleasure
   With me, to do the will of thy mind,
If I can without hazard,
   And fear of my being persecuted.
If the villain knew,
2120   Immediately I should be killed.

(Let Bathsheba go home with king David.)

KING DAVID

Bathsheba, flower of all the world,
   Certainly, for thy love,
Sir Uriah shall be put to death;
   I swear it to thee by my truth.
For all my love always
   To thee shall be truly ever.
Thou shalt be my wife,
   And I will live with thee.

BATHSHEBA

I cannot deny thee,
2130 Now every thing to grant
   From me what thou askest.
My sweet Lord, kill all,
Else he will spit at me
   If he shall hear of our sport.

KING DAVID

My dear beloved heart,
   God made a rose, flower of her sex,
He shall be, without fail,

Dead for thy love.

——————[This line in the manuscript
probably indicates a scene division,
but no stage direction is given.]

KING DAVID

Uriah, my best knight,
2140   I would pray thee,
To take with thee a host well armed,
    To fight, as thou lovest me.
A great enemy is to me,
    Over my land doing violence.
I cannot ride,
    There is a disease in my body.

URIAH

Dear sir lord, as thou wishest,
I will do at once, without refusal,
    All in my power ever.
2150 And as I am a trusty knight,
    Never will I come from the place
      Until I take that fellow.

KING DAVID

O, Uriah, thou art excellent,
I love thee much, on my peril,
    For thy answer is fair.
Take care to be forth in advance,
That thou be not held a coward,
    Nor fearful of any man.

URIAH

My lord, I swear it to thee,
2160 By the order I have received,
    No man shall prove me of cowardice,
For I will be the first
To give a blow on the journey,
    And to do my duty.

Farewell, my best lord,
I will not stay longer;
    Bless me before I go, I pray thee.

KING DAVID

My blessing on thee ever;
My messenger goes with thee,
2170   And my butler also, armed.

URIAH

I must speak, really,
   To my wife before going from home,
If I should go without speaking to her,
   She would break her heart.

(He speaks to Bathsheba.)

Bathsheba, my sweet of me,
   Need is to me to labour
At a battle, certainly,
   But very soon it will be ended.

(Here Uriah is prepared and armed.)

BATHSHEBA

Do not you go, on my soul,
2180   From me ever,
My heart is separating
   When I hear you talk so.
My lord, by my truth,
   I will break my neck, crack;
If you go away from home,
   Never will I taste bread.

URIAH

Bathsheba, my faithful wife,
It is necessary to do immediately
   The will of our sovereign lord.
2190   I cannot longer stay;
I will kiss thee;
   And pray with me very earnestly.

(She goes up, and exit.)

(Here Uriah comes down.)

BATHSHEBA

Oh! alas! that I was born!
With sorrow I am filled,
  Behind thee, my sweet lord.
But always that thou return,
I will pray with thee;
  And that will be pleasing.

(Here Gabriel comes down.)
————[See note after line 2138]

URIAH

I pray thee now, messenger,
2200 Carry my banner valiantly,
  As thou wishest to be rewarded.
And thou also, butler,
I pray thee to be bold,
  Like a good horseman armed.

(Here he mounts a horse.)

MESSENGER

I tell thee, Uriah,
Bear no doubt of me,
  Certainly, ever.
For there is no reason to bear doubt,
I tell you,
2210   Upon my soul.

And then they shall ride out of the stage.
————[see note after line 2138]
And afterwards the messenger comes, and says to David
the king:—

My lord, hail to thee!
Behold me come
  Again home,
But sir Uriah is killed,
And thy butler also,
  Unfortunately for them.

KING DAVID

Alas! sir Uriah is dead;
Tell me, as thou lovest me,
   When death reached him,
2220   And how he was killed;
For he was stout and proud,
   And felt himself a strong man.

MESSENGER

He is dead, by God's day;
He wished to do a deed,
   And he gave sharp strokes;
But a horseman slew him,
And soon drove him to the earth,
   And hacked him to pieces.

*Then the angel shall come to king David, and ask him
a question; and he says:—*

GABRIEL

Answer me, thou mighty king:
2230   A man may possess a hundred sheep,
   And his neighbor only one;
If he steal it from him,
What punishment is due to him?
   Tell me the truth, certainly.

KING DAVID

I will answer thee at once;
   Certainly there is no hindrance.
By truth surely judgment should fall
   On him to suffer to be killed.
     Very positively,
2240   Whoever has acted
      In that way,
   Death is due to his body.

GABRIEL

In that way thou hast acted,
And from Uriah hast taken

His one wife, David, certainly.
And to thee there are
Wives enough and plenty;
 Suffer thy judgment thyself.

KING DAVID

Lord, pardon to my soul;
2250 Alas! that I have done sin
 With the body of the wicked woman.
O God, have mercy upon me,
According to thy grace and thy pity;
 Let not my punishment be to the end.

*And then, under the tree . . . , he begins
the Psalter, viz. Beatus vir.* [The dots indicate
an illegible word in the manuscript.]

APPENDIX C

From Bale's *God's Promises*

As a source of this selection, I have used the Tudor Facsimile Text of *The Chief Promises of God unto Man* (London, 1908). The reproduction in facsimile is not a good one, as the editor, John S. Farmer, admits, but Act V, which contains the David episode, is legible. Only the punctuation presents difficulty, but the difficulty is easily resolved. On the rare occasions when the printer used a macron instead of an *n* I have inserted the *n* and underscored it.

Incipit actus quintus. [C4ᵛ]

Pater coelestis.

For all the fauer, I haue shewed Israel,
Delyuerynge her, from Pharaoes tyrannye,
And geuynge the lande, fluentem lac & mel,
Yet wyll she not leaue, her olde ydolatrye,
Nor knowe me for God. I abhorre her myserye.
Vexed her I haue, with battayles and decayes,
Styll must I plage her, I se non other wayes.

Dauid rex pius.

Remembre yet lorde, thy worthye seruaunt Moses,
Walkynge in thy syght, without rebuke of the.
Both Aaron, Jetro, Eleazar, and Phinees,
Euermore feared, to offende thy mageste.
Moch thu acceptedest, thy seruaunt Josue,
Caleb and Othoniel, sought the with all their hart,

Aioth and Sangar, for thy folke ded their part.
Gedeon and Thola, thy enemyes put to smart,
Jayr and Jephte, gaue prayses to thy name.   [D1]
These to leaue ydolles, thy people ded coart,
Samson the strongest, for hys part ded the same.
Samuel and Nathan, thy messages did proclame,
What though fearce Pharao, wrough myschef in thy syght:
He was a pagane, laye not that in our lyght.

 I wote the Beniamytes, abused the wayes of ryght,
So ded Helyes sonnes, and the sonnes of Samuel.
Saul in hys offyce, was slouthfull daye and nyght,
Wycked was Semei, so was Achitophel.
Measure not by them, the faultes of Israel,
Whom thou hast loued, of longe tyme so inteyrlye,
But of thy great grace, remyt her wycked folye.

Pater coelestis.

 I can not abyde, the vyce of ydolatrye,
Though I shuld suffer, all other vyllanye.
Whan Josue was dead, that sort from me ded fall,
To the worshyppynge of Asteroth and Baal,
Full vncleane ydolles, and monsters bestyall.

Dauid rex pius.

 For it they haue had, thy ryghteouse ponnyshment,
And for as moch as they, ded wyckedly consent,
To the Palestynes, and Chananytes vngodlye,
Idolaters takynge, to them in matrymonye,
Thu threwest them vndre, the kynge of Mesopotamye,
After thu subduedest them, for their Idolatrye.

 Eyghtene years to Eglon, the kynge of Moabytes,
And xx years to Jabin, the kynge of Chananytes.
Oppressed they were, vii years of the Madyanytes,
And xviii years vexed, of the cruell Ammonytes.
In iii great battayles, of iii score thousand and fyue,
Of thys thy people, not one was left a lyue.

Haue mercye now lorde, and call them to repentaunce. [D1ᵛ]

Pater coelestis.

So longe as they synne, so longe shall they haue greuaunce.
Dauid my seruaunt, sumwhat must I saye to the,
For that thu latelye, hast wrought soch vanyte.

Dauid rex pius.

Spare not blessed lorde, but saye thy pleasure to me.

Pater coelestis.

Of late dayes thu hast, mysused Bersabe,
The wyfe of Vrye, and slayne hym in the fyelde.

Dauid rex pius.

Mercye lorde mercye, for doubtlesse I am defyelde:

Pater coelestis.

I constytute the, a kynge ouer Israel,
And the preserued, from Saul whych was thy enemye.
Yea, in my fauer, so moch thu dedyst excell,
That of thy enemyes, I gaue the vyctorye.
Palestynes and Syryanes, to the came trybutarye.
Why hast thu then wrought, soch folye in my syght:
Despysynge my worde, agaynst all godlye ryght.

Dauid rex pius.

I haue synned lorde, I besyche the, pardon me.

Pater coelestis.

Thu shalt not dye Dauid, for thys inyquyte,
For thy repentaunce, But thy sonne by Bersabe,
Shall dye, for as moch, as my name is blasphemed,
Amonge my enemyes, and thu the worse estemed.
From thy howse for thys, the swerde shall not depart.

Dauid rex pius.

I am sorye lorde, from the bottom of my hart.

Pater coelestis.

To further anger, thu doest me yet compell.

Dauid rex pius.   [D2]

For what matter lorde: I besyche thy goodnesse tell.

Pater coelestis.

Why dedest thu numbre, the people of Israel:
Supposest in thy mynde, therein thu hast done well:

Dauid rex pius.

I can not saye naye, but I haue done vndyscretelye,
To forget thy grace, for a humayne pollycye.

Pater coelestis.

Thu shalt of these iii, chose whych plage thu wylt haue,
For that synnefull acte, that I thy sowle maye saue.
A scarsenesse vii years, or els iii monthes exyle,
Eyther for iii dayes, the pestylence most vyle.
For one thu must haue, there is no remedye.

Dauid rex pius.

Lorde at thy pleasure, for thu art full of mercye.

Pater coelestis.

Of a pestylence, then iii score thousand and ten,
In iii dayes shall dye of thy most puysaunt men.

Dauid rex pius.

Oh lorde, it is I, whych haue offended thy grace,
Spare them and not me, for I haue done the trespace.

Pater coelestis.

Though thy synnes be great, thy inwarde hartes contrycyon,
Doth moue my stomake, in wonderfull condycyon.
I fynde the a man, accordynge to my hart,
Wherfor thys promyse, I make the ere I depart.

A frute there shall come, forth yssuynge from thy bodye,
Whom I wyll aduaunce, vpon thy seate for euer.
Hys trone shall become, a seate of heauenlye glorye,
Hys worthy scepture, from ryght wyll not dysseuer,
Hys happye kyngedome, of faythe, shall perysh neuer.
Of heauen and of earthe, he was autor pryncypall,   [D2ᵛ]
And wyll contynue, though they do perysh all.

Thys sygne shalt thu haue, for a token specyall,
That thu mayst beleue, my wordes vnfaynedlye.
Where thu hast mynded, for my memoryall,
To buylde a temple, thu shalt not fynysh it trulye.
But Salomon thy sonne, shall do that accyon worthye,
In token that Christ, must fynysh euery thynge,
That I haue begunne, to my prayse euerlastynge.

Dauid rex pius.

Immortall glorye, to the, most heauenlye kynge,
For that thu hast geuen, contynuall vyctorye,
To me thy seruaunt, euer sens my anoyntynge,
And also before, by manye conquestes worthye,
A beare and lyon, I slewe through thy strength onlye,
I slewe Golias, whych was vi cubites longe.
Agaynst thy enemyes, thu madest me euer stronge.

My fleshlye fraylenesse, made me do deadlye wronge,
And cleane to forget, thy lawes of ryghteousnesse.
And though thu vysytedest, my synnefulnesse amonge,
With pestylent plages, and other vnquyetnesse.
Yet neuer tokest thu, from me the plenteousnesse,
Of thy godly sprete, whych thu in me dedyst plant.
I hauynge remorce, thy grace coulde neuer want.

For in conclusyon, thy euerlastynge couenaunt,
Thu gauest vnto me, for all my wycked synne.
And hast promysed here, by protestacyon constaunt,
That one of my sede, shall soch hygh fortune wynne,
As neuer ded man, sens thys worlde ded begynne.
By hys power he shall, put Sathan from hys holde,
In reioyce wherof, to synge wyll I be bolde.

Canora uoce tunc incipit Antiphonam, O Adonai, Quam [D3]
(ut prius) prosequetur chorus cum organis.

Vel sic Anglice.

O lorde God Adonai, & gyde of the faythfull howse of Is
rael, whych sumtyme aperedest in the flamynge bushe to Mo
ses, and to hym dedest geue a lawe in mounte Syna, come
now for to redeme vs in the strengthe of thy ryght hande.

Finit actus Quintus.

THE OLD WIVES TALE

ACKNOWLEDGMENTS

For their assistance I am grateful to the general editor, Professor Charles T. Prouty; to my colleagues J. Burke Severs and William Digel; and to the editorial staff of the Yale University Press. The librarians have, as usual, lived up to the best traditions of an unsung profession. Either in person or in correspondence, I have received the kindest of receptions from the Columbia University Library, the Bodleian Library, the British Museum, the Henry E. Huntington Library and Art Gallery, the National Library of Scotland, the Pforzheimer Library, the University of Pennsylvania Library, the Victoria and Albert Museum, and, certainly not least, the Lehigh University Library. The Institute of Research of Lehigh University has generously provided funds to assist in the preparation of this edition. The photograph of the title page of *The Old Wives Tale* is reproduced with the permission of the Henry E. Huntington Library and Art Gallery from its copy of the quarto of 1595.

F. S. H.

Bethlehem, Pennsylvania
June 1969

ABBREVIATIONS AND SHORT TITLES

Abridgements	Greg, W. W., *Two Elizabethan Stage Abridgements*, Oxford, 1922.
Arber	*A Transcript of the Registers of the Company of Stationers of London, 1554–1640 A.D.*, ed. Edward Arber, 5 vols., London, 1875–94.
B	*The Works of Peele*, ed. A. H. Bullen, 2 vols., London, 1888.
BM	British Museum copy of Q (162.d.53).
Baldwin	Baldwin, T. W., *On the Literary Genetics of Shakespeare's Plays, 1592–1594*, Urbana, Ill., 1959.
Blair	Blair, Robert L., "An Edition of George Peele's *Old Wives Tale*," dissertation, University of Illinois, 1936.
Bradbrook	Bradbrook, Muriel C., "Peele's *Old Wives Tale*," *English Studies, 43* (1962), 323–330.
Brooke	Brooke, C. F. T., and N. B. Paradise, eds., *English Drama 1580–1642*, New York, 1933.
Cady	*The Old Wives Tale*, ed. Frank W. Cady, Boston, 1916.
Chambers	Chambers, E. K., *The Elizabethan Stage*, 4 vols., Oxford, 1923.
Cheffaud	Cheffaud, P. H., *George Peele (1558–1596?)*, Paris, 1913.
Cooper	Cooper, Thomas, *Thesaurus linguae Romanae & Britannicae*, London, 1578 (STC 5688).
Crow	Crow, John, "Folklore in Elizabethan Drama," *Folk-Lore, 58* (1947), 297–311.

D	Dyce copy of Q (Victoria and Albert Museum).
Diary	*Henslowe's Diary*, ed. W. W. Greg, 2 vols., London, 1904–08.
Dyce 3	*The Dramatic and Poetical Works of Robert Greene & George Peele*, ed. Alexander Dyce, London, 1861, rep. 1874.
Gummere	*The Old Wives Tale*, ed. F. B. Gummere, in Vol. 1 of *Representative English Comedies*, ed. C. M. Gayley, 4 vols., New York, 1903.
H	Henry E. Huntington Library copy of Q.
Horne	Horne, David H., *The Life and Minor Works of George Peele*, New Haven, 1952.
McIlwraith	McIlwraith, A. K., ed., *Five Elizabethan Comedies*, Oxford, 1934.
Nares	Nares, Robert, *A Glossary*, ed. J. O. Halliwell and T. Wright, 2 vols., London, 1859.
OED	*Oxford English Dictionary*.
P	Pforzheimer copy of Q.
Q	Quarto of 1595.
SD	Stage Direction.
Thompson, *Motif*	Thompson, Stith, *Motif-Index of Folk-Literature*, Bloomington, Ind., 1955 (cited by Motif number, e.g., Motif F601).
Thompson, *Types*	Thompson, Stith, *The Types of the Folk-Tale*, Helsinki, 1961 (cited by Type number, e.g., Type 450).
Tilley	Tilley, Morris P., *A Dictionary of the Proverbs in England in the Sixteenth and Seventeenth Centuries*, Ann Arbor, Mich., 1950.

Unless noted otherwise, references to Shakespeare are to the Yale edition, references to Jonson are to the Herford and Simpson edition, references to Chaucer are to the Robinson edition, and references to Nashe are to the McKerrow edition; Greene's plays are cited from Malone Society Reprints, and citations of Peele are to Volumes 1 and 2 and the present volume of the Yale edition. Classical authors are cited from the Loeb Classical Library editions.

Throughout, *The Old Wives Tale* is printed without an apostrophe, a convention that derives from Q. Wherever the title appears in quotations from scholarly works, it has been silently emended to bring it into conformity with this convention.

INTRODUCTION

1. AUTHORSHIP, DATE, AND STAGE HISTORY

The earliest edition of *The Old Wives Tale* has on its title page the legend "Written by G. P." For two hundred years the play was said to be anonymous by all commentators except Edward Phillips, who through a misreading of Francis Kirkman's catalog (1661) attributed both it and *Orlando Furioso* to one Thomas May, and William Winstanley, who followed Phillips in his error. In 1782 Isaac Reed, compiling his revision of David Erskine Baker's *Biographia Dramatica*, remarked of the still anonymous play, "I am informed, it is in the collection of a gentleman now residing in London, but it has not fallen in my way to see it" (2, 262). Before his edition was published, Reed apparently managed to get a look at the London gentleman's copy, for in "Additions and Corrections to the Second Volume" (2, 441), he reprinted the title page, adding after the author's initials "i.e., George Peele." Reed was thus the first to attribute *The Old Wives Tale* to Peele in print; the suggestion for the attribution evidently came to him from George Steevens.[1]

1. Details are given in T. Larsen, "The Growth of the Peele Canon," *The Library*, Ser. 4, *11* (1930), 301–302, 305–306, and Robert H. Wilson, "Reed and Warton on the Old Wives Tale," *PMLA*, *55* (1940), 605–608. After discussing Reed's 1782 entry, Larsen says that the "play was formally added to the canon" in Egerton's *Theatrical Remembrancer* (London, 1788). This is evidently a technicality based upon the point that Reed's attribution is in an appendix. But *Theatrical Remembrancer* (p. 9) merely lists the titles of the plays attributed to Peele; it adds nothing to Reed. Moreover, Egerton's attribution was anticipated by Thomas Warton's description of the play in his edition of Milton's *Poems upon Several Occasions* (London, 1785), but, as Wilson shows, Warton is plagiarizing from

Since 1782 no one apparently has wished to deny that Peele wrote the play, but that need not count for much since a considerable portion of the history of Elizabethan drama is the perpetuation of guesses. Curiously enough, there has not been, so far as I am aware, any attempt to judge the accuracy of the Reed-Steevens attribution. Except for the initials "G. P." on the title page, there is no external evidence. Yet the internal evidence for Peele's authorship is, if not overwhelming, at least convincing.

One may advance, first of all, certain verbal echoes of other undisputed Peele compositions. The phrase "these chalkie Cliffs of Albion" (l. 132), a favorite with Peele, also appears in the holograph of *Anglorum Feriae* (l. 43) and with minor variations in l. 3 of *A Farewell* and l. 183 of *Polyhymnia*. The phrase "loadstar of my life" (l. 434) is similar to "loadstarre of my delight" in *Edward I* (l. 938).[2]

In addition to verbal parallels, there is a certain duplication of manner to be noted between *The Old Wives Tale* and *Edward I*. In the introduction to *Edward I* (p. 53), I remarked that a characteristic of Peele's style is his use of the various figures of repetition. In *The Old Wives Tale* this characteristic style recurs, as in the extended use of anadiplosis in ll. 137–139:

> O fortune cruell, cruell and unkind,
> Unkind in that we cannot find our sister;
> Our sister haples in hir cruell chance,

Reed. One detail in Larsen needs correction. He says that Stephen Jones, in his 1812 edition of *Biographia Dramatica*, follows Reed, but does not include the play in the canon. In fact, Jones expands Reed's list of four plays assigned to Peele by including *The Old Wives Tale* after *Edward I* (1^2, 565).

2. See note to l. 434. There are other minor similarities between *The Old Wives Tale* and *Edward I:* cf. "runs madding" (l. 198) and "ranne madding" (l. 839) with "that makes me madding run" in *Edward I*, l. 1110; cf. "what all amort" (l. 1) with *Edward I*, l. 1127. The use of "good countriman" in its comic context at ll. 266 ff. is rather like the repetition of the phrase at ll. 401 ff. in *Edward I*. At l. 847, in pert response to the rubric of Eumenides ("God speed faire maide sitting alone"), Delya says, "Not so good sir, for you are by." Both in point and in tone this exchange is similar to Elinor's retort to Mortimer in *Edward I*, ll. 1331–34.

or the anaphora in l. 135:

> To seeke our sister, to seeke faire Delya forth.

Related to anaphora is the figure in l. 432:

> Tell me Time, tell me just Time,

which F. G. Hubbard describes as "repetition of a word or words with an added epithet." Of this figure Hubbard says: "This is a very rare form; I have found it outside Peele's work only in *Misfortunes of Arthur* (three times), *1st Henry VI* (once), and *Locrine* (ten times); in Peele I have noted eighteen cases." [3] The use of this, as well as other figures of repetition, strongly supports the case for Peele.[4]

In *The Old Wives Tale* each of the prophecies uttered by Erestus is repeated by the hearers, as if to impress them upon the minds of the audience.[5] The same technique is used in *Edward I* with the prophecy of the Welsh Harper (ll. 516–533). The use of jingling verse for the prophecies also has its parallel in *Edward I*.[6] The jingles involving dog Latin at ll. 281–284 may be compared with ll. 1376–77 of *Edward I*. In both plays there are frequent descents into rhyme, though one would hardly call the passages verse. Finally, for what it is worth, one may note that there is a perfectly gratuitous slap—slight though it may be—at Spain in l. 364 and again in l. 385, which suits well with a point of view that made her Spanish ancestry a primary element of the villainy of the proud Queen Elinor in *Edward I*. The Friar is also described as a "knave infinit" (l. 388), which agrees with the portrayal of Friar

---

3. "Repetition and Parallelism in the Earlier English Drama," *PMLA*, 20 (1903), 373. Hubbard gives no references, but I find the following instances of the device in Peele's work: *Alcazar*, ll. 43–44, 113–114, 175–176, 233–234, 382, 976–977, 1157, 1221, 1227; *Araygnement*, l. 980; *David*, ll. 329–330, 1128–29, 1378–79, 1529, 1534–35, 1586–87; *Edward I*, ll. 112, 581, 585, 599, 646, 765–766, 852, 916, 934, 1457, 2022, 2055, 2097, 2445, 2606; *Anglorum Feriae*, l. 113; *A Farewell*, ll. 23, 50; *Polyhymnia*, l. 263.

4. For other figures of repetition see ll. 433–435, 687–689.

5. See ll. 158–174, 445–453.

6. Cf. ll. 329–332 and passages just cited with *Edward I*, ll. 455–463, 516–533, 2378–91.

David in *Edward I* and the anticatholicism of *The Battle of Alca-zar*.

Thus the internal evidence supports the conjecture based upon the initials on the title page. I think we need not doubt that Peele was the author of *The Old Wives Tale*.

Of the date of composition one cannot, unfortunately, be so certain. The *terminus ad quem* is provided by entry in the Stationers' Register on April 16, 1595 (Arber, *2*, 296):

Raphe Hancock   Entred for his Copie vnder th[e h]andes of bothe the wardens a booke or interlude intituled *a pleasant Conceipte called the owlde wifes tale* . . . . vj^d.

Except for this entry, there is not much to go on. The information on the title page that *The Old Wives Tale* was "played by the Queenes Maiesties players" gives little assistance. The Queen's Men were founded in 1583. If the Symons connection with the play is valid, which seems unlikely (see below, Sec. 4), it could not have been written for the company before he joined it in 1588 (Chambers, *2*, 111). In 1591 two touring companies are recorded under the name of Queen's (ibid., p. 112), which might be significant if one accepted the theory that the extant text was prepared for provincial performances. But since the company toured the provinces every summer, one cannot argue the point with much conviction. From about 1591 the company appears to have been in trouble, and Henslowe tells us on May 8, 1594, that the Queen's players "broke & went into the contrey to playe" (Chambers, *2*, 114; *Diary*, *1*, 4); they can be traced in the provinces until the end of Elizabeth's reign. After 1594 a number of their plays, including *The Old Wives Tale*, were printed. Historians have said, plausibly enough, that financial difficulties led to the sale of playbooks, but this is merely conjecture. We do not know enough about how plays fell into the hands of publishers to do any more than guess. If we assume that the Queen's Men would not buy plays after breaking early in 1594, we can move the latest possible date for the play back to 1593. The Queen's company connection can carry us no further.

One clue that provides more promise than substance is the relationship between *The Old Wives Tale* and Greene's *Orlando Furioso*. The two share one passage too close to be coincidence (see note to ll. 853–856) and another phrase which is no doubt traditional (see note to l. 657). The name Sacrapant (spelled differently) is common to both. Though it is impossible to be absolutely certain which was the borrower, the shared passage seems somewhat more at home in Greene's context,[7] and, since there is ample evidence elsewhere that Peele was an eclectic and imitative writer, we probably will be right to assume that Greene's is the original. I would not wish to press the argument too far, but Peele's Sacrapant possibly owes something to Greene's character. Among the liberties Greene took with Ariosto's story is the transformation of Sacrepant into a villain, who pursues Angelica and by his treachery brings on Orlando's madness. Peele goes one step further and turns Sacrapant into a particular kind of villain: a sorcerer who ensnares the fair heroine by his enchantments. It should be noted, however, that the ludicrous self-conceit of Greene's Sacrepant brings the character closer to Peele's Huanebango than to his sorcerer. Certainly the two plays are so closely related that one might hope to date the one by dating the other. Unfortunately, no precise date can be assigned to *Orlando Furioso*. A clear Armada reference (ll. 90–96) allows us to place it after mid–1588,[8] and a record of a performance at the Rose sets a terminal date of February 1592 (*Diary, 1,* 13). Baldwin argues at length for a date "after the Armada, August, 1588, but before *Bacon,* the summer of 1589" (p. 78), and he may very well be right. But his argument, far too intricate to review here, with its display of erudition that awes the reader into submission as much as it convinces him, may disguise a crucial point: it depends upon assumptions about the relationship of recurring images in Greene's work that cannot be proved

7. Harold M. Dowling, "The Date and Order of Peele's Plays," *Notes and Queries, 164* (1933), 183, argues convincingly that the itinerary outlined in the speech is suited to Mandrecard's journey in *Orlando,* but not for the trip from Thessaly to England in Peele's play. His conclusion is supported by the learned—and one may safely, I think, call it definitive—discussion of the point by Baldwin (pp. 61–64).

8. Noted by C. M. Gayley (Gummere, *1,* 408–411). The careful student will agree that the rest of Gayley's argument is worthless.

beyond question. About the only thing that seems quite certain is that both *Orlando* and *The Old Wives Tale* are post-Armada pieces.

Argument based upon the spelling of Sacrapant's name is worthless. In the introduction to his Malone Society Reprint (1908) of *The Old Wives Tale*, W. W. Greg argues that the question of priority of the two plays "is settled by the name Sacrapant in the *Tale*, corresponding to Sacrepant in *Orlando*. Greene, of course, took the name from Ariosto (Sacripante), and Peele must therefore have borrowed from Greene" (p. vii). Why Peele, who quoted a passage in Italian from Ariosto in *Edward I* (ll. 2588–91) and therefore must have known the original, could not have derived Sacrapant from the original Sacripante as well as from Greene's Sacrepant is not explained. But the problem is complicated by the fact that we do not know for sure how Greene spelled the name. In the printed text it is Sacrepant, but in the Alleyn manuscript of Orlando's part, the name is Sacrapant,[9] as it is in the Harington translation published in 1591. Greg later said that Greene must have copied Harington (*Abridgements*, p. 126), but his argument is negated by the fact that in *Perimedes* (1588) Greene had already used the name and spelled it Sacrapant.[10] This latter work has been cited as a possible source for Peele's play. While I consider the possibility remote (see below, Sec. 3. A.), one must admit that Peele could have encountered the spelling he uses either in *Perimedes*, in some manuscript version of *Orlando*, or in Harington. It seems to me most likely that Greene, Harington, and Peele independently anglicized Ariosto's Sacripante in the same way. Whatever theory one inclines to, it is clear that the possibilities cancel one another out, and no argument for dating *The Old Wives Tale* can be based upon the spelling of Sacrapant.

The easiest and most obvious way of accounting for the relationship between the two plays would be to assume that Peele used the 1594 quarto of Greene's play. *Orlando* was originally entered in the Stationers' Register on December 7, 1593, but on May 28,

9. See ll. 355, 359, 404, 494 in Greg's edition (*Abridgements*).

10. Robert Greene, *The Life and Complete Works in Prose and Verse*, ed. A. B. Grosart (London, 1878), 7, 83.

1594, figured in a transfer (Arber, 2, 641, 650). Presumably, therefore, the play was not printed before June 1594. Peele might have
seen the quarto and written his own play before the end of the
year. The chief problem with this explanation is that just before
Orlando was printed, the Queen's Men went bankrupt and retired
to the country. It is unlikely, therefore, that a play written late in
1594 would belong to the Queen's Men. But if Peele did not use
the printed text, how are we to account for the common passage?
One may always call into use that "widely circulated manuscript"
that figures so often in the history of Elizabethan literature, and
one might support the theory by the fact that in at least one manuscript Sacrapant's name was spelled in the way Peele was to spell
it. It is also barely possible that Peele himself is not responsible for
the common passage. The extant text has long been considered a
curtailed version prepared for playing in the provinces; such a
theory allows for the intrusion of alien material. About the curtail-
ment I argue quite differently below (Sec. 4); the reader must
judge for himself. But whatever his decision, it is clear that the relationship between *The Old Wives Tale* and *Orlando Furioso* does
not give any firm basis for dating either play.

A final argument rests upon the identification of Huanebango as
a satiric portrait of Gabriel Harvey. This problem is sufficiently
important to warrant special treatment, and in the next section I
shall endeavor to show that there is really no basis for the view
that Harvey is the original of Huanebango. But because my challenge to it may not be accepted, we shall here explore the implications of the orthodox view for dating the play.

What is beyond question is that in ll. 646 ff. Peele is poking fun
at efforts to torture the English language into the pattern of the
classical hexameter. In l. 647 he parodies the strange vocabulary of
one notorious attempt, Stanyhurst's translation of the *Aeneid*, and
in l. 654 he quotes a hexameter from Harvey's "Encomium Lauri."
Cheffaud (pp. 121–128), arguing that the quotation (with other
evidence to be examined in the next section) proves that Huanebango is Gabriel Harvey, suggests that the occasion of the caricature was the quarrel between the Harvey brothers and Lyly in
1589–91 and that the play was probably written in 1591.

Accepting Cheffaud's identification of Huanebango with Harvey
but denying his conclusions about the occasion, Thorleif Larsen
argues that because there is no evidence that Peele was a friend of
Lyly and because the Harvey-Lyly quarrel was a private affair,
Peele would have had no occasion to join the fray. Further, if the
attack by Peele had come before 1592, surely Harvey would have
answered; after that, Harvey was busy dealing with Greene and
Nashe. Larsen then argues that Peele's attack is a part of the
Harvey-Greene-Nashe imbroglio in 1592–93 and that the attack
on Harvey as a hexametrist establishes the position of the play in
the affair. In *Foure Letters* (1592) Harvey laid claim to fame as
the inventor of the English hexameter and spoke admiringly of
Stanyhurst. Nashe responded in *Strange Newes* by ridiculing Harvey's hexameter effusions. Peele is following Nashe's lead. Therefore, *The Old Wives Tale* "must have been written between January, 1593, when Nashe published his *Strange Newes*, and May,
1594, when the Queen's Company left London for the last time." [11]

In his edition of the play Blair accepts Larsen's argument except
for the conclusion that Peele was following Nashe's lead. Since no
connection is made between Harvey and Stanyhurst in *Strange
Newes*, Blair concludes that Peele was operating on his own and
that the best we can say is that the play was written after Harvey's
claim in *Foure Letters* that he was the father of the hexameter.
This, according to Blair (p. 12), moves Larsen's earliest date back
to December 1592. Actually, he might have moved the date back
to September, for, although *Foure Letters* was entered on December 4, it was apparently published earlier.[12]

All this argument is very ingenious, and that perhaps is its great
fault: it is too ingenious to be convincing. Even if one accepted
the identification of Huanebango with Harvey, there seems no
reason to assume that Peele could not have made fun of Harvey as

11. T. Larsen, "The Date of Peele's *Old Wives Tale*," *Modern Philology*,
30 (1932), 23–28.

12. F. R. Johnson, "The First Edition of Gabriel Harvey's *Foure Letters*," *The Library*, Ser. 4, *15* (1934–35), 212–223; "Gabriel Harvey's *Three
Letters*: A First Issue of His *Foure Letters*," *The Library*, Ser. 5, *1* (1946),
134–136.

a hexametrist without having a leader to follow. The argument over the advisability of using classical meters in English had been going on for about half a century,[13] and Harvey had been involved in the discussion publicly ever since the appearance of *Three proper, and wittie, familiar Letters* in 1580; indeed, it is from a poem in that early work of Harvey's that Peele quotes the line in the play. Peele was a learned man, a poet, doubtless interested in the great critical debate of his day, and I see no reason why he could not have identified Harvey with that debate at any time after 1580. It seems clear that we will not be able to date *The Old Wives Tale* by relating it to the Harvey-Nashe affair.

To sum up, one can say with certainty no more than that the play is a post-Armada piece written before its entry in the Stationers' Register in 1595, probably before the Queen's Men left London in 1594.

Little as we know about the date, we know even less about the play's stage history. For the early period, we have only the statement on the title page that it was "played by the Queenes Maiesties players." The first recorded performance was in 1911 at Middlebury College; the text used for that performance was printed a few years later.[14] Professors Parrott and Ball refer to a performance at Bryn Mawr.[15] Doubtless some other college theaters have tried the play, but their efforts have not come to my attention.[16]

2. HUANEBANGO AND GABRIEL HARVEY

The identification of Huanebango with Gabriel Harvey may, without undue exaggeration, be described as orthodox, even though not all critics have accepted it. But since those who do not accept it merely ignore it or, at best, make a brief statement, it seems advis-

13. *Cambridge History of English Literature*, 3, 333. See also R. B. McKerrow, "The Use of So-Called Classical Meters in Elizabethan Verse," *Modern Language Quarterly* (London), 4 (1901), 172–180; 5 (1902), 6–12.

14. *The Old Wives Tale*, ed. Frank W. Cady (Boston, 1916).

15. *A Short View of Elizabethan Drama* (New York, 1943), p. 68.

16. After this section was written, the play was performed in 1965 at the Tufts University Arena Theatre by The Magic Circle, the children's acting company.

able to review the evidence and attempt to set a perturbed spirit to rest.[1]

There are two undeniable satiric portraits of Harvey. Nashe, indeed, did such an effective job of depicting Harvey as a silly ass that only recently are students coming to a more just estimate of Harvey's place in Renaissance literature.[2] Nashe's Harvey is a lean, meager, swarthy man with a sparse beard (McKerrow, *3*, 38, 93, 129). He is vain about this unprepossessing appearance (*3*, 68), vain about his association with the great men of the time (*1*, 294), vain about his family and their accomplishments (*1*, 257). The

1. Dyce was the first to suggest "that Peele intended to ridicule and mortify Harvey" (Dyce *3*, p. 342), but he is referring only to the quotation of the line from "Encomium Lauri"; he does not further identify Huanebango with Harvey. The first to suggest that "Huanebango . . . is palpably Harvey" was F. C. Fleay (*A Biographical Chronicle of the English Drama 1559–1642*, London, 1891, *2*, 155). But Fleay's evidence is limited to the quoted line from "Encomium Lauri" and his preposterous "translation" of the comic names in Huanebango's pedigree. It was left for Cheffaud to develop the case fully. The identification has been accepted by virtually everyone who has discussed the play in any detail. Notable exceptions are Crow (p. 308) and Bradbrook (p. 324). Chambers, with characteristic caution, says only, "The hexameters of Huanebango are a burlesque of Gabriel Harvey" (*3*, 461). Neither *CHEL* nor C. S. Lewis in the *Oxford History of English Literature* mentions Peele in connection with Harvey.

2. The rehabilitation of Harvey began with R. B. McKerrow's balanced discussion in his edition of Nashe (*5*, 65–110). This is the classic account of the great quarrel; all subsequent scholars have started from McKerrow's version, and I am heavily indebted to it. G. C. Moore Smith continued the work in *Gabriel Harvey's Marginalia* (Stratford-upon-Avon, 1913). The most recent treatment of the quarrel is an excellent lively account in G. R. Hibbard, *Thomas Nashe* (Cambridge, 1962), chap. 7. For further efforts to show that Harvey was something more than a bumptious pedant, see P. A. Duhamel, "The Ciceronianism of Gabriel Harvey," *Studies in Philology, 49* (1952), 155–170; H. Oppel, "Gabriel Harvey," *Shakespeare-Jahrbuch, 82–83* (1946–47), 34–51; D. Perkins, "Issues and Motivations in the Nashe-Harvey Quarrel," *Philological Quarterly, 39* (1960), 224–233; H. S. Wilson, *Gabriel Harvey's Ciceronianus*, University of Nebraska Studies in the Humanities, No. 4 (1945); H. S. Wilson, "The Humanism of Gabriel Harvey," *John Quincy Adams Memorial Studies* (Washington, 1948), pp. 707–721; H. S. Wilson, "Gabriel Harvey's Orations in Rhetoric," *Journal of English Literary History, 12* (1945), 167–182.

family background is one of Nashe's chief weapons, for over and over again he reminds his victim that his father is a ropemaker, and Harvey seems to have been touchy about this humble calling. Harvey was also vain about his literary ventures, for which Nashe, justly enough no doubt, puts him in the pillory. His "ill english Hexameters" (*1*, 278) are ridiculed, and he is coupled with the unfortunate Dr. Stanyhurst (*1*, 299):

> Master *Stannyhurst* (though otherwise learned) trod a foule lumbring boystrous wallowing measure, in his translation of *Virgil*. He had neuer been praisd by *Gabriel* for his labour, if therein hee had not bin so famously absurd.

Nashe ridicules (*3*, 66) other stylistic tricks, especially the use of the Ciceronian clausulae: [3]

> Some there be (I am not ignorant) that, vpon his often bringing it in at the end of euerie period, call him by no other name but *esse posse videatur*.

And Harvey's own rather charming confession of his Ciceronian sins suggests that Nashe did not exaggerate.[4]

Such a character seems created for the comic stage. Indeed, it was no secret that Harvey was the model for the chief character in *Pedantius*, a play that had been performed at Cambridge probably in 1581, though not published until fifty years later.[5] The play is in the manner of Roman comedy. Its chief characters are, as Moore Smith has demonstrated (pp. xxvii ff.), Renaissance additions to or adaptations of classical types. As the name indicates, the hero's main characteristic is his pedantry; as a lover, he preposterously includes references to points of grammar in his discourses on love (e.g., ll. 861–876). Pedantius is also a satiric portrait of the

3. In rhetoric, the rhythm pattern of the ending of a period: "Those Orators that lived about his [Cicero's] age, reproved also in him the curious care he had of a certaine long cadence, at the end of his clauses, and noteth these words, *Esse videatur*, which he so often useth" (Montaigne, *Essays*, tr. Florio, ii.10, ed. T. Seccombe, London, 1908, *2*, 121–122).

4. *Harvey's Ciceronianus*, ed. Wilson, pp. 63 ff.

5. *Pedantius*, ed. G. C. Moore Smith, p. iii, in *Materialen zur Kunde des älteren Englischen Dramas*, ed. W. Bang, Vol. 8 (Louvain, 1905). This edition of the play is the one cited throughout.

Ciceronian. His speeches are a pastiche of phrases culled from authors favored by the Renaissance humanists, particularly Tully. This Ciceronian dialogue is interlarded with quotations from Harvey's own work.[6] Pedantius is extremely vain. The plot contains situations that hit at Harvey's pretensions to court preferment. The piece is brilliant and devastating, and there seems no reason to doubt Nashe's statement (3, 80) that its effect was enhanced in production by having the actor dress like Harvey and mimic his mannerisms in both action and speech.

In these two satiric representations of Harvey there is a remarkable consistency. One feels, indeed, that Nashe could have created his Harvey from having seen the play and without ever actually knowing the man.

Huanebango does not resemble this figure in the least. Like Pedantius, he is a stock character—but not the same one. He descends from that long line of military braggarts which stems ultimately from Plautus; that Peele was quite aware of this direct connection appears in the Plautine names given to Huanebango's ancestors. The character is sketched so briefly that it seems idle to argue about the possibility that it is more akin to the Italian adaptations than to the classical original. But there is no question that it is in the braggart tradition.[7] From what we know of Harvey's life and from what we see in two comic renditions, there seems no reason to suppose that someone wishing to use him as a satiric butt would naturally make him a huffing character. The pedant is the obvious stock character to start with, and there is nothing of the pedant in Huanebango.[8] Moreover, as far as I can see, Huane-

6. E.g., "Cogit amare jecur" (l. 1079), which is a quotation from *Gratulationum Valdensium*, IV; the reference to "Tusculano meo" (l. 2903), which parallels Harvey's reference to Saffron Walden as "in Tusculano nostro" in *Ciceronianus* (ed. Wilson), p. 44. See also Moore Smith's notes to ll. 1073, 2368, and 2426, among others.

7. That tradition includes the long train of huffing characters in the mystery and morality plays and in the ritual St. George plays. See below, Sec. 3. G.

8. This seems to me the case despite the assertion to the contrary by T. Larsen, " 'The Old Wives Tale' by George Peele," *Transactions of the Royal Society of Canada, 29* (1935), 160.

bango gives no evidence of being painted from life; everything that he does or says can be traced either to the ruffler tradition from which he comes or to the folklore milieu in which he operates throughout the play.

The burden of proof, of course, is upon those who would identify Huanebango with Harvey. The most elaborate argument is that of Cheffaud; the case which generations of scholars have taken as proved can reasonably be said to stand or fall with it. For convenience of reference and clarity I enumerate Cheffaud's points:

(1) His first, and indisputable, point is that one of Harvey's hexameters is put into the mouth of Huanebango (l. 654). The significance is debatable, however. It seems clear that in this passage Peele is taking a position in the argument about the use of hexameters in English. What is held up to ridicule is not a particular author but the whole preposterous idea of writing verse as if English were Latin. Huanebango begins, in the best fashion of the modern structural linguist, with a nonsense hexameter—to define the "beat," as it were; in l. 647 he parodies the strange language of Stanyhurst's *Aeneid;* there follow three original lines that are splendidly ridiculous. Only in the next speech does he quote Harvey. In all, there are seven hexameters, one of which makes fun of Stanyhurst and one of which quotes Harvey. Is it not reasonable to assume that Peele is more concerned with ridiculous poetry than with particular authors? (See note to l. 647.) In *2 Henry IV* (II.4.192) Shakespeare puts a fatuous line from Peele's *Battle of Alcazar* into the mouth of Pistol, but no one has ever argued that Pistol is, therefore, a caricature of George Peele.

(2) Huanebango's prose, like his verse, is an attack on Harvey's "lourdes périodes contournées," "rhétorique pompeuse," "étrange vocabulaire." As evidence, Cheffaud cites ll. 321–323: "whoo he comes uppon me with a superfantiall substance, and the foyson of the earth, that I know not what he meanes." The passage is a bit puzzling, but it has generally been interpreted as the clown's ridicule of Huanebango's inflated language. The words are, however, the Clown's, and one may note that Huanebango himself, while a bombastic speaker, is not especially given to strange words in his own dialogue. Cheffaud (p. 122) adds that "le langage par trop

affecté d'Huanebango imite la manière d'Harvey" in *Three Proper,
and wittie, familiar Letters*. He cites no particulars, and I do not see
the similarity. One cannot accept the point as proven.

(3) Cheffaud (p. 122) tells us that "le feu et le soufre, le tonerre
et les éclairs dont il étoffe ses discours" are direct references to a
work on earthquakes which made Harvey the butt of ridicule about
1580. He is referring to the second of the *Three Proper, and wittie,
familiar Letters* and apparently thinking of ll. 263–264 of the play,
but in these lines there is no connection with earthquakes, only a
very real spoof of romance enchanters.

(4) There is a reference to Harvey's ropemaker father. If this
were true, the case would be closed in Cheffaud's favor; but unfortunately his evidence is one of the aberrations of Fleay, who chose
to translate the name of Huanebango's grandfather Polimackeroeplacydus as "Polly-make-a-rope-lass" and his father Pergopolyneo
as "Perg-up-a-line-oh." Fleay knew that the names were from
Plautus, but that did not stop him. Gummere's laconic comment
concluding his note recording this fantasy should suffice: "Mr.
Fleay is bold."

(5) Huanebango has a self-conceit matched only by Harvey's.
The point is undeniable, but, since vanity is not limited to Harvey,
its significance is another matter.

(6) Harvey's love of parading his high connections, especially
his relationship to Sir Thomas Smith, is caricatured in Huanebango.
Cheffaud refers here to ll. 291–294. But the jest seems to lie more in
the preposterous name of Bustegustecerydis than in his connection
with the court. The mouth-filling name is another Plautine touch.
Again the satire, if such it be, is certainly not pointed.

(7) Harvey tells us that his own complexion is dark; in *Gratulationum Valdinensium* he makes much of the Italianate coloring that
brought him to the Queen's attention. Huanebango, according to
Cheffaud, is similarly dark. He cites for authority Zantippa: "Foe,
what greasie groome have wee here? Hee looks as though hee crept
out of the backeside of the well" (ll. 651–652). She may mean
that he is dark, but the dominant impression is dirt. One may also
note that Harvey (following the Queen) spoke of his "vultu Itali,"
but Huanebango, if we may judge by his name (Huan y Bango), is
Spanish. Certainly Cheffaud's point is not a striking one.

(8) Harvey was tall; Huanebango is a giant. The evidence for both points is equivocal. Nashe (3, 38) indicates that Harvey was skinny, but it does not follow that he was tall. Nashe also says (3, 94):

> For his stature, he is such another pretie *Jacke a Lent* as boyes throw at in the streete, and lookes, in his blacke sute of veluet, like one of these ieat droppes which diuers weare at their eares in stead of a iewell.

The dominant characteristic of the Jack-a-Lent seems to have been its meager, spare quality, rather than anything that would justify calling it a giant.[9] Elsewhere Nashe refers to "this *Timothie Tiptoes*" (*1*, 276), which Moore Smith uses as evidence that Harvey was tall. Moore Smith also cites *Pedantius:* "non sum rotundus, sed quadratus" (l. 1652). A pun is apparently involved; the common meaning of "quadratus" is four-sided, but Cooper's *Thesaurus* has these entries: "Corpus quadratum . . . A body well compact and of good stature" and "Quadrati boues grantibus membris . . . great and strong oxen with bigge limbes." Quite possibly Harvey was a big man. The evidence is even less clear for Huanebango, though since Cheffaud everyone has talked as if there were no question about his being a giant. The only evidence I find for calling him a giant is his "Fee, fa, fum," which is the giant's leitmotiv in fairy tales. However, Edgar says it in *King Lear*, but we do not assume therefore that he is disguised as a giant bedlamite. Perhaps critics

---

9. According to W. C. Hazlitt's edition of *Brand's Popular Antiquities* (London, 1905), *2*, 344, the Jack-a-Lent is "a puppet, formerly thrown at, in our country, in Lent"; a Cornish account in 1871 describes it: "a figure, made up of straw and cast-off clothes, was carried around the town, amid much noise and merriment, after which it was either burnt, shot at, or brought to some other ignominious end. This image was called 'Jack o'Lent,' and was doubtless intended to represent Judas Iscariot. A dirty slovenly fellow is often termed a 'Jack o'Lent'." Earlier references imply that the Jack-a-Lent was a skinny, scrawny figure. This is clearly the case in *How a Man may choose a Good Wife from a Bad* (1602), sig. E1ᵛ (Tudor Facsimile Text): "that lean chittiface, that famine, that lean Envy, that all bones, that bare anatomy, that Jack a Lent, that ghost, that shadow." Less definite, but in the same vein, are two references in Jonson (*A Tale of a Tub*, IV.2.49; *The Staple of News*, V.5.35).

have been influenced by the fact that one of the sources of the play, though not of Huanebango, may be the tale of Jack the Giant-Killer. Cheffaud may be right in both cases, but the evidence is not clear, nor is the point a very striking one.

(9) Harvey was a "bon escrimeur" and proud of it; Huanebango always carries his two-hand sword. Cheffaud is apparently referring to Harvey's threat in *Pierce's Supererogation*,[10] which is answered by Nashe (*3*, 134). But the braggart is always armed, and I see no reason to find a specific application in anything so conventional as Huanebango's great sword. If Peele is satirizing Harvey, he is certainly doing it ineptly.[11]

(10) Finally, Harvey was of a "temperament amoureux," though unsuccessful in his pursuits; according to Nashe (*3*, 81) he wrote the first English hexameters for a lady, and Huanebango is excited to hexameter verse by his passion for Zantippa. But all braggarts from Plautus down through Ralph Roister Doister are amorous and unsuccessful. Their passions generally produce extravagant language.[12] We are dealing again with convention.

Such is the argument, which seems to me to be no argument at all. In this I differ from many writers. The most recent treatment of the subject accepts the identification without question and refers to Cheffaud for "convincing arguments."[13] A curiously irrational

10. *The Works of Gabriel Harvey*, ed. A. B. Grosart (London, 1884), *2*, 237.

11. See note to l. 253 SD.

12. Ralph Roister Doister writes verse that is almost as silly as Huanebango's effusions (II.1.33–34).

13. W. Schrickx, *Shakespeare's Early Contemporaries* (Antwerp, 1956), p. 260, n. 2. This weight on Cheffaud's side may not count for much when one considers what Schrickx himself offers as evidence. He would identify Harvey with Huanebango because: "'Appertain' and its derivatives seem to have been deliberately used [in *The Old Wives Tale*] to suggest Harvey to an Elizabethan audience" (p. 26). He is thinking of ll. 283–284, where Booby uses the phrase "*cum apurtinantibus gibletes* and all." The connection with Harvey comes about because in *Pedantius* a character says, " . . . si tradas cum appertinentibus etiam" (l. 648). But *cum appertinentibus*, a variant of *cum pertinentiis suis* ("with its appurtenances"), is a common legal term that occurs again and again in documents relating to transfer of properties. To attempt to connect the term with any individual on the basis of one passing occurrence is simply fantastic.

process occurs when scholars are confronted with an argument like Cheffaud's. Blair is a case in point. After demolishing Cheffaud, he capitulates and summarizes (p. 7):

> Cheffaud's combination of possibilities by itself is far from being conclusive, and acquires strength only by virtue of Dyce's identification of the line from the "Encomium Lauri." Taken in conjunction with Dyce's work, Cheffaud's catalogue is quite impressive, although one may question seriously each separate detail of it; nevertheless, our knowledge that Peele intended Huanebango to be a satirical caricature of Harvey, the prince of pedants, is virtually absolute.

Seldom does one find so naïvely stated what actually underlies many critical judgments of this kind: a sufficient amount of non-evidence can by some mysterious alchemic reaction be transmuted into incontrovertible evidence.

From Cheffaud's catalogue, the only point that can be considered evidence is the quotation of the hexameter from Harvey. This, as has been suggested above, I do not consider sufficient to erect a case upon. One might argue almost as cogently that Huanebango is meant to be Dr. Stanyhurst because his peculiar vocabulary is parodied in l. 647. The glance at the folly of English hexameters is a mere by-blow, having no real relation to the Huanebango character. Huanebango is simply a stock figure adapted from the ruffler tradition for a role in a folklore comedy; no personal satire is involved. Huanebango is not Gabriel Harvey.

3. SOURCES

To anyone who, either as child or parent, has gone through the customary nursery curriculum in fairy tales, much of *The Old Wives Tale* will have a vaguely familiar sound, for it is based upon folk motifs, supplemented with bits and snatches from the vast literature of romance. Study of folk literature is a comparatively new discipline, and the tales with which we are concerned are often not extant in written form earlier than the eighteenth century. This means that our study of Peele's sources will be pervaded by a great degree of uncertainty. On the one hand, we cannot be sure that extant versions of folktales traceable in his plot correspond exactly to those that Peele knew; and, on the other hand, the fact that Peele was working for the most part with an oral literature allows for the introduction of all sorts of alterations, resulting from tricks of memory as much as conscious intent.

To place the matter in the context of Peele's own work, the problem of sources in *The Old Wives Tale* corresponds to the use of traditional lore in the Greenwood sequence of *Edward I* rather than to the use of historical materials in that play or in *The Battle of Alcazar*.[1] Peele's imagination was obviously well-stocked with tales from folklore and romance, which are both composed of motifs susceptible to infinite combination and variety. Peele used the motifs, but his combination and manipulation are original. Even in the few cases where we can with some assurance identify the underlying story, it is misleading to think of it as a book source from which Peele diverged consciously for a specific dramatic purpose.

This point is worth emphasizing because most of the critical commentary dealing with the subject assumes that in this play Peele was attempting to combine a group of tales and that departures from a source are consciously made for some discernible dramatic purpose. Critics proceeding upon this assumption appear to see no difference between the source problem in *The Old Wives Tale* and, let us say, in Shakespeare's history plays. The failure to make a distinction gives an entirely erroneous impression of the manner in which Peele worked. If it were simply a matter of rendering justice to Peele, the problem would be worth investigating, but something even greater is at stake: our understanding and critical judgment of the play must rest ultimately upon the conclusions we reach about the source materials and their use.

For purposes of analysis it is necessary to separate the various strands of the plot. Critics often assume that the play is loosely constructed, but when one attempts to dissect the tissue of narrative, he discovers that it is more closely woven than appears on the surface. Therefore, some of the separations made below are the result of severe wrenching, rather than mere lifting.

1. See my introduction to *Edward I*, Yale ed., *2*, 17–19.

A. THE FRAMEWORK

The first readily separable section of the play is the framework—those portions in which Madge, Clunch, and the pages appear. Cheffaud (p. 107) suggests that Peele got the idea for the framework from Greene's *Perimedes the Blacksmith* (1588). In that book the wife of a smith entertains visitors by telling stories; the woman's name is Delia. In one of the stories a minor character is named Sacrapant, but he has no resemblance to Peele's evil sorcerer.[2] Neither the situation nor the stories resemble in any way the plot of Peele's play. Since we cannot enter Peele's mind, there is, of course, no way of proving or disproving Cheffaud's thesis; but if Peele is here indebted to Greene, it is for no more than the germ of an idea. Moreover, the framework device had a long history in prose and verse narrative before Peele's time and was popular in contemporary English drama. But Peele's use of the framework is unique in the way the play within the play develops out of the surrounding story. This is the only play in which characters act out a tale begun as a narrative in the framework. Perhaps the nearest contemporary approach to Peele's device is the part of the citizen and his wife in *The Knight of the Burning Pestle* (1607), but one must really wait for the twentieth century and the extensive use of flashback in movies to find an exact parallel.

B. THE ABDUCTED MAIDEN

The first portion of the play within the play that can be detached for purposes of discussion is the series of events revolving around the abduction and enchantment of Delya and the quest for her. Several writers have suggested that the source underlying this part of the plot is the story of Childe Rowland.[3] In that story the sister,

2. See above, Sec. 1.
3. The most elaborate argument is that of Friedrich Brie, "Das Märchen von Childe Rowland und sein Nachleben," *Anglica*, 2 (1925), 118–143 (published as *Palaestra*, No. 148). Brie argues that Peele used the Childe Rowland story; that Christopher Middleton's romance, *The Famous Historie of Chinon of England* (1597), shows a dependence upon both the Childe Rowland story and Peele's play; and, finally, that Milton used both the old story and the play in *Comus*. The argument does not seem to me to be convincing. See also Gummere, p. 345; Sarah L. Clapp, "Peele's Use

Burd Ellen, who has been carried off by fairies to the king of Elf-land, is sought by her brothers in turn. When the two elder do not return from the quest, the youngest, Childe Rowland, acting on advice from the warlock Merlin, goes to find her. By following Merlin's injunctions to kill everyone who speaks to him in Elfland and to avoid taking any food, Childe Rowland evades the enchant-ments of the place. When the Elfking confronts him

> With, *fi, fi, fo,* and *fum!*
> I smell the blood of a Christian man!
> Be he dead, be he living, wi' my brand
> I'll clash his harns frae his harn-pan,

Childe Rowland defeats the king in combat and forces him to restore not only the sister but also the two elder brothers, who, not having the good offices of Merlin, have also fallen prey to the en-chantments of Elfland.[4]

There is, of course, some similarity between Peele's plot and this folktale, but the differences are more impressive. In the play Delya is carried off by a sorcerer, disguised as a dragon, who is motivated by love. Burd Ellen is transported by fairies; the motivation is not clear. The nature of Delya's enchantment renders her a kind of slave to her abductor and causes her to lose her memory. Burd Ellen, though completely in the power of the Elfking, does nothing corresponding to Delya's fetching water or goading her brothers at work; she recognizes her brother when he appears before her, though she is powerless to aid or advise him. Delya's two brothers go together on the quest; Burd Ellen's three brothers travel singly. Delya's brothers are made slaves, but they do not appear to be enchanted otherwise. Burd Ellen's older brothers are in a trance when Childe Rowland appears. Delya's rescue is effected, not by a

of Folk-Lore in *The Old Wives Tale,*" *University of Texas Studies in English, 6* (1926), 148; and C. S. Adams, "The Tales in Peele's *Old Wives Tale," Midwest Folklore, 13* (1963), 17–18.

4. I follow here the oldest extant version as given by R. Jamieson in *Illustrations of Northern Antiquities* (Edinburgh, 1814), pp. 398–403. This is the source underlying the more familiar version in Joseph Jacobs, *English Fairy Tales* (3rd ed. rev., New York, n.d.), pp. 122–129.

brother, but by a servant of her lover. Sacrapant is destroyed; the Elfking is only defeated.

One way of describing the relation between the two plots is to say that the substance is similar but virtually all the accidents have been changed; in other words, we may be dealing with a case of literary transubstantiation. Folklorists are, of course, particularly concerned with substances (which they call motifs or types), but by the time the accidents have all been changed, often only a trained folklorist can see the substantial similarity—and Elizabethan dramatists were not folklorists. The dramatist—and therefore the student of sources—is properly concerned with accidents. In other words, I do not for a moment think Peele started to tell the tale of Childe Rowland, for the only thing shared by the tale and Peele's plot is the sister, lost through magic arts, being sought by three people. And here we are dealing with motifs common in folklore and romance. The abducted princess occurs in many tales,[5] and romances have even more instances (see, for example, *Orlando Furioso*, 8.29 and 26.128). The amnesia motif (Motif D2000, Magic Forgetfulness) occurs in a number of folktales, but under quite dissimilar circumstances. Three searchers on a quest is a motif so common that documentation would be idle, but Peele has mixed in a touch of romance by making the third searcher a lover. Thus, even though one admits that the play and Childe Rowland share a number of motifs, they share nothing unique.

Nor am I impressed by the argument that Erestus, the man-bear who gives prophecies and advice, is the counterpart of Merlin in the Childe Rowland story.[6] Stripped of his transformation, Erestus is one of the most common figures in folk stories. At every cross-roads he stands, waiting to aid kindly passersby with words of wisdom (Motif N825.2, Old Man Helper). Moreover, Peele had

5. See, e.g., Thompson, Type 301, 302, and especially 312D. In the latter, a sister abducted by a dragon is saved by her youngest brother after the two elder have perished in the quest. Involved here: Motifs R11.1, Princess Abducted by Monster; R111.1.7, Rescue of Princess from Magician; and H1385.1, Quest for Stolen Princess.

6. According to Crow (p. 305), Erestus is "Merlin, who was, according to certain Arthurian legends, the last of England's bears." See also Gummere, p. 345.

already used prophecies in a similar manner in *Edward I* (ll. 455–463; 516–533; 2378–91). The transformation itself is a common motif, though I have found no parallel for the double transformation by which Erestus not only is changed into an old man, so that the aged Sacrapant can enjoy his youth, but is further compelled to be a bear by night.[7] The usual folklore transformation is one in which a man is an animal or monster by day, but resumes his own form by night (Motif D621.1), though the reverse also occurs (Motif D621.1.1). There seems no need to seek any specific source for either the transformation or the prophetic nature of Erestus. However, the coupling of Erestus with the raging Venelia—for, we must remember, this play has not one, but two abducted females—and the enchantments of Sacrapant may suggest that this strand in the plot has a particular story underlying it. If so, no one has yet discovered it.

Nothing in this argument demonstrates—nor is it intended to—that Peele did not know the Childe Rowland story. I am arguing only that Peele is not *telling* the Childe Rowland story (and messing it up in the process). Nor would I wish to deny that the man-bear figure of Erestus has a Merlin connection. I argue merely that the relation, if such there be, is not of Peele's making. The study of this relation is a perfectly proper one for folklore, but it has no bearing on the sources or the interpretation of the play.

C. THE GRATEFUL DEAD

Eumenides brings into the play one of the oldest themes of folk literature, the Grateful Dead. The Grateful Dead is apparently not itself a tale, but a kind of framework within which some half-dozen different stories are told.[8] Here, though, we are concerned more

7. Crow remarks (p. 308): "One comes across everywhere the situation in which the magician takes the youth of a man and gives him his old age and youth returns to the victim when the magician's spells are broken." I have not encountered this motif elsewhere, nor do I find it in Thompson, *Motif*, where entries involving aging do not fit the circumstances here (cf. Motifs Q551.12, Premature Aging as Punishment; D1890, Magic Aging; D1891, Transformation to Old Man to Escape Recognition).

8. The most familiar study of the motif is in Gordon H. Gerould, *The Grateful Dead* (London, 1908), but this has been superseded by Sven Liljeblad, *Die Tobiasgeschichte und andere Märchen von toten Helfern* (Lund,

with the framework than the story imbedded in it, for, curiously enough, nothing more than a point or two from the tale proper survives in the play. In the approximately one hundred and fifty occurrences of the Grateful Dead framework, there are many variations, but scholars agree that the basic motif runs something like this: a kindly traveler arranges for a pauper's burial by paying debts owed by the dead man; at a later stage of his journey the traveler meets a stranger who offers to become his servant; they agree that they will share equally any gains; the prize of the journey is a wife for the hero; the servant demands that she be divided, but withdraws his demand and identifies himself as the ghost of the buried man when the traveler demonstrates his willingness to sacrifice his wife rather than break his promise. The tale proper, which the Grateful Dead motif enfolds, relates how the wife is won. In northern and western Europe, this tale is most frequently the Monster's Bride (Type 507A), the bride who must be released from enchantment before the hero can safely wed her. We need not here go into details of the story proper, except to note that it comes to its climax when the helpful ghost, invisible for the moment, beheads the enchanter with a magic sword. All that remains of this story in the play is Jack's invisibility at the crucial moment and the decapitation of Sacrapant. We will return to these details later.

It is obvious that Peele knew some version, indeed a relatively "pure" one, of the Grateful Dead motif, for his only significant departure from the essentials listed above is that Eumenides pays the parish charges for the burial, rather than debts contracted by the corpse as a living man. This change enables Peele to have a bit of fun with the veniality and selfishness of parish officials. But it is impossible to say precisely where Peele encountered the motif, for the most likely sources either vary or fail to preserve essential elements employed by Peele.

It has been suggested that Peele met the Grateful Dead in the medieval romance *Sir Amadas.*[9] Quite apart from questions that

1927). A convenient résumé of the problem is in Stith Thompson, *The Folktale* (New York, 1951), pp. 50–53.

9. F. Holthausen, "*Sir Amadas* und Peele's *The Old Wives Tale*," *Archiv für das Studium der neueren Sprachen und Literaturen, 119* (1917), 177.

may arise about the availability to Peele of a medieval story which lay in manuscript until the nineteenth century,[10] the motif appears in *Amadas* in a variant form. Although Amadas does spend all his money to bury a stranger's body, the ghost appears, not as a servant, but as a White Knight, who provides money, horse, and armor for Amadas to use in a tournament in which the prize is a king's daughter. Amadas wins, marries the princess, and undergoes the test of his word when the White Knight demands that the wife be divided. Peele's source is surely not the knight-tournament variant [11] but some version in which the ghost acts as a servant and helps win a wife by disenchanting a maiden.

The Grateful Dead in a rather disguised form appears also in one of the most familiar of English folktales, Jack the Giant-Killer, which some have assumed to be Peele's source, though not necessarily in the form that has come down to us.[12] In the extant version Jack encounters King Arthur's son, who is seeking out a beautiful lady possessed by evil spirits (the Monster's Bride theme). The prince spends his last penny to satisfy a group of creditors so that a corpse can be buried. However, no ghost appears. Instead, so impressed is Jack by this act of generosity that he becomes the prince's servant, thus taking upon himself what in purer forms of the tale is the duty of the ghost. By his cleverness, Jack obtains from giants the cloak of invisibility, the shoes of swiftness, and the sword of strength. With these instruments he manages to destroy the enchanter and free the lady, who marries the prince. (This account of winning the lady is a straightforward version, somewhat condensed, of the Monster's Bride.) There is no agreement that spoils will be shared and, hence, no demand that the lady be divided.

10. Laura A. Hibbard, *Mediaeval Romance in England* (New York, 1924), p. 78.

11. Type 508 (The Bride Won in a Tournament) is one class of tales using the Grateful Dead motif; see Gerould, pp. 37–39, and Liljeblad, pp. 39, 58–63.

12. Gummere, p. 345; Gerould, pp. 72–73; Clapp, p. 150. The earliest extant version of Jack the Giant-Killer is a chapbook printed in 1711. It has been reprinted several times. I have used the version in J. O. Halliwell-Phillips, *Popular Rhymes and Nursery Tales* (London, 1849), pp. 67–77, as well as the modernized version in Jacobs, *English Fairy Tales*, pp. 102–116.

The points of contact between the tale and Peele's play should be clear: the prince, like Eumenides, is on a quest for an enchanted lady; both provide for the burial of a corpse (the circumstances differ); both have a helper named Jack, who decapitates an enchanter, thereby freeing the lady. But even more striking are the points of difference: Jack the Giant-Killer has no ghost, no agreement to share the prize, and no demand to divide the lady. These omissions, particularly that of the ghost, cannot have been supplied by any lost version of Jack the Giant-Killer, which has no room in it for a ghost. Instead of being a source, Jack the Giant-Killer is at best an analogue, itself perhaps based on the story Peele knew.

Rather more striking are the similarities between Peele's play and three appearances of the Grateful Dead in Irish stories, each of which contains a better version of the motif than does Jack the Giant-Killer. In "Jack the Master and Jack the Servant," [13] the kindly corpse burier meets a stranger at a crossroads and shares food with him; the stranger becomes the servant Jack. They get the giants' magic properties and save the lady. There is no sharing of spoils; the servant identifies himself as the brother of the buried man. In "The King of Ireland's Son," [14] a prince sets out to find a lady white as snow, red as blood, and black as a raven. He buries a corpse, but does not spend all his money. He acquires servants with special abilities (Type 513; Motif F601, Extraordinary Companions), including a Green Man, who asks the first kiss of his wife. They get the giants' magic properties. The maiden is freed when they bring her the head of the enchanter, but she demands water from the well of the western world. When this is obtained, she still must be disenchanted. The Green Man kisses her and draws out poison serpents. The Green Man identifies himself as the spirit of the dead man, but there is no demand for division of the spoils. In "Beauty of the World," [15] there occur the white-red-black motif, the burial, the search for the lady. The assistant is a red-haired man. The magic properties are obtained from the giants; with them the head of the giant enchanter is procured for the

13. In Patrick Kennedy, *Legendary Fictions of the Irish Celts* (London, 1891), pp. 28–35.

14. In Douglas Hyde, *Beside the Fire* (London, 1890), pp. 19–47.

15. In William Larminie, *West Irish Folk-Tales and Romances* (London, 1890), pp. 155–167.

lady. She is beaten to remove the devils which still possess her. A year later a division of spoils (a child) is called for. The red-haired man identifies himself as the spirit of the dead man.

Scholars have been attracted to these stories as possible sources because they contain motifs besides the Grateful Dead that appear in *The Old Wives Tale*, especially the white as snow and red as blood motif (Z65.1), the stranger at the crossroads, and the sharing of food.[16] However, these motifs are so widespread that one would hardly expect to locate any specific source for them; furthermore, the sharing of food occurs in another story that Peele certainly knew (see below, Sec. 3. F). Fascination with these details must not cause us to overlook an essential point: in the first two Irish tales there is no division of spoils, and in the last the division is not at all like that in the play.

We must conclude, therefore, that while Peele may very possibly have known the Grateful Dead in a version which, like the Irish ones, has the white-red motif, the meeting at the crossroads, and the food sharing, neither these tales nor any of the versions treated above can be considered a source for the play. It follows, I think, that Peele knew some "purer" version of the Grateful Dead motif than any of those preserved in English.[17] I see no reason to doubt that the tale imbedded in the framework, as Peele met it, was the Monster's Bride.[18] We may guess that he discarded all the mechanism of securing the magic properties with which the bride is released because of complications involved in dramatizing and staging this section of the story. Instead he has gathered around the framework other motifs: the quest by the brothers and the

16. Gummere, p. 345; Crow, p. 305.

17. Cf. Hans Dutz, "Der Dank des Todten in der englischen Literatur," *Jahres-Bericht der Staats-Oberrealschule in Troppau für das Schuljahr 1893–1894* (Troppau, 1894), p. 13: "Peeles Quelle für den Dank des Todten wird also ein bis jetzt noch nicht bekannten Märchen gewesen sein."

18. As Gerould (chap. 5) and Liljeblad (pp. 39, 63 ff.) show, the Grate-ful Dead also appears with Type 506, the Rescued Princess. Miss Clapp (pp. 151–152) argues that this compound also underlies Peele's play, but since she admits that "the rescue of an enchanted princess is about all *The Old Wives Tale* has left" of the Rescued Princess as well as of the Monster's Bride, there seems no reason to complicate matters by bringing in still an-other tale.

Magic Providing Purse (Motif D1451; Type 564), the latter a common motif but not elsewhere used in connection with the Grateful Dead.

D. THE GIANT AND THE KING'S DAUGHTER

Scholars have been fond of pointing out that the magic horn which Jack blows is "a touch out of 'Jack the Giant Killer'." [19] This, I think, misses the point. That tale is (like the play) a mélange of motifs—one could almost call it an anthology—and it shares with Peele's play some that have not been hitherto noted. In one of the adventures Jack comes, late at night and lost, to the house of an aged man, who invites him to stop in and upon learning his identity tells him that atop a nearby mountain is an enchanted castle kept by a giant. The giant, aided by an old conjurer, captures knights and ladies and transforms them into various beasts. Above all, there is a duke's daughter, who had been brought to the castle in a chariot drawn by fiery dragons; she is now transformed into a white hind. To gain access to the castle, Jack blows a golden trumpet, which hangs by the gate; the winding of the horn breaks the enchantment. Jack beheads the giant, and the conjurer is carried away in a whirlwind. The castle vanishes, and the prisoners are restored to their proper shapes.

There are points of contact between this portion of Jack the Giant-Killer and both the beginning and end of Peele's play. In the induction to the play one of the pages asks Madge to tell the story of the "Gyant and the Kings Daughter," and she begins to tell a rather disconnected story about a conjurer who turned himself into a dragon "and carried the Kinges Daughter away in his mouth to a Castle that hee made of stone." When the actors enter to act out the story, we learn from Sacrapant himself that Delya is daughter of the King of Thessaly and that he turned himself into a dragon to steal her away. The enchanter is an aged man. At the end of the play Jack twice blows a horn to signal the destruction of the magic light and the end of the enchantment, and he decapitates the enchanter (rather unnecessarily since he is already dead). Thus, scattered through the play are several details clustered in a small portion of Jack the Giant-Killer. That section of the tale is

19. Clapp, p. 149; Crow, p. 308.

very brief, only about two pages, and one suspects that it is a summary of an adventure from one of the romances, like *Huon of Bordeaux*, that were so popular in the sixteenth century. There is something close to an analogue in the magic castle of Atlas in Cantos 2 and 4 of *Orlando Furioso*, a poem that Peele knew well.

Can we then regard this section of Jack the Giant-Killer as a source? Peele has no giant, no enchanted castle, no transformation of the lady. What is left is an aged conjurer who in the guise of a dragon abducts a high-born lady; a magic horn; and a decapitation (though of a different character). Magic horns and decapitation are far too frequent to enable one to rest any case upon them. There remains the striking detail of the circumstances of the lady's abduction to form a close connection between play and tale. This is, I think, symptomatic of much of the source problem in the play. One cannot be sure he is dealing with a specific source, for although there is a striking detail and an interesting cluster of motifs common to both the tale and the play, the circumstances of the story, if it is the source, have been altered beyond recognition. This would suggest that, while the tale might be the germ of Peele's plot, he can hardly be said to be making a serious attempt to retell it.

E. THE DESTRUCTION OF THE ENCHANTER

The peculiar mélange that occurs at the end of the play gives us further clues to Peele's way of working. When Jack and Eumenides arrive before the conjurer's house, Jack stuffs wool into his master's ears so that he will "not be intised with his inchanting speeches" (ll. 800–801). The motif is as old as Homer's account of Odysseus and the sirens, but the precise origin from which Peele imported it into his play cannot be identified. It does not appear as a part of the mechanism of disenchanting the Monster's Bride, although in that story the hero is usually passive (as Eumenides is) while the supernatural agent goes about his business of destruction.

When Sacrapant enters, he speaks to Eumenides, who does not hear him. The conjurer says (l. 808), "Then Sacrapant thou art betraide." Precisely why Sacrapant interprets the deafness of Eumenides as a sign of doom is not clear, but we may be dealing with another motif (perhaps connected with Motif K911.5, Feigning Deafness to Lure Enemy Close and to Kill Him). Then comes this stage direction: *"Enter Jack invisible, and taketh off Sacrapants wreath from his head, and his sword out of his hand."* Sacrapant dies—at some length—when the wreath and sword are removed, as if they are involved in some mysterious way with his life. But his magic persists even after his death until the light is blown out by Venelia. After Sacrapant is dead and the magic light is destroyed, Jack, quite unnecessarily, cuts off his head.

This is all rather strange—as if two versions of the destruction of the enchanter were being fitted together. That is, when Jack gets possession of the sword, we expect him to decapitate Sacrapant, because in the Monster's Bride the hero's agent, having used his magic shoes and cloak of invisibility to get at the demon enchanter, destroys him with the magic sword. Thus it is surprising that the invisible Jack with sword in hand, clearly a residue of the Monster's Bride, merely watches Sacrapant die.

But in view of the preparation earlier in the play, we might have assumed that Sacrapant would expire at the moment the light is extinguished. For although Sacrapant, in announcing that he is to die by a dead man's hand and that his magic will endure as long as the flame burns, actually makes a distinction between his life and his magic, we are dealing with a variant of the life-token, or external soul (Motif E710), in which a person's life is magically bound up with the welfare of something quite outside it.[20] It would not be surprising to see Sacrapant die when Venelia blows out the light, as many an ogre does when his life-token is destroyed, indeed as Sacrapant does in the play when Jack takes the wreath from his head. But things are turned about. When we expect Sacrapant to be beheaded, he merely dies. When we might expect him to die—if, of course, he were not already dead—Jack brings in his head. Two traditional methods of disposing of enchanters or villains are mixed together here.[21] Moreover, they are combined with motifs

20. On the life-token see J. G. Fraser, *The Golden Bough* (New York, 1919), *10*, chaps. 10, 11, and Edwin S. Hartland, *The Legend of Perseus* (London, 1895), *2*, 1–54.

21. Cf. Crow, p. 308. Perhaps some of the confusion is to be traced to problems of staging. Decapitation is, I think, never represented on the Elizabethan stage (for fairly obvious reasons), but the display of heads severed in an offstage decapitation is virtually *de rigueur*, particularly for

(ear-stopping and deafness as an ill omen) brought in from some unknown source.

The confusions in the death of Sacrapant may be connected with the Erestus-Venelia part of the plot, for which no source has been found. Sacrapant seems to be something of a compulsive rake. Not only did he carry Delya away but he abducted Venelia, being, as Erestus tells us, "besotted" with love of her. So at the very start we have not one but two enchanted and abducted females. Venelia's enchantment is a raging madness, and her lover undergoes a dual transformation. At the close Venelia ends the enchantment by blowing out the light. It may be that this Erestus-Venelia-Sacrapant strand is a fossil of an undiscovered tale. Perhaps, then, one might conclude that Peele is telling two stories at once and, in the process, not quite telling either.

One more source of confusion must be noted. When Venelia blows out the magic light, according to the stage direction (l. 843), Jack "*draweth a curten, and there Delia sitteth asleepe.*" Eumenides awakens her by a thrice repeated rubric, "God speed faire maide," obviously intended as a kind of counterspell. The use of this device suggests that the form of Delya's enchantment is the magic trance (like the spell cast upon the brothers in Childe Rowland), but this is quite different from the form of enchantment which she undergoes earlier in the play.

The peculiar mixture of elements represented in the death of Sacrapant and in the disenchantments does not seem to me to be explicable on the assumption that Peele is fitting particular stories together. It is comprehensible, however, if one assumes that the playwright was not telling a particular story of abduction and enchantment with their consequences, but drawing upon familiar folklore motifs stored in his memory since childhood.

F. THE HEADS IN THE WELL

To complete our examination of the main narrative strands in Peele's play, we must move into the subplot. The fate of the

---

rebels and other such deep-dyed villains (see *Edward I*, l. 2673, where a head most mysteriously and inappropriately appears). Given the folklore tradition and the stage convention, it was inevitable that we should be treated to the sight of Sacrapant's severed head. But *when* is it cut off?

daughters of Lampriscus points with reasonable clarity to the story of "The Princess of Colchester," usually called in modern versions "The Three Heads in the Well." [22] In this story a king has a daughter beautiful and kind; he marries a woman who has a daughter ugly and surly. When life with her new stepmother becomes unbearable, the beautiful daughter sets out from home with a bag of coarse food. This food she shares with an old man, who gives her a magic wand and advises her to do exactly as requested when she encounters the heads in the well. With the aid of the wand, the girl easily penetrates a thick hedge and seats herself by the well. One after another three heads arise, asking her to comb them and lay them down softly on the bank to dry. This she does, and they reward her by making her even more beautiful and sweet. Proceeding on her journey, she encounters a prince who is so struck by her beauty that he marries her. When her stepsister hears of this good fortune, she sets out on the same journey. She refuses rudely to share her food with the old man, who curses her. With great difficulty she climbs through the hedge and seats herself by the well. As the heads arise, she bangs each with a bottle. The heads cause her to be struck by leprosy, and she wanders on to a town where she meets a poor cobbler who offers to cure the leprosy if she will marry him. She agrees, and when she is cured and married, she returns to her father's court. Her mother, enraged at this stroke of fortune, hangs herself, and the king pays the cobbler to take his wife to a remote part of the kingdom.

It is apparent that Peele knew this story,[23] even though he has

22. I have used the version in Edwin S. Hartland, *English Fairy and Other Folk Tales* (London, n.d.), pp. 20–24, which is said to be printed from a chapbook, *The History of the Four Kings of Canterbury, Colchester, Cornwall, and Cumberland, their Queens and Daughters* (Falkirk, 1823). The story is retold by Jacobs, pp. 232–237. It is one of many variants of Type 480, the Kind and Unkind Girls.

23. One cannot, of course, be sure that the version Peele knew paralleled the chapbook version in every detail. Yet there seems little reason to doubt that both versions are essentially the same; at least the chapbook is closer to the play than is any other extant version. The story has been studied in detail by Warren E. Roberts, *The Tales of the Kind and the Unkind Girls* (Berlin, 1958). Roberts has found no oral version that could repre-

changed nearly all the details and kept only the central motif: the Kind and Unkind (Motif Q2) united with Victorious Younger Daughter (Motif L50). In "Three Heads," as in other occurrences of the motif, the elder is ugly and surly, the younger beautiful and sweet; they are rewarded according to their natures. Peele has divided the sisters' characteristics, making one beautiful and shrewish, the other ugly and sweet. The rewards are probably intended to follow generally those of the tale, though with a difference. Certainly marriage to Huanebango is to be regarded as a fittingly unpleasant end for the elder,[24] while marriage to Corebus is probably supposed to augur happiness for the younger. The fool in folklore is often a fortunate character, and Corebus is a kindly person.[25] Indeed, Corebus and Huanebango also represent the kind and unkind motif. Corebus shares his cake with the old man while Huanebango refuses to give alms to Erestus. Thus they take over roles given to the sisters in the tale of "Three Heads," and they demonstrate their natures, just as their wives do, and receive appropriate rewards. Peele has provided us with a double instance of poetic (or folkloric) justice, which improves upon the single instance in the tale.

This section is not, however, without confusions of its own. In the tale each of the sisters encounters three heads. In the play Zantippa meets one head and Celanta two; it is not clear—though it makes no great difference—whether we are to regard the total number in the play as two or three. Zantippa gets a husband at the

sent the specific source used by Peele. Conversely, Peele's version—the oldest literary version in English—"has had no influence on oral forms of the tale" (p. 121).

24. In his analysis Roberts (p. 13) says that there is no punishment in the play, but I think he rather underestimates Huanebango.

25. For Corebus, see note to l. 538 SD. Crow will not allow Peele any credit for originality in the matter of reassorting characteristics and providing husbands for the girls; though he can cite no parallel, he does "not for a moment believe that way out is one which Peele has invented. It smacks to me far too much of the folk-tale and I shall not be in the least surprised if someone better informed than myself quotes many parallels" (p. 309). Miss Clapp, on the other hand, finds the solution to be Elizabethan (and, therefore, original with Peele), not folk. Well, one man's Rescued Princess is another's Monster's Bride.

well, but Celanta gets hers somewhere else—we never know where —before she receives gold at the well. In a minor way, this confusion is not unlike that which attends the death of Sacrapant.

G. HUANEBANGO AND THE RUFFLERS

Huanebango is, as I noted earlier, out of the braggart tradition. There seems no need to belabor his obviously Plautine background: his ranting, his rhetoric, his amorous adventures, his absurd weapon, his cowardice, his grandiose names for his ancestors. One may even argue—quite inconclusively—about his relation to the Italian descendants of the *miles gloriosus*. Clearly, Huanebango is from a long, dishonorable line. But he may also be related to a native version of the braggart who appears in the huffing characters in mystery and morality plays and in the ritual St. George plays. The Herods, Beelzebubs, Vices, and assorted devils in this tradition are familiar enough, but perhaps a word may be added about the St. George plays.

In nearly all these plays is to be found a huffing character who has an elder-brother resemblance to Huanebango. One might compare with ll. 545–550 the Giant Blunderbore in the Oxfordshire St. George play:

> I am Giant Blunderbore, fee, fi, fum!
> Ready to fight ye all,—so I says, "Come!" . . .
> I'll fight King Alfred, I'll fight King Cole,
> I'm ready to fight any mortal soul! [26]

Blunderbore is accompanied by a boy who may be compared with Huanebango's Clown. One may even see a resemblance between Huanebango and Prince George himself in the Leicestershire play:

> I am Prince George, the champion bold,
> And with my sword I won three crowns of gold;
> I slew the fiery dragon and brought him to the slaughter,
> And won the King of Egypt's only daughter.[27]

There are many parallels in the texts that have been collected. These are, of course, late texts, but they preserve ancient tradition.

26. I quote from the text in J. Q. Adams, *Chief Pre-Shakespearean Dramas* (Cambridge, Mass., 1924), p. 353.
27. Adams, p. 355.

How ancient is a matter of uncertainty. E. K. Chambers dates the St. George plays at the very end of the sixteenth century.[28] Even if that surprisingly late date should be correct, the ruffler tradition itself, which was incorporated into the mummers' play, is far older.[29]

H. THE AMOROUS HARVESTERS

The play is divided into three not quite equal sections by the two appearances of an unspecified number of harvest men. Despite their identification with the harvest season, they sing first a song of sowing; only at their second appearance do they sing the song of reaping. While I do not propose to find any deep meaning in this progression, it suits well with what a modern reader might like to think of as the anthropological aura of the play. It is well known that our ancestors, far more attuned than we to the relentless revolution of the seasons, celebrated the changing year with festivals that ranged from appalling human sacrifices in ancient times to the relatively harmless, though still decidedly pagan, Maying customs of Peele's own day, customs about which we hear a great deal but know very little. Peele's songs of sowing and mowing inevitably suggest some contact with these seasonal festivities (see note to l. 249). This seems appropriate in a play so permeated by folklore as this one. The seasonal element in the songs is particularly interesting in view of the peculiar nature of the heads that arise before Celanta. One has "eares of Corne," which she combs into her lap, and as the other rises, the song tells her that "every haire, a sheave shall be, / And every sheave a goulden tree" (ll. 785–786). The heads also have golden beards. These attributes clearly suggest some fertility or harvest symbol, and there is another fertility connection in the reference to cockle bread in the song which the heads sing (see note to l. 639).

At the same time, these songs, which seem rooted in folk experience, are sufficiently sophisticated in presentation to suggest that folk material has been transmuted by coloration of the courtly masque. The masque connection is more pointedly suggested by the

28. *The English Folk-Play* (Oxford, 1933), p. 192.
29. This tradition has been worked out by R. J. E. Tiddy, *The Mummer's Play* (Oxford, 1923), pp. 108–110.

stage direction that, at their second appearance, the harvesters are to have "women in their hands," which clearly implies that the song is to be followed by dancing. This may be compared with the dancing and singing shepherds of *David and Bethsabe* (l. 753 SD). Peele's relation to the masque tradition has been explored in the introduction to *The Araygnement of Paris*, the play in which that tradition is most pervasive, and more will be said later about the relationship of *The Old Wives Tale* to courtly entertainments in general.

I. THE GOLDEN ASS

As Warton long ago noted,[30] the name of Meroe (mother of Sacrapant, l. 341) appears in *The Golden Ass* of Apuleius, which Peele may have read either in the original or in the Adlington translation (1566). But Apuleius had no monopoly upon the name, although he and Peele are the only ones to apply it to a person.[31] Warton also thought the transformation motif derived from Apuleius (p. 592), but the metamorphoses of Lucius are a far cry from the fate of Erestus, and so common is the motif in both folklore and romance that one cannot make a convincing argument for a particular source unless the parallels are exact and detailed. Dutz (p. 13) suggested that the title of the play is derived from the Adlington translation. The famous retelling of "Cupid and Psyche" is put by Apuleius into the mouth of an old woman, who introduces her story by saying, "Sed ego te narrationibus lepidis anilibusque fabulis protinus avocabo" (IV.27). Adlington renders this passage: "But I will tell thee a pleasant old wives' tale to put away all thy sorrow and to revive thy spirits." But the translator is merely availing himself of a proverbial phrase very common in Elizabethan English.

30. In his edition of Milton's *Poems upon Several Occasions,* pp. 126–127.
31. In Greene's *Arbasto, The Anatomie of Fortune* (1584), Meroe is an island where virgins "are suffered to see none but him whome they shall marrye" and women see no men but their husbands until they are past fifty (*Works, 3,* 195). It is also a place name in the anonymous *Caesar's Revenge* (ll. 329, 911, 1447, Malone Society Reprint). Lucan, 4.333, is probably the source for this latter reference and for Cooper's description of it in his *Thesaurus* as "an yle in the great riuer of Nilus in Aegipt." See also Greg's note to l. 1182 of *Orlando Furioso* in *Abridgements* and the discussion in Baldwin, pp. 215–216.

Faustus, for example, thinks the pains of hell "are trifles and mere old wives' tales" (ed. F. S. Boas, London, 1932, II.1.136).

Another detail has been traced by at least one scholar to Apuleius. In *The Golden Ass*, Lucius travels to Thessaly and there encounters the magic that transforms him into an ass and sets off the series of adventures he passes through. Larsen suggests that this portrayal of Thessaly as the home of witchcraft and enchantment perhaps explains why it is the home of the characters in the play.[32] But the unsavory reputation of Thessaly is of ancient origin and was widely known among Elizabethans with a classical education.[33] Cooper's *Thesaurus* reports that "the women there being woonderfull witches, transformed men into the figure of beastes."

The positive residue of this excursus into Peele's use of his source materials can be summarized thus: Peele used in a fairly straightforward manner as a primary strand in his story some version of the Grateful Dead that is no longer extant; in a subplot he used "Three Heads in the Well," but modified it almost beyond recognition; he may possibly have used motifs from a portion of Jack the Giant-Killer. Further identification of specific sources (except for details like names) is unsafe.[34]

32. *Trans. Royal Soc. Canada*, *29*, 162, n. 24.

33. See the references in the note to Lyly's *Endimion*, III.1.47 (ed. R. W. Bond, Oxford, 1902).

34. The danger has been no deterrent to some intrepid scholars. Some, like Miss Clapp, would trace the almsgiving of Corebus and Huanebango to "Red Ettin," a quite unnecessary endeavor for such a common motif. Since the daughters of Lampriscus are sent to the "well for the water of life," it is not surprising to find that the tale of "The Well of the Water of Life" has been suggested as a source (Clapp, pp. 153 ff.), but there is no correspondence between the tale and the adventures of the damsels in the play. Peele very probably knew the story, but it supplied nothing to the play except the phrase quoted. Gummere (p. 345) also thought—for reasons he did not trouble to explain—that Peele knew "The Well of the World's End." Miss Clapp, following Gummere faithfully (though somewhat myopically), says there is "a hint" of this story (p. 153), but in a footnote she admits that "there is really no resemblance between Peele's action" and that of the tale. Crow (p. 307) struggles with the possibility

It is possible, as most scholars who have examined this matter seem to assume, that recovery of sixteenth-century versions of Jack the Giant-Killer, Childe Rowland, and other tales would provide us with the play's sources. As I have indicated, this is clearly the case with the Grateful Dead theme, but it is probably not so with the other stories mentioned. This is not to say that Peele knew none of those tales or even to say that he made no use of them. But I return to the thesis that has, both explicitly and implicitly, pervaded the discussion: the sources for the play are all the tales Peele knew—doubtless a great many—from which he drew sporadically and not systematically (perhaps one should say unconsciously) motifs that he combined in his own way.

This thesis is supported by the catalog of folk materials in Peele's play provided by Sylvia Lyons-Render.[35] She lists over ninety motifs in the plot and points out folk beliefs and sayings in the dialogue. Although the catalog is overextended, Miss Lyons-Render has managed to give a quantitative value to this important element of the play, and more significant than the accuracy of her interpretation of particular points is the incontrovertible demonstration that *The Old Wives Tale* is permeated by folklore.[36]

The thesis has been anticipated in what is the most perceptive piece of criticism yet to deal with this aspect of the play. John

---

that "The Golden Bird" (an analogue to "The Water of Life") is a source, but he is, I think, beating a dead ass (see note to l. 777).

35. "Folk Motifs in George Peele's *The Old Wives Tale*," *Tennessee Folklore Society Bulletin, 26* (1960), 62–71. The value of this study is marred by its lack of discrimination in citing motifs, its innocence about Elizabethan language, and some errors that are difficult to account for. For instance (a few from many), the daughters of Lampriscus finding their husbands at the well is said to be Motif T35.1, Fountain of Lovers' Rendezvous. The "huffe snuffe" (l. 647) coupled with the "stickes and strawes" (l. 143) reminds the author of the materials used by the Three Little Pigs and the Bad Wolf's huffing and puffing. And the curious comment on l. 214 is: "Since there is no St. Luke's Day, this must be an oblique reference to one of Christ's disciples."

36. In this section I have discussed only the folk background for the major narrative strands. For minor elements related to folk material see notes to ll. 54, 183, 214, 372, 526, 639, 657, 777, 797.

Crow says, "My suggestion is that Peele had in his mind a number of odd ends together without really knowing at all what odd end came from what story" (p. 305). Elsewhere he refers to the play as a "strange jumble of folk stories" and comments that Peele "showed a remarkable ability to leave things unworked out." He cites a number of examples of jumbling. We have already explored the duplication of the abducted maiden motif in Delya and Venelia and the strange conglomeration of motifs in the death of Sacrapant. To these Crow would add the confusion in the motif of the "fairest for white, and the purest for redd." At the start this refers to Delya, but later we hear no more of her complexion, and the motif is transferred to Zantippa and Celanta. Delya's brothers are urged to "Blow a blast at every flame," but they make no attempt to destroy the magic light when they find it. Instead, they merely replace it and leave to Erestus the task of getting it put out; he has to summon Venelia to do the job, but we have not been prepared for her ability to accomplish the feat. Huanebango is carried off by the furies to be a prey to crows and kites, but it turns out that he is merely afflicted by deafness and becomes prey only to Zantippa.

These complications and others may, Crow says, be due either to Peele or to a corrupt text, but in either case, his conclusion is that Peele's approach to his folklore material is completely naïve. One may grant Crow his conclusion without accepting all his evidence, though much of it seems incontrovertible. To some extent the play is a jumble and presents difficulties not to be explained away by attributing them to high art; that is, by maintaining that Peele has constructed his play as Madge with her jumbled mind might tell the story. This strikes me as a sophistication which, if not beyond the reach of all Renaissance dramatists, is certainly beyond the capabilities of Peele. While working with the play, I have been forcibly struck by what other critics have noted: a curious vagueness that makes the plot difficult to follow; a good deal of close study is required to fix it in one's mind. This elusive quality is not easy to explain, but it has something to do with what Crow refers to as Peele's "remarkable ability to leave things un-worked out." However, before we can deal finally with this and other critical problems, we must examine the text to determine how much of the difficulty is due to corruption by an alien hand or to cutting.

4. THE PRINTER'S COPY

Since the textual critic always feels most comfortable when he can rely on evidence that does not involve aesthetic judgment, *The Old Wives Tale* is likely to make him uneasy. Because the play proper is a dramatization of Madge's tale, it can be argued that the naïveté, the incoherence, the rush of events, the confusion—much that might in another play be evidence of textual corruption—are the results of consummate artistry: Peele is dramatizing the story just as Madge might be expected to tell it. Yet, when all allowances have been made for the effect of the Old Wife on the text, most critics have felt that there is still something unsatisfactory about it. However, they do not usually go beyond a few general remarks about mutilation or cutting. The only study that can claim thoroughness is that of Harold Jenkins, who argues that the extant text is a cut version prepared for a reduced troupe acting in the provinces.[1]

Jenkins argues that the text has characteristics that lay it open to the suspicion of mutilation: "Is it not *too* huddled, do not the figures come and go *too* abruptly, are not one or two of the themes *too* slightly handled? . . . The general impression left by a rapid reading of the play is of an abridgment. Every incident . . . is told as barely and as briefly as possible" (p. 178). He cites particularly the curiously pointless incident involving the Spanish friar. In response to a question from Sacrapant, the Friar answers that the usurer is the "most greediest Englishman" (l. 390). Jenkins comments (p. 178):

> Usurers were stock material for satire in both play and novel, and we await some satiric character sketch or at least a witty epigram at their expense. But the friar is told to "hold thee there," a rather unnecessary caution to one who, far from showing any signs of garrulity, has answered one direct question in a mere six words.

1. "Peele's 'Old Wives Tale'," *Modern Language Review*, 34 (1939), 177–185.

Jenkins has, I think, misinterpreted the "holde thee there." It means
"hold to that opinion," not "hold your tongue." But his point is
well taken; if the Friar is to do no more than this, there seems
little reason to go to the trouble of finding a costume for him. A
somewhat different kind of problem occurs in the Huanebango-
Corebus-Zantippa-Celanta plot. We see Zantippa winning her
husband, but we do not have a corresponding scene for Celanta.
Of course, Zantippa's winning her husband is joined with her
violence to the heads in the well, and there is a parallel scene
for this latter motif when Celanta combs "eares of Corne" and gold
from the heads that arise. The husbands are enchanted, and one
might suppose that they are restored to their original states when
the magic light is blown out. It would surely be dramatically
satisfying to see what happens when Huanebango can hear his
beautiful shrew and Corebus can see his sweet ill-favored mate.
This does not occur.[2]

Yet, one wonders if Jenkins has accurately described the whole
play when he says (p. 180):

> the fine blending of diverse legends and the haphazard progress
> of the story . . . [are] not . . . inseparable from the parsi-
> mony of treatment. I say parsimony here rather than economy
> because the style is not terse, only sketchy. It is not, of course,
> that everything is told in a minimum of words—that would have
> been inappropriate for an old wive's tale and was assuredly no
> part of the dramatist's intention—but that certain things are not
> told at all.

Two things are involved here: (1) the completeness of the plot
and (2) the style of what is represented. Of the first, it is fair, I

2. Jenkins (p. 180) notes also that at the end "Erestus and Venelia . . .
speak no word." Miss Bradbrook (p. 323) adds to the list of loose ends
that the prophecy made to the brothers is fulfilled by Eumenides and that
the prophecy made to Eumenides is "fulfilled, but not noted." This rather
cryptic remark refers, I presume, to the winning of Delia, which occurs,
but is not, as one might have expected, the subject of a prophecy. This
seems to be reading somewhat too curiously. More puzzling is the mysterious reference to "our yong master" and his "faire Lady" in the induction
(l. 11).

think, to say that everything *essential* to the very complicated action is included. Perhaps, with Jenkins, we might like something to come of the Spanish friar, and we might like to find out what happens when the enchantments are lifted from Huanebango and Corebus, but neither can be said to be essential to the action. We might like to know more about Venelia and to hear something from Erestus after his transformation is ended; both are disappointingly silent. But we can understand the story without these things. As Jenkins admits, our feeling that something may have been omitted or that inclusion of other scenes might satisfy certain expectations raised by the action does not *prove* that anything has been cut.

The problem of style—whether we are dealing with parsimony or economy—is more difficult. Jenkins himself has described the first Huanebango scene (ll. 254–334) as "quite leisurely" (p. 183). Nor is it the only one. The induction, as he suggests, is similar; indeed, it is as long as any scene in the play. I detect no different treatment in the scene between Erestus and Lampriscus (ll. 200–242), the interview between Eumenides and Erestus (ll. 432–453), the scene in the churchyard (ll. 454–527), the scene of the daughters at the well (ll. 611–686), the scenes between Eumenides and Jack (ll. 687–768), or Celanta's treatment of the heads (ll. 769–794). Some of these scenes are short, especially Celanta at the well and the exchange between Eumenides and Erestus; but they do not seem hurried. They do what they need to do without any waste, and the scene changes. In the last of these scenes, one might expect three heads to appear, the usual number in folktales, but there seems no reason to suspect that because there are only two any decapitation has occurred. If we exclude these scenes and the soliloquies of Erestus and Sacrapant, not many places remain in which to find problems. In the scene between Erestus and the brothers, an inadvertent omission, discussed more fully below, occurs at l. 154; otherwise the manner does not differ from that of the Huanebango scene. In the scene that runs from the entrance of Delya (l. 353) to the enchantment of the brothers (l. 431), except for the strangely inconclusive bit with the friar there is no problem of haste, and the same can be said for the subsequent scene with the brothers (ll. 574–610). Huanebango and Corebus are handled in very brief fashion in ll. 539–565, but the essentials are there; the action and dialogue are all in character, and one is at a loss to say what else to expect in the scene.

In the final scene everything proceeds at a rapid pace. Nothing is wasted; in particular, we hear no explanation of what the audience already knows, even though the characters might not be expected to be as fully informed as we are. It would be possible to conceive of this scene being done in a manner comparable to the interminable closing scenes of *Measure for Measure* or *Cymbeline*, but that would not be in keeping with the movement of the rest of the play. In short, what Jenkins describes as parsimony can equally well be called economy.

But our general impressions of economy or parsimony, our suspicions about what might have been or what ought to be in the play cannot prove anything about the nature of the text. We must look for further evidence; it is not easy to find.

The play is unusually short. It is almost exactly half the average length calculated from over fifty plays;[3] it is some three hundred lines shorter than *The Araygnement of Paris*, more than five hundred lines shorter than the corrupt extant text of *The Battle of Alcazar*, both of which are also short plays. Jenkins takes this brevity as proof that we are dealing with a curtailed text. But the proposition that a particular play must be of some customary length is difficult to support. If *The Old Wives Tale*, like the *Araygnement*, was written as a court divertissement instead of as a play for the public stage, length would have nothing to do with the argument. A play, like Antony's crocodile, is of its own length, and no forceful argument, certainly no proof of cutting, can be based upon comparison with the length of other plays. Therefore, although the brevity of the play may allow us to look upon it with suspicion, we are forced back into the text for evidence about its nature.

The play contains a number of peculiarities and characteristics that any theory about the nature of the text must take into account. Some of these have long been noted by scholars; others have not.

(1) At l. 154 Erestus, talking with Delya's brothers about their mission, abruptly asks, "Was shee fayre?" Although Gummere

3. The estimates of length are from Jenkins, pp. 180–181.

tried to defend the text as it stands by arguing that the lack of transition is in keeping with the seer quality of Erestus, it is perfectly clear, as Jenkins says, that something has been dropped out at this point.[4] But the omission is not clear evidence (*pace* Jenkins) of cutting. It may equally well be an inadvertent omission by the compositor, whose eye skipped one or more exchanges between the characters. This explanation seems the more likely because the error occurs at the top of a page (B2[v]). Since type was set up by the page, errors of omission or repetition frequently occurred in the process of moving from one page to the next.[5] In this case it is easy to assume that in making the transition the compositor somehow missed several speeches. Certainly the possibility vitiates the strength of the passage as evidence of deliberate cutting.[6]

(2) One of the most enigmatic problems in the text is the triple confusion of Booby-Clown, Corebus-friend-of-Jack, and Corebus-Clown.[7] It is obvious that the Clown is one character,

4. Gummere, p. 356; Miss Bradbrook (p. 325), agreeing that something has been omitted, points out that the omission causes no problem because of the curious we-have-seen-it-all-before atmosphere of the play. Thus she mediates between Jenkins and Gummere.

5. R. B. McKerrow, *An Introduction to Bibliography* (Oxford, 1928), p. 65, n. 1.

6. For a similar case see the top of sig. C1[v] of Greene's *Alphonsus*, where something—probably only a speech tag—is missing. A speech may have been omitted between H2 and H2[v] of *Selimus* (ll. 1957–58, Malone Society Reprint). One might wish to argue that some speeches are dropped between ll. 307 and 308 of *Old Wives Tale*. At ll. 365–374 three successive speeches are given, apparently correctly, to Sacrapant; this is unusual, but there is no clear indication that anything is missing. A similar instance occurs at ll. 804 and 809. Cf. *David and Bethsabe* (l. 1105), where one sign of textual dislocation is the ascription of two successive speeches to David.

7. One might even argue that there is a quadruple confusion, for when he first enters (l. 453) and in the first speech tag for him, Corebus-friend-of-Jack is called Corobus; both spellings are on C4[v] in Q. In the remainder of the scene (D1, D1[v], and D2), he is Corebus, and the speech tags are "Core" and "Coreb," five occurrences in all. It would be handy if one could attribute this variation to a change of compositors, but the evidence is that all the pages in question were set by the same man. The Corobus spelling does not appear outside of Peele, to my knowledge. On the other hand, Coroebus is the proper form, of which Corebus is a common variant

though he operates under two names, and it is equally obvious that Corebus-friend-of-Jack is a different character, though he shares his name with the Clown. Jenkins puts it succinctly: "The one is bold and defiant, vigorous in speech, and, though humble in station, delightfully independent in spirit: the other is timid, awkward, naïf" (p. 184). How are we to explain the confusion in names? Jenkins offers an ingenious solution which supports his argument for a curtailed text.

When Huanebango and the Clown enter for the second time (at l. 538 SD), Madge introduces them as if they had not already appeared at l. 253 SD. Madge's second introduction is redundant, for it merely summarizes Huanebango's character as he had himself demonstrated it in the earlier scene. Jenkins concludes that the reviser, desirous of cutting the play, saw that the earlier scene was not essential because it contained no action, only preparation for action; he therefore marked it for omission, supplanting it with a single-line summary at l. 540. The printer misunderstood the mark and retained the original scene along with the revised introduction to the later scene. Thus, according to Jenkins, the very brief extant play is actually longer than was intended by the reviser.

The most attractive thing about this theory is that it explains how two names for the Clown survive. Booby appears only in the section that was to have been omitted. The change to Corebus in the later section was made by the reviser, who expected—Jenkins supposes—that the role would be doubled by the actor who played Corebus-friend-of-Jack.

This ingenious argument explains what otherwise may seem inexplicable, yet there are difficulties in accepting it. First, the introduction of Huanebango is not, as Jenkins says, an isolated example of redundancy in the play. At l. 244 Frolicke asks whether Erestus is the Man-Bear, though less than a hundred lines earlier Erestus has given a complete briefing on the nature of his dual transformation. Sacrapant identifies Delya's brothers for us (ll. 421–422), even though their identity has been made clear, not

when the name appears in vernacular literature (as Corebo in Ariosto's *Orlando Furioso*, 13.24). Therefore, I concur with other editors in assuming that, whatever the source of the two *o* spellings, the name intended for the friend of Jack is Corebus.

once but twice before (ll. 132 ff., 394 ff.). One might almost say that redundancy is the rule in the play. Second, as noted above, the "leisurely pace" of the Huanebango scene does occur elsewhere. Third, it is not quite true to say that the earlier scene only prepares for action. So far as Huanebango's little part in the Sacrapant-Delya plot is concerned, this may be true. But Huanebango and the Clown figure primarily in the subplot with Zantippa and Celanta. In that story—which is, as we have seen, a version of the traditional kind-unkind motif—Huanebango's refusal to give alms and the Clown's kindness to Erestus are actions that result in the punishment and reward of the later scenes. If, therefore, a reviser actually did think the earlier scene unnecessary, he was mistaken.

There are also difficulties in the way of the portion of the theory that explains the duplication of names. First, it is not clear why a reviser would introduce the complication of giving the same name to two characters; if the play is to be acted by a small cast, surely there must be a great deal of doubling, none of it indicated elsewhere by duplication of names. Second, there is some evidence, not strong to be sure, that the use of different names for the Clown is to be traced to the author. Booby, as Jenkins points out, is a traditional name, sometimes actually a synonym for clown. In the play it is obviously intended as a name, for the stage direction calls for the entrance of "*Booby the Clowne*," and the name occurs also in the prose dialogue. But Corebus is another traditional name for a fool (see note to l. 538 SD), and that name likewise appears in the dialogue. At l. 565 "And robbed poore Corebus of his sight" can be scanned as iambic pentameter by making "robbed" disyllabic. If we assume that Corebus is a reviser's change, the line must originally have read "And robbed poore Booby of his sight." By making "robbed" a monosyllable, this line can be scanned as iambic, but it is not a pentameter. Elsewhere both Booby and Corebus appear in prose except at l. 793: "So Corebus things have well hit." The line does not scan well,[8] but substitution of Booby only makes things worse. The state of the play's verse will not allow any very forceful argument from scansion, but I am inclined

8. By accenting "Corebus" on the first syllable and eliding the first two words in the following line, one can make a passable octosyllabic couplet.

to think that these lines demonstrate that Corebus was the name originally used there. If this is the case, we must find some explanation different from that offered by Jenkins to account for the duplication of names.[9]

If we assume the manuscript used by the printer represented something earlier than a final draft, we can perhaps account for the confusion as a change of mind on Peele's part. He started with Booby, the traditional name for a fool. When he introduced Corebus-friend-of-Jack (and who can possibly guess what possessed him to choose that name for a rustic?), he remembered from his school days that Corebus was also a fool and decided to use the name for the Clown, probably intending to make changes that would eliminate the confusion. For some reason we cannot hope to know, the alterations were not made in the manuscript that eventually went to the printer. I do not pretend that this is a neat explanation, but it does show that the problem may without strain be traced to the author.

(3) Another puzzling confusion of names occurs in the scene in which Jack's burial is settled. The stage direction after l. 453 calls for "*Wiggen, Corebus, Churchwarden and Sexten.*" The second speech in the scene has a tag for "*Simon*"; it is reasonably certain that the speaker is the Churchwarden, who has a number of other speeches in the scene, and all editors have given the speech

9. Miss Bradbrook has a different explanation. She finds sufficient similarity in a number of Queen's plays of the period to suggest that there was a "general habit of building up scenes fairly freely upon the basis of a scenario or 'plot'" (p. 326). This appears to envision a mode of performance somewhat like *commedia dell'arte*. Moreover, in a play like *The Old Wives Tale*, "each figure was so familiar that as he came forward to give his sequence, it would have been natural for the audience, if pleased, to demand a little more—to cry for the braggart to come back" (p. 325). Thus she explains the first Huanebango scene as an addition to supply this demand. Rejecting Jenkins' theory, she says (note 7): "It seems to me more likely to be an accretion; the later writer has forgotten the Clown's grand name of Corebus, which he perhaps was meant originally to assume on becoming a knight errant." But Miss Bradbrook does not go into any greater detail, and it is not clear how an audience's demand for more (implying impromptu gags) would result in the text as it stands—or, indeed, any written text.

to him. But his name is apparently not Simon but Steeven Loache, for at ll. 494–495 he says: "he shall lie above ground till he daunce a galliard about the churchyard for Steeven Loache." Although, as the note to the passage indicates, I am willing to entertain the possibility that his name is not actually Steeven Loache, there is certainly no evidence that it is Simon. H. M. Dowling suggested "for what it is worth" that the name might refer to John Symons, the long famous tumbler who joined the Queen's Men about 1588 or 1589.[10] The diffidence with which the suggestion was made indicates that Dowling did not really believe there was much in it, nor do I. The most likely explanation of the confusion seems to be that the author had not quite made up his mind about what to call the character.

(4) There are confusions in the spelling of some other names. In the first scene in which she appears, the younger daughter of Lampriscus is Celanta, but when she returns later, she is Zelanta or Zelanto. There are three possible explanations of this variation: (a) it represents an intentional change on the part of the author; (b) it is an inadvertent change by the author, the source of which we cannot hope to penetrate; or (c) it results from the printer's difficulty in reading the manuscript. If my division of the printed text between two compositors is correct (see Sec. 7), the confusion may be the result of different readings of a curiously made letter; "Celanta" appears in Compositor A's stint, and "Zelanta(o)" in Compositor B's. A similar confusion occurs in naming Delya's brother; at ll. 400 and 417 he is Calypha, but at l. 874 he is Kalepha. These two passages, however, were set by the same compositor.

(5) In the Delya-Sacrapant relationship some confusion occurs. At l. 353 Sacrapant says that Delya is a source of sorrow for him; he does not explain why, but we gather that his love for her is unrequited (a situation that must rather undermine our respect for his powers of enchantment). At ll. 423–424 he says he has given

10. *Notes and Queries, 164* (1933), 184. See also Chambers, *2*, 111. Baldwin takes up the point: "This structure suggests that the play was in fact designed for Simonds and Stanley's boys, as there is other evidence to indicate" (p. 211). But there is no other evidence except the speech tag for Simon, and we know nothing of his boys except that they tumbled.

Delya a potion to make her "forget her selfe." It is not clear
whether the potion has taken effect or not, but at ll. 566–568, as if
he had forgotten the earlier statement, he says:

> Now I have unto Delya
> Given a potion of forgetfulnes,
> That when shee comes shee shall not know hir Brothers.

At l. 571 he is going to give her another name, and she will never
know herself again until he is dead. When four lines later he calls
her Delya and orders her to whip her enslaved brothers, she says,
"Good sir I know not what you meane." One's first impression is
that she does not recognize her name, and Sacrapant's response
("She hath forgotten to be Delya") supports this reading. But he
goes on with what seems to be a contradiction (ll. 580–583):

> But not forgot the name [Q same] she should forget:
> But I will change hir name.
> Faire Berecynthia so this Country calls you,
> Goe ply these strangers wench, they dig for gold.

In the light of this passage we can only assume that forgetting to
be Delya means that she has forgotten her identity and her family
but not yet her name. As the following lines indicate, she is now
quite impressed with Sacrapant, though whether she can be said
to love him is not clear.

The relationship between these two is a fairly murky business.
Peele faced a problem: Sacrapant's power could not be made too
strong, because Delya must be kept pure for her rescuer. Even so,
one can raise questions about the presentation: Does she love him
or not? Just how enchanted is she? When does she get the potion?
But once raised, the questions must not be allowed a significance
beyond their merit. The slight obfuscation does not offer any real
barrier to understanding the plot. Nor are these peculiarities different in kind from those that occur in many Elizabethan plays.
Bradley found in *King Lear* many "defects" in the way Shakespeare tells (or does not tell) his story, but it is perfectly clear that
these "defects" have no bearing on the play. No more do these
elements in Peele's play. If there is muddling, it is of the sort that

may be traced to the author (without any prejudice to his art) rather than to an alien hand.[11]

(6) The most important evidence for the nature of the text has never before been noted. The stage directions and speech tags in *The Old Wives Tale* indicate clearly that an authorial manuscript is not far beneath the printed text. The author's sign is the great inconsistency in the way characters are identified. Sometimes a descriptive word or phrase replaces the name. Erestus is never identified by name in the directions or speech tags. In the tags he is always "*Old Man*," and in the directions he is at first "*Senex*," later "*the old man at the crosse*" (l. 431) or "*he that was at the crosse*" (l. 872). Similarly, the brothers are never named in the directions or tags, though they acquire names in the text at ll. 417 and 874. Sacrapant is usually named, but at ll. 415 SD and 559 SD he is "*Conjurer*." Sometimes both name and descriptive phrase are used: At l. 196 there is an entrance for "*Venelia his Lady*." At his first entrance (l. 431) and again at l. 686 the direction calls for "*Eumenides the wandring Knight*"; at ll. 794 SD and 803 SD he is called only "*the wandring knight*." At her first entrance (l. 610) the daughter of Lampriscus is "*Zantyppa the curst Daughter*." Her sister is "*the fowle wench*" (l. 614 SD) when she first enters, but at l. 768 SD she is "*Celanta* [Zelanto Q] *the foule wench*." We have already noted the character who at l. 253 SD is "*Booby the Clowne*" and at l. 538 SD "*Corebus the clowne*." These directions scattered throughout the play suggest an authorial manuscript.[12]

An unusual number of stage directions describe business (other than entrance and exit); I count twenty-eight in all. One might argue that this is simply the result of the elaborate action of the piece, but many of these directions are unusually full, even literary. Most significant is this one: "*Here they dig and descry the light under a litle hill*" (l. 603 SD). In the following line, the second brother says, "Stay brother what hast thou describe?" The use of such a literary word as "descry" in a stage direction and its duplication in the text are clear indications of the author. Again, at l. 614

11. Similar questions arise about the relationship of Erestus and Venelia; see note to l. 183.

12. Cf. these directions with the lists in W. W. Greg, *The Shakespeare First Folio* (Oxford, 1955), esp. pp. 124–132.

a stage direction echoes the dialogue of ll. 612–613: When Zantippa comes to the well, the direction (l. 610) is "Enter Zantyppa the curst Daughter *to the well* with a pot in hir hand." She then explains to the audience: "My father hath sent me *to the well for the water of life* . . ." At that moment, "Enter the fowle wench *to the well for water* with a pot in hir hand." Clearly the phrase added to the second direction comes from the immediately preceding dialogue. To these examples may be added the use of "wandring knight" in stage directions at ll. 431, 686, 794, and 803, and finally in the dialogue at l. 881. The source of such echoes is surely the author.[13]

There are many other directions in which the discursive style suggests the author, rather than a theatrical hand:

> *She covers it agen.*
>
> [l. 606]
>
> *Here she strikes hir Pitcher against hir sisters, and breakes them both and goes hir way.*
>
> [l. 624]
>
> *Heere she offers to dip her Pitcher in, and a head speakes in the Well.*
>
> [l. 634]
>
> *Shee breakes hir Pitcher uppon his heade, then it thunders and lightens, and Huanebango rises up: Huanebango is deafe and cannot heare.*
>
> [l. 645]
>
> *Enter the Hostes and Jack, setting meate on the table, and Fidlers come to play, Eumenides walketh up and downe, and will eate no meate.*
>
> [l. 734]
>
> *A head comes up with eares of Corne, and she combes them in her lap.*
>
> [l. 777]

13. Peele makes something of a habit of such echoes in the *Araygnement;* see ll. 52–53, 68–69, 163–164, 165–166, 355–356, 456–457, 461. See also *David,* ll. 212–213. A similar echo of a stage direction in the text occurs in Greene's *Alphonsus,* where the direction calls for entry of the Muses, "Calliope onely excepted, who comming last, hangeth downe the head." Venus then remarks: "Only excepted faire *Calliope?* / Who coming last & hanging downe her head" (ll. 53–54, Malone Society Reprint).

A head comes up full of golde, she combes it into her lap.

[l. 782]

Enter Jack invisible, and taketh off Sacrapants
wreath from his head, and his sword out of his hand.

[l. 808]

He pulles the Wooll out of his eares.

[l. 822]

He digs and spies a light.

[l. 825]

He windes the horne.
Heere enters Venelia and breakes the glasse, and blowes
out the light, and goeth in againe.

[l. 838]

He draweth a curten, and there Delia sitteth asleepe.

[l. 843]

Such directions suggest an author visualizing the action of his piece.

An unusually high number of entrance directions (ten in all) include a property to be carried by the actor.[14] According to McKerrow, mention in an entrance direction of a property not needed until later is a sign of prompt copy.[15] But, like most matters involving stage directions, there is nothing inevitable about this, and the discursive nature of many of these directions suggests the authorial hand. Eight more properties, omitted from entrance directions, are called for in later directions or must be deduced from the dialogue: the cake (l. 311), the pike staff (l. 478), the goad (l. 577 SD), the purse (l. 745), the wool (l. 801), the wreath and sword (l. 808 SD), and the horn (ll. 838, 872). This casual treatment of properties points to the author.

The stage directions are fairly complete. I have supplied ten, including a final exeunt; of these, five are exit directions, all of which are quite obviously needed.[16] Such omissions may be laid at the door of the author or even someone connected with the stage, the assumption in Elizabethan repertory companies apparently being that once a character is on stage it is up to him to get himself

14. See SD at ll. 27, 199, 253, 352, 373, 587, 610, 614, 629, 863.
15. "The Elizabethan Printer and Dramatic Manuscripts," *The Library,* Ser. 4, *12* (1931), 271.
16. See SD at ll. 22, 300, 395, 417, 520, 559, 561, 753, 849, 928.

off. Entrance directions are more significant. Three are missing from the quarto text. At l. 300 an entrance must be supplied for Erestus, who left the stage at l. 240. The point is marked in the dialogue by "Soft, here is an olde man at the Crosse." If the cross is a station, one might argue that Erestus is actually on stage all the time (see Sec. 6). At l. 559 a direction must be added for the Furies to enter and carry off Huanebango. Since only business is involved, this point would be easy for an author to overlook, but a copy connected with the stage should clear up such matters. At l. 753 the hostess must enter. Again, the author might easily over-look her exit some lines earlier (l. 741 SD), but theatrical copy needs to be careful about such matters. There is, as has been noted, some confusion about the beheading of Sacrapant; just what hap-pens to his body is not clear. This confusion should have been settled if the copy had gone through theatrical hands, but it is something the author might easily miss. The evidence from the stage directions is clear, strong, and consistent: it points directly to the author and away from a reviser, especially a reviser connected with the theater.[17]

(7) Instead of being especially adapted to a small troupe, as Jenkins and Miss Bradbrook believe, the play seems to me to be composed without any concern for the troupe's capabilities to perform it, for its demands are almost as prodigal as those made by *Edward I*, if one considers the difference in length.[18] The play has twenty-three speaking roles (not including Echo, Head, and Voice), three mutes (Venelia, two Furies), fiddlers, and an unspec-ified number of singing harvesters with their female partners. No doubt many parts could be doubled, but the final scene, in which doubling would be impracticable, requires nine speaking actors (Frolicke, Fantasticke, Madge, two brothers, Eumenides, Sacra-pant, Delya, Jack) and two mutes (Erestus and Venelia). This

17. I think this is a fair assessment of the evidence. Yet one must remem-ber that, as Sir Walter Greg reminds us in *The Editorial Problem* (Oxford, 1954), "With regard to stage directions the chief lesson to be learned from the prompt-books is caution" (p. 36). We much need a thorough study of the textual implications of stage directions.

18. *Edward I* has thirty-four speaking parts and even more walk-ons; see Yale ed., 2, 46–47, 70–71.

does not suggest that the play was set up for a *very* small troupe. We do not know much about the personnel of the Queen's Men, particularly in its later years. When the company was founded in 1583, it was composed of twelve players (Chambers, 2, 106; 4, 296). In 1588 a list includes only nine names, but Chambers suggests that it is incomplete (2, 107); there is, however, no likelihood that the total was more than twelve. This number, of course, does not include boys and journeymen. How many of this group might have composed a touring company one can only guess. By assuming that boys would play the pages as well as female roles (and perhaps even Jack and the Clown), one could reduce sharply the number of adult actors required to produce the play, but this kind of speculation is unlikely to prove anything. The one hard fact about the personnel required is the heavy demand in the final scene.[19] To be coupled with this is the disposition of characters in the induction. Anticke and Clunch go to bed—primarily, one supposes, to release two actors for doubling and to keep the stage from being cluttered with silent spectators. But if one were preparing the play for a skeleton group, surely he would send another of the pages to bed with Clunch and so save one more actor. This kind of extravagance—at least, so it seems to me—appears also in the requirement of an unspecified number of singing men with women partners. All this taken together suggests that the mind behind this text is more concerned with the effects to be achieved than with the personnel available. This sort of concern points to the author, rather than to any theatrical source.

Such, then, is the evidence upon which one must base his conclusions about the sort of manuscript that underlay the printed text. It falls into three groups: First, represented by (1) and perhaps (4), are those peculiarities which may most likely be traced to the printer but might conceivably be explained as the result of

19. Miss Bradbrook says that the play "for a company of seven men and two boys needed much doubling" (p. 323), but she gives no authority for her numbers. Baldwin includes the play among those written with "six principal parts for men . . . and one for a boy" (p. 204). How one decides which are the major roles in this play and how many of them there are, I do not know; but obviously the cast demands at least five boys (at one time Madge, two pages, Celanta, and Zantippa are all on stage; and the final scene requires five boys).

a reviser's work. Second, represented by (2), (3), and (5), are those peculiarities which might be the result of a reviser but could just as readily be traced to the author. Third, represented by (6) and (7), are characteristics which point clearly to the author.

Weighing all the evidence leads me to the conclusion that the eccentricities of *The Old Wives Tale* can be satisfactorily explained on the assumption that the printer made some gaffes and had occasional difficulty in reading his copy; that copy was an authorial manuscript in a state before final revision—foul papers, but not very foul. To take a position supporting the essential integrity of the extant text flies in the face of orthodoxy, but I am comforted by the support that the critical discussion in the next section will give. Indeed, considering the careful way in which the extant text is written, it is incredible that it should be the work of either a hack or a hacker.[20]

5. A CRITICAL VIEW

The first critical notice of *The Old Wives Tale* was Thomas Warton's full description in his notes to *Comus*.[1] For more than a century, scholars contented themselves with a comparison between the play and the poem, a comparison in which the play was inevitably found wanting. John Addington Symonds is typical: "Peele's

20. After this section was written, S. Musgrove published a study in "Peele's 'Old Wives Tale': An Afterpiece?," *Journal of the Australasian Universities Language and Literature Association*, 23 (1965), 89–95, in which he argues against Jenkins and supports the integrity of the text. Musgrove suggests that the play is a brief afterpiece intended to be performed following a romantic comedy and that many of the mysteries of the text are to be explained as allusions to the main play of the evening. Musgrove summarizes his argument conveniently (p. 93): ". . . let us recall that the play is extremely short, that Peele tells us that it is meant to run for an hour [ll. 85–86], that there are what seem to be clear references in the induction to a preceding comedy [ll. 11–14], that the play is by definition a semi-parody, that there are difficulties in it which might best be explained by the hypothesis of a preceding play on a similar theme, and that the whole thing has the air of being written for an occasion and for an audience of literary sophisticates. I find it hard to believe that it was written for the public theatre . . ."

1. John Milton, *Poems upon Several Occasions*, pp. 126, 591–593.

'Old Wives Tale' deserves to be remembered because of its resemblances to 'Comus'." And after describing the resemblances, he
adds: "So far the coincidence with 'Comus' is manifest. But Peele
takes no advantage of these romantic circumstances, either to point
a moral or to lift his subject into the heavens of poetry." [2]

It apparently never occurred to Symonds to reflect upon what
place Clunch and Madge, Huanebango and Corebus, Celanta and
Zantippa might have in those heavens. A. W. Ward, about the
same time, was describing the play as a "farcical extravaganza, not
devoid of occasional touches of a true poetic fancy," but still much
inferior to *Comus*, which is "one of the loftiest, most sustained, and
most refined of moral allegories in our own or any other literature." [3] One can only wonder at the blindness which could not see
that *The Old Wives Tale* written in the style of *Comus* would be
quite as preposterous as *Comus* written in the style of *The Old
Wives Tale*.

In the introduction to his edition of Peele's plays (*1*, xxxix), Bullen pointed out the injustice of comparing the play to *Comus*, but
the honor of establishing the orthodox critical point of view of the
early twentieth century goes to Gummere. He says (p. 341) that
Peele

> was the first to blend romantic drama with a realism which turns
> romance back upon itself, and produces the comedy of sub-
> conscious humour. . . . Realism in diction was no new thing;
> romance in plot was not an innovation; it was the clash, the
> interplay, the subjective element, the appeal to something more
> than a literal understanding of what is said and done, a new
> appeal to a deeper sense of humour—here lay the new vein
> discovered by George Peele.

Gummere sees the play as a forerunner of *The Knight of the
Burning Pestle* in its "dramatic irony, springing from contrast of
romantic plot and realistic diction" (p. 342).

Gummere's view has been echoed by the influential surveys of
the Elizabethan drama, though most writers content themselves

2. *Shakespere's Predecessors* (London, 1900), p. 452.
3. *A History of English Dramatic Literature* (London, 1875), *1*, 211.

with only a passing comment.[4] It has been sensitively expanded by Cady, who argues (pp. 9–10) that the point of view of the play is at once childlike and sophisticated. Chivalry is seen from the point of view of the child listening to Madge's tale; the effect is a double-edged satire, as the chivalric excesses are refracted through the eyes of Madge and this distortion is in turn judged by the child's point of view that Peele invites in his audience.

More recently it has been argued that what Gummere saw as the basis of the comedy—the ironic contrast between realistic speech and romantic subject matter—is only one of a number of such contrasts in the play. There is a constant intermixing from different kinds of literary worlds: the folklore princess is also a cruel Petrarchan mistress; the grateful folklore ghost turns up among a group of realistic villagers. The play contains a mélange of character types and motifs, and the comedy arises from this juxtaposition of disparate stereotypes. Yet they are somehow fused into a unified whole, so that the piece dramatizes "by means of interplay the working of the imagination and [shows] how it enlarges, unifies, and yet refreshingly complicates human life." [5] This might seem a heavy philosophical burden for so fragile a creation to bear, even if one were disposed to accept the argument.

The essence of Gummere's thesis—that the play juxtaposes romance and realism for satiric purposes—has long been under attack. Gwenan Jones argued that the play contains nothing heroic or romantic, and consequently no burlesque; instead, it is composed almost entirely of popular material appropriate to the homely setting.[6] It is "just what it purports to be, a straightforward representation of a folk-tale" (p. 93). Far from being burlesque, it is rather *less* exaggerated than the heroic plays themselves. Larsen argued

---

4. *CHEL*, 5, 146; Felix E. Schelling, *Elizabethan Drama 1558–1642* (Boston, 1908), *1*, 136, 201, 240; Schelling, *Elizabethan Playwrights* (New York, 1925), pp. 59, 94; C. F. Tucker Brooke, *The Tudor Drama* (Boston, 1911), pp. 242, 279; T. M. Parrott and R. H. Ball, *A Short View of Elizabethan Drama* (New York, 1943), pp. 67–68.

5. Herbert Goldstone, "Interplay in Peele's *The Old Wives Tale*," *Boston University Studies in English*, 4 (1960), 213.

6. "The Intention of Peele's 'Old Wives Tale'," *Aberystwyth Studies*, 7 (1925), 79–93.

in the same vein a decade later,[7] and more recently John Crow (p. 305) has echoed the appeal for a naïve reading.

So the critical lines are drawn, the cleavage absolute: on the one hand, those who see the play as a sophisticated juxtaposition of romance and realism for the purpose of satire; on the other, those who see it as a childlike retelling of old tales. My own reading of the play is rather in the latter tradition, though I have not hesitated to pillage from the first group whatever seems of value.

It can be said quite dogmatically that the play, except for that portion involving Huanebango, is not satire or burlesque. The Huanebango episodes must not be allowed to confuse the issue. No one has ever denied that Huanebango is a satiric figure, though there is disagreement about precisely what he is intended to satirize. But Huanebango, even if one admits that he is a parody of a hero in romantic drama, does not turn *The Old Wives Tale* into the kind of sophisticated spoof that the followers of Gummere find it to be. The mood and tone of the play as a whole are something quite different.

A telling point made by both Gwenan Jones and Larsen is well worth emphasizing. If the play were a satire, the author surely would have made his attitude clear in the commentary by the characters of the induction. Indeed, if Peele were writing satire, one would suppose that a primary function of the courtly pages would be to make the attack explicit in something like the manner of the courtly observers of the play of Pyramus and Thisbe in *Midsummer Night's Dream*. But far from making fun of the story unfolded before them, the pages are entranced, and their uncomplicated and sympathetic acceptance of the tale is an invitation to the audience to take the same point of view.

Equally telling is the point developed at length by Miss Jones: the play can hardly be a burlesque of romance because the action is less exaggerated than that in the romantic plays themselves. She argues that the subject matter of the play is not romantic at all, but folklore. Though the argument is, on the whole, convincing, one must move cautiously here. It is easy for a modern reader to make distinctions between folklore and romance, distinctions that Peele

7. *Trans. Royal Soc. Canada, 29,* 157–170.

himself would probably not have been aware of. After all, what we call romance draws heavily upon folk motifs. The difference lies primarily in the point of view. Romance, particularly as it evolves in sixteenth-century drama, emphasizes a heroic code of behavior; the hero may be impelled by love of his lady, but his actions demonstrate the strength of his arm. In folklore the hero may achieve much the same end as the romantic hero (i.e., a beautiful princess and much gold), but the emphasis is less on the code of behavior than on simple poetic justice. In folklore the underestimated younger brother rescues a princess by the superiority of his wits or by the superiority of his morality; often he does not do much, but is instead a relatively passive character assisted by supernatural beings. The romantic hero is good, but he conquers by strength. The folk hero conquers merely by goodness. This is all very generally stated, but it does get at a basic distinction between the two: the romantic protagonist must be heroic, the folk protagonist is likely not to be.

The Old Wives Tale is in the folklore camp. As has been shown, the sources are folktales and motifs. There are no heroic deeds in the play—not even one good swordfight. The hero is passive to the point of being positively helpless. Victory comes to him through a superhuman agent, who helps him simply because he is good. There is a certain aura of romance in the play, but it is superficial, residing mainly in the names. It seems perfectly clear that if the play does not represent heroic deeds or romantic attitudes, it can hardly be said to burlesque them.

Critics following Gummere have had a good deal to say about the realistic language of the play; some, like Goldstone, have been aware that "realistic" is an inadequate description of language that ranges from the earthiness of Madge to the rodomontade of Huanebango. A more searching analysis than has yet been made will show, I think, that for all its variety the total effect of the language of the play is one of harmony and that the harmony extends to the way the language is suited to the characters and the plot. In short, Gummere's theory that the humor of the play arises from disparity between language and plot and a consequent disparity between the induction and the play proper is a quite erroneous reading.

As their names suggest, the three pages, who appear first and therefore contribute heavily to establishing the mood of the piece, are fanciful, their point of view courtly. They serve a master who is himself devoted to the religion of Cupid. Their diction is simple enough, but the language is mannered. They play with words ("Doth this sadnes become thy madnes?"—l. 2). They quote Terence in an offhand, even off-key, manner ("*O coelum! O terra! O maria! O Neptune!*"—l. 10). They pun ("a dogge in the wood, or a wooden dogge"—l. 23). The tone is light, charming, whimsical. This trio would be comfortable with a set of Lyly's pages. Into this atmosphere comes a man carrying a lantern; he is invoked in the same tone (ll. 29–31): "In the name of my own father, be thou Oxe or Asse that appearest, tell us what thou art." The answer is a straightforward, no-nonsense kind of speech (ll. 32–34): "What am I? Why I am Clunch the Smith, what are you, what make you in my territories at this time of the night?" But though straightforward, the speech is not altogether realistic: would any real Clunch ever say, "what make you in my territories"? The fanciful note continues in the page's pun on "make" ("What doe we make . . . ? why we make faces for feare"—ll. 35–36), in the equally fanciful statement (l. 37) of the earthy threat that they might frighten him enough to make him "water the long seames of thy side slops," and in the whimsical description of the fate that appears to await the lost trio ("wee are like to wander with a sorrowfull hey ho, among the owlets, and Hobgoblins of the Forrest"—ll. 40–41). In this mood Clunch is addressed as "good Vulcan." He responds with a prosaic reduction of their fantastic language ("Well Masters it seemes to mee you have lost your waie in the wood"—ll. 45–46) and issues an invitation for the night, to which they reply in what can hardly be described as a realistic manner ("O blessed Smith, O bountifull Clunch"). Madge is rather more earthy than her husband, but even she does not disrupt the mood. Her speech is marked by something of a rustic fancy, as when she assures the pages that Clunch is "a cleane skind man . . . without either spavin or windgall" (ll. 94–95). And she too makes puns (l. 117).

Peele is not here contrasting types of language or characters. The fusion is more significant than the fission. The pages use on the whole a vocabulary simple enough not to jar with Clunch's, and

Clunch in turn uses expressions here and there that would not be
out of place in the mouth of the pages ("in my territories," "in
consideration whereof," "for your further entertainment"). The
effect of this leveling of vocabulary and idiom is to soften the distinction between the pages and Clunch, to create a harmony rather
than a disparity. This harmony of language is reflected in the
harmonious relation of the pages with Clunch and Madge. The
pages are not condescending or patronizing; Clunch and Madge
are not obsequious. The pages respond to Madge and Clunch like
children, and they are accepted by the old couple in the same manner. This childlike point of view is reinforced by the pages' request
for a tale (ll. 83, 88–90): "a merry winters tale would drive
away the time trimly" and "I have seene the day when I was a
litle one, you might have drawne mee a mile after you with such
a discourse." When Madge starts her "old wives winters tale" the
language has the authentic ring of a folktale. Thus we are invited to
give ourselves up like children to the story to be unfolded by the
actors.

When the two brothers appear, they speak first in a blank verse
that is simple in diction. It is perhaps going too far to suggest that
the formulaic quality of the folktale is suggested by such stereotyped phrases as "O fortune cruell, cruell and unkind" (l. 137).
For the modern reader it is undoubtedly true that such a line,
which in another context would simply be a cliché, has a quaintness that is right in this context. Whether Peele (or his audience)
was aware that he was dealing in cliché is a question that cannot be
answered; he did know that he was using anadiplosis.[8] However
that may be, the language is not elaborate enough to create any
clash when we descend into prose. The ease of descent results not
only from the unelevated diction of the verse but also from the
elevated level of the prose, as in "if I speede in that I goe for, I
will give thee as good a Gowne of gray as ever thou diddest
weare" (ll. 148–150). The formulaic quality of folktale language is
certainly evoked in the next line when the first brother echoes this
speech: "if I speede in my journey, I will give thee . . ." Then we

8. Although his statement is ambiguous, W. Clemen seems to believe this
speech is burlesque (*English Tragedy before Shakespeare*, London, 1961,
p. 177).

move into the rhymed doggerel of the prophecies, which is exactly right: it does not jar with its context, it sets off the prophecies from that context, and it contributes to the folk tone of the play as a whole.

When the brothers leave, Erestus is left to tell his story. He speaks blank verse interspersed with several rhyming couplets, a way of softening the distinction between the blank verse and the rhymed prophecies. The diction is once again tinged with stereotyped phrases, but is not on the whole elaborate. When Lampriscus enters, Erestus switches to prose that scans about as well as some of the verse in the play. Contrary to the view of some critics, the speech of Lampriscus is not realistic but the most highly mannered prose in the play. Note for instance the parallelism (ll. 204–205):

> if you do anything for charity,
>> helpe me;
> if for neighborhood or brotherhood,
>> helpe me.

The jingle on "neighborhood or brotherhood" is like the page's playful sadness-madness line. The careful parallelism occurs again in the description of the first wife (ll. 217–220):

> whose tongue wearied me alive,
>> and
>>> sounded in my eares . . .
> whose talke was a continuall torment to all that dwelt by her
>>> or
>>>> lived nigh her.

Again the jingle. Of his fair shrewish daughter Lampriscus says (ll. 224–226, 229–231):

> poore shee is,
> and
>> proude shee is, as poore as a sheepe new shorne,
>>> and
>>>> as proude of her hopes, as a Peacock . . .
>>>> As curst as a waspe,
>>> and
>>>> as frowarde as a childe . . .

shee is to my age,
     as smoake to the eyes,
  or
     as vinegar to the teeth.

This is obviously a very carefully contrived prose.

It is not necessary to carry this detailed analysis through the play, but it should be emphasized that nowhere can the language be described accurately as realistic. Even in those places which come nearest, we are dealing with artfully constructed, playful dialogue. In the graveyard scene Wiggen intersperses his rustic speech with formulae from scholastic disputation. In the scene at the well the formulaic quality of the folktale is preserved in the close parallels of the sisters' opening statements (ll. 612–614, 617–618):

My father hath sent me to the well for the water of life, and tells mee if I give faire wordes I shall have a husband.

My father hath sent mee to the well for water, and he tells me if I speake faire, I shall have a husband . . .

The daughters have inherited the eloquence of their father. Celanta describes her sister (ll. 626–627): "you see what she is, a little faire, but as prowd as the divell, and the veriest vixen that lives upon Gods earth." And Zantippa comments upon her father's advice (ll. 632–634): "now my father sayes I must rule my tongue: why alas what am I then? a woman without a tongue is as a souldier without his weapon." In the scene where Jack and Eumenides strike their bargain, Jack uses a kind of mumming jingle (l. 709): "Are not you the man sir, denie it if you can sir." Throughout, the prose is ingeniously fanciful.

If it is inaccurate to describe the prose as realistic, it is equally inaccurate to describe the blank verse as bombastic. There are only about 150 lines of blank verse in the play, most of it in a straightforward style. Sacrapant's dying speech is bombastic, as is the speech of Eumenides adapted from *Orlando Furioso*, but to single out these two passages is to draw the contrast with the rest of the verse. In some scenes it is not always easy to say whether a given passage is prose or verse: some lines which scan are short, and some lines of the right length do not scan properly; sometimes the prose scans almost as well as the verse. This uncertainty in the poetic line, as much as anything else, has given rise to the frequent comments about textual corruption. Curiously, the effect is not so much to impress one with the inadequacy of the verse as to blur the distinction between verse and prose, much as the distinction between what is fanciful and what is realistic is blurred in the induction. The use of doggerel contributes to the effect. The result of the writing down of the verse and the writing up of the prose is to make the language, despite some surface disparity, very much a unity. Throughout the play, as in the induction, the result is fusion, not fission, and the whole piece has a remarkably harmonious tone.

Once again we find the only exception in Huanebango. He speaks a bombastic prose most of the time; in the scene with Zantippa there is a clear contrast between his "poetical" effusions and her comment (l. 651): "Foe, what greasie groome have wee here?" But, as has already been pointed out, these scenes are clearly intended as a special satire and, as such, are apart from the rest of the play.

Now to say that the author's attitude toward his work is naïve and that the play calls for a childlike acceptance is not, at least in my reading of it, to deny it a sophistication. Indeed, in the light of what I have been attempting to show about the language, such denial would involve contradiction. But the kind of sophistication is not that suggested by Gummere, Goldstone, or Cady, though the latter comes close to the truth.

What I mean by sophistication in the naïve work can be made clear by an analogy, though perhaps an inexact one. Any father who has read his children into a state of euphoria knows that the bulk of what appeals to the child is not likely to appeal to him. He is indeed fortunate if the effect upon himself is only soporific; he is at least escaping nausea. But there are some things he can read with endless delight, among them, by almost universal agreement, *Winnie the Pooh*. This book appeals to the eternal child in all of us, and the appeal is pure. We love Eeyore, but we do not also see him as a satiric picture of our querulous in-laws. We adore Pooh, but we do not see him as an edged portrait of our lazy neighbor. We delight in Owl, but he is not an acid portrayal of the Expert with a Ph.D. Our fondness for these characters is not in spite of their faults but because of them. We accept these stories as children do, for what they are, but we recognize their sophistication in language, in characterization, in plot. When Pooh engages in one of his illogical conversations with Piglet, we are amused, not only as children but also as adults watching children. The book is sophisticated because of this two-level appeal. Indeed, were it not for this sophistication, we would not like it nearly so much. And so it is with many of what parents call the "really good children's books."

To come closer to *The Old Wives Tale*, I once heard Sean Mac-Manus hold a college crowd enthralled for an hour or more as he told his own old wives' tales. The simplicity and the naïveté, the child appeal, were there, but so was the sophistication; and the spell MacManus cast lay in that sophistication, that is to say in the art of telling the story—the language, the tone, the timing. But the art did not make the stories something different from their real nature; it only heightened the appeal. I do not mean for a moment to suggest that any primitive art (like the folktale) needs sophistication to make it effective. But in an age when African statues are used by interior decorators and folk singers perform in swank night clubs, it is not revolutionary to suggest that primitive art can be sophisticated without turning it into a kind of ironic attack upon itself.

What I am suggesting, then, is that *The Old Wives Tale* is essentially naïve: it presents an amalgam of folktales and motifs cleverly joined together. The resulting story has no hidden meaning, no ironic overtones; it is simply itself. Nevertheless, the manner of presentation is highly artful, or sophisticated, but not in such an obvious way that the art calls attention to itself. This approach explains the diverging critical views of the past. One school had eyes only for the naïveté; the other school detected the sophistication, but misread its use.

In some ways the clearest validation of this reading is Cady's edition of the play. His acting version takes liberties with the text that may offend purists, but it is a sympathetic reading; its chief value is, as Cady puts it, that the "elaborate stage directions, so unlike the antique practice, have been inserted that those who read and see not may possibly get some of that same spirit as they read" (p. 17). To demonstrate the point, I shall quote some of Cady's directions that describe characters. Erestus (p. 26) is

> an old man, half wizard and half friar, in gown of grey with rosary and crucifix. He walks head down and counts his beads and begs an alms, while Madge points him out to her companions; and yet he is the power for good within the play, who puts to naught the plans of sorcery. Fittingly he stands by the cross where meet three ways to warn the passers-by against the sorcerer.

Sacrapant, we are told (p. 36),

> appears in his cell and there does magic. He is clad in the dark robes of sorcery and is in form majestic. In his hand he bears a wand and on his head he wears a wreath, the signs of his magic power. Without these he is impotent and doomed to death. At his first word there are signs of intense fear in the three spectators, which die down as the incidents unfold.

Delya enters (p. 37), a pot in her hand,

> drawn, it seems by the magic in the wand of Sacrapant for she walks as one fixed in a dream, modestly and with a charming innocence.

The Ghost of Jack (p. 56) is

> the shadow of a sprightly young fellow full of attitudes and the play of wit and fancy in many poses. This is no somber and mysterious ghost, except when bent upon undoing evil. Even then he goes about his business somewhat more cheerfully than do many.

All of this seems to me to be exactly right. It takes the story and the characters at face value without being patronizing or condescending. It takes account of the conflict between good and evil, yet it does not pretend that we are seeing Armageddon. The good humor of the piece gets full play. Folk literature comes to life before our eyes. Certainly Cady's edition demonstrates that *The Old Wives Tale* can be a highly attractive vehicle for actors.

A few points remain. The plot calls for some comment. As noted earlier, many have complained about its confusion or, at least, its lack of clarity. The complaints have not gone unanswered; defenders have tried to demonstrate that the piece is a model of tight construction. One can analyze the plot as Cady did (p. 7):

> When [Madge's story] is well under way it is seen to consist of at least two stories. Each of these centers about a double quest. In the main story two brothers are searching for their sister who has been spirited away by a sorcerer. The other part of the double quest in this main story is taken up by a lover of the sister who comes seeking her. In the minor story two crude fellows aping the chivalry of their betters enter upon a quest for one whom we are allowed to believe is the same young woman; but they are satisfied each with one of the two daughters of Lampriscus, a villager, whose quest for husbands for his daughters is the second part of the minor story. All of these quests are bound together by the presence in the plot of the story of Erestus, who is the prophet of good, and foretells to each seeker what he may hope from his quest. Erestus himself is under the power of the sorcerer in the play who has stolen his lady and driven her mad.

This indeed sounds very neat. Everything is perfectly balanced, and the characters representing the juxtaposition of good and evil provide the unifying elements in the plot. The plot is, however, much less orderly than the analysis. And the analysis has one serious flaw: it does not mention the character who resolves the action. A number of scholars who have studied the sources have maintained that the Grateful Dead motif is the center of the story; while one may not wish to pick a center for an anthology, one is surely safe in arguing that an analysis of the plot which ignores that very important motif does not give an accurate picture. And here may lie a clue to the difficulty noted, but not defined adequately, by critics.

The hero is Eumenides, but he does not appear until l. 432, just before the halfway mark, surely a late entry. And when he finally appears, he does nothing. The other characters share the hero's lassitude. Only at l. 692 does the active agent (Jack) appear, and he does not clash with his opponent until the final scene of the play, nor is the coming showdown forecast in any way. Thus, though it may be accurate enough to say that the play is organized around an opposition of a good to an evil principle, the conflict is not presented dramatically. It cannot be because the figure who represents the good principle (Erestus) is not the agent who finally is victorious over the evil. Until the final scene, the good principle is as quiescent as everyone else in the cast. Things do happen in the early part of the play, but there is no sense that we are getting anywhere. There is also a good deal of haziness about Venelia; probably it is a mistake to give a mute character so important a function in resolving the plot. Certainly our inability to anticipate her role at the end is a flaw—unless one wishes to argue that the surprise itself is a coup de theatre. The static quality of the plot, despite the almost furious action, contrasts violently with the usual ordered movement in a folktale. The lack of progress perhaps accounts for the fact that some critics have spoken of a dreamlike atmosphere in the play.[9] The comment is just enough; one's judgment of the results will be a matter of individual taste. But there is not much point in trying to pretend that the play is really very clearly plotted, even though it can be analyzed and even though the various elements are so tightly enmeshed that one can hardly disentangle them.

But it may, after all, turn out that analysis of the dramatic technique of a piece like *The Old Wives Tale* is irrelevant. It is, perhaps, not a play—or not quite a play. Miss Bradbrook (p. 323) has suggested that the piece stands halfway between the show and the drama. Certainly Peele's other work lends plausibility to this approach. He did produce Lord Mayor's pageants (as his father had before him). His court poems show a lively interest in pageantry. His earliest stage piece, *The Araygnement of Paris*, reverts at the end to the pure masque form upon which the work as a whole is based. *The Battle of Alcazar* has elaborate dumb shows and a spectacular display at the beginning of the last act. I have already commented upon Peele's concern with pageantry in *Edward I* (see Yale ed., 2, 46). It should not, therefore, be surprising to find that *The Old Wives Tale* is a vehicle for show. We might profitably consider it as an entertainment, a kind of subdramatic form, rather than a play.

Elizabethan entertainments were of many kinds, all of which had

9. Janet Spens, *Elizabethan Drama* (London, 1922), p. 53; Horne, p. 90.

some influence, either generic or peripheral, upon the developing drama. At the folk level there were seasonal festivities like May games, morris-dances, and mummings; their influence has already been traced in *The Old Wives Tale* (see above, Sec. 3, G, H). At a more sophisticated level, a variety of forms developed for entertainment at Court: the masque, the pastoral, the tournament, the debate, the pageant.[10] If from this variety we distill the pervasive elements, we find an entertainment tradition marked by songs, dances, pageantry, and spectacle. *The Old Wives Tale* participates in this tradition.

The Old Wives Tale is a highly musical play, rather more so than the casual reader may suspect, for not all the songs are marked as such, and those that are marked occupy a deceptively small portion of the printed text. The pages sing a catch (ll. 19–22)[11] and another song, which is one of the most charming lyrics of the period (ll. 75–81). The harvest men have two songs; although each of them is only four lines long, the stage directions call for them to be doubled and repeated. The second song is evidently followed by a dance, else there would be no reason for the *"women in their hands"* called for at l. 532 SD. The harvesters' share in the entertainment is thus far greater than the eight lines of song in the printed text would suggest. Fiddlers play during the tavern scene (l. 734 SD).

Elsewhere music is not specifically called for, though there are many possibilities for introducing it that would surely not be overlooked in a period when music played such an important role both in social life and in theatrical production. The heads in the well are called upon to speak (l. 634 SD), but their speeches are in a form suggesting they are sung by an offstage voice. Huanebango has what might very well be a comic song (ll. 670–675). Sacrapant's incantation over his magic table (ll. 367–373) could be set to mu-

10. For the masque and pastoral, see Introduction to *The Araygnement of Paris* in this volume. There is an excellent discussion of the whole entertainment tradition in chap. 3 of G. K. Hunter's *John Lyly* (Cambridge, Mass., 1962).

11. There is nothing in the text to indicate that the catch is not a part of Anticke's speech, but Q prints it in italics like the other songs. It therefore seems likely that it is to be sung. Could it be that Peele used three pages in the play so that there can be "Three merrie men"? See note to l. 19.

sic, and the prophecies of Erestus (ll. 158–165, 330–332, 445–448) might have musical accompaniment. A musical background for the echo scene (ll. 400–408) would be effective. In a number of places dancing might be introduced into the stage business. The pages in the induction, the clown, and Jack are all frolicking characters who might easily break into dancing at any moment. Sacrapant's conjurations might involve dancelike movements. In short, one supposes that adequate production would turn *The Old Wives Tale* into a kind of musical entertainment.

If we keep in mind the long tradition of the spectacular, ranging from fireworks for the devils in the mystery plays to the elaborate scenic devices for court masques and a play like Peele's *Araygnement*, we may suspect that a performance of *The Old Wives Tale* would be a good deal more lively than even the stage directions indicate. Thunder and lightning are called for in connection with Sacrapant's conjuring (l. 415 SD) and again to accompany Huanebango's appearance at the well (l. 645 SD). A *"flame of fire"* is specified for striking Huanebango down (l. 555 SD), and one would suppose that Sacrapant would need another flash of lightning to blind Corebus (l. 559 SD). Although the stage direction does not say so, surely the appearances of the Furies should be marked by some sort of smoke and fire (ll. 417, 559, 629). Similarly the Friar might appear in a puff of smoke (l. 373 SD). The death of Sacrapant, the destruction of his magic glass, and perhaps even Jack's appearance with the head should be marked by some spectacular display.

Nor is the spectacle limited to fireworks. Everything we know about Elizabethan stage practice and courtly entertaining indicates that productions were as lavishly costumed as a Broadway musical.[12] *The Old Wives Tale* offers many possibilities: The pages would have colorful court costumes; Sacrapant's sinister qualities might be enhanced by an elaborate conjurer's costume, and his

12. The Elizabethan taste for splendid costume in both real life and theater has been widely commented upon. A recent interesting discussion, which also covers scenery, properties, and lighting, is Morton Paterson, "The Stagecraft of the Revels Office during the Reign of Elizabeth," in *Studies in the Elizabethan Theatre*, ed. C. T. Prouty (New Haven, Shoe String Press, 1961).

attendant furies should be fantastically garbed. The most obvious place for costly display slips by virtually unnoted in the text. The harvesters and their women, whose only function is to add to the entertainment, would certainly be dressed in the kind of splendor that transformed many an evening in the hall into a time of enchantment, a splendor whose faded glory we can now perceive but dimly in the musty pages of the Revels Accounts.

What scenic display might have enhanced the production one can only guess at, but the obvious possibilities are the conjurer's cell, the well, and the little hill with Sacrapant's vital flame burning inside it. Exploitation of these opportunities would be in keeping with what the stage directions of the *Araygnement* and *Alcazar* demand.

It should be clear that to think of *The Old Wives Tale* as a mutilated piece to be performed by a poverty-stricken troupe before a rustic audience is wrong. Whatever may have been its fate in the declining days of the Queen's Men, the author had in mind a splendid evening of sophisticated entertainment. One may even suspect, though of course he cannot prove, that Peele originally conceived the piece for performance by a company of children. In any Elizabethan performance, a large number of roles would be played by boys (the three pages and the six women). The major roles of the Clown and Jack seem particularly suited to boys, and, indeed, all the remaining parts could be better rendered by children than by adults. Even Huanebango, whom all recent critics think to be a giant, would fit the mood better if he were a diminutive giant instead of a Falstaff. The atmosphere of the play is delicate and demands a naïve surrender on the part of the audience. It has a quaintness that is genuine, not merely the patina of three hundred years. To convey that atmosphere requires a stylization that would be enhanced if it were performed by boys. Therefore, despite what the title page tells us of the play's provenance, *The Old Wives Tale* finds its proper place in the tradition of court comedy and entertainment; its natural affinity is with Lyly and the Peele of the *Araygnement*, or, to use Professor Harbage's terms, with the select rather than the popular tradition.[13]

13. *Shakespeare and the Rival Tradition* (New York, 1952).

Even though we place *The Old Wives Tale* in a tradition, we must not lose sight of the fact that it is unique. There is nothing else quite like it in the whole range of Elizabethan drama, and it is in the unique qualities, rather than in the use of tradition, that Peele's genius lies.

6. STAGING

At the beginning of his chapter on "Staging in the Theatres," Chambers (*3*, 48) excludes *The Old Wives Tale* from consideration because the stage implied by its action and directions seemed to him more akin to the Court than to the playhouse. Clearly the stagecraft is not typical of contemporary plays presented on the public stage, but exactly what kind of stage is assumed is an open question. Since the printed text is an author's version rather than a theatrical version, it represents what the author thought might be or should be done at certain points, rather than what was actually done. Even though Peele had had practical experience as a "producer" and probably would not have demanded impossibilities, he was not producing this play and certainly did not concern himself with detailed staging. One may therefore expect a certain amount of fuzziness about the play's stagecraft.

It is clear that Peele was thinking of what may be called simultaneous staging; that is, various locales would be identified and visible to the audience throughout the play. One such location is the cross, which is clearly indicated in these directions:

> *Enter Senex at the Crosse . . .*   [l. 140]
>
> *Enter Eumenides . . . and the old man at the crosse.*
>   [l. 431]
> *Enter . . . he that was at the crosse.*   [l. 872]

There are also dialogue references to the cross (ll. 127, 301, 870). Whether the spot should be marked with a large upright cross (with its connotations of good to contrast with Sacrapant's evil) or merely with something to suggest a crossroads is open to question, but there is clearly to be a place on stage which is "the cross." An indication that Peele had not thought through all the details is the exit for Erestus at l. 240, which necessitates a direction for re-entry at l. 300; it would be more effective for him to remain at the cross.[1]

Another fixed location is the "litle hill" under which the magic light is hidden. It is indicated by these directions:

> *He remooves a turfe, and shewes a light in a glasse.*
>
> [l. 424]
>
> *Here they dig and descry the light under a litle hill.*
>
> [l. 603]
>
> *He digs and spies a light.*
>
> [l. 825]

Still another location appears in these directions:

> *Enter Zantyppa . . . to the well . . .*
>
> [l. 610]
>
> *Enter the fowle wench to the well . . .*
>
> [l. 614]
>
> *Enter two Furies . . . and laies Huanebango by the well of life.*
>
> [l. 629]
>
> *Enter Corebus and Celanta . . . to the well . . .*
>
> [l. 768]

So much is certain: the play requires a cross, a hill, and a well. These properties could easily be set in place at the beginning of the play; they could be used equally well in performances in a great hall, at Court, or on the public stage.[2]

The author's plan requires at least one trap. The heads must rise from the well, and the most convenient way of managing this

1. If "the cross" were a mansion, the exit might be interpreted as a direction for Erestus to go inside it and thus exit from the sight of the audience. For other places which suggest that Peele has not completely thought out his stagecraft see notes to ll. 520 SD, 559 SD, and the trouble over beheading Sacrapant (see above, Sec. 3.E).

2. A much-cited well appears in *Documents Relating to the Office of the Revels in the Time of Queen Elizabeth*, ed. A. Feuillerat (Vol. 21 of *Materialen zur Kunde des Alteren Englischen Dramas*, ed. W. Bang, 1908), p. 277: "ffor the Cariadge of the partes of ye well counterfeit from the Bell in gracious strete to St Johns to be performed for the play of Cutwell xd." This was in February 1576/7.

effect is to locate the well over a trap. A trap is indicated for the final exit of Jack, who "leapes downe in the ground" (l. 909 SD).

More debatable is the need for mansions. Miss Bradbrook requires two (smith's cottage and Sacrapant's study), and Chambers requires three (smith's cottage, an inn, and Sacrapant's study). Peele does not *require* any. For, while the play can be done in the Bradbrook-Chambers manner (and may so have been done at Court), it can also be performed on the public stage without any equipment other than that already discussed. I assume (perhaps rashly, in view of the current argument about the structure of the theaters) that the public theater had a forestage, some kind of area at the rear before which a curtain could be drawn, and an "above" (not required for this play).

Sacrapant must have a lair; it is called a cell in a stage direction (l. 629). Perhaps it should have a curtain before it, since some curtained-off area that is probably, but not necessarily, identified with the cell is required at l. 843 SD when Jack "*draweth a curten*" to disclose the sleeping Delya. At his first entrance the stage direction is "*Enter Sacrapant in his studie*" (l. 334); the study is the name given to that area we usually call the inner stage. I see no reason to suppose that Peele is thinking of anything more than such an area when he speaks of the study, the cell, and the curtain. In other words, on the public stage the study makes a hut for Sacrapant unnecessary. At Court a hut could be provided.

No special equipment is necessary for the pages and Madge, though it might be effective to show a hut for them. Clunch, after leading the pages through the forest to his house, calls to Madge to open the door; she enters. This sort of action occurs frequently on the Elizabethan stage. Editors used to explain that "we are to imagine that the stage now represents the interior of the hut," or one might say that Madge brings the inside of the house onstage with her. But such explanation gives a false impression of the workings of the Elizabethan stage. The audience does not imagine that the scene changes to an interior, because it had not imagined the previous scene taking place in an exterior. Unless something in the scene made necessary a specific reference to the locale, a scene merely occurred. Here no real door need be involved. Clunch, Madge, and the pages may act out their scene near the rear of the stage, to one side, where they will sit through the rest of the performance. When at the end (l. 922) Madge says, "come, let us in," we need not suppose she is inviting them into a hut (as Chambers seems to think); she is really inviting them off the stage. At Court a hut might well be supplied.

Chambers is surely wrong in requiring "an inn before which a table is set." The table at l. 734 SD might be Sacrapant's magic table from l. 367. Sacrapant's table probably would be within the study, which in the later scene would for the moment become the inn. Or, as sometimes happens in Elizabethan plays, the inn might enter at l. 734. Jack leaves the stage to go to the inn; Eumenides continues his journey (around the stage), and in the space of one line he meets the inn, which appears when a table is carried on. So the scene might be performed, either on the public stage or at Court. But it is dangerous to argue too curiously here: I don't suppose that Peele ever gave a moment's thought to the actual staging of these scenes with the table. Although it may seem incredible to academic critics, always lamentably literal minded about stagecraft, even the most uninspired theatrical troupe could rise to this situation without even realizing it had faced a problem.

It is clear, I think, that the play could be performed equally well on the public stage or at Court, and the Queen's Men, like all major companies, performed on both stages. The use of "studie" suggests that, for the moment at least, Peele was thinking of the public stage.[3]

3. It is of some interest to note that the stage for the Middlebury production of the play was an adaptation of the public stage; Cady (pp. 13–14) describes it thus: "A word should, perhaps, be said about the stage. Its construction is an easy matter, requiring a very moderate outlay. The only essentials are an open front stage and a back stage, before which a curtain is hung. There should be two entrances to the open front stage, one on either side of the curtain hung before the back stage. The entrances to the back stage can be arranged to suit the convenience of the play which is to be given. For instance, it was found that the fireplace made an effective entrance and exit for the characters in Madge's interrupted tale. . . . it was necessary to place the house of Clunch, the magic well, and the cell of Sacrapant behind the curtain. The cross where three roads met and the mound of earth with the magic glass would as necessarily be on the open stage. At the beginning of the play the open stage is a wood into which the

7. THE TEXT

A. EARLIEST EDITION

[Ornamental bar] / THE / Old Wiues Tale. / A pleasant conceited Come- / die, played by the Queenes Ma- / iesties players. /
Written by *G. P.* / [Device] / Printed at London by *Iohn Danter,*
and are to / be sold by *Raph Hancocke,* and *Iohn* / *Hardie. 1595.* /

HT] [Ornamental bar] / The old VViues / Tale. /

RT] *The Old VViues Tale.* [*The old VViues tale.* on A4ᵛ, B1,
C3, C4, E3, E4; *The Old VViues tale.* on B3, C1, C2, E1, E2,
F2]

Colophon] Printed at London by *Iohn Danter,* for *Raph / Hancocke,* and *Iohn Hardie,* and are to / be solde at the shop ouer
against / Saint Giles his Church with- / out Criplegate. /
1595. /

Collation] 4⁰. A–F⁴[–F4].   23 leaves unnumbered.

Contents] A1, blank except for signature; [A2], Title (verso
blank); A3, Text with ornament, HT, and initial; F3ᵛ, Col-
ophon.

Catchwords] A3 *Fan-;* B3 *your;* C3 *Enter;* D3 *this;* E3 *Eum:;*
F3 *Fant:*

Typography] 29 ll. [28 ll. on C1ᵛ, F1, F1ᵛ, F2, F2ᵛ; 27 ll. on
F3, F3ᵛ] plus headline and direction line.
Roman 20 ll. x 94 mm.   137 (148) x 76mm.
(B3, Pforzheimer)

Copies] British Museum 162.d.53 (lacks A1)
        Dyce (lacks F2, F3, which are supplied in facsimile)
        Huntington (lacks A1)
        Pforzheimer (lacks A1)

Variants] Variants are preserved in E[i]:
    E1ᵛ [l. 660] rude (D,P)   rim (BM,H)
    E2   [l. 694] Whose (D,P)   Who's (BM,H)
    E4   [l. 777] goulden bird (D,P) gouldē beard (BM,H)

---

three vagabonds enter, and after Madge is interrupted in her story, that
same open stage becomes the fairy-land where all these strange wonders
happen."

[l. 782]	goulden bird (D,P)	gouldē beard (BM,H)
[l. 789]	tost (D,P)	iust (BM,H)
[l. 790]	quoiners (D,P)	coiners (BM,H)
	quine (D,P)	coine (BM,H)

On A4 (ll. 54–55), there is a problem in spacing. BM prints:

for stumbling on thethreshold, open dore

with a larger than customary space between the comma and "open" and with an en-space at the end of the line, so that it is not justified. In D the line is justified, or nearly so, but there is space in "o pen" and "dor e". Greg, who saw only these two copies, says in a note in his Malone Society Reprint (p. viii): "The error . . . arose in the course of printing off. A space somehow dropped out and the type closed up. In the Dyce copy the last word still stands almost at the end of the line, but the type gradually crept back, and in the B.M. copy there is about an en-space blank at the end. Other copies may perhaps show the space in its right place." But they do not. In H and P the line is justified not, as one would expect, by inserting a space in "thethreshold" but by a wider space in "o pen." Exactly what happened is not clear, but no ambiguity of reading results.

In E[i] there is not much doubt that BM and H preserve the corrected state. "Who's" is clearly a correction of "Whose", and "iust" is an attempt to do something about the obviously impossible "tost". Bullen said that neither reading is intelligible, and he may be right. "Iust" is not quite impossible, but it is not very good; it has the look of a printer's attempt to correct an error without recourse to copy. The other changes are perhaps less obviously necessary, but BM and H are generally preferable. "Coiners" and "coine" are modernizations (and may indicate that the copy had the spellings preserved in D and P). I would, however, not expect the corrections to "rim" and "beard" without recourse to manuscript.[1]

On F2 (l. 869), where H and P have "he see-", something has happened in BM, which preserves only traces of *h* and *e-*; everything between has failed to print, and the paper bulges in a peculiar way. In the Dyce copy, both F2 and F3 are supplied in facsimile. At this point the facsimile reads "he se-". On F3ᵛ (l. 928), the facsimile has "goe to", where BM, H, and P all have "goe, to". If

1. See notes to ll. 777, 789, 790.

these variants are not the error of the facsimile maker, they must come from some copy no longer extant.

The play is printed with two sets of running titles, including three identifiable variants:

> x *The Old VViues Tale.*
> y *The old VViues tale.*
> z *The Old VViues tale.*

A[i], B[i], D[i], D[o], and F[o] use only the x versions, which are indistinguishable from each other. The other set appears as follows, in what was probably the order through the press:

A[o]	B[o]	C[i]	C[o]	E[i]	E[o]	F[i]
	y	x	z	x	z	x
	x	z	x	z	x	z
	z	x	y	x	y	x
y		x	y	x	y	x

The pattern of transfer between formes is the normal one as diagrammed by Moxon, except for B[o] to C[i], where one forme was apparently not turned as usual, producing the variant as diagrammed by McKerrow. There is no way of proving that the inner formes preceded the outer; indeed, the use of the running titles from D (which would presumably be available before the set used in E) for F[o] might suggest that it preceded F[i].[2]

The play was probably set by two compositors, though the evidence is not so extensive as one might wish. No evidence except spelling has been discovered, and in a play so short with so few words per page, spelling evidence is necessarily spread very thin. The variant spellings are given on the accompanying chart. Although the evidence is not extensive, I see no convenient way of explaining the consistency of variation between *hir/her* and *Jacke/Jack* except on the assumption that two compositors are at work. The *doo/do* and *goe/go* preferences also appear consistent except on E3, where B uses the long form of *doo*. Tabulated, the evidence looks impressive enough, but it should be noted that some

2. See F. T. Bowers, "Notes on Running-titles as Bibliographical Evidence," *The Library*, Ser. 4, *19* (1938–39), 315–338.

	A3	A3ᵛ	A4	A4ᵛ	B1	B1ᵛ	B2	B2ᵛ	B3	B3ᵛ	B4	B4ᵛ	C1	C1ᵛ	C2	C2ᵛ	C3	C3ᵛ	C4	C4ᵛ	D1	D1ᵛ	D2	D2ᵛ	D3	D3ᵛ	D4	D4ᵛ	E1	E1ᵛ	E2	E2ᵛ	E3	E3ᵛ	E4	E4ᵛ	F1	F1ᵛ	F2	F2ᵛ	F3	F3ᵛ
Jacke	1																	1							5	1	4	1		9	4	4	5						1	1	8	1
hir			1	1	2	1	1						3	1	1	1						1		1		1	1	1	1				1	1	1		1	1	1	1		1
doo(e)	2		1																					1			2	1					1								
goe	1								1									1					1			1	1	1	1				1								1
Jack																	2	4	8		2	1	1				1		8	1			10	9	7	7	8	2	6	6		
her										1			1	2	1	1	1	3	2		1	1	1	1				1	1	1			9	1	7		1	1	6	7		
do																	1				1					1		1							2	2						
go																		1	2					1			1						2		2							1
be	2		2		1			2	1	1	1	1	1	1	1		1	1	1		2	2	1	2	1	1	2		2	1	1	1	1	1	1	1	4	2	6		1	1
he	1		1		4	1			1	3	1	1	1	2	4	1	1	1	4	5	3	3	1	2	1	1	3		2	1	1	1	1	1	1	1	1	1	2	1	1	1
me	1		2	1	1	1			4		1		2	2	4	1	3	1	5		3	1	1	2	4	1	3	3	3	1			2	2	2	2	1	2	2		1	
she	1		1	1	1				3		1		3		1		1	1			5		3	1	2		3						1	1	2	4	1		1	3		1
we	1	2		2	4					1			5	1			3					5		1	4	2					1	4	1	1	4		1		1			
bee						4					1		5	1									1						1		4		1									
hee	1		1						1		1		1	1	1							1						2	1	1			1									
mee			1	1	1								1	1	3						3				1	3		3	2	1	1	1	1				1		1		1	
shee			1		1		1		3		1		2	1	3	1					2								1	1	1										2	
wee	1	2	1	1		1	2																2						1	1											1	

pages are assigned by virtue of one spelling. That is risky enough when the forms involved are the *her* and *Jack* variants, but highly questionable when *do* or *go* is involved. The conclusions can hardly be called more than tentative, but it appears that Compositor A set from the beginning to B2^v, C1–C3, D3–E2^v, and F3–3^v; Compositor B set B3–4^v, C3^v–D2^v, and E3–F2^v.

If my division of the stints is correct, it is clear that A is more likely than B to use the long form for *be, he, me, she, we*, a tendency that matches his preference for *Jacke, goe, doo*. The total number for each compositor by stints (short form first) is:

					Total
A 33 / 16	24 / 17	33 / 18	6 / 3	96 / 54
B	18 / 6	50 / 3	42 / 4	110 / 13

A different method of tabulation renders the same results:

	be	*bee*	*he*	*hee*	*me*	*mee*	*she*	*shee*	*we*	*wee*	Total
A	20	12	17	11	22	17	18	8	19	6	96 / 54
B	11	2	34	4	33	1	8	4	24	2	110 / 13

But one must be cautious; it is possible that one could add different pages of the -*e* and -*ee* forms and come to different results. I have used them only as a way of substantiating the conclusions reached by the more clearly established preferences.

There is no evidence that copy was cast off. Examination of other works printed by Danter has not helped with compositor determination. Nothing in the division of labor need affect the editor's treatment of his text.

Of the first edition, one can say that it is an undistinguished piece of work, though in justice to the printer one must admit that there is no reason to think that it preserves anything but a reasonably careful rendition of what appeared in the copy. The paucity of emendations demonstrates that it is generally clear of error.

B. MODERN EDITIONS

Dyce edited *The Old Wives Tale* three times: in *The Works of George Peele: Now First Collected* (London, 1828); in *The Works of George Peele* (2d ed., London, 1829–39); and in *The Dramatic and Poetical Works of Robert Greene & George Peele* (London, 1861; several times reprinted; I have used the 1874 reprint). Bullen included the play in *The Works of George Peele* (London, 1888). These editions and their treatment of the text have already been described in Volume 2 of the Yale edition (p. 65). W. W. Greg edited a facsimile from the British Museum copy for the Malone Society in 1909. One of Peele's most popular plays, *The Old Wives Tale* has been included in numerous anthologies. I have used the texts in Volume 1 of *Representative English Comedies* (New York, 1903); in C. F. Tucker Brooke and N. B. Paradise, *English Drama 1580–1642* (New York, 1933); and in A. K. McIlwraith, *Five Elizabethan Comedies* (Oxford, 1934). Robert Blair edited the play for a doctoral dissertation at the University of Illinois in 1936; his edition remains unpublished. The other edition that seems worthy of mention is the acting version by Frank Cady (Boston, 1916), but it is of critical, not textual value.

C. THE PRESENT EDITION

The copy of *The Old Wives Tale* in the Huntington Library is the immediate source of this text, but all four extant copies have been collated. This text follows the original, except that *i, j, u,* and *v* are changed to conform with modern usage, long *s* is altered to modern *s, vv* to *w, æ* to *ae,* and *œ* to *oe.* Distinctions between italic and roman type are disregarded except on the title page, and abbreviations (limited to the ampersand and the bar over vowels to indicate omission of a following nasal consonant) have been silently expanded. Lowercase letters at the beginning of a speech have been silently changed. Obvious printer's errors in spacing have been corrected. Speech tags have been regularized throughout. All other changes are noted. Editorial insertions are enclosed within square brackets.

As is usual with old texts, the punctuation presents some problems. I have tried to keep as close to the original as possible without sacrificing clarity; when an emendation has been necessary, I have tried to make the change conform to what I consider the spirit of the original.

This edition, like Gummere's, follows the lineation of Q more closely than is usual with other modern ones. The rule has been:

when in doubt, follow the original. Thus no changes are made that do not render some positive advantage. At ll. 432–433, where Q has

> Tell me Time, tell me just Time,
> When shall I Delia see?

I find no advantage in Dyce's alteration:

> Tell me, Time,
> Tell me, just Time, when shall I Delia see?

A similar case occurs at ll. 807–808, where Q has

> What, not a word but mum,
> Then Sacrapant thou art betraide,

and Dyce prints

> What, not a word but mum? Then, Sacrapant,
> Thou art betray'd.

Nor does Dyce improve the hypermetrical l. 584 by printing

> O heavens, how
> Am I beholding to this fair young man,

or by printing l. 589 as

> O Delya,
> Happy are we to see thee here!

On the other hand, ll. 605–608, which are printed as prose in Q, are printed in this edition as verse, admittedly irregular, because they are in the midst of a verse passage. Jingles are usually printed as prose in Q and are so printed in this edition. This seems better than following Dyce in rendering ll. 283–284 as

> *O falsum Latinum!*
> The fair maid is *minum*,
> *Cum apurtinantibus gibletis* and all.

If one makes this alteration, to be consistent he should also change the lineation to point up the jingles in "*Meus, mea, meum, in contemptum omnium Grammaticorum*" (l. 281) and "Hips and Hawes, and stickes and strawes" (ll. 143 and 145), all of which are printed as prose by Dyce. Other lineation problems are discussed in the notes.

Line numbers are consecutive throughout the present text, excluding stage directions, which are given the number of the last line of dialogue preceding the direction. Page signatures of the original edition are indicated in brackets at the margin of the text.

In the collations, punctuation readings include the word immediately preceding the mark in question.

THE
Old Wiues Tale.

A pleasant conceited Come-
die, played by the Queenes Maiesties players.

Written by *G. P.*

Printed at London by *Iohn Danter*, and are to
be sold by *Raph Hancocke*, and *Iohn
Hardie.* 1 5 9 5.

Anticke ⎫
Fantasticke ⎬ pages
Frolicke ⎭
Clunch (Smith)
Madge (Old Woman), the old wife who tells the tale

Lampriscus, an unhappy father
Zantippa (Curst Daughter) ⎫
Celanta (Fowle Wench) ⎬ his daughters

Huanebango, a slashing knight
Booby (Clown), also called Corebus, his attendant

Delya, the abducted maiden
Eumenides (the Wandring Knight), her lover
Calypha (Kalepha, 1 Brother) ⎫
Thelea (2 Brother) ⎬ Delya's brothers
Erestus (Senex, Old Man), a young lover transformed
Venelia, his mad lady
Sacrapant (Conjurer)
Friar
Jack, a ghost
Wiggen ⎫
Corebus ⎬ friends of Jack
Churchwarden (Steeven Loache?)
Sexton
Hostess
Head
Voice
Eccho

Two Furies
Harvest Men and dancing partners
Fiddlers] *

  * Q omits the list of characters.

Ant. How nowe fellowe Frolicke, what all amort? Doth this sadnes become thy madnes? What though wee have lost our way in the woodes, yet never hang the head, as though thou hadst no hope to live till tomorrow: for Fantasticke and I will warrant thy life tonight for twenty in the hundred.

Frol. Anticke and Fantasticke, as I am frollicke franion, never in all my life was I so dead slaine. What? to loose our way in the woode, without either fire or candle so un-
10 comfortable? *O coelum! O terra! O maria! O Neptune!*

Fant. Why makes thou it so strange, seeing Cupid [A3ᵛ] hath led our yong master to the faire Lady and she is the only Saint that he hath sworne to serve.

Frol. What resteth then but wee commit him to his wench, and each of us take his stand up in a Tree, and sing out our ill fortune to the tune of O man in desperation.

Ant. Desperately spoken fellow Frollicke in the darke: but seeing it falles out thus, let us rehearse the old proverb.

　　Three merrie men, and three merrie men,
20 　　And three merrie men be wee.
　　I in the wood, and thou on the ground,
　　And Jacke sleepes in the tree.

　　　　[A dog barks.]

Fant. Hush a dogge in the wood, or a wooden dogge, O comfortable hearing! I had even as live the Chamberlaine of the white Horse had called me up to bed.

Frol. Eyther hath this trotting Cur gone out of his cyrcuit, or els are we nere some village, which should not be farre

Enter a Smith with a Lanthorne and Candle.

off, for I perceive the glymring of a Gloworme, a Candle, or a Cats eye, my life for a halfe pennie. In the name of my

1　*Frolicke*]　Franticke Q　　　*amort*]　a mort Q
4　*tomorrow*]　to morrow Q
5　*tonight*]　to night Q
22　SD *A . . . barks.*]　Q omits

30 own father, be thou Oxe or Asse that appearest, tell us what thou art.

Smith. What am I? Why I am Clunch the Smith, what are you, what make you in my territories at this time of [A4] the night?

Ant. What doe we make dost thou aske? why we make faces for feare: such as if thy mortall eyes could behold, would make thee water the long seames of thy side slops, Smith.

Frol. And in faith Sir unlesse your hospitalitie doe releeve
40 us, wee are like to wander with a sorrowfull hey ho, among the owlets, and Hobgoblins of the Forrest: good Vulcan, for Cupids sake that hath cousned us all: befriend us as thou maiest, and commaund us howsoever, wheresoever, whensoever, in whatsoever, for ever and ever.

Smith. Well Masters it seemes to mee you have lost your waie in the wood: in consideration whereof, if you will goe with Clunch to his Cottage, you shall have house roome, and a good fire to sit by, althogh we have no bedding to put you in.

50 *All.* O blessed Smith, O bountifull Clunch.

Smith. For your further intertainment, it shall be as it may be, so and so.

Heare a Dogge barke.

Hearke this is Ball my Dogge that bids you all welcome in his own language, come, take heed for stumbling on the threshold, open dore Madge, take in guests.

Enter old woman.

Old Woman. Welcome Clunch and good fellowes al that come with my good man, for my good mans sake, [A4ᵛ] come on, sit downe, here is a peece of cheese and a pudding of my owne making.

54 *come,*] *come* Q   *the threshold*] thethreshold Q
55 *open dore*] See p. 378.   *Madge,*] Madge Q
57 *man,*] man Q   *sake*] sake Q
58 *on,*] on Q   *downe,*] downe Q

60   *Ant.*   Thanks Gammer a good example for the wives of our
        towne.
      Frol.   Gammer thou and thy good man sit lovingly together,
        we come to chat and not to eate.
      Smith.   Well Masters if you will eate nothing take away:
        Come, what doo we to passe away the time? Lay a crab in
        the fire to rost for Lambes-wooll; what, shall wee have a
        game at Trumpe or Ruffe to drive away the time, how say
        you?
      Fant.   This Smith leades a life as merrie as a King with
70   Madge his wife; Syrrha Frolicke, I am sure thou art not
        without some round or other, no doubt but Clunch can
        beare his part.
      Frol.   Els think you mee ill brought up, so set to it when you
        will.

They sing.

Song.

> When as the Rie reach to the chin,
> And chopcherrie chopcherrie ripe within,
> Strawberries swimming in the creame,
> And schoole boyes playing in the streame:
> Then O, then O, then O my true love said,
80 Till that time come againe,
> Shee could not live a maid.

      Ant.   This sport dooes well: but me thinkes Gammer,   [B1]
        a merry winters tale would drive away the time trimly,
        come, I am sure you are not without a score.
      Fant.   I faith Gammer a tale of an howre long were as good
        as an howres sleepe.
      Frol.   Looke you Gammer, of the Gyant and the Kings
        Daughter, and I know not what, I have seene the day when
        I was a litle one, you might have drawne mee a mile after
90   you with such a discourse.
      Old Woman.   Well, since you be so importunate, my good

66   *what,*] what Q
84   *come,*] come Q

man shall fill the pot and get him to bed, they that ply their
worke must keepe good howres, one of you goe lye with
him, he is a cleane skind man I tell you, without either
spavin or windgall, so I am content to drive away the time
with an old wives winters tale.

Fant.   No better hay in Devonshire, a my word Gammer,
Ile be one of your audience.

Frol.   And I another thats flat.

100 *Ant.*   Then must I to bed with the good man, *Bona nox*
Gammer, Good night Frolicke.

Smith.   Come on my Lad, thou shalt take thy unnaturall rest
with me.

Exeunt Anticke and the Smith.

Frol.   Yet this vantage shall we have of them in the morning,
to bee ready at the sight thereof extempore.

Old Woman.   Nowe this bargaine my Masters must I [B1ʳ]
make with you, that you will say hum and ha to my tale,
so shall I know you are awake.

Both.   Content Gammer, that will we doo.

110 *Old Woman.*   Once uppon a time there was a King or a
Lord, or a Duke that had a faire daughter, the fairest that
ever was; as white as snowe, and as redd as bloud: and once
uppon a time his daughter was stollen away, and hee sent
all his men to seeke out his daughter, and hee sent so long,
that he sent all his men out of his Land.

Frol.   Who drest his dinner then?

Old Woman.   Nay either heare my tale, or kisse my taile.

Fant.   Well sed, on with your tale Gammer.

Old Woman.   O Lord I quite forgot, there was a Conjurer,
120 and this Conjurer could doo anything, and hee turned himselfe into a great Dragon, and carried the Kinges Daughter
away in his mouth to a Castle that hee made of stone, and
there he kept hir I know not how long, till at last all the

98   *of*] of of Q
101   *Good*] God Q
109   *Gammer,*] Gammer Q
120   *anything*] any thing Q

Kinges men went out so long, that hir two Brothers went
to seeke hir. O I forget: she (he I would say) turned a proper yong man to a Beare in the night, and a man in the day,
and keeps by a crosse that parts three severall waies, and he
made his Lady run mad: gods me bones, who comes here?

Enter the two Brothers.

Frol.   Soft Gammer, here some come to tell your tale   [B2]
130 for you.

Fant.   Let them alone, let us heare what they will say.

1 Bro.   Upon these chalkie Cliffs of Albion
We are arived now with tedious toile,
And compassing the wide world round about
To seeke our sister, to seeke faire Delya forth,
Yet cannot we so much as heare of hir.

2 Bro.   O fortune cruell, cruell and unkind,
Unkind in that we cannot find our sister;
Our sister haples in hir cruell chance:
140 Soft who have we here?

Enter Senex at the Crosse stooping to gather.

1 Bro.   Now father God be your speed, What doo you
gather there?

Old Man.   Hips and Hawes, and stickes and strawes, and
thinges that I gather on the ground my sonne.

1 Bro.   Hips and Hawes, and stickes and strawes, why is that
all your foode father?

Old Man.   Yea sonne.

2 Bro.   Father, here is an Almes pennie for mee, and if I
speede in that I goe for, I will give thee as good a Gowne of
150 gray as ever thou diddest weare.

1 Bro.   And Father here is another almes pennie for me, and
if I speede in my journey, I will give thee a Palmers staffe
of yvorie, and a scallop shell of beaten gold.

Old Man.   Was shee fayre?   [B2ᵛ]

128 *bones,*] bones Q
140 *here?*] here. Q

   2 Bro.   I, the fairest for white, and the purest for redd, as the
   blood of the Deare, or the driven snow.
Old Man.   Then harke well and marke well, my old spell:
   Be not afraid of every stranger,
   Start not aside at every danger:
160   Things that seeme are not the same,
   Blow a blast at every flame:
   For when one flame of fire goes out,
   Then comes your wishes well about:
   If any aske who told you this good,
   Say the white Beare of Englands wood.
   1 Bro.   Brother heard you not what the old man said:
   Be not afraid of every stranger,
   Start not aside for every danger:
   Things that seeme are not the same,
170   Blow a blast at every flame:
   [For when one flame of fire goes out,
   Then comes your wishes well about:]
   If any aske who told you this good,
   Say the white Beare of Englands wood.
   2 Bro.   Well if this doo us any good,
   Wel fare the white Bear of Englands wood.

Ex[*eunt brothers*].

Old Man.   Now sit thee here and tel a heavy tale.
   Sad in thy moode, and sober in thy cheere,
   Here sit thee now and to thy selfe relate,
180   The hard mishap of thy most wretched state.
   In Thessalie I liv'd in sweete content,
   Untill that Fortune wrought my overthrow;
   For there I wedded was unto a dame,   [B3]
   That liv'd in honor, vertue, love, and fame:
   But Sacrapant that cursed sorcerer,

155   *I,*] I Q
156   *snow.*] snow: Q
171–172   Q omits
176   SD *Exeunt brothers*] ex. Q

Being besotted with my beauteous love,
My deerest love, my true betrothed wife,
Did seeke the meanes to rid me of my life.
But worse than this, he with his chanting spels,
190   Did turne me straight unto an ugly Beare;
And when the sunne doth settle in the west,
Then I begin to don my ugly hide:
And all the day I sit, as now you see,
And speake in riddles all inspirde with rage,
Seeming an olde and miserable man:
And yet I am in Aprill of my age.

      Enter Venelia his Lady mad; and goes in againe.

See where Venelya my betrothed love,
Runs madding all inrag'd about the woods;
All by his curssed and inchanting spels.

      Enter Lampriscus with a pot of Honny.

200   But here come Lampriscus my discontented neighbour.
How now neighbour, you looke towarde the ground as
well as I, you muse on something.

Lamp. Neighbour on nothing, but on the matter I so often
mooved to you: if you do anything for charity, helpe me;
if for neighborhood or brotherhood, helpe me: never was
one so combered as is poore Lampryscus: and to begin, I
pray receive this potte of Honny to mend your fare. [B3ᵛ]

Old Man. Thankes neighbor, set it downe, Honny is alwaies
welcome to the Beare. And now neighbour let me heere
210   the cause of your comming.

Lamp. I am (as you knowe neighbour) a man unmaried, and
lived so unquietly with my two wives, that I keepe every
yeare holy the day wherein I buried them both; the first was
on saint Andrewes day; the other on saint Lukes.

Old Man. And now neighbour, you of this country say,
your custome is out: but on with your tale neighbour.

Lamp. By my first wife, whose tongue wearied me alive, and

186 *love,*] love: Q
201–202 *as well*] aswell Q

sounded in my eares like the clapper of a great Bell, whose
talke was a continuall torment to all that dwelt by her, or
220   lived nigh her, you have heard me say I had a handsome
daughter.

Old Man.   True neighbour.

Lamp.   Shee it is that afflictes me with her continuall clam-
oures, and hangs on me like a Burre: poore shee is, and
proude shee is, as poore as a sheepe new shorne, and as
proude of her hopes, as a Peacock of her taile well growne.

Old Man.   Well said Lampryscus, you speake it like an Englishman.

Lamp.   As curst as a waspe, and as frowarde as a   [B4]
230   childe new taken from the mothers teate, shee is to my age,
as smoake to the eyes, or as vinegar to the teeth.

Old Man.   Holily praised neighbour, as much for the next.

Lamp.   By my other wife I had a daughter, so hard favoured,
so foule and ill faced, that I thinke a grove full of golden
trees, and the leaves of Rubies and Dyamonds, would not
bee a dowrie aunswerable to her deformitie.

Old Man.   Well neighbour, nowe you have spoke, heere me
speake; send them to the Well for the water of life: there
shall they finde their fortunes unlooked for; Neighbour
240   farewell.

Exit.

Lamp.   Farewell and a thousand, and now goeth poore
Lampryscus to put in execution this excellent counsell.

Exit.

Frol.   Why this goes rounde without a fiddling stick; but
doo you heare Gammer, was this the man that was a Beare
in the night, and a man in the day?

Old Woman.   I, this is hee; and this man that came to him
was a beggar, and dwelt uppon a greene. But soft, who
comes here? O these are the harvest men; ten to one they
sing a song of mowing.

235   *trees,*] trees; Q
242   SD *Exit*] *Exeunt* Q
246   *I,*] I Q

Enter the harvest men asinging, with this Song   [B4^v]
double repeated.

250   All yee that lovely lovers be, pray you for me,
            Loe here we come asowing, asowing,
            And sowe sweete fruites of love:
            In your sweete hearts well may it proove.

Exeunt.

Enter Huanebango with his two hand sword, and Booby
the Clowne.

Fant.   Gammer, what is he?

Old Woman.   O this is one that is going to the conjurer, let
him alone, here what he sayes.

Huan.   Now by Mars and Mercury, Jupiter and Janus, Sol
and Saturnus, Venus and Vesta, Pallas and Proserpina, and
by the honor of my house Polimackeroeplacydus, it is a
260   wonder to see what this love will make silly fellowes adventure, even in the wane of their wits, and infansie of their
discretion. Alas my friend what fortune calles thee foorth
to seeke thy fortune among brasen gates, inchanted towers,
fire and Brimstone, thunder and lightning. Beautie I tell
thee is peerelesse, and she precious whom thou affectest: do
off these desires good countriman, good friend runne away
from thy selfe, and so soone as thou canst, forget her;
whom none must inherit but he that can monsters tame,
laboures atchive, riddles absolve, loose inchantments, mur-
270   ther magicke, and kill conjuring: and that is the great and
mighty Huanebango.

Booby.   Harke you sir, harke you; First know I have   [C1]
here the flurting feather, and have given the Parish the
start for the long stocke: Nowe sir if it bee no more but
running through a little lightning and thunder, and riddle
me riddle me whats this, Ile have the wench from the Conjurer if he were ten Conjurers.

Huan.   I have abandoned the Court and honourable com-

249   SD *asinging*] *a singing* Q
251   *asowing*] a sowing Q

pany, to doo my devoyre against this sore Sorcerer and
mighty Magitian: if this Ladie be so faire as she is said to
bee, she is mine, she is mine. *Meus, mea, meum, in contemp-*
tum omnium Grammaticorum.

Booby. O *falsum Latinum!* the faire maide is *minum, cum*
apurtinantibus gibletes and all.

Huan. If shee bee mine, as I assure my selfe the heavens will
doo somewhat to reward my worthines; shee shall bee allied
to none of the meanest gods; but bee invested in the most
famous stocke of Huanebango Polimackeroeplacidus, my
Grandfather: my father Pergopolyneo: my mother, Dyonora de Sardynya: famouslie descended.

Booby. Doo you heare sir; had not you a Cosen, that was
called Gustecerydis?

Huan. Indeede I had a Cosen, that somtime followed the
Court infortunately, and his name Bustegustecerydis.

Booby. O Lord I know him well: hee is the knight   [C1ᵛ]
of the neates feete.

Huan. O he lov'd no Capon better, he hath oftentimes deceived his boy of his dinner, that was his fault, good Bustegustecerydis.

Booby. Come, shall we goe along?

[*Enter Erestus.*]

Soft, here is an olde man at the Crosse, let us aske him the
way thither. Ho, you Gaffer, I pray you tell where the wise
man the Conjurer dwells?

Huan. Where that earthly Goddesse keepeth hir abode; the
commander of my thougts, and faire Mistres of my heart.

Old Man. Faire inough, and farre inough from thy fingering sonne.

Huan. I will followe my Fortune after mine owne fancie,
and doo according to mine owne discretion.

Old Man. Yet give something to an old man before you goe.

298 *fault,*] fault Q
300 *Come,*] Come Q   SD *Enter Erestus.*] Q omits
310 *something*] some thing Q

Huan. Father mee thinkes a peece of this Cake might serve
your turne.

Old Man. Yea sonne.

Huan. Huanabango giveth no Cakes for Almes, aske of
them that give giftes for poore Beggars. Faire Lady, if thou
wert once shrined in this bosome, I would buckler thee,
haratantara.

Exit.

Booby. Father doo you see this man, you litle thinke heele
run a mile or two for such a Cake, or passe for a   [C2]
320   pudding, I tell you father hee has kept such a begging of mee
for a peece of this Cake, whoo he comes uppon me with a
superfantiall substance, and the foyson of the earth, that I
know not what he meanes: If hee came to me thus, and
said, my friend Booby or so, why I could spare him a peece
with all my heart; but when he tells me how God hath en-
riched mee above other fellowes with a Cake: why hee
makes me blinde and deafe at once: Yet father heere is a
peece of Cake for you, as harde as the world goes.

Old Man. Thanks sonne, but list to mee,
330   He shall be deafe when thou shalt not see;
Farewell my sonne things may so hit,
Thou maist have wealth to mend thy wit.

Booby. Farewell father, farewell; for I must make hast after
my two hand sword that is gone before.

Exeunt omnes.

Enter Sacrapant in his studie.

Sacra. The day is cleare, the Welkin bright and gray,
The Larke is merrie, and records hir notes;
Each thing rejoyseth underneath the Skie,
But onely I whom heaven hath in hate:
Wretched and miserable Sacrapant,
340   In Thessalie was I borne and brought up,
My mother Meroe hight a famous Witch,   [C2ᵛ]

316   *thee,*] thee Q
328   *you,*] you Q

And by hir cunning I of hir did learne,
To change and alter shapes of mortall men.
There did I turne my selfe into a Dragon,
And stole away the Daughter to the King,
Fair Delya, the Mistres of my heart:
And brought hir hither to revive the man,
That seemeth yong and pleasant to behold,
And yet is aged, crooked, weake and numbe.
350   Thus by inchaunting spells I doo deceive,
Those that behold and looke upon my face;
But well may I bid youthfull yeares adue:

Enter Delya with a pot in hir hand.

See where she coms from whence my sorrows grow,
How now fair Delya where have you bin?
Delya.   At the foote of the Rocke for running water, and
gathering rootes for your dinner sir.
Sacra.   Ah Delya, fairer art thou than the running water,
yet harder farre than steele or Adamant.
Delya.   Will it please you to sit downe sir?
360   *Sacra.*   I Delya, sit and aske me what thou wilt, thou shalt
have it brought into thy lappe.
Delya.   Then I pray you sir let mee have the best meate from
the king of Englands table, and the best wine in all France,
brought in by the veriest knave in all Spaine.
Sacra.   Delya I am glad to see you so pleasant, well   [C3]
sit thee downe.
Spred table spred;
Meat, drinke and bred
Ever may I have,
370   What I ever crave:
When I am spred,
For meate for my black cock,

345   *King,*] King; Q
359   *sir?*] sir. Q
367   Q prints as new speech with tag for *Sacr.*
367-368   One line in Q
369-370   One line in Q
371-372   One line in Q

And meate for my red.

Enter a Frier with a chine of Beefe and a pot of wine.

Sacra. Heere Delya, will yee fall to?
Delya. Is this the best meate in England?
Sacra. Yea.
Delya. What is it?
Sacra. A chine of English beefe, meate for a king and a kings
     followers.
380 *Delya.* Is this the best wine in France?
Sacra. Yea.
Delya. What Wine is it?
Sacra. A cup of neate wine of Orleance, that never came
     neer the brewers in England.
Delya. Is this the veriest knave in all Spaine?
Sacra. Yea.
Delya. What is he a Fryer?
Sacra. Yea a Frier indefinit, and a knave infinit.
Delya. Then I pray ye sir Frier tell me before you goe,
390   which is the most greediest Englishman?
Fryer. The miserable and most covetous Usurer.
Sacra. Holde thee there Friar,

Exit Friar.

But soft who have we heere? Delia away, be gon.

Enter the two Brothers.   [C3ᵛ]

Delya away, for beset are we,
But heaven or hell shall rescue her for me.

[Exeunt Delya and Sacrapant.]

1 Bro. Brother, was not that Delya did appeare?
     Or was it but her shadow that was here?

374 *to?*] to. Q
378–379 Q lineates: . . . king / . . . followers.
383–384 Q lineates: . . . Orleance, / . . . England.
393 *heere?*] heere, Q   *away,*] away Q   *be gon*] begon Q
395 SD *Exeunt . . . Sacrapant.*] Q omits

2 Bro.   Sister, where art thou? Delya come again.
He calles, that of thy absence doth complaine.
400   Call out Calypha that she may heare,
And crie aloud, for Delya is neere.
Eccho.   Neere.
1 Bro.   Neere, O where, hast thou any tidings?
Eccho.   Tidings.
2 Bro.   Which way is Delya then, or that, or this?
Eccho.   This.
1 Bro.   And may we safely come where Delia is?
Eccho.   Yes.
2 Bro.   Brother remember you the white Beare of Englands
410   wood:

> Start not aside for every danger,
> Be not afeard of every stranger;
> Things that seeme, are not the same.

1 Bro.   Brother, why do we not then coragiously enter?
2 Bro.   Then brother draw thy sword and follow me.

Enter the Conjurer; it lightens and thunders, the 2. Bro-
ther falles downe.

1 Bro.   What brother doost thou fall?
Sacra.   I, and thou too Calypha.

Fall 1. Brother. Enter two furies [and carry them off].

Adestes Daemones: away with them,
Go cary them straight to Sacrapantos cell,   [C4]
420   There in despaire and torture for to dwell;
These are Thenores sonnes of Thessaly,
That come to seeke Delya their sister forth:
But with a potion, I to her have given,
My arts hath made her to forget her selfe.

He remooves a turfe, and shewes a light in a glasse.

398   *again.*] again Q
407   *is?*] is Q
411   *aside*] a side Q
414   *enter?*] enter Q
417   *too*] to Q   SD *and . . . off*] Q omits

See heere the thing which doth prolong my life,
With this inchantment I do any thing.
And till this fade, my skill shall still endure,
And never none shall breake this little glasse,
But she that's neither wife, widow, nor maide.
430　Then cheere thy selfe, this is thy destinie,
Never to die, but by a dead mans hand.

Exit.

*Enter Eumenides the wandring Knight, and the old man
at the crosse.*

Eumen.　Tell me Time, tell me just Time,
When shall I Delia see?
When shall I see the loadstar of my life?
When shall my wandring course end with her sight?
Or I but view my hope, my hearts delight.
Father God speede, if you tell fortunes, I pray good father
tell me mine.
Old Man.　Sonne I do see in thy face,
440　Thy blessed fortune worke apace;
I do perceive that thou hast wit,
Beg of thy fate to governe it,
For wisdome govern'd by advise,
Makes many fortunate and wise.
Bestowe thy almes, give more than all,　　　　　　　[C4ᵛ]
Till dead mens bones come at thy call:
Farewell my sonne, dreame of no rest,
Til thou repent that thou didst best.

Exit Old Man.

Eumen.　This man hath left me in a Laborinth,
450　He biddeth me give more than all,
Till dead mens bones come at my call:
He biddeth me dreame of no rest,

425　*life,*] life Q
431　SD *Exit.*] *Exeunt* Q
448　SD *Man*] *m.* Q
451　*my*] thy Q

Till I repent that I do best.

Enter Wiggen, Corebus, Churchwarden and Sexten.

Wiggen.   You may be ashamed, you whorson scald Sexton
and Churchwarden, if you had any shame in those shame-
lesse faces of yours, to let a poore man lie so long above
ground unburied. A rot on you all, that have no more compassion of a good fellow when he is gone.

Churchwarden.   What, would you have us to burie him, and
460   to aunswere it our selves to the parishe?

Sexton.   Parish me no parishes, pay me my fees, and let the
rest runne on in the quarters accounts, and put it downe for
one of your good deedes a Gods name, for I am not one
that curiously stands upon merits.

Corebus.   You whoreson sodden headed sheepes-face, shall a
good fellow do lesse service and more honestie to the parish, and will you not when he is dead let him have Christmas buriall?

Wiggen.   Peace Corebus, as sure as Jack was Jack, the   [D1]
470   frollickst frannion amongst you, and I Wiggen his sweete
sworne brother, Jack shall have his funerals, or some of
them shall lie on Gods deare earth for it, thats once.

Churchwarden.   Wiggen I hope thou wilt do no more then
thou darst aunswer.

Wiggen.   Sir, sir, dare or dare not, more or lesse, aunswer or
not aunswer, do this, or have this.

Sexton.   Helpe, helpe, helpe, Wiggen sets upon the parish
with a Pike staffe.

Eumenides awakes and comes to them.

Eumen.   Hould thy hands good fellow.
480   *Corebus.*   Can you blame him sir, if he take Jacks part against
this shake rotten parish that will not burie Jack?

453   SD *Corebus*] Corobus Q
459   *Churchwarden*] *Simon* Q   *What,*] What Q
465   *Corebus*] Corobus Q
468   *buriall?*] buriall. Q
469   *as sure*] assure Q
481   *Jack?*] Jack Q

Eumen.   Why what was that Jack?

Corebus.   Who Jack sir, who our Jack sir? as good a fellow
as ever troade uppon Neats leather.

Wiggen.   Looke you sir, he gave foure score and nineteene
mourning gownes to the parish when he died, and because
he would not make them up a full hundred, they would not
bury him; was not this good dealing?

Churchwarden.   Oh Lord sir how he lies, he was not worth a
490   halfepenny, and drunke out every penny: and nowe his
fellowes, his drunken companions, would have us to burie
him at the charge of the parish, and we make many   [D1ᵛ]
such matches, we may pull downe the steeple, sell the Belles,
and thatche the chauncell: he shall lie above ground till he
daunce a galliard about the churchyard for Steeven Loache.

Wiggen.   *Sic argumentaris domine* Loache; and we make
many such matches, we may pull downe the steeple, sell
the Belles, and thatche the chauncell: in good time sir, and
hang your selves in the Bell ropes when you have done,
500   *Domine oponens praepono tibi hanc questionem,* whether
will you have the ground broken, or your pates broken
first, for one of them shall be done presently, and to begin
mine, ile seale it upon your cockescome.

Eumen.   Hould thy hands, I pray thee good fellow be not too
hastie.

Corebus.   You Capons face, we shall have you turnd out of
the parish one of these dayes, with never a tatter to your
arse, then you are in worse taking then Jack.

Eumen.   Faith and he is bad enough: this fellow does but the
510   part of a friend, to seeke to burie his friend; how much will
burie him?

Wiggen.   Faith, about some fifteene or sixteene shillings will
bestow him honestly.

Sexton.   I, even thereabouts sir.

Eum.   Heere hould it then, and I have left me but one poore
three halfe pence; now do I remember the wordes   [D2]
the old man spake at the crosse:

501   *broken*] broken: Q
514   *I,*] I Q   *thereabouts*] there abouts Q
517   *crosse:*] crosse; Q

Bestowe all thou hast, and this is all,
Till dead mens bones comes at thy call,
520   heare holde it, and so farewell.

[Exit Eumenides.]

Wiggen.   God, and all good, bee with you sir; naie you cor-
morants, ile bestowe one peale of Jack at mine owne proper
costs and charges.
Corebus.   You may thanke God the long staffe and the bilbowe blade crost not your cockescombe; well weele to the
church stile, and have a pot, and so tryll lyll.
Both.   Come, lets go.

Exeunt.

Fant.   But harke you gammer, me thinkes this Jack bore a
great sway in the parish.
530   *Old Woman.*   O this Jack was a marvelous fellow, he was but
a poore man, but very well beloved: you shall see anon
what this Jack will come to.

*Enter the harvest men singing, with women in their
hands.*

Frol.   Soft, who have wee heere? our amorous harvestars.
Fant.   I, I, let us sit still and let them alone.

Heere they begin to sing, the song doubled.

Loe heere we come areaping, areaping,
To reape our harvest fruite,
And thus we passe the yeare so long,
And never be we mute.

Exit the harvest men.

Enter Huanebango, and Corebus the clowne. [D2ᵛ]

Frol.   Soft, who have we here?

518–519   Prose in Q
520   SD *Exit Eumenides.*] Q omits
525   *blade*] blade, Q
527   *Come,*] Come Q
533   *harvestars*] harvest starres Q
535   *areaping*] a reaping Q

540 *Old Woman.*   O this is a cholerick gentleman, all you that
     love your lives, keepe out of the smell of his two hand
     sworde: nowe goes he to the conjurer.
     Fant.   Me thinkes the Conjurer should put the foole into a
     Jugling boxe.
     Huan.   Fee, fa, fum,
     Here is the Englishman,
     Conquer him that can,
     Came for his lady bright,
     To proove himselfe a knight,
550 And win her love in fight.
     Corebus.   Who hawe maister Bango are you here? heare you,
     you had best sit downe heere, and beg an almes with me.
     Huan.   Hence base cullion, heere is he that commaundeth
     ingresse and egresse with his weapon, and will enter at his
     voluntary, whosoever saith no.

          A voice and flame of fire: Huanebango falleth downe.

     Voice.   No.
     Old Woman.   So with that they kist, and spoiled the edge of
     as good a two hand sword, as ever God put life in; now
     goes Corebus in, spight of the conjurer.

          Enter the Conjurer [*and two furies*], *and strike Corebus
          blinde.*

560 *Sacra.*   Away with him into the open fields,
     To be a ravening pray to Crowes and Kites:

               [*Exeunt furies and carry out Huanebango.*]

     And for this villain let him wander up and downe   [D3]
     In nought but darkenes and eternall night.
     Corebus.   Heer hast thou slain Huan a slashing knight

     545–546 One line in Q
     547–548 One line in Q
     555 *voluntary,*] voluntary Q
     559 SD *and two furies*] Q omits
     561 SD *Exeunt . . . Huanebango.*] Q omits

And robbed poore Corebus of his sight.

Exit.

Sacra.   Hence villaine hence. Now I have unto Delya
          Given a potion of forgetfulnes,
          That when shee comes shee shall not know hir Brothers:
          Lo where they labour like to Country slaves,
570   With spade and mattocke on this inchaunted ground.
          Now will I call hir by another name,
          For never shall she know hir selfe againe,
          Untill that Sacrapant hath breathd his last.
          See where she comes.

Enter Delya.

          Come hither Delya, take this gode, here hard
          At hand two slaves do worke and dig for gold,
          Gore them with this and thou shalt have inough.

He gives hir a gode.

Delya.   Good sir I know not what you meane.
Sacra.   She hath forgotten to be Delya,
580   But not forgot the name she should forget:
          But I will change hir name.
          Faire Berecynthia so this Country calls you,
          Goe ply these strangers wench, they dig for gold.

Exit Sacrapant.

Delya.   O heavens! how am I beholding to this faire   [D3ᵛ]
          yong man.
          But I must ply these strangers to their worke.
          See where they come.

*Enter the two Brothers in their shirts with spades dig-
ging.*

566–567 Q lineates: . . . hence. / . . . forgetfulnes,
575 *Delya*,] Delya Q
575–576 Q lineates: . . . gode, / . . . gold,
580 *name*] same Q
583 *wench*,] wench Q   *gold*.] gold Q

1 Bro. O Brother see where Delya is.

2 Bro. O Delya happy are we to see thee here.

590 *Delya.* What tell you mee of Delya prating swaines?
I know no Delya nor know I what you meane,
Ply you your work or else you are like to smart.

1 Bro. Why Delya knowst thou not thy Brothers here?
We come from Thessalie to seeke thee forth,
And thou deceivest thy selfe for thou art Delya.

Delya. Yet more of Delya, then take this and smart:
What, faine you shifts for to defer your labor?
Worke villaines worke, it is for gold you digg.

2 Bro. Peace brother peace, this vild inchanter

600 Hath ravisht Delya of hir sences cleane,
And she forgets that she is Delya.

1 Bro. Leave cruell thou to hurt the miserable;
Digg brother digg, for she is hard as steele.

Here they dig and descry the light under a litle hill.

2 Bro. Stay brother what has thou describe?

Delya. Away and touch it not, it is some thing,
That my Lord hath hidden there.

She covers it agen.

Enter Sacrapant.   [D4]

Sacra. Well sed, thou plyest these Pyoners well,
Goe get you in you labouring slaves.
Come Berecynthia, let us in likewise,

610 And heare the Nightingale record hir notes.

Exeunt omnes.

*Enter Zantyppa the curst Daughter to the well, with a
pot in hir hand.*

Zant. Now for a husband, house and home, God send a
good one or none I pray God: My father hath sent me to

597   *What,*] What Q
605–606   Prose in Q
607–608   Prose in Q

the well for the water of life, and tells mee if I give faire
wordes I shall have a husband.

*Enter the fowle wench to the well for water with a pot
in hir hand.*

But heere comes Celanta my sweete sister, Ile stand by and
heare what she saies.

Celanta.   My father hath sent mee to the well for water,
and he tells me if I speake faire, I shall have a husband and
none of the worst: Well though I am blacke I am sure all
the world will not forsake mee, and as the olde proverbe is,
though I am blacke, I am not the divell.

Zant.   Marrie gup with a murren, I knowe wherefore thou
speakest that, but goe thy waies home as wise as thou
camst, or Ile set thee home with a wanion.

Here she strikes hir Pitcher against hir sisters,   [D4ᵛ]
and breakes them both and goes hir way.

Celanta.   I thinke this be the curstest queane in the world,
you see what she is, a little faire, but as prowd as the divell,
and the veriest vixen that lives upon Gods earth. Well Ile
let hir alone, and goe home and get another Pitcher, and
for all this get me to the well for water.

Exit.

*Enter two Furies out of the Conjurers Cell and laies
Huanebango by the well of life.*

Enter Zantippa with a Pitcher to the Well.

Zant.   Once againe for a husband, and in faith Celanta I have
got the start of you; Belike husbands growe by the Well
side; now my father sayes I must rule my tongue: why alas
what am I then? a woman without a tongue is as a souldier
without his weapon; but ile have my water and be gon.

*Heere she offers to dip her Pitcher in, and a head
speakes in the Well.*

620   *is,*] is Q
633   *tongue*] tongue, Q

Head.   Gently dip, but not too deepe,
　　For feare you make the golden beard to weepe,
　　Faire maiden white and red,
　　Stroke me smoothe, and combe my head,
　　And thou shalt have some cockell bread.
640 *Zant.*   What is this?
　　Faire maiden white and red,
　　Combe me smooth, and stroke my head:
　　And thou shalt have some cockell bread.
　　Cockell callest thou it boy, faith ile give you   [E1]
　　cockell bread.

*Shee breakes hir Pitcher uppon his heade, then it thunders
and lightens, and Huanebango rises up: Huanebango is
deafe and cannot heare.*

Huan.   Phylyda phylerydos, Pamphylyda floryda flortos,
　　Dub dub a dub, bounce quoth the guns, with a sulpherous
　　　　huffe snuffe:
　　Wakte with a wench, pretty peat, pretty love, and my
　　　　sweet prettie pigsnie;
　　Just by thy side shall sit surnamed great Huanebango,
650 Safe in my armes will I keepe thee, threat Mars or thunder
　　　　Olympus.
Zant.   Foe, what greasie groome have wee here? Hee looks
　　as though hee crept out of the backeside of the well; and
　　speakes like a Drum perisht at the West end.
Huan.   O that I might but I may not, woe to my destenie
　　　　therefore;
　　Kisse that I claspe but I cannot, tell mee my destenie where-
　　　　fore?
Zant.   Whoope nowe I have my dreame, did you never
　　heare so great a wonder as this? Three blue beanes in a
　　blue bladder, rattle bladder rattle.
Huan.   Ile nowe set my countenance and to hir in   [E1ᵛ]

636 *beard*] birde Q
640 *this?*] this, Q
640–641 One line in Q
649 *Huanebango,*] Huanebango Q

660 prose, it may be this rim ram ruffe is too rude an incounter. Let me, faire Ladie if you be at leisure, revell with your sweetnes, and raile uppon that cowardly Conjurer, that hath cast me or congealed mee rather into an unkinde sleepe and polluted my Carcasse.

Zant.   Laugh, laugh Zantyppa, thou has thy fortune, a foole and a husbande under one.

Huan.   Truely sweete heart as I seeme, about some twenty yeares, the very Aprill of mine age.

Zant.   Why what a prating Asse is this?

670 *Huan.*   Hir Corall lippes, hir crimson chinne,
Hir silver teeth so white within:
Hir golden locks, hir rowling eye,
Hir pretty parts, let them goe by:
Hey ho hath wounded me,
That I must die this day to see.

Zant.   By gogs bones thou art a flouting knave,
Hir Corral lippes, hir crimson chinne:
ka wilshaw.

Huan.   True my owne and my owne because mine, and
680 mine because mine, ha ha: Above a thousand pounds in possibilitie, and things fitting thy desire in possession.   [E2]

Zant.   The Sott thinkes I aske of his landes, Lobb be your comfort, and Cuckold bee your destenie: Heare you sir; and if you will have us, you had best say so betime.

Huan.   True sweete heart and will royallize thy progeny with my petigree.

Exeunt omnes.

Enter Eumenides the wandring Knight.

Eumen.   Wretched Eumenides, still unfortunate,
Envied by fortune, and forlorne by Fate;

660   *rim*] BM, H; rude D, P   *ruffe*] ruffe, Q
661   *Let me*] Q indents as for a new speech, but without tag.   *me,*]
me Q
672   *locks,*] locks Q
673   *parts,*] parts Q
677   Prose in Q
680   *mine,*] mine Q

Here pine and die wretched Eumenides.

690   Die in the spring, the Aprill of my age?
Here sit thee down, repent what thou hast don.
I would to God that it were nere begon.

Enter Jacke.

Jack.   You are well overtaken sir.

Eumen.   Who's that?

Jack.   You are heartily well met sir.

Eumen.   Forbeare I say, who is that which pincheth mee?

Jack.   Trusting in God good Master Eumenides, that you
are in so good health as all your friendes were at the making hereof: God give you Good morrowe sir, lacke you

700   not a neate handsome and cleanly yong Lad, about the
age of fifteene or sixteene yeares, that can runne by your
horse, and for a neede make your Mastershippes   [E2^v]
shooes as blacke as incke, howe say you sir?

Eumen.   Alasse pretty Lad, I know not how to keepe my
selfe, and much lesse a servant, my pretty boy, my state is
so bad.

Jack.   Content your selfe, you shall not bee so ill a Master
but ile bee as bad a servant: Tut sir I know you though
you know not me; Are not you the man sir, denie it if you

710   can sir, that came from a strange place in the land of
Catita, where Jacke a napes flies with his taile in his mouth,
to seeke out a Ladie as white as snowe, and as redd as
blood; ha, ha, have I toucht you now?

Eumen.   I thinke this boy be a spirit, How knowst thou all
this?

Jack.   Tut are not you the man sir, denie it if you can sir,
that gave all the money you had to the burying of a poore

691   *don.*] don Q
694   *Who's*] BM, H; Whose D, P
699   *Good*] God Q
703   *sir?*] sir. Q
713   *now?*] now. Q
714–715   Q lineates: . . . spirit, / . . . this?

man, and but one three-halfe-pence left in your pursse:
Content you sir, Ile serve you, that is flat.

720 *Eumen.* Well my Lad since thou art so importunate, I am
content to entertaine thee, not as a servant, but a copartner
in my journey. But whither shall we goe? for I have not
any money more than one bare three-halfe-pence.

Jack. Well Master content your selfe, for if my divination
bee not out, that shall bee spent at the next Inne or   [E3]
alehouse we come too: for maister I knowe you are passing
hungrie; therefore ile go before and provide dinner untill
that you come, no doubt but youle come faire and softly
after.

730 *Eumen.* I, go before, ile follow thee.

Jack. But doo you heare maister, doo you know my name?

Eumen. No I promise thee, not yet.

Jack. Why I am Jack.

Exit Jack.

Eumen. Jack, why be it so then.

*Enter the Hostes and Jack, setting meate on the table,
and Fidlers come to play, Eumenides walketh up and
downe, and will eate no meate.*

Hostess. How say you sir, doo you please to sit downe?

Eumen. Hostes I thanke you, I have no great stomack.

Hostess. Pray sir, what is the reason your maister is so
strange, doth not this meate please him?

Jack. Yes Hostes, but it is my maisters fashion to pay be-
740 fore hee eates, therefore a reckoning good hostesse.

Hostess. Marry shall you sir presently.

Exit.

719   *you,*] you Q
720   *importunate*] impornate Q
721   *servant,*] servant; Q
722   *goe?*] goe Q
732   *thee,*] thee Q
733   SD *Exit*] *Exeunt* Q
734   SD *come*] *came* Q
738   *him?*] him. Q

Eumen. Why Jack what doost thou meane, thou knowest I
have not any money: therefore sweete Jack tell me what
shall I doo.

Jack. Well maister looke in your pursse.

Eumen. Why faith it is a follie, for I have no money. [E3ᵛ]

Jack. Why looke you maister, doo so much for me.

Eumen. Alas Jack my pursse is full of money.

Jack. Alas, maister, does that worde belong to this accident?
750   why me thinkes I should have seene you cast away your
cloake, and in a bravado daunced a galliard round about
the chamber; why maister, your man can teach you more
wit than this, come hostis, cheere up my maister.

[Enter Hostess.]

Hostess. You are heartily welcome: and if it please you to
eate of a fat Capon, a fairer birde, a finer birde, a sweeter
birde, a crisper birde, a neater birde, your worship never
eate off.

Eumen. Thankes my fine eloquent hostesse.

Jack. But heare you maister, one worde by the way, are you
760   content I shall be halfes in all you get in your journey?

Eumen. I am Jack, here is my hand.

Jack. Enough maister, I aske no more.

Eumen. Come Hostesse, receive your money, and I thanke
you for my good entertainment.

Hostess. You are heartily welcome sir.

Eumen. Come Jack, whither go we now?

Jack. Mary maister to the conjurers presently.

Eumen. Content Jack: Hostis farewell.

Exeunt omnes.

*Enter Corebus and Celanta the foule wench, to the well
for water.*

Corebus. Come my ducke come: I have now got a   [E4]

753 SD *Enter Hostess.*] Q omits
763 *Hostesse,*] Hostesse Q
766 *Jack,*] Jack Q   *whither*] whether Q
768 SD *Exeunt omnes.*] Exe. om. Q   *Celanta*] Zelanto Q

770   wife, thou art faire, art thou not?

Celanta. My Corebus the fairest alive, make no doubt of that.

Corebus. Come wench, are we almost at the wel?

Celanta. I Corebus, we are almost at the Well now, ile go fetch some water: sit downe while I dip my pitcher in.

Voyce. Gently dip: but not too deepe;
For feare you make the goulden beard to weepe.

A head comes up with eares of Corne, and she combes them in her lap.

Faire maiden white and red,
Combe me smoothe, and stroke my head:
780   And thou shalt have some cockell bread.
Gently dippe, but not too deepe,
For feare thou make the goulden beard to weep.

A head comes up full of golde, she combes it into her lap.

Faire maiden, white, and redde,
Combe me smooth, and stroke my head;
And every haire, a sheave shall be,
And every sheave a goulden tree.

Celanta. Oh see Corebus, I have combd a great deale of golde into my lap, and a great deale of corne.

Corebus. Well said wench, now we shall have just enough,
790   God send us quoiners to quine our golde: but come, shall we go home sweet heart?

Celanta. Nay come Corebus, I will lead you.

773   *wel?*] wel. Q
774   *Corebus,*] Corebus Q
777   *beard*] BM, H; bird D, P
782   *beard*] BM, H; bird D, P   SD Q prints after l. 786
783   *maiden*] maide Q
787   *Corebus,*] Corebus Q
789   *just*] BM, H; tost D, P
790   *quoiners*] D, P; coiners BM, H   *quine*] D, P; coine BM, H
come,] come Q
792   *Corebus,*] Corebus Q

Corebus.   So Corebus things have well hit,   [E4ᵛ]
Thou hast gotten wealth to mend thy wit.

Exit.

Enter Jack and the wandring knight.

Jack.   Come away maister come.
Eumen.   Go along Jack, ile follow thee, Jack, they say it
is good to go crosse legged, and say his prayers backward:
how saiest thou?
Jack.   Tut never feare maister, let me alone, heere sit you
800   still, speake not a word. And because you shall not be
intised with his inchanting speeches, with this same wooll
ile stop your eares: and so maister sit still, for I must to
the Conjurer.

Exit Jack.

Enter the Conjurer to the wandring knight.

Sacra.   How now, what man art thou that sits so sad?
Why dost thou gaze upon these stately trees,
Without the leave and will of Sacrapant?
What, not a word but mum,
Then Sacrapant thou art betraide.

*Enter Jack invisible, and taketh off Sacrapants wreath
from his head, and his sword out of his hand.*

What hand invades the head of Sacrapant?
810   What hatefull fury doth envy my happy state?
Then Sacrapant these are thy latest dayes,
Alas my vaines are numd, my sinews shrinke,
My bloud is pearst, my breath fleeting away,
And now my timelesse date is come to end:
He in whose life his actions hath beene so foule,

795   *come.*] come, Q
801   *speeches,*] speeches; Q
804   *sad?*] sad Q
807   *What,*] What Q
809   Q has a new speech tag for *Sac.*

Now in his death to hell desends his soule.   [F1]

He dyeth.

Jack. Oh Sir are you gon: now I hope we shall have some
other coile. Now maister how like you this? the Conjurer
hee is dead, and vowes never to trouble us more. Now get
820   you to your faire Lady, and see what you can doo with
her: Alas he heareth me not all this while; but I will helpe
that.

He pulles the Wooll out of his eares.

Eumen. How now Jack, what news?
Jack. Heere maister, take this sword and dig with it, at the
foote of this hill.

He digs and spies a light.

Eumen. How now Jack, what is this?
Jack. Maister, without this the Conjurer could do nothing,
and so long as this light lasts, so long doth his arte indure,
and this being out, then doth his arte decay.
830   *Eumen.* Why then Jack I will soone put out this light.
Jack. I maister, how?
Eumen. Why with a stone ile breake the glasse, and then
blowe it out.
Jack. No maister you may as soone breake the Smiths Anfill,
as this little vyoll; nor the biggest blast that ever Boreas
blew cannot blowe out this little light; but she that is
neither maide, wife, nor widowe. Maister, winde   [F1ᵛ]
this horne; and see what will happen.

He windes the horne.

*Heere enters Venelia and breakes the glasse, and blowes
out the light, and goeth in againe.*

Jack. So maister, how like you this? this is she that ranne
840   madding in the woods, his betrothed love that keepes the

818   *this?*] this; Q
836   *blew*] blew, Q
839   *this?*] this; Q

crosse, and nowe this light being out, all are restored to
their former libertie. And now maister to the Lady that
you have so long looked for.

He draweth a curten, and there Delia sitteth asleepe.

Eumen.   God speed faire maide sitting alone: there is once.
   God speed faire maide; there is twise:
   God speed faire maide, that is thrise.
Delya.   Not so good sir, for you are by.
Jack.   Enough maister, she hath spoke, now I will leave her
   with you.

[Exit.]

850   *Eumen.*   Thou fairest flower of these westerne parts:
   Whose beautie so reflecteth in my sight,
   As doth a Christall mirror in the sonne:
   For thy sweet sake I have crost the frosen Rhine,
   Leaving faire Po, I saild up Danuby,
   As farre as Saba whose inhansing streames,
   Cuts twixt the Tartars and the Russians,
   These have I crost for thee faire Delia: [F2]
   Then grant me that which I have sude for long.
Delya.   Thou gentle knight, whose fortune is so good
860   To finde me out, and set my brothers free,
   My faith, my heart, my hand, I give to thee.
Eumen.   Thankes gentle Madame: but heere comes Jack,
   thanke him, for he is the best friend that we have.

Enter Jack with a head in his hand.

Eumen.   How now Jack, what hast thou there?
Jack.   Mary maister, the head of the conjurer.
Eumen.   Why Jack that is impossible, he was a young man.
Jack.   Ah maister, so he deceived them that beheld him: but
   hee was a miserable, old, and crooked man; though to each

843   SD asleepe] *a sleepe* Q
849   SD Exit.] Q omits
859   good] good: Q

mans eye he seemed young and fresh; for maister, this Con-
870   jurer tooke the shape of the olde man that kept the crosse:
and that olde man was in the likenesse of the Conjurer.
But nowe maister winde your horne.

He windes his horne.

*Enter Venelia, the two brothers, and he that was at the
crosse.*

Eumen.   Welcome Erestus, welcome faire Venelia,
Welcome Thelea, and Kalepha both,   [F2ᵛ]
Now have I her that I so long have sought,
So saith faire Delia, if we have your consent.
1 Bro.   Valiant Eumenides thou well deservest
To have our favours: so let us rejoyce,
That by thy meanes we are at libertie.
880   Heere may we joy each in others sight,
And this faire Lady have her wandring knight.
Jack.   So maister, nowe yee thinke you have done: but I
must have a saying to you; you know you and I were part-
ners, I to have halfe in all you got.
Eumen.   Why so thou shalt Jack.
Jack.   Why then maister draw your sworde, part your Lady,
let mee have halfe of her presently.
Eumen.   Why I hope Jack thou doost but jest, I promist thee
halfe I got, but not halfe my Lady.
890   *Jack.*   But what else maister, have you not gotten her, therefore devide her straight, for I will have halfe, there is no
remedie.
Eumen.   Well ere I will falsifie my worde unto my friend,
take her all, heere Jack ile give her thee.
Jack.   Nay neither more nor lesse Maister, but even just
halfe.
Eumen.   Before I will falsifie my faith unto my   [F3]
friend, I will divide hir, Jacke thou shalt have halfe.

869   *he seemed*] See p. 378.   *fresh;*] fresh, Q   *maister,*] maister; Q
891   *halfe,*] halfe Q

1 Bro. Bee not so cruell unto our sister gentle Knight.

900 *2 Bro.* O spare faire Delia, shee deserves no death.

Eumen. Content your selves, my word is past to him, therefore prepare thy selfe Delya for thou must die.

Delya. Then farewell worlde, adew Eumenides.

He offers to strike and Jacke staies him.

Jack. Stay Master, it is sufficient I have tride your constan-
cie: Do you now remember since you paid for the burying
of a poore fellow?

Eumen. I, very well Jacke.

Jack. Then Master thanke that good deed for this good
turne, and so God be with you all.

Jacke leapes downe in the ground.

910 *Eumen.* Jacke what art thou gone? Then farewell Jacke.
Come brothers and my beauteous Delya,
Erestus and thy deare Venelia:
We will to Thessalie with joyfull hearts.

All. Agreed, we follow thee and Delya.

Exeunt omnes.

Fant. What Gammer, asleepe?   [F3ᵛ]

Old Woman. By the Mas sonne tis almost day, and my
windowes shuts at the Cocks crow.

Frol. Doo you heare Gammer, mee thinkes this Jacke bore
a great sway amongst them.

920 *Old Woman.* O man, this was the ghost of the poore man,
that they kept such a coyle to burie, and that makes him
to help the wandring knight so much: But come, let us in,
we will have a cup of ale and a tost this morning and so
depart.

900 *Delia,*] Delia Q
906 *fellow?*] fellow. Q
907 *I,*] I Q
908 *deed*] deed, Q
910 Q lineates: . . . gone? / . . . Jacke.
915 *asleepe*] a sleepe Q
922 *come,*] come Q

Fant. Then you have made an end of your tale Gammer?

Old Woman. Yes faith: When this was done I tooke a peece of bread and cheese, and came my way, and so shall you have too before you goe, to your breakefast.

[*Exeunt.*]

928 *goe,*] BM, H, P; goe D (facsimile leaf)   SD *Exeunt.*] Q omits

EXPLANATORY NOTES

1 *Frolicke*] All modern editors have made this emendation, except for Gummere, who retains Q "Franticke," but adds in a note, "a mistake for Frolic." Perhaps it is a joke, not a mistake, but if so, the point is lost on the audience, who have no way of knowing before l. 17 what Frolicke's name is. Line 7 also loses part of its point if the audience does not realize he is playing on his name.   *all amort*] Spiritless, dejected (from French *à la mort*).

3 *hang the head*] One might expect "thy head," but "the head" occurs in Greene's *Alphonsus*, l. 46, and *Venus and Adonis*, l. 666. Cf. *David and Bethsabe*, l. 36; and *Edward I*, l. 604 and note.

5 *twenty . . . hundred*] Blair points out that this is the normal rate of travel insurance in Elizabethan times; he refers to "putter-out of five for one" (*Tempest*, III.3.48). The system is fully explained by Puntarvolo in *Every Man Out of His Humour* (II.3.243 ff.). The phrase—or more commonly "ten in the hundred"—is also used for stating usury rates; in this connection, see the discussion of the epigrams attributed to Shakespeare in E. K. Chambers, *William Shakespeare, 2*, 139. Cf. Nashe (*1*, 258): "I meane to trounce him after twentie in the hundred"; here the phrase, McKerrow notes, apparently means "thoroughly."

7 *franion*] Gay, reckless fellow (*OED*); Nares defines as "idle, loose, and licentious person," and his citations support him. On omission of the article, see E. A. Abbott, *A Shakespearean Grammar* (London, 1873), §84.

8 *dead slaine*] Not in *OED*, which does, however, cite "dead-struck" with the figurative meaning of "struck with horror, paralyzed." Frolicke may mean that he is frightened nearly to death, or only that he is dead tired.

10 *O . . . Neptune*] Terence, *Adelphoe*, l. 790, has: "o caelum, o terra, o maria Neptuni." Blair considers the misquotation to be intentional and, therefore, an academic joke of the kind that occurs in *Edward I*, l. 1735. But it was apparently a well-known tag; it is also misquoted in *Soliman and Perseda*, IV.2.67 (*The Works of Thomas Kyd*, ed. F. S.

Boas, London, 1901): "O coelum, O terra, O maria, Neptune." See also Plautus, *Trinummus* (l. 1070): "Mare terra caelum"; Horace, *Epode* xvii.30: "O mare et terra."

11 *makes . . . it*] Behave. "Makes" is perhaps phonetic for "makest."

12 *yong master*] This is all we hear of the pages' employer, who makes a saint of his fair lady in the approved manner of Elizabethan love jargon. Musgrove (*Journal Australasian Univ. Lang. and Lit. Assn., 23,* 98), arguing that Peele's play is an afterpiece, assumes that the "yong master" and the "faire Lady" were the lovers in the main play of the evening (see above, Introduction, Sec. 4, n. 20).

16 *O . . . desperation*] A popular tune, often referred to; a large number of broadsides were written to be sung to it.

19 *Three . . . men*] This song is referred to in *Twelfth Night*, II.3.84. In the Variorum Edition, Furness cites four other occurrences, or variations of it, in early Jacobean drama. He also prints music for Peele's words (from E. W. Naylor, *Shakespeare and Music*, London, 1896, p. 189); this version is also given in J. H. Long, *Shakespeare's Use of Music* (Gainsville, Fla., 1961), p. 174. A different arrangement is in William Chappell, *Old English Popular Music*, ed. H. E. Wooldridge (reprinted New York, 1961), *1,* 197.

23 *wood . . . wooden*] Dyce 3 notes: "Let us not fail to observe Fantastic's precious pun, 'a dog *in* the *wood,* or a wooden [*wood in*] dog.'" Perhaps more to the point is the pun on "wood," meaning "mad," as in *Midsummer Night's Dream*, II.1.192: "wood within this wood."

24 *as live*] As lief.

25 *white Horse*] In *Merry Conceited Jests* (B, 2, 386), we learn that "George was invited one night by certain of his friends to supper at The White Horse in Friday Street." According to Kenneth Rogers, *The Mermaid and Mitre Taverns in Old London* (London, 1928), the inn was well-known (p. 17 n.). Later he says, "It is a curious fact, and worthy of remark, that the *White Horse* in Friday Street is today the only surviving representative of the *forty* taverns of 1553" (p. 186) and refers to his own article giving details in *London and Middlesex Archaeological Society, Transactions* (1926–27), but I have not seen it.

32 *Clunch*] A lumpish fellow (*OED*).

37 *long seames . . . side slops*] Slops are the baggy hose (i.e., breeches) fashionable at the time. I have not been able to discover precisely what "side slops" were or the significance of the "long seames," but cf. T. Heywood, *Fair Maid of the West* (*The Dramatic Works*, London, 1874), *2,* 285: "I could wish you to looke to your long seames, fights are dangerous."

42 *cousned*] I.e., cozened (tricked).

51 *shall . . . be*] Cf. Tilley (T202): "Things must be as they may."

Corporal Nym rings the changes on this proverbial expression in *Henry V*, II.i.

54 *stumbling . . . threshold*] From ancient times considered ominous; see *Brand's Popular Antiquities*, ed. Hazlitt, 2, 570.

55 *open dore*] See above, Introduction, Sec. 6.

60–64 Anticke and Frolicke seem to be of two minds about the food. Cady brings this to life by inserting directions for business; Anticke "begins to eat hastily" when Madge offers the food. When Frolicke has refused for the group, "Madge removes food. Antic grievously disappointed."

66 *Lambes-wooll*] A drink made by mixing the pulp of roasted apples, sugared and spiced, with hot ale.

67 *Trumpe or Ruffe*] A card game resembling whist. The names seem to be interchangeable (see *OED* citations).

73 *Els . . . up*] Such was apparently the attitude toward people who could not bear their part. Cf. Thomas Morley, *A Plain and Easy Introduction to Practical Music* (1597): "But supper being ended and music books (according to the custom) being brought to the table, the mistress of the house presented me with a part earnestly requesting me to sing; but when, after many excuses, I protested unfeignedly that I could not, every one began to wonder; yea, some whispered to others demanding how I was brought up . . ." (ed. R. A. Harman, New York, n.d., p. 9).

76 *chopcherrie*] Bob-cherry, a game in which one attempts to catch with his teeth a cherry suspended from a string. Herrick has a poem with this title in *Hesperides*.

83 *winters tale*] A trivial tale to pass away the time on a winter night. The phrase is common in Elizabethan literature. See the New Arden *The Winter's Tale* (ed. J. H. Pafford), p. liii, n. 3.

85 *I faith*] "Aye, faith" or "in faith."   *tale of an howre long*] Taken literally by Musgrove (*Journal Australasian Univ. Lang. and Lit. Assn.*, *23*, 89), who assumes that Peele intended his play (or afterpiece) to be only half the length of the usual "two hours' traffic of our stage."

87 *Gyant . . . Daughter*] See above, Introduction, Sec. 3.D.

95 *spavin*] Hard bony tumor resulting from inflammation of cartilage in the joint of a horse's leg. Some quotations in *OED* seem to apply jocularly to human beings.   *windgall*] Soft tumor just above the fetlock on a horse.

97 *No better hay*] Sounds proverbial, but I have not found it elsewhere. If Peele's family were from Devon (see Horne, p. 10), he might have preserved some local saying. McIlwraith notes: " 'hay' may be either a country dance or an abbreviation of 'have you,' but I do not understand this in either case."   *a*] I.e., on.

100 *Bona nox*] Blair notes that although conversation books offered such parting formulae as "opto tibi faustam noctem," and "precor tibi

noctem placidam," the kind of Latin actually spoken by the boys probably resembled Anticke's farewell.

102 *unnaturall*] Because Anticke is going to bed with Clunch.

105 *extempore*] Immediately.

127 *keeps*] Dwells. It is, of course, the enchanted "yong man" who "keeps by" the cross. For discussion of this story see above, Introduction, Sec. 3.B.   *crosse*] Apparently Erestus takes his stand at a place where three roads meet, and the place is marked by a cross. In view of the wealth of superstitions attached to both the cross and cross-roads, such a location is redolent with suggestion, but no specific significance seems to predominate. See above, Introduction, Sec. 6, for comment on staging.

132 *chalkie Cliffs*] See above, Introduction, Sec. 1, for parallels in Peele's other works.

135 The line does not scan properly. Dyce 3 queries deletion of "faire"; B reads "seek" for "to seeke." But Peele is so often careless in metrics that one cannot be sure the text is in error. The use of anaphora is characteristic of Peele (see above, Introduction, Sec. 1).

140 SD *Senex*] I.e., Erestus, who is called Old Man in the speech tags.

143 *Hips and Hawes*] A phrase to indicate something of no worth. The hip is the fruit of the wild rose, and the haw the fruit of the haw-thorne.

148 *Almes pennie*] A penny given for charity, though Nares is no doubt right in suggesting that it is also given for luck.

149 *Gowne of gray*] Traditional palmer's garb. Cf. Greene, *Farewell to Folly* (ed. Grosart, 9, 276): "imagine thy palmers bonnet a princes diadem, thinke thy staffe a scepter, thy graie weeds costly attire."

152–153 *Palmers staffe . . . scallop shell*] A pilgrim returning from the Holy Land carried a palm branch or leaf and was hence called a palmer. The staff also seems to have been part of the ordinary equip-ment of palmers. The pilgrims returning from the shrine of St. James at Compostella wore as a badge a scallop shell found on the Galician shore. Sir Walter Raleigh in "The Passionate Man's Pilgrimage" makes symbolic use of these characteristic pieces of equipment: "Give me my scallop shell of quiet, / My staff of faith to walk upon."

154 Something is obviously omitted. See above, Introduction, Sec. 4.

155 *I*] I.e., aye.

165 *white Beare*] See above, Introduction, Sec. 3, n. 6.

171–172 Supplied from ll. 162–163. For a similar omission in a cryptic prophecy, see *Edward I*, l. 517.

178 *cheere*] Face.

181 *Thessalie*] See above, Introduction, Sec. 3.I.

183 *wedded*] The relationship of Erestus and Venelia seems confused, but it is not really. Although Erestus says that he "wedded was unto a dame," she is later his "true betrothed wife" (l. 187) and his "be-

trothed love" (l. 197). Since she blows out the magic light, she must have the qualifications for the job: "neither wife, widow, nor maide" (l. 429). Apparently she is in the same equivocal position as Mariana in *Measure for Measure* (V.1.170–180), who has been betrothed and has consummated the marriage, but has not yet had the bond sanctified by the Church. An interesting variant of this motif appears in the *commedia dell'arte* scenario "La Innocentia Rivenuta," where the Duke's wife will be cured by one who is "a woman, widow, wife, and maid" (see K. M. Lea, *Italian Popular Comedy*, Oxford, 1934, p. 579).

189 *chanting*] Enchanting.

194 *rage*] Prophetic fury.

196 *Aprill of my age*] Echoed by Huanebango at l. 668 and Eumenides in l. 690. The phrase was perhaps something of a cliché already. Cf. *Rare Triumphes of Love and Fortune* (Malone Society Reprint, l. 583): "Even in the Aprill of mine age, and May month of my time."

198 *madding*] Frenzied.   *inrag'd*] Maddened.

206 *combered*] Harassed.

214 *saint Andrewes day*] St. Andrew's Day is November 30. It was a day propitious for lovers. In Northamptonshire the day is one of "unbridled license—a kind of carnival" with masquing, transvestism, mumming (*British Calendar Customs, England*, London, 1940, 3, 187). V. S. Lean, *Collectanea* (Bristol, 1902), 2, 362, cites customs used on this day in France for divining the identity of future husbands. (See also *Brand's Popular Antiquities*, ed. Hazlitt, 1, 8.)   *saint Lukes*] St. Luke's Day is October 18. The horned oxen was the medieval symbol for St. Luke, who was patron of horned beasts. His day was observed by Horn Fair (W. S. Walsh, *Curiosities of Popular Customs*, Philadelphia, 1907, p. 641). It was inevitable that the patron of horned beasts should come to be regarded as the patron of cuckolds. The extension of St. Luke's dominion apparently did something for Horn Fair: "The so-called 'Horn Fair,' formerly held on St. Luke's day and two other days, at Charlton, was a strange combination of a revel of a licentious type and a fair. Horns of all kinds, especially those of sheep and goats, were worn, and toys made of horn were sold, and the gingerbread sold at the fair had horns" (*British Calendar Customs, England*, 3, 100–101). "St. Luke's is a lucky day on which to choose a husband" (ibid.); there are rituals like those for St. Agnes Eve that enable a girl to divine her future spouse. Activities of this kind are recorded in "Mother Bunch's Closet Newly Broken Open," a chapbook containing marriage and betrothal lore, reprinted in *Amusing Prose Chapbooks*, ed. R. H. Cunningham (London, 1889). It is not clear whether Peele has in mind anything more specific than the irony of burying wives on these days connected with good luck for lovers.

216 *custome*] Obligatory service; hence, "you have served your turn."

224 *poore . . . proude*] Cf. Ecclesiasticus 25:2: "Three sorts of men my

soule hateth, and I utterly abhorre the life of them: a poore man that is proude, a rich man that is a lyar, and an olde adulterer that doteth" (Geneva version, 1594). Tilley cites many examples of "Poor and proud, fie, fie" (P475).

225 *poore . . . shorne*] Apparently a logical, though unusual form of the proverb. Tilley (S295) cites examples of the ironic "As rich as a new-shorn sheep" and (S299) two instances of "As bare as a new-shorn sheep." He does not include this passage from Peele.

226 *proude . . . Peacock*] Proverbial. Tilley (P157) cites examples of "proud as a peacock."

227 *like an Englishman*] Musgrove (*Journal Australasian Univ. Lang. and Lit. Assn., 23, 93*) takes this to be a "clear reference to Euphuism."

229 *curst*] Shrewish. Tilley (W76) has many examples of "As angry as a wasp." See also W78, W79, and W705.   *frowarde*] Refractory. The whole expression sounds proverbial, but I have not found it elsewhere. Cf. *Romeo*, I.3.26 ff.

231 *smoake . . . teeth*] Cf. Proverbs 10:26: "As vinegar is to the teethe, and as smoke to the eyes, so is the slouthfull to them that send him" (Geneva version, 1594).

232 *Holily*] Because Lampriscus has been quoting the Bible.

238 *Well . . . life*] See above, Introduction, Sec. 3, n. 34.

240 SD See note to l. 300 SD.

241 *Farewell . . . thousand*] "I.e., a thousand times farewell" (Dyce 3).

243 *goes . . . stick*] Surely proverbial, but I have not found it elsewhere. Cf. Tilley (D263): "The devil rides on a fiddlestick," which means "here's a fine commotion."

246 *I*] I.e., aye.

247 *beggar . . . greene*] An allusion to the familiar ballad of "The Beggar's Daughter of Bednall Green" (Thomas Percy, *Reliques*, ed. H. B. Wheatley, London, 1889, 2, 171), but Lampriscus has no discernible similarity to the blind father of "prettye Bessee." The ballad is one of the sources of Day's *Blind Beggar of Bednall Green*.

249 *song of mowing*] Madge loses her wager, for they sing of sowing. It is curious that the singers are referred to as harvest men throughout the entire season. Perhaps they wear some conventional masquing costume that so identifies them. The joining of motifs from various portions of the agricultural year was apparently customary in folk festivals. T. F. Ordish ("English Folk-Drama," *Folk-Lore, 4,* 1893, 169), describes a Plough Monday processional: "Ploughmen from neighboring hamlets joined the procession, dressed in clean smock-frocks, decked out with ribbons by the maids. Some wore branches of corn in their hats. Often 'the procession was joined by threshers carrying their flails, reapers with sickles, and carters with their long whips, which they were ever cracking to add to the noise; while even the smith and the miller were among their number, for the one sharp-

ened the ploughshare, and the other ground the corn.' " See above, Introduction, Sec. 3.H. On the connection with the masque, see Margaret Dean-Smith, "Folk-Play Origins of the English Masque," *Folk-Lore, 65* (1954), 74–86.

250   Dyce divides the line as indicated by the rhyme; except for Gummere, other editors follow him.

253   SD *two hand sword*] See above, Introduction, Sec. 2 and 3.G. Because Huanebango is so armed, because Booby refers to him later as "my two hand sword" (l. 334), and because Nashe calls Harvey "an olde Fencer . . . flourishing about my eares with his two hand sworde of Oratory and Poetry" (*1*, 262), Cheffaud and Blair see in this passage evidence that Huanebango is Harvey. But Harvey (*Works, 2,* 49) refers to Nashe as a "dubble sword-bearer," and Nashe (*3*, 217) uses the phrase in a place that has no connection with Harvey. Finding a personal allusion rather misses the point, which is that the weapon carried by Huanebango is an old-fashioned one. See *2 Henry VI,* II.1.45, and Herford and Simpson's note to *Epicoene,* IV.5.109.

      Booby the Clowne] For the confusions involving this character, see above, Introduction, Sec. 4, and notes to ll. 453 SD and 538 SD.

259   *Polimackeroeplacydus*] In Plautus, *Pseudolus,* the master of Harpax— he does not appear onstage—is named Polymachaeroplagides (l. 988, and passim). See above, Introduction, Sec. 2, for Fleay's fantastic "translation."

261   *wane*] The modern form is "waning." The older form still is current in the phrase "on the wane."

265   *do off*] Take off (doff).

272–274   *First . . . stocke*] A puzzling passage. Dyce appends this note to *stock:* "i.e. sword, I believe. [Booby] means, as it appears to me, that he has run away from the parish, and become a sort of knight-errant." B quotes Dyce and adds: "Dr. Brinsley Nicholson understands the passage differently:—'He has started and they may catch him (if they can) and as a vagabond put him in the stocks.' Neither explanation appears to be satisfactory. It seems to me that the clown is pluming himself on his finery. He points with pride to his feather; and he is equally proud of his fashionable 'long stock' (*i.e.,* the stocking fastened high above the knee). Cf. Middleton's *Blurt, Master Constable,* ii.2, 'I was a reveller in a *long stock.*' The meaning of the passage is, as I take it, 'I have been the first beau in the parish to adopt the long stocking of the town-gallants.' " B is surely on the right track. C. and P. Cunnington, *Handbook of English Costume in the Sixteenth Century* (London, 1954), p. 114, refer to "*Whole Hose* or Long Stocked Hose, [which] consisted of breeches and long tailored stockings sewn together to form a single garment. (1400–1620, but far less common after 1605.)" I suspect the point is that the Clown is preening himself upon his dress, which he considers fashionable but which is actually somewhat outmoded. Presumably Huanebango, in the tradition of the braggart, would be elaborately, even fantastically, dressed, and the Clown is aping him. As Huanebango is a parody of the Knight Errant, so the Clown is a parody of Huanebango.

279 *devoyre*] Duty. The high-sounding phrase is a formula from chivalric romance.

283–284 Dyce arranged the clown's jingle to emphasize the rhymes. He also corrected the "Latin" by printing *gibletis,* and modern editors have usually followed him. *Cum appertinentibus* was apparently sometimes used instead of the more common legal term, *cum pertinentiis suis,* 'with its appurtenances.' It is used in *Pedantius,* l. 648. See above, Introduction, Sec. 2, n. 13, and Sec. 7.

289 *Pergopolyneo*] Pyrgopolynices is a character in the *Miles Gloriosus* of Plautus. "Dyonora de Sardynya" has not been traced.

292 *Gustecerydis*] The jest here, as in l. 294, is simply the tongue-twisting name. Peele is imitating such Plautine effects as the grandson of Neptune in *Miles Gloriosus,* Bumbomachides Clutomistaridysarchides (l. 14).

296 *neates feete*] The neat's (oxen's) foot was used as food. Huanebango's kinsman was evidently a noble trencherman.

300 SD There seems no alternative to following earlier editors in inserting an entrance here for Erestus. If I were staging the play, instead of editing it, I would omit the exit at l. 240 and leave Erestus on stage during the intervening dialogue. But his "Neighbour farewell" (l. 240), which breaks off his dialogue with Lampriscus, is a clear indication that Peele intended him to leave the stage at that point. See above, Introduction, Sec. 6.

311 This speech would perhaps be more fitting for the Clown, but Blair alone of modern editors gives it to him.

316 *buckler*] Shield, protect.

319 *passe for*] Care for.

321–323 *whoo . . . meanes*] This passage becomes clearer if modernized: Whoo! he comes upon me with "a superfantial substance" and "the foison of the earth"—[so] that I know not what he means. It is generally regarded as the Clown's parody of Huanebango's fine language. See above, Introduction, Sec. 2, for discussion of the possible connection with Harvey.

328 *for you,*] I insert the comma to point up the fact that it is the times that are hard, not Booby's cake. Cf. Harvey (*Works, 1,* 129): "And yet haue I on suer frende as harde as the world goith . . . that neuer yet faylid me at a pinche." See also Jonson's *Bartholomew Fair,* II.6.139, and *2 Return from Parnassus* (*The Three Parnassus Plays,* ed. J. B. Leishman, London, 1949), ll. 334–335.

334 SD *Omnes* does not, of course, include Madge and her two guests. Elsewhere there are directions which, like this one, seem to clear the

stage, but the induction characters remain to the very end. See ll. 686
SD and 768 SD. On the significance of "in his studie" see above, Introduction, Sec. 6.

335   *gray*] Blue. The equivalence of blue and grey in the Elizabethan
period seems generally accepted by everyone except *OED*, which has
a special note that *grey* is "said of the sea, sky, and clouds when not illu-
minated by the sun," but it then disproves its statement by citing "as
the sun/In the grey vault of heaven" (*2 Henry IV*, II.3.18–19). The
"grey-eyed morn," a well-established cliché, seems always to refer to a
clear, bright morning, whatever the color (cf. *Romeo*, II.1.230, and
Lyly, *Maid's Metamorphosis*, IV.2.40). It has a long tradition before
Peele's time, as Chaucer demonstrates in "The Knight's Tale" (ll. 1491–
94):

> The bisy larke, messager of day,
> Salueth in hir song the morwe gray,
> And firy Phebus riseth up so bright
> That al the orient laugheth of the light.

One may guess that a "morwe gray" is one in which the exact color is
not quite to be determined; that is, it is a blue-grey, even as Cotgrave
indicates in his *Dictionarie* (1611): "Bluard . . . Gray, skie-coloured,
blewish." Elizabethans often speak of grey eyes. Malone long ago said:
"What we now call *blue* eyes, were in Shakespeare's time called *grey*
eyes, and were considered as eminently beautiful." The curious reader
who wishes to pursue this byway of cultural history will find assistance
in notes to l. 140 of *Venus and Adonis* in the Variorum and Arden
editions.

336   *records*] Sings.
340   *Thessalie*] See above, Introduction, Sec. 3.I.
341   *Meroe*] See above, Introduction, Sec. 3.I.   *hight*] Named.
346   *Delya*] Cooper has this entry: "Delia, One of the names of Diana."
Hence, the name suggests chastity.
357–361. Dyce prints ll. 357–358 as verse:

> Ah, Delia,
> Fairer art thou than the running water,
> Yet harder far than steel or adamant!

and ll. 360–361:

> Ay, Delia, sit and ask me what thou wilt,
> Thou shalt have it brought into thy lap.

One can hardly say out of hand that Dyce is wrong, but since there
is an argument equally strong for maintaining that Q is correct, I

have followed Q. For Dyce's treatment one can argue that since Sacrapant has been speaking blank verse, one might expect him to continue in verse. Moreover, there are two blank verse lines in Dyce's version: "Yet . . . adamant" and "Ay . . . wilt" (if Delia is read as a disyllable, instead of with three syllables as in ll. 346 and 354). "Fairer . . . water" has ten syllables, but it cannot even be tortured into an iambic pattern, and "Thou . . . lap" has only nine syllables. The case for verse is weak —even in a play with a good deal of metrical irregularity. If Sacrapant's speeches are verse, Delya's speech at ll. 355–356 might as well be called verse.

360   *I*] I.e., aye.

367   Q has a speech tag for Sacrapant as if this were a new speech. One might suspect omission or cutting in such cases, but nothing has gone noticeably astray here. See above, Introduction, Sec. 4, and l. 809 and note.

372   *For meate*] Dyce and B omit "For," following a suggestion by J. Mitford, "The Early English Drama," *Gentleman's Magazine, 103* (1833), 104. Other editors, however, retain it. Although no more than a generally sinister connotation is involved here, the colors of the cocks are significant in folklore. See *Standard Dictionary of Folklore, Mythology, and Legend*, ed. M. Leach and J. Fried (New York, 1950), *1*, 239–240.

373   SD *chine*] Backbone.

383   *neate*] Not adulterated with cheaper wine or water.

384   *brewers*] To "brew" is to mix liquors with water (*OED*, v. 2). William Harrison, in his *Description of England* (*Holinshed's Chronicle*, London, 1807, *1*, 281–282), tells us that "in old time" those desirous of the best (i.e., the strongest) wine procured it from religious houses, "being sure that they would neither drinke nor be serued of the worst, or such as was anie waies mingled or brued by the vintener." The practice of adulterating wine produced the unsavory reputation that enabled Nashe to speak of "Brewers, that, by retayling filthy *Thames* water, come in few yeares to bee worth fortie or fiftie thousand pound" (*1*, 173). In *Anything for a Quiet Life* (V.1.98), there is a reference to "*Water Thin* the Brewer" (*Complete Works of John Webster*, ed. F. L. Lucas, London, 1927).

387   Following Q enables me to avoid choosing between the two readings open to modernizing editors: "What, is he a friar?" or "What is he? a friar?"

388   *Frier indefinit*] If there is anything more here than a play with words, it may be the opposite of a "friar limiter," a friar licensed to beg in a restricted area, like Chaucer's "lymytour" ("Prologue," l. 209).

392   *Hold thee there*] Hold fast to that opinion. For another interpretation see above, Introduction, Sec. 4.

392–393   Dyce realigns: "Hold . . . soft / Who . . . gone." This provides one line of seven syllables, vaguely iambic, and one line of blank verse, a dubious improvement of the original.

395   A messy line. B and Brooke read "heaven nor hell"; other editors follow Q. As it stands, the line must mean "some force—good or evil—will rescue Delya from those who now beset us." Reading "nor" does not help unless one goes the next step and makes the line "But heaven nor hell shall rescue her from me." This makes better sense. Cf. *David and Bethsabe* (l. 364): "Nor God nor Time will doe that good for me."   SD *Exeunt . . . Sacrapant*] It is clear from the dialogue that Delya departs at this point. Since Sacrapant re-enters at l. 415 SD, this is the most convenient point for him to leave the stage.

414   Dyce realigns: "Brother / Why . . . enter?" The result can hardly be considered verse; he makes the change apparently because the next line happens to be blank verse.

417   *I*] I.e., aye.   SD *and carry them off*] It seems better to have the furies depart with the brothers while Sacrapant speaks the next three lines, rather than have the whole quartet remain to listen to what is obviously intended as a soliloquy addressed to the audience. See note to 431 SD.

421   Since the brothers were introduced, though not named, at l. 132, these lines seem redundant. The play abounds in such problems. See above, Introduction, Sec. 4.

431   SD *Exit*] The Q *"Exeunt"* suggests that the furies do not carry off the brothers until this point, but this would be awkward. This is another detail that suggests the author at work. See note to l. 417 SD.   *Enter . . . crosse*] Eumenides and Erestus probably do not enter together. The first five lines Eumenides addresses to himself; then he sees Erestus, who has entered at another door. Again, it would be more effective to have Erestus at his cross on stage during the entire action. See above, Introduction, Sec. 6.

432–433   See above, Introduction, Sec. 7, for Dyce's realignment.

434   *loadstar of my life*] See *Edward I*, l. 938, and above, Introduction, Sec. 1; cf. *Alcazar*, l. 104; and *Honour of the Garter*, l. 392. The phrase appears also in *Jew of Malta* (*The Works of Christopher Marlowe*, ed. C. F. Tucker Brooke, Oxford, 1910, l. 681) and Sidney's *Arcadia*, II.2 (*The Prose Works*, ed. A. Feuillerat, Cambridge, 1912; reprinted 1965, *1*, 155). *Caesar's Revenge* has "lodestarre of her looks" (Malone Society Reprint, l. 604); Greene's *Alphonsus* (l. 1951) has "Loadstone of his life."

453   SD Eumenides apparently sits down and goes to sleep at this point; otherwise, it would be difficult to account for the direction at l. 478. The Corebus who now enters is not the same character as Booby-Corebus (see note to l. 538 SD and above, Introduction, Sec. 4).

Wiggen] Variant of *widgeon*, traditionally a stupid bird; hence, a fool. Pigwiggen, another variant, appears several times as a proper name, as "maister Pigwiggen our constable" (*Selimus*, l. 1971, Malone Society Reprint). *OED* has other references.

454 *scald*] Afflicted with scall (a scabby disease of the skin, particularly the scalp); hence, in a figurative sense, "contemptible."

459 *Churchwarden*] Like all modern editors, I give this speech to the Churchwarden. Q has a speech tag for *Simon*. See above, Introduction, Sec. 4.

460 *aunswere*] Be responsible for the cost. Cf. *1 Henry IV*, I.3.184–185: "this proud king, who studies day and night / To answer all the debt he owes to you."

463 *a*] I.e., in.

464 *curiously*] Finically.

465 *sodden*] Soaked in water; hence, of persons, "rendered dull, without expression."

467 *Christmas*] Malapropism for "Christian."

470 *frannion*] See note to l. 7.

471 *funerals*] Singular in meaning, though often plural in form.

475–476 The rhythm of Wiggen's speech, indicating the beating he administers to the Churchwarden, may be compared with that in a speech by Friar David in similar circumstances in *Edward I*, ll. 419 ff.

477–478 *Wiggen . . . staffe*] This part of the speech sounds like a stage direction that has crept into the text, and it is so printed by modern editors except Gummere and McIlwraith. Even though it might serve better as a direction, it is the sort of thing a character might be expected to say under the circumstances. Cf. *David and Bethsabe*, l. 1307, where Q prints a half-line of dialogue as a stage direction, and the mysterious direction in *Edward I*, l. 1644.   *parish*] Brooke and Paradise gloss as "the parochial officers," which may be correct, but no dictionary offers any support.

481 *shake rotten*] An expression of opprobrium not found elsewhere. C. T. Prouty suggests that the reference is to fruit so rotten that it will fall if one shakes the tree.

494 *thatche the chauncell*] A necessary measure after the more substantial roof has been sold. In *The Alchemist* (II.2), Sir Epicure Mammon, concerned about a supply of metal for the projection, is advised to "Buy the couering of o' churches" and replace it with shingles. But Mammon says that he will use thatch, for it "will lie light vp o' the rafters." The spoliation of churches was sufficiently widespread during the early Protestant period for Archbishop Grindal to include in his orders on the duty of churchwardens this injunction: "They shall not sell or alyenate anye bell or other churche goodes without the consent of the ordinarye in writing first had, nor shall putt the money that

shall come of anye suche sale to anye other uses than to the repara-
tions of their churches or chappells" (J. S. Purvis, *Tudor Parish
Documents of the Diocese of York*, Cambridge, 1948, p. 183).

495 *galliard*] A lively dance in triple time.   *Steeven Loache*] Taken
by all commentators to be the name of the Churchwarden; in this they
agree with Wiggen (l. 496). But they should perhaps beware of
aligning themselves with a character whose name indicates that he is a
fool (see note to l. 453). A loach is a "simpleton" (*OED*, which cites
the *Jests of George Peele*), and I suspect that the reference has underlying it some proverbial expression that makes Wiggen's use of the
name for the Churchwarden into a joke revealing his simplicity. (See,
above, Introduction, Sec. 4.)

496 *Sic argumentaris*] "Thus you argue, Master Loache," a formula for
formal disputation; another in l. 500 means, "Sir, in opposition I put
to you this question." Cf. Greene, *Friar Bacon*, l. 911.

497–499 *pull . . . sell . . . hang*] Cf. Captain Jenkins in *Northward Ho!*
(IV.2.25–27): "I know a parish that sal tag downe all the pells and sell
em to Capten *Ienkens*, to do him good, and if pells will fly, weele flie
too, vnles, the pell-ropes hang vs" (*The Dramatic Works of Thomas
Dekker*, ed. F. T. Bowers, Vol. *2*, Cambridge, 1955).

502 *begin mine*] Dyce thought something was missing here, but B explains
satisfactorily as "open the argument from my side (with the aid of
the pike-staff)."

506 *Capons face*] T. Davies, *Supplementary English Glossary* (London,
1881), says that the capon, "like the goose, is taken for an emblem of
stupidity." One may, of course, find in the capon a source for con-
temptuous invective more obvious than its lack of brains.

508 *taking*] Condition.

520 SD *Exit Eumenides*] No doubt the author may have intended the
departure of Eumenides to be covered by the exeunt at l. 527, but the
dialogue indicates that he leaves at this point.

522 *bestowe . . . of*] An obsolete construction now replaced by "bestow
on."

524 *bilbowe*] From Bilbao in Spain. Such swords were highly regarded
for their fine tempering.

526 *church stile*] The meaning is not absolutely clear. Brooke and Paradise gloss: "edge of church property," meaning, presumably, that the
group retire from holy ground to consume their drinks. P. A. Daniel
thought we should perhaps read "church-ale." Before the Reformation,
the sale of ale by the church was apparently customary at Easter and
other festival seasons. The ale was made with malt provided by the
churchwardens and sold with bread contributed by parishioners; profits
were used for parish expenses. (See *Brand's Popular Antiquities*, ed.
Hazlitt, *1*, 126.) When Henry VIII, in a curiously puritanical move,
forbade ales in churches, buildings for the purpose were established

near by. In later times these often became inns (*British Calendar Customs, England, 1*, 94). The vicarage itself was sometimes the ale house. In 1571 Archbishop Grindal felt it necessary to include among his injunctions to the clergy this: "ye shall not kepe nor suffer to be kepte in your parsonage or vicaredge howse anye ailehouses tiplinge houses or tavernes, nor shall sell aile beere or wine" (Purvis, p. 195). Several York diocese vicars were called to account for offending against the injunction. Such activities explain the proverbial proximity of the church and the ale house referred to by Nashe (*3*, 67): "like a Church and an ale-house, God and the divell, they [vice and virtue] manie times dwell neere together." Gummere cites the same proverbial use from Overbury's *Characters* (*The Miscellaneous Works*, ed. E. F. Rimbault, London, 1846, p. 145). *tryll lyll*] Onomatopoeic word for the sound of flowing liquid. Cf. Nashe, *Summer's Last Will*, *l.* 1009: "Try-lill, the hūters hoope to you." *OED* has a number of citations.

527 *Both*] It is apparently not clear to whom this refers. Dyce added an exeunt for Wiggen and Corebus after l. 526, allowing the Churchwarden and Sexton to have this final line. He has been followed by all modern editors except Gummere. But "Both" should refer to Wiggen and Corebus, who are the ones to speak immediately before the indefinite tag occurs. It need not be awkward for the parish officials to remain without a word; after all, they are counting the money that has come in so unexpectedly.

533 *harvestars*] All editors emend Q in this way except Gummere and Blair. Gummere, in a momentary fit of conservatism, retains Q. Blair reads "harvest swaines"; his argument is interesting: "the separately rendered noun 'starres' is *per se* evidence that a separate noun followed the adjective 'harvest,' and not a suffix rendering the adjective substantive." On the significance of the women, see above, Introduction, Sec. 3.H.

534 SD *they*] The "amorous harvestars," of course.

538 SD *Corebus*] The same character who is earlier called Booby (see l. 253 SD), but not the same as the friend of Jack (see l. 453 SD). Although Virgil describes Corebus, suitor to Cassandra, as a brave warrior who dies valiantly in the sack of Troy (*Aeneid* 2.341 and passim), in some manner not quite clear he became in later accounts the symbol of folly, so that Erasmus in his *Adagia* (Chil. II, Centur. IX, Prov. lxiv) could introduce the proverb "stultior Coroebo," upon which he offers this comment: "Proverbialis hyperbole in stupidos & vecordes. Coroebi stultitia vulgi fabula celebrata est, qui maris undas numerare fit conatus, cum non potuerit ultra quinque prosequi supputationem." See "Excursus x ad librum II" in Heyne's edition of *Aeneid* (London, 1830), *2*, 426, and note to 2.341 in J. Conington's edition of Virgil (London, 1876). In *Foure Letters* (Bodley Head Quarto, p. 43), Harvey

has a reference in this tradition, and it is answered by Nashe (*1*, 302). Stanyhurst translates the *Aeneid* 2.407–408: "This sight foule freighted with woodful phrensye Choroebus, / Hee runs too rescu, lyk a bedlem desperat, headlong." Corebo (not a fool) appears in Ariosto, *Orlando Furioso*, 13.24 and passim. See above, Introduction, Sec. 4, for discussion of textual problems arising from use of the name.

540 For textual problems connected with this passage see above, Introduction, Sec. 4.

544 *Jugling boxe*] Juggling is an Elizabethan term for magic or legerdemain. The exact nature of the box is not clear. Lean, *Collectanea, 2,* 278, cites a proverb: "As sure as a juggler's box." *Brand's Popular Antiquities*, ed. Hazlitt, *2,* 350–351, quotes from Bacon, *Sylva Sylvarum,* a description of "the Experiment of Iuglers," which involves a box, but it hardly seems what is meant here.

545 *Fee, fa, fum*] Cry of the folklore giant. See above, Introduction, Sec. 2 and 3.B.

551 *Who hawe*] A cry to attract someone's attention.

553 *cullion*] Abusive term derived from the meaning "testicle," still current in Shakespeare's day.

554 *at his voluntary*] Of his own free will.

559 *spight of*] Shortened form of "in spite of."   SD *and two furies*] The helpless Huanebango must be carried off stage, and the inserted directions here and at l. 561 seem the simplest way of disposing of him. This kind of unfinished business is further evidence of the author at work. See above, Introduction, Sec. 4.

561 *ravening*] Applies to the crows and kites (not to poor Huanebango), as in Kyd's *Soliman and Perseda:* "No, let her lie, a prey to ravening birds" (V.3.55, ed. Boas).

566–567 Lineation follows Dyce.

575 *gode*] I.e., goad.

575–576 Lineation follows Dyce.

580 *name*] Although editors have generally felt restive about Q "same," only Blair emends it. B comments that both Q and the emendation are "far from intelligible." Gummere admits Q is awkward, but explains it: "Sacrapant says she has forgotten her name, but has not forgotten as much as she ought to forget." On the other hand, I assume the lines mean that Delya, while still responding to the name, has forgotten everything else about herself. See above, Introduction, Sec. 4.

582 *Berecynthia*] In *Aeneid* (6.784) "Berecyntia mater" is another name for Cybele (see also 9.82, 619, and Ovid, *Metamorphoses* 11.16, 106), She is discussed by Cooper in several places (see esp. the entry under Cibele). Although Berecynthia-Cybele is what we today call an "earth goddess," it seems doubtful that the name had the anthropological overtones for Peele that it has for us.

584 See above, Introduction, Sec. 7, for Dyce's realignment.

589 See above, Introduction, Sec. 7, for Dyce's realignment.

591–592 These lines demonstrate the futility of trying to make regular verse in this play. In l. 591 read "Delya" with three syllables and the line is an alexandrine; read it as a disyllable and the line limps, suggesting that we should read "I know no Delya nor know what you meane." In l. 592 it is necessary to contract "you are" to "you're" (as Dyce does) to make the line scan.

597 *faine*] I.e., feign.

599 *vild*] Common variant of *vile*.

603 SD For this unusually literary stage direction and its echo in the next line, see above, Introduction, Sec. 4.

605–608 Though printed as prose in Q, these lines in the middle of a verse passage seem intended as verse, even though irregular. Dyce makes l. 605 regular by emending and printing

> Away, and touch it not; 'tis something that
> My lord hath hidden there.

But there is no reason to assume that Q is corrupt. Peele does not always write his verse in decasyllables. Lines 607–608 are probably best read as octosyllabic by reducing "plyest," "Pyoners," and "labouring" to disyllables.

607 *Well sed*] Dyce notes: "Equivalent to—*Well done!*—in which sense, as I was the first to observe, the words are frequently used by our early writers." *OED* does not bear out this interpretation, nor does it seem anything but a forcing of the text. Sacrapant is complimenting Delya on her fidelity to him as demonstrated by what she has just said to her brothers.   *Pyoners*] Those who work with spade and shovel. See *Edward I*, l. 1203 and note.

610 SD *Zantyppa*] Common Elizabethan form for Xanthippe, shrewish wife of Socrates.   *to the well*] See above Introduction, Sec. 6, for comment on the staging. Among the many customs centering about holy wells, their use for procuring husbands is common. See E. K. Chambers, *The Mediaeval Stage* (2 vols., Oxford, 1903), *1*, 123, for references.

621 *though . . . divell*] Proverbial; see Tilley (D297). Black is merely dark-complexioned, a defect by Elizabethan standards of beauty.

622 *Marrie gup*] Exclamation of indignation.   *murren*] Murrain (plague).

624 *with a wanion*] With a vengeance. "Wanion" is an altered form of "waniand"; hence, "in the waniand" (probably with the ellipsis of "moon") means "at the time of the waning moon," i.e., in an unlucky hour.

625 *curstest queane*] Most shrewish jade.

629 SD *Conjurers Cell*] See above, Introduction, Sec. 6.

636 *beard*] All Qq read "birde," and some commentators have assumed
a reference to the Search for the Golden Bird (Type 550), a supposi-
tion that may seem to be supported by l. 613 (see above, Introduction,
Sec. 3, note 34). But when the head reappears, BM and H read
"beard," which is almost surely correct (see l. 777 and note, l. 782).

639 *cockell bread*] W. J. Thoms, *Anecdotes and Traditions* (London,
1839), 5, 94–95, quotes from an Aubrey MS: "Young wenches have a
wanton sport which they call moulding of Cockle-bread, viz. they
get upon a table-board, and then gather up their knees and their
coates with their hands as high as they can, and then they wabble to
and fro, as if they were kneading of dowgh, and say these words, viz.

> My dame is sick and gone to bed,
> And I'le go mould my Cockle-bread,

I did imagine nothing to have been in this but meer wantonnesse of
youth. But I find in Burchardus, in his 'Methodus Confitendi,' printed
at Colon, 1549, (he lived before the Conquest,) one of the Articles
(on the VII. Commandment) of interrogating a young woman is, 'If
she did ever, 'subigere panem clunibus,' and then bake it, and give it
to one she loved to eate, 'ut in majorem modum exardesceret amor.'
So here I find it to be a relique of naturall magick—an unlawful
philtrum.

"White Kennet adds, in a side note—'In Oxfordshire, the Maids,
when they put themselves into the fit posture, sing thus,

> My granny is sick, and now is dead,
> And wee'l goe mould some Cockle Bread,
> Up with my heels and down with my head,
> And this is the way to mould Cockle-bread."

Thoms adds from Burchardus: "Fecisti quod quaedam mulieres
facere solent, prosternunt se in faciem, et discoopertibus natibus jubent,
ut supra nudas nates conficiatur panis, et eo decocto tradunt maritis
suis ad comedendum. Hoc ideo faciunt ut plus exardescant in amorem
illorum." Dyce 3 has some further information that might be of
interest to a folklorist but does not elucidate the passage in the play.

647 There can be little doubt that this line is a parody of Stanyhurst's
"ragged quill" (Nashe, 3, 319). That author's worst excesses were not
in his translation of the *Aeneid* but in the "Other Poetical Devices"
included with it. Here, quoted from Edward Arber's reprint (*The
English Scholars Library*, 10, London, 1880), are samples:

> Lowd dub a dub tabering with frapping rip rap of Aetna.
> A clapping fyerbolt (such as oft, with rounce robel hobble,
> *Iove* toe the ground clattereth).

[p. 137]

now grislye reboundings
Of ruff raffe roaring, mens herts with terror agrysing,
With peale meale ramping,
            with thwick thwack sturdelye thundring.

[p. 138]

Nashe in his preface to *Menaphon* (*3*, 320) parodies Stanyhurst:

Then did he make heauens vault to rebound,
            with rounce robble hobble
Of ruffe raffe roaring,
            with thwicke thwacke thurlerie bouncing.

Making fun of Stanyhurst was a favorite sport; McKerrow (Nashe, *4*, 456) and Arber (*The English Scholars Library*, 10, p. viii) cite other examples. Peele's "huffe snuffe" may also be a glance at Stanyhurst, who has "Linckt was in wedlock a loftye Thrasonical huf snuffe" (p. 143). "Thrasonicall huffe snuffe" is quoted by Nashe (*3*, 320). "Huff-snuff" is a popular late sixteenth century tag. In *Cambises* a trio of soldiers are Huf, Ruf, and Snuf. The father and two sons to whom *Pappe with an Hatchet* is dedicated are called Huffe, Ruffe, and Snuffe. Harvey in Sonnet VI at the end of *Foure Letters* uses the phrase: "I wott not what these cutting Huffe-snuffes meane." Nashe turns the phrase against Harvey in *Foure Letters Confuted* (*1*, 300):

But ah what newes doe you heare
            of that Good Gabriel huffe snuffe,
Knowne to the world for a foole,
            and clapt in the Fleete for a Rimer?

He repeats the lines in *Have with You* (*3*, 127), but alters the phrase to "that good Gabriell Haruey." See above, Introduction, Sec. 1.

648   *peat*] Term of endearment.   *pigsnie*] Little pig; a term of endearment.

654   Dyce noted that this line is a quotation from Harvey's "Encomium Lauri" (see above, Introduction, Sec. 2). The next line is evidently original with Peele.

657   *Three blue beanes*] Since this expression occurs in the MS of Alleyn's part in *Orlando Furioso* (ll. 136–137), it has sometimes been offered as evidence of a connection between the two plays. But the expression is proverbial. See Herford and Simpson's references in their note to *Bartholomew Fair*, I.4.76; see below, note to ll. 853 ff. for a passage in which Peele is indebted to *Orlando Furioso*. Beans "play a prominent part in the ritual and folklore of the world" (*Standard Dictionary of Folklore*, ed. Leach and Fried, *1*, 123); colors are often significant, but I have not been able to trace a specific meaning for the expression in the play, which is probably a remnant of a game.

660 *rim ram ruffe*] There can be little doubt that "rim", the reading of
BM and H, is correct, although the original in Chaucer's Parson's
Prologue (l. 43) is "rum, ram, ruf." One suspects that the correction
may have required consultation of copy. The exact significance of
Chaucer's phrase has been much debated (see W. W. Skeat, ed., *The
Complete Works of Geoffrey Chaucer*, 2d ed., Oxford, 1900, 5, 446),
but Huanebango's meaning (i.e., the alliterating hexameters) is clear
enough. There may also be a glance at Stanyhurst's explosive diction,
as in l. 647.

661 Q indents at "Let me faire Ladie" as if for a new speech, but there is
no separate speech tag. This may be a way of indicating that the preceding sentence is an aside.

668 *Aprill of mine age*] See ll. 196 and note, 690.

676 *flouting*] Jeering.

678 *ka wilshaw*] "Ka" is a variant of "quotha." It is used with sarcastic
force in repeating words used by another. "Wilshaw" is a mystery.
In Gummere, Gayley adds a note: "Qy.: Will ich ha(ve)?" and
refers to l. 684.

682 *Lobb*] Country bumpkin. Zantippa's kindly wish for Huanebango is,
therefore, that his destiny as a cuckold may be somewhat mitigated
by his being too much a simpleton to recognize the horror of his fate.

686 SD *Exeunt omnes*] Except, of course, Madge and her companions (as
at l. 334).   *Eumenides*] Peele knew of the Furies (*Alcazar*, ll.
293 ff.) and was probably also aware that they were often called the
Eumenides, but that did not keep him from using the name for a lover,
as Lyly had done in *Endimion*.

690 *Aprill of mine age*] See ll. 196 and note, 668.

693 ff. Eumenides' reaction suggests that Jack is invisible when he first
appears (if that is possible); but if so, he has materialized by l. 704.

698 *making*] Presumably, at the conception of Eumenides. Cf. *OED*,
"make," v., 17. Falstaff says that Justice Shallow is "like a man made
after supper of a cheese-paring" (*2 Henry IV*, III.2.334).

705 *state*] I.e., the state of my finances.

711 *Catita . . . Jacke a napes*] While its origin is obscure (see *OED*),
jackanapes is often used to refer to an ape or, by extension, to an
impertinent fellow. Catita, where this marvel occurs, is something of
a mystery also. The two words appear in the same context in John
Marston, *The Malcontent* (I.3.74–77): "Sir Tristram Trimtram, come
aloft, Jackanapes, with a whim-wham; here's a knight of the land of
Catito shall play at trap with any page in Europe" (ed. H. Spencer,
Elizabethan Plays, Boston, 1933). Spencer adds this note derived from
Kittredge: " 'Catito' is a coinage from 'cat,' which (like 'trap') is the
name of a boyish game. 'Catito'=sport-land, boys' play-land." But the
Peele reference suggests that the source is a bestiary or story of a
fabulous voyage.

712   *white . . . redd*] See above, Introduction, Sec. 3.C.

728   *faire and softly*] Quietly.

730   *I*] I.e., aye.

734   SD An example of economy in scene-changing made possible by the nature and conventions of the Elizabethan stage. See above, Introduction, Sec. 6.

736   *stomack*] Appetite.

751   *bravado*] An unusual use of the word, which ordinarily has connotations of exaggerated fearlessness by one who is really timorous.   *galliard*] A lively dance.

753   SD An obviously necessary addition.

755   Cf. Dandaline, the Hostess, in *Liberalitie and Prodigalitie* (Malone Society Reprint, ll. 518–522):

> for I assure you at a word,
> A better bird, a fairer bird, a finer bird,
> A sweeter bird, a yonger bird, a tenderer bird,
> A daintier bird, a crisper bird, a more delicate bird,
> Was there neuer set vpon any Gentlemans board.

Liberalitie and Prodigalitie was printed in 1602 and is generally thought to have been performed before the Queen in the previous year, but in style and conception it seems of a much earlier period.

757   *eate off*] Eat (past tense, rhymes with "met") of.

768   SD *Exeunt omnes*] Again, does not include Madge and her companions (see SD at ll. 334 and 686).   *Celanta*] In this scene, Q has "Zelanta" or "Zelanto" throughout. On the uncertain spelling of names in the play, see above, Introduction, Sec. 4.

774   *I*] I.e., aye.

777   *beard*] Although one may wonder exactly how a beard could weep, there seems no reason to bring in a bird—and another tale (see note to l. 636). Perhaps we can understand "beard" as metonymy for head. Floating rather vaguely underneath, and supported by "sheave" in l. 785, is a suggestion of the bearded corn and fertility gods (see above, Introduction, Sec. 3.H; Crow, p. 307).

785   *sheave*] Sheaf.

789   *just*] This is somewhat better than the "tost" of the uncorrected copies, but not much. It looks like a printer's attempt to correct without consulting copy. B queries "grist."

790   *quoiners . . . quine*] "Coiners . . . coin," as in the corrected state, which is evidently the printer's modernization. One must assume that the copy preserved the archaic form; it is unlikely that the printer, whose general tendency is toward modernizing, would have set an archaic form if his copy had the modern form.

797   *go crosse legged . . . prayers backward*] Crossed legs may bring bad luck (Lean, *Collectanea*, 2, 42, 111, 167), but can also produce good

results, especially at card playing or averting some expected punishment (2, 42, 405). See also John Brand, *Observations on Popular Antiquities* (London, 1810), p. 105, and *Edward I*, l. 2263 and note. I have found no such ambiguity about saying prayers backwards. This is the practice of witches and a means of summoning the devil (Lean, 2, 430).   *his*] One's; Dyce 3 and B omit.

807 *not . . . mum*] Proverbial; see Tilley (W767). On the significance of the silence and problems surrounding the death of Sacrapant, see above, Introduction, Sec. 3.E.

807–808 See above, Introduction, Sec. 7, for Dyce's realignment.

809 Q prints a tag for Sacrapant at the beginning of this line as if it were a new speech, but there seems no reason to assume that anything has been omitted. See l. 367 and note.

810 Dyce 3 suggests that to make the line scan we might omit "hatefull." B says either "hatefull" or "happy" should go. But the alliteration and the contrasting adjectives suggest that rhetoric prevailed over metrics.

813 *bloud*] Life (by extension from blood, that vital fluid upon which life depends).   *pearst*] I.e., pierced. While an unusual usage, the meaning is clear enough. Peele is very fond of the word; he uses it at least ten times in *David and Bethsabe*.

814 *timelesse date*] Eternal life (referring to the fact that, since the magic light could be destroyed only by one who was neither wife, widow, nor maid, the conjurer might have anticipated immortality). See above, Introduction, Sec. 3.E. Cf. *Araygnement*, l. 3.

816 SD There is no direction, but Sacrapant's body must be removed from the sight of the audience; otherwise Jack could hardly enter with the head at l. 863.

818 coile] Noisy disturbances.

822 SD The wool was inserted at l. 801.

831 *I*] I.e., aye.

834 *Anfill*] I.e., anvil.

837 See note to l. 183.

847 Delia's response refers to l. 844; she is not alone because Eumenides is with her. A similar joke occurs in *Edward I*, ll. 1332–33. See above, Introduction, Sec. 1, note 2.

853–856 Adapted from Greene, *Orlando Furioso* (ll. 72–76):

> Come from the South, I furrowd Neptunes Seas,
> Northeast as far as is the frosen Rhene,
> Leauing faire Voya crost vp Danuby,
> As hie as Saba whose inhaunsing streames,
> Cuts twixt the Tartares and the Russians.

See above, Introduction, Sec. 1.

863 SD Concerning the head, see above, Introduction, Sec. 3.E.

909 SD See above, Introduction, Sec. 6.
921 *coyle*] See l. 818 and note.
924 *depart*] Part, separate.
928 *to*] For.

ADDITIONAL NOTES TO 'EDWARD I'

Since the publication of Volume 2, a fifth copy of the quarto of 1593 has been located in the Bute Collection of the National Library of Scotland. The title page and B2 are missing, supplied in manuscript; L3 is defective. Collation reveals the following variants, noted in the Introduction to *Edward I* (p. 61):

B1ᵛ State 2: stars,
[B2 missing]
D2 State 2: trie
flies,
L2 State 1: ard

The Bute copy contains no additional variants.

In the text of *Edward I*, ll. 2442 and 2453 should end with periods. These additions should be made to the Explanatory Notes:

263–264 Thetis is sometimes confused with Tethys, the wife of Oceanus; cf. *Pericles*, IV.4.39–41, and *Troilus*, I.3.39. (See also Robert Graves, *The Greek Myths*, 11.2, 33.2.) This is no doubt the source—via Ovid— of the love relation between Phoebus and Thetis, for in *Metamorphoses* (2.68–69), Phoebus, explaining to his son about the journey through the heavens, says

> tunc etiam quae me subiectis excipit undis,
> ne ferar in praeceps, Tethys solet ipsa vereri.

The Phoebus-Thetis connection is well established in Elizabethan literature. See Greene, *Menaphon* (ed. Grosart, 6, 36–37 and passim), *Alphonsus*, l. 574; Nashe, *Summer's Last Will*, ll. 489–490; *Caesar's Revenge*, l. 255; Tourneur, "The Transformed Metamorphosis," ll. 432, 580.

1189 *infracte*] Clearly means "unbroken" in Gascoigne's translation of

Ariosto's *Supposes* (ed. Adams, I.2.36): "O how straight and infracte is this line of life! You will liue to the yeeres of Melchisedech."

1394 *quae negata sunt grata sunt*] Apparently proverbial. Cf. Webster, *White Devil*, I.2.162 (ed. Lucas), and Tilley, F585 ("what is forbidden is desired").

2448 *showres*] Cf. Lodge, *Wounds of Civil War*, l. 772 (Malone Society Reprint): "I late arriude vpon this wished shore."

2509 *Piropes*] Cf. Harvey, *Pierce's Supererogation* (*Works*, ed. Grosart, 2, 284): ". . . Rhetoricall figures, sanguin and resplendishing Carbuncles, like the flamy Pyrops of the glistering Pallace of the Sun." The source is Ovid, *Metamorphoses*, 2.1-2:

> Regia Solis erat sublimibus alta columnis,
> clara micante auro flammasque imitante pyropo."

2514 *eies . . . Cesars*] The terrible eyes are attributed by Lyly to Octavius Caesar Augustus in the prologue to *Gallathea:* "Augustus Caesar had such pearcing eyes, that who so looked on him, was constrained to wincke." See also *Euphues His England* (ed. Bond, 2, 77, l. 12).

2543 The poet is not Virgil but Ovid. Book 4 of *Metamorphoses* (ll. 415 ff.) describes Juno's jealous vengeance upon Ino. She ventures into Avernus to call upon the Furies, "sorores / Nocte . . . genitas" (l. 452; cf. Peele's "Daughter of darkenes"). Their abode before hell's gate is an accursed place ("sedes scelerata vocatur", l. 456). Tisiphone is Juno's agent. She approaches the doomed house of Ino, "solque locum fugit" (l. 488; cf. Peele's "Cimerian darkenes checks the Sun"). There may be a reminiscence of *Metamorphoses*, 11.592 ff.; there Ovid describes the Cave of Sleep, which is "prope Cimmerios,"

> quo numquam radiis oriens mediusve cadensve
> Phoebus adire potest.

Cf. Peele's *Honour of the Garter* (l. 337): "Envy stept from out the deepe Averne." There is possibly some reminiscence also of Ariosto, *Orlando Furioso*, 42.46 ff. The passage is an allegory of Jealousy, figured as a poisonous monster who lives in a dark cave. Rinaldo sees

> uscir fuor d'una caverna oscura
> Un strano mostro in femminil figura.

Building Bridges

Tales from Grace Chapel Inn®

Building Bridges

Carolyne Aarsen

Guideposts

CARMEL, NEW YORK

Acknowledgments

All Scripture quotations are taken from
The Holy Bible, New International Version. Copyright © 1973,
1978, 1984 International Bible Society. Used by permission
of Zondervan Bible Publishers.

www.guideposts.org
(800) 431-2344
Guideposts Books & Inspirational Media Division
Series Editors: Regina Hersey and Leo Grant
Cover art by Edgar Jerins
Cover design by Wendy Bass
Interior design by Cindy LaBreacht
Typeset by Nancy Tardi
Printed in the United States of America

Acknowledgments

To my many lovable nephews and nieces. You made it easy for me to write this book.

—Carolyne Aarsen

Chapter One

I don't usually beg, but I am begging you now. Please help me out."

Jane Howard anchored the phone between her ear and her shoulder. One part of her mind was listening to the slightly breathless woman on the other end, while another part was occupied with a list of groceries she was scribbling on the back of an envelope she had found lying on the butcher-block counter.

Upstairs the vacuum cleaner wheezed and whined as one of her older sisters, Alice, did the final cleaning of the guest rooms. Nearby the washing machine swished through its last cycle of linen.

Multitasking was alive and well at Grace Chapel Inn.

"I am absolutely at my wit's end," Stacy Reddington continued, her voice rising as she grew more upset. "My caterer canceled on me two days ago, and there is no caterer to be had in Potterston, and the hall I booked had a fire in the kitchen, so it's out of commission. I'm expecting ladies from Canada, the Netherlands and all the way from New Zealand and Japan . . ." Stacy stopped, exhaling heavily, and Jane felt a moment of sympathy for this obviously overwrought woman.

"What organization are you with?" Jane asked.

"It's not an organization per se," Stacy replied. "I belong to the Potterston Chamber of Commerce and these women belong to the Chambers of Commerce from towns we've twinned with in different countries. They've been touring, and I was in charge of this dinner, their last one in our area. I want it to be the highlight of the tour, but I think it's going to be a disaster." Stacy continued after she had composed herself, "Could you please, please help me out?"

Jane hesitated, torn between her obligations to running the bed-and-breakfast that she and her sisters owned, and a genuine desire to help this woman. Catering was a small sideline for Jane, and she took on jobs when she could for the extra income to purchase items for the inn.

And high on the list of extra things was a new vacuum cleaner, Jane thought, as the grating sound upstairs was finally silenced.

"What day would you need me and for how many people?" Jane asked, scribbling "ear plugs" at the bottom of the grocery list. If she and her sisters, Louise and Alice, had to use that vacuum cleaner much longer, all three of them would go deaf.

"Twelve women this coming Saturday, and I have no place to go . . ."

As Stacy revisited her problems, Jane pulled off the apron covering her pale-blue shirt and walked to the front desk tucked under the stairs. A quick check of the appointment book showed Jane the other reality of their situation. The inn would be full to bursting from tonight, Tuesday, until Sunday morning. A group of seven young people were in town for a football reunion, which would keep them busy Friday night, all day Saturday and Saturday evening. Catering the event on Saturday would be tight, but with organization she could make it work, especially because the inn's guests were gone all day and a large part of the evening.

"Do you need an answer today?" Jane asked, trying to

buy some thinking space, though she had to admit the idea appealed to her. International guests meant she might experiment with a varied cuisine.

"I'd like to know as soon as possible. I know I'm groveling, but, Ms. Howard, I'm desperate. These women are coming Saturday. I promised I would take care of this. I would make it worth your while," and she named her figure, which gave Jane pause.

Jane tapped her pencil on the desk, contemplating. She loved cooking and baking, and the challenge of doing this for a group of unknown people gave her a delicious tingle.

And, she had to admit, the figure Stacy quoted would add nicely to the inn's quickly depleting maintenance fund.

She had to run it past her sisters before she made a firm commitment, however. Money or not, the busier she was with a catering project, the less she was available for any extra work their inn guests might require.

"I'll see what I can do," Jane said. "I'll call you tomorrow with my answer."

"Thank you. Thank you so much. I really appreciate that you would even consider this, but could you let me know as soon as possible?"

"I'll do my best," Jane assured her. Jane listened to a few more breathless *thank you*s, and then Stacy said good-bye.

Jane closed the appointment book and leaned her elbows on the desk, staring toward the front windows of the inn. Raindrops slithered down the windows, obscuring the dreary day outside. The rain, which had started the day before, had put a damper on her plans to clean out the garden and ready the flowerbeds for fall. Though it was only late August, some of the plants had come to the end of their lifespan and needed to be cleaned out to make room for the still-producing plants.

If the rain continued today, she would have to wait another day just to let the ground dry out.

She had time on her hands, and her thoughts returned to Stacy's phone call and panicked request. Should she do this meal? If the rain continued, she would have time.

If she did cater this meal, what should she serve? Jane could draw on her work as a gourmet chef in San Francisco as well as on her experience from cooking at the inn.

The more she entertained the thought of catering for Stacy Reddington, the more the idea appealed to her. A challenge—just what Jane needed to energize herself.

The thumping of the vacuum cleaner getting moved down the stairs pulled her back to the present. She hurried around the desk to help her sister.

Alice Howard stood on the landing, her usually pleasant face puckered with frustration. She slipped her hands over her auburn hair, then checked her hands as if looking for something. "Are you quite sure you changed the bag on this machine, Jane? It still seems to have minimal suction. In fact, I'm fairly sure it's spitting out dust instead of air." She brushed down the front of her oxford shirt, checking it and her twill pants for more dust. "At any rate, there is something wrong with it."

"Okey dokey," Jane said, hastening to her sister's side. "Let me help you bring that downstairs and I'll have a look at it."

They manhandled the machine the rest of the way down the stairs. At the bottom, Jane opened it up and was immediately enveloped in a dusty cloud. She coughed and tried ineffectually to wave the dust away from her face.

"Oh dear," Alice lamented.

Jane waited for the dust to settle, then took another look inside. "Here's part of the problem." Jane pointed to the place where the hose entered the bag. "This connection is broken."

"Part of the problem? Is there more?"

"Besides causing migraines every time we use it?" Jane asked, brushing off her blue jeans. "This machine is going to make us deaf if we don't replace it."

"We can't do that now," Alice said. "When Fred Humbert came over to do the annual inspection, he said we should replace the gutters and make repairs on the north roof. That will use up most of our maintenance fund."

Jane stared down at the semiuseless piece of equipment, thought of the dollar figure Stacy had quoted and made a sudden decision.

"Don't worry about it. We'll have enough to buy a new vacuum cleaner in a few days."

"I suppose you'll just head out to the money tree we have growing out back?" Alice teased as Jane closed the cover.

"I believe I'll cater a dinner. I just got a phone call from a woman who is desperate." Jane paused, pursing her lips in a thoughtful gesture. "That could either be a compliment or an insult, couldn't it?"

"Take it as a compliment." Alice flicked some lint off her pants. "And what do we use to clean the inn in the meantime?"

"I'm sure Aunt Ethel has a vacuum cleaner we can borrow." Jane poked their moribund vacuum cleaner with the toe of her running shoe. "As for this . . . thing . . . we should banish it immediately."

"We can put it on the back porch for now." Alice closed up the vacuum cleaner. "When did this request to cater a dinner come up? Are you going to have enough time?"

"Of course. I'm a super supper caterer," Jane said flapping her hand at Alice's concern. She opened the door, letting in a gust of cold, damp air, and together they dragged the now-defunct appliance onto the porch. "I'll phone Fred to see if he can send José down to pick this up and take it to the landfill."

Alice stood a moment, looking down at the machine. "It seems a shame to get rid of this vacuum cleaner. Are you sure we can't get it fixed?"

Jane put her arm over her sister's shoulder, giving it a squeeze. "I'm sorry, Alice." She pretended to sniff, her voice taking on a melodramatic tone. "We did all we could. We didn't give up. Even Fred said this faithful cleaner was on its last legs . . . er . . . wheels. But its time has come. We must accept this and move on. It was a good vacuum cleaner in its day. It worked hard, but you have to admit, the last few years it was a bit of a whiner."

Alice started to chuckle. "I suppose even appliances must die."

Jane nodded solemnly.

"Are we done here?" Alice said, shivering. "I'm getting chilly."

"Shame on you, Alice," Jane said with mock severity. "Have some respect."

"I'd sooner have some tea, thank you very much."

"All right then." Jane saluted the appliance, pulled open the door, tucked her arm in her sister's and walked with her to the kitchen. "I'll clean up the dust later."

As Alice filled the kettle, Jane called Stacy to tell her what she had decided.

"Jane, you are a lifesaver," Stacy gushed. "An absolute lifesaver. I can't thank you enough."

"Not a problem. Now, did you have any preferences as to a menu?"

"I discussed that with the other caterer. I still can't believe he just up and quit on me. I had something memorable in mind but not too out there. You know how you can go to these gourmet restaurants, and you get a concoction that looks like it took hours to put together, and you hardly know where to start eating it? I don't want that. Good food, yes, and of course not too plain. Yet I want them to get the idea that care was taken. I want them to think we've put ourselves out a bit, but, as I said, not too out there. Does that help?"

Jane scribbled a few words on a pad. "So, elegant yet simple?"

"Not too elegant. But tasty. Whenever I think of elegant I think of tiny portions that don't fill a person up."

"How about an international flavor? Would that appeal to you?"

"Oh yes. I like that idea."

"Okay, we could go with a mixture of some ethnic foods—"

"Not too ethnic. I'd like every dish to be something anyone would enjoy eating."

"Okay. I think I have an idea of what I can do," Jane said, taking a few more notes. This dinner sounded like a challenge, but Jane was confident in her abilities to pull it off.

"Could you let me know fairly soon what you plan?"

"As soon as possible," Jane said.

They chatted a bit more, and then Jane hung up the phone.

She went to the cupboard holding her library of cookbooks and started pulling some out.

"Planning already?" Alice asked, setting cups out on a tray.

"There's no time like the present," Jane said, laying them out in a fan on the butcher-block counter. "So many recipes, so little time," she said, though with a smile of delight rather than regret.

Quiet reigned once again, broken only by the sound of pages flipping—Jane thumbing through her cookbooks and Alice immersed in a mystery book she had picked up at the library.

Wendell, the inn's resident feline, strolled into the room, looked about as if trying to decide where to sit, then hopped up on a chair, settled in and promptly began purring.

Jane looked up and smiled. For a while all was peaceful, restful.

Then the kettle started whistling, the back door flew open and excited voices spilled into the room. Louise, the oldest of the Howard sisters, and their Aunt Ethel bustled into the kitchen. Ethel looked flustered, Louise slightly annoyed.

"Are you sure you're all right, Louise? That didn't look very good to me," Ethel was saying, holding Louise's arm. "You ran right into that young boy and his truck. My goodness, he wasn't happy with you about the accident."

"What did you say?"

"You had an accident?"

Jane and Alice spoke at the same time.

"Nothing happened more than a very minor smack of bumpers and one flat tire," Louise said, holding up her free hand to keep her sisters at bay. She shrugged out of Ethel's grip, set a stack of papers and envelopes on the table, then removed her raincoat. She took off her glasses, letting them swing from the chain to which they were attached. In spite of her assertion that nothing had happened, Jane saw in her older sister's bright blue eyes that all was not right in Louise's world.

Jane pulled a chair out from the table. "Sit down, Louise, and tell us what happened. Is your car drivable?"

"Nothing and I'm fine, thank you very much," Louise said. "My car is at the mechanic's getting checked over."

"But she won't let herself get checked over," Ethel harrumphed. "Seems a bit odd. Besides, that accident didn't look good from where I was standing."

"You were standing inside Time for Tea and I bumped

into a truck at the other end of the block," Louise said dryly, giving Alice and Jane a quick smile.

"You never mind. I saw it all happen. And I'm a little worried about you," Ethel said, all concern and frowns. "You might want to see Dr. Bentley and have your head examined."

Jane wasn't going to look at Alice or Louise because she was sure if she did, they would burst out laughing.

"I'm sure that that is a given regardless of my circumstances," Louise replied. "Alice, could you please make that kettle stop its infernal whistling?"

Jane was closer so she hurried over and turned off the flame underneath the now strident-sounding kettle.

"Some tea, Louise?" she asked, as she lifted the lid off the teapot.

"Tea would be lovely."

When Jane brought back the tray that Alice had prepared, Ethel was still insisting that Louise see a doctor.

"Truly, Aunt Ethel," Louise said, her voice firm, "My car is worse off than I am, and my car has a mere scratch. The boy's truck had rubber bumpers, so not much chance of damage there."

"But these days you never know. You can get whiplash like that," Ethel snapped her fingers to underline her statement. Only nothing happened. Ethel frowned. "Like that," she repeated, trying to snap her fingers again. "Well now, isn't that something. Whatever is wrong with my fingers? I used to snap them all the time. I hope it's not arthritis."

"I'm sure you would have noticed some pain if it was," said Alice.

Ethel flexed her fingers, frowning. "I think I'm starting to feel a few twinges. Feels like, well, almost like . . ."

"Needles?" suggested Alice helpfully.

Ethel's frown deepened. "Possibly. Yes."

"Sometimes the weather can affect how your hands feel."

Ethel sat up as if something had just occurred to her. "Why just this morning I was having a discussion with Florence about this very thing. I told her the other day my hips were sore and I was sure it was because of the changing weather. She told me that was nonsense, that I was just imagining it. Then I told her that every time the weather changes, I can feel it, and then she said weather has nothing to do with how I'm feeling. I'm afraid we had a bit of a falling out over that. She can be quite opinionated, you know." Ethel looked around at each of her nieces as if seeking confirmation of that very fact.

"Imagine that," Jane said with a wry note in her voice.

Ethel glanced down at her hands. "So I'm sure my problem is arthritis." She looked around the table with a lugubrious expression.

"So tell us about this accident," Jane said, settling down to a cup of tea.

Louise simply shook her head, the overhead light glinting off her silver hair. "It was nothing. My tire went flat and as a result the car veered to one side and I bumped into a young man's truck. Thank goodness his truck is fine. I must confess, however, I felt rather foolish. I've never been in a car accident before. And I was clearly at fault."

"That young man wasn't a happy camper either," Ethel put in, patting her lips with a napkin. "He came storming out of his truck, took one look at the car and the truck and got upset with Louise."

"Oh dear. How unfortunate," said Alice.

"Nerve-racking," Jane agreed.

"Did you have to call the police?" Alice asked.

"We called them for insurance purposes and to be on the safe side," Louise said. "I'm glad to say the young man's truck didn't sustain any damage."

"I wanted to call an ambulance . . ." Ethel put in.

"But I found that unnecessary. As for that young man's attitude, as I said before, he was simply concerned about his truck."

"He still didn't need to be so angry with you," Ethel added, her pale blue eyes darting over the rest of the available brownie squares, trying to decide which one to have next. "I'm sure if you had been hurt, he still would have been more concerned about his precious truck."

"I hope that would not have been the case," Louise said, unbuttoning her peach-colored cardigan.

"Well, he was impolite. I hope I don't have to see him again soon."

The front doorbell rang, and in unison all three sisters pushed their chairs back, put their hands flat on the table and got up in one smooth motion.

Alice laughed. "You could say we've been living together too long."

"The Synchronized Innkeepers," Jane joked. "We could take our show on the road."

"We could become famous."

"We could answer the door," Louise commented, already walking briskly toward the front of the inn.

Jane winked at Alice and followed Louise. They, in turn, were followed by Ethel who was always vitally interested in the comings and goings of the guests at Grace Chapel Inn.

Though Louise had pooh-poohed Ethel's concern over the accident, Jane knew Louise well enough to understand that she would be disappointed with herself, no matter how slight the accident may have been.

Yet in spite of that, she was the consummate hostess. Smile in place, ready to greet and welcome prospective guests, she was the embodiment of Grace Chapel Inn's motto: "A place where one can be refreshed and encouraged, a place of hope and healing, a place where God is at home."

Louise opened the door to the sounds of lively chatter. A group of young people were gathered on the porch.

Behind them Jane heard Ethel's gasp.

"That's him," she said in a stage whisper, plucking at Jane's shirt. "That's the boy Louise hit with her car."

Chapter ⊤ Two

The young man staring back at her appeared as surprised as Louise felt. With his dark brown eyes and thick brown hair, he looked like a young movie star. But a deep frown marred his handsome features.

It was the same frown he directed at her after their collision. Of course, he had done more than frown then. As Ethel said, he seemed quite upset over a minor incident.

And now, here he was on her porch. Had he come to make amends? Or worse, had he come to charge her with something?

But he looked back over his shoulder at a young woman whose short black hair was spangled with rain, as was the bright red windbreaker she wore. She ran up the steps, joining the group of chattering and laughing young people.

Was this the party of seven Jane had booked two months ago? Jane's scribbled note had merely said, "Cobalt high school alumni-reunion," and Louise had drawn her own conclusions about their age. Cobalt was a town near Potterston. *Well, I overestimated,* she thought, taking note of the group's youthfulness.

"Hey, Carita, you sure this is the right place?" the dark-haired young man said.

"Yes, Lynden, it is," Carita replied. "You know, the sign? Grace Chapel Inn? That was the first clue."

The young woman, Carita, shook rain from her hair and favored Louise with a smile. "I am giving the right information, aren't I?"

Louise nodded.

"See. Right place, Lynden." She glanced up at him as if challenging him to question her authority.

Lynden looked back at Louise, then shrugged. His dark leather jacket glistening with moisture, the torn T-shirt, the faded blue jeans, the frown still creasing his forehead, all combined to give him the same edgy look that had made Louise feel uncomfortable in his presence after their accident.

But it appeared that he was now their guest, so Louise stepped aside, pulling the door farther open. "Please, come in out of the rain. And welcome to Grace Chapel Inn."

As the other young people tumbled past Lynden into the front hall, laughing and joking, Louise glanced back at Jane who seemed as surprised as she was at just how young this group of guests was. Why, most of them barely looked old enough to vote.

Obviously, Jane had not verified their ages either.

"My name is Louise Smith, and these are my sisters, Jane Howard and Alice Howard. We're the owners of the inn. And this is our Aunt Ethel. She lives in the carriage house behind us."

"I'm Carita. This is Lynden, Rick, Matthew, Herbie, Isabel and Pete."

Carita reached out and shook Louise's hand, then Jane's, Alice's and Ethel's. The rest of the group nodded their heads in greeting.

Carita smiled. "Okay. That's settled. What's next?" she asked, fingering her damp hair.

"Jane took your reservation, so she will sign you in. Then I'll show you to your rooms upstairs."

"This is a great place," Carita said, glancing around the foyer. "Love the wallpaper. Whaddya think, guys? Did I do good or what?"

"Yeah."

"Great."

"Nice place."

Louise thought that, despite the responses, Carita's friends seemed less than enthusiastic about the accommodations. She wondered what they had expected.

"Rick and Matthew, can you please help me get our luggage from the van?" Carita asked, smiling sweetly at two of the young men.

They spun around, ready to assist the young woman.

Lynden hung back, one hand in the pocket of his blue jeans, looking at the floor, the reception desk, the nails of his fingers, anywhere but at Louise, Jane, Alice or Ethel.

Isabel whispered to one of the other boys and, it seemed to Louise, sent furtive glances her way.

Was there a problem?

Once Jane had them signed in, Louise led the way up the stairs to the guest rooms.

"We have four rooms, and I notice there are seven in the group," Louise said, stopping in the main hall, "so six of you will double up. We do have extra cots if you are uncomfortable with sharing a bed.

"Each room has a name," Louise continued, opening the door of the Garden Room, a room at the front that was decorated in shades of green with a floral border along the wainscoting. She moved across the hall. "This one is called the Sunset Room," she said, then opened the door to a room with terra-cotta ragged paint. "The Sunset and Garden rooms each have a private bath, so I thought either of these might be suitable for the girls."

"The Garden Room looks okay," Isabel said. "Carita told me to pick it. Besides, I kinda doubt the boys will appreciate flowers and stuff."

"Unfortunately, one of the other rooms for the boys is called the Symphony Room and it does have flowers," Louise said. "And stuff."

"Yay for us," one of the boys said. Louise clearly heard the irony in his voice.

Undaunted, she showed them the other rooms, letting them decide. Lynden just hung back, not responding to anything the other boys said.

Louise glanced at him from time to time, but he appeared not to notice her.

She waited while the boys made their choices, growing increasingly uncomfortable with their obvious lack of enthusiasm. It appeared the inn wasn't what they had expected either.

Carita rejoined the group. "So? Everyone got his or her rooms picked out? You pick the Garden Room, Isabel?"

"Just like you told me to," Isabel replied.

"Awesome. My cousin told me about this place. Said it was awesome and you ladies were super-duper hostesses." Carita flashed a smile that Louise was pleased to return. At least Carita seemed enthusiastic about the inn. "Hey, Lynden, whaddya think?"

"Yeah. Good," was all he mumbled.

Louise chose to ignore his reticence as she glanced around the hall at the gathering of young people. She knew she shouldn't care, but for a moment she felt very . . . old. To have so much youth and vitality all gathered in one place seemed to underscore the age difference between her and her guests.

Still undaunted, however, Louise went over the basic house rules, telling them when breakfast was served and how their linen was handled. "We have a number of brochures downstairs by the desk in case you are interested in touring Acorn Hill. I understand you are going to be visiting Cobalt for something called Spirit Night on Friday and a school reunion on Saturday?"

"Go, Cobalt Cougars," one of the young men called out, pumping his fist in the air.

"Herbie and Rick are our reps in the flag-football game on Friday night," Carita said.

"And there are going to be bonfires," another boy said with obvious relish.

"I'm sure you will all have a wonderful time, but if there's anything we can do to make your stay here more comfortable, please don't hesitate to let us know." Louise glanced around the gathered young people. "Does anyone have any questions?"

"Can I check my e-mail here?" a short, slightly overweight young man asked. Louise tried to recall who he was, but the introductions had been such a flurry of names, she could attach only a few names to faces.

Lynden she had already identified. Matthew's hair was cut close to his head and Pete wore a baseball cap. She'd have to work on the others.

"You can use the library downtown."

"You need to limit your surfing, Herbie." Carita wagged her finger in a mock reprimand. "You spend way too much time on MySpace."

"MySpace being . . . ?" Louise asked with genuine interest. She had only recently mastered the rudiments of searching the Web and had discovered the joys of "googling" various topics. She hadn't heard about MySpace yet.

"A huge sprawling mess of interconnected personal Web pages." Carita's dismayed look telegraphed her opinion of said sprawling mess. "If you're really interested, Mrs. Smith, I can show you some time. You have to be a member to log in though."

"I could help you set up a page. For the inn," Herbie offered.

"Would that be helpful?" Louise asked.

"Well, yeah. You could set up a really cool friends' list and then you can post bulletins." Herbie slung the bag he carried over his shoulder onto the floor.

"Give Mrs. Smith a break," Matthew said.

Louise held up her hand. "Please. Feel free to call me Louise. Mrs. Smith makes me feel old."

Herbie frowned, then glanced at Lynden still slouched against the wall. "But she is old," he whispered.

"What do you mean?" Louise asked, delicately placing her hand on her chest. "I'm a mere sixty-five."

"And not deaf either," Matthew shot a warning glance at Herbie who simply shrugged.

"So, if everything is satisfactory, then I shall leave you to your unpacking." Louise's glance touched each one of them and then she turned to leave.

"She seems okay," she heard Herbie whisper. "For an old lady."

"Hey. Remember. Not deaf," she heard Matthew warn.

Louise smiled as she walked down the stairs. So perhaps it was just an age gap that made some of the young guests seem unimpressed with the inn. She resisted the urge to jump a step, just to show them. *One is only as old as one feels*, she reminded herself as she came to the bottom.

"Got our new guests settled in?" Alice asked, looking up from the dishwasher she was filling.

"I hope so. Where is Aunt Ethel?"

"She went to get her vacuum cleaner."

"Why is she doing that?"

"I forgot to tell you. Our vacuum cleaner has expired. It

bit the dust, once literally, but now metaphorically," Jane offered, glancing up from the cookbooks she was paging through.

"But that machine is quite new."

"I bought it eighteen years ago, Louise," Alice said.

Louise frowned. "Are you sure? I had exactly the same type when Eliot and I lived in Philadelphia. I'm sure I bought it when Cynthia was . . ." She stopped there and shook her head, then sighed. "I guess it is old, and I guess I am older than I think."

"Where is this coming from," Jane said, folding her arms over her chest.

"Our guests. They seemed somewhat dismayed."

"At what?" Alice asked. "They seem much like many of our other guests. Tired, excited to be doing something different."

"I am quite sure they were expecting much younger hostesses," Louise replied. "As I was expecting much older guests." She sent a questioning look Jane's way.

Jane lifted her hands in a gesture of surrender. "Mea culpa. When Carita said they were alumni, I pictured older men in scarves and jackets looking all very Harvardish and reserved."

"Wrong picture," Louise said.

"Well, I'm not going to start asking guests' ages when they phone for reservations," Jane said. "Especially not when they use a Platinum credit card."

"Of course not, but they are so young and energetic . . ."

"Now Louise, you know we want to model our Lord here. Everyone is welcome."

"Of course they are. It's just . . ."

Alice wiped her hands and walked over to her sister. "Louise, what is the problem? You seem upset. Could you have hurt yourself in the accident?"

"No, I didn't. Truly, I'm fine." Then Louise sighed and

shook her head. "However, I still feel foolish for running into Lynden's truck, and though nothing serious happened, I'm uncomfortable with how I felt afterward. And then, just a few moments ago one of our guests made a comment about being surprised at how old I was. Usually, I really don't feel old, and I maintain that one is only as old as one feels. But today, I have to confess, I do feel old."

"Now, Louise, we're always going to be older than someone, but the upside is we're always going to be younger than someone too," Jane said, adding an infectious grin.

Alice, however, truly understood Louise's concern. Though she still felt quite fit, there were times, especially when the young, bright and seemingly tireless student nurses would come into the hospital to work under her, that she had "elderly" moments. But that soon subsided when she realized all the experience and wisdom she had to offer these young girls. Often, by the time the students moved on to another ward, or graduated, she and the young women had achieved understanding and mutual respect. They ceased to be young students and an older woman; they were simply nurses, united in a common cause to alleviate suffering.

Other than the half-hour sessions with her piano students, Louise did not have as frequent an opportunity as Alice to interact with young people over longer periods of time.

"You put things quite well, Louise, when you said that you're only as young as you feel. I don't think you're old at all."

"You realize you have a vested interest in consoling me, Alice," Louise said with an ironic tone. "You're only a few years younger than I am."

"And I feel as young as I ever did," Alice said with a decisive nod.

"That may be, but sometimes reality intrudes and today

it has." Louise straightened her shoulders. "I must be realistic. I remember reading an advertisement in the *Acorn Nutshell* about a refresher course for seniors who still drive. I think I should register."

"You don't need that," Jane protested. "There have been no major breakthroughs in the transportation department. We're not strapping on jet packs yet, as I once thought we would be by now." She sighed, looking almost wistful.

But Alice, being just three years younger than Louise, understood her sister. "I think that might be a good idea," Alice said, by way of encouraging her sister. "I have a number of days off coming up. I might take it with you."

"I'll have to look into this course," Louise said, pressing the palm of her hand on the table like a judge considering a sentence. "It would be the prudent thing to do."

"Could someone help me with this?" Ethel's call was followed by some thumping noises punctuated with some unladylike grunts.

Alice scooted across the kitchen to the door, and a few moments later Ethel's ancient vacuum cleaner took up one corner of the kitchen and Ethel sat on a chair, fanning herself. Her hair was plastered to her head and the vacuum was spotted with rain.

"Mercy me, that old thing is heavier than I thought. I had to stop three times between here and my house."

"You should have asked us to help you," Alice chided gently as she maneuvered the machine into a corner.

"Why? I can certainly manage to get a vacuum cleaner from point A to point B. I'm not some helpless little old lady," Ethel protested.

Jane snorted and then covered it up with a cough.

"Are you all right, Jane?" Ethel asked, her bright eyes flicking to her youngest niece.

"I'm fine, really," Jane responded, adding another cough.

"Sounds a bit croupy to me. I would get that checked out." Ethel turned back to Alice. "Now the vacuum should be running like a top. I won't need it for a couple of days, so feel free to use it all you want. The carriage house doesn't get very dusty in this weather."

"You didn't need to bring it over in the rain," Alice said.

Ethel patted her hair and sniffed. She cocked her head, listening. "Those kids still here?"

"They are settling in." Alice made a trip to the laundry room, and when she returned, Ethel was quizzing Louise on their new guests.

"Seems odd a bunch of kids like that wouldn't want to stay in a motel so they can whoop it up till all hours of the night. I remember when Bob and I were traveling. We ended up in a town during a big hockey tournament. We couldn't find a room anywhere. We wound up in a little motel with walls no thicker than my pinky and stayed in a room beside a group of young kids who were louder than a marching band at Macy's Thanksgiving Day Parade. Except without the instruments. They didn't need instruments, the way they were trumpeting on and on and playing music loud enough to wake the dead." She shook her head as if still amazed at the memory. Ethel frowned at Alice. "These kids won't be loud, will they? I mean the carriage house is a ways away, but still, noise does travel at night."

"I don't think so," Alice said reassuringly. "I'm sure if they wanted to whoop it up, as you say, they would have chosen a motel."

"One of the girls, Carita, said her cousin recommended the inn," Louise said. "I think it's always wonderful when previous guests are so satisfied with their stay that they pass that information on."

"Word of mouth. Best advertising in the business," Jane said from her perch, making a note on a piece of paper.

"What are you doing, Jane?" Ethel asked.

"Looking for new and exotic recipes." Jane tucked the pencil behind her ear and paged through another cookbook. "Though I'm coming up empty-handed."

"I'm sure our young guests don't need exotic breakfasts," Louise said.

"That's not the only thing I'm looking up recipes for," Jane said.

"Jane might be catering a dinner Saturday night," Alice put in.

"Won't the extra work leave you in a bind?" Louise frowned, adjusting her glasses. "We will still have all these guests."

Jane shrugged. "They'll be gone most of Saturday and I see this as a challenge."

"Who is the dinner for?"

"A certain Stacy Reddington from Potterston. She sounded desperate and 'really, really, really' wanted me to do this dinner." Jane held up her hand as if to forestall Louise's correction. "Her words, not mine."

"Where would this dinner take place?"

"She hadn't settled on a venue. I'm sure she's checking that out as I speak."

"Are you certain you won't be too tired?

"Stop fretting, Louise. I've got loads of energy."

Louise pushed herself to her feet. "Very well. I see I can't dissuade you. However, I have my own work to do. I'll be in the office." She gathered up the papers she had brought in and left the kitchen.

"How did this lady find you?" Ethel asked, folding her arms on the kitchen table.

Alice could tell that her aunt was settling in for a session of chatting, but she could also see Jane was buried in her cookbooks and preferred not to be distracted.

Seven guests and an upcoming dinner meant hours of planning on Jane's part, and Alice was sure Jane would prefer peace and quiet while she planned.

"I heard June Carter at the Coffee Shop made some raisin pie today," Alice said, getting up from the table. "Why don't I treat you to some, Aunt Ethel?"

Ethel got the hint, and together they left Louise to her bills, Jane to her planning and the group upstairs to their unpacking.

Chapter Ⲧ Three

H i, ladies. What do you want to order?" Hope Collins asked, stopping at Alice and Ethel's booth with a full coffeepot. An array of bobby pins held up her hair in an intricate style.

Ethel had selected a booth by the window to keep her eye on the comings and goings in the town. Light rain fell steadily, obscuring the buildings across the street, drizzling down the glass.

The walk to the Coffee Shop had been damp and cool, and Alice was glad to be inside again.

"I'll have a piece of raisin pie," Ethel said. "With some ice cream on the side, but not too much. I should be watching my weight."

"And you, Alice?"

"I'll also have the raisin pie, but without the ice cream, thank you." Alice too was watching her weight, and in spite of her regular walks with her friend Vera, the struggle was an ongoing one.

"Will do," Hope said as she poured coffee for Ethel and brought the usual tea for Alice. "And how is Louise? I heard about her fender bender."

"More like an embrace of bumpers," Alice said.

Hope frowned, setting the coffeepot on the table. "I heard the police were at Wilhelm's?"

"Just a formality. Neither Louise nor the young man she hit was hurt. Nor were the vehicles damaged."

"Road must have been slippery," Hope said. "I can't imagine Louise being even the teeniest bit careless. She is a lot like your dear father. Rev. Howard was methodical and careful."

"She said something was wrong with her tire. That's what caused the accident."

"I saw the whole thing," Ethel piped up, only too eager to share any bit of news with Hope. "Seeing that car slide into that truck put my heart smack dab in my throat. Very scary, though Louise won't admit it. She's going to take a seniors refresher course now."

"I can't think of her as a senior," Hope said with a chuckle.

"Tell Louise that," Alice said. "She's been feeling a bit elderly today."

"If she's feeling that way, I hope June isn't counting on her."

"Count on her for what?" Ethel asked.

"I'll let her tell you. I should get back to work."

"Do you have any idea, Alice? I can't imagine June would plan something and not tell me. I was talking to her just the other day and she said nary a word about any plans."

Aunt Ethel looked peeved, and Alice tried not to smile. Her dear aunt liked to be in the forefront of any new gossip in town. Of course she would never call it gossip. "Generous sharing of information" was her preferred phrase.

Alice saw June Carter, the shop's owner, walking toward them, wiping her hands on her apron. Flushed cheeks and a smudge of flour decorating her forehead indicated that she had just taken a break from cooking and baking chores.

"Maybe June is coming over to tell us now," Alice assured her aunt.

Ethel twisted around. "*Yoo-hoo*, June, come join us."
Ethel slid closer to the window to give June room.

"Hope told us you have something going on," Ethel said
as June settled next to her. "Is it a big secret or are you
allowed to share?"

"No secret, Ethel, though I don't know if you'd be interested. I'm going to be involved in helping with Habitat for
Humanity. They're building a house for a young couple."

Alice was taken aback. She couldn't imagine June swinging a hammer.

"You look surprised, Alice," June said with a laugh. "I'm
surprised myself. But if first ladies can do it—"

"Who?" Ethel asked.

"A number of first ladies and female governors set up an
affiliate to build houses. They've been doing it for many years
now. In fact, sometimes Habitat for Humanity sets up building crews made up entirely of women—they call it the
Women Build program. Helps give women a safe place to
learn how to use a hammer and operate a skill saw."

Aunt Ethel's eyes lit up. "A skill saw," she said in a rever-
ential tone.

Alice tried not to imagine her dear aunt in possession of
such a tool and the potential havoc she could wreak. As a
nurse who had seen many accident victims in her time, she
knew all too well how much damage a saw, wrongly handled,
could do.

"I imagine they leave the operation of dangerous tools to
experienced people," Alice commented.

"Absolutely. They believe in safety first," June said.

"So this project is a women-only project?"

June shook her head. "We were hoping, but we can't
seem to get enough women. For now, we're just content to
get enough volunteers."

"Can anyone volunteer? Do they have an age limit?"
Ethel put in.

"You have to be over eighteen and, I guess, reasonably fit. I imagine they don't want people having heart failure once they start hammering," June said. Hope set down cups and plates of pie, then bustled away.

Ethel glanced down at her hands, and Alice guessed she was pondering her arthritis. Then Ethel flexed her fingers and straightened her back as if a small thing like twinges and aches wasn't going to keep her away from doing her duty by her fellow man.

"I'd like to volunteer," she said.

"Are you sure you should?" Alice asked, envisioning her usually spry but slightly plump aunt trying to climb a ladder or straddle a roof.

"I could probably do something. Maybe bring water or clean up behind the workers."

"Good afternoon, ladies."

Florence Simpson stood at the end of their booth, her brown hair teased and sprayed to glazed perfection, her deep red earrings and necklace sparkling in the overhead light. Her gaze merely flicked over Ethel, but Alice and June got a full-fledged smile.

"I overheard you talking about this building project, June," Florence said. "I heard about it previously and I am very interested. Could I get some more information?"

"I can only give you what I received from the project co-coordinator," June said.

"I might be interested," Florence's eyes skipped over Ethel and rested on June, "if there's a place for me on the crew."

"Don't worry," June assured her with a laugh. "From what I understand there will be many different jobs to do once they get started building. You might find the perfect place to help."

Though Ethel and Florence were taking great pains to avoid speaking, Alice saw her aunt squirming with curiosity.

"Did you put this information in other places, June?" Ethel asked, pointedly ignoring Florence. "I'm just wondering how people would hear about this." Ethel dug into her pie.

"Martha Bevins told me while I was getting my hair done at the Clip 'n' Curl," Florence said, aiming her comment at June and only June. Florence could ignore a person as well as Alice's aunt could.

June gave Alice a puzzled glance as if trying to figure out why Florence and Ethel were channeling their conversation through her. The two women's relationship could be stormy, but sooner or later Ethel would have something she simply had to tell someone, and Florence, always a willing recipient of any news, big or small, would forgive her.

In the meantime, however, Alice felt uncomfortable and a bit sad for these two friends.

Florence tapped June on the shoulder. "I don't have arthritis, so I could probably help out. What could I do?"

"Lots of things," June said, stifling a smile at the gymnastics she was going through to maintain a conversation with these women. "I'm sure you could handle some of the heavier work. It's always a cooperative effort, so it's not like you have to build the house on your own," June explained, warming to her subject. "In fact, the future owners of the house are required to help, which I think is very interesting."

"Do you need training?" Alice asked, growing curious herself about the project. "I don't believe any of us here has used a hammer for anything more than putting nails in walls or doing minor repairs."

"There is usually a supervisor on the project, and she or he will tell you what you need to do and help you. I'm sure after a few days, you'll get better at it."

"And how do they get the money if they need assistance?" Florence asked.

"The cost of building the house itself is pretty low.

Apparently much of the material and the time to build the house is donated, or provided for Habitat at a deep discount. In addition, as I mentioned, the people who will receive the home have to commit to working at least five hundred hours on the project, either building or collecting funds or whatever else might need to be done to help raise money or raise the house."

"How interesting and how motivating." Florence looked impressed.

"It is. I visited my sister a few years back when she was involved in a similar project. I went to help her for a day and have been wanting to do this ever since. The day I was there, the family had to decide on paint colors. One of the volunteers was helping the woman, a single mother, and the dear girl was so excited and so happy that she was crying while she was picking out the colors."

"I'm in," declared Ethel, slapping her hand—somewhat cautiously—on the table for emphasis. "I think this is a wonderful example of faith in action. I want to be a part of this."

Alice saw an answering spark in Florence's eye. "Well. If some people can forget their disabilities, I am sure I can be of help. I will also volunteer," Florence declared in a loud voice, as if making sure June and Ethel—as well as others in the shop—would not doubt her meaning. Alice glanced from Ethel to Florence, who were still studiously avoiding each other. If Ethel and Florence were helping, it would be prudent if Alice volunteered some time to keep an eye on the two of them.

"I'm interested as well," Alice said.

"This is wonderful," June said, beaming at the assembled group. "I'll let my contact person know and she can give you all the details."

"When do we start?" Ethel said. "I need to prepare myself."

"You can go to the building site tomorrow if you like," June said. "I may not go until Thursday."

Ethel turned to Alice. "If you're coming, I can ride with you."

"I'll ride with you, June," Florence said.

Alice exchanged a smile with June. "I guess that's decided," she said.

"Good, and I better get back to my kitchen. I'm excited about this and so glad Acorn Hill will be well represented."

"I don't know how well Acorn Hill will be represented, but we will be represented," Alice said with a smile.

After June and Florence left the table, Ethel leaned closer to Alice, her blue eyes fairly snapping. "Can you believe that Florence? I think she's deliberately setting out to goad me."

"What makes you say so, Auntie?"

Ethel sniffed. "That comment she made about not having arthritis. Then that one about ignoring disabilities. She's just trying to get me riled up."

"Why would she do that?"

Ethel sat back, crossing her arms over her bosom and glancing out the window, her dyed red hair bouncing with suppressed indignation. "She can be that way, you know," was all Ethel would say.

"I see," Alice said, even though she wasn't sure that she did. Ethel and Florence had fallings-out before, but not over something this trivial. She suspected there was more to the story, but for now Ethel wasn't telling her.

She also suspected she would receive even less information from Florence herself.

However, Alice had hopes for her aunt and for Florence. Working together on this project could be a good opportunity to bring them back together again.

Ethel sighed, glanced over at her niece and was suddenly all smiles. "Are you done with your tea?" Ethel said, leaning closer to peer into Alice's cup.

"Not quite." Alice couldn't help but smile herself. Her aunt could be easily provoked, but she bounced back quickly to her usual sunny nature.

"Okay." Ethel leaned back, drumming her fingers on the tabletop, glancing out the window, then around the Coffee Shop, then back at Alice's teacup.

"Are you in a hurry to leave, Auntie?" Alice asked.

"If we are going to be working on this house tomorrow, we'll need some tools."

"I'm sure they will be provided."

"Are you positive?"

"Well, not positive. I've never done anything like this before."

"Then we should be prepared, shouldn't we?" Ethel's face fairly beamed. "I'd like to stop at Fred's Hardware. The more we provide ourselves, the less they have to, right? And we should probably stop at the Nine Lives Bookstore too. See if Viola has any books on carpentry in stock. Might find some information to help us be better prepared when we get there."

Alice finally caught the gist of where her aunt was headed—shopping.

"I'll be done in a few sips," she said, smiling at her aunt's enthusiasm. One thing about Aunt Ethel, she never stayed down long.

"And when would this course begin?" Louise asked, writing down a figure on the message pad on the reception desk. "And it is every day, starting tomorrow? Then I'm glad I contacted you as soon as I did. I shall see you tomorrow."

Louise hung up the phone and ripped the paper off the pad. She paused a moment, wondering if she was doing the right thing.

Well, of course she was. She had been fortunate nothing worse had happened this morning when she ran into that truck. For what seemed like the twentieth time, she replayed the scene in her head. But what else could she have done?

According to Harlan Green, her tire had been wearing down for a while. Simple maintenance and regular observation would have prevented the tire's going flat, he had said. That was something she should have been aware of.

Louise was always of the opinion that preparation for potential problems limited the potential for future problems.

As a result, she decided to be proactive and find a way to be prepared. And, thankfully, she remembered reading that piece in the *Acorn Nutshell* about this refresher course. Now that she was registered, she felt better.

A blast of music from upstairs gave her an unexpected jolt. Had there been other people staying at the inn, Louise would have asked their current guests to turn down the music. As it was, no one was complaining, and as long as they didn't keep the music playing into the night, she and her sisters would simply have to put up with the noise.

Louise was surprised these young people chose to stay at the inn when there were many other places in Potterston that would seem to have been better suited for their purposes.

Louise tucked the paper into the pocket of her narrow gray skirt and wandered back to the kitchen, where Jane was hunched over her recipe books, talking to someone on the phone.

"I understand. I could make some traditional American recipes," Jane made a note on a pad of paper lying beside the books, nodded, then scratched it out. "We don't *have* to do traditional American. I could try to find something more cosmopolitan . . . no, I don't mean fancy, I just mean . . . more . . . European? I see." She nodded, spoke some more, said good-bye and then hung up the phone.

"Haven't settled on the menu?" Louise asked as the door to the dining room swung back and forth behind her.

Jane pushed her long hair back from her face and sighed. "Stacy specifically said she didn't want exotic ingredients— she's concerned about possible allergies—nor did she want something too 'out there,' wherever 'there' is, or too plain, or something that's been done before. That narrows the list. So I thought of an international menu, but she didn't like the idea, and, well, you heard the rest of the story." Jane gestured at the telephone.

Louise caught a note of frustration. "Are you already regretting taking this on?"

Jane's forehead puckered a moment as she flipped through her recipe books. Then she shook her head. "If anything, I'm becoming more determined."

The timer for the dryer buzzed, and Louise moved toward the utility room to remove a load of clothes.

"I'll get it," Jane said, holding up her hand. "You just sit down."

"And why should I do that?" Louise asked.

"Well, I'm just, you know, a little concerned . . . I mean, you did just have an accident."

"Nothing happened, Jane," Louise said. "I'm fine and I'm not going senile and there is nothing wrong with my coordination." She frowned, glancing upward as a particularly loud measure of music boomed above them. "I didn't realize the ceilings and walls were so thin."

"What do you mean?"

Was she deaf? "That thumping music carries with remarkable effectiveness throughout the inn."

Jane frowned, cocking her head as if to listen. "I hadn't really paid much attention."

"How could you not? That bass chord is practically shaking the floor."

Jane's smile showed Louise once again the differences in their ages. And their musical tastes as well. "Maybe I should get them to play their radios in the parlor."

"They would completely fill up that room. Why would you want to do that?"

"Soundproof walls."

The music stopped, and Louise breathed a sigh of relief. Too soon, it seemed, because only a few moments later, country music wailed through the halls of the inn.

"I'm going to go out for a while," Louise said. "Unless you need any help here?"

Jane smiled at her sister, obviously recognizing the source of her discomfort. "There's not much to do, so go ahead. Maybe by the time you come back, they might have switched to classical."

"I don't think I can be gone that long," Louise said with a wry smile. "I'll be at Viola's bookstore."

"Would you like a ride?"

Louise stared at her sister. "No. Nine Lives is not far. I'm walking."

Jane held her hands up in a gesture of surrender. "Fine. Good. Walking is healthy and invigorating. Make sure you take your umbrella."

Chapter ⊤ Four

A few moments later Louise was striding down the wet sidewalks, inhaling the fresh, albeit damp, air. Dark clouds still hung low over the area, dropping a light drizzle on the town—enough to spangle the trees with moisture and to keep Jane out of her beloved garden, yet not enough to inhibit a good, brisk walk.

She waved at a neighbor, slowed to admire the flowers filling a corner flowerbed near Grace Chapel. *I should appreciate them while I can*, she thought, bending over to touch the bright chrysanthemums. Soon the killing frost would come, the plants would die, and the trees of Acorn Hill would display their glorious colors as a muted song of praise to God for His creation.

But not yet, Louise thought, tucking her hands deeper in the pockets of her raincoat. For now the grass was still green, plants were still alive and the leaves still clung to the trees.

She paused at the street crossing, looked both ways, then looked again as if to make sure she didn't have a second accident this morning. Then she crossed over.

Though she had waved off her sister's concern, her confidence in her own driving ability had been shaken. She realized that drivers made mistakes all the time, but hitting that truck was a reminder of how much power and weight a vehicle had.

Louise paused at the entrance of the bookstore, removed her rain bonnet, shook out the moisture, then pulled open the door of Nine Lives. The faint jangling of the bell created a welcoming, homey sound.

All was quiet inside the store. Louise looked around the crowded shelves and felt a familiar pull of anticipation. The sight of all these new, still unopened books, these potential adventures, and the information stored inside the shiny new covers never ceased to create a gentle thrill. *All this, just waiting to be plucked from a shelf and read.*

"Hello," she called, wondering where her good friend was. Usually when the bell rang, either Viola or one of her many cats were there to greet her.

But no one came, and the only cat Louise saw was resting on Viola's desk in the back of the store.

Where could she be?

She finally heard a faint murmuring of voices and followed the sound to a far corner of the store where the how-to books were shelved, a section Louise seldom visited.

"I need to know if there's a right or wrong way to hold a hammer."

Was that Aunt Ethel's voice?

Louise peered around a bookshelf and there was her aunt squinting at a book as Viola was pointing out something on one of the pages.

"From what it says here you want to hold the hammer near the very end. I would imagine you get better leverage that way."

"This doesn't give a person much information."

"If you want more detailed books, you could check with Nia Komonos at the library," Viola said.

Aunt Ethel snapped the book shut. "Maybe I'll just figure it out on my own. Alice, I'm ready to go to Fred's now."

Alice is here as well?

Louise coughed lightly to make her presence known. "Hello, Viola, Aunt Ethel," Louise said.

Viola spun around, her expression slipping from humor to worry. "Louise. How are you?"

"I am the picture of health and vitality." Louise held up a hand to forestall any concern on Viola's part. She should have known something as minor as two vehicles bumping each other would have already spread across the width and breadth of Acorn Hill. And she should have known that her friend would have already found out. Louise was certain that Ethel had seen to that.

Louise turned to her aunt. "I thought you and Alice were having pie in the Coffee Shop."

Ethel shrugged Louise's comment aside. "Well, we were." She put the book back on the shelf. "But now we're here."

Alice appeared around the end of the bookshelf holding a couple of books in her hand. Mysteries, Louise saw from their covers.

"These just came out, didn't they?" Alice asked.

Viola fiddled with the floral silk scarf draping her shoulders. "Yes. I just finished shelving them." Sharing Louise's less-than-enthusiastic regard for mysteries, she gave her friend a "what can I do" look, which merely made Louise smile.

One would think that after all these years of running a bookstore in Acorn Hill, Viola Reed had resigned herself to the varied and, at times, ordinary tastes of her patrons.

"Wonderful. I wondered when this author's new book would come out. I love reading her stories. They may not be great literature, but they are great fun."

"I set a new anthology of Walt Whitman's poetry on the display table," Viola suggested in an encouraging tone.

Louise gave Viola high marks for maintaining her campaign to raise the literary bar for the residents of Acorn Hill.

Over time some had succumbed and slowly purchased a number of Viola's more challenging suggestions. But by and large, her biggest selling item was popular contemporary fiction.

Alice wrinkled her nose, giving Viola a sly smile. "Thank you, but I prefer a good rollicking read."

Viola shrugged. "Well, then rollick away," she said, leading Alice to the front of the store.

"May I ask why you are looking at books about construction?" Louise asked Ethel, her curiosity piqued.

"Alice and June Carter and I are going to help build a Habitat for Humanity home. It's a wonderful opportunity and it's going to be so much fun."

Louise considered remarking on her aunt's developing arthritis but thought the better of it. "So where is this house being built?" she asked.

"Just outside of Potterston. It's going to be a fulfilling experience. June filled us in on all the particulars. She said the people for whom we are building the house are going to be helping. This is a good chance to use the gifts God has given me to help someone else. That's a good thing, isn't it?" Ethel asked.

"I think it's a wonderful opportunity," Louise agreed though she was secretly relieved Alice would be working with her aunt. Ethel's exuberance could, at times, get in the way of good sense. Though she was not exactly reckless, the picture of Ethel wielding a hammer was somewhat disconcerting. "I hope you will be careful."

"Of course I will." Ethel patted Louise on the arm, reassuring her niece that all would be well. "Now if you'll excuse me it looks like Alice has paid for her book. We've got to get moving. Lots to do before tomorrow. We want to be up at the crack of dawn." Ethel paused a moment, tilting her head to one side. "Your Uncle Bob always said that, but you know I never really knew what it meant. Dawn doesn't exactly crack, does it? I mean the sun, it usually kind of slips up over the horizon. *Hmm.* I wonder where that saying came from. I'll have to check that out when I do some more research on this Habitat program." Ethel's face brightened. "I'm so excited about this. You should come too."

"I have other fish to fry," Louise said with a smile. "But if I have time, I might stop by at the site to see you and Alice at work."

"You do that. Now I need to get going." And Ethel was off.

As the bell above the door provided Alice and Ethel a tinkling send-off, Louise glanced over the how-to books, wondering if she could find something on driving. Not that she needed to start from the beginning, but some helpful tips might come in handy.

"Are you trying to find out how to build a house too?" Viola asked, adjusting her glasses as she looked at Louise.

"I don't think you'll find me scampering about on a building site anytime soon," Louise replied with a smile. "No, I've just come to visit. And to see if you carry any books on driving."

"Because of your accident this morning? Louise, you hardly need to worry about your competence in that department. Accidents are called accidents because they are, by their very nature, unintentional."

Louise felt comforted by her friend's enthusiastic defense of her abilities.

"Nonetheless, I have decided to enroll in a seniors refresher course at the library that I read about in the *Acorn Nutshell*. I was able to get in on such short notice."

"What can they teach you that you don't already know?"

"I believe I could use some brushing up. The longer a person drives the less attentive she gets. I really do not want a repeat of what happened today."

Viola looked thoughtful. "Refresher course? I wonder if I

wouldn't benefit from that as well?" She fingered the fringe of her silk scarf.

"Could you get me the information? Then I can enroll as well." Viola turned, tapping her chin with her fingers as she studied a nearby shelf. "As for books on the subject, I'm afraid you'll have to go to the library. I don't have much demand for material of that sort."

"That's fine. The books were mostly an excuse to come here. The inn is filled with young people, and they were listening to music when I left. Quite loud and noisy music."

"Can't you ask them to turn it down?"

"They are guests, which means we invite them to make themselves at home." Louise simply smiled.

"How old are they?"

"Not that many years out of high school. They seem like an exuberant and friendly group of kids."

"You are using your 'I have my doubts' voice," Viola teased.

"They vastly outnumber Alice, Jane and me."

"You're not expecting a guest insurrection, are you?"

Louise laughed. "No. Usually our guests come to the inn to enjoy the peace and quiet. These guests seem to have other plans."

"Sounds like you need a cup of tea and some conversation," Viola said. "Wilhelm just brought in a new brand of Indian chai, which can be most welcome on a dreary day. I'll be glad to fix some."

Though she had already had a cup of tea at the inn, Louise welcomed the opportunity to visit with her friend. "That sounds lovely. You can tell me which books will be coming out this fall."

Viola's expression brightened. "I just got some new catalogs from two of my favorite publishers. I'll show them to you."

A few moments later a cat lay curled up on Louise's lap,

a cup of tea stood steaming at her elbow and she and Viola were leaning over brightly colored brochures discussing the merits of various authors and publishers.

The bell over the door tinkled, and Viola leaned sideways to look out of the office. Louise also glanced back.

Florence Simpson entered the shop. She caught sight of them and came striding over.

"Hi, ladies. Ah, Viola," Florence said. "I was wondering if you have any books on carpentry."

A cough caught Jane's attention. She looked up from the towel she was folding to see Carita standing in the kitchen doorway, her hands tucked in the pockets of her blue jeans. Herbie stood behind her, peering over her shoulder.

"What can I do for you, Carita?"

"We were wondering if you could recommend a good place to eat." She poked her thumb over her shoulder at Herbie. "He's starving."

"The Coffee Shop has a fine reputation, and it's not expensive."

"Burgers?" Herbie stretched his head to peer more closely into the kitchen.

"Some of the best you'll ever have."

"Score!" Herbie slapped Carita on the shoulder. "I'll go tell the others."

Carita, however, didn't follow him. She stayed in the doorway watching Jane work as if waiting for something.

Jane felt obligated to make some conversation. "How long has this group known each other," Jane asked.

"We all hung out in high school, and most of us now go to college together."

"Most of us . . ." Jane prompted.

"Lynden ducked below everyone's radar the past year.

Didn't phone, e-mail, nothing. Of course he doesn't really need to learn a trade or get a degree. His grandma has oodles of money. Lynden could just hang out the rest of his life and not do anything if he wanted." Carita stopped, pressing her fingers against her lips. "Sorry. I shouldn't be yapping about him. He doesn't like it."

"I won't breathe a word."

Carita stepped farther into the kitchen, fluttering her hand in the direction of the hallway. "I noticed the name on the library door. Was that your dad?"

Jane set the still-warm towel on the pile on the table. "Yes, he was an avid reader." Jane picked up another towel, her mind slipping back to memories of her father sitting at his desk, a book open in front of him, a pad of paper beside him, fountain pen in his hand as he made notes on what he was reading. "The library also holds many valuable concordances of the Bible and reference books he would use to make his sermons."

"So you were a preacher's kid too," Carita said with a grin.

"Too?" Jane asked.

"Yeah. Lynden's dad was a preacher at the church my father and mother went to, until he died and Lynden went to go live with his grandma." Carita leaned against the doorframe, looking like she was settling in for a chat.

Though Jane and her sisters tried to maintain boundaries between their guests and themselves by keeping the kitchen a separate place, occasionally they bent the rules. Talking to Carita across the expanse of the kitchen seemed awkward.

"Come on in," Jane said, lifting her chin in the direction of a chair by the kitchen counter.

"You sure? I don't want to intrude." But even as she put forward her mild protest, Carita pushed herself away from the doorway.

"Please, I'm not doing anything too demanding."

Carita bounded into the room and sat down. "You want a hand with that?" Carita asked, pointing to the still full laundry basket.

"I'm not about to make a guest work." Jane glanced at the oven timer, and her heart gave a quick jump. She'd almost forgotten about the cookies baking in the oven. She dropped the towel she'd been folding, snatched the oven mitts off the counter and yanked the oven door open.

Thank goodness the cookies were a comforting, golden brown.

She drew the cookie sheet out of the oven, and, one by one, scooped the cookies off and set them to rest on a cooling rack.

"Wow! Those look good," Carita said.

"I smell something outrageously wonderful."

Pete stood, licking his lips, his blond hair anchored by a black cap this time. Herbie stood behind him, peering over Pete's shoulder.

Their eyes widened when they saw the cookies. "You just made those?" Pete asked.

"Well, she didn't just pick them up from the store and heat them up in the oven," Carita said, shaking her head at Pete's question.

"I don't think my mom ever baked anything," Herbie said, casting a longing look at the cookies.

"Would you like some?" Jane asked.

Herbie didn't need urging.

Jane piled some cookies on a plate. She had planned on setting the plate on the table and putting out some napkins, but by the time she rounded the end of the counter, Herbie and Pete were there. They each whisked a cookie off the plate faster than she could say "Help yourself."

"You can take two," Jane said.

The words had barely left her mouth when the two boys acted on her offer.

"Things are looking up at Carita's inn," Pete said.

"These are fantastic." Herbie licked his lips and ate the second cookie in three bites. "Butterscotch cookies are my number-one favorite, and yours are the best."

"I appreciate the compliment. These are a favorite of mine too." Jane beamed.

"You two guys don't believe in savoring your food, do you," Carita teased.

"Savor?" Pete asked, his frown indicating his opinion of that particular exercise, his own cookie disappearing in record time.

"You know. Take your time and enjoy it? Like this?" Carita lifted a proffered cookie, took a bite and closed her eyes, chewing slowly.

Jane laughed at the dumbfounded looks on the boys' faces. They looked at each other, then at Carita, shrugged and each took another cookie.

"Thanks, Ms. Howard."

"See ya later, Carita," Pete mumbled around a mouthful of cookie.

"Yeah, thanks. These were the best," added Herbie.

Carita sighed as she watched them leave. "Barbarians," she grumbled.

The sound of feet thumping down the porch stairs drew her and Jane's attention.

"You sure you don't want to go with them?" Jane asked, surprised that this young woman would choose to stay behind.

"I'm tired. I drove the rented minivan most of the way here."

"And Lynden took his own vehicle?"

"He arranged to meet us here." Carita pressed her index finger against a few scattered crumbs lying on the counter and popped them in her mouth.

"Which of you likes to listen to the music?"

"Was it too loud? I told Matthew to turn down the volume.

We thought Mrs. Smith might be annoyed, but he said she told them to make themselves at home. The guys thought that was cool of her."

"If we had other guests, we would probably ask you to tone it down, but if none of your fellow travelers objects, you go ahead and listen to what you want."

"Maybe Matthew should put on earphones." Carita smiled.

"So when do the festivities start?"

"Friday. We're talking about having a tailgate party earlier."

"And what will you be keeping busy with while you are here?"

"I've got some plans. I hope everyone goes along with them. And I really hope Lynden wants to play along."

"He strikes me as a taciturn young man."

"He can be." Carita fiddled with the knife block, shifting it back and forth. "But he's one of these 'still-waters-run-deep' kinds of people. He was pretty smart in school."

"Sounds like you know him well."

Carita ducked her head, popping another cookie crumb in her mouth, the faint blush in her cheeks telling Jane what Carita's silence didn't.

"How long have you and your sisters run this inn?"

Her sudden change of subject made Jane wonder about Carita's relationship with Lynden, but she wasn't going to pry. "We've done this awhile now."

"You don't mind sharing your home with people?"

Jane shook her head as she scooped out more cookie dough. "I enjoy meeting new people and finding out where they come from. But I have to confess I find it interesting that a group of such young people would come to a bed-and-breakfast."

"Totally my idea," Carita said. "I wanted to come to a quiet place and a place that felt more like a home for this reunion. I heard about this inn and this town, and figured this would be a good place to stay." Carita shrugged. "It's fun to be together again."

"Well, I'm glad you came. It's been a while since we've had such a young group." Jane slipped the cookies into the oven and leaned on the counter.

"Trouble is, I didn't think they'd all want to come this soon, and this group needs someone to get them moving, so now I have to come up with something to do on the days there isn't anything planned. I'm trying to make up an itinerary," Carita pulled a small notebook and a pen from her shirt pocket and set it on the counter in front of her. "Do you have any ideas?"

"Acorn Hill doesn't have a lot of things to do, so you will probably have to spend most of your time in Potterston."

"I already have a movie night planned, and we're hoping to check out some of the local tourist stuff in some of the surrounding areas. Matthew was talking about a car show. I was trying to think of something I could do around here. None of us has a lot of dollars except for Lynden, it seems."

Jane scratched her chin. "Paintballing?"

"Possibility," Carita said.

"The only other thing on my list of activities would either be an Easter egg hunt, which is rather out of season, or a town scavenger hunt, which is pretty lame," Jane said with a laugh.

"How does a town scavenger hunt work?"

"That was a joke."

"I'm not joking. That might be something fun. How would you do it?"

"It would require prep work."

"So what would you do?"

As she told Carita, she had thrown the idea out as a joke. Now, it seemed, she actually had to come up with something for the young woman. "I guess you could divide the group into teams, then make a list of things to find in the town.

Maybe pick up a business card from Time for Tea, that's Wilhelm Wood's teashop, a muffin from the Good Apple Bakery, a matchbook from the Dairyland convenience store, describe an item in Humbert's Hardware. That kind of thing." Jane shook her head, and laughed. "Just a silly suggestion. I think Alice did something similar with the girls group she works with, the ANGELs. They're younger than your group, so a scavenger hunt might seem a bit immature for you. Forget I mentioned it."

Carita pursed her lips as she considered the suggestion. Then she smiled. "Trust me, this is exactly what these guys would enjoy. When guys turn nineteen or twenty, it's like they regress. The only trouble is that a scavenger hunt would take some planning."

"If you're serious about this, I could help you. I know the town, and I think Alice still has something lying around from when she and her girls group did the hunt."

"That'd be great." Carita made a quick note in her book, then tapped her pen on the counter. "As long as it's not too much work for you."

"I need to run a bunch of errands tomorrow anyway. If you're not busy with your friends, we could compile a list. Add Alice's stuff and I think we could keep them busy."

The timer started beeping for the second batch of cookies and Jane pushed herself away from the counter to answer the insistent summons.

"You sure it's not too much?"

Jane glanced out the window. The weather was still damp and chilly. She doubted she'd be getting much done in the garden for the next few days. She still had Stacy's dinner to plan, but she was fairly certain that she had that taken care of with a sure-fire menu item. "I have time," Jane assured the engaging young woman.

"Great. I'll see you about it tomorrow." Carita glanced at her notebook, pausing a moment.

"Anything else I can help you with?" Jane asked, setting the cookie sheet on the cooling rack.

Carita looked pensive, and then shook her head. "No. Not really. But I am feeling tired. I think I'll grab a nap. I'm beat from our drive."

Jane watched Carita leave, then turned her attention back to her cookies. But as she took more cookies off the sheet to cool, she sensed Carita wanted to talk about something other than her friends' entertainment.

Before she could ponder more about the young woman's situation, the telephone rang. Jane answered it.

"Jane, have you figured out a menu yet?"

Jane stifled a groan. Stacy Reddington. "I've got a basic concept in place."

"I hope you're not going to do anything with noodles . . ."

Jane sighed as she walked over to her sure-fire menu and scratched her entrée off the list. "Why don't you tell me what you would like," Jane said, settling in for what would be a long chat, as all chats with Stacy were turning out to be. She would never admit this to Louise or Alice, but her second thoughts about taking on this dinner had become third and fourth thoughts two phone calls ago.

Chapter Five

"This one should do," Ethel said, tilting the hammer back and forth, as if testing its weight. "What do you think, Alice?"

"It seems okay now, Aunt Ethel, but I'm sure if you had to wield it all day, you might be sorry you took such a heavy one."

"But Fred said these Estwings are the best."

"For a carpenter, maybe, but I think we might want to stick to something with less heft." Alice held the hammer a moment, then put it back. "We don't need to get the nails in with one blow."

"But I want to be a help, not a hindrance." Ethel grabbed a smaller hammer from the pegboard and pretended to hammer a few nails. "This one seems a bit light. And according to that handyman book in the library, you want a head with cross-hatching." She turned it over to check the head, then put it back with a grimace. "Smooth as glass. No hitting the nail on the head with this hammer. It will be bouncing around all over the place and then there'll be hammer dents in the wood. Won't look professional is all I can say. I want to do the best job I can."

"That's important," Alice agreed, "but if you get too tired using your hammer, you might have the same problem."

"This is true," Ethel said and considered the display in front of her. "So I suggest a compromise. Not too much weight, but not too light." She pulled another hammer off the display. "This one will do quite nicely." She dropped it in the pull-along grocery cart she had taken with her from home. "Now we need pouches."

"I'm fairly sure those will be provided," Alice said, glancing over the list she and Ethel had compiled.

"Cotton things," Ethel said with a dismissive wave of her hand. "We need the real McCoy. The leather ones with the metal hammer handle. After all, that hammer will wear out those cotton aprons in a New York minute. Now mind you, I always thought minutes were minutes. You can't change time in spite of what the daylight saving time people tell us."

Alice looked decidedly puzzled. "Auntie, I—"

"But I figure if I'm going to spend my time wisely, I don't want to bother those Habitat folks every time my hammer falls off my pouch because the hammer sling broke." Her emphatic nod told Alice precisely what Ethel thought of that idea and how far Alice was going to get trying to dissuade her.

Not very far.

Alice decided to humor her aunt. Despite having urged her to consider that Habitat would probably provide tools, she knew that Ethel had enough money to supply her own tools, and her aunt was insistent she do her part on this project to the best of her ability.

"Besides, the more I provide of my own supplies," Ethel continued, striding down the aisle toward the section carrying leather pouches, "the less they have to, and the more money they'll have for the people they're helping."

They made an abrupt halt at the end of the aisle. "Only two to choose from?" Ethel frowned. "That makes it difficult."

Alice actually thought that made deciding much easier and was secretly relieved. She and Ethel had spent a good part of their afternoon at the library, checking Habitat Web sites, reading up on tools usually provided and tools that volunteers might bring along. Even though they weren't told exactly what they were expected to supply, Ethel had a take-no-prisoners attitude and was marching full force into the fray.

Alice was willing to help her aunt and had even purchased a few items herself. She understood that having one's own hammer was beneficial, and even though they had a finishing hammer at the inn, she got a heavier one for herself here. She also decided that a few extra pencils probably wouldn't hurt, but she had put her own spending on hold when it came to pouches, chalk lines, box cutters, hand planes, metal rulers or calculators.

Ethel finally decided on a pouch and dropped it into the basket.

"Can you think of anything else we might need?" she asked, casting a critical eye over her current choices, then glancing down the carpentry aisle again. She shook her head. "All this time, and I never knew half of these things existed. It's like a whole new world of shopping has opened up for me."

"I'm sure you have everything you need and then some," Alice said, glancing surreptitiously at her watch. She didn't want to leave Jane alone to prepare and serve dinner.

Though the inn didn't offer dinner to its guests, they did, on occasion, offer an evening snack. Alice had a feeling the alumni at the inn were a snacking crowd.

"You want to go?" Ethel said.

"You don't miss a thing, do you?"

"That's the third time you've looked at your watch in the past minute. I've been trying to hurry, truly, but we can go now." Ethel marched down the aisle, pulling her well-stocked little cart behind her.

"Looks like you've got some big plans. I've been wondering about your new interest in tools," Fred said as he rang up their purchases. "Doing some renovating at the inn?"

"Alice and I are going to work on the Habitat for Humanity house they're putting up outside of Potterston," Ethel said.

"Now that sounds fascinating," Fred replied. "Does Vera know?"

Alice shook her head. "This just came up. And I mean, just."

"June told us about it at the Coffee Shop," Ethel put in, bending over to take the other items out of her cart.

"I thought I should volunteer," Alice said, and then poked her index finger down at her aunt, who couldn't see what she was doing. "Keep an eye on her," she mouthed to Fred who grinned, then nodded.

"I'll be glad to be one up on Vera," Fred said, bagging their purchases. "You'd think running a store would give me the upper hand on news, but somehow Vera always comes home from teaching school with one anecdote or piece of information that is new to me."

"Little pitchers. Big ears," Ethel said, lifting the last of the items. "People say all kinds of things around children and don't think they hear. When my three were young, they were pretty good at cobbling bits and pieces of information together when Bill and I were talking about things we didn't think they should know."

Fred gave Ethel the final tally, and as she paid, Alice saw her aunt glancing around, as if afraid she had missed something.

"I suppose we'll need a visor," Ethel mused.

"I think they'll provide us with hard hats," Alice replied.

Ethel nodded, but Alice was fairly sure Ethel would be back here again, only too happy to be searching through some aisle of the hardware store she had never explored carefully before.

They packed the crinkly plastic bags back in the cart, and slipped their rain bonnets on, getting ready to venture out into the wet.

As they stepped outside, they almost collided with a young man walking at a brisk clip. His jacket was pulled up around his ears, his hands shoved deep in his pockets.

Lynden, Alice thought, recognizing his dark hair and handsome features.

He skidded to a halt, his blue eyes glancing from Alice to Ethel.

He gave them a curt nod, then stepped around them and kept walking.

Ethel glanced over her shoulder, looking peeved. "He seems like a rather rude young man, don't you think?"

"Maybe he didn't recognize us," Alice said.

"Oh, I'm sure he did. I saw the minute he clapped eyes on us he knew exactly who we were."

Alice had inclined toward the same conclusion as Ethel, though she preferred to give Lynden the benefit of the doubt.

As they walked back to the inn, avoiding puddles and chatting about the project coming up, Alice wondered what was on that young man's mind.

"Wonderful dinner, Jane," Louise said, gently patting her mouth with her napkin. "I especially liked the way you prepared the prawns. An unusual flavor."

"Too unusual or just interesting unusual?" Jane pushed an uneaten prawn around on her plate, suddenly unsure.

"Is this one of the dishes you want to serve at Stacy's dinner?"

"I thought I did, but somehow I think it might be a little

too 'out there,' which Stacy specifically warned me to avoid."
Jane sat back and crossed her arms over her chest. "She's
called me several times today, and each time she had another
suggestion and another idea. It's like she's trying too hard."

"Which in turn puts pressure on you," Alice offered.

Jane nodded, tapping her fingers on her arm. "This
afternoon I was thinking in terms of a simple but elegant
dinner à la Jane Austen. This evening I'm leaning more
toward a meal worthy of Lucretia Borgia."

"Without the complication of poisoning, one would
hope," Louise added.

"Well, I can't say that hasn't crossed my mind." Jane held
up a hand to forestall her older sister's reprimand. "Joking,
dear Louie, just joking."

"Could you call it off?"

Jane rocked back and forth in her chair, shaking her
head. "I'm a gourmet chef, for goodness sake. I help run an
inn. I've fed mothers, daughters, fussy businessmen, easygoing guests and persnickety guests. Surely this dinner
shouldn't confound me."

"And it won't because I think you have a winner with this
meal," Louise said.

"It's superb," Alice added.

"I quite like it myself."

"Then isn't it nice to have that out of the way," Alice said.
"Now all you need to do is decide what to make for dessert."

"I already decided on dessert, lemon ginger cheesecake,
which should complement the flavors of the main course."
Jane released a light sigh of contentment. She had spent quite
a few hours hunting down all the ingredients for this recipe.
Now that she had them in the house and she had already
done a trial run of the meal, her preparation time would go
down considerably. So far so good.

Louise pushed herself back from the table and retrieved

the Bible from its drawer in the buffet and handed it to Alice. "I believe we agreed upon devotions for this evening."

Alice opened the Bible at the last place they had read, cleared her throat and was just about to begin when the doorbell rang.

The sisters glanced at one another, and Jane got up and walked to the door. A woman wearing a light-green raincoat stood outside, her brown hair falling in soft waves back from her pale face. She started when she heard footsteps, then recovered when Jane opened the door.

"Hello. I'm Stacy Reddington." Stacy held out her hand to Jane, her smile bright. "I thought I would stop by and see you face to face. Go over a few things for the dinner."

This was completely unexpected, and for a moment Jane was taken aback. But good manners overruled telling Stacy that it would have been wise to make an appointment. "Please come in. May I take your coat?" Jane held out her hand to do so, but Stacy waved her off.

"No. No. I'm not staying long. I'm running around the area, checking out halls for the dinner." She glanced around the foyer of the inn. "This is a lovely place."

"It's our family home and has worked quite well for our business," Jane said as she led the way down the hall. She kept a smile on her face, trying to keep her voice pleasant. Talking to Stacy every hour on the hour had been bad enough; now she was stopping in unexpectedly?

Stacy paused at the entrance to the dining room. "How many people stay at the inn?"

"We have four bedrooms, and this weekend they are all taken. Seven guests."

"That's a lot."

"My sisters and I are just finished eating," Jane said, leading Stacy toward the kitchen. "In fact the meal was one I was thinking we could make for your dinner."

"Wonderful." Stacy's eyes brightened. "I'm excited to see what you've come up with. I've heard some enthusiastic reports about your cooking. That was one of the reasons I called you."

"Well, I'm flattered."

Jane introduced Stacy to her sisters and then pulled out a chair for her. "If you want to sample dinner, I still have some left."

"I would love to try it out."

While Louise and Alice kept their newest guest occupied, Jane quickly put a plate of food together, and heated it up, added the salad she was going to serve and then set it on the table.

"I have to say it myself—this dish is quite tasty," Alice said as Stacy glanced at the plate.

Stacy only nodded, picked up a fork and isolated a prawn. She frowned as she found another one. "Seafood?" was all she said.

Jane nodded, trying not to feel upset. This was ridiculous. As she said to her sisters, she was a gourmet chef. She shouldn't be so uneasy around this woman.

But the truth was, she was.

"I'm so sorry. I forgot to tell you one of the ladies is allergic to shellfish," Stacy said, giving Jane an apologetic look.

Of course, Jane thought, mentally scratching a black line through much of the work she had done this evening.

"I hope this isn't a problem."

"No. I'll work around it," Jane said, her "pleasant" voice getting a real workout.

"I realize I should have told you when I called earlier. I know you did ask me about allergies, but I've been so busy trying to find a venue. Unsuccessfully, as it turns out." She sighed as she looked around the kitchen of the inn. "My, this really is a lovely place—so welcoming and friendly."

Stacy paused and Jane was fairly sure she knew what was coming next. "I don't suppose you could recommend a place in Acorn Hill?" Stacy's voice held a plaintive note.

Jane felt a tickle of a premonition. She had seen the look on Stacy's face when she saw the size of the dining room and was fairly sure Stacy could count as well.

Twelve chairs around the table and she was going to entertain twelve guests. "I'll see if we can find something for you," Jane said.

She scurried to the reception area, tucked a pen behind her ear, slipped a pad of paper into the pocket of her blue jeans and grabbed the phone book, flipping through it as she walked. By the time she got back, she had found the section of the yellow pages that she wanted.

She laid the open book on the table in front of Stacy, set the pen and paper beside it. "There. This should help."

Stacy nodded slowly, but Jane saw from the set of her mouth and the downward tilt of her eyebrows that she was less than impressed with Jane's solution to her dilemma.

Out of the corner of her eye Jane saw Alice lean forward and she intuitively sensed that her dear, generous sister was going to offer the inn. Jane zeroed in on Alice and gave a quick, tight shake of her head.

Alice sat back and Jane breathed a sigh of relief.

"I can see I have limited options," Stacy mumbled, glancing through the book.

As do I, thought Jane. She was tempted to call off the entire thing, but she couldn't do that to Stacy, knowing that she was a last-minute hire.

And there's still the vacuum cleaner, Jane thought.

This wasn't a major stressor, but the reality of a full inn meant that having a vacuum cleaner was even more pressing than usual. Borrowing Aunt Ethel's machine was strictly a short-term solution. Very short term.

"Obviously I have a number of phone calls to make," Stacy said, scribbling down some numbers. "I'll get back to you when I know more."

"As for the guests, any other food allergies or problems I should know about?" Jane asked, glancing over at her cheesecake, thinking *lactose intolerance*.

"Not that I know of," Stacy said, a distinctly defensive note creeping into her voice.

"I'm sorry, but time is working against us here," Jane replied diplomatically. "And the more information I have, the better I can plan."

"I'm sorry for all the difficulties." Stacy heaved another sigh looking at Alice and Louise as if trying to garner sympathy. "I had so hoped to make a good impression on these women, to give them an experience they've never had before, and every time I turn around, I'm faced with another obstacle."

"And I'm sure your dinner will turn out fine," Alice assured her. "And with Jane's cooking, I'm sure it will be a resounding success."

"Thank you," Stacy said, and Jane saw the tension around the woman's mouth ease.

Alice had that ability, Jane thought. A few words in her mellifluous nurse's voice and you felt as if all your problems had shrunk.

"You simply need a location," Louise put in, adding her own brand of assurance. "For a small group like yours, that shouldn't pose an insurmountable difficulty."

"Thank you so much, ladies." Stacy got up and turned to Jane. "I'll call you as soon as I find something."

Jane kept her smile intact, trying not to glance at the calendar. *Tick tock*, she thought. "That'd be great. In the meantime, I'll continue trying to find a dish everyone will enjoy."

Stacy put her hand on Jane's arm. "Don't get me wrong.

What you made was wonderful. Just . . ." she shrugged, ". . . the prawns. Not such a good idea. You need to be aware there are people who are allergic to seafood."

"I'll take that under advisement," Jane said, trying not to be irked by her unneeded advice.

She walked Stacy to the door, bid her a pleasant farewell, then closed it carefully, looked upward, and offered a prayer for patience and wisdom.

By the time she got back to the kitchen, Alice was clearing the table and Louise was putting out cups for tea and coffee.

"So did you get the problems ironed out?" Alice asked, placing the dinner dishes on the counter.

"If you'll allow me to extend the housekeeping metaphor," Jane said, "there are still a few wrinkles." She gave her sister a quick smile to alleviate the faint concern she had heard in Alice's voice. "I made dessert that was supposed to go with the meal we just had."

"Was?" Louise asked, pouring tea.

Jane pulled the cheesecake out of the refrigerator. The only decorations she had put on the top were curls of lemon, creating a simple yet elegant touch. "Now that prawns are off the menu, I'm thinking I might be better off to go with a simpler dessert. This dessert perfectly complemented that meal. So I don't know. The cheesecake is a bit heavy and wouldn't fit with every meal. However, cheesecake freezes well."

"Why don't you offer two desserts," Louise suggested. "Freeze this one for Saturday and offer it along with a lighter option."

Jane weighed the idea and offered a noncommittal "That could work."

"And for tonight's dessert, we can have some of those cookies you made earlier," Alice suggested.

The tension gripping Jane's neck slowly released. Her sisters were right. She could nicely check off one item for Saturday.

"*Yoo-hoo,*" Ethel's voice called out from the back door. "I'm here."

Louise pulled out another cup and plate for their aunt, and Jane did a double take as Ethel strode into the kitchen.

A bespattered painter's cap held down her red hair, she wore an old pair of denim coveralls over a twill shirt, and circling her waist was a leather carpenter's apron, its pockets bulging with nails and pencils. A tape measure was clipped to one side of the carpenter's pouch, and a hammer swung from the other.

"What do you think?" Ethel asked, doffing her cap and doing a slow twirl so that her nieces could more fully appreciate her transformation.

"I think you look like you mean business," Jane said, scratching her head with one finger. "Are you moonlighting as the town's handyman?"

Ethel wagged a warning finger at her. "Silly girl. This is what I'm going to wear tomorrow for the Habitat job." Ethel shot Alice a frown. "Do you know what you're going to wear?"

"I thought I could get away with blue jeans and a plain shirt," Alice said.

"What happened to your pants?" Jane asked, glancing at the dirt circling the bottoms of Ethel's coveralls.

Ethel glanced down, then took a quick step back toward the porch. "I'm so sorry. I didn't think I would get muddy."

"What were you doing?"

Ethel bent over and brushed off what dirt she could onto the rug just inside the entrance, then bent down and rolled the cuffs of the coveralls up. "I was practicing my nailing. There were some boards loose on your tool shed."

"And you fixed them."

Ethel raised her one hand in a vague gesture that could have meant anything. "I'm sure I'll get better with practice." Ethel double-checked her pants, then walked to the kitchen sink to wash her hands, wincing as the water hit her fingers.

"And what happened to your thumb?" Jane asked, noticing a deep purple mark on her aunt's thumbnail.

Ethel turned pink, and curled her thumb into her palm. "Nothing. Well, just a little tap. I hit the wrong nail on the head."

"Let me see that." Alice reached for Ethel's hand.

"It's just a bruise. It doesn't hurt . . . much." Ethel winced again as Alice gently manipulated the thumb, checking for more injuries.

"You shouldn't be swinging a hammer with such force," Alice said.

"I need the practice . . . as you can tell," Ethel said, holding up her thumb. "It's better now, anyway."

"When did you do this?"

"When we got back from Fred's. I was so excited to try my new hammer, and it works well. Lovely heft, and swings nicely. I'm sure that in time I won't have to hit the nail so many times to get it in." Ethel glanced over the counter. "Well, doesn't that look lovely," Ethel said, her eyes falling on the cheesecake. "Is that for tea?"

"I think Jane wants to freeze the cheesecake," Alice said, sparing Jane from having to douse the expectant light in her aunt's eyes.

"I'll try to save some for you," Jane said.

Just then the front door burst open, slamming against the stopper, and boisterous voices filled the inn with noisy laughter.

Alice was still busy with the dishwasher and Louise with pouring coffee, so Jane volunteered to greet their guests.

The boys stood in the foyer, shaking water off their coats, laughing at a joke one of them had just told. Only Lynden and the girls were missing. Jane wondered about the elusive Lynden.

"Hey, Ms. Howard," Herbie said, his round cheeks shining

with moisture from the rain falling outside. "Sorry about the wet."

"That's fine. How was your evening?"

"Great. Hey, you got any of those cookies left? I was telling the guys about them."

Before she could reply, Herbie turned to the rest of the group. "I'm telling you guys, you have got to try these cookies. Best Pete and I ever had. Homemade."

"Can we take some to eat in our rooms?"

Jane imagined crumbs all over the rooms and thought of Ethel's wheezing vacuum cleaner. She made a snap decision. "Why don't you join us? We were just going to enjoy some coffee and dessert."

As she walked to the kitchen she sensed the boys hot on her heels, as if afraid she would change her mind.

Louise glanced up as the group swept into the room. "Hello, everyone. How was your evening?"

"We went to the Coffee Shop. Great food."

"This is some kind of town, though," Matthew said, rubbing his hand over his buzzed hair. "Saw some woman pushing a baby buggy. When she went past I thought, whoa, that's the ugliest baby I've ever seen. Then I saw it was a pig. Freaked me out."

"Clara Horn and Daisy," Ethel put in. "She loves that pig like a baby. It's a miniature pot-bellied pig."

Matthew pulled back his head as if assimilating this information. Then he grinned. "Cool," was his succinct summation.

"Would any of you like a cup of tea or coffee?" Alice asked.

"Could I have some water instead?" Pete asked, pushing his cap back from his forehead.

Jane gathered what chairs she could, then angled her chin toward the refrigerator. "There's a jug of water in the fridge, just help yourself. The cups are in the cupboard over there," she pointed in another direction.

"Anyone else want some?" Pete asked, pulling open the door and glancing over the contents of the fridge. "Wow! Look at all this good food."

Jane had already prepared a fruit platter for breakfast to go with the French toast she was going to make in the morning. She had decided to forgo gourmet breakfasts for this group, assuming that the heartier food would probably be more welcome. She assumed Pete was interested in the plate of cinnamon rolls and muffins she had prepared and covered in plastic wrap.

"Look at this Rick," he said. The tall, lanky fellow disengaged himself from the wall and sauntered over, his long, dark hair bobbing as he walked.

"Oh . . . my . . . goodness . . . this is better than television." Rick leaned closer to the fridge, the dragon tattoo on the back of his hand looking oddly out of place against the appliance. Jane didn't know how long he would have stayed there, but he had to move when Pete pulled out the water pitcher. He poured a cup for himself and one for his friend.

Matthew joined them, his eyes growing wide at the sight of the food. "Hey, look at that. I haven't seen a fridge so full of good stuff since I lived at home."

"Do you and your sisters eat all this food?" Pete asked.

"Most of that is for breakfast tomorrow morning." Anticipating time to be spent with Carita to work on the scavenger hunt, Jane had done as much prep work for the following day as possible. Unfortunately, this seemed to be creating an irresistible temptation for the boys, and she knew she would be unable to turn them down if they asked for some of it.

"For us? Tomorrow? Whoa, I don't know if I can wait that long." Matthew rubbed his stomach as if underlining his statement.

Jane saw all her hard work disappearing in one fell swoop and made another quick decision.

"I have some cheesecake . . ."

Ethel's eyes lit up. "Yes. Cheesecake. Just the thing."

And so, after a few quick strokes of a knife and a few flips of a serving spoon, the cheesecake began disappearing almost as quickly as Jane could pass it around.

"This is awesome," Pete exclaimed, his hazel eyes beneath the brim of his cap sparkling with pleasure.

"Jane is the best cook in town," Ethel advised, tucking into her own piece of the dessert.

"Why did we go to that Coffee Shop then?" Matthew asked, swiping his finger over the plate, gathering the last of the crumbs and cream.

"I dunno," Herbie said, licking his lips as he settled his bulky figure into a more comfortable position.

"I thought Ms. J doesn't cook dinner for us," Pete said, casting a longing eye at the remaining half of the cheesecake.

"We generally don't serve dinner," Jane agreed, catching the hint and getting up to cut the rest of the cheesecake.

"That's too bad," Herbie said, following her, holding his plate like an oversized Oliver Twist, wanting to ask for "more."

"It would simply make us too busy," Louise said. She followed Jane's lead and, opening up the cookie tin, made up a plate of homemade cookies.

"Fair enough. There are a few good places in Potterston from the looks of it, and Lynden has got something planned for game night on Friday anyway. Tailgate party," Pete said in an aside to Jane. "We should get you to come and cook for us."

"I feel honored to be asked, but I don't think a tailgate party at a football game is somewhere I want to be Friday night," Jane said with a smile.

"Hey, who should we start in the first quarter?" Rick asked, settling with his plate. He was eating a little slower this time, as if savoring the treat.

"Probably Harris. He's a real winner. Quick off the

snap." Herbie leaned against the counter, emphasizing his point with a wave of his fork. "We'd be crazy not to."

Jane served the last of the cheesecake, bemused at the quick change in conversation.

Comments ping-ponged as the young men pontificated on the various strengths of their team and the opposition teams they would be playing. Louise, Jane, Ethel and Alice settled in at the table, listening, while the boys devoured the cheesecake.

Jane enjoyed the energy the young men brought to the kitchen, but as Matthew got up and walked to the fridge to help himself to a glass of orange juice, she wondered if she had too easily erased the carefully guarded boundary she and her sisters had always maintained between the kitchen and the rest of the house.

"Did you boys have some cookies?" Ethel asked, getting up and passing around the plate Louise had arranged.

"Herbie told us about these," Matthew took one quickly. "Gotta be pretty good for him to say they're the best he ever had."

"Jane's baking skills are also quite renowned," Ethel said, seeming only too glad to brag about her niece. "In fact, she's going to be catering a dinner for international guests on Saturday night."

"Wow! Impressive," Rick said, nodding his head as he took another cookie from the plate Ethel was passing around.

"Hey, what happened to your thumb?" Herbie asked when Ethel came by him for the third time.

"I was doing some repair work on the inn's shed," Ethel said, pride sounding in her voice.

"That explains the getup," Pete said. "Nice hammer. Estwing?"

"They are supposed to be the best." Ethel put down the cookies and pulled the hammer out of its metal sling.

"Nice. Well balanced. Perfect hammer for a lady," Pete assured her.

"I'm going to be working on a Habitat for Humanity home."

"Cool!"

"Is that where you get together with a bunch of people and put a house up in one day?" asked Matthew.

"You can't put a house up in one day." Pete punched Matthew on the shoulder, as if reprimanding him for his ignorance.

"Hey. I've seen it on TV." Matthew protested, punching Pete back. "The Amish do it all the time."

"Yeah, well, they can put up a barn really fast."

"How fast?"

"I dunno." Matthew leaned past him to address one of the other boys. "Hey, Rick, you worked construction last year. How fast do you think the Amish could put up a barn?"

From this the conversation switched to construction and jobs and trying to find a job and what jobs they had been doing over the summer to help pay their college tuition.

Jane sipped her coffee, content to listen to the scattershot discussion. She glanced sidelong at Louise, wondering how she felt about this male domination of the kitchen.

Louise was leaning back in her chair, smiling and feeling more comfortable with their guests than she had at their arrival. Ethel was standing beside Herbie, her arms crossed over her chest, looking for all the world like she belonged with this circle of young men.

Alice was laughing at some of the jokes being bandied about.

"Hey, what's with the invasion?"

Carita and Isabel stood in the doorway, their eyes going over the group in the kitchen.

"Come on in," Matthew said, waving his hand. "The

ladies are serving us cookies and cheesecake, and you should see the awesome food they're going to feed us tomorrow."

Carita gave Matthew an indulgent smile. "Where's Lynden?"

Matthew glanced at Pete, then shrugged. "Dunno. Herbie, you know?"

"Yeah. He's up in his room. Reading."

"Is he feeling okay?" Carita sounded concerned.

"Yeah. He's hibernating," Herbie said.

"And missing out on awesome cheesecake." Rick licked his fork, then glanced over at the counter. "I think there's a piece left if you girls want some."

"No thanks." Isabel wrinkled her nose.

Jane motioned for Carita and Isabel to join them. "Come on in."

Isabel shook her head as she took a step away from the doorway. "I think I'll just go to bed, okay?"

"I'll be right up." Carita glanced at Isabel's retreating figure, then at the kitchen, and Jane saw she would have preferred to join the party in the kitchen. "I should go too. We'll see you tomorrow." She walked away, then turned and came back. "Almost forgot. What time is breakfast?"

"I usually start serving breakfast about seven thirty. You can come down anytime after that until about ten," Jane explained.

"Whoa, that's early." Matthew sounded incredulous.

"No, it isn't, you lazybones. Besides, I thought you and the boys were going to check out that car show in Potterston," Carita said. "You'd have to leave early for that."

Matthew snapped his fingers. "Yup. Totally forgot about that." He shot Jane a grin. "Guess I'll be up early tomorrow anyway."

Carita laughed. "See you bright and early boys."

As she left, Pete pushed himself to his feet. "Probably should hit the shower and then bed anyway." He put his plate on the counter and paused, eyeing the last piece of cheese-cake, adjusted his ball cap as if making a decision and grabbed a cookie instead. "Thanks for dessert," he said, waving his other hand at Jane. "Goodnight, ladies. You be careful with that hammer tomorrow, Aunt Ethel."

The rest of the boys soon followed, each of them thanking the sisters and a couple of them taking a last cookie upstairs with them as they left.

Jane shook her head as their conversation faded away up the stairs. So much for her ingenious plan to avoid having them eating in the bedrooms.

"Wasn't that fun," Ethel said, stacking up the plates and bringing them to the dishwasher. "Reminds me of when Bob would get crews in to help on the farm. Always young boys with big appetites and full of stories. My, what fun we used to have when they were around. And, oh, the food they could inhale."

As Jane walked past her refrigerator, she had a sudden flash of misgiving. She certainly didn't think she would see an entire cheesecake, supposed to serve twelve, disappear in minutes.

What if she hadn't planned for enough food for tomorrow's breakfast?

Chapter Six

Wednesday morning dawned sunny and cheerful and found Louise sitting in the parlor, her Bible on her lap. The quiet of the morning surrounded her, creating a sense of sanctuary.

Her only company was the antique doll collection in one corner of the room and Wendell, draped over the tapestry-covered stool pulled out from Louise's grand piano.

The piano had been a gift from her beloved husband Eliot, and Louise treasured it as much as she did the ivory velvet piano shawl, a gift from her sister Alice.

In fifteen minutes she, Jane and Alice would be getting breakfast ready for their guests and then she and Viola were scheduled for the first lesson of their car course.

Besides being a chance to spend time with her friend, the course offered Louise an opportunity to learn something new and useful.

Louise reread her Bible passage for the day from Romans 5:1–2: "Therefore, since we have been justified through faith, we have peace with God through our Lord Jesus Christ, through whom we have gained access by faith into this grace in which we now stand. And we rejoice in the hope of the glory of God."

Louise let the words enter her heart, relishing the peace they gave her. As her gaze rested on the piano, she thought of the moments of sorrow she had felt after her dear husband's death. She had felt as though she could never smile again, as though all the light had been taken out of her life.

Yet, coming back to Acorn Hill and starting up the inn with her sisters had combined to give her a purpose she had thought she would never find again. Together they encouraged each other in their faith and helped each other express that faith to their community and to the guests who stayed at the inn.

She bowed her head, once again thanking the Lord for the love He showered upon her every day and for the blessing of her work. As she prayed, her thoughts and prayers touched on each member of her family, the greater community and each of the guests at the inn. Her prayers included the multitudes in the world who had so much less, reminding her of her blessings and her obligations.

And, as she always did, she asked for a blessing on the day.

She kept her head bowed as she finished, allowing God's peace, the peace offered her in the passage from Romans that she had just read, to settle over her.

She drew a long, deep breath, closed the Bible and looked out the window. The sunshine made little prisms of the droplets of water still clinging to the leaves of the trees, sending out bright showers of light, like little promises.

Today was going to be a good day. Ethel and Alice would have good weather for their building project, and she would have good weather for her newest venture.

She had telephoned Viola last night and made arrangements to meet at her store. Viola would then drive Louise to the garage so Louise could pick up her car. Justine Gilmore was going to cover for Viola at Nine Lives.

She glanced at the brass-faced clock sitting on the mantel

of the fireplace. In twenty minutes Jane would be downstairs working in the kitchen. She still had time to practice some songs.

Louise closed the door, leaving it open only a crack, and took out the music for Sunday's service. As she sat at the piano she felt again the moment of anticipation, just before her fingers touched the keys. Though she had played for orchestras and had accompanied many vocalists in public performances, she still felt a special thrill when she contemplated the music she would choose for a worship service. Knowing that the songs she played helped the members of the congregation to worship God created a combination of responsibility and humility.

She chose the first song, flexed her fingers and slowly, reverently began playing. As the notes filled the room, a smile crept over her lips. Music was for her a purer expression of her faith than that which could be conveyed through the medium of words.

She moved from hymn to hymn, discarding some, studying others. Finally a meowing interrupted her. She glanced over and saw Wendell nudge the door open.

"You don't approve of the music I'm choosing?" Louise asked as she slipped off the piano bench.

As she opened the door a figure detached itself from the shadow of the front entrance and moved up the stairs. Louise started at the same time her mind recognized Lynden's retreating figure.

She stepped out of the parlor, watching him, but he didn't turn around. An equally curious Wendell padded up the steps behind him.

What was he doing outside the parlor, and why did he leave?

Louise waited a moment longer, wondering if he would come back, but no one appeared at the top of the stairs. This was a puzzle indeed, she thought, returning to the piano and tidying up her music. Why had he been standing close by? The parlor was soundproof but, in the morning quiet, had he been disturbed by the faint sounds that made their way outside the room? If he had something to say to her, surely he would have knocked on the door.

Bemused, she walked down the hallway to the kitchen, the hum of the mixer telling her that Jane was already hard at work. Alice stood at the table, wrapping cutlery in napkins.

"Good morning. What can I do?" Louise asked, pulling an apron off a nearby hook.

"Morning, Louise. You could get out the warming trays and turn on the oven," Jane said, breaking a few eggs into the spinning bowl of the mixer. "I think breakfast for this crowd will be a long, drawn out affair, and I want to keep this French toast warm."

Louise went into the storage room off the kitchen and in a few moments had the warming trays set up.

"When are you leaving for the Habitat project?" Louise asked Alice.

"I told Ethel I couldn't leave until our guests ate breakfast, so I guess it depends on when the last ones are done."

Jane shut off the mixer and angled her sister a wry glance. "You might want to rethink that strategy. As I said to Louise, this crowd may use up the entire morning having breakfast."

"I thought those boys had to go early to Potterston for something."

"Maybe, but I'm fairly sure their alarm clock will ring, they'll look at the time and make a sudden change of plans."

"Are you sure?"

"Reasonably. They're students, and from my recollections of my days at college, morning was just a recuperation time from the night before. Especially summer vacation mornings."

"But Louise can't help you because she has a class—"

"And I'm perfectly capable of keeping food warm," Jane said.

"Are you sure?" Louise asked.

"Sure as a plumb line."

Louise frowned and Jane laughed.

"Little carpenter humor there, Louie," Jane said.

"Indeed."

At seven thirty on the dot, Jane had the French toast laid out, dusted with powdered sugar and garnished with orange peel. Another warming tray held sausage patties, seasoned with coriander. Fruit and plates of muffins and cinnamon buns sat ready on the sideboard as well.

At eight, Jane, Louise and Alice sat down to their own breakfast, listening for any signs of life stirring above.

At eight fifteen, Ethel knocked on the door, set her tool belt just inside the entry and joined the sisters for breakfast.

At nine, Alice reluctantly put her and Ethel's dishes in the dishwasher and bid her sisters farewell.

At nine fifteen, Louise put the last dishes into the dishwasher and turned to Jane. "I can cancel my class, if you like."

Jane flapped her hand at her in a shooing motion. "You go. I'll be fine."

"Are you sure?"

"Didn't we just do this?" Jane said with a cheeky wink. "Please, I don't have anything else planned. The garden is still too wet to work in after all that rain. All I had figured on doing today was going on an outing with Carita and planning the menu for the dinner yet again."

"Well then . . ." Louise washed her hands, dried them off, hesitated a moment, and left.

But as she walked to Viola's, she thought of the noise and busyness of last night and felt as if she was abandoning her sister. Her mind slipped from the boys dropping by the kitchen to Lynden, and she remembered that he hadn't been there.

She wondered anew what he was doing at the bottom of the stairs this morning.

One thing was certain—Lynden was a puzzle.

"Hard hats are mandatory. We don't want anyone going home with a concussion and then calling up a lawyer and suing us." The heavy-set, middle-aged man stood on a pile of dirt, arms folded over his massive chest, a tool belt, worn and cracked, hanging low on his hips. His grin showed them all that he was mostly kidding. "For those of you who are new, my name is Cal. Today we've got Jasmine, the owner of the house and her sister Cordy helping us. The sun is out and we've got a good number of volunteers. That's great, so I'll be assigning you different jobs today." He clapped his hands together, rubbing them as if in anticipation of the work ahead. "Let's build a house."

Ethel grabbed Alice's hand. "Isn't this exciting? Let's go get our hard hats."

Ten minutes later Ethel, Alice and a young woman of about eighteen were getting instructions from Cal.

"What I want you ladies to do is nail down this particle-board on the studs. It's been tacked down already, so all you need to do is, essentially, fill in the blanks."

Alice looked at the wall section, puzzled. "But there are no windows in this section."

"That comes later," Cal said. "Once you're done tacking, we'll get a router and cut out the holes for the window. That way you don't waste time cutting and measuring, and the opening for the window is perfectly square." He tapped a stained forefinger to his forehead. "Always thinking, us carpenters."

He gave them a smile and then left.

The pounding of hammers and the whine of the skill saw

filled the air as Alice pulled her hammer out of the pouch and turned to the young woman.

"I'm Alice, and this is my aunt Ethel." Alice had to raise her voice above the noise to make the introductions. "We've come from Acorn Hill to help."

"I'm Cordy."

"So I understand you're Jasmine's sister?"

Cordy simply nodded, her hand resting on the hammer still swinging from the canvas pouch many of the volunteers wore.

"Do you have a preference as to where you want to start?" Alice asked.

Cordy shook her head, the hard hat slipping over her eyes. She pushed it back over her thick red hair, her hazel eyes looking down at her feet encased in boots that looked two sizes too big for her.

"Don't care." She added a half-hearted shrug.

"Why don't you start on that side, Ethel. You can work your way along the top, and I'll start on this side with Cordy," Alice said, realizing someone needed to be in charge.

Cordy nodded, pulled out her hammer and knelt. But she made no move to start.

Ethel glanced from Cordy to Alice, her eyebrows lifted in question.

June Carter had explained that the future owners of the house they were building had to volunteer five hundred hours of their time to help construct the home. They could also bring in family members to contribute their labor. Cordy was one of those members, but no one said anything about making them work.

Alice and Ethel began.

"Now make sure you don't hit your thumb again," Alice warned her aunt as she took a handful of nails out of the pouch.

She carefully rearranged them, making sure she had all the points in the same direction.

"So, where do you live, Cordy?" Alice asked as she pounded the first nail into the particleboard. Though the worksite was noisy, holding a conversation wasn't impossible.

"Around here." Cordy narrowed her eyes as she watched Ethel carefully pounding in a nail.

"And where does your sister live?" Alice continued.

"Apartment. Just down the road."

"She must be excited about the house." Ethel gave the nail one last hit and sat back on her heels, surveying her handiwork.

"Yeah."

But Cordy didn't seem to be excited.

Alice set aside her campaign to get Cordy to talk for now and concentrated on putting the nails exactly the same distance apart along the chalk line laid out for them.

After putting in a few nails, she felt more comfortable wielding the hammer and got a certain satisfaction out of hitting the nail precisely on the head each time.

"You do this before?" Cordy asked after a few minutes of watching Alice and Ethel working. All around them crews were chattering and laughing above the noise. Cal walked around calling out instructions. Everyone else seemed to be having fun.

Alice shook her head. "First time for me."

"I've put a few nails in wood in my day," Ethel said with all the authority of one who had been swinging a hammer since youth.

"That why you are using both hands on the hammer?" Cordy asked.

Ethel gave the young woman a smile. "It's my personal style."

"So, really, neither of you has done much carpentry work."

"Well, okay. Not a lot," Ethel admitted.

"I see." Cordy pulled a nail out of her pouch and set it in the wood. She gave it a few taps, then looked to see what Alice was doing. "So, is there any trick to this?"

Alice shook her head, realizing that Cordy was unsure of herself. "No. There's no trick and there's no wrong way to put in the nail . . . as long as you put it pointy-side down."

Cordy gave the nail a few more taps. "It's wobbling."

"You need to hold the nail steady," Alice said, walking over to show her how.

"Okay, but what if I hit my hand?"

Ethel held up her hand. "See that black mark on my nail? I was practicing my nailing and whacked my thumb good and proper. You don't want to do that. Hurts bad."

"So how do I make sure I don't?"

Ethel shrugged. "Just be careful, I guess."

Cordy sighed and gingerly tapped the nail, her fingers curled around it.

"You only have to hold it until the nail is steady, and just use your fingertips," Alice suggested. Then she took a nail out of her own pouch and demonstrated. "Once it's set, you can hit it without holding on. Then you won't hit your hand."

"Okay." Cordy tried again and this time got the nail in, and twenty taps later the head was flush with the wood. She shook her head when she was done. "There's no way I'm going to get good enough to be any help."

"Maybe if you hit the nail a bit harder," Alice suggested. "Like this."

She demonstrated and ended up bending the nail over. "Well, maybe not like that." Alice laughed and pried it out. "Guess I'll have to try again." She did, and this time the nail went in with five strokes of her hammer.

Cordy angled her head to one side, watching as Alice started another nail. "So you did that first one wrong."

"Yes, I did, but I got the second one right." Alice gave her an encouraging smile. "You're going to make some mistakes, but you shouldn't worry about that."

"But if we make too many mistakes the house won't turn out good."

"That's why Cal is here. To help us prevent the bad mistakes and to help us learn from the small ones. Why don't you try again?"

Cordy caught her lower lip between her teeth, set the nail in place and gave it a few careful taps.

"Good. Now just give it a good whack," Alice suggested.

Cordy wound up and pounded on the nail. Three hits and the nail head was flush with the wood.

"Hey! Look at that," she exclaimed. "I got it in."

"See. Nothing to it." Alice worked beside her for a few more minutes, guiding and giving a few words of encouragement.

"I might be okay at this," Cordy said.

"I think you'll do just fine, and I think helping out your sister is a wonderful thing to do," Alice said.

"Yeah, well, I hope she thinks so. I don't know nothing about building a house," Cordy said, setting another nail in place. "Jasmine told me I had to come . . ." Cordy stopped and narrowed her eyes as though concentrating on putting in the nail.

"Where is your sister?" Alice asked.

"Over there, talking to that man with the paper." Cordy pointed her hammer at a tall, young woman with the same flaming red hair as Cordy, consulting the blueprint held up by Cal.

"You two look a lot alike." Alice set another nail and pounded it in with a few solid hits.

"Mom says we act alike, though that's not true. I never had no kid while I was in high school like Jas did."

"That must have been difficult for her," Alice said. "I understand she is married now."

"Yeah. Though Grainger ain't doin' too well. Lost his arm in an accident. Jas has to work all the time while Grainger stays home with the kids."

"Your sister must be a strong person."

"Strong in lots of ways. Strong headed, strong-minded. Stubborn, kind of. Pushy too." Cordy didn't look at Alice while she listed her sister's traits. The defensive note in her voice made Alice wonder if there was some conflict between the two women.

"Do you two get along?"

Cordy hit the nail she was pounding in a little too hard and it bent over. "Well, there's a question." Cordy sighed as she bent another nail. But she didn't answer.

"It's nice that you're here helping her," Ethel put in.

"Yeah, well, she told me I had to. Don't know why she wanted me here. She always tells me how I'm always doing things wrong. Like she's so perfect." Cordy hit the bent nail once more and it went deeper into the wood. She dropped the hammer and pushed her hard hat back on her head. "I can't do this. This is a waste of time."

Alice walked over and checked the nail with her fingers. "This isn't too hard to fix. You can get the claw part of your hammer underneath the head and pry upward, like this. Then you can use your hammer to get the nail out."

Alice demonstrated and sat back to let Cordy finish. She guided her through the steps and patted her on the shoulder when the nail was out. "See, that mistake isn't so difficult to fix, is it?"

"Well. No. Except I made a mark on the wood now."

"That will be covered over, I imagine," Alice assured her.

"But it's not perfect," Cordy said, her voice holding a mocking tone. Alice wondered where that came from.

"Nothing in this world is perfect," Ethel pronounced, frowning as she gave her nail another hit. "But that shouldn't stop us from trying, should it? It didn't stop your sister from working and staying on course?"

Cordy shook her head. "No. I just wish she didn't think the rest of us have to be better than she is. Have to be perfect." She pulled another nail out of the pouch, looked it over as if checking for defects, set it and tried again.

Alice watched Cordy, her mind processing the tone of the young woman's voice as much as her words. "I have two sisters myself and we don't always get along."

"Really? Even though you're, well, older than me?" Cordy sounded surprised.

"Unfortunately wisdom doesn't automatically come with age." Alice set another nail, watching out of the corner of her eye as Cordy did the same. "But I've found when we disagree I try to see things from their points of view and that helps. I'm sure Jasmine is very happy you are here," Alice continued, trying to find her way through the moment of awkwardness.

Cordy's only response was to swing at the nail and miss.

Alice knew better than to push the matter. Ethel shot her a puzzled glance and Alice gave her aunt a slight shake of her head as if to discourage any questions that Ethel might fire Cordy's way.

For a few moments the only sound coming from their part of the worksite was the steady pounding of hammers. Finally Cordy sat back on her heels and sighed. "I didn't tell you the truth," she said to Alice, rolling a nail between her fingers. "Something is wrong."

Alice simply waited.

Cordy tapped her hammer lightly on the wooden wall. "Me and Jas had a big fight."

"Over what?" Ethel asked, frowning.

"She thinks I need to grow up."

"In what way?" Alice asked.

Cordy shrugged. "The usual. I'm not getting good marks in school, and she says it's because I don't go to classes. Says my mom spoils me."

"Does she?" Ethel asked in her usual no-holds-barred manner.

Cordy shrugged. "No."

"Does she make you go to school?"

"Sometimes, maybe, she lets me sleep in, and I miss some classes. But not many. I mean class can be so boring, and it doesn't always make any sense."

"The only way that the classes will make sense is if you go regularly," Ethel said. "You can't learn if you don't go. And if you don't learn, you'll fail."

Cordy pressed her lips together, as if this was not the answer she was looking for.

"Hey, Cordy, I thought you came here to work."

A tall figure stopped beside them, and Alice squinted toward the sun to see Jasmine standing over her little sister, her arms folded over her chest. The sun backlit Jasmine's hair, giving her an almost ethereal glow.

Cordy didn't look up, but Alice sensed her anger from the set of her jaw.

"I was distracting her with questions," Alice said gently, trying to intercede for the young woman. "She's been working really hard up to now."

"Really?" Jasmine glanced at Alice as if she was surprised. "That's good. I guess." Jasmine frowned, then bent over, brushing her finger over a bent-over nail. "Aren't you supposed to take these out?"

"Probably." Cordy's answer came out sharp, and Alice saw Jasmine wasn't happy with her sister. She wanted to defend the young woman but sensed that neither Jasmine nor Cordy would appreciate a complete stranger getting involved.

"It was just a mistake."

"Well, then, maybe you should try to fix the mistake," was all Jasmine said. She looked as though she was about to say something more when Cal called her over to where he was working.

She left and Cordy picked up her hammer, twisted it around and started digging out the offending nail with jerky movements.

Alice took pity on her and came over to help. "Here, why don't I do that for you, and you can keep nailing."

"I can do this myself," Cordy snapped. Then she gave Alice a troubled look. "I'm sorry. It's just that Jas can get me angry when she gets going on me." She tapped her hammer on the wood.

"I think, in her own way, she's trying to help you."

"Help me have a fit." Cordy scowled. "I'm never good enough for her. She makes me so mad."

"But as Ethel said, you're here, helping her."

"Like I said, Jas told me I had to. Since she got religion, she's been trying to get everyone else to be like her. As if it's done her any good. All her praying and churchgoing didn't stop Grainger from losing his arm. Didn't stop Jas from yelling at me about something that wasn't my fault."

"But now your sister and her husband are getting a home," Alice pointed out, preferring to emphasize the positive. "That could be seen as an answer to your sister's prayers."

"So you guys are church ladies too?" Cordy asked.

"We go to church to worship our God, if that's what you mean," Alice said gently. She had found when guests from the inn asked her about church, those who were not religious themselves often viewed their attendance as a cute quirk of some slightly eccentric older ladies. Now and again she tried to find a way to show whoever asked that attending church was an opportunity to worship God in community, not a habit like brushing one's teeth.

"Well, I guess that is kinda what I meant," Cordy said, looking a bit baffled by Alice's gentle response.

Alice felt a touch of remorse. "I'm sorry. I was just trying to explain that when we go to church, we go out of a conviction and a desire to worship our Savior with fellow believers. We go to hear God's Word and to be encouraged to carry God's name out into the world." Alice gave her a self-deprecating smile. "And now I sound like I'm preaching at you."

"No, you don't," Cordy said quietly. "It sounds nice. I never went to church, but I always liked the idea."

"Maybe you could come with us some time," Ethel piped up. "Rev. Thompson is always a good preacher, and Louise, my niece and Alice's sister, plays the organ. And she's quite talented."

"I might do that. Maybe if Jasmine thinks I got religion, she might lay off me for a change."

"Maybe you just need to show up here regularly. Let your actions speak for themselves," Alice encouraged.

Cordy nodded, as if processing the comment. "Maybe," was all she said.

"Alice, would you like a drink?"

Alice and Ethel both spun around at the sound of the voice behind them. Florence stood holding a thermos flask and some paper cups. "I've got some nice cold juice if you or your helper would like some refreshment."

"Sounds like a plan," Cordy said, putting her hammer down and jogging over to Florence.

Ethel looked over at her friend, as if hoping Florence would catch her eye, but she ignored Ethel.

With a gentle sigh, Alice asked Florence for another cup of juice for her aunt and then waited until Florence moved to the next crew.

Alice handed the cup to Ethel. "Some juice, Auntie?"

"Oh my, yes, I was so busy I didn't notice that Florence

was here." Ethel put down her hammer, wiped her hands on the sides of her pants and took the cup. But Alice could see Ethel felt hurt by Florence's snub.

"That was real kind of her," Cordy said, finishing off her juice.

"She's just doing her job," Ethel said, handing Alice the empty cup when she was done. She opened and closed her fist, grimacing.

"Are you okay?" Alice asked, watching her aunt. She hoped Ethel's arthritis wasn't acting up.

"I'm fine," Ethel said quickly, lowering her hands.

"So who is going to cut out the hole for the window when we're done here?" Cordy asked, her hammer flashing in the sun as she pounded in another nail.

"I doubt any of us will be doing that," Alice said. "I've never handled a saw in my life."

"I'd like to try," Ethel put in, lifting her chin defiantly. "I think it could be fun." She gave Alice a significant look.

"I'm not sure about the fun part, but I am sure about the dangerous part," Alice warned.

Ethel wrinkled her nose in reply and went back to work.

An hour later the sheets of chipboard were all nailed down and the trio was ready for another job.

Alice was about to go looking for Cal when he came striding toward them, carrying a domed tool with a cord wrapped around it.

"Ladies, you ready for the router?" he asked.

"Um, shouldn't you be doing that?" Alice asked.

"It's not hard. One of you can handle this baby. I'll just get you started." He glanced at Cordy. "There's an extension cord lying on the ground behind you. Can you bring it here?"

A few seconds later, Cal had the machine plugged in. It was the oddest tool Alice had ever seen. A small bit poked out of the bottom of a flat, rounded plate. Above that plate was, she assumed, the motor that ran the bit.

"How does this saw work?" she asked.

"It's not a saw. This is a router and it works very simply," he said, crouching down. "What you do is find out where the hole for the window is. Luckily for you ladies, we marked it out with the blue chalk line."

Alice looked where he was pointing and saw the lines, just as he had said.

"So you get this started just a ways away from the edge, like this." He hit a switch and a whining sound filled the air. "Then you push the bit in, slowly."

As he did so, chips of particleboard flew out from the machine in an arc, releasing the pungent smell of cut wood.

"Then you move the router toward the line until it won't go any further, but don't force the tool too much. Like this." He demonstrated and sure enough, the router came to a stop, still whining away. "When you hit resistance, that means you've come to the frame of the window. Then you simply keep sideways pressure on the router and follow the line. The board framing the opening of the window keeps the bit from going the wrong way. Just follow the frame and you've got a nice rectangular hole for the window." He hit the switch, turning it off. "Who wants to try?"

Ethel jumped forward so fast, her hard hat slipped sideways. "I'd love to try."

Cal showed her how to turn on the router and what to watch for. Alice sent up a quick prayer as the machine started whining again, spitting out chips and sawdust.

Ethel pressed her lips together, her tongue poking out as she concentrated on slowly moving the router down. It wobbled a bit but she straightened the cut and with Cal's guidance, she managed to work her way down and then across. "This is great," she called out, clearly enjoying her newfound skill.

"You're doing just fine, miss," Cal said.

Miss Ethel might have appreciated that, Alice thought.

"You and your friend might want to hold the section that's getting cut loose," Cal said, showing Alice and Cordy how to pry the board up with their hammers so they could get their fingers under it.

A few minutes later Ethel had come back to where Cal had started, Cordy and Alice supporting the piece getting cut away.

"Done," Ethel said, pulling the router away just as the board dropped.

Alice and Cordy pulled it aside and stood back to admire what Ethel had done. Before them was a perfectly rectangular hole cut in the particleboard they had just nailed to the wall section.

"Well, isn't that just the cat's pajamas!" Ethel crowed.

"You can trim things up a bit," Cal said, pointing out a few places where the router had slipped to one side. "Just make sure you don't push the router too hard into the frame of the window."

When she was done, Ethel turned off the router, and she, Alice and Cordy stood back again to appreciate their handiwork.

"I think that looks like a very nice wall," Alice said, giving Cordy a quick hug. "Simply perfect."

"Looks good to me too." Cordy beamed, then turned to Cal. "Now what?"

"Lunch time," he said, brushing the wood chips off his blue jeans.

"I think I'm going to be stiff tomorrow morning." Alice rolled her shoulder as they joined the rest of the group for lunch. "This is even harder work than I thought."

"Feels good though," Ethel said.

A cluster of chairs was set out on a vacant lot beside the house, and a group of women handed out bag lunches. One of them was Florence. Alice had to bite her tongue as she followed her aunt through the line. This time Ethel, as if acting on the slight Florence had given her a few moments before, didn't even look at her. She simply took the bag and walked on.

Alice cringed. Whatever was going on between those two seemed to be escalating. She hadn't imagined either Florence or Ethel being able to maintain her silence this long, but somehow they both had.

"Are you volunteering here every day?" Alice asked Florence as she accepted the lunch bag.

"I hope to. I can't work hard, but I am able to help with the food. I think I might even be helping Jasmine with some of her decorating decisions. Some people say I have quite good taste." Florence looked down demurely. "Not that *I* would say so, but other people have."

"I'm sure you can give her good advice," Alice said warmly, trying to offset her aunt's decidedly cool attitude.

"Not that I like to put myself forward, mind you," Florence continued, her gaze ticking to Ethel, then back again. "I know I can be opinionated, but so can other people. And I find it puzzling when other people claim to be unable to help a friend, when they can clearly help someone they don't know."

The subtext in Florence's words was rapidly becoming full-blown text. Alice assumed the "other people" in Florence's little speech referred to Ethel. But she was not going to get involved. Not yet.

Chapter ⊤ Seven

J ane glanced at the clock, then went out to the dining room to check on the warming trays. The French toast was getting limp, the sausages were curling up and some of the fruit was changing color.

Should she wake up the young guests?

She stood in the doorway of the dining room, straining her ears for any sign of life coming from upstairs. But nothing.

Wendell rubbed up against her legs, then strolled into the hallway and flopped down on the carpet with a muffled thud. He yawned, stretched and rested his head on his paws, as if bored by the lack of life at the inn.

Jane glanced over her shoulder at her rapidly deteriorating breakfast. She hated to leave food out so long, but what was she going to do? Start all over?

Wendell's head popped up, his ears perked and he got to his feet, padded over to the stairs, looking up.

A figure was coming down. *What a relief*, Jane thought.

Lynden came around the corner and smiled down at the cat. He bent over and picked him up, stroking Wendell's head with one hand and cradling him to his chest with the other.

Jane was surprised. Lynden didn't seem the animal lover type. He didn't seem the anything type except utterly reserved.

Louise had told her sisters about his being outside the parlor while she went over her songs for the church service.

This was the first time Jane had actually seen him smile since he had arrived.

"Breakfast is ready," she said quietly, hoping she wouldn't startle him. She was fairly sure he hadn't noticed her in the doorway.

He jumped.

"Sorry," Jane said. "I didn't mean to startle you."

"That's okay. I was just . . . somewhere else . . ." He bent over and put Wendell on the ground. "Did any of the rest come down yet?"

"I'm pretty sure they're still sleeping. I doubt they would simply steal away without breakfast."

Lynden frowned. "I thought the other guys were going out early this morning."

"I thought so too. That's why I was cracking eggs at the crack of dawn." Jane gave him a self-deprecating smile. "Innkeeper humor."

Lynden only nodded his head.

Okay, Jane thought. *No wisecracks around this young man.*

"I'll get them up," he said, moving back toward the stairs.

Their phantom guest was on the run again.

"No, that's fine. They're on vacation, let them sleep."

A creak of the stairs made Lynden look back over his shoulder. And blush.

Carita came down, her hand trailing over the banister, a smile teasing out a dimple on her cheek. She wore loose fitting, linen pants topped with a bright yellow shirt. "Morning, Lynden. You sleep okay?"

He nodded, slipping his hands in the pockets of his blue jeans.

"Did you eat breakfast yet?"

He shook his head.

Carita saw Jane, and her smile grew self-conscious. "Morning, Ms. Howard. How are you?"

"I'm fine. Just wondering when your crew is going to be coming down for breakfast."

Carita shrugged, stifling a yawn. "I thought they were all done already."

"You and Lynden are the first."

"Well, that's great. We get dibs on all the best food then, don't we?" Carita said to Lynden with what Jane could only describe as a coy look.

He didn't catch it, however, and with a shrug, ambled into the dining room.

"There's fresh coffee and juice," Jane offered. "The French toast is aging, but it's still warm. If you want I can make a fresh batch."

Carita lifted the lid of the warming tray and grinned. "No need to do that. This looks just great, Ms. Howard. Thanks."

Jane fussed a bit with the cutlery, made sure the coffee-pot was full and retreated to the kitchen. As soon as Louise and Alice had left, she had pulled out her cookbooks and been leafing through them, alternately choosing and discarding recipes to go with the entrée. She had settled on chicken with roasted lemon, a recipe from an obscure cookbook she had bought a few years back. It sounded like it had the right combination of unique and comfortable that Stacy wanted. Chicken was the most versatile of meats and lent itself to a variety of spices and flavors.

She took out the recipe and went over the steps again.

". . . line baking sheets with parchment, arrange lemon slices, brush with olive oil . . ." *So far so good,* she thought. *Not too exotic or unusual.* She pulled out her grocery list and started marking down what she would need.

"Capers, lemons, brine-cured olives . . . I could serve this with a side dish of steamed spinach, possibly a type of stuffed pepper, go with a Mediterranean flavor . . ." Jane muttered to herself, planning, visualizing. She could use that festive look-ing tablecloth Wilhelm brought back for her from a trip to Italy. Possibly use some of those brightly colored canisters with the Greek pictures on them. But what else? Maybe her friend Sylvia Songer would have some ideas. Jane wanted to create warmth, an invitation to sit down and experience a slice of the Mediterranean. She had a decorating budget so she could provide atmosphere as she saw fit.

"We need more syrup, please."

Jane was yanked from visions of warm hillsides covered with olive groves and of sun sparkling on azure waters to the reality of Herbie standing squarely in front of her. He held out an empty syrup pitcher.

"Sorry to bug you but we're all out."

"I'm sorry, I didn't know the rest of you were down here." Jane took the sticky pitcher, wiped down the sides with a warm, wet cloth, and refilled it from the jug in the pantry.

"Not the rest of us, just me, Carita, Lynden and Pete. Matthew and the others are still sleeping."

Jane couldn't help a quick glance at the clock. The time that she could devote to breakfast was running out. What should she do? They had set hours for breakfast and had never extended them like this before. But if she declared breakfast over before the other kids came down, she would have too much food to get rid of.

You have an inn to run, she reminded herself. You need to maintain some semblance of order.

However, Jane also knew what it was like to be a student, pushing yourself all year, then working all summer and only grabbing a few days of rest. Sleeping until noon on days off wasn't abnormal.

She gave Herbie the pitcher. "Do you have any more of that French toast and sausage patties?" he asked.

Jane stared, dumbfounded. She had made enough for seven adults. There were only four people in the dining room, one more than half of their guests. And they were almost finished with the warm food?

But she pulled herself back, gave him a smile as if four people eating enough for seven was perfectly normal. "Sure. I'll get some together lickety split." Looked like leftovers weren't going to be an issue after all.

"That would be great. Good breakfast, Ms. J," he said, hoisting the syrup pitcher in a salute to her cooking.

As soon as the door swung closed behind him, Jane shoved the cookbook aside, jumping into innkeeper-panic mode. The unsliced bread was still frozen; thankfully she had enough eggs and milk, though she would have to make sure to pick up more when she and Carita went through town today.

She pulled a bowl out of the dishwasher, rinsed it and pushed it under the mixer. Then she cracked eggs, poured milk, defrosted bread and started slicing.

"Can I do anything?"

Jane started and turned around.

Carita stood right behind her.

Jane wagged a warning finger at her. "Honey, don't ever sneak up on a woman wielding a knife."

Carita held up her hands. "Sorry. I just wanted to know if I could help you."

Jane frowned. "You are our guest. You shouldn't even be in here."

"Well, I can still help. I told those lazybones if they didn't come down, there wouldn't be any breakfast left." Carita grabbed an apron off one of the hooks and wrapped herself in it. "I can take care of the French toast if you tell me what to do. You can do the sausage patties."

"What I want you to do is go back to the dining room and just relax. I'll be ready in a few minutes," Jane protested.

"In a few minutes the rest of the troop will be down and, trust me, you can't fry fast enough to feed them all." Carita removed the bowl from the mixer and reached for the bread.

Trying to take the bowl away from Carita would create an even more awkward situation. This wasn't right, but it looked like Carita was here to stay.

"It's not done yet. You need to put some vanilla extract in the milk and egg mixture," Jane said with a feeling of resignation.

"Okay. What else?" Carita said, pulling open cupboard doors in an effort to find the vanilla.

"Vanilla is over there," Jane said, pointing with the knife she still held. "And you need a dash of salt and a teaspoon of orange zest."

"Zest?"

"Grated orange peel. Oranges are in the . . ."

"Refrigerator. Got that."

A few minutes later Jane was frying up sausage patties, Carita stood at the stove earnestly cooking French toast and the noise level in the dining room was increasing.

It sounded as though the rest of the guests were downstairs. Jane couldn't help take a quick glance at the clock.

The swinging door flew open and Matthew stood in the kitchen, scratching his head, his fingers running over his short, short hair. "So, what can I do?"

"Nothing. It's all under control," Jane said with a forced smile.

Boundaries. We need to reset the boundaries, she thought.

Matthew sauntered over to the refrigerator. "Got anymore orange juice?"

"Yes." Jane wiped her hands on her apron. "I'll get it for you."

"No worries. I got 'er." Matthew snagged the juice container and carried it to the counter. He walked over to the cupboard that held the glasses, took one out and poured the juice while he was walking back to the dining room.

"I had set out glasses on the sideboard," Jane said, wiping her hands on a towel.

"Oh. Sorry. Didn't see them," he shot over his shoulder as he returned to his friends. "Got juice," he announced, holding the jug aloft.

Jane cringed. Usually she put the juice in a glass pitcher, but she didn't have time to correct the situation.

"I think these things need to be flipped," Carita said.

Jane returned to her cooking, trying to maintain her focus. A few minutes later, another batch of French toast and a plate of fresh sausage patties were ready to be delivered to an appreciative and hungry crowd.

Carita took one plate, Jane another, but they were both intercepted by Matthew and Pete.

"We'll just take those," Matthew said, relieving them both of the plates. Ignoring Jane's protests, he handed one to Pete and the two of them walked around the table, forking slices of toast and sausage patties onto the plates of the others.

Jane stood, dumbfounded, watching her job being taken, literally, right out of her hands.

"Please, boys, let me take care of that."

"You're too busy," Matthew called out, clearly enjoying his stint as a server.

"No thank you," Isabel said quietly as Matthew dropped another slice on her plate.

"I know you'll eat it if I give it to you," he said.

"But I didn't want more."

Matthew gave her another piece. "Keep talking and you'll be eating until lunch time."

Isabel glanced down but said nothing more.

"Good stuff, Ms. J," Rick mumbled, wiping his mouth with a napkin.

Ms. J? Once more Jane thought about boundaries.

"Very delicious," the usually silent Lynden put in.

And under Jane's fascinated gaze, the crowd sitting around the table devoured the French toast and the sausages.

She cast a panicked glance at the muffins and fruit plate. Also empty. She picked up the plate to replenish it, and Carita followed her back into the kitchen.

"What else do we need to do?" she asked.

Jane bit back another protest and decided to embrace the chaos. "There's a white container in the fridge with more muffins and pastry inside. You can refill this plate with those. I'll take care of the fruit."

Carita saluted, took the plate and a few moments later was humming a little song as she arranged the food. "This is kind of fun. I remember when I was little, I always wanted to be a waitress."

"Waitressing has its moments," Jane said, setting the fruit out in a semiorderly fashion. She assumed artistic impression was less important than speed with this bunch. "It's sort of like the girl with the curl right in the middle of her forehead."

Carita cast her a puzzled glance.

"You know the nursery rhyme? When she was good, she was very, very good, but when she was bad, she was horrid?"

Carita shook her head.

For a moment Jane felt her age. She remembered so vividly having Louise read this and various other nursery rhymes to her as a child. She loved the pictures, the rhythm of the words and especially snuggling up next to her sister, Louise's arm around her.

"At any rate, that about sums up my waitressing experiences," she said, carrying the tray into the dining room.

She was spot on with her assumption about the need for

speed. No sooner had she brought the tray in then it was taken from her and plates were filled. Ditto with the plate Carita brought in.

"Honestly, you guys," Carita said, a note of reprimand edging her voice. "You act as if you hadn't eaten for months."

"I haven't eaten this good for months." Matthew pointed his fork at the remnant of French toast swimming in syrup on his plate.

Carita sighed and glanced at Jane. "I'll go mix up another batch."

Half an hour later, appetites sated, the group sat around the table, full but still laughing and joking. Even Lynden, sitting quietly, had a smile on his face.

"So, now what, guys?" Rick said, his hands resting on his stomach.

"Now we head out to Potterston," Matthew said, pushing himself away from the table. He held his hand out to Carita. "Keys please, we depart in fifteen minutes."

"I'll be staying here," Carita said, clearing off the plates.

"What? Why?" Isabel sat up, looking startled.

"I've got plans," was all she said, giving Jane a wink.

Isabel glanced around the table, as if unsure of what to do.

"Just go, Isabel," Carita said. "You'll have fun."

Though Isabel didn't look convinced, she got up and followed the boys up the stairs to get ready.

"That girl," Carita said, shaking her head. "She can't seem to make up her mind until I tell her what to do."

"And now I'm going to tell you what to do, and that's relax," Jane said to Carita. "I don't want you to help me."

"I want to get things cleaned up so we can head into town," she said, waving off Jane's protests. "The sooner this place is clean, the sooner we can go."

Jane couldn't argue with her logic, so she reluctantly gave over yet another job to this young woman and guest.

While they were working Jane could hear the rumble of conversation and the thumping of feet above them.

"Sounds like the inn has been invaded by elephants." Carita shook her head as she scraped and rinsed plates.

"This is probably the most exuberant group we've ever had with us," Jane said.

"They're good guys. Lots of fun. But wait until they're getting ready for Friday night. Right now they're being downright civilized compared to when they're getting pumped to cheer their school on."

"That will be interesting," Jane said, trying to inject a note of enthusiasm into her voice. She couldn't imagine that this group could be busier or noisier. She didn't *want* to imagine this group any busier or noisier.

A few moments later Matthew and Pete poked their heads into the kitchen. "Sure you don't want to come, Carita?" they asked.

Carita looked up from the plates she was stacking in the dishwasher and nodded. "You guys go ahead. I've got a few irons in the fire."

"Isabel seems nervous about being alone with us," Pete said, settling his cap on his head.

"She'll be fine." Carita said, her voice taking on a bit of an edge.

And with a final burst of noise they closed the door behind them and peace fell like a soft blanket over the inn.

As Carita loaded the dishwasher, Jane wiped the counters, the stove and the dining room table. Next she pulled out the mop to clean the floor. *Memo to self*, she thought as she squeezed water out of the mop, *nothing with syrup for the next few breakfasts.*

Tomorrow was a brunch casserole. However, given how much food she had gone through at breakfast, she already knew she would have to double the recipe. As she had watched the boys wolf down their food she had put aside all thoughts of poached pear in crème brûlée sauce or meringue eggs with hollandaise sauce, both of which required smaller appetites than she was faced with.

"I'm all done," Carita said, wiping her hands on her apron. "Anything else?"

Jane leaned on her mop as she looked over the kitchen and dining room. "You know, I think we might actually be done here."

Ten minutes later they stepped outside, the bright sun pouring down like a blessing.

"Oh, it feels wonderful to see the sun again," Jane said, releasing a pent-up sigh and unbuttoning her cropped jean jacket. "I miss working outside."

"Is that your garden?" Carita asked, pointing to the tangled rows of plants edged by mounds of asters, pink lisianthus and orange mimulus.

"Yes. Usually it's much neater, but the rains really beat down my vegetable plants." Jane walked over the damp grass for a better look.

The beans needed one last picking, as did the peas. She could pick some squash too, she noticed. And the weeds had taken advantage of the wet weather to propagate like, well, weeds.

"I'm going to need to get at this as soon as it dries," Jane said, shaking her head at the work lying ahead of her. Then she gave Carita a smile. "But today I am at your disposal."

"Great. I brought along a notebook and some pens so I could write things down," Carita said, slipping a backpack over her shoulders.

"And I've got my grocery list. Let's go."

"I thought we could start with the Coffee Shop," Jane said as they walked down the street toward town. "It's the first place on our way. Oh, there's Pastor Thompson."

He returned her wave before stepping into Grace Chapel.

Jane moved to one side to avoid a puddle just as a young boy zipped by them on his bicycle. "Hey, Ms. Howard," he called out.

"Where are you off to in such a hurry, Bobby?" she called back.

"Errand for Mrs. Humbert," he shouted back over his shoulder.

As they walked, they met a young couple strolling along the sidewalk.

"And a lovely morning to you both. What brings you to this part of town?" Jane asked.

"Just going for a walk," the young woman said.

"Have a nice day," Jane said.

"Who *don't* you know?" Carita asked as she and Jane carried on.

Jane frowned at her. "What do you mean?"

A rueful little smile played about Carita's mouth. "Before my family moved to Cobalt, I don't think I could step out my door there and even be able to say hi to a neighbor, let alone the first three people I'd meet."

"Acorn Hill is a lot different from living in San Francisco, where I was before. Sometimes I miss the city, but mostly I'm quite content to live here." Jane drew in a long breath of fresh, clean air and let it out in a sigh of contentment. "Not lots of excitement, but lots of people who know and care about you."

"Yeah. A person can get lost in the city. Either lost or caught up in the day-to-day business of making a living."

"That happens here too," Jane said. "Doesn't matter

where you live. Bills need to be paid, and money needs to be made, and there are obligations to the community that you are a part of."

"Like your sister working on that Habitat project?"

"Like that."

"Did she see that as an obligation?"

Jane shook her head. "No. She was excited to do it, and knowing my sister, she did it because she wants to help where she can. She wants to be a light, a representative of Christ in this world. As Saint Teresa of Avila said, 'Yours are the eyes through which He looks with compassion on the world. Christ has no body now on earth but yours.' Essentially she was saying Christ uses us to spread His compassion and love. And that's what Alice does and is doing with this project."

Carita didn't reply, and Jane thought she might have been too preachy. She didn't know where this girl stood spiritually. She and her sisters always strove to model Christ in their actions and words but at the same time be aware that not everyone shared their convictions.

"And here's our first stop of the day," Jane said as they rounded the corner onto Hill Street. She held open the door of the Coffee Shop for Carita.

The Coffee Shop was quiet this time of day. The breakfast rush was over, and the lunch crowd wouldn't come for a couple of hours.

"Hey, Jane," Hope called out from behind the counter as they stepped inside. "Be with you in a minute." Hope turned back to the coffee machine. "Things have been crazy here this morning," she said as she scooped coffee into a filter-lined basket. "I don't know if it's the weather or the fact that people have been cooped up so long, but I've never passed out so many breakfasts as I did this morning. It's like they hadn't seen food for days."

"I know what you mean," Jane murmured, giving Carita a conspiratorial wink.

Hope slid the basket into the machine and turned to Jane, grabbing a couple of menus as she slipped around the counter.

"Unfortunately we're not staying for coffee," Jane said holding up her hand to stop Hope. "Our guest Carita and I are planning a town scavenger hunt for the group at the inn. Carita, this is Hope Collins, a genuine, dyed-in-the-wool waitress." Jane saw Hope's faint frown and smiled. "Carita confessed to me this morning that at one time in her life she had aspirations to be a waitress."

"I always wanted to fill up the sugar containers and stack those little cream pitchers," Carita said.

Hope's laughter filled the Coffee Shop. "And I always wanted to be a movie star. Bloom where you're planted, huh?" She looked from Jane to Carita. "So tell me about this town scavenger hunt."

"We want to get the group from the inn to go through town and either pick up clues or some small items from various businesses."

Hope crossed her arms over her chest, her head bobbing as she thought. "Sounds like fun. How old are the little kiddies you're doing this for?"

"Nineteen and twenty."

Hope's eyebrows zoomed up into her bangs. "Now that's going to be an interesting challenge."

"Carita said they would enjoy it," Jane said.

"Trust me, they'll be stoked to try it," Carita put in.

"So, what could you do here?" Hope asked, looking around the Coffee Shop.

"Could you have June put something on the menu board?"

Hope wrinkled her nose. "She always puts that in the

window. I'm thinking you might want them to actually come into the place."

Jane imagined the group pouring into the Coffee Shop, taking it over. Second thoughts about this little venture bombarded her mind. "What do you think, Carita?"

"I had planned on splitting them into teams of two. That way there won't be a stampede. The point was for them to appreciate the town, so I'd really like it if they could do something here to make them take a second look at the place."

"Smaller teams would work." Jane was relieved at Carita's practical suggestion. While she felt a responsibility to her guests, she also was a resident of Acorn Hill and had no desire to jeopardize the inn's goodwill in the town.

Hope snapped her fingers. "I have just the thing. They could do a taste test and pick their favorite dessert."

Jane held up both hands and shook her head as she imagined either Matthew and Rick, or Herbie and Pete descending on the pie case. "I don't think that would work."

Hope glanced around the diner. "They could count the booths."

Jane waggled her hand as if considering this and finding it wanting. "That might be too simple."

"How about if we get them to ask Hope a question about the Coffee Shop?" Carita suggested. "When it started. Who owns it?"

"And what if they wouldn't know what question to ask me?" Hope's eyes widened as she clapped her hands together. "We could put hints on the menu board and they have to decipher the question from that."

Jane was pleased to see Hope buying into the silly scheme. If she was this excited about it, the group was sure to be as well.

Carita slipped off her backpack and pulled out her notebook. "Run that by me again," she said digging out her pen.

Hope and Carita slipped into an available booth and refined the plan, while Jane thought of the next destination. Acorn Hill Antiques was next door. A picture of those rambunctious boys lollygagging in the Holzmanns' store came to mind, and she shivered. Joseph and Rachel were fairly easygoing, but it would be best not to tempt fate.

The Good Apple Bakery would be a great hit. Clarissa, the owner, would be more than pleased to have those boys descend on her.

Sylvia's Buttons was just around the corner from the Bakery. Jane had to talk to Sylvia about decorating for Stacy's dinner anyway. Maybe her friend could give Jane some ideas.

"Okay. I think we got that figured out," Carita said, slapping shut her notebook. "That's great, Hope. Thanks a bunch."

"Any time. If you need more help, let me know."

As Carita and Jane exited the Coffee Shop, they almost ran into Fred Humbert. "Well, hey there, Jane," Fred said, pushing his cap back on his sandy-colored hair as he stepped aside. "Nice day to be out and about."

"I sure am glad to see the sunshine. Any idea if it's going to stick around?"

Fred Humbert dabbled in weather forecasting. He was impressively accurate. "Should stay for a couple days," he said, glancing up at the sky. "Barometer is holding steady and we've got no wind."

"Glad to know. I want to get at my garden in the next few days. If I don't, the weeds are going to stage a hostile takeover." Jane briefly introduced Carita and explained their mission to Fred. "We'll stop by your store on our way back. If you don't mind, we'd appreciate a few moments of your time to plan what we could do at your store."

Fred tapped his temple. "I'll think on that. I'll let you know when you come by."

"That'd be great." They said their good-byes. No sooner had Fred left them when Clara Horn came out of the antique store, pushing her baby buggy.

"That's her," Carita whispered, tugging on Jane's elbow. "The lady with the pig."

Clara waved, then hurried toward them, the baby buggy rattling over the cracks in the sidewalk. "Jane Howard. I need to talk to you."

Jane gave Carita a warning glance and had to stifle her own smile. Then she made brief introductions

"Now, Clara, what can I do for you?"

"Have you heard what Florence is up to? She said she was going to be working on some house. Building things. Should she be doing that?"

"I can't see why not, Clara," Jane said. "I think it's quite safe. Alice and Ethel are also involved."

Clara looked shocked. "Ethel too?" She shook her head. "What were they thinking? Though it would have been nice to at least be told."

"It was rather spur of the moment," Jane assured her. "And how is Daisy?"

"Just fine." Clara angled the buggy so Carita and Jane could see for themselves.

Daisy sat curled up on a blanket, her eyes closed, the picture of porcine peace.

"Does she make a mess?" Carita asked, obviously curious about this pet.

"She's really very clean," Clara said, only too glad to be expounding on Daisy's many virtues. "And quiet."

Carita edged closer. "May I touch her?"

"Oh sure. Once she's down, she sleeps like a log. I just took her shopping, so she's plumb worn out."

Carita reached carefully into the buggy and touched the pig. Then she started to smile. "She's warm. Soft actually."

"I wash her every day. I use a lovely English soap."

Carita's eyes lit up and Jane could almost see the gears turning in her head. "What is it called?"

"I'll have to go home and check. Smells like vanilla."

"Thanks so much, Mrs. Horn."

"You're welcome." And Clara left, a contented smile on her face.

Love my pig, love me, Jane thought. "So I'm guessing you've got another idea for your little scavenger hunt."

"If Mrs. Horn doesn't mind people going to her house, I think I'm going to get the guys asking her the brand and the scent of what she uses on Daisy." Carita scribbled the idea in her notebook. "Now where?"

"Sylvia's Buttons," Jane said, unfastening her denim jacket. The sun gained strength with each passing minute. "My good friend works there. I need to talk to her about the dinner, and I'm hoping she can give us some ideas for the scavenger hunt."

They walked along Hill Street, past Acorn Hill Antiques. Carita paused to inspect the Holzmanns' window display of antique porcelain dolls and doll furniture. "I'm guessing you don't want the boys in here."

"And I'm guessing you're one smart lass," Jane said. "We could make up a riddle to do with the window display, but you're right. I'm sure Isabel would be fine, but best keep the boys out of this store."

Carita laughed. "Not all the boys are that active."

"Well, at least Lynden seems quiet."

Carita turned thoughtful. "Yeah. Like I said, he's a deep one. Though he's not the Lynden I used to know. I've tried to talk to him, but he's not saying much. He's changed a lot in the year we've been apart."

Jane thought of what Louise had said about Lynden's standing outside the door of the parlor. He seemed uncommunicative, and if Carita said he wasn't the same person she remembered . . .

What *was* he all about?

Chapter ⊺ Eight

"Regular washing will maintain the luster of the paint job, but waxing is important as well."

Louise stifled a yawn as Bart Tessier, the instructor for the course, showed them yet another slide of yet another car with yet another poorly maintained paint job.

She didn't want to glance over at Viola who, she sensed, was growing annoyed with the lack of what she regarded to be practical information offered in this hour-and-a-half lecture.

The course was held in a small room in Acorn Hill's library. Besides Louise and Viola, people in attendance included Martha Bevins, a tiny, birdlike, elderly woman; Delia Edwards; Derek Grollier, scowling at the instructor over his glasses; and Harvey Racklin, who provided a mirror image of Derek with his grumpy demeanor.

Louise knew that neither Martha Bevins nor Harvey Racklin even owned a vehicle, but she suspected they were attending merely as a way to fill time. Martha loved nothing more than to find new and unusual things to talk about when she was getting her weekly "do" at the Clip 'n' Curl down the street from the library.

"So you realize you need to be diligent in which type of wax you're going to be using on your vehicle. Harvey, can you get the lights, please?"

Harvey, Bart's assistant, ambled over to the light switch, grumbling as he went. Louise didn't blame him. She felt like doing a bit of grumbling herself. This wasn't what she had in mind when she signed up.

"So, are there any questions about paint and wax jobs?" Bart glanced around the room, rubbing his hands as if anticipating a flood of questions.

Louise kept her eyes averted, Viola huffed, but thankfully no one was dying to know more about the qualities of paint.

"Okay then," Bart said, drawing the two words out as if he couldn't understand why anyone wouldn't want to continue the discussion. "Tomorrow Clyde is coming in to give us some pointers on batteries. I hope you enjoyed today's class." He beamed at the class, and Louise took a chance and put up her hand.

"I appreciate the information you gave us, but when I signed up for this course, I understood it was going to be more about driving than car maintenance?"

Bart frowned. "Well, in order to drive your car properly, you need to learn how to take care of it. That is the first emphasis of this course."

"So we won't be driving?"

"Not right away." He gave her a patronizing look, then glanced around the class. "Any other questions? No? Then be here tomorrow when Clyde will speak to you."

As soon as was polite, Louise got up, and she and Viola beat a hasty retreat.

"I don't know about you, but I think this might be a waste of time," Viola said as she and Louise walked out of the classroom. "I didn't think anyone could hold forth for so long on the properties of car wax."

Much as Louise hated to admit it, Viola was correct. "The course was rather drawn out for what we learned this morning."

"Or maybe we are too old."

"We are not that old," Louise protested.

"I signed up and paid for the course so I feel obligated to go through with it to the end. Besides, this was just the first lecture. Perhaps the rest will be more practical."

Viola shook her head. "I didn't pay good money to learn that improperly applied paint can flake. As if I have any control over that when I buy a vehicle."

While they walked, Louise flipped through the course materials. "From the looks of the outline, we will be getting to the driving portion next week. Tomorrow Clyde will talk about battery and tire maintenance, so perhaps we'll get some valuable information. Maybe it will be more interesting."

"If you find tires interesting, I would say you need to get out more." Viola shook her head as they crossed over Berry Lane, then across Acorn Avenue. "I have to stop at Wilhelm's a moment."

"I'll go with you," Louise said. "I haven't seen Wilhelm for a few days."

The bell above the door tinkled a gentle greeting as they walked in. Strains of classical music soothed away any minor irritation Louise had accumulated listening to an instructor drone on for an hour and a half about paint jobs, glass maintenance and the amazing properties of leather conditioner.

"Good morning, Louise, Viola." Wilhelm greeted them from behind the counter, nattily dressed as usual. Today he wore a beige suit, yellow shirt and gold and brown striped tie.

"Very elegant tie," Viola said.

"Thank you. I purchased it in Sri Lanka," Wilhelm said, touching it briefly as if resurrecting memories of that trip. "Wonderful place. And the sheer variety of tea . . ." he sighed, lifting one hand upward as if mere words could not do the subject justice. "I shipped lots of it back."

"And I imagine we would be well-advised to taste some of the varieties when they arrive?" Louise asked.

"I brought a few sample packages back," Wilhelm said. "In fact, I am willing to give one to you as a prize, if you can—"

"Name that tune?" Louise finished the sentence, cocking an ear to listen to the music playing softly from the speakers located throughout the store. She listened a moment, concentrating. "Wassenaer," she said.

Wilhelm could hardly hide his smug smile. "I don't usually stump you, Louise, but this time I have. It is Giovanni Pergolesi's six concertos."

"They *were* attributed to Pergolesi," Louise said, almost hating to steal his thunder, "but a number of years ago Dutch musicologist Albert Dunning was successful in identifying the composer as a Dutch nobleman, Count Unico Wilhelm van Wassenaer. At one time it was thought that Bach had composed these pieces."

Wilhelm frowned. "I made a CD from an older record my mother had in her collection. When I copied the notes from the record sleeve I clearly remember reading that Pergolesi was the composer."

"Because the information comes from a record sleeve, that is not a surprise," Louise said, warming to the subject. "The record most likely predates the discovery. Dunning discovered this unknown manuscript copy of the score of the concertos. The concertos were made during the first half of the eighteenth century in the Wassenaer palace at Twickel in Overijssel, the Netherlands. The Count wrote the foreword to the score in his own hand."

Wilhelm stroked his thinning hair, a light frown creasing his eyebrows. Perhaps he regretted getting involved in this challenge. "But how is it the mistake was made? And why has the classical music world never heard of this man Wassenaer before these concertos, or afterward?"

"Apparently Count van Wassenaer was dissatisfied with the pieces. They were played initially at a musical gathering and one of the violinists playing with van Wassenaer wanted to make a copy. Van Wassenaer initially refused, but he was prevailed upon by another man, and when he finally gave in, it was on the condition that his name not appear anywhere on the copy. Granted, you are justified in assuming we have never heard of van Wassenaer as a composer before, but the evidence is apparently incontrovertible."

"Fascinating." Wilhelm shook his head, amazed at his friend's knowledge. "How did you know all this?"

"I'm always interested in what goes on in the musical world. I've always enjoyed these concertos, so when the information came out some time ago, I naturally remembered it and stored it away."

"And were able to pull it out at the drop of a note," Wilhelm said, still full of admiration.

"I must say, Louise, you were far more interesting to listen to than the instructor we just had," Viola put in.

"What instructor?" Wilhelm asked.

"Louise decided she needs a refresher course in driving, so she enrolled." Viola gave Wilhelm a wry look, and turned to the bins of tea on display. "I thought I would join her, but for the past hour and a half we were inundated with terminology that I only hear on car commercials. So I'm ready for something more my style." She pointed to a blend of tea Wilhelm had displayed in a sealed glass jar with a note card describing the contents leaning against the jar. "Now that looks new. And interesting."

"It's a Rooibos blend with a hint of caramel and vanilla. I discovered it in South Africa. Very common there, but I thought the unique flavor would translate well to North America."

"I'll take a small package and a three-hundred gram bag of the Earl Grey mixture."

"That is also a new blend. I found a new source of Lapsang Souchong, which brings out a slightly smokier flavor. As well you might want to try . . ."

As Wilhelm expounded on the qualities of other blends, Louise wandered over to the tea sets. Wilhelm had a successful business on the side, selling china over the Internet. He often had several of the sets on display, and every time Louise was in the shop, it seemed he had yet another alluring pattern.

This time she was admiring a set whose hand-lettered sign stated that it came from Morocco. The silver teapot had a high, domed lid, and the small glasses were a lovely, clear sapphire blue, etched with a gold border on the rim.

The doorbell tinkled again and Louise turned. Jane entered the shop, looking over her shoulder as she spoke.

". . . but the real challenge is going to be to make sure we don't make the hunt too long or too easy."

Carita was behind her, scribbling something in a notebook she was carrying.

"Well, this is a pleasant surprise," Louise said. "What brings you here?" As far as she knew the inn was well stocked with tea.

"Looking for ideas," Jane explained, glancing around the shop.

Louise was about to ask for what when Carita scurried over to Louise's side. She gently picked up one of the glasses.

"Oh my, look at those lovely Moroccan tea glasses."

"How did you know what they are?" Louise asked.

"My parents took us on a Mediterranean trip, and we made a two-day stop in Morocco." Carita set down the glass. "They drink sweet mint tea in these glasses. It's great fun to watch them serve it. They lift the pot way up in the air, the higher the better, and the tea foams up in the cup. Everywhere you go, any shop you stop at, you get invited in for a cup. The ultimate expression of Moroccan hospitality, we were told. It's really good, but after a day of shopping and constantly being invited in for tea, you can feel really antsy, it's so laced with sugar."

"So you were in Morocco?" As if drawn by the mere

mention of that ancient country, Wilhelm joined them, his eyes alight as if he were about to relive another one of his own adventures. After introductions he asked, "What parts did you see?"

"We stayed mostly on the coast. We went to a place called Essaouira, Casablanca, of course, and Marrakech. I even went on a camel ride." Carita's eyes sparkled with fun, as if transported back to that particular experience.

"Morocco is on the top of my list of places to go," Wilhelm said. "I would love to find out more about it."

"I'm staying at the inn," Carita said. "Maybe I could stop by, and we can talk."

"That would be wonderful." Wilhelm rubbed his hands together, as if in anticipation. "And you'll have to explain precisely how to make Moroccan tea. I would love to be able to give out those instructions with the tea set."

"When you do, I'd like to know as well," Viola put in.

"I think these glasses would make lovely holders for votive candles. The light would glow quite nicely through these rich colors," Louise said. She glanced over at her sister, who was looking puzzled. "What seems to be the problem, Jane?"

"Carita and I are planning a town scavenger hunt," Jane said. "She wanted to keep our guests occupied one afternoon here in town. We have a number of things planned for the other businesses, but we need something for them to discover here."

"What could you do here?" Louise asked. She didn't want to dampen Jane's enthusiasm, but she was trying to imagine the rambunctious group of boys in this store. The phrase, "bull in a china shop," seemed to fit the situation.

"Not sure." Jane glanced around the shop.

She walked over to the display case, glancing at some of the tea sets displayed under the glass.

"You're not too tired, are you?" Louise asked. From the

sight of Jane's full grocery bag, it seemed that she had also been doing some shopping.

Jane waved away Louise's concern. "I'm fine."

But Louise saw a slight tension in Jane's face that hadn't been there this morning. She resolved to have a sisterly chat with her when they had a free moment.

"What about a quiz?" Wilhelm suggested. "You could give some obscure hints about tea, and they would have to guess or ask me."

Jane nodded, considering.

"How many different kinds of tea, do you have here, Mr. Wood?" Carita asked.

Wilhelm slowly shook his head. "You know, I don't believe I've ever counted."

"They could try to find a dozen different kinds of tea," Carita suggested.

"And ingredients," Wilhelm added. "And where they come from."

"That would mean answering a lot of questions," Louise said. "Are you sure you want to?"

But when she saw Wilhelm's expectant expression, Louise had her answer already. Wilhelm loved expounding on the various kinds of tea and his own special blends. The only thing he liked more was discussing the many places he'd been.

"We could possibly get each group to come up with a name for a new type of tea," Wilhelm said.

"And we could vote on the answer," Carita put in.

Viola put down the glass and glanced at Louise. "We should go. My helper said she had to run a few errands yet."

Louise glanced over at Jane, but she, Wilhelm and Carita were already deep in discussion. So she simply said good-bye and left.

"Jane and Carita's plan sounds like a lot of fun," Viola said as they made their way down Berry Lane. "I wonder if they had decided on coming to the bookstore."

"I'm sure Jane will figure out something," Louise said. "Though I think she's taking on too much. I get tired just thinking of all the things she has to accomplish."

"I don't think you need to worry about Jane," Viola said. "She's smart enough to know when she needs to slow down."

Louise didn't say anything, but she wished she could share Viola's confidence.

"Are you going right back to the inn?" Viola asked.

Louise sensed that Viola was angling for a visit, but she had a few other things to do. "No. I have to stop at the church and go over the music for Sunday with Rev. Thompson."

"Then I'll see you tomorrow." Viola sighed. "Do you think it's worth going?"

"I'll give it one more try," Louise said. "If I don't learn anything, I'll have to chalk it up to experience and lose the money I paid for the rest of the course."

"I'm of the same mind." Viola shrugged. "Let's hope for a more interesting topic tomorrow then. I hate to think I paid good money to be bored to tears."

Louise said good-bye, then made her way back up Chapel Road. As she walked, she tried to formulate a diplomatic way to tell Jane that she might be overextending herself.

"I don't know if I can ever lift a hammer again," Alice said as she got out of the car.

Ethel was unusually quiet as they trudged toward the inn. All the way home, she hadn't said anything and simply stared out the window. Was the physical work too much for her?

"You're not too tired, are you?" Alice asked, trying to mask the concern in her voice.

Ethel merely shook her head, which only confirmed Alice's misgivings.

"I'm looking forward to a long, quiet soak in a hot bath and then bed. I just hope I'm not too stiff tomorrow."

When Alice opened the door to the kitchen, she was immediately inundated with the sound of voices, which grew louder as she and Ethel stepped inside.

What were all these people doing in the kitchen?

Herbie, Pete and Matthew were sitting at the table, large glasses of milk at their elbows. In front of them sat a plate holding only crumbs. Isabel stood by the counter mixing up something as Carita chatted with Jane, who was paging through her recipe books. Again.

"Hello everyone," Alice said, glancing from the boys to Jane.

Jane brightened. "And here come the resident carpenters," she said. "You must be starving. Do you want some tea? I've got a fresh batch of cookies in the oven."

Alice nodded. "That would be lovely." She gave Jane a questioning look, which was answered with a vague shrug of Jane's shoulders.

"Jane's making cookies," Herbie offered as if he caught Alice and Jane's wordless exchange. "And I couldn't resist the smell so I followed my nose and ended up here. Awesome, huh?"

Oh very, Alice thought, giving Herbie a warm smile. "And how was the day for all of you?"

"Tell you the truth, Ms. A, kind of a downer," Matthew volunteered, wiping his mouth with the back of his hand. "We were supposed to go to this car show, but it was only old, antique cars, which was kind of cool, but I wanted to see some souped-up cars. Something a bit more my style." He leaned back in his chair, his arms folded over his hooded sweatshirt. "Tomorrow's supposed to be pretty cool. Carita's got a treasure hunt thingy going on."

Alice accepted the "Ms. A" in stride. Jane had spoken earlier with her sisters, and all three had agreed to allow their young guests more latitude than was usual in addressing them—even if that meant that Louise might soon hear something other than "Mrs. Smith."

"I see," Alice said, though she really didn't.

"A scavenger hunt through Acorn Hill," Jane explained, setting the cookies on a wire rack to cool. "Carita and I made it up."

"In Acorn Hill?" Ethel asked, taking a chair at the table. "How would that work?"

"Well, I hope," Jane said with a rueful expression.

"Those cookies done yet?" Pete asked, looking up from the map he had spread out on the table.

"They're still hot," Isabel said, handing Jane a new tray of cookies to put in the oven.

"Where is Lynden? He might like some cookies," Ethel said, looking around the kitchen as if he might be hiding somewhere.

"On the porch. Reading."

"We probably shouldn't disturb him," Ethel said.

"Actually, I think we should," said Matthew with a mischievous glint in his eyes. "He's been on a downer since he came here, and this was supposed to be all about fun and fellowship and he's not really fellowshipping, now is he?"

Matthew pushed his chair back and grabbed Herbie by the front of his shirt. "C'mon, dude, let's go light a fire under that friend of ours."

Herbie, unable to stop Matthew's momentum stumbled along behind his friend, throwing a beseeching look over his shoulder. "But . . . Matthew . . . cookies."

"Later. C'mon, Pete, let's get in the spirit of the game."

Pete folded up his map, tucked it in his back pocket, slipped his cap on and followed the two other boys.

As the front door closed behind them, silence fell on the kitchen.

"Thank goodness," Isabel said as she laid more cookies

on the cookie sheet, "I'm getting tired of hearing about blue bottle kits—"

"That's lift kits," Carita corrected. "Lift kits and blue bottle mufflers. Those boys love to talk about cars and trucks and all the things they would do if they actually had one."

The curt nod of Isabel's head showed Alice that the young woman wasn't impressed with Carita's correction. However, Isabel didn't say anything and kept working.

"Sorry about these boys taking over, Jane," Carita said with an apologetic look. "I didn't think they would come right into the kitchen."

"That's okay," Jane said. She turned to Alice. "So how was the first day on the job?"

"I don't know about Aunt Ethel, but I'm tired. My hands are sore and my back is sore, and I think I got a bit too much sun," Alice said.

"But you're smiling."

"It was a lot of fun," Alice admitted as she eased her tired body into a chair. She bent over and unfastened her shoes, toeing them off. Her feet burned, her hands had blisters on them. But, as Jane had said, she was smiling. "It was not only a lot of fun, but satisfying to be a part of such a big project."

"How did you make out, Aunt Ethel?"

Ethel simply nodded. "Well. Real well. Looking forward to tomorrow." She pulled her tape measure out of her pouch and pulled out the tape, absently measuring the width of the table.

Alice frowned. "I don't know if you should go, Aunt Ethel. You seem very tired."

"I'm not," was all Ethel said. She let the tape slip back into the case but then pulled it out again.

Alice was certain her aunt was not as well as she claimed, but she also knew not to press her point. Tomorrow would be a determining factor. And, if need be, Alice could give Ethel a way out by claiming exhaustion herself. Yes, she was tired and yes, her feet ached, but it was a good tired. She would sleep well tonight.

"Why don't you girls join the boys," Jane said, taking the bowl of cookie dough away from Isabel. "You don't need to help me here."

"I don't mind helping," Isabel said.

"Besides, the boys just annihilated those cookies," Carita put in, glancing at the few cookies left. "You've hardly gotten anywhere."

"I'll just have to adjust my amounts next time I bake. Now, go." Jane waved her hand in a shooing motion. Carita got up but Isabel lingered.

"Are you sure you don't need help?" Isabel asked.

"Absolutely. Now go have some fun." So Isabel did as she was told.

When the door closed, Jane brought the teapot to the table with a plate of gingersnaps she had kept hidden from the cookie monsters. "Those kids. What a pile of energy. I can hardly keep up with them."

"I can stay home tomorrow and help you," Alice said, seeing her chance to create an excuse for Ethel.

"But what about the house?" Ethel said, sitting up, a frown creasing her forehead.

"Well, I might be too tired . . ."

"Nonsense!" Ethel exclaimed, waving Alice's comment away like she was swatting a pesky fly. "You don't look the least bit tired to me."

Alice's tactic wasn't working, so she faced the situation head on. "But you do, Aunt Ethel. I don't want you to wear yourself out."

"I'm not tired." Ethel set aside her tape, poured the tea, then sat back, her arms folded over her bosom. "I'm just thinking."

"About . . ." Alice offered.

"Florence." Ethel tapped her fingers on her arm, then shook her head.

"I believe I did notice some strain at the building site today," Alice said, hoping Ethel would elaborate.

"She completely ignored me when she brought the juice around," Ethel said. "Didn't even offer me a glass. As if I wasn't there."

Alice didn't mention that Ethel had treated Florence in much the same way previously. "Maybe she didn't notice you."

Ethel wrinkled her nose, then shook her head. "She noticed me all right. I could tell the minute she looked my way."

"Why do you think she would do that?" Jane asked, dropping into a chair.

Ethel did not respond. Instead she stared into the steaming liquid of her cup as if trying to find an answer there.

Jane glanced at Alice, lifting her eyebrows in question. Alice gave a light shake of her head, indicating to Jane that she should hold off. For some reason Florence and Ethel's little pique had deeper roots that Ethel wasn't yet ready to discuss.

"And how is your menu coming along?" Alice asked, curious to see what her sister had planned for Stacy's dinner.

"I haven't had much time to work on it today."

"I can stay tomorrow . . ." Alice began.

Jane held up her hand. "Don't even suggest it. Things are going along just fine."

Alice wasn't sure about that part, but she also knew better than to buck her younger sister when she had a notion.

"I'm making a simple meal tonight. I have some ideas I'm going to try out tomorrow night for supper," Jane continued, stirring some sugar into her tea. "If my family doesn't mind being guinea pigs."

"We'll gladly test anything you come up with," Ethel offered. "You always have the most interesting ideas."

Jane smiled at her aunt. "Thanks for the vote of confidence. I'll do my best to maintain your faith in me."

The ringing of the phone broke into the moment, and Alice answered it.

"Is Jane there? Is Jane available?" The breathless voice on the other end of the line gave Alice a start.

"Yes she is. Just a moment, Stacy." Alice quickly handed the phone to Jane.

Jane's face drooped as soon as she heard Alice mention Stacy's name, but she held out her hand. "Hello, Stacy. No, I'm not terribly busy . . . I see . . . I'm not sure . . . I'll have to ask . . . I can't promise you anything. Sorry. . . . Yes, I'll talk to my sisters and get back to you." Jane nodded, made a few more abbreviated comments as she drummed her fingers on the table, making Alice more concerned the longer she spoke.

"Okay. I'll call you as soon as I know anything. Goodbye." Jane put the phone down and shook her head.

"What does Stacy want now?" Alice asked.

"Stacy can't find a place anywhere in Acorn Hill, in Potterston or any place within driving distance. She wants to use the inn."

"I take it you don't want the dinner here?"

"You take correctly." Jane smacked her hand on the table. "I knew it. I knew this would happen. From the minute she walked into the inn and saw the dining room, she looked as if she was going to have that dinner here no matter what other options were available to her."

"But wouldn't catering be simpler if she had her event at the inn? It would free you from a host of problems," Alice offered helpfully.

"And we could help you," Ethel offered, her eyes bright. Then she frowned as she looked at the calendar on the wall. "Oh, wait. That's Saturday, isn't it? Lloyd wants to take me to Potterston that night. But I'm sure Louise and Alice could help out," she said, glibly offering her nieces' services.

"I can help you," Alice said.

"You'll be too tired from working on the house," Jane said.

"I don't work at the hospital until next week, so I'll have lots of recuperation time."

"And the kids will be busy all day Saturday and Saturday night," Jane mused.

"And you wouldn't have to worry about whether the hall has the proper equipment. You could serve everything fresh and warm."

"I know all that. She's been—for lack of a better expression —a pain in the neck, and I couldn't imagine what she would be like if she got her hands on the inn. She quoted me a generous decorating allowance, but, knowing Stacy, she probably would want me to use some of that to repaint the inn."

"Now, Jane, that's where there's a difference. Here, in the inn, you are in charge. This is your territory, even if she is paying for decorations. Plus you have two partners who can be—and would be—as adamant as she is." Alice got up and patted Jane on the shoulder as she walked past her. "This could turn out just fine. Aunt Ethel, did you want some more tea?"

"I better get home and put my feet up for a while."

"Are you coming back for supper?" Alice asked as she rinsed out the teacups.

To Alice's surprise, Ethel shook her head. "No. I should stay home and cook for myself. Besides, I think I should get to bed early, and you seem to be quite busy with your guests."

Alice watched with concern as Ethel slowly got up from the chair and walked out of the kitchen with measured steps. Doing carpentry work all day was more than enough for Alice, let alone someone of Ethel's age.

Maybe she could talk her aunt into going to the project later in the morning to make a shorter day of work.

Chapter ⌐ Nine

Jane yawned as she made her way down the stairs Thursday morning. As she hitched up the waistband of her khaki cotton capri pants and tucked in her bright yellow shirt, she paused on the landing of the second floor.

The silence on this floor was a direct contrast to the noise the young people made last night as they played a game Isabel had brought along. Though they were playing two floors down in the living room, their cries had filtered up to the third floor where Jane and her sisters lived.

Jane had been tempted to go downstairs and get them to quiet down, but at the same time she didn't feel right about chiding them as if they were unruly children. So she lay in bed, wakeful, fretting that Alice might not be getting enough sleep and hoping Louise wouldn't be upset.

Now, with morning, the inn was utterly quiet.

Nonetheless, she had a schedule to maintain, so she carried on to the main floor, taking a moment to step outside.

The sun was warming off the early morning chill, drying the dew that sparkled on the grass. The faint growl of a car starting up drifted down the street followed by a mother's voice calling her child in for breakfast.

The neighborhood was slowly waking up.

Jane looked around, a smile on her lips.

"Thank You, Lord, for the promise of a new day," she prayed aloud. "For work and for health, for family and friends. For freedom and blessings we can't begin to count."

As she spoke she caught the muted sound of the tinkling of piano keys laying down a tranquil soundtrack to her spoken prayer.

Somehow Louise had slipped downstairs without Jane's knowing it and was already practicing the songs she would be playing in church on Sunday. The door was cracked open a bit, and the melody floated softly through the first floor. Jane should not have been surprised.

In spite of the noise from last night that surely had kept her awake, Louise was maintaining her disciplined schedule.

Jane crossed her arms, giving herself some time outside before diving into the busyness of her own day. She mentally ticked off her jobs, organizing her hours.

Finalize menu for the dinner Saturday night, keeping in mind that Stacy could call at any time with yet another food issue.

Help the kids get started on the scavenger hunt. Though she still had her misgivings about how well it would go over with the college crowd, Carita had assured her that they would have fun.

Get the laundry started and do some more baking to feed the insatiable appetites of these youths for homemade goodies.

Today she was going to make biscotti. Maybe the crunchy twice-baked cookies would slow their jaws down a bit. She had some lovely recipes she hadn't used in a while.

Feeling as if her day was now ordered, Jane opened the door behind her, whistling the same tune Louise had just played.

She stopped as she spied a figure hovering at the bottom of the stairs, outside the partially open parlor door.

Lynden. Today he wore a dark T-shirt and the baggy pants teenage boys often seemed to favor. A small book peeked out of his back pocket.

If she was startled, so was he. He pushed himself away from the wall, looking as if she had caught him with his hand in the cookie jar. *Not that he would have found anything there,* Jane thought. It was as empty as Mother Hubbard's cupboard.

She recovered in time to smile at him, pushing down a slight misgiving she felt at his lurking presence ... once again.

"Good morning, Lynden. How are you?"

He shoved his hands in his pockets and gave her a brief nod. "I'm good," was his terse reply.

"Lovely morning, isn't it?"

"Yeah."

In the background, Louise had stopped playing, and Jane wondered what her sister would think if she came out and found Lynden standing in the foyer as he had the other day.

"I'm glad the weather is cooperating for the scavenger hunt," she said, soldiering on. She was growing increasingly concerned over this young man and was determined to engage him one way or the other, inane conversation or not.

"I guess."

"I hear you're going to be hosting a tailgate party Friday night."

This time he simply nodded.

Way to get him to open up, Jane. "What are you going to serve?"

"The usual."

Four syllables. She was really getting somewhere. Jane was about to ask him another harmless question when Louise started playing again and Lynden's head snapped up, his eyes fixing on the parlor door.

Jane glanced in the same direction, wondering what he was looking at. Then she had a moment of inspiration. Something Carita had said came back to her. A throwaway comment she had made about a doting grandmother.

"She plays well, doesn't she?" Jane said, lowering her voice to a decidedly nonthreatening timbre.

Again Lynden only nodded, but this time Jane caught the faintest glint in his eyes.

"Does your grandmother play the piano?"

A look of sorrow crept across the young man's face. "Used to."

Jane sensed a whole world of pain and hurt wrapped up in those two words. Used to. Past tense. And suddenly everything became much clearer. This young man wasn't odd and he wasn't angry. He was still grieving the loss of someone he must have cared for deeply.

Taking a chance, Jane laid her hand on Lynden's arm. "I'm sorry to hear that. How long ago did she die?"

Lynden blinked and looked away. "Two months ago. She was sick for almost a year before."

She squeezed lightly, a gesture of silent sympathy.

"I lived with her." He spoke so quietly Jane had to strain to hear. "She took care of me since my parents died."

Jane remembered Carita's mentioning this. How her family had lived next door to Lynden and his grandmother. "How old were you when your parents died?"

"Ten."

A wave of sorrow washed over Jane. This poor young man had lost much in his life. No wonder he was taciturn. "Losing your grandmother must make you feel lonely."

He glanced at her, as if surprised she could empathize. "Yeah. Totally."

"I'm surprised you agreed to come along on this trip."

He shrugged. "I thought it would be fun. Didn't think I'd be such a loser." Lynden dragged his hand over his face and gave Jane an apologetic smile. "Sorry if you thought I was stalking your sister, but I like hearing her play."

"I'm glad. I was a little concerned, especially after your accident."

"That freaked me out," he exclaimed. "I thought for sure I'd hurt her or something."

Jane paused, letting his words settle in. "So you were concerned about Louise and not your truck?"

"My truck? Are you kidding? I mean it's a great set of wheels and all, but hey, I didn't want to think I'd hurt her."

And one more mystery was solved.

"Louise was sure you were worried about it."

"Well, yeah. A bit. After I realized she was okay." He ran his fingers through his hair. "I mean, I got the truck from my granny. Before she died."

"So it reminds you of her then."

"I know it's just a truck. But she gave it to me. Said it was a small thanks for helping take care of her."

"Take care of her . . ." Jane let the sentence trail off, hoping he would finish it.

"When she was sick. I was supposed to go to college, but I canceled and stayed home when she got sick."

Jane felt a moment of shame for the negative thoughts she had harbored about this giving and unselfish young man. Amazing what the correct information could do to make a connection between people.

"You are a very remarkable young man," she said quietly.

"She was a great person. For a grandma, she was pretty cool. Taught me a lot. I miss her." He looked embarrassed. "Don't tell the other guys about this, okay? I don't know if they'd get it."

Jane thought of Matthew, Pete, Herbie and Rick. "I think underneath all that chatter, they're pretty decent guys. You might want to tell them, so they understand where you're coming from."

"I'll think about it." He pulled the book out of his back pocket and pointed it at the front door. "If anyone wants to know where I am, I'll be on the porch. Reading."

"You don't want breakfast now?"

"Nah. I'll wait until the rest come."

"Then enjoy the morning," Jane said. "The day is fresh and new."

He gave her an oblique smile. "Yeah. It sure is."

As Jane made her way back to the kitchen, she felt a shadow lift. In spite of Carita's assurances, she'd had her misgivings about Lynden and his reclusive behavior. Now that she knew what was happening in his life, she could regard him differently.

She whispered a quick prayer for him, creating another connection.

She pulled out her recipe book and turned to the marked page. If yesterday was any indication of when the kids would come down for breakfast, she had time to mix up a few batches of puff pastry. She would use part for the dessert for Stacy's dinner. The rest she could freeze for future use.

As she weighed the flour portions and measured out the water, she wondered if Stacy would call today. Since Jane had agreed to do the dinner for her, it seemed that Stacy called every couple of hours to give updates, ask questions and, in general, create an air of tension. Now that the inn was involved, Jane feared Stacy's calls and concern would only increase.

"Is there anything I can do for you?"

"Goodness, Louise, you startled me." Jane pressed a floury hand to her heart, leaving a white imprint on her yellow shirt.

"Jane, you seem rather jumpy."

Jane narrowed her eyes at her sister and caught a glint of humor in Louise's blue eyes. "I'm concentrating. I have a lot on my mind."

"Is that breakfast you're making? Shall I set the table and get the kettle boiling?"

"Please." Jane put the flour and a small amount of butter in the food processor, but before she pushed the button, she turned to her sister. "Lynden was hanging around the foyer again this morning. Listening to you play."

"Again?"

"You don't need to be concerned, Louise. I found out why." Jane craned her neck to look through the door, into the hallway, to see if Lynden or any of the other guests were there, but the hall was empty. "Turns out his grandmother used to play the piano. He is just missing her, and he likes to hear you play."

"Indeed?"

"Yes. His grandmother passed away recently."

"Oh, that poor boy." The genuine sympathy in Louise's voice warmed Jane's heart. "Where is he now?"

"Outside. Reading a book on the porch."

"Do you think it would be a good idea if I joined him?"

Jane shook her head. "I talked to him already. He did say how much he liked your playing. Maybe more music might be the best thing for him."

"Very astute, Jane. I'll do that. And I'll be back to set the table," Louise promised. "So make sure you leave that chore for me."

"Wouldn't dream of taking that away from you," Jane said as her sister left the room. She hit the button on the food processor.

Making puff pastry was time consuming, and Jane could purchase it frozen, but she preferred making the food they served at the inn from scratch. That way she could proudly stand behind the word *homemade* appearing on their Web site and in their brochures.

She rubbed her marble cutting board with ice and wiped off the excess moisture. She rolled out the dough into a cross shape on the board, set the cold butter in the middle, folded the dough over and started rolling, being careful not to let the butter slip out of the cracks.

She folded again, getting lost in the soothing rhythms of the work.

A light knock at the doorway startled her again.

Carita this time.

"Am I bothering you?" she asked.

"No, no," Jane waved the young woman's concern away with a floury hand. "Come in."

Carita looked pensive.

"Is something wrong?" Jane asked.

Carita merely shook her head, but she wouldn't meet Jane's eye.

Jane continued folding and rolling, occasionally glancing at the young woman. Carita shifted, her elbows resting on the counter, her dark eyes staring off into the middle distance. Jane sensed something was wrong, but she had already given Carita an opportunity; the only thing she could do was wait.

After a few quiet seconds Carita sighed, then turned to Jane. "You ever been in love?"

No light topics this morning, Jane thought.

"Yes. I was. I was married once." Jane thought of her ex-husband Justin. Though Jane had reconciled herself with their marriage break-up, there were times when her mind went back to those first few years, wondering if she could have done something differently.

Carita displayed a puzzled frown. "You make it sound like you didn't love him."

Jane brushed the flour off her rolling pin, then smiled. "I wouldn't have married him if I didn't."

"Have you been in love since?"

"No, but I'm quite content with my life."

"You don't want to get married again?"

Jane thought of some of the men that had slipped in and out of her life since Justin, then shook her head. "I've made a decision to focus my desire on my Lord first, to be content in my circumstances and to thank God every day for all the good things He has given me." She folded the dough over on itself and started rolling again. "I don't want to reject the idea that love might come my way, but for now, as I said, I'm content."

Carita folded and unfolded a napkin in front of her, and Jane could almost see the questions wandering through the young woman's mind.

"This is pretty heavy stuff so early in the morning," Jane said with a light teasing tone in her voice, thinking of what she had just discussed with Lynden.

"Yeah, well, it's just I don't know what to do."

"About . . ."

Carita put down the napkin and sighed. "Lynden."

The morning had come full circle. "You like him." Jane stated the fact simply.

Carita nodded. "A lot. I've liked him all through high school. Before that even."

I'm on top of my game this morning, Jane thought. *I should hang up a shingle—Advice. Free.*

"You didn't stay in touch when you left for college?"

"I tried, but he stopped writing."

Jane had promised Lynden she wouldn't tell the boys about his grandmother, but would she be stretching her promise if she told Carita?

She weighed the thought, but discarded it. Lynden's loss was not hers to share. But she could possibly help things along a little.

"Do you know why he stopped?"

Carita shook her head.

"Have you asked him?"

"How could I when he wouldn't answer my letters?"

"He's out on the porch," Jane offered, rolling out the pastry one more time. "Everyone else is still in bed. This might be a good time to catch up."

Carita pressed her lips together. "What if he doesn't want me there? His mind isn't on me at all."

"Maybe you might want to find out what his mind *is* on," Jane hinted. "He could have a lot to think about."

"Do you think he'll tell me?"

"If you are old friends? I'm guessing he would."

Carita's expression brightened. "You might be right." She stood up, but just before she left the room she turned back to Jane.

"Just thought I'd let you know I'm getting everyone up in half an hour so that you don't have to make breakfast twice."

"Thanks for the heads up," Jane said, glancing at the clock. Thirty minutes was not nearly enough time to finish up here, get a breakfast casserole together and bake it.

Scrap that menu item, she thought, thinking on the fly. She'd need something hearty enough yet tasty. Something she could make with ingredients on hand.

She wrapped the pastry dough, and as she set it in the refrigerator, did a quick inventory and came up with bacon, avocado and tomato salsa to make cheese omelets that would be tasty, fiery and full of zippy nutrition. Just what the growing college student needs. And just what the harried innkeeper can make in thirty minutes.

She pulled out two cartons of eggs, bacon and the rest of the ingredients, and set them on the counter. How much would those kids eat? Better to err on the side of generosity.

Once breakfast was over, she might have time to put the final touches on the menu she and Stacy had decided on, and possibly make what she could in advance.

She also had to get hold of Sylvia Songer to help her develop a theme for the evening. Maybe Craig Tracy, at Wild Things, would be willing to rent some plants to fill some of the corners.

"*Yoo-hoo.*" Aunt Ethel stood behind her, dressed for work. "You're busy already."

"And you're up early," Jane said, surprised at how spry her aunt seemed compared to how tired she had been last night.

"I slept like a log," she exclaimed. "Haven't had such a good sleep in a long time. I think it was all that fresh air and exercise. Is Alice up yet?"

"Not yet," Jane said, taking out a bowl and cracking eggs into it. "But I'm getting breakfast ready for the guests, so I should ask Louise to wake her. What time do you have to be at the worksite?"

"Not for two hours," Ethel said, glancing around the kitchen. "I've got time to do a few chores for you. Do you need anything done?" Ethel fingered the hammer hanging from her pouch. "Any loose nails to be pounded in or something like that?"

Jane had nervous visions of her aunt working her way through the inn, flailing away with her hammer, causing more problems than she could fix. "No, Aunt Ethel. Trust me, everything is just fine."

Ethel's eyes flitted around the kitchen again, as if she didn't quite believe Jane's earnest protestations. "All right then. But keep it in mind, I don't mind pitching in where I can."

"I'll do that Auntie." Jane prepared ingredients and scraped them into the bowl holding the eggs. She glanced at the clock. If she let the eggs settle, she had time to make a batch of biscuits to go with the omelet. And then . . .

"Good morning, Aunt Ethel," Louise said as she entered the kitchen.

Jane started at the sound of her sister's voice.

"You seem on edge," Louise said with a frown.

"I've got people hopping in and out of my kitchen like erratic rabbits," Jane said, a defensive tone creeping into her voice. She didn't want to admit that Louise was right.

"Well, this bunny has come to set the table," Louise said, picking up a tray and removing the place settings from the cupboard. "Which tablecloth do you want me to use?"

"The brown one is fine," Jane said, measuring out flour for the biscuits.

"I believe it's dirty."

"Then use the green one." She didn't mean to let the snappy tone enter her voice, but a questioning lift of Louise's eyebrows showed Jane that her sister was less than pleased with her younger sister's response.

While she added salt to the biscuit mixture she kept one cautious eye on Ethel. Her aunt wandered around the kitchen, testing the walls with her index finger, fiddling with the cupboard doors as if determined to find something loose to tighten or crooked to straighten.

"The table is set," Louise said, returning from the dining room with an empty tray. "When do you think our guests will be eating?"

"Carita said she was going to have everyone down here in thirty minutes. Actually, twenty, now." Jane rolled out the biscuits into a rectangle and instead of using the biscuit cutter, simply slashed the rectangle into squares and dropped them on the greased cookie sheet. She suspected the college group wouldn't notice if the biscuits were round or square or flower shaped.

"Where is Alice?" Louise asked, glancing around the kitchen. "I thought she would be up by now."

"I can go get her," Ethel offered, dropping her hammer back in its hook with a metallic click.

"You just sit down," Louise said. "I'll get you some coffee, and then I'll see what Alice is up to."

"And no weapons at the table," Jane said, pointing her whisk at Ethel's tool belt.

Ethel laughed and unhooked the leather apron, setting it

down carefully beside the back door. "Funny how a person gets used to wearing it," she said with all the authority of a full-time carpenter.

Twenty-five minutes later, Alice had meandered down-stairs, the kids were settling in at the dining room table, and Louise and Jane were hustling food back and forth.

Sixty minutes later, the food was gone, the dirty dishes were piled up on the kitchen counter and Jane, Louise, Alice and Ethel were finishing up the last of their own breakfast.

They could hear Carita explaining the rules of the scavenger hunt as they ate.

Jane wondered what Carita and Lynden had talked about, if indeed they had talked at all, but she hadn't had a chance to ask the young woman about what happened. Carita sounded cheerful, though.

Ethel daintily wiped her mouth with a napkin. "That was delicious, as usual, Jane," she said. "I'm sure this breakfast will hold us for the rest of the morning."

"A carpenter's breakfast," Alice agreed.

Jane saw her sister stifling a yawn. Alice looked more tired than Ethel did.

"So, Alice, do you want to do dishes yet?" Ethel said, picking up her plate and bringing it to join the pile of dirty dishes the kids had created.

"I'll take care of the dishes," Jane said. "I'm not planning to go anywhere today."

"I thought you were helping with the scavenger hunt?" Louise asked.

"Carita has that well in hand. I've got enough to do," Jane said.

And as if to underline that comment, the phone rang again. Jane picked it up and the voice on the other end made her clench her teeth.

Stacy. Yet again.

She waved to her sister and aunt as they left. As Stacy expressed still more misgivings about Saturday night and what Jane was going to serve, Jane kept her smile fixed firmly in place while watching Louise clear and scrape and rinse and stack.

Fifteen minutes later she had a new list of marching orders and the beginnings of a headache.

"Everything okay?" Louise asked as Jane forced herself to end the call without shrieking.

Jane flashed her a bright smile. "Just peachy. Just peachy."

Louise's expression told Jane that her older sister was not convinced, but Jane didn't want to listen to another sisterly lecture on how she shouldn't have taken on this job. There was no backing out now.

Ten minutes later the kitchen shone, and Louise was getting ready to leave.

"Are you sure you'll be okay?" Louise asked one more time. "I can certainly skip my course. If the lecturer this morning is anything like the one yesterday, then I'm sure I won't miss much."

Jane answered her sister that all was well. "I just have to do some tidying in the rooms. The laundry is done. Go. Learn about cars." Jane knew her sister would have gladly stayed home to help, but she also knew that her budget-minded sister would want to get her money's worth for a course for which she had already paid.

Louise left and Jane sat at the counter, enjoying the first moment of silence the inn had experienced since she had come downstairs.

She let the quiet settle over her as Wendell padded softly across the kitchen floor and jumped onto an empty chair. He curled up, and the rumble of his purring was the only sound in the peaceful kitchen.

The ringing of the phone cut into the tranquility, and Jane let out a deep sigh.

The person on the other end of the line, however, was Sylvia, Jane's good friend.

"Hey, do you have time to stop by the shop today?" Sylvia asked. "I have some ideas for your dinner."

"I can come in two hours." She had to clean up the bed-rooms and vacuum with Ethel's wheezy vacuum cleaner, which would remind her what the money from Stacy's dinner would help pay for. "Is that soon enough?"

"Absolutely. I'll see you then."

Jane hung up the phone, pushed herself away from the counter and started in on the cleaning for the day.

Chapter Ten

"If you look at the pictures of this battery, you can see the posts are full of corrosion," Clyde Gilroy, the instructor of the day, walked over to the screen, and pointed to the white coating on the battery terminals. "You want to keep these clean so your battery is charging and discharging to its full capacity."

"Many of the things we are going to be talking about this morning, while basic, are important," Clyde was saying. "We're not going to have you doing engine overhauls, but I will be showing you a lot of preventive maintenance. I want you to feel comfortable around the various parts of the engine. I also believe the best way to learn is to do, and I have a few sets of batteries here for you to work on."

Louise glanced at Viola. This was a new twist and not entirely unwelcome.

"I think we actually might be learning something practical," Viola said, speaking Louise's thoughts aloud.

All the way here, Louise had felt bad about leaving Jane alone, and in spite of Jane's assurances that everything was fine, she saw her sister getting more tense every day.

The only thing Jane had requested of her was that she pick up groceries. Nevertheless, Louise had decided that if the course today was in any way a waste of her time, she would excuse herself and return to the inn.

"So if you don't mind breaking up into groups of two, I'll get each couple to stand at a table."

Louise and Viola paired up. On the table in front of them sat a battery, a few tools, rubber gloves and safety glasses.

"You need to remember that a battery is full of acid," Clyde was saying as he walked up and down in front of the tables. "Any time you work on one, you run the risk of exposing yourself to that acid. That's why you'll be putting on the glasses and gloves."

"This makes me feel right at home," Louise said, rolling her eyes.

Viola looked askance at the large, rectangular car battery squatting on the table in front of them. "At home? Perhaps you need to change the inn's décor."

Louise laughed at her friend's comment.

"The battery posts, as you can see, are encrusted with deposits. These deposits are a natural result of using your car," Clyde was saying, pointing out the green-and-white residue on the posts of a battery in front of Martha Bevins.

Louise stifled a smile at the puzzled look on the elderly woman's face. Louise was sure Mrs. Bevins would have been happier to listen to another lecture.

"When your vehicle and battery are operating, very small amounts of gas are released through the vent cap," Clyde continued. "When released, these fumes naturally combine with the heat, dirt and humidity in the air to form corrosion on your battery cables and terminals. One of the ways to get rid of this deposit is with a wire brush and a mixture of baking soda and water. You have to be careful not to get the mixture inside the battery. Baking soda can neutralize the acid in the battery."

"It's safe if you're careful," Clyde assured the class. "But having said that, I do want to caution any of you when handling batteries elsewhere to wear protective clothing. Older batteries can leak and the acid inside can spill onto your clothes."

"What about pennies for the corrosion," Harvey said, his voice gruff. "Mechanic I knew used to use pennies."

"I've heard that pennies can actually draw all the corrosion away, using a chemical reaction between the copper of the penny and the corrosion, but then you need to keep the penny in place. I believe zinc works better than copper. But for now we'll concentrate on simply cleaning the battery."

Clyde gave some further instructions, and Louise picked up the brush and began scrubbing. In less than a minute, the terminals were spotless.

"Well, now, that wasn't difficult," Louise said.

"And a simple cleaning like this, done regularly, will keep your battery running well and, by extension, your car. Once your battery is clean, you want to check how tight the cables are on the posts. A loose cable can keep a car from starting." Clyde said. "You also want to make sure the battery is sitting snug in its bracket. A loose battery can cause excessive vibration, which causes more wear and tear than on one that is properly set." As he spoke, he walked to the side of the room, heaved a tire up from the floor and rolled it toward the tables where everyone stood.

"One of you was talking about pennies," he said. "Does anyone have a Lincoln penny on them?"

"I've got one." Harvey dug into his pocket and brought it over to Clyde.

"If everyone could just come over here a minute, I want to show you something," Clyde said.

When everyone had gathered around, he pointed to the tire. "How worn is this tire?"

Louise was immediately all ears. Worn tires had been

cited as one of the factors in her accident with Lynden. But she hadn't been able to detect the wear from just looking at them.

"How much wear is left?" Clyde looked around the room. "Anyone?"

Louise was comforted to know that neither Harvey Racklin nor Derek Grollier could give Clyde a confident answer.

"If you don't want to put your trust in a tire store, which is, after all, in the business of trying to part you from your money, you might want to take note of this little trick. You first need a Lincoln penny." He squatted down. "If you want to know if your tires are worn beyond what is considered safe, simply stick a penny into one of the tread grooves. Make sure you have President Lincoln's head pointing down. If the tread is lower than Lincoln's hair, the tire needs to be replaced. If his hair is covered, like this . . ." he indicated. Everyone moved closer to have a look, and sure enough, nothing could be seen of Lincoln's hair, "then your tires are fine." He pushed himself to his feet and handed the penny to Louise so she could try for herself.

Louise was impressed by this simple fact. Easy to remember and something she could do on her own.

"You have to check all of your tires though," Clyde was saying as Louise handed the penny to Viola, "Tires may wear at a different rate, even if they're on the same vehicle."

Louise made a mental note to write this down. As she straightened, she had to admit she was feeling much better about the course today.

"Correct inflation is also important. I've got my own car sitting outside, so I'd like us all to head out to the parking lot, where I can demonstrate how to use a pressure gauge."

As they followed him into the bright sunshine, he kept talking. "A decrease in tire pressure of only two pounds can affect your gas mileage by four percent. Now that may not seem a lot, but if you add it up, at today's gas prices, that does have a considerable effect."

They gathered obediently around Clyde's car, a midsize sedan, as he pulled out four pressure gauges.

"Mrs. L. Hey, there, Mrs. Louise!"

Louise stiffened, then glanced around to see who might be calling out her name.

Herbie and Isabel were waving at her from the sidewalk. She waved back and Herbie came charging over, Isabel trailing in his bulky wake. Louise excused herself from her group.

"We need your help," Herbie shouted. He was out of breath by the time he reached her. "We need to know who named Acorn Hill," he panted, bent over, resting his hands on his knees.

"We asked the lady who runs the paper, but she didn't know," Isabel offered quietly, standing a ways back from the group. Louise tried to catch her attention to give her an encouraging smile, but the girl kept her head down, looking at the papers she held. She seemed the most reserved of the guests, a complete opposite of her exuberant roommate Carita.

"Is this for the scavenger hunt?" Louise asked.

"Yeah. The one Carita made," Herbie said.

Louise frowned, trying to think. She glanced at Viola who shrugged. "Sorry, I don't remember," she said. "Though you might be able to find that information in the library."

"Yeah. Library." Herbie sucked in a few more deep breaths. "Where's that?"

"Right here." Louise indicated the building behind them.

"Okay. That's good. Who do we need to talk to at the library?"

"Nia Komonos," Martha Bevins put in, her bright smile taking in the two youngsters. "And what is this about a scavenger hunt? What are you hunting for?" Martha asked, obviously more interested in what the kids were doing than discovering correct tire pressure.

Herbie glanced at his list. "We need to talk to Wilhelm at Time for Tea and name a tea, we have to figure out a puzzle at the Coffee Shop . . ."

"Well now, I love puzzles," Martha said brightly. "Maybe I could help."

Louise caught Herbie's panicked glance.

"I think that would be an unfair advantage to the other teams," Louise said, rescuing the young man. "They divided up in pairs, and I'm sure they're not allowed to take anyone from the town along. You would simply have too much knowledge."

"Well now, that might be," Martha said, her smile smug. "I'm sorry I can't help you, though it sounds like fun."

"It is fun, but busy." Isabel rustled through the papers she held. "We should get going, Herbie."

"Yeah. I don't want Matthew to get ahead of us. Thanks, Mrs. L." Herbie waved good-bye, caught Isabel by the arm and hustled her off to the front of the library.

"What a fun bunch of kids," Martha said. "Where did they come from?"

"They are our guests," Louise said. "There are seven of them staying with us."

"Wouldn't that be fun having all those young people around." Martha's voice held a touch of envy.

Louise thought of the other night. The noise, the busyness and the music that was finally turned off at 11:30 PM. Martha might be singing a different tune if she knew.

Clyde cleared his throat, getting the group's attention. "I'd like each of you to take a pressure gauge . . ."

"Mrs. L, Mrs. L . . ."

Louise sent Clyde an apologetic look and turned in time to see Matthew and Pete rushing toward her.

"More kids?" Martha asked.

"Sorry to bug you, Mrs. L.," Matthew said. "We need to find out . . ."

"Who named Acorn Hill?" Louise asked.

He shook his head. "Nah. We're not that far yet, but if you know . . ."

"Sorry. We just sent Herbie and Isabel to the library to find that out," Louise said.

"Rats! But I'm really thirsty. Do you know where I can buy some water?"

"Go to Dairyland," Harvey said, his tone abrupt as if he was eager to get these young people out of their hair. "Down Berry Lane to Village Road. It's across from the Methodist Church."

"Thanks, Mister," Matthew said, giving him a quick salute. "See you at the inn, Mrs. L.," he called out as he and Pete jogged off.

"Can we continue?" Clyde asked, tapping a gauge against his palm.

"I'm sorry for the interruptions," Louise said. "Please do. This is really interesting. I'm learning a lot."

She gave her fellow classmates an apologetic look.

"Okay. Tire pressure varies from vehicle to vehicle. You can find the correct pressure in the book that comes with your car, or often the number is printed on a door jamb or in the glove box." The group followed Clyde around his car while he showed them. "In the case of my vehicle, the correct pressure is thirty-two pounds per square inch." He demonstrated how to measure this and then gave each of them an opportunity to try it themselves. "I've got a piece of carpet on the ground, so you won't get your clothes dirty."

Louise glanced at the carpet and then at her narrow, gray skirt. With a shrug, she carefully knelt and pressed the gauge over the valve. Immediately the little white ruler popped up and stopped. "And there we have it," she said to Viola. "Thirty-two pounds."

"I keep hearing a hissing sound, but nothing is happening," Viola complained, fiddling with her gauge.

"You have to make sure you push down hard enough to cover the valve stem," Clyde instructed.

He walked around, making sure everyone understood the procedure and then gathered up the tools.

"Hello there, Mrs. L," Another young male voice sang out across the parking lot.

Louise caught an annoyed glance from Clyde as Rick and Lynden walked past them. But Rick only waved and carried on. Louise thought of what Jane had told her about Lynden, and called out to them. "How is the hunt going, boys?"

To her surprise, Lynden stopped. "Goin' okay," he called back. Though he sounded less than enthusiastic about the entire expedition, Louise was pleased to see a faint smile on his face.

"Good luck," she called out.

And when she saw Lynden's careful smile, she knew it was worth risking Clyde's annoyance to make this small connection with the young man.

"How are you feeling today?" Ethel asked Alice as they walked over to the building site. "You seem stiff."

Ethel sounded positively gleeful, Alice thought as she carefully adjusted the buckle on her pouch. Alice's arms were stiff. Her legs were stiff. Even her face was stiff. She had discovered muscles in places she had never studied in any anatomy class she had taken. Tiny muscles and big muscles, all of them stiff and sore and complaining with every move she made.

"I'm fine, Auntie," Alice said with a faint touch of pride. She wondered how her aunt managed. Ethel seemed as spry as she had yesterday, her hammer swinging as she strode up the wooden plank leading to the floor of the house. Two men in blue jeans and stained T-shirts were already at work, pounding nails into what looked like a wall section.

"Good morning, ladies," Cal said with a grin. "Glad you showed up today."

Ethel glanced around the quiet site. "Where is everyone else? Why are there so few people?"

"Oh, this happens once in a while," Cal said. "People offer to come, and then something else comes up and they can't make it. I've got Del and Jim setting out the wall section you'll be working on. You'll be doing the same thing you were doing yesterday."

As he spoke, another vehicle pulled up, and Alice was pleased to see June Carter emerge from the car.

Then she did a double take as Florence got out of the other side of the car wearing brand-new coveralls, a white visor, leather gloves and a new leather pouch.

"And it looks like Florence is going to be joining us on the worksite today." Alice gave her aunt a sidelong glance to see her reaction to this news, but Ethel was suddenly fussing with her pouch.

"I better stock up on nails. Don't want to run out." And off Ethel bustled toward the supply shed.

As Florence and June approached, Alice saw Florence frowning as she watched Ethel leave.

Alice had gently prodded Ethel this morning about her tiff with Florence, but couldn't get much out of her aunt. She wasn't quite sure how to deal with this situation. Usually Ethel or Florence would have discovered some vital and fascinating piece of gossip to pass on by now and would have been chatting away like magpies.

"Good morning, Alice," June said as she slipped on her hard hat.

"Good to see you, June. I imagine we'll get started pretty

soon." Alice stretched her arms over her head, trying to work the kinks out and as she did, she caught sight of Cordy walking gingerly up the gangplank to the foundation of the house.

She gave Alice a forlorn look as she came nearer. "I hurt all over," she said.

"So do I. I'm really glad you made it this morning."

"I didn't want to come, but my mom told me I could just sleep . . ." She gave Alice a sheepish look. "Then I thought of you ladies coming here, and I figured I better get myself out of bed and get over here. Besides, I had fun yesterday."

"I'm glad to hear that."

As Ethel joined them, Cordy looked around. "Jasmine here yet?"

"Not yet."

Cordy's shoulders straightened. "Cool. I beat her here."

"Very cool," Ethel agreed, putting her arm around her young co-worker. "And once she comes she'll be proud to see you working again."

Cordy sighed. "I hope so. She's been on my case more and more lately. I don't like it that she's mad at me."

"I'm sure your showing up here every day will help," Ethel said, her voice growing soft. She looked down, fidgeting with the pocket of her carpenter's apron.

Alice was about to ask her what was wrong when Cal approached and started giving out instructions.

"So ladies. We're short of workers today," he said, glancing around the gathered group. "I thought today you could all work together. Alice, Ethel and Cordy, you can help these other women out. You'll be doing the same thing today as you did yesterday, only on a larger section, so there'll be enough room for all of you."

He pointed with his hammer to where the men were working. "We guys need to put up another wall, and there's too much bracing in the way for you to work on the floor of the house. Just ask Del what you need to do. He'll get you all started."

He gave them a quick nod and left.

"Aunt Ethel, can you and Cordy show Florence what to do?" Alice asked.

Alice left, not taking the time to see Ethel's reaction. She thought Cordy's presence could act as a buffer in case Ethel and Florence were still maintaining their campaigns of silence.

How long could they hold out?

"So, Cordy, are you ready to work through the pain?" Alice asked, turning her attention to the girl.

Cordy rolled her shoulder and grimaced. "This morning it hurt even to roll over in bed."

Alice laughed. "I know how you feel."

"Yeah, but you're old . . ." Cordy flashed her a contrite smile. "Sorry, I didn't mean like you were ancient or anything like that. Just, well . . ."

"I'm a lot older than you," Alice offered, flashing Cordy a smile to show her that she wasn't insulted at all.

Alice peeked over her shoulder and saw Ethel and Florence trailing behind, each making a point of looking in the opposite direction.

This tiff had to come to an end, Alice thought. Ethel couldn't explain the work in sign language.

Cordy moaned as she lifted a box of nails.

"When you use muscles you normally don't use, a person gets stiff. That's just the way the body works. As a nurse, though, I can assure you that once you get working, you'll work out the stiffness."

"I didn't know you were a nurse," Cordy said as she, June and Alice walked over to where Del was waiting.

"Alice works in the hospital in Potterston," June offered.

"Do you like the work?" Cordy asked. "I used to want to be a nurse, but Jasmine said I needed to be smart to do that."

"What are your marks like?"

"They're okay." Cordy said with a shrug.

"What grade are you going into?" June asked.

"Eleven. But I have to redo some of my courses." Cordy flashed June an embarrassed grin. "The cutting thing is catching up on me."

"Then it sounds like you'll have time to make that up," Alice said.

"I'm trying to turn the corner. But it's hard to break bad habits."

Alice patted her on the shoulder. "It's even harder to get up in the morning and help your sister build her house, but here you are."

"Yeah. I should get my own alarm clock. My mother never wakes me up on time. Jas says I shouldn't lay the blame on Mom." Cordy sighed. "And my friends don't always show up at school. And when they do, they're always trying to talk me into leaving early with them."

"Maybe you need to find people who can be a good example for you."

"I know." Cordy shot her a discomfited look. "Not so easy."

Alice wanted to say more, but Del was waving at them to join the other people already gathered around him.

Del was a squat man and his stomach strained against his soiled T-shirt. "So, you ladies know what to do?" he asked, hitching up his pants.

"Cal told us we would be doing the same thing we did yesterday, so I think we'll be okay," Alice said.

"Good. Have at 'er." He dropped his hammer into his pouch and stalked away, as if he couldn't be bothered to spend much more time with them.

"What a rude man," Florence said while he was still in earshot.

Del glanced over his shoulder, his scowl easily visible.

"Okay. Let's get started," Alice said, preferring to let the exchange pass. "What we have here is, as Cal explained, a wall section—"

"An inside wall?" Florence asked.

"No. We are first putting up the outside walls."

"How odd. There are absolutely no windows on this wall," Florence proclaimed.

Alice waited for Ethel to explain the situation, but her aunt said nothing. "We first tack down the wood, then Aunt Ethel will cut out the windows with a router."

"What in the world is a router?" Florence directed her question to Alice.

Again Alice waited for Ethel to explain, but realized the longer her aunt kept quiet, the ruder she looked. "It's like a small saw with a bit that spins around to do the cutting. You'll see, once we get that far. For now we need to nail down the studs behind the particleboard. Space your nails about a hand's width apart."

"That would be Alice's hand width, not mine." Cordy held her hand up and grinned.

"I believe I can do this," Florence said with a tinge of hauteur in her voice.

Alice knelt gingerly on the wall section, muscles in her thighs, calves and back protesting. In spite of her reassurances to Cordy, she wondered herself if she was going to be able to work all day.

Once she started pounding the nails in, however, the stiffness eased off.

"Is your sister coming today, Cordy?" Ethel asked as they started nailing.

"I don't know. The kids might be sick."

Alice watched Cordy working and was pleasantly surprised to see how much more accurate she was with her hammering today than she had been the day before.

"What is your sister's name?" Florence asked.

"Jasmine. Mom got the name off some television show,"

she said. "I'm named after a character she read in a book. My real name is Cordelia."

"That's a lovely name." Florence knelt down and glanced over at Alice as if to see what she was doing.

Alice pressed her lips together, suddenly frustrated with her aunt. Florence seemed to be trying in her own way, but Ethel wasn't responding at all.

"You don't know how to put the nails in?" Cordy asked Florence.

"Actually, I've never done much manual labor," Florence said. "When I signed up I saw myself as more of a consultant. My specialty is decorating. I like to change the décor of my house every year. I thought I could help your sister in that department. But today I thought maybe I would try the basic work."

"It's not rocket science," Cordy said with a light chuckle. "I can show you what to do."

Alice was pleased that Cordy took the initiative, but of course that wasn't her plan when she had put Ethel and Florence to work together.

Cordy walked over to Florence's side and showed her how to set the nails and how to avoid bending them.

"I did a bunch of that yesterday, but I soon got the hang of it."

Ethel was hammering away like an old pro. Almost showing off, Alice thought. If she wasn't careful she was going to hit her finger.

Florence started working, but Alice saw her struggling. "Is there a trick to this?" she asked.

"Nails go pointy side down, you hit the flat top with the hammer," June offered with a laugh.

But Florence was looking at Ethel as she spoke.

Ethel kept working and didn't look up.

Alice stifled a sigh and started nailing. She was here to

help build a house, not build bridges between Ethel and Florence. They would have to figure out their problems by themselves.

For the next fifteen minutes the only sound was the ringing of hammers hitting nails. Alice was pleased to discover how much easier the work was today. She didn't take nearly as long to pound a nail in, and she hardly ever missed.

"You sure you know what you're doing?" Del stood above them, a dark shadow against the sky.

Alice glanced up, squinting into the sun, but Del was addressing Florence.

"You're supposed to follow the red chalk line, lady," he said, his tone disrespectful as he pointed with one stubby finger. "Don't you know that?"

"I wasn't told . . ."

Alice felt a flash of guilt. She should have explained things to Florence herself and not left it up to Ethel—or Cordy.

"It shouldn't be that hard," Del continued.

"I understand but . . ."

"Here. Let me show you." Del pulled the hammer out of Florence's hands and pounded the nail in with a few swift blows. "That's how we do it here."

"I know how to use the hammer," Florence protested.

Del pointed the toe of his grease-stained work boot at a bent nail. "Doesn't look like it. You maybe should try somethin' else."

At that Ethel looked up, frowning at him.

"Somethin' I can help you with, sister?" Del asked.

"I am not your sister, mister. And don't you talk to me or my friend like we're simpletons. You show some respect."

Del stood with his hands on his hips as if he was about to challenge Ethel.

"You might want to watch yourself," Florence put in. "My friend can take quite good care of herself."

Ethel's lips twitched a bit, and Alice took that as a good sign. That and the fact the two women referred to each other as "friend."

"Just trying to help, is all," Del said, holding up his hands as if warding off the two women.

"You are not much help," Ethel said. "I think we can manage on our own. And if we can't, Cal can help us out."

"Suit yourself, you two." And Del stormed away, his hammer swinging at his side.

"I hope that nasty man stays away from us," Ethel said. "I can't believe how rude he was."

"I'm sure I could have taken him," Florence remarked.

"The two of us certainly could." Ethel gave Florence a cautious smile.

Florence held her gaze, then, finally, returned the smile.

Alice relaxed, pleased that these two were speaking again. She did find it interesting that it took someone else's berating Florence for Ethel to stick up for her friend.

Chapter ⊤ Eleven

J ane glanced over her list as she walked down the street to Sylvia Songer's shop. Louise had been willing to take care of the groceries, leaving Jane free to plan for the dinner.

Decorations.

She needed Sylvia's advice on this.

Dishes.

Though Stacy, in one of her many calls, had talked about the possibility of renting dishes, Jane thought she could use her mother's lovely Wedgwood set.

She stopped in front of the Good Apple Bakery and glanced across Hill Street to Craig Tracy's flower shop, Wild Things. He might have some ideas about what to use for the dinner.

She crossed the street and stepped inside the shop, the scent of multitudes of flowers mixed with damp, fresh earth greeting her. A new shipment of houseplants must have arrived.

"Be right with you," she heard Craig call out from the back.

While she waited, Jane wandered around, checking out the new plants. She should get some for the inn, she thought. Some of their other plants were getting root-bound.

"Hello, Jane. Haven't seen you around for a while." Craig came through the door at the rear of the shop, wiping his hands on a small towel, his smile bright and welcoming. The apron he wore over his trim frame had a comical picture of a cartoon flower leaning over to look at itself in a puddle of water.

"I've been busy. Guests in every room of the inn, vacuum cleaners dying, a frantic catering customer and a dinner party to be put on by the hostess with the mostest."

"Ah, the ins and outs of inns."

Jane acknowledged his joke with a groan.

"Lame humor aside, what can I do for you, Jane?"

"For said dinner party, I would like to add a few plants or flowers to the décor. Not too pretty, not too plain, not too . . ." Jane caught herself. Goodness, she was starting to sound like Stacy herself.

"And the theme is . . . ?"

"Food."

Craig gave her a droll look. "Innovative." He put heavy emphasis on the first syllable.

"Please don't make me hurt you," she said, her grin belying the hidden threat in her words.

"So. Plants." Craig rubbed his hands together as if in anticipation of a new challenge. "Tall? Short? Foliage? Joking aside, a theme would help tremendously."

Jane wrinkled her nose. Stacy had provided her with a generous budget, but left the planning on her shoulders. "I'm going over to Sylvia's after this to see what she can help me come up with."

"What type of group are you going to be hosting?"

"The group is part of a Chamber of Commerce twinning program. These women come from towns paired with Potterston. They're coming from Japan, Canada, the Netherlands and New Zealand."

"That's an interesting mix of people," Craig mused, glancing around his shop. "When are they coming?"

"Saturday evening."

Craig whipped his head around. "As in *this* Saturday evening?"

"One and the same."

"That's cutting things very, very close," Craig said.

"Tell me about it. I keep having to change the menu because every time I plan something, my client lets me know about shellfish warnings and obscure allergies and her aversion to pasta."

"We could go with some tall plants in one corner, though if allergies are a consideration we could go with silk . . ."

"As far as I know, no plant allergies," Jane said. "I would prefer real plants."

"I agree. Besides, real plants cleanse the air," Craig said taking an exaggerated sniff. He dug into his apron pocket and pulled out a stub of a pencil and a piece of paper. "Let's make a potential plan," he said.

Twenty minutes later the plan was committed to paper, and Jane was happy with Craig's suggestions. Simple, elegant and not too tropical. They went with small topiaries on the sideboard and down the table with one large one repeating the theme in one corner of the room. Also a possible flower arrangement of lilies and ferns to provide some brightening.

"Thanks so much, Craig," Jane said, tucking her version of the plan into her pocket. "This is a good place to start . . ."

The electronic door chime sounded, and Jane turned in time to see Matthew and Pete scurry into the store, glancing behind them as they entered.

"Oh, hey, Ms. J," Matthew said, tossing off a quick salute as he ducked behind a plant, craning his neck to look down the street. "Has Herbie been here yet?"

"I haven't seen him, but ask Craig. He might know."

Matthew gave another quick glance out the window and moved closer to the counter. "He gave me and Pete totally wrong advice. Messed up our stellar record. I'm trying to get even with him, but don't know how."

"How are you making out with the game?" Jane asked, not sure she should hear about any scheming he and Pete might be indulging in.

"Like I said, we got sidetracked. But we're getting close." Matthew tucked a pen behind his ear and pulled out a sheaf of papers he had rolled up and stuffed in the back pocket of his baggy jeans. "So according to this, we're supposed to talk to Mr. Tracy." Matthew glanced up from his notes, "I'm guessing that would be you," he said to Craig.

"Would be," Craig agreed.

Matthew sighed as he tapped his pen on the paper. "I gotta tell you, Carita has some weird idea going of a scavenger hunt. I thought we'd like be picking up stuff. You know?"

"Maybe she's trying to get you to expand your minds," Jane said.

Pete looked up, frowning. "Can't do that. My hats won't fit then."

Jane laughed. "I'm sure you'll do just fine, and I better get going," Jane said, slipping past the boys. "Thanks for your help, Craig."

"No problem, Jane. I'll be by with the plants and the arrangements on Saturday."

As Jane left, Matthew and Pete were peppering Craig with questions, and Jane had to smile. Carita had been absolutely correct. These boys did truly seem to be enjoying themselves doing something as innocent as a scavenger hunt. She was glad they had taken the time to put it together.

From the sound of Carita's plans, the group would be busy most of Friday. Then there would be the football game and come Saturday they would be gone all day. Then Jane would have the afternoon to prepare for the dinner, do the dinner and then collapse. But next would come Sunday morning, a time of rest. First thing, the kids would leave. And then a reprieve until Wednesday when the next guests arrived.

When Jane entered Sylvia's shop, her friend looked up from the bolts of cloth she had laid out on a large cutting table for the perusal of a couple of customers. Alongside the bolts was a vast array of squares for quilting, also in a rainbow of colors.

Today Sylvia wore a plain, white T-shirt with a cropped jacket in a unique material. Jane guessed Sylvia had been doing some fabric painting to achieve the watery effect on the surface of the jacket.

Very cute and very stylish.

"Be right with you, Jane," Sylvia said, glancing at her friend over her reading glasses, her reddish-blond hair swinging away from her face.

"No worries," Jane said.

Jane recognized the women gazing at the material as members of the local quilters guild. They fingered the delicately patterned fabric, frowned over some choices, aahed over others and in general looked like they were thoroughly enjoying themselves.

While they debated fabric quality and color, listening intently to Sylvia's suggestions, Jane ambled through the store, checking out the newest quilt that Sylvia had completed. She had hung it up for display alongside a couple of Amish quilts she had picked up the last time she had gone to Lancaster.

Jane didn't sew quilts, but as an artist she could appreciate the way Sylvia had arranged the material to set off colors and patterns creating a harmonious grouping. As Jane let the symphony of colors wash over her, she had a momentary urge to take up quilting.

Too many projects, too little time, she thought with a wistful glance at the intricate work of the quilts. Life was too short to do all the things she would like to try.

Sylvia chatted with her customers as she cut and folded, discovering what they were working on and, in the process, finding out about their children and grandchildren.

She had that knack, Jane thought. Though in many social circumstances Sylvia could be somewhat shy and diffident, here in her shop she shone.

The women left, awash in smiles and good humor, their shopping bags rustling.

"And there go two completely satisfied customers," Jane said, as the door closed behind them.

"I love it when a customer knows what she is talking about, yet is willing to take some advice," Sylvia said, rolling up the rest of the fabric on the bolts. "These ladies are avid quilters, so that's great." While she chatted, she hustled from shelf to table, putting back material, sorting out the samples into neat piles and arranging them once again in the boxes they had come from.

When she was done, she picked up her tape measure and slung it back around her neck. "I feel like I haven't seen you in ages," she said,

"I stopped by the other day," Jane protested.

"I know. I'm just trying to tease you," Sylvia said, leaning on the fabric table. "So how is the scavenger hunt going? That's today, isn't it?"

"No one has been by here yet?"

Sylvia shook her head. "Not yet. What clue did you end up giving them?"

"They were supposed to figure out that they had to come here from reading the words of a song that Carita had scrambled up."

Sylvia frowned. "What song would that be?"

"'Needles and Pins.'" Jane said.

"Of course."

"Can you spare some time?" Jane inquired. "Remember I asked if you would be willing to help me do some decorating for this dinner?"

"I'm all yours."

"I was just at Craig's. We are going with small topiaries down the table, rather than more formal centerpieces, the same topiaries on the buffet and one large one as a corner display."

Sylvia thought for a moment, her eyes flitting around her shop, as if looking for inspiration in the myriad colors and textures surrounding her.

"I think you will want to keep things reasonably simple. You only want to create atmosphere for your dinner, not overwhelm it."

Jane and Sylvia discussed a few options, working in the flowers that Craig was supplying and the larger purpose of the dinner.

In the end they decided to go with an eclectic theme. The tablecloth would be a rich brown, set off with a gold linen runner. Sylvia had a variety of napkin rings she had collected over time, some in china, some bamboo, some in wood and some made from brushed metal as well as napkins made from different, patterned fabrics. Each place setting would be unique, but the dishes would tie everything together as would the place cards decorated with stamps from various countries.

As they talked and planned, Jane could visualize the setting and grew more excited about the evening.

"What are you going to serve?" Sylvia asked.

And Jane's excitement became edged with a hint of panic. "Every time I think I have a sure-fire, can't-miss menu Stacy calls and moves the target. So for now, I have three desserts picked out, a salad and possibly a soup or two. But for the main course, to tell you the truth, I'm stumped."

Sylvia frowned. "This isn't like you, Jane."

"I know, I know." Jane pressed the palms of her hands against the side of her head as if restraining her racing thoughts. "I am trying not to feel the pressure. I wish she wasn't paying me so much money. If this were just a simple catered dinner, I would feel far more comfortable. As it is, I feel like I'm not just serving a dinner. I'm putting on a production."

Sylvia patted Jane's arm. "Don't put too much stress on yourself. This woman obviously wanted you badly enough. You'll do a fine job. Just go with your instincts."

"I've been trying to, but she wants a dinner that isn't too 'out there' or too plain, or too simple. No fish, no potatoes, no hamburger—as if I would—and easy on the onions." Jane shook her head. "I can handle all of that, but she phones me constantly."

"I imagine having so many guests at the inn doesn't help."

Jane smiled. "They're not difficult to have around . . ."

"Finish that sentence, my friend," Sylvia said.

"Well, they do tend to take over the place," Jane conceded.

"I suppose they can be very boisterous."

"Emphasis on very," Jane agreed. "Oh well, tomorrow they have their pep rally, and they'll have lots to keep them busy on Saturday."

"Giving you time to concentrate on your dinner."

"Precisely. And I thank you for your help. At least the inn will look warm and welcoming."

"You'll do fine. I'll come by Saturday morning to help you get things ready."

"That would be lovely," Jane said. She glanced at her watch and gathered her lists. "I better run. Alice will be tired when she comes home, and Louise has a couple of extra piano students today, so I want to provide them with a meal that will replenish their strength."

"Their vigor will be completely restored, I'm sure."

With her friend's assurances ringing in her ears, Jane left.

By the time she got back to the inn, she was ready to sit for a few moments before she had to work on supper.

She paused at the garden, mentally choosing which vegetables she could use for Stacy's dinner. String beans with fresh herbs? Too provincial. Carrots. Glazed and honeyed. She could make something with her own tomatoes, cucumbers and lettuce, but that sounded too plain too.

She knelt to pull a weed, found another and yanked it out, then tossed it aside. As she picked, she felt her fluttering nerves relax. A hymn came to mind, and as she entered the inn a short time later, the song was on her lips. She set her list on the kitchen table and became aware of the sound of voices coming down the hallway from the living room.

"I'm just saying this seems pointless." Lynden seemed agitated.

"It's just fun, Lynden. Nothing more," Carita was saying. "We're all going to be diving back into our studies in a couple of weeks. Surely some time off is appropriate."

"And that's the problem. Our whole lives are centered on fun and entertainment. We don't even take school seriously."

Jane felt sorry for Carita. She knew the girl cared for Lynden, and it sounded like they were having a fight.

Jane wondered if she shouldn't leave. But just as she was about to retreat, the voices came closer, toward the kitchen.

"You didn't used to take school seriously," Rick said. "And you didn't even go this year. What's the big deal now?"

"Maybe I've seen what a waste my life has been," Lynden was saying. "Maybe I want something different."

And suddenly they were in the kitchen with her.

Lynden was the first one in, and he stopped short when he saw Jane, Carita almost running into him.

"Sorry, Ms. Howard. I didn't know you were here,"

Lynden said, pushing his hands into the pockets of his leather jacket.

"Sorry, I . . . uh . . . was just going."

"This is your place," Carita said, brushing past Lynden, Rick in her wake. "We're the ones who should feel bad."

"Would you like something to drink? Some soda? Tea?" Jane felt a little awkward in the situation, but Rick seemed completely at ease as he dropped his lanky frame into a kitchen chair.

However, Jane was the hostess and they were her guests. She had to do what she could to make them feel comfortable.

"Thanks, Ms. J. I'll have a soda," Rick said.

"Rick, for goodness' sakes, Ms. Howard isn't here to serve us hand and foot," Lynden said, frowning at his friend.

Rick held his tattooed hand up in a gesture of surrender. "She offered."

"Yes, but . . ."

"I wouldn't offer if I didn't mean it," Jane assured him. "Now, please sit down while I get you something to eat and drink."

Carita held back a moment, then finally walked over to the table and sat down, her arms crossed tightly over her chest.

Jane thought of the conversation she and Carita had enjoyed, when Carita had said how much she liked Lynden. Well, it seemed the romance was not prospering. They sat as far away from each other as they could, not making eye contact.

Rick tapped out a rhythm on the table, bobbing his head in time to a tune only he seemed to hear, oblivious to the waves of animosity swirling around him.

"So, Rick and Lynden, you guys must have finished quickly?" Jane said, trying to make small talk as she pulled out the cinnamon buns she had planned on serving tomorrow for breakfast.

"Can I help you?" Carita asked.

"Could you put out the soda and glasses please," Jane asked.

Carita set everything on the table, then sat down, folding her arms over her chest once again, looking put out.

Rick shrugged as he poured his soda. "Lynden quit. Said it was lame. I thought it was fun. But he's my partner so I go where he goes. He quits, I quit."

"Oh, that's too bad."

"I thought so too," Carita said, shooting Lynden an angry glance. "The hunt was supposed to be for fun."

"And like I said, I think we look for too much fun," Lynden returned quietly. "I'm sorry, Carita. I don't want to be a poor sport."

"I couldn't help overhearing what you were discussing earlier," Jane said, realizing she may as well be up front about what she had heard. "I'm just curious about what you mean, Lynden?"

He pulled in a deep breath, as if trying to decide what to say. "This whole trip was a good idea, that's true enough, and I really appreciate what Carita is doing . . ."

That should make Carita feel somewhat better, Jane thought.

"But the past few days I've been thinking—"

"Always a dangerous proposition," Rick said with a grin as he lifted his glass.

"—and it seems there's no point to what we're doing with our time. We spend money on ourselves, we buy all the newest toys—"

"Like that sweet unit parked outside?" Rick asked with a faint note of cynicism. "What did that set you back?"

"The truck was a gift from my grandmother. But don't kid yourself that it hasn't been on my mind. I feel like I've been wasting my life. Like all I've been doing is trying to find some meaning, some purpose to why I'm here." He shrugged and shot a pained look Jane's way. "I don't know anymore."

"So this is really about you, then," Carita said, relief edging her voice.

"Yeah. I guess."

"And your grandmother?" Carita continued.

Lynden took a can of soda and ran his finger down the side, making a line in the condensation. "She had such high hopes for me. Such big plans. Then when she died, she left me all that money, left me her house. And I guess I went overboard. I went out every night and blew money. When you phoned me about this trip, I thought it was a great idea." He gave a short laugh. "Except for the place you wanted to stay and all. I was all for going to a motel. I wanted to party."

"Instead you ended up here with a bunch of old women," Jane said with a light laugh to show him she was joking.

"Not proud of that comment, either," Lynden said, lifting his gaze to meet hers.

Jane's smile granted him absolution as she brought the plate of cinnamon buns, some extra plates and knives to the table, then decided while she was there, she could start working on the desserts for the dinner.

"So what made you change, dude?" Rick asked, absently scratching the back of his tattooed hand.

"The music Mrs. Smith played," Lynden said quietly. "My grandmother used to play the piano too. Same songs. As soon as I heard them, they came back. Words and everything. And it was like looking at myself through my granny's eyes. I didn't like what I saw." He fell quiet, his focus on the can of soda in front of him.

"And now?" Jane asked after a few moments of silence.

"I don't know what I want. I feel like I'm just marking time."

"That's why you thought this whole scavenger hunt was a waste of time?" Carita asked.

Lynden shot her a pained expression. "I'm sorry. It's just, I feel frustrated. That's why I couldn't finish."

"What was the prize?" Rick asked. "I mean, if there was a really cool prize attached, I could get seriously ticked about missing out."

"Just some tickets to a movie," Carita said. "More entertainment."

"What were you thinking of going to college for, Lynden?" Jane asked, directing the conversation back to the young man's problem. While she asked, she measured out the ingredients for one of the desserts for Saturday, Nanaimo bars, trying to juggle making conversation and concentrating on her recipe.

"See, that's the problem. I've just registered for some general courses. Just filling time."

"Do you know what you would like to do?"

"Not a clue."

"Not knowing makes making a decision more difficult," Jane agreed. "I wish I could give you some solid advice, but I know I wasted a few classes myself in my time. Like you, I'm not proud of that either."

"But you do good work here," Lynden said. "You and your sisters. I read what you had put on that plaque in the front."

"'A place where one can be refreshed and encouraged, a place of hope and healing, a place where God is at home.'" Jane smiled as she repeated the motto. "My sisters and I strive to live up to that every time guests come here. When I was your age, however, running an inn was hardly in my long-term plan. There was a time that all I wanted was to make a big success out of my life. To be famous for my cooking."

"What happened?" Rick asked.

"Life. Disappointments. I returned here feeling a bit bitter and disillusioned. But God granted me healing through my sisters and through my community and my church, and I thank Him every day that He brought me back here to find my purpose."

Silence greeted this comment, and Jane wondered if maybe she had come across too strong. But the faint smile hovering at the corner of Lynden's mouth made her realize she might have said exactly the right thing.

"That's your church next door?" Lynden asked.

"Yes. My late father preached there. He taught me a lot."

"Your dad preached too?"

Jane nodded.

"I went to church all the time when my dad was preaching," Lynden said, a surprising note of wistfulness in his voice. "After he and Mom died, my granny used to take me till she was too ill. Then I quit going too."

"We could go to church here instead of leaving first thing Sunday morning," Carita suggested. "Isabel didn't want to leave so early anyway."

"Could." Lynden just looked thoughtful.

"And Saturday? We're still going to the reunion?"

"I don't know," Lynden said.

"I'd just as soon not do it," Rick said, brushing the crumbs off his hand.

"Are you guys kidding me?" Carita asked. "The reunion was the main reason we came out here."

Jane kept the smile on her face even as her heart plunged as plans were changed on the fly. But what could she say? These young people were their guests and if they wanted to change their plans, she couldn't really say much.

But she also had the dinner for Stacy on Saturday night. How could she juggle the two? She simply had to find a way to make sure they were out Saturday evening.

"Hey, ho, we're the winners." Pete and Matthew's voices rang out as the front door slammed shut behind them. "We get the prize . . ."

But their voices faded away as they entered the kitchen and saw Lynden, Carita and Rick sitting at the table.

"Or not," Matthew said, scratching his head. "How did you guys get ahead of us?"

"They didn't finish," Carita said with a heavy sigh.

"Well, we are the winners then, cause we snuck past Herbie and Isabel still trying to figure out the menu at the Good Apple." Matthew exchanged high fives with Rick. "Number one, mister." He turned to Jane. "What are you working on?"

Jane glanced down at the chocolate mixture she was pressing into the pan. "Something called Nanaimo bars. They're for the dinner I'm having here tomorrow night," she added, just in case he might think they were going to be the recipients.

"Too bad," he said with a sigh. "But I'm sure we can find something else. There's always lots of food at Grace Chapel Inn," he said flashing a winning smile at Jane.

Chapter Twelve

Louise checked over the list of groceries and other items that Jane had asked her to pick up after her course, double-checking to make sure she had purchased everything.

Some of the items seemed rather exotic, but Jane knew what she was doing. The rest of the list was straightforward, though Louise hoped that the containers of milk and the yogurt she had purchased were meant for their young guests. There was no way she and her sisters could gulp their way through that ocean of dairy produce.

She had originally planned on walking to the auto course and taking their pull-along grocery cart, but when Jane handed her the list, Louise did a double take and took her Cadillac instead.

She and Viola had been pleased with what they learned in the course, but Louise was less than optimistic about tomorrow. They were supposed to be learning about the care and feeding of windshield wipers. Viola had talked about not attending, but Louise was growing more dedicated. She was determined to learn something useful, one way or the other.

They were slated to do some actual driving on Monday with an instructor beside them to give them pointers and tell them what they might be doing wrong. Louise felt somewhat nervous about that, but at the same time, it was what she had signed up for.

Satisfied she had everything on the list, she got in her car and drove back to the inn. She would have time to help Jane before she had to go to the church to go over the songs she had chosen for Sunday's service.

As Louise gathered what bags she could and carried them to the house, she looked forward to a few moments of quiet with Jane. It seemed that since the college students had arrived, she and her sisters hadn't had much time to sit and go over the events of the day together.

When she set the grocery bags down on the floor of the porch to open the kitchen door, instead of silence she heard people talking. Lynden, Rick and Carita she figured, recognizing the various voices.

Louise stifled a sigh as she opened the door and carried rustling plastic bags into the kitchen. No sooner did she set the bags on the counter, then Lynden jumped up from the table where he sat with Carita and Rick.

"Would you like us to help, Mrs. Smith?" he asked.

Louise was about to say no when she caught Jane's pained look, and right behind her sister she spotted a pan of some dark substance on a cooling rack, probably the same something that was filling the air with a burnt smell.

Though it went against her concept of hospitality to have her guests do any chore, however small, she guessed Jane wanted a few moments alone with her.

"Thank you, Lynden," Louise said. "There are more bags in my car. Maybe the others could help too."

"Sure. Of course." Carita called out to Matthew to come and help, and Rick followed Lynden outside. As the door closed behind them, Louise hurried to her sister's side.

"What is the matter, Jane?"

Jane cast a quick look past Louise as if to make sure the

kids were out of earshot. "They're changing their plans constantly," she whispered, panic edging her voice. "Sounds like
they might not be gone all day Saturday . . ." Jane's dejected
expression clearly showed her turmoil.

"And you have a dinner to prepare, and they've been
hanging around the kitchen all afternoon."

"I was going to make Nanaimo bars, especially for the
Canadian women, but I burnt them."

"That's understandable," Louise said, consoling her sister. "Easy enough to do." Louise had burned enough things
in her life to allow her to envision how that could happen.

"But they're a no-bake bar." Jane bit her lip, looking
distraught. "I can't concentrate. I keep losing track of ingredients. I keep forgetting where I am in the recipe."

"You're under stress, Jane." Louise shook her head. "You
never should have—"

Jane held up one finger. "No. You're not going to say it."

"All right, then I'll say this. We can all help on Saturday,
Jane. Maybe find a way to keep the kids busy in case they
change their plans."

But Jane's skeptical look showed Louise how much confidence she had in that course of action.

"Here you go," Matthew led the troupe, all of them
carrying bags. "Do you want us to put this stuff away?"

"No. I can take care of the rest."

"Maybe it's time to try to find Isabel and Herbie?" Jane
suggested with a hopeful note in her voice.

"Yeah. Sounds like a plan. Tell the losers they can quit
now," Matthew said with a grin.

As they left, Jane settled back against the counter, rubbing
her forehead. "I'm trying not to get flustered. Sometimes I
wish I had been firmer in setting boundaries, but we always
wanted the inn to be a place of refuge and peace. I've always
hoped I could model the Lord to our guests."

"And you have," Louise assured her. "These kids love

being in the kitchen because they feel at home, and they feel welcome here. As for the dinner, it will all work out. I think you need to relax, trust your own instincts."

Jane gave her sister a smile. "Thanks for the pep talk, Louise. You're right. I've faced bigger problems when I was at the Blue Fish Grille in San Francisco. I can do this."

"Of course you can." Louise's gaze slipped past Jane to the clock on the wall. "I better go. I need to go over my songs for Sunday."

"And I need to try once again to make these Nanaimo bars," Jane said as she started unpacking the groceries. "At least Stacy and I have that part of the menu figured out."

"What are you having?" Louise couldn't help asking.

"It's quite innovative, really. Kumara soup from New Zealand and miso soup from Japan for starters, followed by a spinach and strawberry salad. Dessert will be Nanaimo bars invented in Nanaimo, British Columbia, something called stroop waffles or treacle cookies from Holland and apple galette, which is more French than anything, but I figured it didn't hurt to try to be as cosmopolitan as I can."

"And the entrée?"

Jane shrugged. "I haven't come up with anything that strikes any chord with Stacy. Though I'm leaning toward something Asian and, well, adjustable on the fly. Hence the special groceries on your list."

"I think you might be trying too hard to please this woman," Louise said.

"She's paying me such a large sum of money to do this, I feel like I have to give her as much say as possible."

"Still, if you are going to get this dinner under control, you'll just have to trust your own instincts and maybe even be a bit firmer with her."

While Louise spoke the telephone rang. Jane picked it up, said hello and when she winced, Louise knew who was calling.

Louise gathered her music from the parlor and exited out the front door. She wished she could help Jane. She was no cook, but she could pray. So as she walked to the chapel, she sent up a prayer for patience and forbearance for her sister.

And later, in the church, while her fingers drew songs of praise and thanksgiving from the keys of the pipe organ, she wove additional prayers for her sister through the songs.

"Are you sure you're not too tired?" Ethel asked as she and Alice made their way back to Alice's car.

"Actually, I'm feeling pretty good." Alice glanced back at the worksite, pleased to see what they had accomplished. Three exterior walls were up and braced. One of those walls was one she, Ethel and Cordy had worked on yesterday.

Ethel yawned as she slipped into the car. "Too bad we had to quit early today," she said. "I would like to have seen those men put up another wall."

"And it sounds like they won't be back tomorrow," Alice said as she started the car. "I know Jasmine was disappointed to hear that."

Jasmine had come by the worksite later in the day. She had been inordinately pleased to see her little sister there, and Alice was glad Jasmine took the time to tell Cordy so.

Cordy beamed the rest of the day.

"I wonder if it's worth coming tomorrow if it's only going to be us women and Cal," Ethel said. "Florence may not be able to make it either."

"Speaking of Florence, I was glad to see the two of you make up."

Ethel nodded, looking rather discomfited.

"If I may play the part of a nosy niece, what was your disagreement about?" Alice turned onto the highway, settling into an easy speed. They had some distance until Acorn Hill and therefore had time to chat. She tuned the radio to a classical station for a comfortable ambiance, but kept the volume low.

"I feel foolish about our spat now," Ethel said, crossing her arms. "You know the saying, there's no fool like an old fool. Well, that sums me up just dandy. However, I wasn't the only one at fault. Florence didn't make things much easier. As I said before, she can be very opinionated. And very stubborn." Ethel stopped there and looked out her window.

The green hills slipped past them as Alice drove toward home. She waited, sensing that while Ethel wanted to talk about the problem, she also had her pride. The confession would have to come on her own time.

A mile later, Ethel sighed, took a breath and turned to Alice.

"Do you remember the day I brought you the vacuum cleaner? The day yours quit?"

Alice nodded.

"Florence had invited me to her place that morning. I thought we were going to have a cup of tea and chat about, well, things. I wanted to ask her opinion of a tie I was planning to buy Lloyd. And I had just found out that Nia had told Carlene that she had heard Patsy Ley saying that when she was in the Good Apple Bakery, Clarissa had told her that Betsy Long had gone on a date. With a man in Potterston. So naturally I thought Florence might have some more information because she had told me, when she got her hair done at the Clip 'n' Curl, that Rose Bellwood had said Ned Arnold had been in Potterston that same evening at the same place."

Alice tried to follow Ethel but got lost in the Good Apple Bakery and was content to let her aunt meander along. Alice would catch up sooner or later.

"But when I got to Florence's ready to have a good chat, she told me she wanted me to help her carry some things up to her attic. Now Florence is a good friend and all, but I thought making someone my age tote stuff was taking advantage of our friendship, and I told her so. I understand that maybe she can't always get people to help her. She's hired women from time to time to help her clean her house, but I suspect that they just get tired of Florence's sharp tongue, and I don't blame them. Florence sometimes lets her mouth run off on her, and you can try to tell her and tell her, but she won't listen."

"I understand the feeling," Alice said.

"Oh, you don't know Florence like I do," Ethel said, wagging her finger for emphasis. "Anyhow, I told her that my arthritis was acting up and that I didn't think it was right to take advantage of our friendship."

"And that was what the fight was about?" Alice said, underlining the point.

"Not really a fight. More of a disagreement."

"But you carried it on for a while."

"When she found out I was going to work on this Habitat job, she phoned and asked why I was more than able to help with this house, but wasn't able to help her with her attic. And I said some things are more important." Ethel turned to Alice. "I didn't mean for it to come out the way it did, but you know me. Sometimes what's in my head doesn't always come out in my words. Well, she took offense in a big way. I tried to make things up to her, but she wouldn't let me, and that made me mad."

And around and around it went, Alice thought, Florence ignoring Ethel, which got Ethel's back up, which made her ignore Florence. "But I was glad to see you stand up for her this afternoon," Alice said.

"When I heard that man pushing Florence around, I got angry. That's all."

"Well, your defense seemed to be just what was needed to break the tension," Alice said. "She seemed very pleased that you were willing to intervene."

"I'm glad I did. Because when we started talking again, after I grilled her all about Betsy Long and her date, I found out why she wanted me to carry stuff to her attic. Seems she had a lot of items she wanted me to have but was afraid that if she out and out gave them to me, I'd be upset." Ethel sat back and blew out a breath. "And in spite of how angry Florence can make me, I realized I probably make her angry too. Not a good thing to see yourself like that. I like to think I'm easy to be with and easy to get along with."

"And you are, Auntie," Alice assured her, laying her hand on Ethel's arm for emphasis. "It's just that you and Florence, well, you have a complicated relationship. But I'm glad that you made up. I'm sure she missed your friendship too."

"I know I missed her. But we're working together now, and that's nice."

"As you said earlier, it might not be worth going tomorrow," Alice said as she made the turn off the highway toward Acorn Hill. "I guess I could phone Cal in the morning to see."

"That would be too bad. The house is really coming along. And Cordy's shown up two days in a row now. I'm sure Jasmine will be pleased to see that kind of progress in her little sister. Wouldn't be good for her to lose the momentum."

They pulled into the inn lot, and Alice parked the car beside Louise's Cadillac.

"How long are those students going to be around?" Ethel asked as she slowly got out of the car.

"They've got their rally tomorrow, some activities planned for Saturday during the day and evening, and then they're gone first thing Sunday morning."

"That will be nice for Jane if they are busy all day Saturday," Ethel said. "She'll have time to work on her dinner."

"She has been troubled about it. I wish she hadn't taken the job, but she wanted to make sure we could add to our funds and afford to buy a new vacuum cleaner."

"Well, that's just silly. I mean, you girls are more than welcome to use my vacuum cleaner as long as you need to."

Not exactly a long-term solution, Alice thought.

"My goodness, I didn't think seven kids could generate this much noise." Ethel raised her voice as she and Alice entered the kitchen. "I thought the worksite was loud, but this is way worse."

Alice had to agree.

"Well good afternoon, Ms. A, Aunt Ethel," Matthew said, looking up from the plate of cinnamon buns he was putting together. "You fine ladies are just in time to see what kind of culinary masterpiece I've concocted today."

"He didn't make them," Herbie protested, trying to filch one as Matthew walked past him. "Ms. Jane did."

"Would you like some tea, coffee, soda?" Carita asked, setting plates out on the table. "Isabel, we'll need two more plates," she called out.

Alice looked around at the bodies draped over kitchen chairs and was surprised Jane had allowed things to get this far.

"I'd love some tea," Alice said.

"Nothing for me, thank you." Ethel stretched.

"Here. Sit down." Lynden got up from his chair, and poked Pete who jumped up from his, offering it to Ethel, then perched himself on the kitchen counter.

"You're back early," Jane said, bringing the butter dish to the table.

"We ran out of workers." Alice accepted the plate with a large cinnamon bun resting on it from Matthew.

"Don't sit on the counter, Pete," Carita said, giving him a light hit on his shoulder.

"How do you run out of workers?" Pete asked as he made a face at Carita, but slid off the counter and moved to a chair anyway.

"Not as many people came out as yesterday. The work is

strictly volunteer, so I guess that happens at times." The scent
of warm cinnamon made Alice reach for her bun.

"Are you going tomorrow?" Lynden stood beside the
table, leaning against the wall.

"I think Ethel and I will go. Cordy, the sister of the lady
who will be getting the house, is going to show up, so we'll
see what we can do with the three of us. And Cal, the supervisor. I'm pretty sure he'll be there. Maybe some more people will come, but Cal wasn't optimistic. He said Fridays are
always a bad day."

"So can anyone just come?" Lynden asked. "Don't you
need to have some experience?"

"It is helpful," Ethel said before Alice had a chance to
reply. "I had quite a bit before I went to work on this project."

Alice didn't contradict her aunt, though Ethel's misad-
venture with the tool shed hardly counted as "quite a bit" of
experience.

"I didn't have any, and I managed okay," Alice added just
so they wouldn't get the wrong impression of what was
required. "They are allowing some latitude on this project."

Lynden looked thoughtful, and Alice wondered what was
going through his mind.

"So, Carita, what's up for tomorrow?" Pete asked, licking
some icing off his fingers.

"I had planned a tour of Lancaster County."

Herbie pretended to snore loudly and Carita gave him a
quelling look.

"Well, really, Carita. I bet it's all cultural and interesting,
but kinda . . ." Matthew lifted his hands, as if he didn't know
how to finish the sentence.

"Okay, okay, I get the message," Carita said, a sharp tone
edging her voice. "Lynden was just talking about how so
much of what we do is silly—"

"I didn't mean to offend anyone," he said.

"I thought we could do something more cultural. But I

guess that was a waste of my time. And I suppose now that we're at it, Saturday's plans will get canceled too. I honestly don't know why I bother." She got up, stuffed her papers into her bag, swung it over her shoulder and stalked out of the kitchen leaving behind a quietly stunned group.

Alice had to force herself to stay in her chair and not follow the obviously distraught young woman. Her sisters often teased her about being too involved with their guests.

But when she caught a glimpse of the pitying look on Jane's face, she realized she wasn't the only one concerned about Carita.

Matthew sighed. "Okay, guys, I guess we should go on this Amish thing."

Lynden pushed himself away from the wall and left the kitchen too.

"Bit of a downer," Rick said, scratching his tattoo. "So what do we do now?"

"Well, we got the tailgate party and a flag football game tomorrow night, so that's all good," Matthew said. "So we won't have to be on that tour all day."

"As long as we're back in time for the alumni barbecue, I'm good," Herbie said.

"And what about Saturday?" Isabel asked.

"We're going, aren't we?" Herbie asked.

"We better. That was the reason we came," Pete said, yanking his hat farther down his head as if emphasizing his point.

"Well I'm hungry, so I'm going to head to that Coffee Shop place and get some food." Matthew glanced around the kitchen. "Rest of you game?"

"Food is good," Herbie said. "Once we've got food in our stomachs, we can figure more stuff out."

As they left, Alice could feel the momentary tension ease.

"That was too bad." Ethel said. "I thought those kids all got along so well."

"They usually do, which is good to see," Jane said, leaning her elbows on the counter. "I think Lynden is frustrated about something, however, and doesn't know what to do about it."

Alice remembered what Jane had said about Lynden's grandmother. "Do you suppose he's still grieving?"

"I'm sure he is," Jane replied, "But he seems at a loss about his life in general. It sounds as if he has money, but no purpose."

"Which is interesting," Alice said. "We like to think money will solve problems, when, in fact, it creates its own problems."

"But money does buy vacuum cleaners."

Alice waved her sister's comment away. "I wasn't trying to make a point at your expense, Jane."

"I know. But I am. I just hope the kids don't figure on hanging around here tomorrow if they can't agree to go on that tour."

"Why don't we take them to the site tomorrow?" Ethel asked. "That Lynden boy seemed like he might enjoy it."

Alice glanced over at her aunt. "I suppose we could. I don't know if all of them would be interested."

"Interested in what?" Louise entered the kitchen, carrying a bundle of music books.

"The kids don't have anything definite planned for tomorrow, and Aunt Ethel suggested they come to help on the Habitat site," Alice said.

"Marvelous idea," Louise said heartily. "I am positive they would enjoy that, and it would keep them busy."

"Sounds to me like you want to get rid of our guests, Louie," Jane teased.

Louise fiddled with the chain of her reading glasses. "I have three music students coming tomorrow, and I don't want them to get scared off by all those college kids hanging around. One of the students is quite shy. So, yes, I wouldn't mind if the young folks were someplace else."

"Tell you the truth, I wouldn't mind either," Jane said. Then she hastened to add, "I really like them, and they're pleasant and fun, just rather . . . overwhelming."

"Then we'll try to convince them to go," Alice said. "I've been wanting to help you in some way, Jane, and if this is how I can accomplish that, I'll do my best."

"They'll need tools," Ethel warned.

"There are more than enough hammers on site, and I'm sure there are things they can do that don't require skilled labor. I know Cordy might appreciate having more people her age working."

"So our plan is to get them helping?"

"If they're interested, yes."

"Is the project going on Saturday as well?" Jane asked, a hopeful note in her voice.

"We'll see," Alice said, though she really didn't know if she could get herself to the worksite four days in a row.

Chapter ⊤ Thirteen

As Louise opened the door into the darkened kitchen, she heard a hinge creak, but over the rest of the inn silence reigned.

She had gone out after supper to a book-club meeting at Viola's bookstore and the discussion went on for longer than usual. However, she had expected that even coming home this late, their guests would still be up and about as they usually were, laughing, joking and consuming vast amounts of food.

But the lights upstairs were out when she came home, and the only sounds permeating the silence was the low hum of the refrigerator and the muffled sound of Wendell's feet padding toward her.

A few moments later she heard soft voices outside the front of the inn, and she wondered who was on the porch.

With Wendell trailing behind, she walked to her father's study and took a few moments to straighten the desk. The past few days, when she had to do bookkeeping for the inn, she had taken refuge there to avoid any interruptions from the kids. She flipped through the accumulated envelopes and made a note to pay their bills and decide how much they could budget for a new vacuum cleaner. Though she still felt that the dinner was making Jane too busy, she had to admit she was thankful for the extra money.

Louise sorted the envelopes in order of importance, then set them on top of the checkbook as a reminder to pay the bills.

As she left the study, she heard the murmur of voices once more from the front porch. She listened.

Lynden and Carita. What were they discussing at this hour?

Just as she was about to slip up the stairs to give them some privacy, the front door opened and the two of them came inside.

"Oh, hello, Mrs. Smith. I didn't know you were still up." Carita glanced back over her shoulder at Lynden. "I had something I needed to talk to Lynden about," she said as Lynden followed her into the inn, closing the porch door behind him.

Ever the hostess Louise said, "Would you like something to eat?"

Lynden laughed. "It seems like all we've been doing since we got here is eat your food."

"You are our guests. We are here to make your stay as comfortable as possible."

"I'd kinda like some juice," Carita said, glancing sidelong at Lynden. "How about you?"

"Juice sounds good."

As Louise led them to the kitchen, she hoped Jane had done some baking.

She was pleased to find the refrigerator well stocked and the cookie jar filled to the brim. In spite of Jane's difficulties with organizing Stacy's dinner, she seemed to be on top of the day-to day-running of the inn.

Louise poured the juice, made up a plate of cookies and joined her guests.

As she sat at the table, she found herself at a loss for words. She didn't possess Jane's facility for making small talk with the younger set. Though she had regular piano students, they were usually much younger and, as a consequence, easier to talk to. In addition, they had the music she was teaching them as a conversation starter. That made Louise think of Lynden's appreciation of her music.

"I understand your grandmother played the piano," Louise said to Lynden.

He nodded, a wistful smile curving his well-shaped lips. "I used to listen to her all the time." He glanced up at Louise. "I hope you didn't think I was some kind of stalker when I was hanging around outside the parlor while you played," he said.

"No, certainly not. I was sorry to hear that she had died. I'm sure you must miss her."

Lynden nodded. "I do."

Carita reached over and covered his hand with her own. "I keep forgetting she didn't die that long ago."

Lynden's smile seemed to absolve her. He turned his attention back to Louise. "Only trouble is, like we were talking about the other day with Jane, I mean, Ms. Howard, I feel like I've been wasting my time. Not sure what I want to do. This Amish trip is a good idea . . ."

"But you'd like to do something with some purpose?" Louise put in.

"Yeah."

"This is a vacation," Carita said with a smile. "Vacations are supposed to be about wasting time."

"I've done enough of that already," Lynden said.

Louise thought this was a perfect opportunity to bring up what she and her sisters had been discussing earlier in the day. "If you want to do something with meaning and purpose, and that could still be fun, why don't you consider helping out on the Habitat for Humanity project tomorrow?"

Lynden toyed with his cup, his expression thoughtful.

"You know, that sounds like a great idea." He glanced sidelong at Carita. "I mean, you could still do your tour thing with the rest, but I'd like to help out on the house."

Carita took a sip of juice, her forehead furrowed. She put down her glass, then gave Lynden a shy smile. "You know, in a way you're right about the summer break. It's not like we never have a chance to take it easy or relax." Carita looked down at her hands. "I think I'd like to help with the project too."

"So, what about the others? What do you think they'll want to do?"

"I'll bring it up tomorrow at breakfast," Carita said. "If they don't want to help, I'll take them on the tour. But the more I think about it, the more I like the idea."

"They might want to come." Lynden curled his hands around his cup. "Who knows? Maybe I'll find my calling by volunteering there," he said with a faint smile.

"Volunteering is an admirable place to start," Louise said, her heart warming at the thought of these kids taking time from their holiday to help someone else. She waited a beat, then got up and bid the two goodnight.

She could hear their voices as she made her way up the stairs to her bedroom.

Lying in bed, she sent up a quiet prayer of thanks to the Lord for His faithfulness through all generations.

"Fantabulous breakfast, Ms. J," Matthew said, carrying a stack of plates into the kitchen Friday morning. "I don't know if we should stay all weekend. I'm gonna get superfat and in my line of work, that's suboptimal."

Jane looked up from the sandwiches she and Alice were assembling. "Don't you go to school?"

"That is my line of work, yes," Matthew said, dropping the plates on the counter with a clatter. "And if I get too fat,

I won't be able to sit in the desks. 'Course I'll be working some of this off today." He swung his hand as if already wielding a hammer. "How many calories does carpentry work burn off?"

"I can't say."

This morning, Jane had been surprised to hear the youths' change of plans. When Lynden got up and suggested they all go to help Alice and Ethel on the worksite, the group, with the exception of Isabel, agreed that this would be a great thing to do.

Eventually, Carita managed to talk her friend into coming along.

And when Jane offered to pack a lunch for them, the entire group was convinced beyond a doubt.

Matthew glanced at the clock. "Not bad. I think we'll get to that site in time to do some serious damage."

"I thought the idea was to do some serious work," Jane teased, packing up the last of the sandwiches.

"Well, yeah. Same thing," Matthew said in a puzzled tone.

For a moment Jane felt every day of her fifty years. Sometimes these kids made her feel young, and then, in a matter of seconds, she keenly felt the gap between them.

Herbie followed Matthew into the kitchen, carrying a pitcher full of cutlery, and behind him came Pete and Rick, expressing their thanks and appreciation for breakfast as they brought in the empty warming trays and the fruit platters.

Jane stared at the clean trays and platters. Seconds ago they were heaped with breakfast burritos and fruit, and for a split second she wondered if the inn was going to realize any profit on this group the way they rocketed through food.

"You don't have to clean up, you know," she protested as Carita and Isabel came behind, bringing the rest of the mugs, cups and utensils.

"Want to. After all, you're making us lunch," Isabel said.

"You make sure to add lunch to the bill," Carita said.

"I will gladly feed workers heading out to do a good deed."

Lynden entered the kitchen. "Truck and van are full of gas. Oil checked. We're ready to roll."

Alice packed up the remaining snacks and put them in a cooler.

"I think we have everything."

"Did you and Ethel pack a lunch yesterday?" Lynden asked.

Alice shook her head. "Yesterday and the day before people came and brought lunch, but Cal warned us that the women who brought lunches for us the past few days wouldn't be able to come today."

"Sounds good to me," Matthew said, leaning over the cooler to inspect its contents. "I don't think anyone can beat the lunch you and Ms. J made for us."

The back door opened and Ethel stepped inside. "So, everyone ready to make some rafters? Put together some headers? Nail some drywall?"

Aunt Ethel must have found a carpentry manual at the library, Jane thought.

"I think we're ready," Alice said, closing the lid on the cooler. "Matthew, can you bring this out to the van? Pete, you and Herbie can take the other cooler, the one holding the juice and soda."

A few minutes later, Jane stood by the driveway, waving off the van, the truck and Alice's car, feeling like a mother sending her children off to school.

And then, like most mothers, she was sure, she returned to the quiet of her kitchen, enjoying the utter silence.

Until she saw the piles of dishes.

She suppressed a sigh, tied back her hair with an elastic she found in her pocket and got to work.

This too will pass, she reminded herself as she started rinsing dishes.

"Brought your own crew, did you?" Cal teased as Alice strapped on her leather pouch.

Alice glanced at the boys who were checking out the supply trailer, trying out some of the hammers, their laughter and joking streaming across the yard like banners of joy.

"I did. They're staying with us at our inn."

Cal frowned. "They a carpentry crew?"

"No. Our guests."

Cal gave her an odd look as if to say he would have second thoughts about staying at Grace Chapel Inn. Alice massaged her neck. Yesterday she'd been stiff; this morning weariness pulled at her limbs with a numbing force. How was she going to get through this day?

Ethel, however, looked as chipper as if she were ready to frame up the entire house on her own.

Matthew strode toward Alice and Cal and stopped, his hands on his hips as he glanced around the building site. "So, where do we start?"

"What do you know about carpentry work?" Cal asked.

"My friend Rick, he's worked construction before. I've helped my dad put up a shed. I can hit a nail without hitting my thumb." Matthew grinned.

"Okay. I need to get a few more outside walls framed up and braced and after that we can look at putting together the inside walls. I've been getting Alice and her crew to tack down the particleboard . . ." While he gave instructions, Alice looked around for Cordy.

She wasn't here yet, and Alice hoped the young woman hadn't changed her mind. Though yesterday Cordy talked about turning over a new leaf, Alice knew how difficult it could be to change when one didn't get much encouragement. Alice got the impression that while Cordy's mother meant well, she might not be the best person to create incentive in young Cordy.

An older car pulled up to the lot, bumping over the dried

ruts, and Jasmine got out. Alice also saw her look around the worksite, then shake her head as she put on her hard hat.

As Jasmine came toward them, Alice saw her disappointment in not finding her younger sister, but she had a smile for Ethel and Alice.

"Thanks so much for coming again," Jasmine said. "Sorry I'm late. The kids were fussing as I was leaving, and I had to get them settled for Grainger before I came."

"I'm surprised you're here as early as you are. Can't be easy to get up on time with all you have to balance."

"And for some of us it seems impossible to get up, period." Jasmine's voice held a faint note of bitterness and Alice guessed she was referring to Cordy.

"I'm sure your sister will be coming," Alice said. "She was here early yesterday."

"Cordy is a good girl," Ethel put in.

Jasmine only nodded, then noticed the rest of the crew. "Who are these people?"

"They're staying at our inn," Alice explained. "They heard about the project and decided to help out."

"They didn't have anything else to do?"

"They're on vacation before school starts. The football team from their old school is having a rally tonight, and they have a reunion tomorrow."

"They came to work on my house on their vacation?" Jasmine's incredulous look made Alice proud of her young guests. And especially proud of Lynden, who was the motivator.

"They wanted to do something meaningful and helpful, and when we told them about this project, they thought they would come and help."

As Alice spoke, she saw a lone figure walking down the sidewalk toward the house.

And Alice's heart swelled with pride. She nudged Jasmine and pointed toward Cordy. "And look who else is here."

Jasmine's pleased expression said more than words could.

"She's a wonderful girl," Alice continued. "She just needs some guidance and direction."

"Something she doesn't get much of from our mother, I'm afraid," Jasmine said with a light sigh.

"But she gets it from you."

"She doesn't want guidance or help or advice from me." Jasmine pulled her hand over her face in a gesture of frustration.

"I'm sure she resents what you tell her, but at the same time, I get a sense that she knows you're right." Alice touched Jasmine's shoulder. "What you think about her matters to her in spite of her reactions. She's still a teenager."

"I know." Jasmine gave Alice a grateful look. "I'm glad you ladies are spending time with her."

"Cordy simply needs a good example, and you've been able to give her one. But what she probably needs more than anything is encouragement when she does something good."

While she spoke, Alice glanced at Cordy. The girl seemed to be whistling as she walked, looking around. But as soon as she saw Jasmine, her steps slowed.

She kept coming, but more tentatively this time. Alice saw her gaze flick from Jasmine to Alice as if suspicious that she was their topic of conversation.

Perceptive little thing, Alice thought.

Cordy lifted her chin, a challenge in her eyes as she stopped in front of her sister. "I'm sorry I'm late."

Alice sensed Jasmine's hesitation. *Just hug her*, she thought, mentally urging Jasmine to do the right thing.

And, to her surprise and pleasure, Jasmine did exactly that. "I'm really glad you came, Cordy. I'm proud of you," Jasmine said.

Cordy's smile blossomed and Alice felt her joy.

"Don't tell me we have to do all that chick stuff." Matthew

stood beside them, his arms folded over his chest. "'Cause if we do, then I'm gonna find myself a different place to work."

Jasmine glanced over her shoulder, laughing at Matthew's comment. "Hello, there. My name is Jasmine and this . . ." Jasmine caught her sister by the shoulders and pulled her forward, "is Cordy. She's been helping me on the house."

"Cool." Matthew inclined his head toward Jasmine, then winked at Cordy. "So, what are we supposed to be doing here?"

"Cal didn't tell you?" Cordy glanced past him to where Cal stood by the other boys, waving his hand and pointing.

"Yeah, but he told me he only pretends to be the boss. Said you're the one I need to be talking to."

A flush crept up Cordy's neck, and Alice flashed a warning frown at Matthew, who gave her a cheeky wink back. She made a note to talk to him later. Matthew was an attractive young man and Cordy an impressionable high school student.

"I . . . uh . . . just work here," Cordy managed to squeak out.

"Well, that's great," Matthew said. He turned to Jasmine. "So, lovely lady, what's the plan?"

Alice resisted the urge to roll her eyes. Matthew was really pouring on the charm.

"Jasmine and her husband will be the future owners of the house," Alice said, putting extra emphasis on husband.

"Okay. That's cool." Matthew nodded, still grinning. "Is he here now?"

"He's home with the kids," Jasmine said, the beginnings of a smile teasing one corner of her mouth. "By the way, I'd like to thank you and your friends for helping out today. That's really neat."

"Well, it was either that or go check out the farms of some Amish people . . ."

He snapped his fingers. "That's what they're called. Thanks, Ms. A. Anyhow, none of us were too stoked about doing that trip, but we wanted to help here. This is a great project."

"Matthew, get over here," Rick called. "We're ready to go."

"Talk to you ladies later," Matthew said, tipping his hard hat in their direction. Then he turned and jogged off.

"What a character," Jasmine said with a laugh. "I think he could be a lot of fun."

"Oh, that he is," Alice said dryly. "And now we better get some work done ourselves."

Alice saw Cordy look with a tinge of envy at Matthew, Rick and company and made a quick decision. "Cordy, I don't know if Aunt Ethel and I will be able to keep up with you. Might be better if you worked with the other group."

She laughed self-consciously. "No. That's okay."

Alice didn't want to press the matter, but as soon as she had an opportunity, she pulled Carita aside and asked her if she would invite Cordy to join them.

Carita had considerably more tact than Matthew, and a few minutes after Alice had asked her, she came over to where Alice, Ethel and Cordy were working.

"Hey, Ms. Howard," she asked, her shadow falling over the board they were nailing down. "I was wondering if you could you spare Cordy? Isabel and I aren't quite sure what to do, and Cal is busy and the boys just laugh at us when we ask them."

Alice squinted up into the sun and grinned back at Carita. "I think that would be fine." She turned to Cordy, who was watching Carita with longing in her face. "Cordy, you wouldn't mind helping over there?"

"But then you and Mrs. Buckley will be working on your own."

A movement up the plank to the house caught Alice's

eye. Florence was painstakingly making her way toward them.

"Here's Florence. I think we'll be okay."

Cordy gave another feeble protest, but when Florence came and Carita added her encouragement, she scrambled to her feet and followed Carita, grinning from ear to ear.

"That was nice of Carita to think of Cordy," Ethel said. "I'm sure she'll have more fun working with them than with us." As Florence joined them Ethel gave her a quick smile. "I thought you might not show up today."

Florence's only rejoinder was a pained look. "I hurt all over. I have muscles I was never aware of before this morning. But I'll meet the challenge."

"You've simply done some very minor straining of your muscles," Alice assured her. "If you slowly start working again, the stiffness will ease."

"I realize this is your area of expertise, but somehow that doesn't make sense. In fact, I thought of staying home and soaking in a warm tub of water."

"Trust me, Florence, the best thing you did was to come back and get moving again."

As Florence slowly eased herself down, Alice saw she remained skeptical.

Soon the whine of power saws and the smacks of hammers blended with voices and laughter and snatches of singing. Now and again a burst of laughter would come from the group of young people. Alice saw Cordy joining in and felt a surge of almost maternal pride.

This pride increased when they quit for lunch and Cal sauntered up to Ethel, Florence and Alice. "That is a great group of kids," he said, poking his thumb over his shoulder. "We're going to get lots done today."

"And even better, they seem to be enjoying themselves," Ethel said.

"Always makes for good production. Yesterday I was

wondering how far we were going to get today, but now I'm real happy."

As he spoke, Herbie and Rick surged past. "Find a place to sit," Herbie called out. "We're getting the lunch."

"Come join us," Ethel said to Florence.

"I was thinking of finding a restaurant . . ." Florence said, obviously wavering.

"Nonsense," Ethel scoffed. "Jane packed us our lunch."

"Well, in that case I'll accept. I don't believe any meal I can buy in a restaurant could compare to a lunch put together by Jane."

A few minutes later Alice, Florence and Ethel were perched on a makeshift bench that Pete had hastily assembled —a plank of wood resting on concrete blocks. Carita, Isabel, Lynden and Matthew parceled out the food.

"I think I could get used to this," Alice said, accepting a paper plate full of food from Pete. "Thank you so much."

"Anything else I can do for you lovely ladies?" Rick asked, folding his hands in front of him as if eagerly waiting their next request.

"You can tell me what you have on the back of your hand?" Florence asked, her expression clearly telegraphing what she thought of the tattoo.

Rick held up his dragon. Now that he wasn't wearing a long-sleeved shirt, Alice could see it snaking halfway up his arm.

"I got this done last year. You like it?"

Florence hesitated long enough for Rick to draw his own conclusion.

"Neither does my mom." He laughed. "Anything else?"

"If you don't mind, I would love something to drink," Ethel said.

Rick placed his hand on his chest. "I have a servant heart. Your wish is my command."

This elicited a guffaw from his friends.

"He's pulling your leg, Aunt Ethel," Matthew called out.

"Some respect, please," Rick said in an aggrieved tone as he went to get some cups.

"How are you making out over there?" Alice asked. "Cal is quite impressed with your work."

"It's going real well," Lynden said, looking up from his sandwich. "I'm enjoying it a lot. Cordy's been explaining how Habitat works. I think it's so cool that she can help out."

Cordy beamed. "When school starts, I won't be able to, though."

"What grade you in?" Herbie asked, wiping the back of his mouth with his hand.

"I'm going into eleventh, but . . ." she gave them a shamefaced look, "I'll probably have to redo some classes."

"Too tough?"

"No. Didn't show up."

"Oh, no. A skipper," Matthew called out in mock horror. "I don't know if we can be here guys. It might be catching."

Pete punched Matthew on the shoulder. "Says the king of school skedaddling." He glanced Cordy's way. "Don't let him get you down. He had a lousy attendance record last year."

"And I was a sorry, sorry student come finals." Matthew shook his head as if still regretting his impulses. "Let me be an object lesson to you, missy. Don't skip. I spent way too much time trying to catch up. Totally wasted a year, a whole year of my life. Not worth it."

"Right on," Herbie agreed. "I was a nervous wreck come exam time. The whole hour I'm writing I'm wishing I could do the year over and not skip so much."

Alice watched as Cordy absorbed these nuggets of information. She hoped Cordy took them to heart.

"What do you want to do when you graduate?" Pete asked her.

"I dunno. I like animals but I'm not sure what kind of job I could have working with animals."

"Be a vet," Pete called out.

"Dog walker," was Rick's contribution.

"Pet groomer."

The rest of them called out various suggestions, and Cordy laughed as they got sillier and sillier.

"I'm not smart enough to be a vet," Cordy said.

"Maybe you could be a vet assistant," Lynden put in. "That way you can work with animals, and you won't have such a long studying period."

Cordy perked up. "I never thought of that before."

"I think it's an excellent idea," Ethel said. "You could probably do your studies at a local community college."

The conversation drifted from colleges to vocations and studying, and as the kids talked, Alice saw Cordy thinking through the various suggestions. She wondered if Cordy's friends ever talked about the future and the possibilities available to them.

Too soon lunch was over, and with exaggerated groans, everyone got up and went back to work.

Isabel rose and started clearing.

"I'll take care of that," Carita said, taking the plates from the girl's hands. "Why don't you help Cordy? Alice and I can finish this up."

"Things are going well, aren't they?" Carita asked.

"Looks like the boys are enjoying themselves," Alice remarked as Carita opened the back door of the van.

"They are, actually. In fact, Lynden's been asking a lot of questions about this organization. Seems like he's interested in doing some kind of longer-term volunteer work."

"I sensed he's been searching for something in his life." Alice and Carita slipped the cooler inside and closed the door.

"We talked last night." Carita said quietly. "He spent a lot of time taking care of his grandmother, and now he feels a bit lost. She left him a lot of money, as did his parents, so he doesn't have to work. Trouble is, he doesn't want to hang around and do nothing."

"That's extremely admirable and mature on his part," Alice said. She glanced over at the boys. From here she saw Lynden's frown as he concentrated on what he was doing.

"I think so too . . ." but Carita's tone told Alice another story.

"But you were hoping he had other plans?" Alice asked, injecting a sympathetic tone into her voice.

"Yeah. I guess I hoped he would enroll in college, and we could spend more time together."

"Just because his plans might take him in a different direction than college doesn't mean you can't keep in touch."

"I suppose." Carita rubbed the side of her nose with her finger. "But I feel so shallow. All the things I did this week were, like Lynden said, just about having fun. About entertaining ourselves. And going to school for another year feels equally shallow."

"Not a chance. Education is a gift you give yourself and others. It broadens your horizons."

"Not when you're taking a general arts curriculum." Carita gave Alice a sad little smile. "And please don't bother telling me it will expand my mind. I'm only taking it because my parents wanted me to go to college, and I didn't know what else to take. I'm not even that committed to school." She folded her arms and leaned back against the van. "When Matthew was teasing Cordy about not going to classes, he could have been talking about me."

"Are you enrolled for this year?"

Carita nodded.

"What if you change your courses?"

"What if I just don't go?"

"And then what?" Alice asked.

Carita pushed back her dark hair, clutching her head with her hands. "Maybe do what Lynden is doing."

Alice felt lost at this point. She wasn't sure of how to advise this young woman. In her day women didn't go chasing after men. At least not openly.

But things change, and it seemed Carita really cared about Lynden.

"Your silence tells me you're underwhelmed by the idea," Carita put in.

Alice had to dwell on the comment. Then she laughed. "It's not my business to be overwhelmed, underwhelmed or simply whelmed. But I do question the wisdom of planning your life around a young friend."

"I know. And I know exactly what my mother would say."

"And that would be?"

"Nice girls don't chase after boys. But I'm not sure Lynden even knows how I feel."

"Maybe you better tell him. Be upfront and then wait and see what he does with it," Alice suggested.

"Maybe. I don't know." Carita pushed her fingers through her hair. "This whole trip turned out completely different. Nothing turned out the way I planned."

"Welcome to life," Alice said with a light laugh. She put her arm around Carita and gave her a quick hug. "You obviously have things to think about, but in the meantime, let's have fun putting this house together."

"This work is fun, isn't it," Carita admitted as they walked back to the house. "I didn't think I'd enjoy building as much as I am. And it's great to know that we're helping out Cordy's sister. Cordy has been telling us a few things about what Jasmine has had to deal with. She's amazing, really."

"Jasmine has had to be a fighter," Alice admitted. "But so are you." Alice stopped, catching Carita by the arm. "I do want to tell you that I really admire what you've done for your friends. This vacation was not a waste of time at all. You showed them a good time, and you showed them a better way to have fun. I think that's worth more than you might realize."

Carita's smile widened. "Thanks for that, Alice."

Alice squeezed her arm. "You're welcome. You're a wonderful girl, Carita. And I don't think you're shallow at all."

Carita nodded, accepting the compliment, then returned to her friends.

"You and Carita seemed to have a lot to talk about," Ethel said, her tone suggesting that Alice had better spill the beans as soon as she could.

"Yes. We did." And that was all Alice was going to tell her dear aunt.

But while she worked, she surreptitiously glanced over to see what was going on elsewhere at the worksite.

Carita and Lynden were now working side by side, and when Alice caught Lynden watching Carita when the young woman wasn't looking, she suspected that it was possible that Carita's future might be in good hands.

Chapter Fourteen

Sh . . . you'll wake them up—"
"Your shushing is louder than my talking—"
"Could you all just hush up—"
"Shhh . . ."

Jane stared at the ceiling listening to teenagers, one floor below, trying to be quiet and failing dismally.

They came back from the Habitat for Humanity site exhausted and complaining how stiff and sore they were. They left for their Spirit Night, a listless and worn-out group. Jane wondered how much spirit they would be able show. In fact she thought for sure they would come home early from their evening and fall into bed.

But they must have caught their second wind at the rally. They stayed out until 1:00 AM, and now they were back at the inn.

She just hoped Louise and Alice weren't disturbed by the noise. Though as tired as Alice looked when she came home this afternoon, Jane suspected her sister was currently in a deep sleep.

Jane slipped out of her room and paused by Louise's door, listening. A faint sound of slow, steady breathing was the only sound coming out of her sister's room.

Well, that was good, Jane thought, creeping back to her bedroom. She crawled back into bed, fluffed her pillow, rolled to her side, pulled the blankets around her and waited for sleep to fuzz her thoughts and lift her off into dreams.

Fifteen minutes later she flopped onto her back, her arms crossed over her chest. A floor below, things grew more and more quiet.

She moved onto her other side, glaring at the alarm clock set to ring in five hours. She winced at the thought of all she had to do. Had she set the alarm properly? She grabbed the clock, checked and double-checked it. Though she doubted the kids would be up early for breakfast, she still had Louise and Alice to take care of.

And then there was the dinner.

Well, at least her challenge provided an opportunity to practice patience. Stacy had called almost every hour on the hour to double-check the arrangements. To fine-tune the menu. To tell Jane how stressed she was, how busy she was, how worried she was.

Jane had tried not to take on Stacy's fretting, but with each phone call Jane grew more anxious. She went over the menu again and again, rechecked her supplies, and finally satisfied that she had everything well in hand, she went to bed.

And started tossing and turning. She was just drifting off when the kids came back and here she lay, wide awake again.

The soup was made and ready to be heated up tomorrow. The salad had to wait to be mixed up. She had the chicken breasts prepared. Tomorrow morning . . . no, this morning, she would mix the stuffing for the chicken breasts, get the dry mixture ready for the biscuits and prepare the salad dressing. The more she could do in advance, the better prepared she would feel when the time came for the dinner.

The Nanaimo bars and the stroop waffles were done. Apple galette couldn't be made until the last moment. She had the vegetables cut up and ready to be cooked. The only thing left to do was . . .

Jane pressed her fingertips against her eyes to control her worries. She had gone over this dinner so many times, she was getting dizzy.

"*Sufficient for the day* . . ." she reminded herself.

But when she rolled onto her side, her worries intruded once more. Had she prepared enough chicken breasts? Enough vegetables?

Stifling a sigh of frustration at her spinning thoughts, she snapped on her bedside light, sat up and wrapped her arms around her knees. She needed to rest, to find comfort. And while she knew the stress from the dinner was nothing compared to some of the things going on in people's lives around the world, she did send up a prayer that the dinner would be a success.

Then she took her Bible off her bedside table, opening it to the passage she'd been reading just the other day, Galatians 5:22–23.

"But the fruit of the Spirit is love, joy, peace, patience, kindness, goodness, faithfulness, gentleness and self-control. Against such things there is no law."

As Jane read the words she felt her focus shift from herself and the worries she carried to the Lord who loved her. She had opportunities to show that love to those around her, and there were times, she had to confess, she had fallen short.

"Forgive me, Lord," she prayed. "Give me the fruit of patience, gentleness and self-control." She read on and stopped at a passage that especially resonated with her.

"Since we live by the Spirit, let us keep in step with the Spirit" (Galatians 5:25).

Jane kept the Bible open, letting the words settle into her mind and recenter her thoughts.

I am put on this earth to serve the Lord and to serve others, she thought. *But I must make sure that in serving others, I don't lose track of serving the Lord.*

She took a deep breath, and bowed her head to pray. And as she prayed, she felt peace settle upon her.

"Where is Jane?" Louise asked Saturday morning, glancing at the clock in the kitchen. "I thought for sure she would be up by now."

Alice eased herself into a chair, nursing her cup of tea. "I didn't hear her get up this morning. Of course, I didn't hear much. I am still tired."

Louise gave her sister a look of sympathy. "You certainly should be. I am full of admiration for all the physical work you've been doing."

"I won't need to go for a walk with Vera for over a month," Alice groaned.

Louise finished her coffee and got up, pausing at the entrance to the hallway, listening. Upstairs, no one was stirring. Not Jane, not Carita, not Isabel and certainly none of the boys.

She rinsed her cup, put it in the sink and returned to the hallway entrance. "Do you think we should wake up Jane?" Louise asked, tapping her fingertips against her arm.

"I say if she can sleep, let her sleep." Alice yawned.

"My goodness, Alice, you look as if you should have stayed in bed yourself."

"I thought Jane was already whipping eggs and making whatever she had planned for breakfast this morning, so I dragged myself out of bed to help."

Louise glanced down the hallway. She didn't know what to do if the young people came downstairs before Jane.

While Louise could breeze through a Chopin Prelude in F Sharp Major, any breakfast beyond boiled eggs and toast confounded her.

She walked back to the kitchen table and perched on the edge of her chair, fiddled with the cloth napkins already prepared for breakfast, straightened the plant sitting on the bright yellow cloth mat, pinched off a dead leaf, then got up and threw it in the trash can.

She wiped the counters, inspected the refrigerator in the faint hope that her usually organized sister had already prepared breakfast and that it only needed heating up. Surely Jane wouldn't be sleeping if she hadn't?

A plate of fruit, already cut up and covered, sat beside two casserole dishes covered in tin foil which, in turn, sat beside a plate of muffins and pastries. Aha! Breakfast.

"I would imagine these need to be heated up?" Louise asked pulling out the tinfoil covered dishes.

"Probably," Alice said, stifling another yawn. "I know she said she was going to make a breakfast casserole for this morning."

"Should we put them in the oven for her? That would save her some time."

Alice didn't reply.

"I'm sure she wouldn't want the kids to come downstairs to no breakfast at all," Louise fretted.

Still no reply from Alice. Louise glanced over and saw her sister with her arms folded and her head down. She was sleeping.

Louise was about to put the pans back in the fridge when she heard footsteps above her. Then the sound of running water. Someone was up.

She looked from the pans to Alice to the hallway and made an executive decision. Jane had been busy enough the past few days. It wouldn't hurt for her to sleep a little longer, and if she already had breakfast here and all that needed doing was for it to be heated up, then Louise would do it.

She turned on the oven, put the pans inside and then went back to the refrigerator to get the rest of breakfast. She was about to wake Alice, then decided to let her sleep.

Feeling on top of things, Louise mixed up the orange juice, got the coffeepot going and set the table. A few more noises emanated from upstairs, but no one came down.

No matter. By the time anyone did, breakfast would be ready.

When the coffee was done burbling, Louise poured it into one of the carafes, set the carafe on the sideboard and immediately started another pot of coffee. A quick survey of the table satisfied her that all was in readiness. The only thing missing were the guests.

And Jane.

Louise allowed herself a smug smile while thinking of her sister. She would be surprised mightily when she came downstairs to find that breakfast was well in hand. Of course, Jane had done all the prep work, but Louise still felt quite proud of her own initiative.

She reached for the oven door to check on the casseroles.

"*Yoo-hoo*," Ethel sang out, entering the kitchen. She wore her cap, her overalls, carpenter's apron and a huge smile. "How is everyone this lovely summer morning?"

Louise waved to Ethel and put her finger over her lips, then indicated Alice, miraculously, still sleeping at the kitchen table.

"Oh, the poor dear," Ethel whispered, covering her mouth with her hand as if trying to recapture her words. "Has she been there all night?"

Louise shook her head and indicated that Ethel should follow her to the front room.

As they walked past the reception desk, Louise glanced

up the stairs, but in spite of the muffled noises above them, no one came down.

"What happened to Alice?" Ethel asked, settling herself into one of the chairs in the living room. She shifted, then moved her hammer so it wasn't banging against the leg of the chair.

"The poor dear is so tired. She got up because she felt she should help with breakfast, then promptly fell asleep at the kitchen table." Louise took a seat across from Ethel, but where she could still keep an eye out in case their guests came downstairs.

"Should we make her go back to bed?"

"We'd have to wake her to do that. I'll wake her up before the kids come down, though. I'm sure she wouldn't appreciate their finding her sleeping." Louise glanced at Ethel's attire. "I thought no one was working at the Habitat project today."

"Florence said she needed some work done on her fence today. So I offered to help."

"That's a wonderful idea," Louise said approvingly. Obviously the feud between the two women was over. Alice had said as much, but with Ethel and Florence one never knew. Sometimes hostilities would cease only to flare up at the slightest provocation. "Is her husband going to help?"

Ethel waved away that question. "Ronald may be a successful businessman, but he has no idea which end of a nail is up."

Louise somehow doubted that, but if fixing a fence would mend proverbial fences between Florence and Ethel, who was she to argue with her aunt?

They chatted for a bit about the Habitat project and Louise was pleased to know Ethel and Alice were going back again the following week.

"Alice has to work a couple of hospital shifts next week,

so I don't think she'll be going to the worksite as often. I'll have to get a ride from Florence—but now that we're getting along again I'm sure she won't mind coming here to get me, especially if I help her with her fence."

Louise nodded, half listening to Ethel, half listening to what was going on upstairs.

"Where's Jane?" Ethel asked. "I thought she would be up by now."

"I thought so too, but I have breakfast well in hand," Louise said.

"Do you now?" Ethel gave her a feeble smile. "I see."

"Are you going to join us?"

At the question, Ethel glanced at her watch, then jumped to her feet. "Oh my goodness! Look at the time. I promised Florence I would be there early. I should probably get going." She adjusted her tool belt, then sidled toward the back entrance. "I mean, we're just starting to get along again, and I don't want her to be angry with me if I come late. You know how she can be sometimes."

Her niece knew exactly what was going on in Ethel's mind. Her aunt was fully aware of Louise's culinary shortcomings.

"Jane prepared the breakfast in advance," Louise assured her. "I just put it in the oven."

"I see. Jane made it. So you're just heating it up."

"Which is happening as we speak."

"In that case, I'm sure Florence will understand if I don't come precisely at the time I said I would be there. What time will breakfast be ready?"

"In about twenty minutes. When the casseroles are done."

The sound of whistling came from the top of the stairs, followed by the thumping of a pair of feet taking the stairs two at a time.

"Morning Mrs. L," Matthew sang out as he landed on the floor of the hallway. His hair still glistened from a shower, and his shirt was partially unbuttoned. "Morning Aunt E." He stopped, pulled his head back as if realizing what he had said. "Hey. That's like a joke or something. Aunt E . . . Auntie. And it's not even ten o'clock yet."

"Actually you are up bright and early this morning."

"Yeah, well, I couldn't sleep. I am still pumped from the game we had last night. Our boys won."

"Well, that's nice," Ethel said. "Did you have a good time?"

"We had a rocking time. Even the band was pretty good. And the bonfire. Whoa! Thought the fire department was going to have to come out."

"Sounds like fun."

"Way more than fun. It was awesome. We met up with some old friends, swapped some old stories. Even Lynden was laughing, and, hey, he doesn't laugh much. And how was your course? Learn how to fix a transmission?"

"That's for next week," Louise said. "Our focus yesterday was windshield wipers."

"Hey, you gotta crawl before you can run. You'll be lifting trannies yet." He headed down the hallway toward the kitchen as if this was the most normal thing in the world. "Do you need any help this morning?"

Too late Louise realized where he was going. What if he woke up Alice . . .

"Hey, Ms. A," Matthew called out. He stopped, looked from the still-sleeping Alice back to Louise who had followed him. "She okay?" he asked, scratching his head.

Alice slowly lifted her head, blinking as consciousness returned. The imprint of her hand blazed bright red on her cheek and her hair listed to one side.

"Good morning, Matthew," Alice said. "How did you sleep?"

"In my bed. How about you? Don't tell me you spent the night here?"

"I must have dozed off. Someone should have woken me before you came down." Again Alice gave Louise a reprimanding look.

"Someone didn't know you would fall asleep at the kitchen table," Louise said in her own defense.

Alice frowned but then her usually sunny nature reasserted itself and she laughed. "I suppose it's not the best place to catch forty winks. I hope I wasn't snoring."

"I can't imagine that you snore," Matthew said.

Alice gave him a quick smile. "And how was your evening?

"Like I told Aunt E, great, fun and fantastic. I probably smell a bit like smoke." He then sniffed the air. "But that smells better. Smells like breakfast is cooking. I made sure we all got up so you don't have to feed us forever and ever. Besides, we got plans for the day."

"That's very considerate of you," Louise said. "I believe breakfast will be ready in about fifteen minutes."

"Great. I'll tell the gang." He paused a moment. "Isn't Ms. J up yet?"

"She's still sleeping," Louise said.

"Oops. If I'd known that, I would have told everyone to be quiet."

"I'm sure she'd like to be awake by now," Louise assured him. "In fact, I think I'll make certain of that immediately."

"Nah. Let her sleep," Matthew said. "She's been working real hard."

"So have you, I hear. Did you enjoy working on the house yesterday?"

Matthew scratched his head, as if contemplating the question. "Yeah. It was a lot of fun building the house. It's not a real big one, but looks like it'll be cozy. It was interesting talking to that Cordy girl. She's the sister of Jasmine, the lady who is getting the house. That Jasmine has had a real tough gig."

"Gig?"

"Yeah, you know, life I guess." He shrugged. "But now she's getting a house, and it's cool. She only has to pay back what she can afford. I think that's supercool."

"Good morning." Carita appeared in the doorway of the kitchen looking bright and chipper, followed by Herbie and Isabel. "Can I do anything?"

"No, you cannot," Louise said, giving her a gentle smile to offset a comment that might be construed as short. "You've done more than enough to help out."

"Smells like you've got breakfast cooking already." Herbie rubbed his hands in anticipation.

"Yes. I do. But I can't take any credit. Jane had it already prepared and ready to go. Now why don't you sit in the living room or enjoy the early morning on the front porch while breakfast is heating."

The group took her advice and left. Soon Louise could hear them boisterously reliving the events of the previous evening. She even caught a glimpse of Herbie backing into the hall, pretending to hold a football as he most probably reenacted a portion of the game.

"Those casseroles smell different," Alice said, sniffing the air.

Louise couldn't remember what the casseroles should smell like. "Maybe Jane used different ingredients this time." She opened the oven door, sniffed again, just because she felt she should. Seemed fine to her.

Fifteen minutes later the kids were gathered around the table and Louise brought out the casseroles. Too late she realized that Jane often used the warming trays for the heated portion of the guests' breakfast, so still holding the hot dishes, she hurried back to the kitchen.

"Where are you going with our breakfast?" Herbie cried out in dismay. "I worked pretty hard last night and need sustenance for today."

"Alice, I forgot the warming trays," she whispered as the doors flapped shut behind her.

"It's too late to get them going." Alice tugged open a drawer and pulled out a few hot pads. "We can use these. I'll put these on the table for you."

As Alice preceded her, the heat of the dishes was making itself known. "Hurry," Louise urged, her hands growing uncomfortably hot.

The pads went down, the dishes followed them with a "thunk" and Louise quickly shook off the overheated oven mitts. She gave the gathered group a weak smile. "There you go."

"I'm so hungry, I could eat a horse," Herbie announced.

Ethel scooted in behind Louise, carrying the fruit and pastry trays, which she set on the sideboard. Alice and Ethel went back to the kitchen and returned with bowls of yogurt, granola and cottage cheese. All was ready.

"Enjoy your breakfast," Louise said, feeling quite proud of herself as she peeled back the foil from the first of the casseroles.

And stopped. And frowned.

"What's wrong, Mrs. L?" Matthew asked.

Louise couldn't answer him. Her eyes were fixed on the strange looking casserole before her. She sniffed, bent closer.

"That doesn't look like breakfast casserole," Ethel said, peering past Louise.

Alice came to inspect as well and clapped her hand over her mouth, stifling her cry of dismay.

"What is it, Alice?" Louise asked.

"I think those are the chicken breasts Jane was going to serve for the dinner tonight," Alice said.

"They were right between the other breakfast foods. Why did she put them where she did if they weren't for breakfast?" Louise struggled to stifle a surge of misgiving.

She gingerly peeled back the foil from the second pan, hoping against hope that it was a breakfast casserole.

But all that faced her was a limp assortment of peppers, olives, celery decorated with blobs of melted feta cheese and the fast-growing smell of scorched vegetables.

"I suppose this was also for tonight?" Louise asked in a faint voice.

"I would think so." Alice said.

Silence fell over the table as realization hit the gathered group of guests.

"So this isn't really our breakfast," Pete asked.

"I'm so sorry," Louise said. "I don't think so."

"We can eat the yogurt . . ."

"If indeed it is yogurt," Louise said, no longer trusting her own instincts. She felt her shoulders slump as she stared at the casserole dishes. Jane was stressed enough over this meal. Now Louise had destroyed the entrée.

So much for feeling on top of things, she thought, wondering how Jane was going to react.

"This is yogurt, all right," Ethel announced from behind her.

Louise turned to see her aunt holding a small bowl and taking another sample.

"And I'm sure this other stuff is fruit," Ethel said gesturing toward the cut-up melon, mangoes and grapes with her spoon.

"I'm sure they are," Louise replied dryly.

"I could make toast for you," Alice said. "Won't take but a minute."

"I can fry eggs," Matthew offered.

"Nah. Scramble them," Pete said, getting to his feet as if he was going to do that very thing. "Goes way faster and you don't have to be as fussy."

"But . . . you . . ." Louise, still discombobulated from her breakfast faux pas, couldn't gather her thoughts fast enough to formulate a coherent objection.

"You must have eggs," Pete said, already walking toward the kitchen.

"If you put seasoning salt in them, that's really tasty," Rick offered, rushing to catch up to his friend.

"Don't put that in mine," Isabel protested, following them. "I like them just plain."

Alice stood by as the kids strode past her and then turned to Louise with a resigned expression.

So they gathered up the dishes holding what was supposed to be portions of Jane's dinner, brought them into the kitchen and found a place for them on a counter.

Pete was cracking eggs into a bowl, Carita was setting up the mixer and Rick had a pan on the stove by the time Louise and Alice got back into the kitchen. Herbie and Matthew were going through a cupboard, calling out the names of various spices.

"What can I do?" Isabel asked, tugging on Louise's sleeve.

"I don't mind helping either," Lynden offered.

"Toast?" Louise said, still trying to gather her thoughts. "Maybe you can take care of the toast?"

In a matter of minutes the pan on the stove was sizzling, toast was toasting and getting buttered, and Louise, Alice and Ethel were sitting at the kitchen table watching the spectacle.

"So how about that touchdown?" Herbie said, opening up another loaf of bread. "I don't think I played that well in high school."

"It was an awe-inspiring play," Matthew said. "Here, dragon man. Use this." He tossed Rick a container of spices.

"And the band did a great job," Carita said. "I really liked that last song they played."

The chatter continued, upbeat and positive and loud.

"Good thing Jane is still sleeping," Ethel commented, her

arms folded over her coveralls. "I don't know that she would appreciate having all these kids running amok in her kitchen."

"Well, at least *they* seem to know what they're doing," Louise said, forcing herself to relax. There was nothing she could do now except watch breakfast unfold.

A few minutes later they were instructed to follow the food into the dining room.

Ethel was already sitting at the table by the time they got there, so Alice and Louise gave in and sat down.

"So, dig in," Matthew urged, waving his fork at the huge platter of eggs and the mound of toast, and everyone did just that.

As their guests laughed and chatted, Louise, Ethel and Alice were treated to yet another account of strategic plays during the football game, a recap of the bonfire and the band and general college-age conversation.

The noise level grew and grew the longer they sat. Conversation was animated and punctuated by laughter and teasing.

Lynden joined in, and occasionally his glance would slip to Carita, and his expression would soften. Then, as if she sensed his gaze on her, Carita's eyes would turn to his, and she would return his look with a gentle smile.

Louise's heart melted at the sight. She wondered what lay ahead for them, but for now, it seemed they both truly cared for each other.

As quickly as the breakfast had been made, the food was consumed. The kids cleaned up, and as they did, the noise level in the kitchen rose dramatically.

"My goodness, what is going on here?"

Louise saw Jane standing in the doorway of the kitchen, blinking at the gathering. A few strands of hair had escaped her hastily tied ponytail.

"Hey, Ms. J, you missed breakfast, but we can make you more," Matthew sung out.

"Good morning, Jane," Louise said, forcing a cheery tone to her voice. "I hope you slept well."

"For some reason my alarm clock didn't go off." She blinked again and pushed the wayward strands of hair back over her ear. "Why didn't you wake me?"

"We thought you needed the sleep," Louise said, hoping that Alice would come to her assistance.

"Yes. You have been working very hard," Alice said. "So we took care of breakfast."

"Among other things," Ethel put in.

Louise saw Alice give her aunt a quick poke.

"What do you mean, other things?" Jane asked, stifling a yawn.

Louise sighed. She should have known Ethel was unable to keep anything she deemed interesting to herself.

"We can fix the problem, though," Louise assured her.

"It's not a huge problem," Alice put in helpfully.

"Whoa! What are you talking about?" Jane put up her hand as if to indicate she would tolerate no further delay.

Louise glanced at Alice who was trying to smile at Jane.

"I think they're talking about the chicken . . ." Ethel informed her.

Louise shot Ethel a frown.

"Chicken?" Jane's confused gaze flicked from Ethel, to Alice, to Louise.

"I'm sure you can do something with it," Louise said, walking to her sister's side. "You must have some kind of recipe you could use—"

"Recipe? Do something?" Jane tried to absorb what her sister was saying. "Could someone please tell me what happened?"

"Louise cooked your chicken."

"I thought it was a breakfast casserole—"

"—and the vegetables."

"Same excuse." Louise shot Ethel a warning look.

Jane scooted past Louise, glancing around the kitchen. Louise could tell the minute her sister laid eyes on the pan. Her expression became pained. "Oh no. Louise, what have you done?"

"I am *so* sorry, Jane. It was an accident."

Jane dropped into a nearby chair and blew her breath out in a sigh. "What am I going to do?"

"Change menus?" Carita said hopefully.

"I can't think of anything else to make," Jane said. "It took me about four days of wrangling to come up with this one, and I'm tired and worn out." Jane waved her fingers as if dismissing the entire menu out of hand. "I made suggestion after suggestion, and this was the only thing Stacy agreed to."

"That's rough." Matthew said, flinging a damp towel over his shoulder.

Jane nodded listlessly.

Louise felt even worse than Jane looked. "I'm so sorry, Jane. I should have been more attentive. I shouldn't have made such a quick presumption."

"Louise, you didn't mean any harm. I'll just have to think of something else."

"That's lousy. Can you do it?" Matthew put in.

Jane glanced across the kitchen counter and gave him a feeble smile. "I hope so. This was supposed to be a gourmet meal. Something unusual, yet not too—" Jane held up her hand and made air quotes with her fingers, "—out there."

"I hate to be the social planner yet again," Carita said with a smile. "But the clock is ticking and we need to get going."

Pete quickly wiped the counter and tossed the cloth into the sink. Matthew finished putting away the dishes, and the rest were leaving the kitchen when Isabel piped up.

"I'm going to stay."

Carita gave her a patient look. "I know you don't like this

stuff, but you bought a ticket for the barbecue and you should come."

Isabel looked from Jane to Carita and then shook her head. "No. I'm going to stay and see if I can help Jane."

Jane was surprised to hear Isabel speak up. The girl had been quiet and withdrawn most of the visit, preferring, it seemed, to let Carita do all the talking. "Don't worry, Isabel," Jane said. "I don't need any help."

"You do," Isabel protested, again surprising Jane with her vehemence. "You've been so great to us. You've let us invade your kitchen. And now I want to help you."

"I can help too," Matthew said suddenly. "I gabbed with all my buddies last night."

"I could stay," Pete said, adjusting the fit of his ball cap.

"No, don't do that," Jane said, raising her hands in a gesture of protest. She would get absolutely nothing done with the kids hanging around. Now more than ever she counted on their being away from the inn. "You have planned this for weeks. I don't want to ruin the day."

"You won't ruin my day," Isabel said quietly. "I don't need to go and be ignored by the same people who ignored me in high school."

Her voice held a plaintive note that called to Jane. She wavered and that was her undoing.

"That's it," Matthew said, returning to the kitchen and slapping his hands on the counter. "We're stayin' and we're helpin'." He turned to Isabel. "So, what should we do?"

Frowns met his question followed by some muttering as they talked among themselves.

"Where are your recipe books?" Pete finally spoke up. "I can look for some ideas."

"I can surf the Web," Herbie offered.

"We could come up with something," Isabel said. "I used to do a lot of cooking for my mom."

Jane was about to protest again, when the sight of seven earnest faces did her in. They weren't going to quit, and she didn't have the energy to buck them. So she simply pointed out the cupboard that held her recipe books, and while the kids bustled around the kitchen, she leaned her elbows on the counter, wishing she could think clearly.

"Should I go get some more groceries?" Louise offered.

Jane shook her head.

"Well, I'll be in the parlor going over my songs for tomorrow," Louise said. "Let me know if you need anything at all."

Jane nodded. Then she sighed.

Chapter | Fifteen

She simply couldn't think. Jane glanced around the kitchen. Carita and Isabel were hunched over a set of cookbooks at the counter, while Herbie, Pete and Rick were surfing the Web at the front desk, printing out possibilities and running them back to Jane for approval.

The kids meant well and she appreciated their enthusiasm for the project, and their sacrifice in staying with her, but if she was supposed to come up with something else for the dinner, she needed quiet.

So she looked over the recipes Herbie had printed out and tried to sort them into piles. Maybe, Definitely Not and Impossible to Do Before Five O'Clock Tonight. While she sorted, she struggled to keep her feelings under control, hoping the kids would eventually find something else to occupy themselves.

She had the dining room to decorate, the flowers to organize, the table to set. And a brand-new entrée to plan.

What happened to that moment of peace she'd had last night? She stopped herself, stopped her fussing as she remembered the words from Galatians. "The fruit of the Spirit is love, joy, peace, patience, kindness, goodness . . ."

She took a long slow breath, letting the passage once again still her soul, until the phone started ringing.

She darted a nervous glance at the clock. Seven hours and fourteen minutes till the dinner.

"Jane, it's for you," Alice said with an apologetic look. "It's Stacy."

"The fruit of the Spirit is love, joy, peace . . ." Jane repeated the words to herself as she took the phone from Alice, forced a smile, then said, "Hello, Stacy." She kept the smile intact while Stacy quizzed Jane again about the menu, about the place settings, the china.

"I might have to make a change," Jane said, knowing that she had to prepare Stacy in advance. "No, no shellfish or MSG . . . I'm fully aware of that . . . No potatoes. Of course. . . . Yes I realize you'll be here at five tonight . . . Yes, I'll be ready . . . I understand the pressure you're feeling. Everything will turn out just fine," Jane said with overly hearty emphasis. Then she made the mistake of looking over at Matthew who was shaking his head while spinning one finger in circles at his temple.

Jane almost burst out laughing at his irreverence. She shook her finger in reprimand, but he just grinned back and handed her another stack of recipes.

"But I should get back to the dinner, Stacy. You'll want everything just so, I'm sure. Bye." Jane hung up the phone.

"How many times does that lady call?" Matthew said. "Every time we're here, you're on the phone with her."

"She's just nervous about this meal," Jane said.

"It's just food," Matthew replied.

"You're right, Matthew, but she's also paying me quite a bit of money to serve that food and decorate the inn, so I am obligated to give my very best."

"As long as it's not too 'out there,'" Alice interjected.

"Precisely."

Jane scanned the recipes Matthew had given her and sorted them into her piles, then she flipped through the pile of Maybe's, setting aside the ones that might fit in with Stacy's criteria.

The pile was disappointingly small. And of those recipes, Jane could only realistically do one. She read through the recipes with a critical eye, mentally going over what she had in the house and what she might still need to purchase.

Would she have time?

"I've got it," Isabel exclaimed. "I've got the perfect recipe."

"Where did you find it?" Jane asked.

"I didn't. This recipe here reminded me." Isabel held up an older recipe book Jane hadn't used for years. "My mom used to make this for us once in a while. She called it Fourteen Boy Rice Dish."

"The name sounds intriguing," Jane asked. "What's in the dish?"

"Everything you have in the house. And the best part, you start with cooked chicken and make a curry sauce, which goes over cooked rice. Then you set out bowls of diced pineapple, banana, mandarin oranges, mango, peanuts, cashews, coconut, raisins, dried cranberries, bird's eye peppers, green onion and diced lemongrass. People can then put any combination of these condiments on their rice that they want." She grew excited as she talked, showing more animation in the past half hour than she had during the whole visit. Jane wondered if Isabel had simply been overshadowed by the more outspoken and exuberant Carita.

"Sounds a bit weird to me," Rick said with a note of skepticism.

"No way. Sounds awesome," Matthew cried. "All those different things, like a sweet and sour."

"And we could serve," Isabel continued. "Each of us could bring in a couple of bowls and set them on the table, which would add a little bit of drama to the meal."

While Isabel spoke, Jane imagined the combination of flavors, then envisioned the table filled with a dozen bowls of colorful and varied condiments. Hope flickered within her. This could work!

And having the kids serve? Genius.

"And the best part," Isabel continued, "is that the chicken curry is easy to make ahead because the longer it sits, the better the flavor. So if you're concerned, we can make the curry now and you can try it right away."

"We could have it for lunch," Matthew said, his eyes lighting up.

"No," Isabel and Carita said in unison. They looked at each other, then laughed, and it was as if an unseen barrier broke down between them.

"We could all help slice and dice the condiments before the meal," Carita said. But then she turned to Isabel. "Sorry. You figure out what we should do."

Isabel gave her a thankful smile. "I like the idea of us all serving the bowls for you. I mean, presentation is often a big part of a meal, right?"

"What do you think, Jane?" Alice asked with a worried look on her face. "It seems like a marvelous plan, plus it would use up the chicken breasts that Louise cooked this morning."

Jane nodded, still thinking. Making it ahead of time appealed to her, as did the idea of being able to taste it right away. If she didn't like it, she might, just maybe, have time to make the recipe she had set aside.

"Do you know how to make this recipe?" Jane asked.

"I can phone my mom. She would know." Isabel pushed herself away from the table, but just as she picked up the phone, it rang. She glanced at the call display. "It says Stacy Reddington," Isabel said.

"Didn't she just call?" Lynden asked.

"Let the phone ring," Alice said. "You just spoke to her. What on earth could she possibly have to say to you?"

Carita stood up just as Isabel was about to hand the phone to Jane. "I'll take care of this," she said. "Hello, Grace Chapel Inn, how may I direct your call? . . . I'm sorry, Ms. Howard is unavailable at this time. Can I take a message?"

Jane shook her head and held her hand out for the phone, when she felt Alice's hand on her arm. "Carita has the right idea," Alice said. "Stacy's constant phone calls are making you more nervous than the dinner itself is. You don't need to talk to her every time she calls."

Jane looked from Alice to Carita who was ending the phone call.

"You've been catering to this woman far too much," Alice said.

"I hope you're not making a pun, Alice."

Alice laughed. "No, but I am giving you some sisterly advice."

"You're probably right. Every time I talked to her I got more nervous." Jane gave Carita a grateful smile. "Thanks for running interference for me."

"Hey, if I'm going to be bossy, may as well be bossy for a good cause."

Half an hour later the chicken had been transferred to a larger casserole dish, and Jane was adding a rich blend of ingredients to prepare her new entrée. Isabel and Carita were going through the pantry, seeking out the other ingredients for the meal.

The boys were sent to Potterston to pick up whatever was missing and to stop at a thrift shop to see if they could find enough black pants and white shirts to add to those already on hand for the crew. Craig and Sylvia had shown up and were in the dining room with Alice, setting up.

Stacy had called two more times and each time Carita answered the phone, shielding Jane. While this did make Jane feel like she was hiding behind Carita, the respite from Stacy's constant worrying and dithering was a relief.

"I think you can give the curry its first taste," Isabel said. She had a small bowl and spoon ready for Jane.

Jane couldn't help taking a quick glance at the clock as she walked toward the stove. *If this doesn't taste good . . .* she stopped herself right there. The curry will be fine. She'd made enough different meals that she knew which ingredients would create which flavors and this one sounded like a winner.

Nonetheless, she was apprehensive as she took the steaming bowl and spoon from Isabel. She blew some steam away, then took her first taste.

And smiled.

"This tastes wonderful," she said, relief washing over her.

She took another taste, enjoying the delightful flavors. "Though I would like to see a hint more cumin." She shook in some more, stirred the pot and sampled it again. "It will be a while yet before the flavor comes out more fully, but this should work quite well."

Isabel beamed. "I'm glad you like it. Adding all the other condiments makes the whole meal taste really good."

"Jane, come and see what you think," Sylvia said, standing by the swinging door between the kitchen and the dining room.

Jane walked over and stopped, her eyes wide. "This looks amazing."

Sylvia had draped gold silk cloth over the buffet, bunching it here and there to allow for placement of the small topiaries Craig had brought. The same gold cloth hung in one corner of the dining room from the ceiling to the floor, serving as a backdrop for a grouping of bamboo plants and a larger topiary. Sylvia had set the table with the bronze tablecloth and gold runner, complementing the dishes Alice was now setting out.

Four small topiaries, matching the ones on the buffet, marched down the long table, creating a formal, yet welcoming effect.

"All we need is the place cards and a menu card," Sylvia said. "I brought along some paper for the menu. You said you didn't have it settled the last time I spoke to you." She picked up a stack of dark brown paper and cream vellum. "I thought we could print the menu on the vellum and stick it to the brown paper using decorating brads."

"Brads?"

"Little buttonlike clips that hold paper together. Decorative and fun. I found some that look like postage stamps to match the place cards." Sylvia looked up as Isabel and Carita joined them. "Maybe these girls could help me put them together?"

"They've done more than enough already," Jane said.

"No way," Isabel protested. "I love working with paper. Carita and I can easily put these together."

"But you're here to have fun," Jane put in. She felt worse and worse at the amount of work her guests were doing for this dinner.

"And this is fun," Isabel said, smiling away Jane's protestations.

"While we're cutting," Sylvia said, "We can make up the place cards. I thought we could decorate them with these used stamps I found . . ." As they walked out of the dining room, Sylvia, Carita and Isabel talked about glue, placement and sizes.

"I didn't think this dinner party was going to take over

the way it has," Jane said to Alice who carefully laid out the last place setting. "I thought I could do the whole thing on my own, and here I not only have you helping, I have our guests pitching in too."

Alice adjusted a spoon, straightened a glass, then glanced at her sister. "They wouldn't help if they didn't want to. I haven't seen Lynden as happy and satisfied as he was yesterday. And today, I see that same satisfaction on the face of these kids. They appreciate what you've done for them, and they want to repay you."

"All I did was cook and bake . . ."

"And allow them into your life. And into your kitchen." And now, look how Isabel seems to have come out of her shell. And it's all because you let her help you."

Jane felt a flush of guilt at Alice's warm praise. There were many times she wished she hadn't been so open armed, yet, at the same time, she knew that these kids appreciated being in a kitchen where food was being prepared and where someone was around. She suspected, whether they wanted to admit it or not, some of them might be missing their families and missing the comfort of a home.

"'A place where one can be refreshed and encouraged, a place of hope and healing, a place where God is at home,'" Jane said as the strains of the music that Louise was playing filtered into the dining room.

"Exactly," Alice said, patting Jane on the shoulder. She glanced around the room. "And now, anything else we can do to make this place look welcoming and comfortable?"

"I have to say, the decorations look wonderfully elegant."

"I think even Stacy would approve."

"I hope so," Jane said, her fingers crossed.

"Avast, me maties. Vehicles approaching at ten o'clock," Matthew called out from the porch.

"Well, it's going on five now. What do we do till then?" Rick joked.

Jane gave a feeble laugh, wiped her hands on a tea towel and gave a quick glance at her reflection in the window.

She had opted for a more formal look for herself and had put on a soft, black-and-gray dress, spangled with tiny discs, which she had bought at one time for a formal dinner. The bias cut dress was shorter in the front, falling just below her knees, and longer in the back, creating a flowing look. She had topped it with a short black, collarless jacket. Alice had helped her with her hair, pulling it up into a sleek chignon. Carita and Isabel took care of makeup, something Jane seldom bothered much about.

But the effect was rather glamorous, she had to admit. She was about to lick her lips, when she felt the flick of a finger on her arm.

Carita frowned at her. "Don't. You'll smudge the lipstick."

"Sorry." She took a long, slow breath to steady her nerves, glanced in the dining room one more time, allowing the soft glow of the tapers to soothe her. The room had been transformed into an elegant, but not too elegant, setting worthy of an international gathering.

She tried to distance herself from the whispering and giggling emanating from the kitchen. Even though the kids had exuded a laissez-faire attitude all day, now that the moment had come she knew they were nervous.

Louise was in the parlor, with the door open, playing some light classical pieces on the piano, the gentle music adding to a welcoming ambience.

Finally the moment arrived. The doorbell chimed and Jane hurried to greet her guests. Pete stood by the entrance looking quite elegant in his second-hand pants and shirt. His hair, up until now covered by a baseball cap, shone and lay flat against his head.

Jane gave them a nod and with a wink, Pete opened the door. "Good evening," he said to the gathering, "and welcome to Grace Chapel Inn."

The group of women standing on the porch beamed back at him, then at Jane, who had come down to the entrance to greet them in person. Jane was relieved to see that they had all dressed up. Stacy stood to one side, clutching her purse, biting her lips as she glanced from Jane to their guests.

"Come in, please," Jane said, standing aside as the group filed in. They murmured amongst themselves as they entered and looked around. Jane recognized some Dutch, caught the twang of a New Zealand accent and the singsong cadence of the Japanese women. She knew the Canadian women by the English they spoke.

All of them looked around the foyer of the inn with interest, their faces lighting up when Lynden bowed and escorted them into the dining room.

Stacy introduced the group to Jane, who had found out in advance all the names and the proper spellings for the place cards, so she was able to greet most of the women personally.

As Lynden and Pete held out the chairs for the women, working their way around the table, she caught Stacy's worried gaze flicking around the room. Jane had to turn away for a moment. Everything looked wonderful. If Stacy could find fault with this, she could find fault with anything.

But the woman's anxious expression slowly mellowed as the women oohed and aahed over the décor and the table. When they were all seated and had a chance to get settled, Jane glanced into the kitchen tilting her chin up. Isabel caught her signal and made a motion to Herbie to stop stirring the soup.

Jane clasped her hands in front of her and looked around

the assembled group. Blonde women, dark-haired women, short and tall, plump and slender, women from all over the globe had gathered under her roof, and for a moment, she felt the weight of Stacy's responsibilities.

"If you would each care to look at the menu, I will try to make clear what we will be serving." Jane picked up a copy of the menu she had laid on the buffet and read it aloud, making explanations as she did so. When she was finished, she looked up to see the women smiling.

"You will also notice beside each plate we have placed a small gift bag that contains mementos of your visit here."

The gift bags had been Stacy's idea, and she had contributed most of the items, but Alice thought it was such a wonderful concept that she and Vera had put their heads together and come up with a few items from Acorn Hill to put in the bags as well. Wilhelm donated a few tea packets; the Holzmanns a pen with their store's logo on it; Lloyd Tynan, the mayor of Acorn Hill, gave them each a pin; Craig a package of seeds; and Sylvia had made up little sachets with soaps inside.

The women fell upon the bags, pulling items out and laughing as they compared the souvenirs. Jane was reminded of the young guests and their scavenger hunt. Games and presents seemed to transcend all age lines. Though these women had probably spent large sums of money to make this trip, they were tickled with items costing only a few dollars.

Once they settled down again, Jane announced, "Our first course, as you can see from the menu, is a choice of Miso soup or Kumara soup."

Pete and Matthew walked around the table politely asking the women their preferences. The boys were properly solemn, but Jane had to stifle a smile when Matthew winked at her once.

While the women were eating their soup and chattering away, Alice and Louise stayed out of traffic, relaxing in the parlor with a light repast. Jane hurried back to the kitchen to oversee the girls assembling the salads on individual plates.

The conversation in the dining room rose slowly with each course and Jane saw Stacy relax.

Jane herself, however, had a moment of misgiving when the girls put out the main course in bowls. She bit her lip as she looked over the meal. *Was it too plain?* But now was not the time to have second thoughts.

Go with it, she reminded herself. *Serve with confidence. As Isabel said, drama and presentation will carry this off.*

She returned to the dining room as Lynden and Rick cleared away the salad dishes. She gave them a moment to divest themselves of the plates and pick up the bowls they would be bringing in.

Jane cleared her throat and avoided looking at Stacy, preferring to zero in on a brightly smiling Japanese woman she vaguely remembered as Etsuko Yamada. Jane held her sparkling, dark eyes.

"This evening we are serving a unique dinner. We have researched this meal and found that it has two names. One is Fourteen Boy Rice Dish. The other is Snow on the Mountain." As she spoke, the youths filed in as they had been practicing all afternoon, and carefully placed the bowls of rice and the bowls of curry within reaching distance of the two ends of the table.

"The one bowl holds a chicken curry sauce, the other rice . . ."

She paused while the many small bowls with the condiments were set out.

"You may add whatever you wish to your sauce. The bowls hold mandarin oranges, pineapple chunks, banana slices, mango pieces, peanuts, cashews, slivered almonds, tomato, peppers, chopped celery, chives, raisins, dried cranberries and coconut."

She saw the women looking from her to the servers to the bowls gradually proliferating around them.

Jane nodded and the young people started serving the rice and curry. Then they showed the women what they might do next.

Slowly the noise level increased as women debated the various merits of each topping, trying to decide. One of the Dutch women was scooping merrily out of every bowl, spreading everything on her rice.

Another, from New Zealand, had taken a small portion of rice and curried chicken, and was cautiously adding minuscule amounts of the various fruits, nuts and vegetables, as if unsure of the finished product.

Jane allowed herself a quick glance Stacy's way, but Stacy was so busy watching the women's reaction to the unorthodox entrée that she didn't even notice Jane's look.

The sounds of cheerful conversation and, as the women started eating, the very positive comments about the food made it clear that they truly were enjoying the meal.

Stacy gave Jane a careful smile, then started putting together her own dish. Jane retreated, relief flowing through her.

In the kitchen, Isabel and Herbie helped Jane put out the desserts on plates. Then they put the plates on a cart to be wheeled in at the proper time. Jane sat down and let out a long sigh.

"I think we did it, people," she said quietly, with a satisfied smile as she glanced around the gathered group. "I think this meal went over remarkably well."

"I'll say," Matthew whispered, rinsing off the dinner plates. "That one Dutch lady would have licked the curry bowl clean if she could have."

"And how about the one Japanese woman?" Isabel said. "I don't think she stopped smiling the whole time."

Jane looked back, watching Herbie and Isabel bring out the cart and let another sigh escape. Almost done, and the best part of all, Stacy looked relaxed and contented.

When all the desserts had been served and coffee and tea had been taken around, Jane wondered what was expected now. Should they retire to the living room with this group? Make small talk?

But then Stacy came into the kitchen, found Jane and hurried over to her side. She caught her by the hands, giving them a light shake. "Thank you so much for making this meal so memorable," she said, truly beaming. "And the kids helping you, they all did a standout job." Stacy glanced around the room, including each one of the youngsters in her praise. "The women will never forget this meal, I'm sure."

"I'm so glad you're pleased," Jane said.

"Pleased? My goodness, I'm thinking of asking you to do this meal again."

Jane's heart plummeted. Plan another meal with Stacy hovering over her? "I did say we don't do this on a regular basis—"

"You made that clear the first time, but this went so well—"

"And Jane's not going to have her hired help next time," Carita put in. "We're only on contract for this one time."

"Really?" Stacy's frown showed her complete puzzlement.

"Yes. We're college students and we, uh . . ." Carita glanced around, as if pleading for help.

"We prefer to pick and choose our jobs," Lynden put in.

"Yeah. Yesterday we volunteered at Habitat, but we never know where we're going to be from week to week," Matthew added.

"I . . . see." The way Stacy drew out the two words showed Jane that she clearly did not see. She turned back to Jane. "Would you be able to work without these kids?"

Jane shook her head decisively. "I couldn't do this without them. They are part of the package."

Stacy tapped one manicured fingernail against her chin. "I'm so sorry to hear that. The meal was a such a hit."

"I'm glad you have satisfied customers," Jane said, getting to her feet. "And I'm glad we could provide them with a memorable experience."

Stacy glanced back at Lynden and Carita, as if hoping they would change their minds. Then, with a long, drawn out breath, she pulled an envelope out of her purse and handed it to Jane. "Thanks again. And if you ever change your mind about the dinner . . ." she let the sentence hang as if giving Jane a chance to do just that.

"Thank you for your patronage," Jane said. "I had an enjoyable evening."

Stacy gave her a quick smile. "You've all been marvelous."

Jane thanked her as she handed the envelope to Alice, who had been supervising the kitchen clean up.

Alice signaled to Lynden and Pete. In a matter of minutes they were back at the entrance, chatting with the women, and in general just being their charming selves as they bid them all farewell.

Jane was thanked again and again for the lovely dinner and her charming staff.

Once they were gone, Jane leaned against the door and closed her eyes. *Done*, she thought.

"I think some tea is in order," Alice said, tucking her hand in her sister's arm and leading her to the living room, where Louise joined her sisters.

"But the kitchen needs to be cleaned up—" Jane protested.

"The 'servants' have that well in hand," Louise said.

Jane allowed herself to be guided as she settled into one of the chairs. She eased her high heels off her feet and sighed as she wiggled her toes. "Were you terribly inconvenienced?" she asked her sisters.

"Not at all." Louise's decisive reply showed Jane her sister wasn't just being polite.

Alice handed her the envelope. "Aren't you even a little bit curious what she paid you?"

"I know what she was going to pay me," Jane said, but took the envelope anyway. "We decided before I agreed to do this."

She slit it open, drew out the check and blinked. Read it again. Blinked again.

"She paid me far more than we had agreed on." Jane looked up at her sisters. "I can't accept this."

Alice got up and her eyes widened when she saw the amount.

"She put this with it." Jane pulled out a small note, cleared her throat and read, "'I know I was hard to deal with, so I let the check reflect that. Thank you again for being so gracious with me, when I have to confess, I was not always so gracious with you. You truly are an example of your inn's guiding principle.'"

Jane felt a moment of guilt. She knew she had not always felt gracious toward Stacy. "This could buy us four vacuum cleaners with lots of money left over. I don't deserve this," Jane said, letting the note fall into her lap.

"Nonsense," Louise said. "You put up with a lot for this occasion, and she made this dinner much harder than it needed to be."

Jane looked at the check again. "But still—"

"But nothing," Alice declared. "She gave it to you. Think of it as a gift."

"I suppose I could do that," Jane said, but she still felt uncomfortable with the final amount.

That night, as she lay in bed, Jane couldn't stop replaying the evening in her head, nor could she stop feeling a slight twinge of guilt at how much Stacy seemed to think Jane was worth.

She rolled over on her side, thinking, and as she thought, she knew exactly what she was going to do with the extra money.

Chapter ⊤ Sixteen

L ouise finished the last bars of the doxology Sunday morning, then glanced toward the front of the chapel, where Jane, Alice, Ethel and Lloyd sat along with Lynden, Carita, Matthew and Isabel. The others had elected to stay at the inn and sleep.

No matter, Louise thought. She was quite impressed that these young people changed their plans to leave early and instead came with them to church. Rev. Kenneth Thompson had a wonderful, thought-provoking sermon about servant-hood and how God uses us and our talents and calls us to build bridges across the chasms that can separate us from one another—chasms of age, abilities, resources.

Louise knew that she was challenged by the message and when she saw the light of hope shining in Lynden's eyes, she knew he had received guidance and strength for the decisions lying ahead of him.

Louise started the prelude, watching as people came to greet the inn's guests and welcome them.

When the service ended and the majority of worshippers had left, Louise closed up the organ and went to join the others, who were already talking to the pastor. "You haven't had a chance to meet our guests," Alice was saying, introducing him to Lynden, Carita, Matthew and Isabel.

"Thanks for your message," Lynden said, shaking Rev. Thompson's hand and gazing earnestly into the minister's eyes. "I've been doing a lot of soul searching the past few weeks, and you really helped me clarify a lot of stuff."

Rev. Thompson looked pleased. "I'm thankful I could be a servant to you."

"Hey, I got that. Servant. Like you were preaching about." Matthew said, raising his hand as if he was going to give a high five to the pastor.

Louise's gaze flew to Rev. Thompson, but their pastor smiled and raised his hand to meet Matthew's.

Matthew slapped their pastor's hand, then rocked back on his heels looking quite pleased with himself.

Louise gave him an indulgent smile. The boy was like a large Labrador puppy at times, but his heart was good and true. She was going to miss him and the others.

"How long are you staying at the inn?" the pastor asked, looking around the group.

"We're leaving right after this," Carita said with a note of regret.

"I'm glad you decided to come."

"I didn't realize how much I missed church and worship until I came here today."

Silence greeted her heartfelt statement.

Then the pastor put his hand on her shoulder, as if in benediction. "I pray you will be blessed by the service."

"I was. Thank you."

The pastor removed his hand and then looked beyond them. "I'm sorry, but I must excuse myself. Again, I'm so glad you came."

"And we should get going too," Isabel said. "Good-bye, Rev. Thompson. We have a long drive ahead of us."

The group walked together to the inn, the kids ahead, talking quietly amongst themselves, Louise, Alice and Jane following behind.

Louise smiled when she saw Lynden's hand slip side-ways, capturing Carita's.

"So this has been an enlightening week," Jane said, simultaneously patting each of her sisters on the arm. "We certainly can't complain about lack of challenges."

Alice massaged her right shoulder. "I know I've been challenged in more ways than one."

"I think we've managed to meet them all head on," Louise said.

"And how nice to know we don't do this alone," Jane said. She gave her sisters' arms a light shake. "Thanks again for all your help last night. The dinner went well and Stacy was so pleased that she called me again this morning to tell me, though I have to confess when I saw her name on call display, I almost let it ring."

"Well, that challenge has come to an end for you," Louise said. "And I am pleased with how our guests conducted themselves."

"They were a huge help," Jane said. "I'd like to give them a discount on their stay. Stacy paid me enough money that I think we can easily do that."

"Excellent idea," Alice said. "Though you make sure that you keep some of that money for yourself."

"No. It's going into the vacuum cleaner fund."

"There is more than enough for that," Alice said. "You should buy something fun. Something just for you."

"What I think would be fun would be to make a contri-bution to the home you are building, Alice," Jane said as they walked up the steps to the inn.

"I'm sure that would be greatly appreciated," Alice said warmly.

Inside, Herbie, Rick and Pete were finishing up their breakfast. Carita, Lynden, Isabel and Matthew chatted with them a moment, then went upstairs to pack.

"And once again, great breakfast," Herbie said to Jane as

he carried a precarious stack of dishes into the kitchen. "I don't know if I can go back to dorm food after this." He set the plates on the counter and cast a curious glance around the kitchen, as if making sure he hadn't missed out on any culinary experience.

"Would you like me to pack a lunch for you and your friends?" Jane asked.

The joy on his face made Louise smile.

"That would be totally awesome, Ms. J."

"When you come downstairs, I'll have it ready."

Herbie disappeared around the corner, and Louise got up. "Do you want some help?"

"That would be great."

Fifteen minutes later Jane, Louise and Alice brought out the bag lunches. The kids were gathered outside. Matthew and Rick were tossing suitcases into the van and Lynden's truck.

Herbie was the first to say good-bye. He took his lunch, glanced inside, then clutched it to his chest, his eyes closed in anticipation.

"This is for *lunch*," Jane emphasized. "That comes later in the day."

"Of course." His wounded look made Louise chuckle.

Rick and Pete were next. "Thanks so much for everything," Rick said as he took his lunch. "You really made us feel welcome and made us feel at home."

"I was going to say the same thing," Isabel said with a wide smile. "I enjoyed helping out."

"And what a help you were. Your meal suggestion saved the day," Jane told her.

"That's kind of you to say. I'm glad the menu worked out."

"Perfectly," Jane said. "Thank you again."

Matthew gave them all a bearish hug. "I'm gonna miss

this place like crazy," he said, pretending to wipe away an imaginary tear. "But, hey, I'll send you a postcard from school. Just so you won't forget me."

"As if that would happen," Louise said with a wry tone.

Matthew grinned, then waved and jumped into the van.

Carita and Lynden were the last.

"Thanks again," Carita said. "For everything. I had a wonderful visit with you. You ladies were awesome." She gave them all a quick hug, her eyes glistening.

"Again, thanks," Lynden said, shaking their hands. "I am really humbled by what I learned from you ladies." He held Louise's hand a moment longer. "Thank you so much for your music and for sharing it with us."

Louise felt a motherly rush of love for this young man. She gave in to an impulse and gave him a hug, which he returned with endearing enthusiasm.

When they pulled away, they were smiling at each other.

"So, a new year lies ahead of you," Louise said. "Do you know what you want to do?"

Lynden nodded. "I think I'm going to go to see about enrolling in a program that lets me help people build a better life for themselves. I don't know what form or shape that will take. I'm counting on the college guidance counselors to point me in the right direction."

"That's admirable," Louise said. "I'm sure your grandmother would be very proud of you."

"I hope so." Lynden gave her a shy smile, then took a step backward, taking Carita with him. "We should get going. The crew is going to mutiny if we don't get moving."

Lynden and Carita walked to his truck and Rick ran toward the van. "Shotgun!" he called out, claiming the front passenger seat.

Doors slammed shut, windows rolled down and as the kids shouted out good-byes, Isabel got in the driver's seat.

She fiddled with something, then frowned. After a few moments, she lifted her hands.

"What's up, Isabel?" Louise asked.

"This van won't start," she said

A collection of groans greeted that remark. Matthew, Pete and Herbie all piled out, then Matthew held up his hand.

"You know, I think we need to give the resident car expert a chance to look at this."

He stood, waiting while Louise wondered who the "car expert" was. He crooked a finger at Louise, his grin lighting up his face.

"Hey, Mrs. L. Why don't you help us out here?"

Louise shook her head, raising her hand in a gesture of denial. "I'm afraid my expertise is limited to tire wear, paint jobs, windshield wipers and, well, batteries."

"See. There you go." Matthew lifted up the hood, stepped back, waving Louise on.

Louise looked from the boys to her sisters, who weren't helping her at all, then with a light sigh, walked over to the van. She hoped she could remember what she had learned, though she doubted she could offer any help at all.

She glanced at the engine. Oil dipstick. Transmission fluid dipstick. Windshield washer fluid container. And there was the battery. She frowned and jiggled the posts. Loose. In fact, the entire battery was loose in its casing.

"And the diagnosis is . . ." Matthew prompted.

"The battery housing needs to be tightened and the battery cables are loose. And, I might add, the posts are quite corroded." Louise gave him a wry look. "But then I'm guessing you knew that already."

Matthew shrugged, looking a little shamefaced. But not much. "I just wanted you to show off your knowledge," he said.

"And what if we hadn't gotten to the battery portion of the course yet?"

"Well, then, I would have given you a hint."

"Thank you for that." She stepped back and took a handkerchief that Lynden had been thoughtful enough to supply. "You might want to check your tire pressure too," she said, glancing at the one low tire on the front.

"See? A veritable font of mechanical know-how," Matthew proclaimed.

Louise shook her head as the other boys went into action. They procured a small tool kit from the back of the van. While Pete tightened the battery cables and housing, Herbie checked the tire pressure, and Matthew offered advice and encouragement from the sidelines.

A few minutes later the battery was secure, the cables tightened, the van was running. Both vehicles left the yard trailing a chorus from within of thank-yous and good-byes.

Louise, Jane and Alice stood watching them as they drove down Chapel Road and then disappeared onto Berry Lane.

The silence they left in their wake was almost deafening. Louise let it settle around them, then sighed lightly.

"I do think I am going to miss them," she said.

"I agree." Alice nodded.

"Do you think they'll write?" Jane asked.

"Who knows? But it doesn't matter if they don't. Maybe they'll send some other guests our way," Louise said.

"Maybe." Jane agreed. "But if they do, I'm going to make sure I don't overschedule myself."

"Really?" Louise asked, raising one eyebrow.

"Really." Jane gave them both a smile. "Now, let's go have some tea and cookies."

"You have some left?" Louise asked.

Jane nodded. "Found four broken ones in the bottom of the cookie jar. The kids must have missed them in their final sweep of the kitchen."

"Sounds . . . tasty," Alice said.

"Bet your boots, Ms. A," Jane said.

They laughed and together walked back to the peace and quiet of the inn.

Jane's Butterscotch Cookies

MAKES THREE TO FOUR DOZEN

1½ cups dark brown sugar
1½ cups butter
1½ cups flour
2 eggs
¼ teaspoon salt
1¼ teaspoons baking powder
12 ounces butterscotch chips
½ cup chopped walnuts or pecans

Combine brown sugar, butter, flour, eggs, salt and baking powder in a mixer. Remove bowl from mixer, and stir in chips and nuts, using a wooden spoon. Place a teaspoonful of batter for each cookie on baking sheet. Bake at 350 degrees for ten to fifteen minutes. Remove from oven and allow cookies to cool before transferring from sheet to serving plate.

About the Author

After twenty years of city living, life changed drastically for Carolyne Aarsen when she married and moved with her husband to a farm two hours away from the nearest mall. Neerlandia, the Canadian hamlet where they went to church and shopped, was so far from New York City, the hub of publishing, that her "someday" plans of writing a book seemed to belong to another world.

The dream wouldn't die, however, and while raising four of their own children and numerous foster children, Carolyne took a writing correspondence course. From that experience came a weekly column that ran for nine years in a number of northern Alberta newspapers. More writing courses and conferences finally led to her attaining her dream of publication.

She has published more than a dozen books that have combined her love of story with her love of the Lord. Carolyne is thankful that her writing permits her to show how God's extraordinary power can shape and change the lives of ordinary people.

Please visit www.carolyneaarsen.com and send her an e-mail if you have the time.

A Note from the Editors

This original book was created by the Books and Inspirational Media Division of Guideposts, the world's leading inspirational publisher. Founded in 1945 by Dr. Norman Vincent Peale and his wife Ruth Stafford Peale, Guideposts helps people from all walks of life achieve their maximum personal and spiritual potential. Guideposts is committed to communicating positive, faith-filled principles for people everywhere to use in successful daily living.

Our publications include award-winning magazines such as *Guideposts*, *Angels on Earth* and *Positive Thinking*, best-selling books, and outreach services that demonstrate what can happen when faith and positive thinking are applied in day-to-day life.

For more information, visit us online at www.guideposts.org, call (800) 431-2344 or write Guideposts, 39 Seminary Hill Road, Carmel, New York 10512.